The Coptic Orthodox Patriarchate of Al
Diocese of New York & New Eng

Holy Pascha
BOOK 1 of 2
Last Friday – Covenent Thursday

According to the original Scriptures of Greek Septuagint
and Coptic Bible in modern English

Ⲡϫⲱⲙ ⲛ̀ⲧⲉ Ⲡⲓⲡⲁⲥⲭⲁ Ⲉⲑⲟⲩⲁⲃ

البصخة المقدسة
الجزء الأول
من جمعة ختام الصوم الى يوم خميس العهد
حسب الترجمات الاصلية القبطية و اليونانية السبعينية للكتاب المقدس باللغة الانجليزية الحديثة

Edited by:
Fr. Abraham Azmy
Virgin Mary and Archangel Michael Coptic Orthodox Church
Of Connecticut
English - Coptic - Arabic
2024 Edition

Both parts include:	يتكون من جزئين بهما:
1- Last Friday of the Great Lent	**1-** جمعة ختام الصوم
2- The Holy Unction Prayer	**2-** صلاة القنديل
3- Lazarus Saturday	**3-** سبت لعازر
4- Palm Sunday (and procession)	**4-** أحد الشعانين (ودورة الشعانين)
5- The Holy Pascha	**5-** اسبوع الآلام
6- Book of Psalms (According to Coptic & Septuagint)	**6-** سفر المزامير (حسب القبطية و السبعينية)
7- Bright Saturday	**7-** سبت النور
8- Book of Revelation	**8-** سفر الرؤيا
9- Resurrection Feast Liturgy	**9-** قداس عيد القيامة

HOLY PASCHA
BOOK 1 of 2
From Last Friday – Day of Great Thursday

BOOK 2 of 2
From Eve of Great Friday – Liturgy of the Resurrection Feast

According to the original languages, the Coptic and Greek Septuagint of the Holy Bible in modern English
English - Coptic - Arabic
Edited by Fr. Abraham Azmy

ISBN: 9798322395133

Publisher:
Virgin Mary and Archangel Michael Coptic Orthodox Church of Connecticut
400 Ridge Rd, Hamden, CT 06517
U.S.A.
www.coptnet.com

His Holiness Pope Tawadros II
118th Pope of Alexandria and Patriarch of the See of St. Mark

His Grace Bishop David
Bishop of the Coptic Orthodox Diocese of New York & New England

Table of Contents

Preface

In the Name of the Father, the Son, and the Holy Spirit, One God, Amen.

We thank our Good Savior, Who gave us unutterable grace to complete this project. I could not find the words to describe how I felt, or how anyone may feel, when I began searching through the rites of the Holy Pascha week. These rites sere passed on from the breath of the Holy Spirit in the first centuries and were treasured by our great and blessed church, the Coptic Orthodox Church.

The miracle of the rites of the Holy Pascha:

Whoever searches in the rites of the Holy Pascha will find that it speaks to the human soul with non-human language. It captures the soul and draws it to one person who is Christ the Savior. The soul enters to Him through His injuries then it settles underneath the Cross.

All the readings of the Week of the Holy Pascha, that were inspired by the whispering of the Holy Spirit, from Genesis to Revelation, are in harmony. They meet together, with all symbols and prophecies, centralizing around the crucified the Lord Jesus.

The hymns of the Week of the Holy Pascha were inspired by the Holy Spirit through the saints, who contemplated in the passion of their beloved Christ. It moves any human soul, even if it is of the evilest sinner, to praise the King who is raised on the Cross.

The scriptures used in the Book of the Holy Pascha:

While preparing the Book of the Holy Pascha, we came across the origins of the scriptures of the Holy Bible, and of the Holy Pascha Katameros. We searched extensively about the most accurate translations that would be in harmony with our Coptic scriptures that were kept since the early centuries. These accurate translations were used in this book of the Holy Pascha.

Regarding the Old Testament:

The Coptic translation: It is in the Katameros of the Holy Week of the Pascha of our Coptic church.

The Arabic translation: It is translated from the Coptic scripture, and taken from the Katameros of the Holy Week of the Holy Pascha of the Coptic church.

The English translation: We used the Septuagint that was translated into modern English from the Greek language by Minister Paul Esposito in 2004, and was published as "The Apostles Bible". We found that this translation is compatible with the Coptic translation.

نشكر مخلصنا الصالح الذى اعطانا نعمة لا يُعبر عنها لاتمام هذا العمل . لا تسعفنى الكلمات لأصف المشاعر الفياضة التى ملكتنى و يمكن ان يعيشها اى انسان عندما يبحث فى طقس اسبوع آلام الرب الذى وضعته كنيستنا العظيمة القبطية الارثوذكسية فى القرون الاولى بانفاس الروح القدس .

الأعجاز فى ترتيب أسبوع الآلام:

أن الذى يبحث فى ترتيب اسبوع الآلام ليجده يخاطب اى نفس بشرية بلغة غير بشرية و يأسرها و يجذبها نحو شخص واحد وهو المخلص المسيح ، و تدخل اليه النفس من خلال جراحاته و تنسكب انسكاباً تحت اقدام الصليب.

فقراءات اسبوع الآلام المقدس التى وُضعت بهمسات الروح القدس من سفر التكوين الى سفر الرؤيا ، نجدها تتوافق و تلتقى جميعها بكل رموزها ونبواتها فى شخص الرب يسوع المصلوب.

والحان اسبوع الآلام التى عمل الروح القدس فيها مع القديسين الذين تأملوا فى آلام حبيبهم المسيح تحرك اى نفس بشرية حتى ولو كانت اشر الخطاة لتسبح الملك المرفوع على الصليب.

النصوص الكتابية فى كتاب البصخة:

فى الإعداد لنصوص كتاب البصخة المقدسة تعرضنا لأصول ترجمات الكتاب المقدس و اصول قطامارس البصخة المقدسة و بحثنا باجتهاد عن ادق الترجمات التى توافق ترجمتنا القبطية المحفوظة منذ العصور الأولى . ثم وضعنا هذه الترجمات فى كتاب البصخة الذى بين يديك.

العهد القديم :

النص القبطى: تم استخدام النص القبطى الموجود بقطامارس اسبوع الآلام بكنيستنا القبطية .

النص العربى: و هو ترجمة للنص القبطى و قد أُخذ من قطامارس اسبوع الآلام بكنيستنا القبطية.

النص الانجليزى: و قد تم استخدام الترجمة الانجليزية الحديثة للسبعينية و التى قام بها القس بول ايسبوزيتو سنة 2004 و نشرها بحقوق طبع بأسم "كتاب الرسل المقدس" و الطبعة السبعينية هذه مطابقة للاصل القبطى.

Regarding the New Testament:

The Scriptures in Arabic and Coptic: are taken from Katameros of the Holy Week of our Coptic church.

English translation: we used the New King James translation of the New Testament as being the closest translation to the Coptic and Arabic translation of the New Testament.

In your hands is "**the Book of the Holy Pascha, from Last Friday of Great Lent to Resurrection Feast Eve.**" It contains: **Last Friday of Great Lent** with the Holy Unction, **Lazarus Saturday, Palm Sunday** with Palm Sunday Procession, **Holy Week**, **complete Book of Psalms** according to the Coptic translations, collected from Arabic-Coptic Psalms book that was published in 1744 A.D., and it is compatible with the Septuagint, **Bright Saturday** with **Book of Revelation**, and the **Resurrection Feast Liturgy**.

We added extra column containing the Coptic text, written in Arabic so that we may help any one unable to read Coptic and came to the land of immigration.

Special thanks to:

+ All servants who worked hard to publish this book.

+ Mr. George Topalidis, of the Holy Trinity Greek Orthodox Church of Bridgeport, CT, U.S., who helped us in all aspects of the original old Greek Septuagint. May God reward him.

+ Minister Paul W. Esposito, the minister and founder of Stauros Ministries, U.S.A., who has given us a written permission to use his modern translation of the Septuagint for all English Old Testament scriptures. May God reward him.

We ask our Good Savior to make this book a blessing to everyone uses it, for the glory of His Holy name, through the intercessions of the Theotokos, the Virgin St. Mary and Archangel Michael; and through the prayers of H.H. Pope Tawadros II and his partner in the Apostolic service, H.G. Bishop David, and Glory be to God, Amen.

Fr. Abraham Azmy
Virgin Mary and Archangel Michael Coptic Orthodox Church of Connecticut, U.S.A.

Babah 12, 1724 A.M.
October 22, 2007 A.D.

بالنسبة للعهدالجديد:

النص القبطى والعربى: أخذا من قطماروس اسبوع الآلام بكنيستنا القبطية.

النص الإنجليزي: قد استخدمنا ترجمة نيو كنج جيمز لانها أقرب الترجمات الانجليزية من الترجمة القبطية والعربية للعهد الجديد.

و ها هو بين يديك "كتاب البصخة المقدسة من جمعة ختام الصوم الى قداس عيد القيامة" اى انه يحتوى على : جمعة ختام الصوم مع صلاة القنديل - سبت لعازر - أحد الشعانين مع دورة الشعانين - اسبوع الآلام - سفر المزامير كاملاً حسب الترجمة القبطية و الذى تم جمعه من طبعة سفر المزامير القبطى و العربى سنة 1744 م و هو يتوافق مع السبعينية - سبت النور - سفر الرؤيا كاملاً - ليلة عيد القيامة .

و قد اهتممنا بإضافة نهر للغة القبطية مكتوباً باللغة العربية و ذلك لكى نساعد كل من لايستطيع قراءة اللغة القبطية من الذين هاجروا الى الخارج .

شكر خاص لكلٍ من:

+ الخدام الذين تعبوا كثيراً لأصدار هذا الكتاب.

+ السيد جورج توباليديس بكنيسة الثالوث الأقدس اليونانية الأرثوذكسية ببريدجبورت بكونيكتيكت بأمريكا لمساعدته لنا فى الأصل اليونانى القديم للطبعة السبعينية ، ليعوضه الرب عن ذلك .

+ القس بول ايسبوزيتو رئيس هيئة خدمة ستوروس بأمريكا الذى أعطانا التصريح الكتابى بأستخدام ترجمته الأنجليزية الحديثة للأصل السبعيني لنصوص العهد القديم ، ليعوضه الرب عن ذلك .

و نسأل مخلصنا الصالح أن يجعل هذا الكتاب سبب بركة لكل من يستخدمه لمجد اسمه القدوس ، بشفاعات والدة الاله القديسة مريم العذراء و رئيس الملائكة الجليل ميخائيل و صلوات قداسة البابا المعظم الانبا تواضروس الثاني وشريكه في الخدمة الرسولية نيافة الانبا دافيد و لإلهنا المجد الدائم الى الأبد ، آمين.

القمص ابراهام عزمى
كنيسة السيدة العذراء و رئيس الملائكة ميخائيل بولاية كونيكتيكت ، الولايات المتحدة الامريكية

12 بابه 1724 للشهداء
22 اكتوبر 2007 م

الصلوات المتكررة فى أسبوع الآلام

Repeated Prayers of Every Hour

Index

Rites of the Holy Pascha	(طقس البصخة المقدسة)

+ The day is divided into five daylight hours (First – Third – Sixth – Ninth – Eleventh) and five hours for the evening (First – Third – Sixth – Ninth – Eleventh) hours. The twelfth hour is added in the Great Friday.

+ ينقسم اليوم إلى خمس ساعات نهارية (باكر – الثالثة – السادسة – التاسعة – الحادية عشر) وخمس ساعات ليلية (الأولى – الثالثة – السادسة – التاسعة – الحادية عشر) وفى يوم الجمعة العظيمة تضاف الساعة الثانية عشر.

+ The day starts from its vesper till the following vesper.

+ يحسب اليوم من الغروب إلى غروب اليوم التالى .

+ The prayers are held outside the first chorus, as our Lord Jesus suffered and was crucified on the Golgotha, outside Jerusalem. *"Let us go forth therefore unto him outside the camp, bearing his reproach. For here have we no continuing city, but we seek one to come."* (Heb 13:13-14)

+ تقام صلوات البصخة خارج الخورس الأول ، لأن السيد المسيح تألم وصُلب على جبل الأقرانيون خارج أورشليم" فلنخرج إذاً إليه خارج المحلة حاملين عاره " (عب 13 : 12 ، 13) . " ولأن ذبيحة الخطية كانت تُحرق خارج المحلة " (عب 3 : 11)

+ We cover the lecterns and the pillars of the church with black cloths and curtains. The icon of our Lord Jesus Christ on the cross is placed in the middle.

+ يُوضَع ستر أسود على المنجلية وتوشّح أعمدة الكنيسة بالستور السوداء ، وتوضع صورة السيد المسيح المصلوب .

+ The priests, deacons and congregation do not kiss each other from Wednesday Eve till the end of Bright Saturday liturgy in reference to Juda's kiss.

+ من ليلة الأربعاء إلى نهاية قداس سبت الفرح لا يُقبّل الكهنة والشمامسة والشعب بعضهم بعضاً لأجل قبلة يهوذا .

+ In the past, when they used to suspend all jobs during the Pascha week, the church used to hold the prayer of each hour at the same hour. The Coptic monasteries, some churches and the Ethiopian churches are still following this tradition.

+ فى الأزمنة الأولى التى كانت الأعمال والمصالح تُعطل طول أسبوع الآلام ، كانت الكنيسة تقيم صلاة كل ساعة فى وقتها . ومازالت الأديرة القبطية وبعض الكنائس والكنيسة الأثيوبية تتبع هذا النظام إلى الآن .

Order of the Readings

(1) Prophecies.
(2) Thok Teti Gom.... (Thine is the Power... 12 times)
(3) Psalm and introduction of the Gospel, then the Gospel in Coptic, and in English or Arabic.
(4) Introduction to the Exposition, Exposition, and conclusion.
(5) The Litanies, then Evnouti Nai Nan..., Epouro.., etc.
(6) The final Blessing.

(Every day has one subject in both morning and evening readings, e.g.. Monday morning and Tuesday eve share the same one subject, and not Monday Eve and Monday Morning)

ترتيب القراءات

(1) النبوات .
(2) ثوك تيه تى جُم (لك القوة والمجد 12 مرة).
(3) المزمور ومقدمة الإنجيل ، ثم الإنجيل قبطياً ثم بالعربية او بالانجليزية.
(4) مقدمة الطرح والطرح وختامه .
(5) الطلبة ثم " إفنووتى نان ناى ، إبؤورو ...
(6) البركة .

(كل يوم له موضوع واحد فى قراءاته الصباحية و المسائية ، مثلا يوم الاثنين صباحا و ليلة الثلاثاء لهما نفس الموضوع الواحد و ليس ليلة الاثنين و يوم الاثنين)

5

Introduction to the Prophecies مقدمة النبوات

A reading from (........) the Prophet, may his holy blessing be with us. Amen.	إيفول خين (فلان) بى بروفيتيس إريه بيف إسموو إثؤواب شوبى نيمان آمين . إفجو إمموس .	Ⲉⲃⲟⲗ ϧⲉⲛ (. . .) ⲡⲓⲡⲣⲟⲫⲏⲧⲏⲥ ⲉⲣⲉ ⲡⲉϥⲥⲙⲟⲩ ⲉⲑⲩ : ϣⲱⲡⲓ ⲛⲉⲙⲁⲛ ⲁⲙⲏⲛ : ⲉϥϫⲱ ⲙⲙⲟⲥ .	من (.......) النبي بركته المقدسة : تكون معنا آمين .

□

Conclusion of the Prophecies خاتمة النبوات

Glory be to the Holy Trinity, our God, forever and unto the ages of all ages. Amen.	أو أ أو إنتيه ترياس إثؤواب بين نووتى شا إينيه إنتيه نى إينيه تيروو آمين .	Ⲟⲩⲱⲟⲩ ⲛ̀ϯⲧⲣⲓⲁⲥ ⲉⲑⲩ ⲡⲉⲛⲛⲟⲩϯ ϣⲁ ⲉ̀ⲛⲉϩ ⲛⲉⲙ ϣⲁ ⲉ̀ⲛⲉϩ ⲛ̀ⲧⲉ ⲛⲓⲉ̀ⲛⲉϩ ⲧⲏⲣⲟⲩ ⲁⲙⲏⲛ.	مجداً للثالوث المقدس إلهنا إلى أبد الأبدين كلها أمين .

Introduction to the Homily مقدمة العظة

+ Ⲟⲩⲕⲁⲑⲏⲭⲏⲥⲓⲥ ⲛ̀ⲧⲉ ⲡⲉⲛⲓⲱⲧ ⲉⲑⲟⲩⲁⲃ ⲁⲃⲃⲁ (Ϣⲉⲛⲛⲟⲩϯ ⲡⲓⲁⲣⲭⲏⲙⲁⲛⲇⲣⲓⲧⲏⲥ - Ⲓⲱⲁ Ⲡⲓⲭⲣⲩⲥⲟⲥⲧⲟⲙⲟⲥ - Ⲁ̀ⲑⲁⲛⲁⲥⲓⲟⲥ ⲡⲓⲁⲡⲟⲥⲧⲟⲗⲓⲕⲟⲥ - Ⲥⲉⲩⲏⲣⲓⲁⲛⲟⲥ) Ⲉⲣⲉ ⲡⲉϥⲥⲙⲟⲩ ⲉⲑⲟⲩⲁⲃ ϣⲱⲡⲓ ⲛⲉⲙⲁⲛ ⲁⲙⲏⲛ.

+ A homily of our Holy Father (Abba Shenouti the Archmanedrite, St. John Chrysystom, St. Athanasius the Apostolic, St. Sawiros) May his holy blessings be with us. Amen.

+ أوو كاتي شيسيس إنتيه بين يوت إثؤواب أفا (شينوتى بى أرشي مانيذريتيس , يوأنّيس بى خريصوسطوموس , أثاناسيوس بى أبوسطوليكوس , ساويريانوس) إريه بيف إسموو إثؤواب شوبى نيمان آمين .

+ عظة لأبينا القديس أنبا (شنودة رئيس المتوحدين , يوحنا فم الذهب , أثناسيوس الرسولي , ساويرس) بركته المقدسة فلتكن معنا آمين.

The Conclusion of the Homily وفى ختام أى عظة يقال

We conclude the homily of our Holy Father (.......), who enlightened our minds and our hearts. In the name of the Father, and the Son, and the Holy Spirit, one God. Amen.	مارين إس إفراجيزين إنتى كاتي شيسيس إنتيه بين يوت إثؤواب أفا (...) في إيطاف إر أوؤوينى إمبين نوس نيم نى فال إنتيه نين هيت : خين إفران إم إفيوت نيم إبشيرى نيم بى بنيفما إثؤواب أوونووتى إن أووأوت آمين .	Ⲙⲁⲣⲉⲛ ⲥ̀ⲫ̀ⲣⲁ̀ⲅⲓⲍⲓⲛ ⲛ̀ⲧⲕⲁⲑⲏⲭⲏⲥⲓⲥ ⲛ̀ⲧⲉ ⲡⲉⲛⲓⲱⲧ ⲉⲑⲟⲩⲁⲃ ⲁⲃⲃⲁ (..) ⲫⲏ ⲉ̀ⲧⲁϥⲉⲣ ⲟⲩⲱⲓⲛⲓ ⲙ̀ⲡⲉⲛⲛⲟⲩⲥ ⲛⲉⲙ ⲛⲓⲃⲁⲗ ⲛ̀ⲧⲉ ⲛⲉⲛϩⲏⲧ : ϧⲉⲛ ⲫ̀ⲣⲁⲛ ⲙ̀ⲫ̀ⲓⲱⲧ ⲛⲉⲙ ⲡ̀ϣⲏⲣⲓ ⲛⲉⲙ ⲡⲓⲡⲛⲉⲩⲙⲁ ⲉⲑⲟⲩⲁⲃ ⲟⲩⲛⲟⲩϯ ⲛⲟⲩⲱⲧ ⲁⲙⲏⲛ.	فلنختم عظة أبينا القديس أنبا (......) الذى أنار عقولنا وعيون قلوبنا باسم الأب والإبن والروح القدس إله واحد أمين.

Introduction to the Paschal Praise - مقدمة تسبحة البصخة

PRIEST:	الكاهن:	Ⲡⲓⲟⲩⲏⲃ:	الكاهن:
Lord have mercy upon us. Amen. Alleluia.	ابشويس ناي نان: امين. الليلويا.	Ⲡ̅ϭⲟⲓⲥ ⲛⲁⲓ ⲛⲁⲛ: Ⲁ̇ⲙⲏⲛ. Ⲁ̇ⲗⲗⲏⲗⲟⲩⲓⲁ:	يارب إرحمنا. آمين. الليلويا.
In the name of the Father, the Son and the Holy Spirit, one God. Amen.	خين افران ام افيوت نيم ابشيري نيم بي ابنيفما اثواب اونوتي ان اواوت. امين.	Ϧⲉⲛ ⲫⲣⲁⲛ ⲙ̇Ⲫⲓⲱⲧ ⲛⲉⲙ Ⲡϣⲏⲣⲓ ⲛⲉⲙ Ⲡⲓⲡ̀ⲛⲉⲩⲙⲁ ⲉⲑⲟⲩⲁⲃ ⲟⲩⲛⲟⲩϯ ⲛ̇ⲟⲩⲱⲧ : ⲁ̀ⲙⲏⲛ.	بإسم الآب والإبن والروح القدس إله واحد. أمين.
Glory be to the Father and the Son, and the Holy Spirit, now and ever and unto, the ages of the ages. Amen.	ذوكصابنتري كي ايو: كي اجيو ابنفماتي: كي نين كي آ اي كي استوس: اي اوناس تون اي اونون: امين. الليلويا.	Ⲇⲟⲝⲁ Ⲡⲁⲧⲣⲓ ⲕⲉ Ⲩⲓⲱ: ⲕⲉ ⲁ̀ⲅⲓⲱ Ⲡⲛⲉⲩⲙⲁⲧⲓ : ⲕⲉ ⲛⲩⲛ ⲕⲉ ⲁ̀ⲓ ⲕⲉ ⲓⲥⲧⲟⲩⲥ: ⲉ̇ⲱⲛⲁⲥ ⲧⲱⲛ ⲉ̇ⲱⲛⲱⲛ : ⲁ̀ⲙⲏⲛ. ⲁ̀ⲗ.	المجد للآب والابن والروح الفدس، الأن وكل أوان وإلى دهر الدهور. أمين.
The doxology of the (…) hour of (eve / day) of (…) of Holy Pascha. May its blessings be with us. Amen.			تسبحة الساعة (...) من (يوم / ليلة) (...) من البصخة المقدسة بركته علينا. آمين.
Make us worthy to pray thankfully: Our Father…			اللهم اجعلنا مستحقين أن نقول بشكر: أبانا الذي في السماوات...

تسبحة البصخة (ثوك تي تيجوم - Pascha Praise (Thine is the power

Pascha Praise – A: From Palm Sunday Pascha to the Ninth Hour of Tuesday

تسبحة البصخة- A : من بصخة احد الشعانين الى الساعة التاسعة من نهار يوم الثلاثاء

Thine is the power, the glory, the blessings, the majesty forever. Amen; Emmanuel our God and King.	ثوك تيه تى جُم نيم بى أوؤو نيم بى إسمو نيم بى أماهى شا إينيه آمين . إمانوئيل بين نووتى بين أوورو .	Ⲑⲱⲕ ⲧⲉ ϯϫⲟⲙ ⲛⲉⲙ ⲡⲓⲱⲟⲩ ⲛⲉⲙ ⲡⲓⲥ̀ⲙⲟⲩ ⲛⲉⲙ ⲡⲓⲁⲙⲁϩⲓ ϣⲁ ⲉ̀ⲛⲉϩ ⲁⲙⲏⲛ Ⲉⲙⲙⲁⲛⲟⲩⲏⲗ ⲡⲉⲛⲛⲟⲩϯ ⲡⲉⲛⲟⲩⲣⲟ .	لك القوة والمجد والبركة والعزة إلى الأبد آمين إلهن عمانوئيل وملكنا .
Thine is the power, the glory, the blessings, the majesty forever. Amen; My Lord Jesus Christ.	ثوك تيه تى جُم نيم بى أوؤو نيم بى إسمو نيم بى أماهى شا إينيه آمين . باتشويس إيسوس بي خرستوس.	Ⲑⲱⲕ ⲧⲉ ϯϫⲟⲙ ⲛⲉⲙ ⲡⲓⲱⲟⲩ ⲛⲉⲙ ⲡⲓⲥ̀ⲙⲟⲩ ⲛⲉⲙ ⲡⲓⲁⲙⲁϩⲓ ϣⲁ ⲉ̀ⲛⲉϩ ⲁⲙⲏⲛ : Ⲡ̅ϭⲟⲓⲥ Ⲓⲏⲥⲟⲩⲥ Ⲡⲓⲭⲣⲓⲥⲧⲟⲥ .	لك القوة والمجد والبركة والعزة إلى الأبد آمين ياربى يسوع المسيح .
Thine is the power, the glory, the blessings, the majesty forever. Amen.	ثوك تيه تى جُم نيم بى أوؤو نيم بى إسمو نيم بى أماهى شا إينيه آمين .	Ⲑⲱⲕ ⲧⲉ ϯϫⲟⲙ ⲛⲉⲙ ⲡⲓⲱⲟⲩ ⲛⲉⲙ ⲡⲓⲥ̀ⲙⲟⲩ ⲛⲉⲙ ⲡⲓⲁⲙⲁϩⲓ ϣⲁ ⲉ̀ⲛⲉϩ ⲁⲙⲏⲛ .	لك القوة والمجد والبركة والعزة إلى الأبد آمين
Our Father Who art…		ϫⲉ Ⲡⲉⲛⲓⲱⲧ…	ابانا الذى فى ....

Pascha Praise – B: *From the Eleventh Hour of Tuesday to the Eleventh Hour of Thursday*

تسبحة البصخة - B : من الساعة الحادية عشر من نهار يوم الثلاثاء الى الساعة الحادية عشر من نهار يوم الخميس

English	Transliteration	Coptic	Arabic
Thine is the power, the glory, the blessings, the majesty forever. Amen; Emmanuel our God and King.	ثوك تيه تى جُم نيم بى أوؤو نيم بى إسموو نيم بى أماهى شا إينيه آمين . إمانوئيل بين نوتى بين أوورو .	Ѳⲱⲕ ⲧⲉ ϯϫⲟⲙ ⲛⲉⲙ ⲡⲓⲱⲟⲩ ⲛⲉⲙ ⲡⲓⲥⲙⲟⲩ ⲛⲉⲙ ⲡⲓⲁⲙⲁϩⲓ ϣⲁ ⲉⲛⲉϩ ⲁⲙⲏⲛ Ⲉⲙⲙⲁⲛⲟⲩⲏⲗ ⲡⲉⲛⲛⲟⲩϯ ⲡⲉⲛⲟⲩⲣⲟ.	لك القوة والمجد والبركة والعزة إلى الأبد آمين عمانوئيل إلهنا وملكنا .
Thine is the power, the glory, the blessings, the majesty forever. Amen; My Lord Jesus Christ, my good Savior.	ثوك تيه تى جُم نيم بى أوؤو نيم بى إسموو نيم بى أماهى شا إينيه آمين . باتشويس إيسوس بي خرستوس باسوتير إن أغاثوس .	Ѳⲱⲕ ⲧⲉ ϯϫⲟⲙ ⲛⲉⲙ ⲡⲓⲱⲟⲩ ⲛⲉⲙ ⲡⲓⲥⲙⲟⲩ ⲛⲉⲙ ⲡⲓⲁⲙⲁϩⲓ ϣⲁ ⲉⲛⲉϩ ⲁⲙⲏⲛ : Ⲡϭⲟⲓⲥ Ⲓⲏⲥⲟⲩⲥ Ⲡⲓⲭⲣⲓⲥⲧⲟⲥ Ⲡⲁⲥⲱⲧⲏⲣ ⲛ̀ⲁⲅⲁⲑⲟⲥ.	لكَ القوة والمجد والبركة والعزة إلى الأبد آمين ياربى يسوع المسيح مخلصى الصالح .
Thine is the power, the glory, the blessings, the majesty forever. Amen.	ثوك تيه تى جُم نيم بى أوؤو نيم بى إسموو نيم بى أماهى شا إينيه آمين .	Ѳⲱⲕ ⲧⲉ ϯϫⲟⲙ ⲛⲉⲙ ⲡⲓⲱⲟⲩ ⲛⲉⲙ ⲡⲓⲥⲙⲟⲩ ⲛⲉⲙ ⲡⲓⲁⲙⲁϩⲓ ϣⲁ ⲉⲛⲉϩ ⲁⲙⲏⲛ.	لكَ القوة والمجد والبركة والعزة إلى الأبد آمين
Our Father Who art...		ⲭⲉ Ⲡⲉⲛⲓⲱⲧ ...	ابانا الذى فى ....

Pascha Praise – C: *From the First Hour of the Great Friday Eve to the end of the Pascha*

تسبحة البصخة - C : من الساعة الأولى من ليلة الجمعة العظيمة الى نهاية البصخة المقدسة

English	Transliteration	Coptic	Arabic
Thine is the power, the glory, the blessings, the majesty forever. Amen; Emmanuel our God and King.	ثوك تيه تى جُم نيم بى أوؤو نيم بى إسموو نيم بى أماهى شا إينيه آمين . إمانوئيل بين نوتى بين أوورو .	Ѳⲱⲕ ⲧⲉ ϯϫⲟⲙ ⲛⲉⲙ ⲡⲓⲱⲟⲩ ⲛⲉⲙ ⲡⲓⲥⲙⲟⲩ ⲛⲉⲙ ⲡⲓⲁⲙⲁϩⲓ ϣⲁ ⲉⲛⲉϩ ⲁⲙⲏⲛ Ⲉⲙⲙⲁⲛⲟⲩⲏⲗ ⲡⲉⲛⲛⲟⲩϯ ⲡⲉⲛⲟⲩⲣⲟ.	لك القوة والمجد والبركة والعزة إلى الأبد آمين عمانوئيل إلهنا وملكنا .
Thine is the power, the glory, the blessings, the majesty forever. Amen; My Lord Jesus Christ, my good Savior. The Lord is my strength, my praise, and has become my salvation.	ثوك تيه تى جُم نيم بى أوؤو نيم بى إسموو نيم بى أماهى شا إينيه آمين . باتشويس إيسوس بي خرستوس باسوتير إن أغاثوس طا جُم نيم با إسموو بيه إبتشويس أفشوبى نى إف سوتيريا إفؤواب .	Ѳⲱⲕ ⲧⲉ ϯϫⲟⲙ ⲛⲉⲙ ⲡⲓⲱⲟⲩ ⲛⲉⲙ ⲡⲓⲥⲙⲟⲩ ⲛⲉⲙ ⲡⲓⲁⲙⲁϩⲓ ϣⲁ ⲉⲛⲉϩ ⲁⲙⲏⲛ : Ⲡϭⲟⲓⲥ Ⲓⲏⲥⲟⲩⲥ Ⲡⲓⲭⲣⲓⲥⲧⲟⲥ Ⲡⲁⲥⲱⲧⲏⲣ ⲛ̀ⲁⲅⲁⲑⲟⲥ : ⲧⲁϫⲟⲙ ⲛⲉⲙ ⲡⲁⲥⲙⲟⲩ ⲡⲉ Ⲡϭⲟⲓⲥ : ⲁϥϣⲱⲡⲓ ⲛⲏⲓ ⲉⲩⲥⲱⲧⲏⲣⲓⲁ ⲉϥⲟⲩⲁⲃ.	لك القوة والمجد والبركة والعزة إلى الأبد آمين ياربى يسوع المسيح مخلصى الصالح . قوتى وتسبحتى هو الرب و صار لى خلاصاً مقدساً .

Thine is the power, the glory, the blessings, the majesty forever. Amen.	ثوك تيه تى جُم نيم بى أوؤو نيم بى إسموو نيم بى أماهى شا إينيه آمين .	Ѳⲱⲕ ⲧⲉ ϯϫⲟⲙ ⲛⲉⲙ ⲡⲓⲱⲟⲩ ⲛⲉⲙ ⲡⲓⲥⲙⲟⲩ ⲛⲉⲙ ⲡⲓⲁⲙⲁϩⲓ ϣⲁ ⲉ̀ⲛⲉϩ ⲁⲙⲏⲛ ⲉ	لك القوة والمجد والبركة والعزة إلى الأبد آمين
Our Father Who art...		ⲝⲉ Ⲡⲉⲛⲓⲱⲧ...	ابانا الذى فى ....

Introduction to the reading of the Holy Gospel in Coptic
مقدمة الانجيل المقروء باللغة القبطية

We beseech our Lord and God, that we may be worthy to hear the Holy Gospel. In wisdom, let us attend to the Holy Gospel.	كيه إبيرتوو كاطا كسيو ثينا إيماس . تيس أكرو آسينوس طوو أجيوو إف أنجيليوو . كيريون طون ثيئون إيمون إيكيتيف صومين صوفيا أورثى : ألك أووصومين طوو أجيوو إف أنجيليون .	Ⲕⲉ ⲩ̀ⲡⲉⲣⲧⲟⲩ ⲕⲁⲧⲁⲝⲓⲱ ⲑⲏⲛⲉ ⲏ̀ⲙⲁⲥ : Ⲧⲏⲥ ⲁⲕⲣⲟ ⲁ̀ⲥⲉⲱⲥ ⲧⲟⲩ ⲁ̀ⲅⲓⲟⲩ ⲉⲩⲁⲅⲅⲉⲗⲓⲟⲩ : ⲕⲩⲣⲓⲟⲛ ⲕⲉ ⲧⲟⲛ ⲑⲉⲟⲛ ⲏ̀ⲙⲱⲛ : ⲓⲕⲉⲧⲉⲩⲥⲱⲙⲉⲛ ⲥⲟⲫⲓⲁ̀ ⲟⲣⲑⲓ ⲁ̀ⲕⲟⲩⲥⲱⲙⲉⲛ ⲧⲟⲩ ⲁ̀ⲅⲓⲟⲩ ⲉⲩⲁⲅⲅⲉⲗⲓⲟ.	لكى نكون مستحقين لسماع الإنجيل الإلهى المقدس. نتوسل من ربنا وإلهنا . إصغوا وإنصتوا بحكمة للانجيل المقدس .
A reading from the Holy Gospel according to St. (....)	أوو أناغنوسيس إيفول خين بى إيف أنجيليون إثؤواب كاطا (.....) أجيوو .	Ⲟⲩ̀ⲁⲛⲁⲅⲛⲱⲥⲓⲥ ⲉ̀ⲃⲟⲗ ϧⲉⲛ ⲡⲓⲉⲩⲁⲅⲅⲉⲗⲓⲟⲛ ⲉⲑⲟⲩⲁⲃ ⲕⲁⲧⲁ (....) ⲁ̀ⲅⲓⲟⲩ.	فصل من الانجيل المقدس حسب قول (......) .

Introduction to the reading of the Holy Gospel in English or Arabic
مقدمة الانجيل باللغة العربية او الانجليزية

O God have mercy and compassion upon us, and make us worthy to hear Your Holy Gospel. A reading according to Saint (Matthew, or Mark, or Luke, or John). May his blessings be with us. Amen.	اللهم تراءف علينا و ارحمنا و اجعلنا مستحقّين لسماع انجيلك المقدس ، فصل من بشارة الانجيل لمعلمنا (مار متى أو مرقس أو لوقا أو يوحنا) البشير ، بركاته علينا آمين.

Introduction to the Exposition at the Daytime Hours
مقدمة الطرح فى ساعات النهار

English	Arabic transliteration	Coptic	Arabic
-In the name of the Trinity,	- خين إفران إن تى إترياس :	- Ϧⲉⲛ ⲫ̀ⲣⲁⲛ ⲛ̀ϯⲧⲣⲓⲁⲥ :	- باسم الثالوث
- One in Essence,	- إن أوو مووؤوسيوس :	- ⲛ̀ⲟⲩⲙⲟⲟⲩⲥⲓⲟⲥ :	- المساوى
- The Father and the Son,	- إفيوت نيم إبشيري :	- ⲫⲓⲱⲧ ⲛⲉⲙ ⲡ̀ϣⲏⲣⲓ :	- الآب والإبن
- And the Holy Spirit	- نيم بى بنيفما إثؤواب .	- ⲛⲉⲙ ⲡⲓⲡⲛⲉⲩⲙⲁ ⲉⲑⲟⲩⲁⲃ .	- والروح القدس .
- O true light,	- بى أووأوينى إنطافمى :	- Ⲡⲓⲟⲩⲱⲓⲛⲓ ⲛ̀ⲧⲁⲫ̀ⲙⲏⲓ :	- أيها النور الحقيقى
- Who enlightens,	- في إتنر أووأوينى :	- ⲫⲏ ⲉⲧⲉⲣⲟⲩⲱⲓⲛⲓ :	- الذى يضىئ
- Every man,	- إيه رومى نيفين :	- ⲉ̀ⲣⲱⲙⲓ ⲛⲓⲃⲉⲛ :	- لكل إنسان
- Who comes into the world	- إثنيوو إيه بى كوزموس .	- ⲉⲑⲛⲏⲟⲩ ⲉ̀ⲡⲓⲕⲟⲥⲙⲟⲥ .	- آتٍ إلى العالم .

Introduction to the Exposition at the Nighttime Hours
مقدمة الطرح فى ساعات الليل

English	Arabic transliteration	Coptic	Arabic
-In the name of the Trinity	- خين إفران إن تى إترياس :	- Ϧⲉⲛ ⲫ̀ⲣⲁⲛ ⲛ̀ϯⲧⲣⲓⲁⲥ :	- باسم الثالوث
- One in Essence	- إن أوو مووؤوسيوس :	- ⲛ̀ⲟⲩⲙⲟⲟⲩⲥⲓⲟⲥ :	- المساوى
- The Father and the Son	- إفيوت نيم إبشيري :	- ⲫⲓⲱⲧ ⲛⲉⲙ ⲡ̀ϣⲏⲣⲓ :	- الآب والإبن
- And the Holy Spirit	- نيم بى بنيفما إثؤواب .	- ⲛⲉⲙ ⲡⲓⲡⲛⲉⲩⲙⲁ ⲉⲑⲟⲩⲁⲃ .	- والروح القدس
- Hail to you Mary	- شيريه نيه ماريا :	- Ⲭⲉⲣⲉ ⲛⲉ Ⲙⲁⲣⲓⲁ :	- السلام لك يا مريم
- The fair dove	- تى تشرومبى إثنيسوس :	- ϯϭⲣⲟⲙⲡⲓ ⲉⲑⲛⲉⲥⲱⲥ :	- الحمامة الحسنة
- Who has born unto us	- ثي إطاس ميسى نان :	- ⲑⲏ ⲉⲧⲁⲥⲙⲓⲥⲓ ⲛⲁⲛ :	- التى ولدت لنا
- God the Logos	- إم إفنووتى بى لوغوس .	- ⲙ̀Ⲫⲛⲟⲩϯ ⲡⲓⲗⲟⲅⲟⲥ .	- الله الكلمة

The Conclusion of the Exposition, at both Nighttime and Daytime hours
ختام الطرح فى ساعات الليل و ساعات النهار

English	Arabic transliteration	Coptic	Arabic
- Christ our Savior	- بيخرستوس بين سوتير :	- Ⲡⲓⲭ̀ⲣⲓⲥⲧⲟⲥ ⲡⲉⲛⲥⲱⲧⲏⲣ :	- المسيح مخلصنا
- Has come and has borne suffering	- أفنى أفشيب إمكاه :	- ⲁϥⲓ̀ ⲁϥϣⲉⲡ̀ⲙⲕⲁϩ :	- جاء وتألم عنا
- That through His Passion	- هينا خين نيف إمكاه :	- ϩⲓⲛⲁ Ϧⲉⲛ ⲛⲉϥⲙ̀ⲕⲁϩ :	- لكى بألامه
- He may save us	- إنتيف سوتى إممون .	- ⲛ̀ⲧⲉϥⲥⲱϯ ⲙ̀ⲙⲟⲛ .	- يخلصنا
- Let us glorify Him,	- مارين تى أوأوو ناف :	- Ⲙⲁⲣⲉⲛ ϯⲱ̀ⲟⲩ ⲛⲁϥ :	- فلنمجده
- And exalt His Name,	- تين تشيسى إمبيف ران :	- ⲧⲉⲛϭⲓⲥⲓ ⲙ̀ⲡⲉϥⲣⲁⲛ :	- و نرفع إسمه
- For He has done us mercy	- جيه أفئر أوونا ى نيمان :	- ⲭⲉ ⲁϥⲉⲣⲟⲩⲛⲁⲓ ⲛⲉⲙⲁⲛ :	- لأنه صنع معنا رحمة
- According to His great mercy	- كاطا بيف نيشتى إن ناى .	- ⲕⲁⲧⲁ ⲡⲉϥⲛⲓϣϯ ⲛ̀ⲛⲁⲓ .	- كعظيم رحمته

The Daytime Litanies

طلبة الصباح

The priest prays these litanies with Metanoia (worships) and all are fasting.

يقول الكاهن طلبة الصباح مع المطانيات و الكل صائماً.

Priest	Priest الكاهن	يقول الكاهن
Let us bow our knees	К̀лінῶмєη ταϩοηατα	نحنى ركبنا .
Congregation	Congregation الشعب	يقول الشعب
Have mercy upon us O God the Father, the Pantocrator.	наі наη Ф̀ηογϯ Ф̀іῶτ піпантократῶр	إرحمنا يا الله الآب ضابط الكل .
Priest	Priest الكاهن	يقول الكاهن
Let us stand. Let us bow our knees.	анαϲτῶμєη К̀лінῶμє ταϩοηατα	نقف ثم نحنى ركبنــا .
Congregation	Congregation الشعب	يقول الشعب
Have mercy upon us O God our Savior.	наі наη Ф̀ηογϯ пєηϲῶτηρ	إرحمنا يا الله مخلصنــا .
Priest	Priest الكاهن	يقول الكاهن
And let us stand. Let us bow our knees.	кєанαϲτῶμєη К̀лінῶμєη ταϩοηατα	ثم نقف و نحنى ركبنــا .
Congregation	Congregation الشعب	يقول الشعب
Have mercy upon us, O God, have mercy upon us.	наінаη Ф̀ηογϯ ογο8 наі наη	إرحمنا يا الله ثم إرحمنــا .

Priest
(Congregation prays, Lord have mercy, after each litany)

يقول الكاهن
(يرد الشعب يارب ارحم بعد كل صلاة)

+ Let us pray that God may have mercy and compassion on us, hear us, help us, and accept the supplications and prayers of His saints for that which is good on our behalf at all times, and forgive us our sins.

+ اطلبوا لكى يرحمنا الله ويتراءف علينا ويسمعنا ويعيننا ويقبل سؤالات وطلبات قديسه منهم عنا بالصلاح فى كل حين . ويغفر لنا خطايانا.

+ Let us pray for the peace of the one, holy, catholic, and apostolic church, and for God's salvation and comfort to abide in all places, and forgive us our sins.

+ اطلبوا عن سلام كنيسة الله الواحدة الوحيدة المقدسة الجامعة الرسولية. وخلاص الله فى الشعوب والطمأنينة بكل موضع . ويغفر لنا خطايانا.

+ Let us pray for our fathers and our brethren who are sick with any sickness, whether in this place or in any place, that the Lord our God may grant us, with them health and healing, and forgive us our sins.

+ اطلبوا عن أبائنا وأخوتنا المرضى بكل الأمراض فى هذا الموضع وكل مكان لكى ينعم لنا الرب إلهنا وإياهم بالعافية والشفاء . ويغفر لنا خطايانا.

+ Let us pray and ask for our fathers and brethren in all places who are traveling or planning to travel, that God may ease their ways, whether by seas, rivers, lakes, roads, air or other means, and may the Lord our God guide them, return them in safety, and forgive us our sins.

+ صلوا واطلبوا عن أبائنا وأخواتنا المسافرين والذين أضمروا السفر بكل مكان ليسهل طرقهم جميعاً إن كانوا فى الجو او البحار أو الأنهار أو الينابيع أو الطرق المسلوكة والذين جعلوا سفرهم بكل نوع لكى يرشدهم الرب إلهنا ويرجعهم إلى مساكنهم بسلام ويغفر لنا خطايانا .

+ Let us pray and ask for the air of heaven, the fruits of the earth, the trees and vineyards, and all fruit-bearing trees everywhere, that Christ our God may bless them, and forgive us our sins.

+ صلوا واطلبوا عن أهوية السماء وثمرات الأرض وكل الأشجار والكروم وكل شجرة مثمرة فى جميع المسكونة لكى يباركها الرب إلهنا ويكملها بسلام . ويغفر لنا خطايانا .

+ Let us pray and ask that God may grant us mercy before leading authorities, incline their hearts with goodwill towards us always, and forgive us our sins.

+ صلوا واطلبوا لكى يعطينا الله رحمة ورأفة أمام السلاطين الأعزاء ويعطف قلوب المتولين علينا بالصلاح فى كل حين . ويغفر لنا خطايانا .

+ Let us pray and ask for our fathers and brethren who have fallen asleep and reposed in the faith of Christ since the beginning, our holy fathers the patriarchs, metropolitans, bishops, hegumens, priests, our brethren the deacons, our fathers the monks and our brethren the laymen, and for the rest of all departed Christians, that the Lord our God may repose all their souls, and forgive us our sins.

+ صلوا واطلبوا عن أبائنا واخوتنا الذين رقدوا وتنيحوا فى الإيمان بالمسيح منذ البدء آبائنا البطاركة وآبائنا المطارنة وآبائنا الأساقفة وآبائنا القمامصة وآبائنا القسوس واخوتنا الشمامسة وآبائنا الرهبان واخوتنا العلمانيين وعن كل الذين تنيحوا من المسيحين لكى ينيح الرب إلهنا نفوسهم أجمعين . ويغفر لنا خطايانا .

+ Let us pray and ask for those who care for the sacrifices, offerings, wine, oil, incense, coverings, reading books, and all the altar vessels, that the Lord our God may reward their labors in the heavenly Jerusalem, and forgive us our sins.

+ صلوا واطلبوا عن المهتمين بالصعائد والقرابين والخمر والزيت والبخور والستور وكتب القراءة وكل أوانى المذبح لكى يعوضهم الرب إلهنا عن أتعابهم فى أورشليم السمائية . ويغفر لنا خطايانا.

+ Let us pray and ask for the catechumens of our people, that our Lord may bless them, open the eyes of their hearts, and confirm them in the Orthodox faith until their last breath, and forgive us our sins.

+ Let us pray and ask for this church and for all churches of the Orthodox people, for the desert monasteries and their elders, and for the peace of the whole world, that the Lord our God may protect both us and them from all evil, and forgive us our sins.

+ Let us pray and ask for the life and standing of our honorable father, the Patriarch and Archbishop Pope Abba (...), [and his partner in the apostolic liturgy, our father the bishop (metropolitan), Abba that the Lord may preserve his life, and confirm him (them) in his (their) see(s) for many years and peaceful times, and forgive us our sins.

+ Let us pray and ask for our Orthodox fathers everywhere, the metropolitans, bishops, hegumens, priests, deacons, and all the orders of the Church, that Christ our God may preserve and strengthen them, and forgive us our sins.

+ Let us pray and ask for this assembly of ours and for all assemblies of the Orthodox people, that the Lord our God may bless them and fulfill them in peace, and forgive us our sins.

+ Let us pray and ask for the hierarchs of the holy Church, and for all the orders of the clergy, that the Lord our God may bless and strengthen them, and forgive us our sins.

+ Let us pray and ask for those who toil in the holy Church and for the Orthodox people, that the Lord our God may have mercy on them, and forgive us our sins.

+ Let us pray and ask for all Christ-loving rulers who asked us to pray for them by name, that the Lord our God may remember them in His mercy and grant them favor before powerful rulers, and forgive us our sins.

+ صلوا واطلبوا عن موعظى شعبنا لكى يباركهم الرب ويفتح عيون قلوبهم ويثبتهم على الإيمان الأرثوذوكسى إلى النفس الأخير . ويغفر لنا خطايانا .

+ صلوا واطلبوا عن هذا المسكن وكل مساكن وديارات الشعوب الأرثوذوكسيين فى البرارى والشيوخ السكان فيها وعن طمأنينة كل العالم معاً . لكى يحفظنا الرب إلهنا وإياهم من كل سوء ومن كل شر . ويغفر لنا خطايانا .

+ صلوا واطلبوا عن حياة وقيام أبينا المكرم رئيس الأساقفة الآب البطريرك أنبا (.....) (وكذلك شريكه فى الخدمة الرسولية الآب المطران أو الأسقف) لكى يحفظ الرب لنا حياتهم ويثبتهم على كراسيهم سنين عديدة وأزمنة سالمة هادئة مديدة ويغفر لنا خطايانا .

+ صلوا واطلبوا عن آبائنا المطارنة والأساقفة الأرثوذوكسيين بكل مكان والقمامصة والقسوس والشمامسة وكل طغمات الكنيسة لكى يحفظهم المسيح إلهنا ويقويهم . ويغفر لنا خطايانا .

+ صلوا واطلبوا عن إجتماعنا هذا وكل إجتماع الشعوب الأرثوذوكسيين لكى يباركهم الرب إلهنا ويكملهم بسلام . ويغفر لنا خطايانا .

+ صلوا واطلبوا عن تدبير البيعة المقدسة وكل رتب الكهنوت لكى يباركهم الرب إلهنا ويقويهم. ويغفر لنا خطايانا .

+ صلوا واطلبوا عن كل نفس لها تعب فى الكنيسة المقدسة ومع الشعب الأرثوذوكسى لكى يصنع الرب إلهنا معهم رحمة . ويغفر لنا خطايانا .

+ صلوا واطلبوا عن محبى المسيح الرؤساء الذين أمرونا أن نذكرهم بأسمائهم لكى يباركهم الرب إلهنا ويذكرهم بالرحمة ويعطيهم النعمة أمام السلاطين الأعزاء . ويغفر لنا خطايانا .

+ Let us pray and ask for the poor, the weak, the farmers, and for every soul in any type of hardship, that the Lord our God may have compassion on them and on us, and forgive us our sins.

+ صلوا واطلبوا عن المساكين والفلاحين والضعفاء وعن كل نفس متضايقة بكل نوع لكى يتراءف الرب إلهنا عليهم وإيانا . ويغفر لنا خطايانا.

+ Let us pray and ask for those in the distress of jails, prisons, captivity, or exile, and for those bound by devils, that the Lord our God may free them from their hardships, and forgive us our sins.

+ صلوا واطلبوا عن كل المتضايقين الذين فى السجون وفى المطابق والذين فى النفى أو فى السبى والمربوطين من جهة رباطات الشياطين لكى يعتقهم الرب إلهنا من متاعبهم . ويغفر لنا خطايانا .

+ Let us pray and ask for all those gathered with us today in this place, seeking mercy for their souls, that the Lord's mercy may encompass both us and them, and forgive us our sins.

+ صلوا واطلبوا عن كل النفوس المجتمعة معنا اليوم فى هذا الموضع يطلبون الرحمة لنفوسهم لكى تدركنا مراحم الرب إلهنا وإياهم . ويغفر لنا خطايانا .

+ Let us pray and ask for each person by name who asked us to remember them in our prayers, that the Lord our God may always remember them in His goodness, and forgive us our sins.

+ صلوا واطلبوا عن الذين أوصونا أن نذكرهم كل واحد بإسمه لكى يذكرهم الرب إلهنا بالصلاح فى كل حين . ويغفر لنا خطايانا .

+ Let us pray and ask for the rising of the waters of the rivers this year, that Christ our God may bless them and raise them according to their measure, give joy to all the earth with the rivers (Nile), sustain us and deliver man and animal, and spare the world from death, scarcity, plagues, devastation, the sword of the enemies, and that He may grant calm, peace, and security to the holy Church, and raise the state of Christians in every place on earth until the last breath, and forgive us our sins.

+ صلوا واطلبوا عن صعود مياه الأنهار فى هذه السنة لكى يباركها المسيح إلهنا ويصعدها كمقدارها ويفرح وجه الأرض بالنيل (بالانهار) ويعولنا نحن البشر ويعطى الناجاة لشعبه والبهائم ويرفع عن العالم الموت والغلاء والوباء والفناء والجلاء وسيف الأعداء ويجعل الهدوء والسلام والطمأنينة فى البيعة المقدسة ويرفع شأن المسيحيين فى كل مكان وفى كل المسكونة إلى النفس الأخير . ويغفر لنا خطايانا .

+ Let us pray and ask for this holy Pascha of our good Savior, that He may complete it for us in peace and bring us the joy of His holy Resurrection in safety, and forgive us our sins.

+ صلوا واطلبوا عن هذه البصخة المقدسة التى لمخلصنا الصالح لكى يكملها لنا بسلام ويرينا بهجة قيامته المقدسة ونحن جميعاً سالمين . ويغفر لنا خطايانا.

Priest - الكاهن

+ Ⲫⲛⲟⲩϯ ⲛⲁⲓ ⲛⲁⲛ ⲑⲉϣⲟⲩⲛⲁⲓ ⲉⲣⲟⲛ ⲁⲣⲓⲟⲩⲛⲁⲓ ⲛⲉⲙⲁⲛ ϧⲉⲛ ⲧⲉⲕⲙⲉⲧⲟⲩⲣⲟ ⲁ

+ إفنووتى ناى نان ثيه شووناى إرون أرى أووناى نيمان خين تيك ميت أوورو.

+ God, have mercy on us, settle your mercy upon us, show us mercy in Your Kingdom.

+ اللهم ارحمنا . قرر لنا رحمة . اصنع معنا رحمة فى ملكوتك.

Congregation replies Kirye Elison 12 times, saying: ويجاوبه الشعب كيرى ليسون 12 دفعة صارخين:

English	Coptic (transliteration)	Coptic	Arabic
O King of peace, grant us Your peace, establish for us Your peace, and forgive us our sins.	إبؤورو إنتيه تى هيرينى : موى نان إنتيك هيرينى : سيمنى نان إنتيك هيرينى : كا نين نوفى نان إيفول .	Ⲡ̀ⲟⲩⲣⲟ ⲛ̀ⲧⲉ ϯⲉⲓⲣⲏⲛⲏ : ⲙⲟⲓ ⲛⲁⲛ ⲛ̀ⲧⲉⲕϩⲓⲣⲏⲛⲏ : ⲥⲉⲙⲛⲓ ⲛⲁⲛ ⲛ̀ⲧⲉⲕϩⲓⲣⲏⲛⲏ : ⲭⲁ ⲛⲉⲛⲛⲟⲃⲓ ⲛⲁⲛ ⲉ̀ⲃⲟⲗ ⲁ	+ يا ملك السلام : إعطنا سلامك : قرر لنا سلامك . وإغفر لنا خطايانا .
Lord have mercy	كيريه ليسون	**Ⲕⲩⲣⲓⲉ̀ ⲉ̀ⲗⲉ̀ⲏⲥⲟⲛ**	يارب ارحم
Disperse the enemies, of the Church, and fortify her, that she may not be shaken forever.	جور إيفول إن نى جاجى : إنتيه تى إككليسيا : أرى صوبت إروس إن نيسكيم شا إنيه .	Ⲭⲱⲣ ⲉ̀ⲃⲟⲗ ⲛ̀ⲛⲓϫⲁϫⲓ : ⲛ̀ⲧⲉ ϯⲉⲕⲕⲗⲏⲥⲓⲁ : ⲁⲣⲓⲥⲟⲃⲧ ⲉ̀ⲣⲟⲥ ⲛ̀ⲛⲉⲥⲕⲓⲙ ϣⲁ ⲉ̀ⲛⲉϩ ⲁ	+ فرق أعداء الكنيسة : وحصنها فلا تتزعزع إلى الأبد
Lord have mercy	كيريه ليسون	**Ⲕⲩⲣⲓⲉ̀ ⲉ̀ⲗⲉ̀ⲏⲥⲟⲛ**	يارب ارحم
Immanuel our God, is now in our midst, with the glory of His Father, and the Holy Spirit.	إممانوئيل بين نووتى : خين تين ميتى تينور : خين إبؤوو إنتيه بيف يوت : نيم بى بنيقما إثؤواب	Ⲉⲙⲙⲁⲛⲟⲩⲏⲗ ⲡⲉⲛⲛⲟⲩϯ : ϧⲉⲛ ⲧⲉⲛⲙⲏϯ ϯⲛⲟⲩ : ϧⲉⲛ ⲡ̀ⲱⲟⲩ ⲛ̀ⲧⲉ ⲡⲉϥⲓⲱⲧ : ⲛⲉⲙ ⲡⲓⲡ̀ⲛⲁ ⲉⲑ	+ عمانوئيل إلهنا : فى وسطنا الآن : بمجد أبيه : والروح القدس .
Lord have mercy	كيريه ليسون	**Ⲕⲩⲣⲓⲉ̀ ⲉ̀ⲗⲉ̀ⲏⲥⲟⲛ**	يارب ارحم
May He bless us all, and purify our hearts, and heal the sicknesses, of our souls and bodies.	إنتيف إسموو إرون تيرين : إنتيف طوفوو إننين هيت : إنتيف طالتشو إن نى شونى : إنتيه نين بسيشى نيم نين صوما .	Ⲛ̀ⲧⲉϥⲥⲙⲟⲩ ⲉ̀ⲣⲟⲛ ⲧⲏⲣⲉⲛ ⲛ̀ⲧⲉϥⲧⲟⲩⲃⲟ ⲛ̀ⲛⲉⲛϩⲏⲧ ⲛ̀ⲧⲉϥⲧⲁⲗϭⲟ ⲛ̀ⲛⲓϣⲱⲛⲓ : ⲛ̀ⲧⲉ ⲛⲉⲛⲯⲩⲭⲏ ⲛⲉⲙ ⲛⲉⲛⲥⲱⲙⲁ ⲁ	+ ليياركنا كلنا ويطهر قلوبنا : ويشفى أمراض : نفوسنا وأجسادنا
Lord have mercy	كيريه ليسون	**Ⲕⲩⲣⲓⲉ̀ ⲉ̀ⲗⲉ̀ⲏⲥⲟⲛ**	يارب ارحم
We worship You O Christ, with Your good Father, and the Holy Spirit, for You were crucified and saved us.	تين أووأوشت إمموك أو بيخرستوس نيم بيك يوت إن أغاثوس : نيم بى بنيفما إثؤواب : جيه أف أشك أك صوتى إممون .	Ⲧⲉⲛⲟⲩⲱϣⲧ ⲙ̀ⲙⲟⲕ ⲱ̀ Ⲡⲓⲭ̀ⲣⲓⲥⲧⲟⲥ ⲛⲉⲙ ⲡⲉⲕⲓⲱⲧ ⲛ̀ⲁⲅⲁⲑⲟⲥ : ⲛⲉⲙ ⲡⲓⲡ̀ⲛⲉⲩⲙⲁ ⲉⲑⲟⲩⲁⲃ : ϫⲉ ⲁⲕϣⲱⲕ ⲁⲕⲥⲱϯ ⲙ̀ⲙⲟⲛ ⲁ	+ نسجد لك أيها المسيح : مع أبيك الصالح : والروح القدس : لأنك صلبت وخلصتنا .

Amen. Alleluia. Glory to the Father and to the Son and to the Holy Spirit. Now and ever and unto the ages of the ages. Amen.

We proclaim and say, O our Lord Jesus Christ, who was crucified on the Cross, trample Satan under our feet. Save us and have mercy on us. Lord have mercy. Lord have mercy. Lord bless us. Amen. Bless me. Bless me. Lo, the repentance (metanoia). Forgive me. Say the blessing.

آمين الليلويا ، ذوكسابترى كى ايو كى اجيو ابنيفماتى ، كينين كى أ أى كى استوس اى اوناس تون اى اونون ، آمين.

تين اوش ايفول انجو اموس : جى اوبينشويس ايسوس بى اخريستوس : فى اطاف أشف ابيسطافروس : إك إيه خُمخيم إم إبصاطانّاس صا بيسيت إنين تشالافج : سوتى امون اووه ناينان : كيرى ليسون كيرى ليسون كيرى افلوجيسون آمين ، ازمو اى روى ازمو اى روى اس تى روى اى تى ماتانويا : كونى ايفول جو امبى اسمو.

Ⲁⲙⲏⲛ ⲁⲗ : ⲇⲟⲝⲁⲡⲁⲧⲣⲓ ⲕⲉ Ⲩⲓⲱ ⲕⲉ ⲁ̀ⲅⲓⲱ Ⲡⲛⲉⲩⲙⲁⲧⲓ : Ⲕⲉ ⲛⲩⲛ ⲕⲉ ⲁ̀ⲓ ⲕⲉ ⲓⲥ ⲧⲟⲩⲥ ⲉ̀ⲱⲛⲁⲥ ⲧⲱⲛ ⲉ̀ⲱⲛⲱⲛ : ⲁ̀ⲙⲏⲛ.

Ⲧⲉⲛⲱϣ ⲉ̀ⲃⲟⲗ ⲉⲛⲭⲱ ⲙ̀ⲙⲟⲥ : ϫⲉ ⲱ̀Ⲡⲉⲛⲟ̅ⲥ̅ Ⲓⲏⲥ Ⲡⲭⲥ . Ⲫⲏ ⲉⲧⲁⲩⲁϣϥ ⲉ̀ⲡⲓⲥⲧⲁⲩⲣⲟⲥ : ⲉⲕⲉ̀ϧⲟⲙϧⲉⲙ ⲙ̀ⲡⲥⲁⲧⲁⲛⲁⲥ ⲥⲁ ⲡⲉⲥⲏⲧ ⲛ̀ⲛⲉⲛⲃ̀ⲁⲗⲁⲩⲭ : ⲥⲱϯ ⲙ̀ⲙⲟⲛ ⲟⲩⲟϩ ⲛⲁⲓⲛⲁⲛ : Ⲕⲩⲣⲓⲉ̀ ⲉ̀ⲗⲉⲏⲥⲟⲛ Ⲕⲩⲣⲓⲉ̀ ⲉ̀ⲗⲉⲏⲥⲟⲛ Ⲕⲩⲣⲓⲉ̀ ⲉⲩⲗⲟⲅⲏⲥⲟⲛ ⲁ̀ⲙⲏⲛ. ⲥⲙⲟⲩ ⲉ̀ⲣⲟⲓ ⲥⲙⲟⲩ ⲉ̀ⲣⲟⲓ : ⲓⲥ ϯⲙⲉⲧⲁⲛⲟⲓ̀ⲁ : ⲭⲱⲛⲏⲓ ⲉ̀ⲃⲟⲗ ⲭⲱ ⲙ̀ⲡⲓⲥⲙⲟⲩ.

آمين الليلويا المجد للآب و الابن و الروح القدس ، الآن و كل اوان و الى دهر الداهرين ، آمين .

نصرخ قائلين يا ربنا يسوع المسيح الذى صلب على الصليب ، إسحق الشيطان تحت أقدامنا خلصنا و ارحمنا. يارب ارحم ، يارب ارحم ، يارب بارك آمين . باركوا علىّ باركوا علىّ ها الميطانية اغفروا لى . فلتنقل البركة.

Priest
الكاهن

May Jesus Christ, our true God, who through His own goodwill accepted sufferings, and was crucified on the cross for our sakes, bless us with all spiritual blessings, and support us, and complete for us the Holy Pascha, and bring forth upon us the joy of His Holy Resurrection for many years and peaceful times. Through the supplications and prayers which our lady, the lady of us all, the holy Theotokos Saint Mary makes for us at all times, and those of the three great holy luminaries, Michael, Gabriel and Raphael; and all the angels and heavenly ranks. And through the prayers of the Patriarchs, prophets, Apostles, martyrs, the whole choir of the cross-bearers; the justs, the righteous and the angel of this blessed day. And through the blessing of this Holy Pascha of our Good Savior. May their holy blessings, their benediction, their power, their gift, their love, and their help be with us all forever. Amen.

يسوع المسيح إلهنا الحقيقى الذى قبل الآلام بإرادته وصلب على الصليب من أجلنا . يباركنا بكل بركة روحية ويعيننا ويكمل لنا البصخة المقدسة ويرينا فرح قيامته المقدسة سنين كثيرة وأزمنة سالمة . بالسؤلات والطلبات التى تصنعها عنا كل حين سيدتنا وملكتنا كلنا والدة الإله القديسة مريم والثلاثة المنيرين الأطهار ميخائيل وغبريال ورافائيل . وجميع مصاف الملائكة وكل الطغمات السمائية . وصلوات رؤساء الآباء والأنبياء والرسل والشهداء ومصاف لباس الصليب والأبرار والصديقين وملاك هذا اليوم المبارك ، وبركة البصخة المقدسة التى لمخلصنا الصالح . بركتهم المقدسة ونعمتهم وقوتهم وهبتهم ومحبتهم ومعونتهم تكون معنا كلنا إلى الأبد آمين .

O Christ our God

Ⲡⲓⲭ̅ⲣⲓⲥⲧⲟⲥ Ⲡⲉⲛⲛⲟⲩϯ

ايها المسيح الهنا

Amen. So be it

Ⲁ̀ⲙⲏⲛ ⲉⲥⲉϣⲱⲡⲓ

آمين يكون

Priest	الكاهن
O King of peace, give us your peace, settle your peace upon us, and forgive us our sins. For Thine is the power, the glory, the blessings, and the majesty forever. Amen.	يا ملك السلام : إعطنا سلامك : قرر لنا سلامك . وإغفر لنا خطايانا . لان لك القوة والمجد والبركة والعزة إلى الأبد آمين .
Make us worthy to pray thankfully:	**اللهم اجعلنا مستحقين ان نقول جميعا بشكر**
Our Father Who art in Heaven.......	**أبانا الذى فى السموات .....**
Go in peace, and may the peace of the Lord be with you all, Amin.	**أمضوا بسلام و سلام الرب يكون معكم ، آمين.**

Nighttime Litanies
(Without Metanoia)

طلبة المساء
(بدون ميطانيات)

+ We ask and entreat You, O Lord God the Father, the Pantocrator, and the holy Only-Begotten Son, who created and ordered all things, and the Holy Spirit, the Giver of life, the Holy Trinity, before whom every knee bows in heaven and on earth. We ask You, O Lord, hear us and have mercy on

+ For the heavenly peace and unity of all churches in the world, monasteries, and for those dwelling in and caring for all holy places, O God, have compassion on Your creation and deliver it from all evil. We ask You, O Lord, hear us and have mercy on us.

+ O You who by Your power planned the life of man before his creation, and created all that exists by Your wisdom, and adorned the heavens with stars, and the earth with plants, trees, and vineyards, and the valleys with meadows and flowers. O our King, accept now the supplication of Your servants who place themselves in Your hands and say, "We ask You, O Lord, hear us and have mercy on us."

+ O great and holy God, who created man in His image and likeness, and gave him a living and reasoning soul, have mercy, O Lord, on Your creation which You have made, show us compassion, and send down upon us Your mercy from the height of Your holiness and Your prepared dwelling. We ask You, O Lord, hear us and have mercy on us.

+ O You who saved Your servant Noah the righteous, and delivered him from the flood, with his sons and their wives, and also the clean and unclean animals, for the sake of the earth's renewal. We ask You, O Lord, hear us and have mercy on us.

+ O Maker and Provider of all, deliver Your people from the flood of the sea of this passing world, and protect them and all animals from harm, and provide for the needs of the birds, for You give to all birds, animals, and ravens their sustenance. We ask You, O Lord, hear us and have mercy on us.

+ نسأل ونتضرع إليك أيها السيد الله الآب ضابط الكل والإبن الوحيد القدوس ، خالق الكل ومدبرهم والروح القدس المحيي الثالوث المقدس الذى تجثو له كل ركبة ما فى السموات وما على الأرض . نسألك يارب إسمعنا وإرحمنا .

+ من أجل السلامة العالية وتآلف سائر البيع التى فى العالم والأديرة والمجامع المقدسة والسكان فيها والقيام بأحوالها . يا الله تحنن على خليقتك ونجها من كل سوء . نسألك يارب إسمعنا وإرحمنا .

+ يا من بقدرته دبر حياة الإنسان قبل خلقته وصنع له الموجودات بحكمته وزين السماء بالنجوم والأرض بالنباتات والأشجار والكروم والأودية ، أنت الآن يا ملكنا إقبل طلبات عبيدك الواقفين بين يديك القائلين . نسألك يارب إسمعنا وإرحمنا .

+ يا الله العظيم القدوس الذى خلق الإنسان على صورته ومثاله وجعل فيه نفساً حية عاقلة ناطقة . إرحم يارب جبلتك التى خلقتها وتحنن عليها وإرسل علينا رحمتك من علو قدسك ومسكنك المستعد . نسألك يارب إسمعنا وإرحمنا .

+ يا من خلصت عبدك نوح البار ونجيته من الطوفان هو وبنيه ونساءهم وأيضاً الحيوانات الطاهرة والغير الطاهرة لأجل تجديد الأرض مرة أخرى . نسألك يارب إسمعنا وإرحمنا .

+ أيها البارى رازق الكل . نج شعبك من طوفان بحر العالم الزائل وإرفع عنهم كل مكروه . وكل الحيوانات أيضاً وسائر الطيور أعطها قوتها لأنك تعطى للبهائم رزقاً ولفراخ الغربان قوتاً . نسألك يارب إسمعنا وإرحمنا .

+ O You who were received as a guest by Your servant Abraham the patriarch, and ate at his table and blessed his Seed, O our King, accept now the supplications of Your servants and priests who place themselves in Your hands, have compassion on the world and save Your people from every hardship, abide in them and accompany them. We ask You, O Lord, hear us and have mercy on us.

+ We ask You, O Lord, to guard us from all evil, to have compassion on Your creation and all Your people, for the eyes of everyone wait upon You, for You give them their food in due season. O sustainer of all flesh, the help of the helpless, and the hope of the hopeless. We ask You, O Lord, hear us and have mercy on us.

+ O You who look to the humble with watchful eyes of protection, who saved Joseph from his master's wife, set him as a ruler over Egypt, and spared him in the days of hardship, so that his brothers and father Jacob came and knelt before him, and took from him wheat for the sustenance of their children and animals, we also bow our heads and kneel before You, O our Creator and Provider, and we thank You for everything, concerning everything, and in everything. We ask You to save us from every tribulation. We ask You, O Lord, hear us and have mercy on us.

+ O God, Logos of the Father, who works in the law, the prophets, and the Old Testament, and fulfills them, save Your people from every hardship, manage their lives according to Your goodwill, and spare them from famines and calamities. We ask You, O Lord, hear us and have mercy on us.

+ O You who supported the people of Israel forty years in the desert of Sinai, though they had no houses or storehouses, O my Lord, keep now Your people, and bless their houses and storehouses with Your heavenly blessings. We ask You, O Lord, hear us and have mercy on us.

+ O You who accepted the prayer of Elijah the Tishbite when the sky rained and the earth produced vegetation, and blessed the barrel of wheat and the vessel of oil in the widow's house, accept the prayers of Your people through the intercessions of Your holy saints and prophets. We ask You, O Lord, hear us and have mercy on us.

+ يا من ضيف عند عبده إبراهيم رئيس الآباء وإتكأ على مائدته وبارك فى زرعه ، أنت الآن يا ملكنا إقبل طلبة عبيدك الواقفين بين يديك وتراءف على العالم وخلص شعبك من كل شدة وحل فيهم وسر بينهم . نسألك يارب إسمعنا وإرحمنا .

+ نطلب إليك يارب لكى تحرسنا من جميع الشرور . وتراءف على خليقتك وجميع شعبك لأن أعين الكل تترجاك وأعطهم طعامهم فى حينه . المعطى طعاماً لكل ذى جسد . يا عون من لا عون له . يارجاء من لا رجاء له . نسألك يارب إسمعنا وإرحمنا.

+ أيها الناظر إلى المتواضعين بعين عنايتك التى لا تغفل وخلصت يوسف من إمرأة سيده وجعلته ملكاً على مصر وأحوالها وأجزت عليه أيام الشدة . فأتى إليه اخوته وأبوه يعقوب وسجدوا بين يديه وأخذوا منه حنطة لقوت بنيهم ومواشيهم . نحن الجميع أيضاً نخضع لك برؤوسنا ونسجد لك بين يديك ونشكرك يا خالقنا ورازقنا على هذا الحال وفى كل حال ومن أجل سائر الأحوال ونجنا يا الله من كل شدة . نسألك يارب إسمعنا وإرحمنا .

+ أيها الإله كلمة الآب الفاعل فى الناموس والأنبياء والعهد القديم ومكملهم خلص شعبك من كل ضيقة ودبر حياتهم كحسب إرادتك الصالحة وإرفع عنا كل القحط والبلية . نسألك يارب إسمعنا وإرحمنا .

+ يا من عال الشعب الإسرائيلى أربعين سنة فى طور سيناء ولم يكن لهم بيوت ولا مخازن . أنت يا سيدى إحفظ شعبك وعلهم وبارك فى منازلهم ومخازنهم بالبركات السمائية . نسألك يارب إسمعنا وإرحمنا .

+ يا من قبلت طلبة إيليا التسبيتى عندما أمطرت السموات وأنبتت الأرض وباركت فى كيلة الدقيق وقسط الزيت فى بيت الأرملة . إقبل طلبة شعبك بصلوات قديسيك وأنبيائك الأطهار . نسألك يارب إسمعنا وإرحمنا .

+ O God, have compassion on the world with kind and merciful eyes, bless their crops and storehouses and the little they may have, raise the waters of the rivers according to their measure, grant moderation to the winds, bless the Nile of Egypt this year and every year, give joy to the face of the earth and to us men. We ask You, O Lord, hear us and have mercy on us.

+ O You who accepted the repentance of the Ninevites when they fasted together, and received the confession of the right-hand thief upon the cross, make us also worthy of pleasing You and receiving Your compassion, crying and saying, "Remember us, O Lord, when You come into Your kingdom; and receive from Your servants their repentance, their confessions, their fasting, and their offerings which are offered upon Your holy altar as acceptable incense, and have mercy on them. We ask You, O Lord, hear us and have mercy on us.

+ O You, the mighty Provider, Chastiser, Healer, and Physician of our souls and bodies, who tested His servant Job and healed him of his calamities, and recompensed him for his losses with more than what he had, have mercy on Your people and save them all from calamities, tribulations, trials, and hardships, O upholder of those who trust in You. We ask You, O Lord, hear us and have mercy on us.

+ O Christ our God, Logos of the Father, who sanctified His pure disciples, washed their feet, and made them leaders of the believers and a light for the faith, who by them satisfied hungry souls, and taught them to pray, saying, "Our Father who art in heaven.... Lead us not into temptation, but deliver us from the evil one." We ask You, O Lord, hear us and have mercy on us.

+ O worker of wonders and miracles, who fed the thousands with five loaves, raised the dead, blessed the wedding in Cana of Galilee, O Lord, bless now the bread, oil, plants, beehives, trades, products, and all the works of Your servants. We ask You, O Lord, hear us and have mercy on us.

+ O Lord, save Your people, and surround them on every side by the sign of Your life-giving Cross, raise the state of Christians in all the world, and fill the hearts of their rulers with kindness toward them, soften their hearts toward our poor and needy brethren, and keep every evil thing far from them. We ask You, O Lord, hear us and have mercy on us.

+ يا الله ترائف على العالم بعين الرحمة والرأفة وبارك فى كيل غلاتهم ومخازنهم وفى القليل الذى عندهم وأصعد مياه الأنهار كمقدارها وهب اعتدالاً للأهوية ، ونيل ارضنا (مصر) باركه فى هذا العام وكل عام وفرح وجه الأرض وعلنا نحن البشر . نسألك يارب إسمعنا وإرحمنا .

+ يا من قبلت توبة أهل نينوى عندما صام الجميع . وقبلت إليك إعتراف اللص اليمين على الصليب . هكذا نحن ايضاً إجعلنا مستحقين لرضاك وتحننك لندعوك قائلين اذكرنا يارب إذا جئت فى ملكوتك . وإقبل توبة عبيدك وصومهم وصلواتهم وقرابينهم المرفوعة على مذابحك المقدسة بخوراً طيباً وإرحمهم . نسألك يارب إسمعنا وإرحمنا .

+ أيها المدبر القوى المؤدب الشافى طبيب الأرواح والأجساد الذى إمتحن عبده أيوب وشفاه من بلاياه ورد عليه ما فقد منه أزيد مما كان. إرحم شعبك وخلصه من جميع البلايا والمحن والتجارب والشدائد . يا ناصر جميع المتوكلين عليك . نسألك يارب إسمعنا وإرحمنا .

+ أيها المسيح الهنا كلمة الآب الذى عاهد تلاميذه الأطهار وغسل أقدامهم وجعلهم رؤساء للمؤمنين ومناراً للدين وأشبع بهم النفوس الجائعة وعلمهم الصلاة قائلين : أبانا الذى فى السموات لا تدخلنا في التجارب لكن نجنا من الشرير . نسألك يارب إسمعنا وإرحمنا .

+ ياصانع العجائب والمعجزات ومن أشبع الألوف من الخمس خبزات وأقام الأموات وبارك فى العرس بقانا الجليل الآن أيها السيد بارك لعبيدك فى خبزهم وزيتهم وزرعهم ونحلهم وفى متاجرهم وصنائعهم وكل أعمالهم . نسألك يارب إسمعنا وإرحمنا.

+ يارب خلص شعبك وأحطهم من كل ناحية بإشارة صليبك المحيي وإرفع شأن المسيحيين فى المسكونة كلها وحنن عليهم قلوب المتولين عليهم وعطف قلوبهم على اخوتنا المساكين والمعوزين بالإحسان وأبعد عنهم كل مكروه . نسألك يارب إسمعنا وإرحمنا .

+ O You who entrusted us with Your holy covenant, Your Body and Blood present with us every day upon the altar, through the descending of Your Holy Spirit on the bread and wine, and commanded us saying, "This do in remembrance of me." We ask You, O Lord, hear us and have mercy on us.

+ O Christ our God, have mercy on Your people and the successors of Your Apostles, bless the fruits of the earth, and give gladness to the heart of man through the abundance of fruits and blessings. We ask You, O Lord, hear us and have mercy on us.

+ O begotten of the Father, who was incarnate of the blessed Virgin Saint Mary in the fullness of time, who said to His saintly disciples, "Go and make disciples of all the nations, and baptize them, teaching them all that I have commanded you; and behold, I am with you always, even unto the end of the world." Be also with Your people who cry out to You saying, "We ask You, O Lord, hear us and have mercy on us."

+ O forgiver of sins and giver of all things, forgive the sins of Your people, purify them from every blemish, and cleanse them from every deceit, and keep them from bearing false witness and from all envy and slander, and uproot from their hearts every evil thought, murmuring, doubts and hardness of heart arising from pride. We ask You, O Lord, hear us and have mercy on us.

+ You are the rampart of our salvation, O Mother of God, the invincible fortress; bring to naught the counsels of the adversaries, turn the mourning of your servants into joy, defend our cities, fight for the orthodox kings and leaders, and intercede for the peace of the world and the churches. We ask You, O Lord, hear us and have mercy on us.

+ O God of mercy and compassion, Lord of all comfort, do not be angry with us, nor rebuke us for our wicked deeds nor for our many sins. Do not be wrathful with us, nor let Your wrath endure forever. Hear us, O God of Jacob, and look on us, O God our Helper. Spare the world from death, scarcity, plagues, devastation, the sword of enemies, earthquakes, horror, and all fearsome events. We ask You, O Lord, hear us and have mercy on us.

+ يا من ترك لنا عهده القدوس جسده ودمه حاضراً عندنا كل يوم على المذبح خبزاً وخمراً بحلول روح قدسه وأوصانا قائلاً : هذا إصنعوه لذكرى . نسألك يارب إسمعنا وإرحمنا .

+ أيها المسيح إلهنا إرحم شعبك وخليفة رسلك وإعط بركة لثمرات الأرض وإبهج قلب الإنسان بكثرة ثمرات القمح والخمر والزيت . نسألك يارب إسمعنا وإرحمنا .

+ أيها المولود من الآب الذى تجسد من البكر البتول العذراء مرتمريم فى آخر الأيام الذى قال لتلاميذه القديسين إمضوا وتلمذوا كل الأمم وعمدوهم وعلموهم جميع ما أوصيتكم به . هوذا أنا معكم كل الأيام وإلى إنقضاء العالم . كن أيضاً مع شعبك الصارخين إليك قائلين . نسألك يارب إسمعنا وإرحمنا .

+ يا غافر الخطايا ومانح العطايا إغفر خطايا شعبك وطهرهم من كل دنس وإغسلهم من كل غش وأبعد عنهم اليمين الحانثة وكل حسد وكل نميمة وإنزع من قلوبهم الفكر الردئ والوسواس وكل الشكوك والكبرياء وكل قساوة وتجبر . نسألك يارب إسمعنا وإرحمنا .

+ أنتِ هى سور خلاصنا يا والدة الإله الحصن المنيع غير المنثلم ، إليكِ نسأل ، مشورة المعاندين لنا إبطلى . وحزن عبيدك إلى فرح ردى ولمدينتنا صونى وعن الملوك و الرؤساء الأرثوذوكسيين حاربى وعن سلام العالم والكنائس إشفعى . نسألك يارب إسمعنا وإرحمنا .

+ يا إله الرحمة والرأفة ورب كل عزاء لا تسخط علينا ولا تؤاخذنا بسوء أعمالنا ولا بكثرة خطايانا ولا تغضب علينا ولا يدوم غضبك إلى الأبد . أنصت يا إله يعقوب وأنظر يا إله عوننا وإرفع عن العالم الموت والغلاء والوباء والجلاء وسيف الأعداء والزلازل والأهوال وكل أمر مخيف . نسألك يارب إسمعنا وإرحمنا .

+ For the sake of our protection under Your high and mighty hand, O God, we ask You to keep for us the life of our honored father and patriarch, Pope Abba [and his partner in the apostolic liturgy, our father the bishop (metropolitan) Abba and to confirm him (them) upon his (their) throne(s) for many years and quiet and peaceful times. We ask You, O Lord, hear us and have mercy on us.

+ O Christ our God, we ask of Your graciousness and Your great mercy to keep for us the life of our fathers: the metropolitans, the bishops, and all the leaders of the flock. Confirm the sheep of Your flock; grant protection to the priests, purity to the deacons, strength to the elders, understanding to the young, chastity to the virgins, asceticism to the monks, purity to the married, and protection for women. We ask You, O Lord, hear us and have mercy on us.

+ Again, we ask for the lost and the travelers, bring back; the widows and orphans, support; the hungry and thirsty, satisfy; and those who are in debt, pay their debts and forgive them; and those who are in prisons and distress, give them release. Heal the sick and repose the departed. We ask You, O Lord, hear us and have mercy on us.

+ O God of our holy fathers, do not forsake those whom You have created with Your holy hands, You who manifested Your love for mankind, O Merciful One, accept from Your mother an intercession on our behalf, and save, O Savior, a humble people. Do not leave us to the end, nor forsake us forever. For the sake of Your holy name, do not break Your covenant nor take away from us Your mercy, for the sake of Abraham Your beloved, Isaac Your servant, and Jacob Your saint. We ask You, O Lord, hear us and have mercy on us.

+ من أجل حفظنا تحت اليد العالية المقدسة التى لك يا الله ، نطلب اليك أن تبقى لنا وعلينا حياة ابينا المكرم بطريركنا المعظم الأنبا (.....) وأن تحفظ لنا حياته وتثبته على كرسيه سنين عديدة وأزمنة سالمة هادئة مديدة . نسألك يارب إسمعنا وإرحمنا .

+ ايها المسيح إلهنا نطلب من جودك ومراحمك العالية أن تبقى لنا وعلينا حياة آبائنا المطارنة والأساقفة ، وكل الرؤساء والرعاة إحفظهم ، وغنم رعيتهم ثبتهم . إعط حفظاً للكهنة ، طهارة للشمامسة ، قوة للشيوخ ، فهماً للأطفال ، عفة للأبكار ، نسكاً للرهبان والراهبات ، نقاوة للمتزوجين صوناً للنـــساء . نسألك يارب إسمعنا وإرحمنا .

+ وأيضاً الضالين والمسافرين ردهم ، والأرامل والأيتام علهم ، والجياع والعطاش إشبعهم ، والذين عليهم دين أوف عنهم وسامحهم ، والمحبوسين والذين فى الشدائد إفرج عنهم ، والمرضى إشفهم والراقدين نيحهم . نسألك يارب إسمعنا وإرحمنا .

+ يا إله آبائنا القديسين لا تتخل عنا ، ولا تخيب رجاء الذين خلقتهم بيدك الطاهرة . يا من أظهرت حبك للبشرية ، أيها الرحوم ، إقبل من والدتك شفاعة من أجلنا . خلصنا يا مخلص شعباً متواضعاً . لا تغفل عنا إلى الغاية ولا تسلمنا إلى الإنقضاء من أجل إسمك القدوس . لا تنقض عهدك ولا تنزع عنا رحمتك من أجل إبراهيم حبيبك وإسحق عبدك ويعقوب إسرائيل قديسك . نسألك يارب إسمعنا وإرحمنا .

Priest - الكاهن

+ Ⲫⲛⲟⲩϯ ⲛⲁⲓ ⲛⲁⲛ ⲑⲉϣⲟⲩⲛⲁⲓ ⲉⲣⲟⲛ ⲁⲣⲓⲟⲩⲛⲁⲓ ⲛⲉⲙⲁⲛ ϧⲉⲛ ⲧⲉⲕⲙⲉⲧⲟⲩⲣⲟ .

+ إفنووتى ناى نان ثيه شووناى إرون أرى أووناى نيمان خين تيك ميت أوورو.

+ God, have mercy on us, settle your mercy upon us, show us mercy in Your Kingdom.

+ اللهم ارحمنا . قرر لنا رحمة . اصنع معنا رحمة فى ملكوتك.

Congregation replies Kirye Elison 12 times, saying : ويجاوبه الشعب كيرى ليسون 12 دفعة صارخين :

English	Coptic transliteration	Coptic	Arabic
O King of peace, grant us Your peace, establish for us Your peace, and forgive us our sins.	إبؤورو إنتيه تى هيرينى : موى نان إنتيك هيرينى : سيمنى نان إنتيك هيرينى : كا نين نوفى نان إيفول .	Ⲡⲟⲩⲣⲟ ⲛ̀ⲧⲉ ϯ̀ⲓⲣⲏⲛⲏ : ⲙⲟⲓ ⲛⲁⲛ ⲛ̀ⲧⲉⲕϩⲓⲣⲏⲛⲏ : ⲥⲉⲙⲛⲓ ⲛⲁⲛ ⲛ̀ⲧⲉⲕϩⲓⲣⲏⲛⲏ : ⲭⲁ ⲛⲉⲛⲛⲟⲃⲓ ⲛⲁⲛ ⲉ̀ⲃⲟⲗ .	+ يا ملك السلام : إعطنا سلامك : قرر لنا سلامك . وإغفر لنا خطايانا .
Lord have mercy	كيريه ليسون	Ⲕⲩⲣⲓⲉ̀ ⲉ̀ⲗⲉⲏⲥⲟⲛ	يارب ارحم
Disperse the enemies, of the Church, and fortify her, that she may not be shaken forever.	جور إيفول إن نى جاجى : إنتيه تى إككليسيا : أرى صوبت إروس إن نيسكيم شا إنيه .	Ⲭⲱⲣ ⲉ̀ⲃⲟⲗ ⲛ̀ⲛⲓϫⲁϫⲓ : ⲛ̀ⲧⲉ ϯⲉⲕⲕⲗⲏⲥⲓⲁ ⲁⲣⲓⲥⲟⲃⲧ ⲉ̀ⲣⲟⲥ ⲛ̀ⲛⲉⲥⲕⲓⲙ ϣⲁ ⲉ̀ⲛⲉϩ .	+ فرق أعداء الكنيسة : وحصنها فلا تتزعزع إلى الأبد
Lord have mercy	كيريه ليسون	Ⲕⲩⲣⲓⲉ̀ ⲉ̀ⲗⲉⲏⲥⲟⲛ	يارب ارحم
Immanuel our God, is now in our midst, with the glory of His Father, and the Holy Spirit.	إممانوئيل بين نووتى : خين تين ميتى تينوو : خين إبؤوو إنتيه بيف يوت:نيم بى بنيقما إثؤواب	Ⲉⲙⲙⲁⲛⲟⲩⲏⲗ ⲡⲉⲛⲛⲟⲩϯ : ϧⲉⲛ ⲧⲉⲛⲙⲏϯ ϯⲛⲟⲩ : ϧⲉⲛ ⲡ̀ⲱⲟⲩ ⲛ̀ⲧⲉ ⲡⲉϥⲓⲱⲧ : ⲛⲉⲙ ⲡⲓⲡ̀ⲛⲁ ⲉⲑⲩ	+ عمانوئيل إلهنا : فى وسطنا الآن : بمجد أبيه : والروح القدس .
Lord have mercy	كيريه ليسون	Ⲕⲩⲣⲓⲉ̀ ⲉ̀ⲗⲉⲏⲥⲟⲛ	يارب ارحم
May He bless us all, and purify our hearts, and heal the sicknesses, of our souls and bodies.	إنتيف إسموو إرون تيرين إنتيف طوفوو إننين هيت إنتيف طالتشو إن نى شونى : إنتيه نين بسيشي نيم نين صوما .	Ⲛ̀ⲧⲉϥⲥⲙⲟⲩ ⲉ̀ⲣⲟⲛ ⲧⲏⲣⲉⲛ ⲛ̀ⲧⲉϥⲧⲟⲩⲃⲟ ⲛ̀ⲛⲉⲛϩⲏⲧ ⲛ̀ⲧⲉϥⲧⲁⲗϭⲟ ⲛ̀ⲛⲓϣⲱⲛⲓ : ⲛ̀ⲧⲉ ⲛⲉⲛⲯⲩⲭⲏ ⲛⲉⲙ ⲛⲉⲛⲥⲱⲙⲁ .	+ ليباركنا كلنا : ويطهر قلوبنا : ويشفى أمراض : نفوسنا وأجسادنا
Lord have mercy	كيريه ليسون	Ⲕⲩⲣⲓⲉ̀ ⲉ̀ⲗⲉⲏⲥⲟⲛ	يارب ارحم
We worship You O Christ, with Your good Father, and the Holy Spirit, for You were crucified and saved us.	تين أووأوشت إمموك أو بيخرستوس نيم بيك يوت إن أغاثوس : نيم بى بنيفما إثؤواب : جيه أف أشك أك صوتى إممون .	Ⲧⲉⲛⲟⲩⲱϣⲧ ⲙ̀ⲙⲟⲕ ⲱ̀ Ⲡⲓⲭ̀ⲣⲓⲥⲧⲟⲥ ⲛⲉⲙ ⲡⲉⲕⲓⲱⲧ ⲛ̀ⲁⲅⲁⲑⲟⲥ : ⲛⲉⲙ ⲡⲓⲡ̀ⲛⲉⲩⲙⲁ ⲉⲑⲟⲩⲁⲃ : ϫⲉ ⲁϥⲁϣⲕ ⲁⲕⲥⲱϯ ⲙ̀ⲙⲟⲛ .	+ نسجد لك أيها المسيح : مع أبيك الصالح : والروح القدس : لأنك صلبت وخلصتنا .

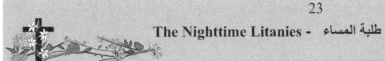

English	Coptic (transliteration)	Coptic	Arabic

Amen. Alleluia. Glory to the Father and to the Son and to the Holy Spirit. Now and ever and unto the ages of the ages. Amen.

آمين الليلويا ، ذوكسابترى كى ايو كى اجيو ابنيفماتى ، كينين كى أ أى كى استوس اى اوناس تون اى اونون ، آمين.

Ⲁⲙⲏⲛ ⲁⲗ: ⲗⲟⲍⲁⲡⲁⲧⲣⲓ ⲕⲉ Ⲩⲓⲱ ⲕⲉ ⲁⲅⲓⲱ Ⲡⲛⲉⲩⲙⲁⲧⲓ: Ⲕⲉ ⲛⲩⲛ ⲕⲉ ⲁⲓ ⲕⲉ ⲓⲥ ⲧⲟⲩⲥ ⲉⲱⲛⲁⲥ ⲧⲱⲛ ⲉⲱⲛⲱⲛ: ⲁⲙⲏⲛ.

آمين الليلويا المجد للآب و الابن و الروح القدس ، الآن و كل اوان و الى دهر الداهرين ، آمين .

We proclaim and say, O our Lord Jesus Christ, who was crucified on the Cross, trample Satan under our feet. Save us and have mercy on us. Lord have mercy. Lord have mercy. Lord bless us. Amen. Bless me. Bless me. Lo, the repentance (metanoia). Forgive me. Say the blessing.

تين اوش ايفول انجو اموس : جى اوبينشويس ايسوس بى اخريستوس : فى اطاف أشف إبيستافروس : إك إيه خُمخيم إم إبصاطاناس صا بيسيت إنين تشالالج : سوتى امون اووه ناينان : كيرى ليسون كيرى ليسون كيرى افلوجيسون امين ، ازمو اى روى ازمو اى روى اس تى ماتانويا : كونى ايفول جو امبى اسمو.

Ⲧⲉⲛⲱϣ ⲉⲃⲟⲗ ⲉⲛⲭⲱ ⲙⲙⲟⲥ: ϫⲉ ⲱⲠⲉⲛⲟ̅ⲥ̅ Ⲓⲏⲥ Ⲡⲭⲥ. Ⲫⲏ ⲉⲧⲁⲩⲁϣϥ ⲉⲡⲓⲥⲧⲁⲩⲣⲟⲥ: ⲉⲕⲉϧⲟⲙϧⲉⲙ ⲙⲡⲥⲁⲧⲁⲛⲁⲥ ⲥⲁ ⲡⲉⲥⲏⲧ ⲛⲛⲉⲛϭⲁⲗⲁⲩϫ: ⲥⲱϯ ⲙⲙⲟⲛ ⲟⲩⲟϩ ⲛⲁⲓⲛⲁⲛ: Ⲕⲩⲣⲓⲉ ⲉⲗⲉⲏⲥⲟⲛ Ⲕⲩⲣⲓⲉ ⲉⲗⲉⲏⲥⲟⲛ Ⲕⲩⲣⲓⲉ ⲉⲩⲗⲟⲅⲏⲥⲟⲛ ⲁⲙⲉⲛ. ⲥⲙⲟⲩ ⲉⲣⲟⲓ ⲥⲙⲟⲩ ⲉⲣⲟⲓ: ⲓⲥ ϯⲙⲉⲧⲁⲛⲟⲓⲁ: ⲭⲱⲛⲏⲓ ⲉⲃⲟⲗ ⲭⲱ ⲙⲡⲓⲥⲙⲟⲩ.

نصرخ قائلين يا ربنا يسوع المسيح الذى صلب على الصليب ، إسحق الشيطان تحت أقدامنا خلصنا و ارحمنا. يارب ارحم ، يارب ارحم ، يارب بارك آمين . باركوا علىّ باركوا علىّ ها الميطانية اغفروا لى . فلتقل البركة.

Priest

May Jesus Christ, our true God, who through His own goodwill accepted sufferings, and was crucified on the cross for our sakes, bless us with all spiritual blessings, and support us, and complete for us the holy Pascha, and bring forth upon us the joy of His holy Resurrection for many years and peaceful times. Through the supplications and prayers which our lady, the lady of us all, the holy Theotokos Saint Mary makes for us at all times, and those of the three great holy luminaries, Michael, Gabriel and Raphael; and all the angels and heavenly ranks. And through the prayers of the Patriarchs, prophets, Apostles, martyrs, the whole choir of the cross-bearers; the justs, the righteous and the angel of this blessed night. And through the blessing of this Holy Pascha of our Good Savior. May their holy blessings, their benediction, their power, their gift, their love, and their help be with us all forever. Amen.

الكاهن

يسوع المسيح إلهنا الحقيقى الذى قبل الآلام بإرادته وصلب على الصليب من أجلنا . يباركنا بكل بركة روحية ويعيننا ويكمل لنا البصخة المقدسة ويرينا فرح قيامته المقدسة سنين كثيرة وأزمنة سالمة . بالسؤلات والطلبات التى تصنعها عنا كل حين سيدتنا وملكتنا كلنا والدة الإله القديسة مريم والثلاثة المنيرين الأطهار ميخائيل وغبريال ورافائيل . وجميع مصاف الملائكة وكل الطغمات السمائية . وصلوات رؤساء الآباء والأنبياء والرسل والشهداء ومصاف لباس الصليب والأبرار والصديقين وملاك هذه الليلة المباركة ، وبركة البصخة المقدسة التى لمخلصنا الصالح . بركتهم المقدسة ونعمتهم وقوتهم وهبتهم ومحبتهم ومعونتهم تكون معنا كلنا إلى الأبد آمين .

| **O Christ our God** | ⲠⲓⲬⲣⲓⲥⲧⲟⲥ Ⲡⲉⲛⲛⲟⲩϯ | ايها المسيح الهنا |
| **Amen. So it is** | Ⲁⲙⲏⲛ ⲉⲥⲉϣⲱⲡⲓ | آمين يكون |

Priest	الكاهن

O King of peace, grant us Your peace, establish for us Your peace, and forgive us our sins. For Yours is the power, the glory, the blessing, and the might, for ever. Amen.

Make us worthy to pray thankfully:

Our Father Who art in Heaven.......

Go in peace, and may the peace of the Lord be with you all, Amin.

يا ملك السلام : إعطنا سلامك : قرر لنا سلامك . وإغفر لنا خطايانا . لان لك القوة والمجد والبركة والعزة إلى الأبد آمين .

اللهم اجعلنا مستحقين ان نقول جميعا بشكر

أبانا الذى فى السموات .....

أمضوا بسلام و سلام الرب يكون معكم ، آمين.

جمعة ختام الصوم

Last Friday of the Great Lent

قراءات و احداث هذا اليوم

قراءات هذا اليوم و هو جمعة ختام الصوم تتكلم عن **"نهاية يعقبها بداية"** و هو تمهيد لنهاية الصوم الذى تعقبه بداية آلام المخلص.

انجيل باكر يتكلم عن المجئ الثاني لمخلصنا الصالح.

البولس من 2 تيموثاوس 3 و 4 يتكلم عن نهاية العالم ثم ظهور المسيح الديان

الكاثوليكون من يعقوب 5 يتكلم عن انتظار مجئ الرب

انجيل القداس من لوقا 13 يتكلم عن نهاية الامة اليهودية واورشليم والوعد بمجئ الرب عند ايمانهم بالرب يسوع " يا أورشليم يا أورشليم يا قاتلة الأنبياء وراجمة المرسلين إليها كم مرة أردت أن أجمع بنيك مثل الطائر يجمع فراخه فى عشه تحت جناحيه ولم تريدوا . هوذا بيتكم يترك لكم خراباً . وأقول لكم انكم لا ترونى منذ الآن حتى تقولوا مبارك الآتى باسم الرب "

و فيه ايضا تصلى الكنيسة صلاة مسحة المرضى

Today's Readings and Events

Today's readings of the last Friday of the great lent talk about **"An End followed by a beginning".** This is to end the fast and to start the suffering of our Lord.

The Gospel of the Morning Prayer talks about the second coming of our Savior.

The Pauline Epistle from 2 Timothy 3, 4 talks about the end of the world and the coming of the Judge, the Lord Jesus Christ.

The Katholicon from James 5, talks about the waiting of the coming Christ.

The Gospel of the Liturgy from Luke 13, talks about the end of the Jewish nation and Jerusalem and the promise to see the Lord when they believe in Him as the Messiah. "O Jerusalem, Jerusalem, which kills the prophets, and stones them that are sent unto you; how often would I have gathered your children together, as a hen does gather her brood under her wings, and you would not! Behold, your house is left unto you desolate: and verily I say unto you, you shall not see me, until the time comes when you shall say, Blessed is he that comes in the name of the Lord."

The church also prays the sacrament of Holy Unction.

Matins of The Last Friday of the Great Lent

باكر يوم جمعة ختام الصوم

Genesis 49:33-50:26

(التكوين ص 49 : 33 - 50 : 26)

And when Jacob had made an end of commanding his sons, he gathered up his feet into the bed, and died, and was gathered unto his people. And Joseph fell upon his father's face, and wept upon him, and kissed him. And Joseph commanded his servants the physicians to embalm his father: and the physicians embalmed Israel. And forty days were fulfilled for him; for so are fulfilled the days of those who are embalmed: and the Egyptians mourned for him three score and ten days. And when the days of his mourning were past, Joseph spoke unto the house of Pharaoh, saying, If now I have found grace in your eyes, speak, I pray you, in the ears of Pharaoh, saying, My father made me swear, saying, Lo, I die: in my grave which I have dug for me in the land of Canaan, there shall you bury me. Now therefore let me go up, I pray you, and bury my father, and I will come again. And Pharaoh said, Go up, and bury your father, according as he made you swear. And Joseph went up to bury his father: and with him went up all the servants of Pharaoh, the elders of his house, and all the elders of the land of Egypt, And all the house of Joseph, and his brothers, and his father's house: only their little ones, and their flocks, and their herds, they left in the land of Goshen. And there went up with him both chariots and horsemen: and it was a very great company. And they came to the threshing floor of Atad, which is beyond Jordan, and there they mourned with a great and very strong lamentation: and he made a mourning for his father seven days. And when the inhabitants of the land, the Canaanites, saw the mourning in the threshing floor of Atad, they said, This is a mourning to the Egyptians: therefore the name of it was called Abelmizraim, which is beyond Jordan. And his sons did unto him according as he commanded them: For his sons carried him into the land of Canaan, and buried him in the cave of the field of Machpelah, which Abraham bought with the field for a possession of a burying place from Ephron the Hittite, before Mamre. And Joseph returned into Egypt, he, and his brothers, and all that went up with him to bury his father, after he had buried his father. And when Joseph's brothers saw that their father was dead, they said, Joseph will perhaps hate us, and will certainly pay back to us all the evil which we did unto him. And they sent a messenger unto Joseph, saying, Your father did command before he died, saying, So shall you say unto Joseph, Forgive, I pray you now, the trespass of your brothers, and their sin; for they did unto you evil: and now, we pray you, forgive the trespass of the servants of the God of your father. And Joseph wept when they spoke unto him. And his brothers also went and fell down before

فلما فرغ يعقوب من وصيته لبنيه ضم رجليه إلى السرير وفاضت روحه وصار إلى قومه . فوقع يوسف على وجه أبيه وبكى عليه وقبله وأمر عبيده الأطباء أن يحنطوا أباه فحنط الأطباء إسرائيل وكملت له أربعون يوماً لأنه كذلك تكمل أيام المحنطين وبكى عليه المصريون سبعين يوماً . ولما انقضت أيام بكائه كلم يوسف آل فرعون وقال إن كنت قد وجدت نعمة فى عيونكم فتكلموا على مسامع فرعون وقولوا له . إن أبى قد استحلفنى وقال لي ها أنا مائت فادفننى فى قبرى الذى حفرت لنفسي فى أرض كنعان هناك تدفننى والآن أصعد لأدفن أبي وأرجع فقال فرعون ليوسف إصعد فادفن أباك كما استحلفك . فصعد يوسف ليدفن أباه وصعد معه جميع عبيد فرعون وشيوخ بيته وجميع شيوخ أرض مصر . وجميع آل يوسف وإخوته وآل أبيه وتركوا أطفالهم وغنمهم وبقرهم فى أرض جاسان . وصعدت معه مركبات وفرسان فكان الموكب عظيماً جداً . فأتوا إلى بيدر أطاد الذى فى عبر الأردن وندبوه ندباً عظيماً جداً . وأقام لأبيه مناحة سبعة أيام فرأى سكان أرض كنعان فى بيدر أطاد فقالوا هذه مناحة عظيمة للمصريين ولذلك دعوا اسم ذلك الموضع مناحة المصريين الذى فى عبر الأردن . وصنع له بنوه هكذا كما أوصاهم . فحملوه إلى أرض كنعان ودفنوه فى مغارة حقل المكفيلة التى اشتراها إبراهيم مع الحقل ملك قبر من عفرون الحثى أمام ممرا . ثم رجع يوسف بعد ما دفن أباه إلى مصر هو وإخوته وسائرمن صعد معه لدفن أبيه . فلما رأى إخوة يوسف أنه قد مات أبوهم قالوا ألعل يوسف يضطهدنا ويرد علينا جميع الشر الذى فعلناه به . فدنوا إلى يوسف وقالوا له إن أباك قد أوصانا قبل موته وقال لنا . هكذا تقولون ليوسف إغفر لإخوتك ذنبهم وخطيتهم فقد فعلوا بك سوءً والآن نسألك أن تصفح عن ذنب عبيد إله أبيك . فبكى يوسف حين قيل له ذلك وجاء إخوته أيضاً فوقعوا بين يديه وقالوا ها نحن عبيد لك فقال لهم يوسف لا تخافوا أليس

his face; and they said, Behold, we are your servants. And Joseph said unto them, Fear not: for am I in the place of God? But as for you, you thought evil against me; but God meant it unto good, to bring to pass, as it is this day, to save many people alive. Now therefore fear not: I will nourish you, and your little ones. And he comforted them, and spoke kindly unto them. And Joseph dwelt in Egypt, he, and his father's house: and Joseph lived a hundred and ten years. And Joseph saw Ephraim's children of the third generation: the children also of Machir the son of Manasseh were brought up upon Joseph's knees. And Joseph said unto his brothers, I die: and God will surely visit you, and bring you out of this land unto the land which he swore to Abraham, to Isaac, and to Jacob. And Joseph took an oath of the children of Israel, saying, God will surely visit you, and you shall carry up my bones from here. So Joseph died, being a hundred and ten years old: and they embalmed him, and he was put in a coffin in Egypt.

Glory be to the Holy Trinity. Amen.

أنى تحت مشيئة الله . أنتم نويتم على شر والله نوى بى خيراً لكى يصنع ما ترونه اليوم ويحيى شعباً كثيراً . والآن لا تخافوا أنا أعولكم وأطفالكم وعزاهم ولاطف قلوبهم . وأقام يوسف بمصر هو وآل أبيه وعاش يوسف مئة وعشر سنين . ورأى يوسف من بنى افرايم الجيل الثالث وأيضاً بنو مكير إبن منسى ولدوا على ركبتيه . وقال يوسف لإخوته أنا مائت والله سيفتقدكم ويصعدكم من هذه الأرض إلى الأرض الذى أقسم عليها لإبراهيم واسحق ويعقوب . واستحلف يوسف بنى إسرائيل وقال إن الله سيفتقدكم فإصعدوا عظامى من ههنا . ومات يوسف وهو إبن مئة وعشر سنين فحنطوه ووُضِعَ فى تابوت بمصر .

مجداً للثالوث القدوس .

Proverbs 11:27-12:22

He that diligently seeks good procures favor: but he that seeks evil, it shall come unto him. He that trusts in his riches shall fall: but the righteous shall flourish as a branch. He that troubles his own house shall inherit the wind: and the fool shall be servant to the wise of heart. The fruit of the righteous is a tree of life; and he that wins souls is wise. Behold, the righteous shall be recompensed on the earth: much more the wicked and the sinner. Whosoever loves instruction loves knowledge: but he that hates reproof is stupid. A good man obtains favor of the LORD: but a man of wicked intentions will he condemn. A man shall not be established by wickedness: but the root of the righteous shall not be moved. A virtuous woman is a crown to her husband: but she that makes ashamed is like rottenness in his bones. The thoughts of the righteous are right: but the counsels of the wicked are deceitful. The words of the wicked are to lie in wait for blood: but the mouth of the upright shall deliver them. The wicked are overthrown, and are not: but the house of the righteous shall stand. A man shall be commended according to his wisdom: but he that is of a perverse heart shall be despised. He that is despised, and has a servant, is better than he that honors himself, and lacks bread. A righteous man regards the life of his animal: but the tender mercies of the wicked are cruel. He that tills his land shall be satisfied with bread: but he that follows vain persons is void of understanding. The wicked desires the net of evil men: but the root of the righteous yields fruit. The wicked is snared by the transgression of his lips: but the just shall escape from trouble. A man shall be satisfied with good by the fruit of his mouth: and the recompense of a man's hands shall be rendered unto him. The

(من أمثال ص 11 : 27- 12 : 22)

من يطلب الخير يلتمس الرضا ومن يطلب الشر فالشر يلحقه . من اتكل على غناه يسقط والصديقون يزهون كالأغصان . من يكدر بيته يرث الريح والاحمق يصير عبداً لحكيم القلب . ثمرة الصديق شجرة الحياة ومن يهتم بالنفوس فهو حكيم . ها أن الصديق يُجزى على الأرض فبالأحرى المنافق والخاطئ . الذى يحب التاديب يحب المعرفة والذى يبغض التوبيخ فهو بليد . الصالح ينال رضى من الرب وإنسان المكايد فيُحْكَمُ عليه . لا يثبت الإنسان بالنفاق أما أصل الصديقين فلا يتزعزع . المرأة الفاضلة إكليل لرجلها . وذات الفضائح كنخر فى عظامه . أفكار الصديقين عدل . تدابير المنافق غش . كلام المنافقين مكون للدم وفم المستقيمين ينقذهم . ينقلب المنافقون فلا يكونون وبيت الصديقين فيثبت . الإنسان يحمد بحسب فطنته أما الملتوى القلب فيكون للهوان . الحقير وله عبد خير من ذى كرامة وليس له خبز . الصديق يعرف نفس بهيمته أما أحشاء المنافقين فقاسية . من يفلّح أرضه يشبع خبزاً ومن يتبع البطالين فهو فاقد الفهم . من تنعم فى محلات الخمر أبقى فى حصونه الهوان . المنافق يشتهى صيد الأشرار وأصل الصديقين ينشأ . بمعصية الشفتين شرك الشرير والصديق يخرج من المضائق . الإنسان من ثمرة فمه يشبع خيراً ومكافأة أيدى البشر ترد إليهم . طريق الجاهل مستقيم

way of a fool is right in his own eyes: but he that hearkens unto counsel is wise. A fool's wrath is at once known: but a prudent man covers shame. He that speaks truth shows forth righteousness: but a false witness, deceit. There is one that speaks like the piercings of a sword: but the tongue of the wise beings health. The lip of truth shall be established forever: but a lying tongue is but for a moment. Deceit is in the heart of them that imagine evil: but to the counselors of peace there is joy. There shall no evil happen to the just: but the wicked shall be filled with trouble. Lying lips are abomination to the LORD: but they that deal truly are his delight. Glory be to the Holy Trinity. Amen.

Isaiah 66:10-24

Rejoice with Jerusalem, and be glad with her, all you that love her: rejoice for joy with her, all you that mourn for her: That you may nurse, and be satisfied with the breasts of her consolations; that you may drink deeply, and be delighted with the abundance of her glory. For thus says the LORD, Behold, I will extend peace to her like a river, and the glory of the Gentiles like a flowing stream: then shall you nurse, you shall be borne upon her sides, and be dandled upon her knees. As one whom his mother comforts, so will I comfort you; and you shall be comforted in Jerusalem. And when you see this, your heart shall rejoice, and your bones shall flourish like the grass: and the hand of the LORD shall be known toward his servants, and his indignation toward his enemies. For, behold, the LORD will come with fire, and with his chariots like a whirlwind, to render his anger with fury, and his rebuke with flames of fire. For by fire and by his sword will the LORD plead with all flesh: and the slain of the LORD shall be many. They that sanctify themselves, and purify themselves in the gardens following one in the midst, eating swine's flesh, and the abomination, and the mouse, shall be consumed together, says the LORD. For I know their works and their thoughts: it shall come, that I will gather all nations and tongues; and they shall come, and see my glory. And I will set a sign among them, and I will send those of them that escape unto the nations, to Tarshish, Pul, and Lud, that draw the bow, to Tubal, and Javan, to the coastlands afar off, that have not heard my fame, neither have seen my glory; and they shall declare my glory among the Gentiles. And they shall bring all your brethren for an offering unto the LORD out of all nations upon horses, and in chariots, and in litters, and upon mules, and upon camels, to my holy mountain Jerusalem, says the LORD, as the children of Israel bring an offering in a clean vessel into the house of the LORD. And I will also take some of them for priests and for Levites, says the LORD. For as the new heavens and the new

فى عينيه وأما الحكيم فيستمع المشورة . الجاهل يعرف غيظه فى يومه وذو الدهاء يكتم هوانه . الناطق بالحق يظهر العدل والشاهد بالزور يظهر غشاً . رب ذى هذر كضارب السيف وألسنة الحكماء شفاء . شفة الحق تثبت إلى الأبد ولسان الزور إنما هو إلى لمحة العين . المكر فى قلوب الذين ينشئون الشر والمشيرين بالسلام فلهم فرح . ولا يصيب الصديق شر والمنافقون يمتلئون شراً . شفتا الزور رجس عند الرب والعاملون بالصدق مرضاته . مجداً للثالوث القدوس .

(من أشعياء النبى ص 66 : 10 – 24)

إفرحوا مع أورشليم وابتهجوا معها يا جميع محبيها إفرحوا معها فرحاً يا جميع النائحين عليها . لكى ترضعوا وتشبعون من ثدى تعازيها وتحلبوا وتتنعموا من درة مجدها . لأنه هكذا قال الرب هاانذا أدير إليها السلام كالنهر ومجد الأمم كالوادى الطافح فترضعون وفى الحضن تحملون وعلى الركبتين تدللون . كمن تعزيه أمه كذلك أعزيكم أنا فى أورشليم تعزون وتنظرون فتنسر قلوبكم وتزهو عظامكم كالعشب وتعرف يد الرب مع عبيده ويغضب على أعدائه . لأنه هوذا الرب يأتى ومعه النار وعجلاته كالزوبعة ليبلغ غضبه بحنق وانتهاره بلهيب نار لأن الرب بالنار والسيف يخاصم كل البشر يكونون قتلى الرب كثيرين . إن الذين يقدسون نفوسهم ويطهرونها فى الجنات وراء واحد فى الوسط ويأكلونه لحم الخنزير والرجس والفأر يفنون جميعاً يقول الرب . فإنى عالم بأعمالهم وأفكارهم . قد حان أن أجمع كل الأمم والألسنة فيأتون ويرون مجدى . وأجعل بينهم آية وأبعث ناجين منهم إلى الأمم إلى ترشيش وفول ولود النازعين فى القسى وتوبال وياوان والجزائر البعيدة الذين لم يسمعوا بسمعتى ولم يروا مجدى فينادون بمجدى بين الأمم ويأتون بجميع إخواتكم من جميع الأمم تقدمة للرب على الخيل والعجلات والهوادج والبغال والهُجُن إلى جبل قدسى أورشليم قال الرب كما يأتى بنو إسرائيل بالتقدمة فى إناء طاهر إلى بيت الرب ومنهم أيضاً اتخذ كهنة ولاويين قال الرب . لأنه كما أن السموات الجديدة

earth, which I will make, shall remain before me, says the LORD, so shall your descendants and your name remain. And it shall come to pass, that from one new moon to another, and from one sabbath to another, shall all flesh come to worship before me, says the LORD. And they shall go forth, and look upon the corpses of the men that have transgressed against me: for their worm shall not die, neither shall their fire be quenched; and they shall be an abhorrence unto all flesh. Glory be to the Holy Trinity. Amen

Job 42:7-17

And it was so, that after the LORD had spoken these words unto Job, the LORD said to Eliphaz the Temanite, My wrath is kindled against you, and against your two friends: for you have not spoken of me the thing that is right, as my servant Job has. Therefore take unto you now seven bullocks and seven rams, and go to my servant Job, and offer up for yourselves a burnt offering; and my servant Job shall pray for you: for him will I accept: lest I deal with you after your folly, in that you have not spoken of me the thing which is right, like my servant Job. So Eliphaz the Temanite and Bildad the Shuhite and Zophar the Naamathite went, and did according as the LORD commanded them: the LORD also accepted Job. And the LORD restored the fortunes of Job, when he prayed for his friends: also the LORD gave Job twice as much as he had before. Then came there unto him all his brethren, and all his sisters, and all they that had been of his acquaintance before, and did eat bread with him in his house: and they consoled him, and comforted him over all the trouble that the LORD had brought upon him: every man also gave him a piece of money, and everyone a ring of gold. So the LORD blessed the latter end of Job more than his beginning: for he had fourteen thousand sheep, and six thousand camels, and a thousand yoke of oxen, and a thousand female donkeys. He had also seven sons and three daughters. And he called the name of the first, Jemimah; and the name of the second, Keziah; and the name of the third, Keren-happuch. And in all the land were no women found so beautiful as the daughters of Job: and their father gave them inheritance among their brethren. After this lived Job a hundred and forty years, and saw his sons, and his sons' sons, even four generations. So Job died, being old and full of days. Glory be to the Holy Trinity. Amen.

Then the priest and the congregation chant the litanies for the Great Fast with metanias, followed by the Litany of the Gospel.

والأرض الجديدة التى أصنعها تدوم أمامى يقول الرب كذلك تدوم ذريتكم واسمكم . ومن رأس شهر إلى رأس شهر ومن سبت إلى سبت كل بشر يأتى ليسجد أمامى قال الرب . ويخرجون ويرون جثث الناس الذين عصونى لأن دودهم لا يموت ونارهم لا تطفأ ويكونون رذالة لكل بشر . مجداً للثالوث القدوس .

(من أيوب الصديق ص 42 : 7 – 17)

وكان بعد أن كلم الرب أيوب بهذا الكلام أن قال الرب لأليفاز التيمانى إن غضبى قد اضطرم عليك وعلى كلا صاحبيك لأنكم لم تتكلموا أمامى بحسب الحق كعبدى أيوب . والآن فخذوا لكم سبعة ثيران وسبعة كباش إنطلقوا إلى عبدى أيوب واصعدوا محرقة عنكم وعبدى أيوب يصلى من أجلكم فانى أرفع وجهه لئلا أعاملكم بحسب حماقتكم لأنكم لم تتكلموا أمامى بحسب الحق كعبدى ايوب . فانطلق أليفاز التيمانى وبلدد الشوحى وصوفر النعمانى وصنعوا ما أمرهم الرب به ورفع الرب وجه أيوب . ورد الرب ايوب من بلائه حين صلى لأجل أصحابه وزاد الرب أيوب ضعف ما كان له قبلاً . وزاره جميع إخوته وكل من كان يعرفه من قبل وأكلوا معه خبزاً فى بيته ورثوا له وعزوه عن كل البلوة التى أنزلها الرب به وأهدى له كل منهم نعجة وقرطا من ذهب . وبارك الرب آخرة أيوب أكثر من أولاه فكان له من الغنم أربعة عشر ألفاً ومن الإبل ستة آلاف وألف فدان من البقر وألف أتان . وكان له سبعة بنين وثلاث بنات . وسمى الأولى يميمة والثانية قصيعة والثالثة قرن هفوك ولم توجد نساء فى الحسن كبنات أيوب فى الأرض كلها وأعطاهن أبوهن ميراثاً بين اخوتهن . وعاش أيوب بعد هذا منة وأربعين سنة ورأى بنيه وبنى بنيه إلى أربعة أجيال . ثم مات أيوب شيخاً قد شبع من الأيام . مجداً للثالوث القدوس .

ثم يقوم الكاهن والشعب بصلاة طلبة الصوم الكبير مع الميطانيات، وبعدها يصلون اوشية الانجيل.

Psalms 97:5-6

Shout joyfully to the LORD, all the earth; Break forth in song, rejoice, and sing praises. Sing to the LORD with the harp, With the harp and the sound of a psalm, With trumpets and the sound of a horn. Alleluia

Luke 17:20-37

Now when He was asked by the Pharisees when the kingdom of God would come, He answered them and said, "The kingdom of God does not come with observation; nor will they say, 'See here!' or 'See there!'For indeed, the kingdom of God is within you." Then He said to the disciples, "The days will come when you will desire to see one of the days of the Son of Man, and you will not see it. And they will say to you, 'Look here!' or 'Look there!' Do not go after them or follow them. For as the lightning that flashes out of one part under heaven shines to the other part under heaven, so also the Son of Man will be in His day. But first He must suffer many things and be rejected by this generation. And as it was in the days of Noah, so it will be also in the days of the Son of Man: They ate, they drank, they married wives, they were given in marriage, until the day that Noah entered the ark, and the flood came and destroyed them all. Likewise as it was also in the days of Lot: They ate, they drank, they bought, they sold, they planted, they built; but on the day that Lot went out of Sodom it rained fire and brimstone from heaven and destroyed them all. Even so will it be in the day when the Son of Man is revealed. "In that day, he who is on the housetop, and his goods are in the house, let him not come down to take them away. And likewise the one who is in the field, let him not turn back. Remember Lot's wife. Whoever seeks to save his life will lose it, and whoever loses his life will preserve it. I tell you, in that night there will be two men in one bed: the one will be taken and the other will be left. Two women will be grinding together: the one will be taken and the other left. Two men will be in the field: the one will be taken and the other left." And they answered and said to Him, "Where, Lord?" So He said to them, "Wherever the body is, there the eagles will be gathered together." Glory be to God forever. Amen.

(المزمور 97 : 5، 6)

هَلِّلوا للرَّبِّ يا كُلَّ الأرضِ. سَبِّحوا، وهَلِّلوا، ورَتِّلوا. رَتِّلوا للرَّبِّ بالقيثار، بالقيثار وصَوتِ المزمور. بأبواقٍ خافقةٍ، وصَوتِ بوق القَرْن. هلليلويا .

(الانجيل من لوقا ص 17 : 20 – 37)

ولمَّا سألهُ الفرِّيسيُّونَ: " متى يأتي ملكوتُ اللَّهِ؟ " أجابهُم وقال: " لا يأتي ملكوتُ اللَّهِ بترقب، ولا يقولونَ :إنه هنا، أو هناك! فهوذا ملكوتُ اللَّهِ داخلكم." ثم قال لتلاميذهُ: "ستأتي أيَّامٌ إذ تشتهون أن تروا يوماً من أيَّام ابن الإنسان فلا ترون. ويقولون لكم: ها هو هناك! أو هنا! فلا تذهبوا ولا تسعوا، فإنَّهُ كما أنَّ البرق يظهرُ مِن السَّماء، ويُضيء تحت السَّماء، كذلك يكون ابن الإنسان في يومهِ. ولكن ينبغي له أوَّلاً أن يتحمل مشقات كثيرة ويرذله هذا الجيل. وكما كان في أيَّام نوح كذلك يكون في أيَّام ابن الإنسان: وكانوا يأكُلون ويَشربون، ويَتزوَّجون ويتزوَّجنَ ، إلى اليوم الذي دخلَ فيه نوحٌ السفينة، فجاء الطُّوفان وأهلكَ الجميعَ .وكما كان أيضاً في أيَّام لوطٍ: كانوا يأكُلون ويَشربونَ، ويشترونَ ويبيعونَ، ويَغرسونَ ويبنونَ. وفي اليوم الذي خَرجَ فيه لوط من سدومَ، أمطر ناراً وكبريتاً مِن السَّماء فأهلك الجميع. على نحو هذا أيضاً يكون في اليوم الذي يظهر فيه ابن الإنسان. وفي ذلك اليوم مَن يكون على السَّطح وأمتعتُهُ في البيتِ فلا ينزل ليأخُذها، ومَن يكون في الحقل أيضاً فلا يرجع إلى ورائه. اذكروا امرأة لوط! مَن يطلب خلاص نفسه يُهلكها، ومن يُهلكها يُحييها. وأقولُ لكُم: إنَّهُ يكون في اللَّيلةِ اثنان على سرير واحدٍ، فيؤخذُ الواحدُ ويُترك الآخَر. تكونُ اثنتان تطحنان معاً، فتؤخذُ الواحدةُ وتُترك الأخرى". فأجابوا وقالوا لهُ: "في أي مكان ياربُّ؟ ". فقال لهم: " حيثُ تكونُ الجُثَّةُ هناك تجتمعُ النُّسور أيضاً ." والمجد لله دائماً.

| Sacrament of the Holy Unction (Anointing the Sick) | صـلاة مسحة المرضى (القنديل) |

| A paten filled with pure oil and with seven cotton wicks is placed in the middle. The priest lights one wick at the start of each prayer. | يوضع فى الوسط قنديل به سبع فتايل ، توقد واحدة فى بداية كل صلاة . |

(1) FIRST PRAYER

(الصلاة الأولى)

The priest starts the prayer saying "Elison Emas...", "Our Father ...", "Thanksgiving Prayer, and Psalm 50."

يبدأ الكاهن الصلاة بقوله ثم ελεηϲοη ημac الصلاة الربية ، وصلاة الشكر ، والمزمور الخمسين ثم يقول :

THE PRAYER OF THE SICK

أوشية المرضى

PRIEST:

Again, let us ask God the Pantocrator, the Father of our Lord, God and Savior, Jesus Christ. We ask and entreat Your goodness, O Lover of Mankind, remember, O Lord, the sick among Your people.

وأيضاً فنسأل الله ضابط الكل ، أبا ربنا وإلهنا ومخلصنا يسوع المسيح . نسأل ونطلب من صلاحك يا محب البشر : أذكر يارب مرضى شعبك .

DEACON:

Pray for our fathers and our brethren who are sick with any sickness, whether in this place or in any place, that Christ our God may grant us, with them, health and healing, and forgive us our sins.

يقول الشماس

أطلبوا عن آبائنا واخواتنا المرضى بكل مرض ، ان كان فى هذا المسكن أو بكل موضع ، لكى ينعم المسيح إلهنا عليهم وعلينا بالعافية والشفاء ، ويغفر لنا خطايانا .

CONGREGATION: Lord have mercy.

يقول الشعب : يارب ارحم

PRIEST:

Take away from them, and from us, every sickness and every malady; the spirit of sicknesses, chase away. Those who have long lain in maladies, raise up and comfort. Those who are afflicted by unclean spirits, set them all free. Those who are in prisons or dungeons, those who are in exile or captivity, or those who are held in bitter bondage, O Lord, set them all free and have mercy upon them. For You are He who loosens the bound and lifts up the fallen; the hope of those who have no hope and the help of those who have no helper; the comfort of the fainthearted; the harbor of those in the storm. All souls that are distressed or bound, grant them mercy, O Lord; grant them rest, grant them refreshment, grant them grace, grant them help, grant them salvation, grant them the forgiveness of their sins and their iniquities. As for us, too, O Lord, the sicknesses of our souls, heal; and also those of our bodies, cure. O You, the true physician of our souls and bodies, the Bishop of all flesh, visit us with Your salvation.

يقول الكاهن

تعهدهم بالمراحم والرأفات ، اشفهم . انزع عنهم وعنا كل مرض وكل سقم ، وروح الأمراض اطرده . والذين أبطأوا مطروحين فى الأمراض أقمهم وعزهم ، والمعذبون من الأرواح النجسة اعتقهم جميعاً . الذين فى السجون أو المطابق . أو الذين فى النفى أو السبى ، أو المقبوض عليهم فى عبودية مرة . يارب اعتقهم جميعاً وارحمهم . لأنك أنت تحل المربوطين وتقيم الساقطين . يا رجاء من ليس له رجاء ، ومعين من ليس له معين . عزاء صغيرى القلوب ، ميناء الذين فى العاصف . كل الأنفس المتضايقة أو المقبوض عليها : اعطها يارب رحمة . اعطها نياحاً . اعطها برودة . اعطها نعمة . اعطها معونة . اعطها خلاصاً . اعطها غفران خطاياها وآثامها . ونحن أيضاً يارب أمراض نفوسنا اشفها ، والتى لأجسادنا عافها ، أيها الطبيب الحقيقى الذى لأنفسنا وأجسادنا يا مدبر كل جسد تعهدنا بخلاصك .

CONGREGATION: Lord have mercy.

يقول الشعب : يارب ارحم

PRIEST says this prayer, and the congregation responds `Lord have mercy', each time.

يقول الكاهن هذه الطلبة ويرد الشعب فى كل مرة : يارب ارحم

O Longsuffering and Lover of Mankind, You gave our grace into the hands of Your holy Apostles that by Your holy anointing, they may heal every affliction and every disease of those who come to ou with faith in Your gifts. Now also, purify us from every sickness with our right hand; and make us worthy of Your unfading joy through Your goodness; and anoint those who come to You faithfully that they may receive deliverance and healing from the sickness of soul and body when Your priests anoint them, as You have commanded on the mouth of St. James Your disciple (James 5:14—16). ou, O Lord, declared in the beginning by the olive branch that the flood was passed; [now], O Compassionate and Merciful One, heal Your servant (...) who believes in Your name, by Your holy anointing and Your name; through the intercessions of the Virgin, Mother of Salvation. **Lord have mercy.**

أعطيت نعمتك أيها المتأنى على أيدى رسلك الأطهار يا محب البشر ، لكى يشفوا بمسحتك المقدسة كل ضربات وكل أسقام الآتين إليك ، وإلى مواهبك بأمانة ، فالآن أيضاً طهرنا بيمينك من كل مرض ، واجعلنا مستحقين بصلاحك ، لفرحك غير الفانى ، وارشم الآتين إليك بأمانة ، ليكون لهم خلاص ونجاة من أمراض النفس والجسد ، عندما يدهنهم كهنتك ، كما قلت على فم يعقوب تلميذك . أنت يارب من البدء ، بغصن الزيتون ، قد أظهرت أنه قد مضى الطوفان وبمسحتك المقدسة وباسمك أيها الرؤوف الرحيم خلص عبدك (فلان) المؤمن باسمك ، بشفاعة العذراء أم الخلاص . يارب ارحم .

O You who commanded the sick to call for the priests of the Church, those who are the servants of Your divinity, to anoint them with holy oil to be healed. Save, O Good One, Your servant (...) by this holy anointing, through the intercession of the Virgin, Mother of Salvation. **Lord have mercy.**

يا من أمر المرضى أن يدعوا قسوس الكنيسة الذين هم خدام لاهوتك وبدهنوهم بالزيت المقدس ليخلصوا ، نج أيها الصالح عبدك (فلان) من قبل هذه المسحة المقدسة ، بشفاعة العذراء أم الخلاص . يارب ارحم .

Heal, O Lord, our souls and bodies by Your divine signing and exalted hand, for You are the Lord of us all; through the intercessions of the Virgin, Mother of Salvation.. **Lord have mercy.**

اشف يارب أنفسنا وأجسادنا برشمك الإلهى ويدك العالية ، لأنك أنت هو ربنا كلنا . بشفاعة العذراء أم الخلاص . يارب ارحم .

O Savior and Lover of Mankind, as You gave grace to the prophets, kings, and highpriests, likewise give healing in this divine oil to those who are anointed by it. Protect them from every demonic assault and look towards them with Your mercy. Look at them with the eye of Your goodness and bless them; and stretch out the might's hand and grant Your servant (...), and those who are present with us, the healing of soul and body; through the intercessions of the Virgin, Mother of Salvation. **Lord have mercy.**

أيها المخلص محب البشر ، يا من أعطيت النعمة للأنبياء والملوك ورؤساء الآباء ، اجعل فى هذا الزيت الشفاء للذين يدهنون منه . واسترهم من جميع المحاربات الشيطانية ، أمل إليهم بوجه رحمتك . وباركهم بعين صلاحك . وابسط يد قوتك وامنح عبدك (فلان) والحاضرين معنا الشفاء النفسانى والجسدانى بشفاعة العذراء أم الخلاص . يارب ارحم .

O Physician of the sick and the Forgiver of sins; who delivers those who come to Him from afflictions; O harbor of rescue from the disturbance of waves. Have mercy on those who are afflicted with sicknesses, and deliver them from the evil of death. Fulfill Your priests' prayer for Your servant (...), and shower him from

يا طبيب المرضى وغافر الخطايا ، المنقذ من الشدائد كل الآتين إليك . يا ميناء الخلاص من حركات الأمواج وهياجها . اصنع رحمة مع المتضايقين بالأمراض ، ونجهم من الموت الردئ ، وكمل طلبة كهنتك

on high with Your mercy. Wash away his impurities, and sprinkle his wounds with the oil and wine of Your healing, that we may praise You in harmony, saying, "Bless the Lord all you works of the Lord." Through the intercessions of the Virgin, the Mother of Salvation, whom we praise, saying, "Blessed are you among women, and blessed is the Fruit of your womb." Now and at all times and unto the age of all ages. Amen.

Doxology

- God is light, He abides in light, and the angels of light, sing unto Him.
- The light has shone, from Mary, and Elizabeth gave birth, to the forerunner.
- The Holy Spirit, woke up in David, and said "Arise and sing, for the light has shone."
- So David the Psalmist, and the saint, rose up and took, his spiritual stringed instrument.
- He went to the temple, the house of the angels, he praised and sang to, the Holy Trinity.
- Saying "In Your light, O Lord shall we see light, let Your mercy come, to those who know You."
- True Light, that gives light, to every man, that comes into the world.
- You came into the world, through Your love for mankind, and all the creation rejoiced, at Your coming.
- You have saved Adam, from deception, and delivered Eve, from the pangs of death.
- You gave unto us, the spirit of sonship, we praise and bless You, with Your angels.
- Blessed are You indeed, with Your good Father, and the Holy Spirit, for You have come and saved us. Have mercy on us.

PRIEST prays, (making the sign of the cross, and CONGREGATION responds, *Lord have mercy,* each time)

+ For the peace that is from above, let us entreat the Lord.
Lord have mercy.
+ For the sanctification of this oil, let us entreat the Lord.
Lord have mercy.
+ For the sanctification of this house and all those who dwell in it, let us entreat the Lord. **Lord have mercy.**
+ For the sanctification of our Christian fathers and brethren, let us entreat the Lord. **Lord have mercy.**
+ For the blessing of this oil, and its sanctification, let us entreat the Lord. **Lord have mercy.**
+ For Your servant (...), let us entreat the Lord.
Lord have mercy.

لعبدك (فلان) . وأرسل عليه من العلو غيث رحمتك . وأغسل أدناسه ، وانضح من زيت وخمر شفائك على جراحاته . لنسبحك باتفاق واحد قائلين : باركى الرب يا جميع أعمال الرب . بشفاعة العذراء أم الخلاص ، تلك التى نسبحها قائلين : مباركة أنتِ فى النساء ، ومباركة هى ثمرة بطنك من الآن وكل ...

الذكصولوجية

- الله هو نور ، ساكن فى النور ، وتسبحه ملائكة النور .
- النور أشرق من مريم ، واليصابات ولدت السابق .
- والروح القدس أيقظ داود قائلاً : قم رتل لأن النور قد أشرق .
- فقام داود المرتل وأخذ قيثارته الروحانية.
- ومضى إلى الكنيسة بيت الملائكة ، وسبح ورتل للثالوث المقدس.
- قائلاً بنورك يارب نعاين النور ، فلتأتِ رحمتك على الذين يعرفونك.
- أيها النور الحقيقى الذى يضئ لكل إنسان آتِ إلى العالم.
- أتيت إلى العالم بمحبتك للبشر وكل الخليقة تهللت بمجيئك.
- وخلصت أبانا آدم من الغواية، وعتقت أمنا حواء من طلقات الموت.
- اعطيتنا روح البنوة، نسبحك ونباركك مع الملائكة.
- مبارك انت بالحقيقة مع أبيك الصالح والروح القدس لأنك أتيت وخلصتنا .

يقول الكاهن وهو يرشم بالصليب وفى كل مرة يرد الشعب : يارب ارحم .

+ من أجل السلام السمائى من الرب نطلب . **يارب ارحم .**
+ من أجل تقديس هذا الزيت من الرب نطلب . **يارب ارحم .**
+ من أجل تقديس هذا البيت والسكان فيه من الرب نطلب . **يارب ارحم.**
+ من أجل تقديس آبائنا واخواتنا المسيحيين من الرب نطلب . **يارب ارحم .**
+ من أجل بركة هذا الزيت وتقديسه من الرب نطلب . **يارب ارحم .**
+ من أجل عبدك (فلان) من الرب نطلب . **يارب ارحم .**

PRIEST

O compassionate and merciful Lord, declare Your mercy to everyone, and reveal Your power by delivering those who come to You faithfully for the anointing by Your priests, and heal them by Your grace. And all those who were struck by pains, guard them from the arrows of the adversary, from the afflictions of the mind, from the sufferings of the body, and from every hated thing, hidden and manifest. Through the intercessions of the Theotokos; and the supplication of the angels; and the blood of the martyrs; and the prayers of the saints, the highpriests, and the chorus of martyrs; we entreat You, O Lord, for Your servant (...) that the grace of Your Holy Spirit may dwell on him; and cleanse him from all his sins; and forgive all his transgressions; and deliver him from every affliction; and save us all from wickedness and the evil one. Amen.

The PRIEST prays this prayer on oil inaudibly.

O compassionate Lord, the Healer of the impairment of our souls and bodies; sanctify this oil that it may become a healing to all those who are anointed with it from the abominations of the spirit and the pains of the body, that as in this, Your holy name be glorified. For Yours is the glory and salvation, and we send up glory to You, O Father, Son, and Holy Spirit, now and at all times and unto the age of all ages. Amen.

The Catholic Epistle of James (5:10-20)

My brethren, take the prophets, who spoke in the name of the Lord, as an example of suffering and patience. Indeed we count them blessed who endure. You have heard of the perseverance of Job and seen the end intended by the Lord—that the Lord is very compassionate and merciful. But above all, my brethren, do not swear, either by heaven or by earth or with any other oath. But let your "Yes" be "Yes," and your "No," "No," lest you fall into judgment. Is anyone among you suffering? Let him pray. Is anyone cheerful? Let him sing psalms. Is anyone among you sick? Let him call for the elders of the church, and let them pray over him, anointing him with oil in the name of the Lord. And the prayer of faith will save the sick, and the Lord will raise him up. And if he has committed sins, he will be forgiven. Confess your trespasses to one another, and pray for one another, that you may be healed. The effective, fervent prayer of a righteous man avails much. Elijah was a man with a nature like ours, and he prayed earnestly that it would not rain; and it did not rain on the land for three years and six months. And he prayed again, and the heaven gave rain, and the earth produced its fruit. Brethren, if anyone among you wanders from the truth, and someone turns him back,

الكاهن

أيها الرب الرؤوف المتحنن ، أعلن رحمتك لكل أحد وأظهر قوتك فى خلاص الآتين إلى مسحة كهنتك بأمانة واشفهم بنعمتك . وكل الذين سقطوا فى سهام الأوجاع انقذهم من سهام العدو ، ومضايقة الأفكار ، وألام الجسد ، وسائر المكروهات الخفية والظاهرة . بشفاعة والدة الإله ، وسؤال الملائكة ، ودم الشهداء وطلبات القديسين ورؤساء الآباء ومصاف الشهداء نسألك يارب من أجل عبدك (فلان) لتحل عليه نعمة روح قدسك ، وطهره من جميع خطاياه ، واغفر له جميع زلاته ، ونجه من كل شدة ، وخلصنا كلنا من الشر والشرير . آمين .

يقول الكاهن هذه الصلاة سراً على الزيت

ايها الرب الرؤوف الشافى أنفسنا وأجسادنا ، قدس هذا الزيت ليكون لكل الذين يمسحون به شفاء لهم من أدناس الروح وآلام الجسد ، لكى بهذا يتمجد اسمك القدوس . لأن لك المجد والخلاص . ونرسل لك إلى فوق التمجيد أيها الآب والإبن والروح القدس الآن وكل أوان و إلى دهر الدهور آمين .

(الكاثوليكون من يعقوب 5 : 10 – 20)

خذوا يا اخوتى مثالاً لإحتمال المشقات والاناة الأنبياء الذين تكلموا باسم الرب . ها نحن نطوب الصابرين . قد سمعتم بصبر أيوب ، ورأيتم عاقبة الرب ، لأن الرب كثير الرحمة ورؤوف . ولكن قبل كل شئ يا اخوتى لا تحلفوا لا بالسماء ولا بالأرض ، ولا بقسم آخر ليكن كلامكم نعم نعم ولا لا لئلا تقعوا تحت دينونة . أعلى أحد بينكم مشقات فليصل . أمسرور أحد فليرتل . أمريض أحد بينكم فليدع قسوس الكنيسة ، فيصلوا عليه ويدهنوه بزيت باسم الرب . وصلاة الإيمان تشفى المريض والرب يقيمه ، وان كان قد فعل خطية تغفر له . اعترفوا بعضكم لبعض بالزلات وصلوا بعضكم لأجل بعض لكى تشفوا . طلبة البار تقتدر كثيراً فى فعلها . كان إيليا إنساناً تحت الآلام مثلنا وصلى صلاة أن لا تمطر السماء ، فلم تمطر على الأرض ثلاث سنين وستة أشهر . ثم صلى أيضاً فأعطت السماء مطراً و أخرجت الأرض ثمرها . أيها الاخوة ، ان ضل أحد بينكم عن

let him know that he who turns a sinner from the error of his way will save a soul from death and cover a multitude of sins. (Love not the world...)

The Trisagion is said, followed by the Litany of the Gospel.
Psalm (6:1,2)

O Lord, rebuke me not in Your indignation: neither chasten me in Your displeasure. Have mercy upon me. O Lord, for I am weak. O Lord, heal me for my bones are vexed. Alleluia.

John (5:1-17)

After this there was a feast of the Jews, and Jesus went up to Jerusalem. Now there is in Jerusalem by the Sheep Gate a pool, which is called in Hebrew, Bethesda, having five porches. In these lay a great multitude of sick people, blind, lame, paralyzed, waiting for the moving of the water. For an angel went down at a certain time into the pool and stirred up the water; then whoever stepped in first, after the stirring of the water, was made well of whatever disease he had. Now a certain man was there who had an infirmity thirty-eight years. When Jesus saw him lying there, and knew that he already had been in that condition a long time, He said to him, "Do you want to be made well?" The sick man answered Him, "Sir, I have no man to put me into the pool when the water is stirred up; but while I am coming, another steps down before me." Jesus said to him, "Rise, take up your bed and walk." And immediately the man was made well, took up his bed, and walked. And that day was the Sabbath. The Jews therefore said to him who was cured, "It is the Sabbath; it is not lawful for you to carry your bed." He answered them, "He who made me well said to me, 'Take up your bed and walk.' " Then they asked him, "Who is the Man who said to you, 'Take up your bed and walk'?" But the one who was healed did not know who it was, for Jesus had withdrawn, a multitude being in that place. Afterward Jesus found him in the temple, and said to him, "See, you have been made well. Sin no more, lest a worse thing come upon you." The man departed and told the Jews that it was Jesus who had made him well. For this reason the Jews persecuted Jesus, and sought to kill Him, because He had done these things on the Sabbath. But Jesus answered them, "My Father has been working until now, and I have been working. Glory Be to God forever and ever.

The three short Litanies are prayed followed by the Creed then this prayer

---

الحق فرده أحد ، فليعلم أن من يرد خاطئاً عن ضلال طريقه ، يخلص نفساً من الموت ويستر كثرة من الخطايا . لاتحبوا العالم ، ولا الأشياء التى فى العالم ...

تقال الثلاثة التقديسات وأوشية الانجيل
(المزمور 6 : 1 ، 2)

يارب لا تبكتنى بغضبك ، ولا تؤدبنى برجزك . ارحمنى يارب فانى ضعيف. اشفنى يارب فان عظامى قلقت . الليلويا .

(الانجيل من يوحنا 5 : 1 – 17)

وبعد هذا كان عيد لليهود ، فصعد يسوع إلى أورشليم وفى أورشليم عند باب الضأن بركة يقال لها بالعبرانية بيت حسدا لها خمسة أروقة . فى هذه كان مضطجعاً جمهور كثير من مرضى وعمى وعرج وعسم ، يتوقعون تحريك الماء . لأن ملاكاً كان ينزل أحياناً فى البركة ويحرك الماء ، فمن نزل أولاً بعد تحريك الماء كان يبرأ من أي مرض اعتراه . وكان إنسان به مرض منذ ثمان وثلاثين سنة . هذا رآه يسوع مضطجعاً ، فعلم أن له زماناً كثيراً . فقال له تريد أن تبرأ ؟ أجابه المريض : يا سيد ليس لى إنسان يلقينى فى البركة متى تحرك الماء ، بل بينما أنا أتِ ينزل قدامى آخر . قال له يسوع : قم أحمل سريرك وامش . فحالاً برئ الإنسان وحمل سريره ومشى . وكان فى ذلك اليوم سبت . فقال اليهود للذى شفى : أنه سبت لا يحل لك أن تحمل سريرك . أجابهم أن الذى أبرأنى هو قال لى أحمل سريرك وامش . فسألوه : من هو الإنسان الذى قال لك أحمل سريرك وأمش . أما الذى شفى فلم يكن يعلم من هو ، لأن يسوع اعتزل . إذ كان فى الموضع جمع . بعد ذلك وجده يسوع فى الهيكل وقال له : ها أنت قد برئت ، فلا تخطئ أيضاً لئلا يكون لك أشر . فمضى الإنسان وأخبر اليهود أن يسوع هو الذى أبرأه . ولهذا كان اليهود يطردون يسوع ، ويطلبون أن يقتلوه ، لأنه عمل هذا فى سبت . فأجابهم يسوع : أبى يعمل حتى الآن ، وأنا أعمل . والمجد لله دائماً .

يقول الكاهن الثلاثة أواشى الصغار وقانون الإيمان ثم هذه الطلبة

PRIEST

O Master, Lord, Jesus Christ, the King of the ages, who brought all things into existence out of nothing, visible and invisible; ho came willingly, and emptied Himself according to the Economy, out of His great mercy, to save us from the death of sin and the victories of the adversary; The Doer of good with haste, the Longsuffering in discipline, and who is greatly fearsome for the sake of good things. Remember, O Lord, Your mercies, and do not turn away Your compassionate face from us, we ho have been called by Your goodness, but give ear to our supplication and to the lowliness of our prayer, we Your sinful servants. and give healing to Your servant (...) who took refuge in the shadow of Your wings, for You are the Lover of Mankind, and forgive his trespasses, and all that he had done in his entire life. d pardon his transgressions, those he committed willingly or unwillingly, whether by his actions alone, or by another foreign, whether in thought or in deed, for the sake of those who please You. O Master, as You forgave the debtor the talents he owed, forgive Your servant his trespasses and pardon all his transgressions. And as You cleansed the leper by Your word, and took away the leprosy from his body by Your will, likewise, take away the sickness from Your servant (...)'s body, and sanctify and purify him. O You who healed the Canaanite girl at the moment her mother prayed, now also, through Your priests' supplications, we who dare, not having boldness in ourselves, but by Your grace on us, free Your servant (...) from every diabolical scheme or work. O You who resurrected from death the widow's son and the official's daughter when You commanded them to rise, and raised Lazarus from Hades after he had been dead for four days by the authority of Your divinity; raise up Your servant from the death of sin; and if You command to raise him up in another time, give him support and help that he may please You while [in this world] and all the days of his lifetime.

(Inaudibly: And if You advocate that his soul be taken, let it be by powerful hands of angels of light to save him from the demons of darkness. Transform him to the Paradise of joy to be with all the Saints.)

Through Your Blood that was shed for our salvation, and by which You purchased us, for You are our hope, we Your servants; Through the intercessions of the Virgin, the Theotokos, and the prayers of all the saints. For glory, honor, and worship are due to the Father, the Son, and the Holy Spirit, now and at all times and unto the age of all ages. Amen.

الكاهن

أيها السيد الرب يسوع المسيح ملك الدهور ، مخرج كل الموجودات من العدم إلى الوجود ، ما يرى وما لا يرى ، الذى جاء بارادته وبكثرة رحمته قد تنازل بالتدبير ، ليخلصنا من موت الخطية وغلبة المضاد . السريع الاحسان ، والمتأنى فى العقاب ، المخيف مراراً كثيرة من أجل الخيرات العتيدة. أذكر يارب مراحمك ، ولا تمل عنا بوجه تحننك نحن الذين دعينا إلى صلاحك . بل اسمع طلباتنا ومسكنة دعائنا نحن عبيدك الخطاة وامنح الشفاء لعبدك (فلان) هذا الذى التجا تحت ظلال كنفك لأنك أنت محب البشر . اغفر له ما عليه ، وما صنعه فى سائر عمره واترك له جميع زلاته التى صنعها بارادته وبغير ارادته . ان كان من حركاته وحده او من جهة آخر غريب. ان كان بالفكر أو بالفعل ، من أجل الذين أرضوك . وكما تركت للغريم ايها السيد الدين الذى لك عليه ، هكذا أيضاً أترك لعبدك ما عليه وسامحه بجميع زلاته . وكما طهرت الأبرص بكلمتك ونزعت البرص من جسمه بارادتك ، هكذا انزع كل مرض من جسم عبدك (فلان) وقدسه وطهره . يا من ابرأ ابنة الكنعانية بسؤال أمها ، الآن أيضاً بسؤال كهنتك الذين هم نحن المتجاسرون إذ ليس لنا دالة من قبل أنفسنا ، بل من جهة نعمتك علينا ، اعتق عبدك (فلان) من كل المؤامرات وجميع المحاربات الشيطانية . يا من أقام إبن الأرملة وإبنة يايرس من الموت لما أمرهما بالقيام . واقام لعازر من بعد موته بأربعة أيام بسلطان لاهوته ، أقم عبدك هذا من موت الخطية . وان أمرت باقامته إلى زمان آخر . فامنحه مساعدة ومعونة لكى يرضيك فى كل أيام حياته .

(وان أمرت أن تأخذ نفسه ، فليكن هذا بيد ملائكة نورانيين يخلصونه من شياطين الظلمة. انقله إلى فردوس الفرح ليكون مع جميع القديسين)

بدمك الذى سفك من أجل خلاصنا. الذى به اشتريتنا لأنك أنت رجاؤنا نحن عبيدك بشفاعة العذراء والدة الإله وسؤال جميع القديسين. لأن لك المجد والكرامة والقوة والسجود يليق بك ايها الآب والإبن والروح القدس الآن وكل أوان وإلى دهر الدهور آمين .

(2) SECOND PRAYER

The priest lights the second wick and says "Elison Emas..."
"Our Father..."

THE PRAYER OF THE TRAVELERS
PRIEST:

We ask and entreat Your goodness, O Lover of Mankind, remember, O Lord, our fathers and our brethren who are traveling.

DEACON:

Pray for our fathers and our brethren who are traveling, or those who intend to travel anywhere. Straighten all their ways, whether by sea, rivers, lakes, roads, or those who are traveling by any other means that Christ our God may bring them back to their own homes in peace, and forgive us our sins.

CONGREGATION: Lord have mercy.

PRIEST:

And those who intend to travel anywhere, straighten all their ways, whether by sea, rivers, lakes, roads, air, or those who are traveling by any other means, everyone anywhere. Lead them into a haven of calm, a haven of safety. Graciously accompany them in their departure and be their companion in their travel. Bring them back to their own, rejoicing with joy and safety in security. Be a fellow worker with Your servants in every good deed. As for us, too, O Lord, keep our sojourn in this life without harm, without storm, and undisturbed to the end...

The Pauline Epistle from Romans (15:1-7)

We then that are strong ought to bear the weaknesses of the weak, and not to please ourselves. Let every one of us please his neighbor for his good to edification. For even Christ pleased not himself; but, as it is written, The reproaches of them that reproached you fell on me. For whatever things were written before were written for our learning, that we through patience and comfort of the scriptures might have hope. Now the God of patience and consolation grant you to be like minded one toward another according to Christ Jesus: That you may with one mind and one mouth glorify God, even the Father of our Lord Jesus Christ. Therefore receive one another, as Christ also received us to the glory of God. The grace of God the Father be with us all. Amen.

(الصلاة الثانية)

توقد الفتيلة الثانية ويقول الكاهن Ⲉⲗⲉⲏⲥⲟⲛ Ⲏⲙⲁⲥ وأبانا الذى فى السموات ثم يقول .

أوشية المسافرين

وايضاً فنسأل الله ضابط الكل ، أبا ربنا وإلهنا ومخلصنا يسوع المسيح ، نسأل ونطلب من صلاحك يا محب البشر : أذكر يارب آبائنا واخوتنا المسافرين .

يقول الشماس

أطلبوا عن آبائنا واخواتنا المسافرين ، الذين يضمرون السفر فى كل موضع ، لكى يسهل طرقهم أجمعين ، ان كان فى البحار أو الأنهار أو البحيرات أو الطرق المسلوكة أو المسافرين بكل نوع ، لكى يردهم المسيح إلهنا إلى مساكنهم سالمين ، ويغفر لنا خطايانا .

يقول الشعب : يارب ارحم

يقول الكاهن

والذين يضمرون السفر فى كل مكان سهل طرقهم أجمعين ، ان كان فى البحار أو الأنهار أو البحيرات أو الطرق المسلوكة أو السالكين بكل نوع ، كل أحد بكل موضع ، ردهم إلى ميناء هادئة ميناء الخلاص . تفضل اصحبهم فى الاقلاع واصحبهم فى المسير . ردهم إلى منازلهم بالفرح فرحين ، وبالعافية معافين . اشترك فى العمل مع عبيدك فى كل عمل صالح . ونحن أيضاً يارب غربتنا التى فى هذا العمر ، احفظها بغير ضرر ولا عاصف ولا قلق إلى الانقضاء . بالنعمة والرأفة...

(البولس من رسالة رومية 15 : 1 – 7)

فيجب علينا نحن الأقوياء أن نحتمل ضعف الضعفاء و لا نرضى أنفسنا . فليرضى كل واحد منا قريبه للخير لأجل البنيان ، لأن المسيح أيضاً لم يرض نفسه ، بل كما هو مكتوب تعييرات معيريك وقعت على ، لأن كل ما سبق فكتب ، كتب لأجل تعليمنا . حتى بالصبر والتعزية بما فى الكتب يكون لنا رجاء . وليعطيكم إله الصبر والتعزية أن تهتموا اهتماماً واحداً فيما بينكم بحسب المسيح يسوع لكى تمجدوا الله أبا ربنا يسوع المسيح بنفس واحدة وفم واحد . ذلك اقبلوا بعضكم بعضاً كما أن المسيح ايضاً قبلنا لمجد الله . نعمة الله الآب تحل على جميعنا آمين .

 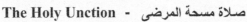 

The Trisagion is said, followed by the Litany of the Gospel.

تقال الثلاثة التقديسات
وأوشية الانجيل

Psalm (101:1,2)

Hear my prayer, O Lord: and let my cry come unto You. In the day that I call, answer me speedily. Alleluia.

(المزمور 101 : 1 ، 2)

يارب استمع صلاتى وليصعد أمامك صراخى . فى اليوم الذى أدعوك فيه استجب لى سريعاً . الليلو يا .

Luke (19:1-10)

Then Jesus entered and passed through Jericho. Now behold, there was a man named Zacchaeus who was a chief tax collector, and he was rich. And he sought to see who Jesus was, but could not because of the crowd, for he was of short stature. So he ran ahead and climbed up into a sycamore tree to see Him, for He was going to pass that way. And when Jesus came to the place, He looked up and saw him, and said to him, "Zacchaeus, make haste and come down, for today I must stay at your house." So he made haste and came down, and received Him joyfully. But when they saw it, they all complained, saying, "He has gone to be a guest with a man who is a sinner." Then Zacchaeus stood and said to the Lord, "Look, Lord, I give half of my goods to the poor; and if I have taken anything from anyone by false accusation, I restore fourfold." And Jesus said to him, "Today salvation has come to this house, because he also is a son of Abraham; for the Son of Man has come to seek and to save that which was lost. Glory Be to God forever and ever. Amen

(الانجيل من لوقا 19 : 1 – 10)

ثم دخل واجتاز فى أريحا . وإذا رجل اسمه زكا وهو رئيس للعشارين وكان غنياً . وطلب أن يرى يسوع من هو ، ولم يقدر من الجمع لأنه كان قصير القامة . فركض متقدماً وصعد إلى جميزة لكى يراه . لأنه كان مزمعاً أن يمر من هناك . فلما جاء يسوع إلى المكان نظر إلى فوق فرآه وقال له: يا زكا أسرع وانزل لأنه ينبغى أن أمكث اليوم فى بيتك . فأسرع ونزل وقبله فرحاً ، فلما رأى الجميع ذلك تذمروا قائلين: أنه دخل ليبيت عند رجل خاطئ . فوقف زكا وقال للرب : ها أنا يارب أعطى نصف أموالى للمساكين ، وان كنت قد وشيت بأحد ارد أربعة أضعاف . فقال له يسوع: اليوم حصل خلاص لهذا البيت ، إذ هو ايضاً إبن إبراهيم. لأن إبن الإنسان قد جاء لكى يطلب ويخلص ما قد هلك . والمجد لله دائماً.

PRIEST:

O Lord, the Compassionate and Lover of Mankind, who accepts those who repent; who knows that man's mind is perverse with evil from his youth; who does not desire the sinner's death but rather to return and live; who became man for the salvation of mankind; who said: "I did not come to call the righteous, but sinners, to repentance"; who sought after, and found, the strayed sheep and the lost coin; who said: "The one who comes to Me I will by no means cast out"; who forgave the adulteress after she repented, and likewise also, You granted the lame man forgiveness of his sins and healing of his body, You have said that there is joy in heaven over one sinner who repents. You have also said that every time you fall, rise up and you shall be saved. Behold O Compassionate One from Your holy high place, and dwell in Your servant (...) who confesses his transgressions and comes to You in faith and hope, and forgive is mistakes, whether in deed or in word or in thought. Purify him from every sin, and keep him the rest of his life, abiding by Your commandments that the enemy may not once again rejoice; that as in this, Your holy name be glorified, and to You, glory, majesty, and worship are

ثم يقول الكاهن هذه الطلبة

ايها الرب الرؤوف محب البشر ، القابل إليه التائبين ، العارف أن فكر الإنسان مائل إلى الشر منذ صباه ، الذى لا يشاء موت الخاطى حتى يرجع إليه ويحيا ، الذى تأنس من أجل خلاص البشر ، الذى قال أنى لم آتِ لأدع الصديقين بل الخطاة إلى التوبة ، الذى طلب الخروف الضال والدرهم المفقود ووجدهما ، الذى قال ان من يقبل إلى لا أخرجه خارجاً ، الذى غفر خطايا الزانية التى تابت قديماً ، وهكذا المقعد أعطيته غفران خطاياه وصحة جسده . أنت الذى قلت أنه يكون فرح فى السماء بخاطئ واحد يتوب . وقلت ايضاً ان كل مرة تسقط قم فتخلص . أطلع ايها المتحنن من سمائك المقدسة ، وحل فى عبدك (فلان) المعترف بزلاته ، المقبل إليك بأمانة ورجاء . واغفر له غلطاته ، ان كان بالفعل أو بالقول أو بالفكر . طهره من كل خطية ، واحفظه بقية زمان حياته سالكاً فى وصاياك ، لكى لا يفرح به العدو دفعة أخرى . وبهذا يتمجد اسمك القدوس ،

due, now and at all times and unto the age of all ages. Amen.

ويليق بك المجد والعز والسجود الآن وكل أوان وإلى دهر الدهور آمين.

(3) THIRD PRAYER

(الصلاة الثالثة)

The priest lights the third wick and says "*Elison Emas…*" "*Our Father…*"

توقد الفتيلة الثالثة ويقول الكاهن Ⲉ̀ⲖⲈⲎⲤⲞⲚ ⲎⲘⲀⲤ وأبانا الذى فى السموات ، ثم أوشية الأثمار التى تناسب .

THE PRAYER OF THE FRUITS
PRIEST:
Graciously accord, O Lord, the air of heaven, the fruits of the earth, the waters of the rivers, the seeds, the herbs and the plants of the field this year, bless them.

أوشية الأثمار
الكاهن
تفضل يارب : أهوية السماء وثمرات الأرض فى هذه السنة باركها .

DEACON:
Pray for the air of heaven, the fruits of the earth, the rising of the waters of the rivers, the seeds, the herbs and the plants of the field, that Christ our God may bless them, bring them to perfection in peace without harm and forgive us our sins.

يقول الشماس
أطلبوا عن أهوية السماء وثمرات الأرض والشجر والكروم وكل شجرة مثمرة فى كل المسكونة ، لكى يباركها المسيح إلهنا ، ويكملها سالمة بغير آفة ، ويغفر لنا خطايانا .

CONGREGATION:
Lord have mercy. Lord have mercy. Lord have mercy.

يقول الشعب : يارب ارحم . يارب ارحم . يارب ارحم .

PRIEST:
Raise them to their measure according to Your grace. Give joy to the face of the earth. May its furrows be abundantly watered, and its fruits be plentiful. Prepare it for sowing and harvesting. Manage our life as deemed fit. Bless the crown of the year with Your goodness for the sake of the poor of Your people, the widow, the orphan, the traveler, the stranger, and for the sake of all of us who entreat You and seek Your holy name. For the eyes of everyone wait upon You, for You give them their food in due season. Deal with us according to Your goodness, O You who give food to all flesh. Fill our hearts with joy and gladness, that we, too, having sufficiency in everything always, may abound in every good deed.

ثم يكمل الكاهن
أصعدها كمقدارها كنعمتك . فرح وجه الأرض ، ليرو حرثها ، ولتكثر أثمارها . أعدها للزرع والحصاد . ودبر حياتنا كما يليق. بارك اكليل السنة بصلاحك ، من أجل فقراء شعبك ، من أجل الأرملة واليتيم والغريب والضيف ، ومن أجلنا كلنا نحن الذين نرجوك ونطلب اسمك القدوس لأن أعين الكل تترجاك ، لأنك أنت الذى تعطيهم طعامهم فى حين حسن. اصنع معنا حسب صلاحك . يا معطياً طعاماً لكل جسد . املأ قلوبنا فرحاً ونعيماً ، لكى نحن أيضاً إذ يكون لنا الكفاف فى كل شئ كل حين نزداد فى كل عمل صالح .

The Pauline Epistle from 1 Corinthians (12:28-13:8)
And God has appointed these in the church: first apostles, second prophets, third teachers, after that miracles, then gifts of healings, helps, administrations, varieties of tongues. Are all apostles? Are all prophets? Are all teachers? Are all workers of miracles? Do all have gifts of healings? Do all speak with tongues? Do all interpret? But earnestly desire the best gifts. And yet I show you a more excellent way. Though I speak with the tongues of men and of angels, but have not love, I have become sounding brass or a clanging cymbal. And though I have the gift of prophecy, and

(كورنثوس الأولى 12 : 28 — 13 : 8)
فوضع الله فى الكنيسة أولاً رسلاً ، ثانياً أنبياء ، ثالثاً معلمين ، ثم قوات ، وبعد ذلك مواهب شفاء ، أعواناً ، تدابير ، وأنواع ألسنة . ألعل الجميع رسل . ألعل للجميع مواهب شفاء . ألعل الجميع يتكلمون بألسنة . ألعل الجميع يترجمون . ولكن جدوا للمواهب الحسنى . وأيضاً أريكم طريقاً أفضل . ان كنت أتكلم بألسنة الناس والملائكة ، ولكن لى ليس لى محبة ، فقد صرت نحاساً يطن أو صنجاً

understand all mysteries and all knowledge, and though I have all faith, so that I could remove mountains, but have not love, I am nothing. And though I bestow all my goods to feed the poor, and though I give my body to be burned, but have not love, it profits me nothing. Love suffers long and is kind; love does not envy; love does not parade itself, is not puffed up; does not behave rudely, does not seek its own, is not provoked, thinks no evil; does not rejoice in iniquity, but rejoices in the truth; bears all things, believes all things, hopes all things, endures all things. Love never fails. But whether there are prophecies, they will fail; whether there are tongues, they will cease; whether there is knowledge, it will vanish away. The grace of God the Father be with us all. Amen.

Trisagion is said,
followed by the Litany of the Gospel.

Psalm (37:1,2)

O Lord, put me not to rebuke in Your anger; neither chasten me in Your displeasure. For Your arrows stick fast in me; and Your hand is heavy upon me. Alleluia.

Matthew 10:1-8

And when He had called His twelve disciples to Him, He gave them power over unclean spirits, to cast them out, and to heal all kinds of sickness and all kinds of disease. Now the names of the twelve apostles are these: first, Simon, who is called Peter, and Andrew his brother; James the son of Zebedee, and John his brother; Philip and Bartholomew; Thomas and Matthew the tax collector; James the son of Alphaeus, and Lebbaeus, whose surname was Thaddaeus; Simon the Cananite, and Judas Iscariot, who also betrayed Him. These twelve Jesus sent out and commanded them, saying: "Do not go into the way of the Gentiles, and do not enter a city of the Samaritans. But go rather to the lost sheep of the house of Israel. And as you go, preach, saying, 'The kingdom of heaven is at hand.' Heal the sick, cleanse the lepers, raise the dead, cast out demons. Freely you have received, freely give. Glory Be to God forever and ever. Amen.

PRIEST:

Blessed are You, O Lord, our God, the Holy One, the Physician of our souls; by Your bruises we were healed, O good Shepherd who sought the strayed sheep; who gives comfort to the fainthearted; who healed Simon's mother-in-law from her severe fever, and the woman who bled from her long-standing sickness. who freed the Canaanite girl from the unclean spirit; who forgave

يرن . وان كانت لى نبوة وأعلم جميع الأسرار وكل علم . وان كان لى الإيمان حتى أنقل الجبال ، ولكن ليس لى محبة فلست شيئاً , وان أطعمت كل أموالى وان سلمت جسدى حتى أحترق ، ولكن ليس لى محبة فلا أنتفع شيئاً . المحبة تتانى وترفق . المحبة لا تحسد . المحبة لا تتفاخر ، ولا تنتفخ ، ولا تقبح ، ولا تطلب ما لنفسها ، ولا تحتد ، ولا تظن السوء ولا تفرح بالاثم ، بل تفرح بالحق ، وتحتمل كل شئ ، وتصدق كل شئ ، وترجو كل شئ ، وتصبر على كل شئ . المحبة لا تسقط أبداً . نعمة الله الأب تحل على جميعنا أمين .

تقال الثلاثة التقديسات
وأوشية الانجيل

(المزمور 37 : 1 ، 2)

يارب لا تبكتنى بغضبك ولا برجزك تؤدبنى ، لأن سهامك قد انغرست فيّ ، وثقلت عليّ يدك . الليلو يا .

(الانجيل من متى 10 : 1 - 8)

ثم دعا تلاميذه الاثنى عشر ، وأعطاهم سلطاناً على الأرواح النجسة لكى يخرجونها ويشفوا كل الأمراض وكل العلل , هذه أسماء الاثنى عشر رسولاً : الأول سمعان المسمى بطرس واندراوس أخوه ويعقوب بن زبدى ويوحنا أخوه ، فيلبس وبرثولماوس . توما ومتى العشار . يعقوب بن حلفى وتداوس . سمعان القانوى ويهوذا الاسخريوطى الذى أسلمه. هؤلاء الاثنا عشر أرسلهم يسوع وأمرهم قائلاً : لا تسلكوا طريق الأمم ، ولا تدخلوا مدينة للسامريين . بل انطلقوا خاصة إلى الخراف الضالة من بيت إسرائيل وفيما أنتم ذاهبون اكرزوا قائلين : أنه قد اقترب منكم ملكوت السموات . اشفوا المرضى طهروا البرص اقيموا الموتى . اخرجوا الشياطين . مجاناً أخذتم مجاناً اعطوا . والمجد لله دائماً .

يقول الكاهن هذه الطلبة

تباركت أيها الرب إلهنا الصالح طبيب أنفسنا ، بجراحاتك شفينا ايها الراعى الصالح الذى طلب الخروف الضال . يا معزى صغيرى القلوب . الذى إبرأ حماة سمعان من حمتها الصعبة ، والنازفة الدم من مرضها القديم . الذى عتق إبنة الكنعانية من الروح النجس . الذى ترك

the debtor what he owed; who forgave the adulteress and the lame man; who justified the tax-collector; who accepted the thiefs confession at the end of his life, and granted him the Paradise; who takes away the sin of the world; who was nailed to the Cross of His own will. We entreat You, we pray to You, we call on You, and we cry unto You to forgive and us, we Your servants, all our iniquities, whether personal or impersonal, whether knowingly or unknowingly, those of the night and those of the day, those that arise from within ourselves and those that come from others, those of the visible senses and those of the hidden consciences, and those of the actions of the spirit and body. For You are God, the Good One and Lover of Mankind. Cleanse all our transgressions, and lead and help us that we may walk in the ways of eternal life, and not the way of eternal death. Yes, O Lord, pardon Your servant (...) for all his transgressions, fill his mouth with Your praise, and direct his hands to do Your commandments. Guide his feet to the path of salvation; fortify his body parts and thoughts with Your power. You have said to us O Lord through Your holy Apostles, "Whatever you bind on earth will be bound in heaven, and whatever you loose on earth will be loosed in heaven". And again, You have said, "If you forgive the sins of any, they are forgiven them". As You heard Hezekiah when his soul was afflicted in the hour of his death, and did not neglect his prayer, likewise also in this hour, hear me, I Your poor servant, and have mercy on Your servant (...) even if his sins are many, for You have commanded forgiveness up to seventy times seven. And we send up thanksgiving for Your mercies and greatness, and glory to You, and Your good Father who is without beginning, and Your Holy Spirit, the Giver of Life, now and at all times and unto the age of all ages. Amen.

للغريم الدين الذى عليه . الذى غفر للزانية خطاياها . الذى برر العشار . الذى قبل إليه اعتراف اللص فى آخر حياته ، وأنعم عليه بالفردوس . الذى حمل خطاياالعالم . الذى سمر على الصليب بإرادته وحده . نسأل ونطلب إليك ، ونتضرع ونصرخ نحوك ، لكى تغفر لعبدك (فلان) ولنا نحن عبيدك جميع آثامنا . الذاتية وغير الذاتية ان كان بمعرفة أو بغير معرفة ، الليلية والنهارية ، التى أتت منا والتى وردت علينا من آخرين ، التى من الحواس الظاهرة أو الضمائر المخفية ، التى من حركات الروح أو الجسد ، لأنك إله صالح محب للبشر . طهرنا من كل زلاتنا ، واهدنا وساعدنا لكى نسلك فى طريق الحياة الأبدية , لا طريق الموت الدهرى . نعم يارب سامح عبدك (فلان) بجميع زلاته . وأملأ فاه من تسبيحك . وأبسط يديه إلى فعل وصاياك . وهيئ أقدامه إلى سبيل الخلاص . وحصن أعضائه وأفكاره بقوتك أنت يارب قلت لنا على أيدى رسلك الأطهار : ان كل ما تربطونه على الأرض يكون مربوطاً فى السموات ، وما تحلونه على الأرض يكون محلولاً فى السموات . وأيضاً قلت ان من غفرتم له خطاياه غفرت له . وكما سمعت لحزقيا عند ضيقة نفسه فى ساعة موته , ولم تعرض عن طلبته ، كذلك أيضاً اسمعنى أنا عبدك المسكين فى هذه الساعة . وارحم عبدك (فلان) وان كانت خطاياه قد كثرت جداً ، لأنك أمرت بالغفران سبع مرات فى سبعين مرة . ونرسل الشكر لمراحمك ولعظمتك . ولك المجد مع أبيك الصالح غير المبتدئ، وروحك القدوس المحيى الآن وكل أوان وإلى دهر الدهور آمين .

(4) FOURTH PRAYER
(الصلاة الرابعة)

The priest lights the fourth wick and says "Elison Emas..." "Our Father..."

THE PRAYER OF THE PRISEDENT

PRIEST:

Again, let us ask God the Pantocrator, the Father of our Lord, God, and Savior Jesus Christ. We ask and entreat Your Goodness, O Lover of Mankind: remember, O Lord, the ruler of our land, Your servant.

DEACON:

توقد الفتيلة الرابعة ويقول الكاهن Ⲉⲗⲉⲏⲥⲟⲛ ⲏⲙⲁⲥ وأبانا الذى فى السموات ، ثم يقول :

أوشية الرئيس
وأيضاً فلنسأل الله ضابط الكل ، أبا ربنا وإلهنا ومخلصنا يسوع المسيح . نسأل ونطلب من صلاحك يا محب البشر ، أذكر يارب رئيس أرضنا عبدك .

يقول الشماس

Pray that Christ our God may give us mercy and compassion before the mighty sovereigns, and soften their hearts towards us, for that which is good at all times, and forgive us our sins.

أطلبوا لكى يعطينا المسيح إلهنا رحمة ورأفة أمام الرؤساء الأعزاء ، ويعطف قلوبهم علينا بالصلاح فى كل حين ، ويغفر لنا خطايانا .

CONGREGATION: Lord have mercy.

يقول الشعب : يارب ارحم

PRIEST:

Keep him in peace, truth and strength. Subject under him all the barbarians, the nations who desire war against all our fertile lands. Speak to his heart concerning the peace of Your One, Only, Holy, Catholic and Apostolic Church. Give him that he may think peacefully towards us and towards Your holy name, that we too may lead a quiet and peaceable life, and may be found in all piety and all chastity in You...

يقول الكاهن

أحفظه فى سلام وعدل وقوة، وتخضع له كل الأمم الذين يريدون الحرب فى جميع ما لنا من الخصب . تكلم فى قلبه من أجل سلام كنيستك الواحدة الوحيدة المقدسة الجامعة الرسولية . أعطه أن يفكر بالسلام فينا وفى اسمك القدوس ، لكى نعيش نحن أيضاً فى سيرة هادئة ، ونوجد ساكنين بكل تقوى وكل عفاف بك . بالنعمة ...

The Pauline Epistle from Romans (8:14-21)

For as many as are led by the Spirit of God, these are sons of God. For you did not receive the spirit of bondage again to fear, but you received the Spirit of adoption by whom we cry out, "Abba, Father." The Spirit Himself bears witness with our spirit that we are children of God, and if children, then heirs—heirs of God and joint heirs with Christ, if indeed we suffer with Him, that we may also be glorified together. For I consider that the sufferings of this present time are not worthy to be compared with the glory which shall be revealed in us. For the earnest expectation of the creation eagerly waits for the revealing of the sons of God. For the creation was subjected to futility, not willingly, but because of Him who subjected it in hope; because the creation itself also will be delivered from the bondage of corruption into the glorious liberty of the children of God. The grace of God the Father be with us all. Amen.

(البولس من رومية 8 : 14 - 21)

لأن كل الذين ينقادون بروح الله فأولئك هم أبناء الله . إذ لم تأخذوا روح العبودية ايضاً للخوف ، بل أخذتم روح التبنى الذى به نصرخ يا أبا الآب . الروح نفسه أيضاً يشهد لأرواحنا أننا أولاد الله . فان كنا أولاداً فاننا ورثة ايضاً ، ورثة الله ووارثون مع المسيح . ان كنا نتألم معه ، فانى أحسب آلام الزمان الحاضر لا تقاس بالمجد العتيد أن يستعلن فينا . لأن انتظار الخليقة يتوقع استعلان ابناء الله . إذ أخضعت الخليقة للباطل ، ليس طوعاً بل من أجل الذى أخضعها على الرجاء . لأن الخليقة نفسها أيضاً ستعتق من عبودية الفساد إلى حرية مجد أولاد الله . نعمة الله الآب تحل على جميعنا آمين .

The Trisagion is said, followed by the Litany of the Gospel.

تقال الثلاثة التقديسات وأوشية الانجيل

Psalm (50:1,2)

Have mercy upon me, O God, after Your great mercy: and according to the multitude of Your mercies do away with mine offenses. Wash me thoroughly from my sin. Alleluia.

(المزمور 50 : 1 ، 2)

ارحمنى يا الله كعظيم رحمتك . ومثل كثرة رأفتك امح ذنبى . أغسلنى كثيراً من اثمى ، ونقنى من خطيتى . الليلويا.

Luke 10:1-9

After these things the Lord appointed seventy others also, and sent them two by two before His face into every city and place where He Himself was about to go. Then He said to them, "The harvest truly is great, but the laborers are few; therefore pray the Lord of the harvest to send out laborers into His harvest. Go your

(الانجيل من لوقا 10 : 1 - 9)

وبعد ذلك عين الرب سبعين آخرين أيضاً ، وأرسلهم اثنين اثنين أمام وجهه إلى كل مدينة وموضع حيث كان هو مزمعاً أن يأتى . فقال لهم : ان الحصاد كثير ولكن الفعلة قليلون، فاطلبوا من رب الحصاد أن يرسل

way; behold, I send you out as lambs among wolves. Carry neither money bag, knapsack, nor sandals; and greet no one along the road. But whatever house you enter, first say, 'Peace to this house.' And if a son of peace is there, your peace will rest on it; if not, it will return to you. And remain in the same house, eating and drinking such things as they give, for the laborer is worthy of his wages. Do not go from house to house. Whatever city you enter, and they receive you, eat such things as are set before you. And heal the sick there, and say to them, 'The kingdom of God has come near to you. Glory be to God forever.

PRIEST:

O Lord, who teaches and heals; who raises the poor from the dust, and lifts the beggar from the ash heap; the Father of orphans and the Judge of widows; the harbor of those in the storm; the Physician of the afflicted; who bears our sicknesses, and takes away our iniquities; who is near to help and is longsuffering in chastisements; who breathed in the face of His Disciples, and said to them, "Receive the Holy Spirit. If you forgive the sins of any, they are forgiven." You are He who accepts the sinners' repentance, and heals from sicknesses, considering Your servant's lowliness, and my prayer—I the unworthy, who have been called by Your grace to the priesthood in Your holy place, yet made worthy by Your grace to serve Your holy mysteries, and to offer prayers and sacrifices for the forgiveness of Your people's sins; and [to be] a mediator to bring Your rational flock closer to You. O good Shepherd, accept my prayer for Your servant (...); send him healing speedily, forgive him his iniquities, give health to his whole body, all his members, and his spirit from every disease, relieve him from his bodily pains, and take away his distresses, O You in whom we hope and none other. As You informed John's two disciples, saying, "Go and tell John the things you have seen and heard: that the blind see, the lame walk, the lepers are cleansed, the deaf hear, the dead are raised, the poor have the gospel preached to them. Blessed is he who is not offended because of Me." We do not doubt the power of Your divinity, O Christ, the only-begotten Son of God, and the Lamb of God who takes away the sin of the world. Remember Your mercies and compassions that exist from the beginning, for man's heart is perverse with evil from his youth since no one is found without sin though his life on earth may be a single day. If You, O Lord, should mark iniquity, O Lord, who would stand? For forgiveness is from You. If You judge, who would provide a justification? For every mouth would be closed and not be able to speak. Do not remember the sins of my ignorance, O Lord, the refuge of those who repent, the hope of those who have no hope, and the comfort

فعلة إلى حصاده . اذهبوا ها أنا أرسلكم مثل حملان بين ذئاب . لا تحملوا كيساً ولا مزوداً ولا أحذية . ولا تسلموا على أحد فى الطريق . وأى بيت دخلتموه فقولوا أولاً سلام لهذا البيت . فان كان هناك إبن السلام يحل سلامكم عليه ، وإلا فيرجع إليكم . واقيموا فى ذلك البيت آكلين وشاربين مما عندهم ، لأن الفاعل مستحق أجرته . لا تنتقلوا من بيت إلى بيت . وأى مدينة دخلتموها وقبلوكم فكلوا مما يقدم لكم . واشفوا المرضى الذين فيها ، وقولوا لهم قد اقترب منكم ملكوت الله . والمجد لله دائماً.

يقول الكاهن هذه الطلبة

أيها الرب المؤدب الشافى ، الذى يقيم المسكين من الأرض ويرفع الفقير من المزبلة ، أب الأيتام وقاضى الأرامل ، ميناء الذين فى العاصف، طبيب السقماء، الذى حمل أمراضنا ورفع آثامنا القريب فى المعونة المتأنى فى العقاب ، الذى نفخ فى وجه تلاميذه وقال لهم : اقبلوا الروح القدس من غفرتم لهم خطاياهم غفرت لهم . أنت الذى تقبل إليك توبة الخطاة أيها الشافى من الأمراض . من أجل مسكنة عبدك ، وطلبتى أنا غير المستحق ، المدعو بنعمتك إلى الكهنوت فى موضعك المقدس ، المستحق بنعمتك لخدمة أسرارك المقدسة ، وتقدمة الصلوات والقرابين من أجل غفران خطايا شعبك. والتوسط فى تقريب خرافك الناطقة إليك . أيها الراعى الصالح ، اقبل إليك طلبتى من أجل عبدك (فلان). أرسل له الشفاء سريعاً. واغفر له آثامه . وامنح الصحة لسائر جسده وجميع أعضائه . أرحه من كل سقم وحل كل آلامه الجسدانية . وأزل ضيقاته وأحزانه ، يا من لا نرجو آخر سواك. كما اعلمت تلميذى يوحنا وقلت لهما : أمضيا واعلما يوحنا بما رأيتما وسمعتما ، ان العميان يبصرون ، والصم يسمعون ، والعرج يمشون، والمرضى يعافون والبرص يتطهرون، والموتى يقومون ، والمساكين يبشرون فطوبى لمن لا يشك فى ، فلسنا نشك فى قوة لاهوتك أيها المسيح إبن الله الوحيد ، حمل الله ، حامل خطايا العالم . أذكر مراحمك ورأفاتك التى منذ البدء . لأن فكر الإنسان مائل إلى الشر منذ صباه ، ولا يوجد إنسان بغير خطية ولو كانت حياته يوماً واحداً على الأرض . وان أخذت بالآثام يارب، من يستطيع الوقوف أمامك، لأن المغفرة هى من عندك . وان حاكمت فمن يقدر أن يحتج ، لأن كل فم يسد ولا يستطيع الكلام.

of those who are burdened. And we send up to You glory, honor, and worship, with Your good Father, and the Holy Spirit, now and at all times and unto the age of all ages. Amen.

يارب لا تذكر خطايا جهلى، يا ملجأ التائبين ورجاء من لا رجاء لهم وراحة التعابى. نرسل لك إلى فوق المجد والكرامة والسجود مع أبيك الصالح والروح لقدس الآن وكل أوان وإلى دهر الدهور آمين.

(5) FIFTH PRAYER

(الصلاة الخامسة)

The priest lights the fifth wick and says "Elison Emas..." "Our Father..."

توقد الفتيلة الخامسة ويقول الكاهن ⲈⲖⲈⲎⲤⲞⲚ ⲎⲘⲀⲤ وأبانا الذى فى السموات ، ثم يقول :

THE PRAYER FOR THE DEPARTED

أوشية الراقدين

PRIEST:

Again, let us ask God the Pantocrator, the Father of our Lord, God, and Savior Jesus Christ. We ask and entreat Your goodness, O Lover of Mankind, remember, O Lord, the souls of Your servants who have fallen asleep, our fathers and our brethren.

وأيضاً فلنسأل الله ضابط الكل أبا ربنا وإلهنا ومخلصنا يسوع المسيح . نسأل ونطلب من صلاحك يا محب البشر ، أذكر يارب أنفس عبيدك آبائنا واخواتنا الذين رقدوا .

DEACON:

يقول الشماس

Pray for our fathers and our brethren who have fallen asleep and reposed in the faith of Christ since the beginning: our holy fathers the archbishops, our fathers the bishops, our fathers the hegumens, our fathers the priests, our brethren the deacons, our fathers the monks, and our fathers the laymen, and for the full repose of Christians that Christ our God may repose all their souls in the paradise of joy, and we too, accord mercy unto us and forgive us our sins...

أطلبوا عن آبائنا واخواتنا الذين رقدوا وتنيحوا فى الإيمان بالمسيح منذ البدء . آبائنا القديسين رؤساء الأساقفة وآبائنا الأساقفة آبائنا القمامصة ، وآبائنا القسوس ، واخواتنا الشمامسة. آبائنا الرهبان وآبائنا العلمانيين ، وعن نياح كل المسيحيين . لكى ينيح المسيح إلهنا نفوسهم أجمعين فى فردوس النعيم . ونحن أيضاً يصنع معنا رحمة ويغفر لنا خطايانا.

CONGREGATION: Lord have mercy.

يقول الشعب : يارب ارحم

PRIEST:

يقول الكاهن

Graciously, O Lord, repose all their souls in the bosom of our holy fathers Abraham, Isaac, and Jacob, sustain them in a green pasture, beside still waters in the Paradise of joy, the place out of which grief, sorrow, and groaning have fled away in the light of Your saints. Raise up their bodies also on the day which You have appointed, according to Your true promises which are without lie. Grant them the good things of Your promises that which an eye has not seen nor ear heard, neither have come upon the heart of man, the things which You, O God, have prepared for those who love Your holy name. For there is no death for Your servants, but a departure. Even if any negligence or heedlessness has overtaken them as men, since they were clothed in flesh and dwelt in this world, O God, as the Good One and Lover of Mankind, graciously accord, O Lord, to repose and forgive them,

تفضل يارب نيح نفوسهم جميعاً ، فى أحضان آبائنا القديسين إبراهيم واسحق ويعقوب. علهم فى موضع خضرة على ماء الراحة فى فردوس النعيم. الموضع الذى هرب منه الحزن والكآبة والتنهد فى نور قديسيك. أقم أجسادهم فى اليوم الذى رسمته ، كمواعيدك الحقيقية غير الكاذبة . هب لهم خيرات مواعيدك ، ما لم تره عين ولم تسمع به أذن ولم يخطر على قلب بشر ، ما أعددته يا الله لمحبى اسمك القدوس. لأنه لا يكون موت لعبيدك بل هو انتقال وان كان قد لحقهم توان أو تفريط كبشر ، وقد لبسوا جسداً وسكنوا فى هذا العالم ، فأنت كصالح ومحب للبشر أللهم تفضل عبيدك المسيحيين الأرثوذكسيين الذين فى

Your servants, the orthodox Christians who are in the whole world from the east to the west and from the north to the south, each one according to his name and each one according to her name. For no one is pure and without blemish, even though his life on earth be a single day. As for those, O Lord, whose souls You have taken, repose them, and may they be worthy of the kingdom of the heavens. As for us all, grant us our Christian perfection that would be pleasing to You, and give them and us a share and inheritance with all Your saints.

المسكونة كلها ، من مشارق الشمس إلى مغاربها ومن الشمال إلى الجنوب . كل واحد باسمه وكل واحدة باسمها ، يا رب نيحهم وإغفر لهم . فانه ليس أحد طاهراً من دنس ولو كانت حياته يوماً واحداً على الأرض. أما هم يا رب الذين أخذت نفوسهم فنيحهم ، ليستحقوا ملكوت السموات . أما نحن كلنا فهب لنا كمالنا المسيحى الذى يرضيك أمامك . وأعطهم وأيانا نصيباً وميراثاً مع كافة قديسك . بالنعمة والرأفة ..

The Pauline Epistle from the Galatians (2:16-20)

knowing that a man is not justified by the works of the law but by faith in Jesus Christ, even we have believed in Christ Jesus, that we might be justified by faith in Christ and not by the works of the law; for by the works of the law no flesh shall be justified. "But if, while we seek to be justified by Christ, we ourselves also are found sinners, is Christ therefore a minister of sin? Certainly not! For if I build again those things which I destroyed, I make myself a transgressor. For I through the law died to the law that I might live to God. I have been crucified with Christ; it is no longer I who live, but Christ lives in me; and the life which I now live in the flesh I live by faith in the Son of God, who loved me and gave Himself for me. The grace of God the Father be with us all. Amen.

(البولس من غلاطية 2 : 16 - 20)

إذ نعلم أن الإنسان لا يتبرر بأعمال الناموس بل بإيمان يسوع المسيح ، آمنا نحن أيضاً بيسوع المسيح ، لنتبرر بإيمان يسوع لا بأعمال الناموس . لأنه بأعمال الناموس لا يتبرر جسد ما . فان كنا ونحن طالبون أن نتبرر فى المسيح نوجد نحن أنفسنا أيضاً خطاة ، أفالمسيح خادم للخطية ؟ حاشا . فانى ان كنت أبنى أيضاً الذى قد هدمته فأنى أظهر نفسى متعدياً ، لأنى مت بالناموس للناموس لأحيا لله . مع المسيح صلبت فأحيا لا أنا بل المسيح يحيا فىّ ، فما أحياه الآن فى الجسد فانما أحياه فى الإيمان إيمان إبن الله الذى أحبنى وأسلم نفسه لأجلى . نعمة الله الآب تحل على جميعنا أمين .

The Trisagion is said, followed by the Litany of the Gospel.

تقال الثلاثة التقديسات
اوشية الانجيل

Psalm (41:7)

Bring my soul out of prison, that I may praise Your name, O Lord: the righteous resort unto my company until You reward me. Alleluia.

(المزمور 41 : 7)

إخرج نفسى من الحبس لكى اعترف لاسمك يا رب . ينتظرنى الأبرار حتى تعطينى مجازاة . الليلو يا .

John (14:1-19)

Let not your heart be troubled; you believe in God, believe also in Me. In My Father's house are many mansions; if it were not so, I would have told you. I go to prepare a place for you. And if I go and prepare a place for you, I will come again and receive you to Myself; that where I am, there you may be also. And where I go you know, and the way you know." Thomas said to Him, "Lord, we do not know where You are going, and how can we know the way?" Jesus said to him, "I am the way, the truth, and the life. No one comes to the Father except through Me. "If you had known Me, you would have known My Father also; and from now on you know Him and have seen Him." Philip said to Him, "Lord, show us the Father, and it is sufficient for us." Jesus said to him,

(الانجيل من يوحنا 14 : 1 - 19)

لا تضطرب قلوبكم ، أنتم تؤمنون بالله فآمنوا بى . فى بيت أبى منازل كثيرة ، ولا فإنى كنت قد قلت لكم . أنا أمضى لأعد لكم مكاناً . وان مضيت وأعددت لكم مكاناً آتى أيضاً وآخذكم إلىَّ . حتى حيث أكون أنا تكونون أنتم أيضاً . وتعلمون حيث أنا أذهب وتعلمون الطريق. قال له توما : يا سيد لسنا نعلم أين تذهب ، فكيف نقدر أن نعرف الطريق . قال له يسوع: أنا هو الطريق والحق والحياة . ليس أحد يأتى إلى الآب إلا بىَّ . ولو كنتم عرفتمونى لعرفتم أبى أيضاً . ومن الآن تعرفونه وقد رأيتموه . قال له فيلبس : يا سيد أرنا الآب

"Have I been with you so long, and yet you have not known Me, Philip? He who has seen Me has seen the Father; so how can you say, 'Show us the Father'? Do you not believe that I am in the Father, and the Father in Me? The words that I speak to you I do not speak on My own authority; but the Father who dwells in Me does the works. Believe Me that I am in the Father and the Father in Me, or else believe Me for the sake of the works themselves. "Most assuredly, I say to you, he who believes in Me, the works that I do he will do also; and greater works than these he will do, because I go to My Father. And whatever you ask in My name, that I will do, that the Father may be glorified in the Son. If you ask anything in My name, I will do it. "If you love Me, keep My commandments. And I will pray the Father, and He will give you another Helper, that He may abide with you forever, the Spirit of truth, whom the world cannot receive, because it neither sees Him nor knows Him; but you know Him, for He dwells with you and will be in you. I will not leave you orphans; I will come to you. "A little while longer and the world will see Me no more, but you will see Me. Because I live, you will live also. Glory Be to God forever Amen

PRIEST:

We thank You, O Lord, God of powers, for everything You have done because You manage our life with Your mercy. You are the Teacher; You are the Healer. Heal Your servant (...) from his sicknesses, and cleanse him from every evil, that he may rise up whole to confess Your mercy and glorify You with Your people in Your Church all the days of his life.

(6) SIXTH PRAYER

The priest lights the sixth wick and says
"Elison Emas…" "Our Father…" then:
THE PRAYER FOR THE OBLATIONS

PRIEST:

We ask and entreat Your goodness, O Lover of Mankind, remember, O Lord, the sacrifices, the offerings, and the thanksgivings of those who have offered to the honor and glory of Your holy name.

DEACON:

Pray for those who provide for the sacrifices, offerings, first fruits, oil, incense, coverings, reading books, and altar vessels,

وكفانا. قال له يسوع : أنا معكم زماناً هذه مدته ولم تعرفنى يا فيلبس ! الذى رآنى فقد رأى الآب. فكيف تقول أنت أرنا الآب ! ألست تؤمن انى أنا فى الآب والآب فىَّ . الكلام الذى أكلمكم به لست أتكلم به من نفسى ، لكن الآب الحال فىَّ هو يعمل الأعمال . صدقونى انى فى الآب والآب فىَّ ، وإلا فصدقونى لسبب الأعمال نفسها . الحق الحق أقول لكم من يؤمن فى فالأعمال التى أعملها يعملها هو أيضاً ويعمل أعظم منها ، لأنى ماض إلى أبى . ومهما سألتم باسمى فذلك أفعله ، ليتمجد الآب بالابن . ان سألتم شيئاً باسمى فانى أفعله . ان كنتم تحبوننى فاحفظوا وصاياى ، وأنا أطلب من الآب فيعطيكم معزياً آخر ليمكث معكم إلى الأبد ، روح الحق الذى لا يستطيع العالم أن يقبله لأنه لا يراه ولا يعرفه . وأما أنتم فتعرفونه لأنه ماكث معكم ويكون فيكم. لا أترككم يتامى ، انى آتى إليكم . بعد قليل لا يرانى العالم أيضاً ، وأما أنتم فترونني. انى أنا حى فأنتم ستحيون . والمجد لله دائماً .

يقول الكاهن هذه الطلبه

نشكرك أيها الرب إله القوات على كل ما صنعت ، لأنك برحمتك دبرت حياتنا . أنت هو المؤدب . أنت هو الشافى . اشف يارب عبدك (فلان) من أمراضه ، وأنقذه من كل شر . أقمه صحيحاً ليعترف برحمتك ، ويمجدك مع شعبك فى كنيستك جميع أيام حياته . بالنعمة والرأفة ومحبة البشر اللواتى لإبنك الوحيد يسوع المسيح ربنا هذا الذى ..

(الصـلاة السادسه)

توقد الفتيلة السادسة ويقول الكاهن
ελεΗϲΟΝ Ημαϲ وأبانا الذى فى ... ثم
أوشية القرابين

الكاهن

وأيضاً فلنسأل الله ضابط الكل أبا ربنا وإلهنا ومخلصنا يسوع المسيح . نسأل ونطلب من صلاحك يا محب البشر ، أذكر يارب صعائد وقرابين وشكر الذين يقربون كرامة ومجداً لاسمك القدوس .

يقول الشماس

أطلبوا عن المهتمين بالصعائد والقرابين والبكور والزيت والبخور والستور وكتب

that Christ our God may reward them in the heavenly Jerusalem, and forgive us our sins.

CONGREGATION: Lord have mercy.

PRIEST:

Receive them upon Your holy, rational altar in heaven as a sweet savor of incense before Your greatness in the heavens, through the service of Your holy angels and archangels. As You have received the gifts of the righteous Abel, the sacrifice of our father Abraham, and the two mites of the widow, so also receive the thank offerings of Your servants, those in abundance or those in scarcity, hidden or manifest; those who desire to offer to You but have none, and those who have offered these gifts to You this very day. Give them the incorruptible instead of the corruptible, the heavenly instead of the earthly, and the eternal instead of the temporal. Their houses and their stores fill them with every good thing. Surround them, O Lord, by the power of Your holy angels and archangels. As they have remembered Your holy name on earth, remember them also, O Lord, in Your kingdom, and in this age, too, leave them not behind.

The Pauline Epistle from Colossians (3:12-17)

Therefore, as the elect of God, holy and beloved, put on tender mercies, kindness, humility, meekness, longsuffering; bearing with one another, and forgiving one another, if anyone has a complaint against another; even as Christ forgave you, so you also must do. But above all these things put on love, which is the bond of perfection. And let the peace of God rule in your hearts, to which also you were called in one body; and be thankful. Let the word of Christ dwell in you richly in all wisdom, teaching and admonishing one another in psalms and hymns and spiritual songs, singing with grace in your hearts to the Lord. And whatever you do in word or deed, do all in the name of the Lord Jesus, giving thanks to God the Father through Him. The grace, of God the Father be with us all. Amen.

The Trisagion is said, followed by the Litany of the Gospel.

Psalm (4:1)

When I called the God of my righteous, He heard me; when I was in trouble you did set me at liberty: have mercy upon me, O Lord, and hearken unto my prayer. Alleluia.

القراءة وأوانى المذبح ، لكى يكافئهم المسيح إلهنا فى أورشليم السمائية ، ليغفر لنا خطايانا.

يقول الشعب : يارب ارحم

يقول الكاهن

اقبلها إليك على مذبحك المقدس الناطق السمائى ، رائحة بخور تدخل إلى عظمتك التى فى السموات ، بواسطة خدمة ملائكتك ورؤساء ملائكتك المقدسين . وكما قبلت إليك قرابين هابيل الصديق ، وذبيحة أبينا إبراهيم وفلسى الأرملة ، هكذا أيضاً نذور عبيدك اقبلها إليك أصحاب الكثير وأصحاب القليل ، الخفيات والظاهرات . والذين يريدون أن يقدموا لك وليس لهم والذين قدموا لك فى هذا اليوم هذه القرابين ، اعطهم الباقيات عوض الفانيات ، السمائيات عوض الأرضيات ، الأبديات عوض الزمنيات ، بيوتهم ومخازنهم املأها بالخيرات . احطهم يارب بقوة ملائكتك ورؤساء ملائكتك الأطهار . وكما ذكروا اسمك القدوس على الأرض أذكرهم أيضاً يارب فى ملكوتك وفى هذا الدهر لا تتركهم عنك . ...

(البولس من كولوسى 3 : 12 - 17)

فالبسوا مثل اصفياء الله المطهرين الأحباء مراحم ، رأفات ، صلاح ، تواضع قلب ، وداعة، وطول روح . تحتملون بعضكم بعضاً ، وتغفرون لبعضكم بعضاً . وإذا كان لوم بين واحد وآخر منكم فكما غفر المسيح لكم كذلك أنتم أيضاً . وعلى هذه جميعها المحبة التى لها رباط الكمال . وسلام المسيح فليثبت فى قلوبكم ، هذه التى لها دعيتم بجسد واحد فكونوا شاكرين وكلمة الرب فلتسكن فيكم بغنى ، وبكل حكمة تعلمون وتؤدبون نفوسكم بالمزامير والتسابيح وتراتيل روحية . تسبحون الله فى قلوبكم بشكر . وكل ما تعملونه بالقول أو بالفعل، كل شئ باسم ربنا يسوع المسيح إذ تشكرون الله الآب من جهته . نعمة الله الآب تحل على جميعنا آمين .

تقال الثلاثة التقديسات وأوشية الانجيل

(المزمور 4 : 1)

إذ صرخت سمعتنى يا اله برى . وفى الشدة فرجت عنى تراءف على يارب واسمع صلاتى . الليلويا .

Luke 7:36-50

Then one of the Pharisees asked Him to eat with him. And He went to the Pharisee's house, and sat down to eat. And behold, a woman in the city who was a sinner, when she knew that Jesus sat at the table in the Pharisee's house, brought an alabaster flask of fragrant oil, and stood at His feet behind Him weeping; and she began to wash His feet with her tears, and wiped them with the hair of her head; and she kissed His feet and anointed them with the fragrant oil. Now when the Pharisee who had invited Him saw this, he spoke to himself, saying, "This Man, if He were a prophet, would know who and what manner of woman this is who is touching Him, for she is a sinner." And Jesus answered and said to him, "Simon, I have something to say to you." So he said, "Teacher, say it." "There was a certain creditor who had two debtors. One owed five hundred denarii, and the other fifty. And when they had nothing with which to repay, he freely forgave them both. Tell Me, therefore, which of them will love him more?" Simon answered and said, "I suppose the one whom he forgave more." And He said to him, "You have rightly judged." Then He turned to the woman and said to Simon, "Do you see this woman? I entered your house; you gave Me no water for My feet, but she has washed My feet with her tears and wiped them with the hair of her head. You gave Me no kiss, but this woman has not ceased to kiss My feet since the time I came in. You did not anoint My head with oil, but this woman has anointed My feet with fragrant oil. Therefore I say to you, her sins, which are many, are forgiven, for she loved much. But to whom little is forgiven, the same loves little." Then He said to her, "Your sins are forgiven." And those who sat at the table with Him began to say to themselves, "Who is this who even forgives sins?" Then He said to the woman, "Your faith has saved you. Go in peace. Glory Be to God forever and ever, Amen.

PRIEST:

O God of spirits and bodies, Lord of powers, God of every comfort, and King of all kings; who hears everyone who cries to You for help. We, Your servants, entreat and pray that You may remember Your servant in Your great mercy; visit him with Your salvation; take away from him all sicknesses; raise him up from his bed of disease. Grant him to Your Church, healed in body, soul, and spirit. Raise him up that he may speak of the glory through the love-of-mankind of Your only-begotten Son, with whom You are blessed, and the Holy Spirit, the Giver of Life and coessential with You, now and at all times and unto the age of all ages. Amen.

(الانجيل من لوقا 7 : 36 - 50)

فطلب إليه واحد من الفريسيين أن يأكل معه ، فدخل بيت ذلك الفريسي وجلس . وكان فى المدينة امرأة خاطئة . فلما علمت أنه متكئ فى بيت ذلك الفريسى ، أخذت قارورة طيب ووقفت من ورائه عند رجليه باكية . وبدأت تبل قدميه بدموعها ، وتمسحهما بشعر رأسها . وكانت تقبل قدميه وتدهنهما بالطيب . فلما رأى ذلك الفريسى الذى دعاه فكر قائلاً فى نفسه : لو كان هذا نبياً لعلم ما هذه وكيف هذه المراة التى لمسته ، انها خاطئة . فأجاب يسوع وقال له : يا سمعان عندى كلام أقوله لك . أما هو فقال : قل يا معلم . فأجاب يسوع وقال له : يوجد غريمان عليهما لإنسان دين ، على الواحد خمسمائة دينار وعلى الآخر خمسون . ولم يكن لهما ما يوفيان فوهب لهما ما عليهما . فأيهما يكون أكثر حباً له ؟ أجاب سمعان وقال : أظن أن الذى وهب له الأكثر . قال له : بالحق حكمت . ثم ألتفت إلى المرأة وقال لسمعان : أترى هذه المرأة ، انى دخلت بيتك فلم تسكب على رجلى ماء ، هذه بلت رجلى بدموعها ومسحتهما بشعر رأسها . أنت لم تقبلنى ، وهذه منذ دخلت لم تكف عن تقبيل قدمى . أنت لم تدهن رأسى بزيت ، وهذه دهنت بالطيب قدمى . من أجل ذلك أقول لك أن خطاياها الكثيرة مغفورة لها لأنها أحبت كثيراً ، والذى يترك له قليل يحب قليلاً . ثم قال لها : مغفورة لكِ خطاياكِ . فبدأ المتكئون يقولون فى أنفسهم : من هذا الذى يغفر الخطايا ؟ فقال للمرأة اذهبى بسلام ، إيمانك خلصكِ . والمجد لله دائماً .

يقول الكاهن هذه الطلبة

يا إله الأرواح والأجساد ورب القوات ، إله كل عزاء ، ملك جميع الملوك ، سامع كل الذين يصرخون نحو معونتك . نحن عبيدك نسأل ونتضرع إليك ، لكى تذكر عبدك (فلان) برحمتك الكثيرة ، تعهده بخلاصك . انزع عنه كل مرض . أقمه من رقاد سقمه . انعم به على كنيستك معافى النفس والجسد والروح . انهضه لينطق بالمجد بمحبة البشر التى لإبنك الوحيد، هذا الذى تباركت معه ومع الروح القدس المحيى المساوى معك الآن وكل أوان وإلى دهر الدهور آمين .

| (7) SEVENTH PRAYER | (الصلاة السابعة) |

The priest lights the sixth wick and says
"Elison Emas…" "Our Father…"

توقد الفتيلة السابعة ثم يقول الكاهن
ελεнсονημας وأبانا الذى فى .. ثم:

THE PRAYER OF THE CATECHUMENS
PRIEST:

Again, let us ask God the Pantocrator, the Father of our Lord, God, and Savior Jesus Christ. We ask and entreat Your Goodness, O Lover of Mankind: remember, O Lord, Your servants, the catechumens of Your people.

أوشية الموعوظين
وأيضاً فلنسأل الله الضابط الكل أبو ربنا وإلهنا ومخلصنا يسوع المسيح ، نسأل ونطلب من صلاحك يا محب البشر ، أذكر يارب موعوظى شعبك ، ارحمهم وثبتهم فى الإيمان المستقيم بك .

DEACON:

Pray for the catechumens of our people that the Lord may bless them and confirm them in the Orthodox Faith, to the last breath, and forgive us our sins.

يقول الشماس
أطلبوا عن موعوظى شعبنا، ليرحمهم الله ويثبتهم على الإيمان الأرثوذكسى إلى النفس الأخير، ليغفر لنا خطايانا .

CONGREGATION: Lord have mercy.

يقول الشعب : يارب ارحم

PRIEST:

Have mercy on them; confirm them in the faith in You. All traces of idolatry cast out of their heart. Your law, Your fear, Your commandments, Your truths, and Your holy ordinances, establish in their heart. Grant them that they may know the certainty of the words with which they have been instructed. At the appointed time, may they be worthy of the washing of the new birth, unto forgiveness of their sins, preparing them to be a temple of Your Holy Spirit.

يقول الكاهن
وكل بقايا عبادة الأوثان انزعها من قلوبهم. ناموسك ووصاياك وحقوقك وأوامرك المقدسة ثبتها فى قلوبهم. امنحهم أن يفهموا ثبات الكلام الذى وُعظوا به. وفى زمن محدود ليستحقوا حميم الميلاد الجديد ومغفرة الخطايا. أعدهم هيكلاً لروحك القدوس . بالنعمة والرأفة ... ألخ .

The Pauline Epistle from Ephesians (6:10-18)

Finally, my brethren, be strong in the Lord and in the power of His might. Put on the whole armor of God, that you may be able to stand against the wiles of the devil. For we do not wrestle against flesh and blood, but against principalities, against powers, against the rulers of the darkness of this age, against spiritual hosts of wickedness in the heavenly places. Therefore take up the whole armor of God, that you may be able to withstand in the evil day, and having done all, to stand. Stand therefore, having girded your waist with truth, having put on the breastplate of righteousness, and having shod your feet with the preparation of the gospel of peace; above all, taking the shield of faith with which you will be able to quench all the fiery darts of the wicked one. And take the helmet of salvation, and the sword of the Spirit, which is the word of God; praying always with all prayer and supplication in the Spirit, being watchful to this end with all perseverance and supplication for all the saints. The grace of God the Father be with us all. Amen.

(البولس من أفسس 6 : 10 - 18)
أخيراً يا اخوتى تقووا فى الرب ، وفى عزة قوته . وألبسوا سلاح الله الكامل ، لكى تقدروا أن تقفوا قبال حيل إبليس . لأن حربنا ليس كائن لنا قبال لحم ودم ، بل ضد الرؤساء ، وقبال السلاطين . ضد ضابطى عالم الظلمة . قبال روحانيات الشر فى جو السماء . من أجل هذا خذوا لكم جميع سلاح الله ، لكى تستطيعوا أن تقفوا فى يوم السوء . وإذا فعلتم كل شئ انهضوا وقوموا على أرجلكم ، مشتدين على حقويكم بالحق . والبسوا درع البر . والبسوا حذاء فى أرجلكم باستعداد انجيل السلام . وفى كل شئ خذوا لكم ترس الإيمان ، هذا الذى به تقدرون أن تطفئوا جميع سهام الشرير الملتهبة ناراً . وخذوا لكم خوذة الخلاص وسيف الروح ، الذى هو كلام الله . وبكل صلاة وطلبة تصلّون فى كل حين بالروح . نعمة الله الآب تحل على جميعنا آمين.

The Psalm

Ⲯⲁⲗⲙⲟⲥ ⲕ̅ⲇ̅ : ⲓ̅ⲍ̅ ، ⲓ̅ⲏ̅

Psalm 24:17,18		(مز 24 : 17 و 18)
Look upon my affliction and my misery: and forgive me all my sins. O keep my soul and deliver me: let me not be confounded, for I have put my trust in You. Alleluia.	Ⲭⲟⲩϣⲧ ⲉⲡⲁⲑⲉⲃⲓⲟ ⲛⲉⲙ ⲡⲁϭⲓⲥⲓ : ⲭⲁ ⲛⲁⲛⲟⲃⲓ ⲧⲏⲣⲟⲩ ⲛⲏⲓ ⲉⲃⲟⲗ : ⲁⲣⲉϩ ⲉⲧⲁⲯⲩⲭⲏ ⲟⲩⲟϩ ⲛⲁϩⲙⲉⲧ : ⲙ̅ⲡⲉⲛⲑⲣⲓϭⲓ ϣⲓⲡⲓ ϫⲉ ⲁⲓⲉⲣϩⲉⲗⲡⲓⲥ ⲉⲣⲟⲕ . ⲁⲗ .	أنظر إلى تواضعى وتعبى واغفر لى جميع خطاياى . احفظ نفسى ولا تحزنى فانى عليك توكلت . هلليلويا .

The Gospel

Ⲉⲩⲁⲅⲅⲉⲗⲓⲟⲛ Ⲕⲁⲧⲁ Ⲙⲁⲧⲑⲉⲟⲛ Ⲕⲉⲫ ⲋ̅ : ⲓ̅ⲇ̅ - ⲓ̅ⲏ̅

Matthew 6:14-18		(متى 6 : 14 - 18)
For if you forgive men their trespasses, your heavenly Father will also forgive you. But if you do not forgive men their trespasses, neither will your Father forgive your trespasses. "Moreover, when you fast, do not be like the hypocrites, with a sad countenance. For they disfigure their faces that they may appear to men to be fasting. Assuredly, I say to you, they have their reward. But you, when you fast, anoint your head and wash your face, so that you do not appear to men to be fasting, but to your Father who is in the secret place; and your Father who sees in secret will reward you openly. Glory be to God forever.	Ⲉϣⲱⲡ ⲅⲁⲣ ⲛ̅ⲧⲉⲧⲉⲛⲭⲱ ⲉⲃⲟⲗ ⲛ̅ⲛⲓⲣⲱⲙⲓ ⲛ̅ⲛⲟⲩⲡⲁⲣⲁⲡⲧⲱⲙⲁ : ⲉϥⲉⲭⲱ ⲛⲱⲧⲉⲛ ⲉⲃⲟⲗ ⲛ̅ϫⲉ Ⲡⲉⲧⲉⲛⲓⲱⲧ ⲉⲧ ϧⲉⲛ ⲛⲓⲫⲏⲟⲩⲓ ⲛ̅ⲛⲉⲧⲉⲛⲡⲁⲣⲁⲡⲧⲱⲙⲁ . Ⲉϣⲱⲡ ⲇⲉ ⲛ̅ⲧⲉⲧⲉⲛϣⲧⲉⲙⲭⲱ ⲉⲃⲟⲗ ⲛ̅ⲛⲓⲣⲱⲙⲓ ⲛ̅ⲛⲟⲩⲡⲁⲣⲁⲡⲧⲱⲙⲁ : ⲟⲩ ⲇⲉ Ⲡⲉⲧⲉⲛⲓⲱⲧ ϥⲛⲁⲭⲱ ⲛⲱⲧⲉⲛ ⲉⲃⲟⲗ ⲁⲛ ⲛ̅ⲛⲉⲧⲉⲛⲡⲁⲣⲁⲡⲧⲱⲙⲁ . Ⲉϣⲱⲡ ⲇⲉ ⲛ̅ⲧⲉⲧⲉⲛⲉⲣⲛⲏⲥⲧⲉⲩⲓⲛ ⲛ̅ⲛⲉⲧⲉⲛⲉⲣ ⲙ̅ⲫⲣⲏϯ ⲛ̅ⲛⲓϣⲟⲃⲓ : ⲉϣⲁⲩⲱⲕⲉⲙ ⲛ̅ⲛⲟⲩϩⲟ : ϣⲁⲧⲧⲁⲕⲉ ⲛⲟⲩϩⲟ ⲅⲁⲣ ϩⲓⲛⲁ ⲛⲥⲉⲟⲩⲱⲛϩ ⲉⲃⲟⲗ ⲛ̅ⲛⲓⲣⲱⲙⲓ ⲉⲧⲉⲣⲛⲏⲥⲧⲉⲩⲓⲛ : ⲁⲙⲏⲛ ϯϫⲱ ⲙ̅ⲙⲟⲥ ⲛⲱⲧⲉⲛ ϫⲉ ⲁⲩⲕⲏⲛ ⲉⲧϭⲓ ⲙ̅ⲡⲟⲩⲃⲉⲭⲉ . Ⲛⲑⲟⲕ ⲇⲉ ⲉⲕⲉⲉⲣⲛⲏⲥⲧⲉⲩⲓⲛ ⲑⲱϩⲥ ⲛ̅ⲧⲉⲕⲁⲫⲉ ⲟⲩⲟϩ ⲓⲁ ⲡⲉⲕϩⲟ ⲉⲃⲟⲗ : ϩⲓⲛⲁ ⲛ̅ⲧⲉⲕϣⲧⲉⲙⲟⲩⲱⲛϩ ⲉⲃⲟⲗ ⲛ̅ⲛⲓⲣⲱⲙⲓ ⲉⲕⲉⲣⲛⲏⲥⲧⲉⲩⲓⲛ : ⲁⲗⲗⲁ ⲙ̅Ⲡⲉⲕⲓⲱⲧ ⲉⲑⲛⲁⲩ ϧⲉⲛ ⲡⲉⲧϩⲏⲡ ⲉϥⲉϯ ϣⲉⲃⲓⲱ ⲛⲁⲕ . Ⲟⲩⲱϣⲧ ⲙ̅ⲡⲓⲉⲩⲁⲅⲅⲉⲗⲓⲟⲛ ⲉⲑⲩ .	فان غفرتم للناس خطاياهم يغفر لكم أبوكم السماوى خطاياكم . وان لم تغفروا للناس سيئاتهم فلا يغفر لكم أبوك أيضاً خطاياكم . إذا صمتم فلا تكونوا كالمرائين ، لأنهم يعبسون وجوههم ويغيرونها لكى يظهروا للناس صائمين . الحق أقول لكم لقد أخذوا أجرهم . وأنت إذا صمت فادهن رأسك وأغسل وجهك . لئلا يظهر للناس صيامك ، لكن لأبيك الذى فى الخفاء . وأبوك الذى ينظر فى الخفاء يجازيك علانية . والمجد لله دائماً .

PRIEST:	يقول الكاهن هذه الطلبة
Again, we ask You, O Lord, God of powers, the Compassionate, the Almighty, to look upon Your servant Raise him up from his sickbed and his evil seat, as You suddenly raised up Simon's mother-in-law from her severe fever; grant him to Your Church. That he may glorify Your holy name, O Father, Son, and Holy Spirit, now and at all times and unto the age of all ages. Amen.	وأيضاً نسألك أيها الرب إله القوات ، المتحنن القادر على كل شئ ، لكى تطلع على عبدك (فلان) . وتقيمه من سرير مرضه وفراشه ، كما أقمت حماة سمعان من حمتها الصعبة . أنعم به على كنيستك ، لكى يتمجد اسمك القدوس أيها الأب والإبن والروح القدس الآن وكل أوان وإلى دهر الدهور آمين .

Another prayer:

O Lord, the Compassionate, and the great in mercy; who does not desire the sinner's death, but rather to return and live; who does not lay my hand on the head of those who come to You, I the sinner, asking You for forgiveness of his sins because of us, we Your priests, but through the mighty hand of the Gospel, we ask considering Your love-of-mankind, O longsuffering Lord. O You who accepted David's repentance through Your prophet Nathan, and accepted Manasseh's repentance; O our Savior, accept Your servant (...)'s repentance, according to the commandment of Your love-of-mankind, through the mediation of Your priests. You have commanded forgiveness up to seventy times seven, and Your mercy is as much as Your power. Glory is due to You, O Father, Son, and Holy Spirit, now and at all times and unto the age of all ages. Amen.

Another prayer:

O God, the Father, the Good One, the Physician of our bodies and spirits, who sent His only-begotten Son, Jesus Christ, to heal every sickness, and to rescue from death. Heal Your servant (...), from his bodily sicknesses, and give him to live a righteous life, that he may glorify Your greatness and give thanks for Your grace and may fulfill Your will through the grace of Your Christ, and the intercessions of the Theotokos, and the prayers of Your saints. For You are the Spring of healing; and we send up to You glory and honor, with Your only-begotten Son, and the Holy Spirit, now and at all times and unto the age of all ages. Amen.

The priest anoints the sick person with oil as he says:

O saints who have the spring of healing offered without a price, give healing to everyone who prays, for the Lord Himself said to you and the Apostles, "Lo, I am with you to the end of the ages." **(Glory to the Father, ...).** "Lo, I have given you authority to cast out unclean spirits, and to heal every sickness and disease. Freely you have received, freely give." **(Now and ever and unto the ages of the ages. Amen.)** O holy Virgin, the Theotokos without man's seed, intercede for the salvation of our souls.

Then we pray the Gloria.., Our Father ...,
The Orthodox Creed,
Lord have mercy 41 times.
The PRIEST prays the three absolutions,
and the final blessing,
then he anoints the congregation with the Holy Oil.
The sick person is anointed with the Holy Oil for one week.

طلبة أخرى

أيها الرب المتحنن الكثير الرأفات ، الذى لا يشاء موت الخاطئ حتى يرجع إليك ويتوب ويحيا . الذى ليس بوضع أيدينا نحن كهنتك الخطاة على رأسه ، متوسلين إليك عن غفران خطاياه ، لكن باليد العزيزة التى لهذا الانجيل . نطلب إليك يا محب البشر ، أيها الرب المتأنى ، يا من قبل إليه توبة داود على يد نبيك ناثان . أيها المخلص الذى قبل إليه توبة منسى ، أقبل إليك توبة عبدك (فلان) كعظيم محبتك للبشر ، وبواسطة كهنتك أنت أمرت بالغفران سبعة فى سبعين وكمقدار رحمتك ومقدار عظمتك يليق بك المجد ، ايها الآب والإبن والروح القدس الآن وكل أوان وإلى دهر الدهور آمين .

طلبة أخرى

الله الآب الصالح طبيب أجسادنا وأرواحنا الذى أرسل إبنه الوحيد يسوع المسيح ليشفى كل الأمراض وينقذ من الموت. اشف عبدك (فلان) من أمراضه الجسدية . وامنحه حياة مستقيمة ، ليمجد عظمتك ويشكر احسانك وتكمل مشيئتك من أجل نعمة مسيحك . بشفاعة والدة الإله وطلبات قديسيك ، لأنك أنت ينبوع الشفاء . ونرسل لك إلى فوق المجد والاكرام مع إبنك الوحيد والروح القدس الآن وكل أوان وإلى دهر الدهور امين .

يدهن الكاهن المريض بالزيت وهو يقول:

أيها القديسون الذين لكم ينبوع الشفاء بغير فضة ، امنحوا الشفاء لكل الطالبين ، لأن الرب قال لكم مع الرسل: هوذا أنا معكم إلى كمال الدهور. **(المجد للآب...)** ها أنا أعطيكم سلطاناً على الأرواح النجسة لتخرجوها وتشفوا كل مرض وكل سقم. مجاناً أخذتم مجاناً أعطوا **(الآن وكل أوان...)** أيتها القديسة العذراء والدة الإله بغير زرع ، اشفعى من أجل خلاص نفوسنا

تقال تسبحة الملائكة وأبانا الذى...
وقانون الإيمان
وكيرى ليصون 41 مرة
ويقول الكاهن التحاليل الثلاثة
والبركة
ثم يرشم الحاضرين بالزيت المقدس
أما المريض فيدهن بالزيت سبعة أيام .

Liturgy Readings

(قراءات قداس جمعة ختام الصوم)

2 Timothy 3:1-4:5

But know this, that in the last days perilous times will come: For men will be lovers of themselves, lovers of money, boasters, proud, blasphemers, disobedient to parents, unthankful, unholy, unloving, unforgiving, slanderers, without self-control, brutal, despisers of good, traitors, headstrong, haughty, lovers of pleasure rather than lovers of God, having a form of godliness but denying its power. And from such people turn away! For of this sort are those who creep into households and make captives of gullible women loaded down with sins, led away by various lusts, always learning and never able to come to the knowledge of the truth. Now as Jannes and Jambres resisted Moses, so do these also resist the truth: men of corrupt minds, disapproved concerning the faith; but they will progress no further, for their folly will be manifest to all, as theirs also was. But you have carefully followed my doctrine, manner of life, purpose, faith, longsuffering, love, perseverance, persecutions, afflictions, which happened to me at Antioch, at Iconium, at Lystra—what persecutions I endured. And out of them all the Lord delivered me. Yes, and all who desire to live godly in Christ Jesus will suffer persecution. But evil men and impostors will grow worse and worse, deceiving and being deceived. But you must continue in the things which you have learned and been assured of, knowing from whom you have learned them, and that from childhood you have known the Holy Scriptures, which are able to make you wise for salvation through faith which is in Christ Jesus. All Scripture is given by inspiration of God, and is profitable for doctrine, for reproof, for correction, for instruction in righteousness, that the man of God may be complete, thoroughly equipped for every good work. I charge you therefore before God and the Lord Jesus Christ, who will judge the living and the dead at His appearing and His kingdom: Preach the word! Be ready in season and out of season. Convince, rebuke, exhort, with all longsuffering and teaching. For the time will come when they will not endure sound doctrine, but according to their own desires, because they have itching ears, they will heap up for themselves teachers; and they will turn their ears away from the truth, and be turned aside to fables. But you be watchful in all things, endure afflictions, do the work of an evangelist, fulfill your ministry. The Grace of God the Father be with you all. Amen.

البولس إلى تيموثاوس الثانية 3 : 1 - 4 : 5

إعلم هذا انه ستأتى فى الأيام الأخيرة أزمنة شريرة صعبة لأن الناس يكونون محبين لأنفسهم محبين للمال مفتخرين متكبرين مجدفين غير طائعين لوالديهم , غير شاكرين دنسين بلا حنو ولا عهد ثالبين عديمى النزاهة شرسين مبغضين للصلاح خائفين مقتحمين متصلفين محبين للذات دون محبة الله . لهم صور التقوى لكنهم ينكرون قوتها . فاعرض عن هؤلاء فان منهم من يدخلون البيوت ويسبون النساء الجميلات للخطايا منساقات بشهوات شتى . يتعلمن فى كل حين ولا يستطعن أن يقبلن إلى معرفة الحق أبداً . وكما أن ينيس ويمبريس قاوما موسى كذلك هؤلاء أيضاً يقاومون الحق أناس أراؤهم فاسدة مرذولة من جهة الإيمان . لكنهم لا يتقدمون أكثر لأن حمقهم سيكون واضحاً للجميع كما كان حمق ذينك أيضاً. أما أنت فقد أتبعت تعليمى ومثالى ورسمى الأول وإيمانى وأناتى ومحبتى وصبرى والاضطهادات والامى وقد أنقذنى الرب من جميعها . وجميع الذين يريدون أن يعيشوا بالتقوى فى المسيح يسوع يضطهدون. ولكن الناس الأشرار الخداعين سيتقدمون فى الشر بالأكثر ضالين ومضلين . وأما أنت فاثبت على ما تعلمته وائتمنت عليه عارفاً ممن تعلمت . وانك منذ الطفولة تعرف الكتب المقدسة القادرة أن تحكمك للخلاص بالإيمان الذى فى المسيح يسوع . لأن جميع الكتب الموحى بها من الله نافعة للتعليم والتوبيخ للتقويم والتأديب الذى فى البر لكى يكون رجل الله مستعداً ثابتاً فى كل عمل صالح . أنا أشهد أمام الله والرب يسوع المسيح الذى سيدين الأحياء والأموات عند ظهوره وملكوته. أكرز بالكلمة وأعكف على ذلك فى وقت مناسب وغير مناسب . وبّخ وانتهر وعظ بكل أناة وتعليم . لأنه سيكون وقت لا يقبلون فيه التعليم الصحيح بل حسب شهواتهم الخاصة يجمعون لهم معلمين ويسدون أذانهم فيصرفون مسمعهم عن الحق ويميلون إلى الخرافات . وأما أنت فاستيقظ فى كل شئ واقبل الآلام . واعمل عمل المبشر . وتمم خدمتك . نعمة الله الآب.

James 5:7-16

Therefore be patient, brethren, until the coming of the Lord. See how the farmer waits for the precious fruit of the earth, waiting patiently for it until it receives the early and latter rain. You also be patient. Establish your hearts, for the coming of the Lord is at hand. Do not grumble against one another, brethren, lest you be condemned. Behold, the Judge is standing at the door! My brethren, take the prophets, who spoke in the name of the Lord, as an example of suffering and patience. Indeed we count them blessed who endure. You have heard of the perseverance of Job and seen the end intended by the Lord—that the Lord is very compassionate and merciful. But above all, my brethren, do not swear, either by heaven or by earth or with any other oath. But let your "Yes" be "Yes," and your "No," "No," lest you fall into judgment. Is anyone among you suffering? Let him pray. Is anyone cheerful? Let him sing psalms. Is anyone among you sick? Let him call for the elders of the church, and let them pray over him, anointing him with oil in the name of the Lord. And the prayer of faith will save the sick, and the Lord will raise him up. And if he has committed sins, he will be forgiven. Confess your trespasses to one another, and pray for one another, that you may be healed. The effective, fervent prayer of a righteous man avails much. Do not love the world, nor the things which are in the world.

Acts 15:1-18

And certain men came down from Judea and taught the brethren, "Unless you are circumcised according to the custom of Moses, you cannot be saved." Therefore, when Paul and Barnabas had no small dissension and dispute with them, they determined that Paul and Barnabas and certain others of them should go up to Jerusalem, to the apostles and elders, about this question. So, being sent on their way by the church, they passed through Phoenicia and Samaria, describing the conversion of the Gentiles; and they caused great joy to all the brethren. And when they had come to Jerusalem, they were received by the church and the apostles and the elders; and they reported all things that God had done with them. But some of the sect of the Pharisees who believed rose up, saying, "It is necessary to circumcise them, and to command them to keep the law of Moses." Now the apostles and elders came together to consider this matter. And when there had been much dispute, Peter rose up and said to them: "Men and brethren, you know that a good while ago God chose among us, that by my mouth the Gentiles should hear the word of the gospel and believe. So God, who knows the heart, acknowledged them by giving them the Holy Spirit, just as He did to us, and made no distinction between us and them, purifying their hearts by faith. Now therefore, why do you test God by putting a yoke on the

(الكاثوليكون من يعقوب 5 : 7 - 16)

فتأنوا أيها الاخوة إلى مجئ الرب . هوذا الفلاح ينتظر ثمر الأرض الكريم متأنياً عليه حتى ينال المطر المبكر والمتأخر . فتأنوا أنتم أيضاً وثبتوا قلوبكم فان مجئ الرب قد اقترب . لا يئن بعضكم من بعض يا اخوتى لئلا تدانوا . هوذا الديان واقف على الأبواب . خذوا لكم يا اخوتى مثالاً لاحتمال المشقات والاناة وتعب الأنبياء الذين تكلموا باسم الرب . ها نحن نطوّب الصابرين وقد سمعتم بصبر أيوب ورأيتم عاقبة الرب معه لأن الرب متحنن جداً ورؤوف . وقبل كل شئ يا اخوتى لا تحلفوا لا بالسماء ولا بالأرض ولا بقسم آخر . بل ليكن كلامكم نعم نعم ولا لا لئلا تقعوا فى الدينونة . فان كان أحدكم فى شدة فليصلّ أو فرح القلب فليرتل . إن كان أحد مريض بينكم فليدع قسوس الكنيسة فليصلوا عليه ويمسحوه بالزيت باسم الرب . فان كان قد فعل خطية تغفر له . اعترفوا بعضكم لبعض بزلاتكم وصلوا بعضكم لأجل بعض لكى تبرأوا . لا تحبوا العالم...

(الابركسيس ص 15 : 1 - 18)

وانحدر قوم من اليهودية وجعلوا يعلمون الاخوة قائلين : إن لم تختتنوا حسب عادة موسى فلا يمكنكم أن تخلصوا . وإذ جرت لبولس وبرنابا منازعة ومباحثة معهم ليست بقليلة ، رتبوا أن يصعد بولس وبرنابا وآخرون منهم ليذهبوا إلى الرسل والقسوس الذين بأورشليم لينظروا فى هذه المسألة فهؤلاء بعد أن شيعتهم الكنيسة اجتازوا فى فينيقية والسامرة يخبرونهم برجوع الأمم وكانوا يسببون سروراً عظيماً لجميع الاخوة . ولما حضروا إلى أورشليم قبلتهم الكنيسة والرسل والقسوس فأخبروهم بجميع ما صنع الله معهم . فقام قوم من شيعة الفريسيين الذين آمنوا قائلين : انه ينبغى أن يختتنوا ويوصوا بأن يحفظوا ناموس موسى . فاجتمع الرسل والقسوس لينظروا فى هذا الأمر . فبعد ما حدثت مشاجرة عظيمة قام بطرس وقال لهم أيها الرجال الاخوة انكم تعلمون انه منذ أيام قديمة اختار الله من بيننا انه بفمى يسمع الأمم كلمة الانجيل ويؤمنون . والله العارف القلوب شهد لهم معطياً الروح القدس كما أعطى لنا أيضاً . ولم يميز بيننا

neck of the disciples which neither our fathers nor we were able to bear? But we believe that through the grace of the Lord Jesus Christ we shall be saved in the same manner as they." Then all the multitude kept silent and listened to Barnabas and Paul declaring how many miracles and wonders God had worked through them among the Gentiles. And after they had become silent, James answered, saying, "Men and brethren, listen to me: Simon has declared how God at the first visited the Gentiles to take out of them a people for His name. And with this the words of the prophets agree, just as it is written: 'AFTER THIS I WILL RETURN AND WILL REBUILD THE TABERNACLE OF DAVID, WHICH HAS FALLEN DOWN; I WILL REBUILD ITS RUINS, AND I WILL SET IT UP; SO THAT THE REST OF MANKIND MAY SEEK THE LORD, EVEN ALL THE GENTILES WHO ARE CALLED BY MY NAME, SAYS THE LORD WHO DOES ALL THESE THINGS.' "Known to God from eternity are all His works. The word of the Lord shall grow, multiply, be mighty and be confirmed in the holy church of God. Amen

Psalms 97:8-9

Let the hills be joyful together before the Lord For He is coming to judge the earth. With righteousness He shall judge the world, And the peoples with equity. Alleluia

Luke 13:31-35

On that very day some Pharisees came, saying to Him, "Get out and depart from here, for Herod wants to kill You." And He said to them, "Go, tell that fox, 'Behold, I cast out demons and perform cures today and tomorrow, and the third day I shall be perfected.' Nevertheless I must journey today, tomorrow, and the day following; for it cannot be that a prophet should perish outside of Jerusalem. "O Jerusalem, Jerusalem, the one who kills the prophets and stones those who are sent to her! How often I wanted to gather your children together, as a hen gathers her brood under her wings, but you were not willing! See! Your house is left to you desolate; and assuredly, I say to you, you shall not see Me until the time comes when you say, 'BLESSED IS HE WHO COMES IN THE NAME OF THE LORD!' Glory be to God forever. Amen

The liturgy is completed as usual in the days of the Great Lent

بشئ إذ طهر بالإيمان قلوبهم . فالآن لماذا تجربون الله بوضع نير على عنق التلاميذ لم يستطيع آباؤنا ولا نحن أن نحمله . ولكن بنعمة الرب يسوع المسيح نؤمن أن نخلص كما أولئك أيضاً . فسكت الجمع كله . وكان يستمع لبرنابا وبولس وها يحدثان بجميع ما اجرى الله من الآيات والعجائب فى الأمم بواسطتهم . وبعد أن سكتا أجاب يعقوب قائلاً: أيها الرجال اخوتنا اسمعوا لي . قد تكلم سمعان كيف افتقد الله الأمم أولاً ليتخذ منهم شعباً لاسمه . وهذا ما توافقه أقوال الأنبياء كما هو مكتوب: انى من بعد هذا سأرجع وأقيم خيمة داود الساقطة وأبنى ما هدم منها وأنصبها ثانية. حتى تطلب الرب بقية الناس وجميع الأمم الذين دعى اسمى عليهم يقول الرب الصانع هذا ومعلوم عند الرب منذ الأزل جميع أعماله. لم تزل كلمة الرب .

(المزمور 97 : 8 و 9)
الجبال تبتهج أمام وجه الرب لأنه آتى ليدين الأرض . يدين المسكونة بالعدل والشعوب بالإستقامة . هلليلويا .

(الانجيل من لوقا ص 13 : 31 ألخ)
وفى ذلك اليوم جاء فريسيون قائلين له : إذهب واخرج من هنا فان هيرودس يريد أن يقتلك . فقال لهم إمضوا فقولوا لهذا الثعلب هأنذا أخرج شياطين وأتمم الشفاء اليوم وغداً وفى اليوم الثالث أكمل . ولكن ينبغى لي أن أعمل اليوم وغداً وما يليه فانه لا يهلك نبى خارجاً عن أورشليم . يا أورشليم يا أورشليم يا قاتلة الأنبياء وراجمة المرسلين إليها كم مرة أردت أن أجمع بنيك كما يجمع الطائر فراخه فى عشه تحت جناحيه ولم تريدوا . هوذا بيتكم يترك لكم خراباً . وأقول لكم انكم لا ترونى منذ الآن حتى تقولوا مبارك الآتى باسم الرب . والمجد لله دائماً.

يكمل القداس كأى يوم من أيام الصوم الكبير

سبت لعازر

Lazarus Saturday

احداث هذا اليوم

انجيل باكر يخبرنا عن معجزة شفاء الاعمى بالقرب من اريحا و فيها نرى رحمة الرب يسوع على هذا الانسان.

الرب يذهب لبيت عنيا ليقيم لعازر الذى احبه وهى آخر المعجزات الكبار و العامة التى صنعها الرب قبل ذهابه الاخير لاورشليم و فيها يظهر الرب رحمته و حبه للذين يحبونه و سلطانه على الموت قبل موته .

Today's Events

In the Gospel of the Morning Prayer, the Lord heals the blind man near Jericho. It shows the mercy of the Lord on this man.

The Lord goes to Bethany to raise Lazarus, whom He loved, from death. This is the last big and public miracle the Lord performed before His last journey to Jerusalem. The Lord shows His mercy and love to all who love Him, and shows His authority over death before His death.

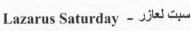

(Lazarus Saturday)   (سبت لعازر)

(The Vesper prayer)   (عشية سبت لعازر)

It is prayed as usual, in addition to the Doxology of St. Lazarus.

تصلى العشية كالعادة ، ولكن يضاف إليها ذكصولوجية تقال خصيصاً للعازر .

Come together all nations: to praise our Lord Jesus Christ: Who raised Lazarus: with the power of His divinity.

Ⲑⲱⲟⲩϯ ⲧⲏⲣⲟⲩ ⲱ̀ ⲛⲓⲗⲁⲟⲥ : ⲛ̀ⲧⲉⲛϩⲱⲥ ⲙ̀ⲡⲉⲛ Ⲓⲏⲥ Ⲡⲭⲥ : ⲫⲏⲉ̀ⲧⲁϥⲧⲟⲩⲛⲟⲥ ⲛ̀Ⲗⲁⲍⲁⲣⲟⲥ: ϧⲉⲛ ϯϫⲟⲙ ⲛ̀ⲧⲉ ⲧⲉϥⲙⲉⲑⲛⲟⲩϯ .

ثؤؤوتى تيروو أو نى لاؤس : إنتين هوس إمبين إيسوس بيخرستوس : في إيطافطوونوس إن لازاروس : خين إتجُم إنتيه تيفميث نووتى .

إجتمعوا يا جميع الشعوب لنسبح ربنا يسوع المسيح الذى أقام لعازر بقـوة لاهوته .

Raise us with Your power: from the shadow of death: like the righteous Lazarus: whom You raised after his death.

Ⲙⲁⲧⲟⲩⲛⲟⲥ ϧⲉⲛ ⲧⲉⲕϫⲟⲙ ⲉ̀ⲃⲟⲗ ϧⲉⲛ ⲧ̀ϧⲏⲃⲓ ⲙ̀ⲫⲙⲟⲩ : ⲙ̀ⲫⲣⲏϯ ⲙ̀ⲡⲓⲑⲙⲏⲓ Ⲗⲁⲍⲁⲣⲟⲥ : ⲉ̀ⲧⲁⲕⲧⲟⲩⲛⲟⲥϥ ⲙⲉⲛⲉⲛⲥⲁ ⲡⲉϥⲙⲟⲩ .

ماطوونوس خين تيك جُم إيفول خين إتخيفى إمفموو : إمفريتى إمبى إثمي لازاروس : إيطاكطوونوسف مينينصا بيفموو .

أقمنا بقوتك من ظلال الموت مثل البار لعازر الذى اقمته من بعد موته .

You are the way and life: O Jesus Christ the creator: You are God Who gave life: to Lazarus the righteous.

Ⲛ̀ⲑⲟⲕ ⲡⲉ ⲡⲓⲙⲱⲓⲧ ⲛⲉⲙ ⲡⲓⲱⲛϧ : ⲱ̀Ⲓⲏⲥ Ⲡⲭⲥ ⲡⲓⲁ̀ⲣⲙⲓⲟⲩⲣⲅⲟⲥ : ⲛ̀ⲑⲟⲕ ⲡⲉ Ⲫϯ ⲉⲧϯ ⲙ̀ⲡⲱⲛϧ : ⲛ̀Ⲗⲁⲍⲁⲣⲟⲥ ⲡⲓⲇⲓⲕⲉⲟⲥ .

إنثوك بيه بى مويت نيم بى أونخ : أو إيسوس بيخستوس بى ذيميورغوس : إنثوك بيه إفنـووتى إنتى إمبؤنـخ : إن لازاروس بى ذيكيوُس .

أنت هو الطريق والحياة يا يسوع المسيح الخالق أنت هوالإله المعطى الحياة للعازر الصديق .

You are the resurrection: Who raised the righteous Lazarus : we ask You to save us from our afflictions: and give us a share with him.

Ⲛ̀ⲑⲟⲕ ⲡⲉ ϯⲁⲛⲁⲥⲧⲁⲥⲓⲥ : ⲁⲕⲧⲟⲩⲛⲟⲥ ⲙ̀ⲡⲓⲑⲙⲏⲓ Ⲗⲁⲍⲁⲣⲟⲥ : ⲧⲉⲛϩⲟ ⲛⲁϩⲙⲉⲛ ⲉ̀ⲃⲟⲗ ϧⲉⲛ ⲛⲉⲛⲑⲗⲩⲯⲓⲥ : ⲙⲟⲓ ⲛⲁⲛ ⲛⲉⲙⲁϥ ⲛ̀ⲟⲩⲙⲉⲣⲟⲥ .

إنثوك بيه تى أناستاسيس: أكطوونوس إمبى إثمي لازاروس : تين تيهو ناهمين إيفول خين نين إثليبسيس : موى نان نيماف إنؤوميروس .

أنت هو القيامة أقمت البار لعازر نسأل أن تخلصنا من شدائدنا واعنا معه نصيباً .

Let us go O faithful: to the mount of Olives to Bethany: to sea the righteous Lazarus : and to praise and to sing.

Ⲙⲁⲣⲉⲛϣⲉⲛⲁⲛ ⲱ̀ ⲛⲓⲡⲓⲥⲧⲟⲥ : ⲉ̀ⲡⲓⲧⲱⲟⲩ ⲛ̀ⲧⲉ ⲛⲓϫⲱⲓⲧ ϣⲁ Ⲃⲏⲑⲁⲛⲓⲁ : ⲛ̀ⲧⲉⲛⲛⲁⲩ ⲉ̀ⲡⲓⲑⲙⲏⲓ Ⲗⲁⲍⲁⲣⲟⲥ : ⲟⲩⲟϩ ⲛ̀ⲧⲉⲛϩⲱⲥ ϧⲉⲛ ϩⲁⲛⲯⲁⲗⲓⲁ .

مارين شينان أو نى بيسطوس : إبى طووؤو إنتيه نى جويت شا بيت أنيا : إنتين ناف إبى إثمي لازاروس : أووه إنتين هوس خين هان بصاليا.

لنذهب أيها المؤمنين إلى جبل الزيتون إلى بيت عنيا لننظر البار لعازر ونسبح ونرتل .

Let us praise and glorify: and worship the Holy Trinity: the coessential: and everlasting forever.

Ⲙⲁⲣⲉⲛϩⲱⲥ ⲛ̀ⲧⲉⲛϯⲱⲟⲩ : ⲧⲉⲛⲟⲩⲱϣⲧ ⲛ̀ϯⲧⲣⲓⲁⲥ ⲉⲑⲟⲩⲁⲃ : ⲉⲥⲟⲓ ⲛ̀ⲟⲩⲙⲟⲟⲩⲥⲓⲟⲥ : ⲉⲑⲙⲏⲛ ⲉ̀ⲃⲟⲗ ϣⲁ ⲉ̀ⲛⲉϩ .

مارين هوس إنتين تى أوأوو: تين أووأوأوشت إنتى إترياس إثؤواب : إسوى إنؤموأووسيوس : إثمين إيفول شا إينيه .

فلنسبح ونمجد ونسجد للثالوث القدوس المساوى الدائم إلى الأبد .

(Matin of Lazarus Saturday)

(باكر سبت ألعازر)

Genesis 49:1-28

And Jacob called unto his sons, and said, Gather yourselves together, that I may tell you that which shall befall you in the last days. Gather yourselves together, and hear, you sons of Jacob; and hearken unto Israel your father. Reuben, you are my firstborn, my might, and the beginning of my strength, the excellency of dignity, and the excellency of power: Unstable as water, you shall not excel; because you went up to your father's bed; then you defiled it: he went up to my couch. Simeon and Levi are brothers; instruments of cruelty are in their habitations. O my soul, come not into their secret; unto their assembly, my spirit, be not united: for in their anger they slew a man, and in their self-will they dug down a wall. Cursed be their anger, for it was fierce; and their wrath, for it was cruel: I will divide them in Jacob, and scatter them in Israel. Judah, you are he whom your brothers shall praise: your hand shall be on the neck of your enemies; your father's children shall bow down before you. Judah is a lion's whelp: from the prey, my son, you are gone up: he stooped down, he crouched as a lion, and as a lioness; who shall rouse him up? The scepter shall not depart from Judah, nor a lawgiver from between his feet, until Shiloh comes; and unto him shall the gathering of the people be. Binding his foal unto the vine, and his donkey's colt unto the choice vine; he washed his garments in wine, and his clothes in the blood of grapes: His eyes shall be red with wine, and his teeth white with milk. Zebulun shall dwell at the shore of the sea; and he shall be for a haven of ships; and his border shall be unto Sidon. Issachar is a strong donkey crouching down between two burdens: And he saw that rest was good, and the land that it was pleasant; and bowed his shoulder to bear, and became a servant unto forced labor. Dan shall judge his people, as one of the tribes of Israel. Dan shall be a serpent by the way, an adder in the path, that bites the horse's heels, so that his rider shall fall backward. I have waited for your salvation, O LORD. Gad, a troop shall overcome him: but he shall overcome at the last. Out of Asher his food shall be fat, and he shall yield royal dainties. Naphtali is a hind let loose: he gives beautiful words. Joseph is a fruitful bough, even a fruitful bough by a well; whose branches run over the wall: The archers have fiercely attacked him, and shot at him, and hated him: But his bow abode in strength, and the arms of his hands were made strong by the hands of the mighty God of Jacob; (from there is the Shepherd, the Rock of Israel:) Even by the God of your father, who shall help you; and by the Almighty, who shall bless you with blessings of heaven above, blessings of the deep that lies beneath, blessings of the breasts, and of the womb: The blessings of your father have prevailed above the blessings of my ancestors unto the utmost bounds of the everlasting hills: they shall be on the head of

من سفر التكوين 49 : 1 - 28

ودعا يعقوب بنيه وقال اجتمعوا لانبئكم بما يصيبكم فى آخر الأيام . اجتمعوا واسمعوا يا بنى يعقوب واصغوا إلى إسرائيل أبيكم . رأوبين بكرى أنت قوتى ورأس أولادى تماديت فى القساوة وتوغلت فى الفظاظة , هدرت مثل الماء الفائر . لأنك صعدت على مضجع أبيك. حينئذ دنست الفراش الذى صعدت عليه . شمعون ولاوى الاخوان قد أكملا الظلم بارادتهما . سيوفهما الات جور . لا تسر بمشورتهما وباجتماعهما لا تبتهج كليتاى . لأنهما فى غضبهما قتلا رجلاً وبشهوتهما عرقبا ثوراً . ملعون غضبهما ما أفظعه وحمية قلوبهما ما أقساها . أقسمهما فى يعقوب وأفرقهما فى إسرائيل . يهوذا تباركك اخوتك . تكون يداك على قفا أعدائك . ويسجد لك بنو أبيك . يهوذا شبل أسد . من غصن زاهر يا بنى قد صعدت واتكأت ورقدت مثل أسد ومثل شبل من ينهضه . لا يزول رئيس من يهوذا ولا مدبر من صلبه حتى يأتى الذى له وهو الذى تنظره الأمم . يربط جحشه عند الكرمة وإبن أتانه بالجفنة . ويغسل بالخمر لباسه وثوبه بدم العنب . عيناه تفرح من الخمر وأسنانه تبيض أكثر من اللبن . زبولون يسكن عند ساحل البحر وهو عند مرفأ السفن ويمتد إلى صيدون . يساكر اشتهى الحسن واستراح بين الانصبة رابض . ورأى الراحة انها حسنة والأرض دسمة فاحنى عنقه للتعب وصار رجلاً فلاحاً . دان يدين شعبه كسبط فى إسرائيل . ويكون دان حية على الطريق . يجلس على السبيل يلدغ عقب الفرس فيسقط الفارس إلى الوراء . ينتظر خلاص الرب . جاد يناضله الغزاة وهو يناضلهم سيقانهم . أشير خبزه دسم وهو يطهر الرؤساء . نفتالى غصن زاهر يمنح جمالاً للثمرة . الإبن النامى يوسف الإبن النامى إبنى الجديد المحسود ارجع إلى الذين تشاوروا عليه ومرروه وغضب عليه أرباب السهام وتكسرت بالقوة سهامهم وانحلت عضلات سواعد اذرعتهم بيدىّ عزيز يعقوب من هناك الذى شدد إسرائيل. من قبل إله أبيك وأعانك الله إلهى علىّ ويباركك ببركة السماء من فوق وبركة الأرض التى عليها كل الأشياء ببركة الثديين والرحم . بركات أبيك وأمك فاقت على بركات الجبال الراكنة وعلى بركات الآكام

Joseph, and on the crown of the head of him that was separate from his brothers. Benjamin is ravenous as a wolf: in the morning he shall devour the prey, and at night he shall divide the spoil. All these are the twelve tribes of Israel: and this is it that their father spoke unto them, and blessed them; every one according to his blessing he blessed them. Glory be to the Holy Trinity. Amen

Isaiah 40:9-31

O Zion, that brings good tidings, get you up into the high mountain; O Jerusalem, that brings good tidings, lift up your voice with strength; lift it up, be not afraid; say unto the cities of Judah, Behold your God! Behold, the Lord GOD will come with strong hand, and his arm shall rule for him: behold, his reward is with him, and his work before him. He shall feed his flock like a shepherd: he shall gather the lambs with his arm, and carry them in his bosom, and shall gently lead those that are with young. Who has measured the waters in the hollow of his hand, and measured out heaven with the span, and known the dust of the earth in a measure, and weighed the mountains in scales, and the hills in a balance? Who has directed the Spirit of the LORD, or being his counselor has taught him? With whom took he counsel, and who instructed him, and taught him in the path of justice, and taught him knowledge, and showed to him the way of understanding? Behold, the nations are as a drop of a bucket, and are counted as the small dust of the balance: behold, he takes up the isles as fine dust. And Lebanon is not sufficient to burn, nor its beasts sufficient for a burnt offering. All nations before him are as nothing; and they are counted to him less than nothing, and worthless. To whom then will you liken God? or what likeness will you compare unto him? The workman melts a graven image, and the goldsmith spreads it over with gold, and casts silver chains. He that is so impoverished that he has no offering chooses a tree that will not rot; he seeks unto him a skillful workman to prepare a graven image, that shall not move. Have you not known? have you not heard? has it not been told you from the beginning? have you not understood from the foundations of the earth? It is he that sits upon the circle of the earth, and its inhabitants are as grasshoppers; that stretches out the heavens as a curtain, and spreads them out as a tent to dwell in: That brings the princes to nothing; he makes the judges of the earth as nothing. Yea, they shall not be planted; yea, they shall not be sown: yea, their stock shall not take root in the earth: and he shall also blow upon them, and they shall wither, and the whirlwind shall take them away as stubble. To whom then will you liken me, or shall I be equal? says the Holy One. Lift up your eyes on high, and behold who has created these things, that brings out their host by number: he calls them all by names by the greatness of his might, for he is strong in power; not one is missing. Why say you, O Jacob, and speak, O Israel, My way is hidden from the LORD, and my right is

الدهرية . تكون على رأس يوسف وعلى هامة اخوته الذين قادهم. بنيامين الذئب الخاطف فى الصباح يأكل وفى المساء يعطى الطعام . هؤلاء جميعهم بنو يعقوب الاثنا عشر . وهذا ما كلمهم به أبوهم وباركهم كل واحد حسب البركة التى باركهم بها . مجداً للثالوث القدوس

(من أشعياء النبى ص 40 : 9 ألخ)

على جبل عال اصعد يا مبشر صهيون . ارفع صوتك بقوة يا مبشر أورشليم. ارفع ولا تخف . قل لمدن يهوذا هوذا إلهك هوذا الرب يأتى بالقوة وذراعه متسلطة . هوذا أجرته معه وعمله قدامه . كراع يرعى قطيع غنمه وبذراعه يجمع الحملان ويعزى الحبالى . من كال الماء بيده وقاس السماء بشبره والأرض كلها بقبضته . من وزن الجبال بالمثقال والآكام بالميزان . من علم قلب الرب أو من كان معه مشيراً فعلمه . من إستشار وعلمه أو من علمه من أراه الحكم أو طريق الفهم من عرفها له . أو من سبق فأعطاه حتى عوضه . إنما الأمم كلها عنده مثل نقطة ماء تنقط من قادوس . ومثل ميلان الميزان حُسبوا . جميعهم كالبصاق يعدون . وخشب لبنان لا يعد للحريق وجميع البهائم لا تعد شيئاً للمحرقة . جميع الأمم لديه كلاشئ وعنده كالعدم حسبوا . فيمن شبهتم الرب وبأى مثل مثلتموه . هل بصورة صنعها النجار وصفحة الصائغ بالذهب وركب فيه الذهب وشبهه يتلف . إنما خشبة لا تسوس اختارها النجار وبحكمة يطلب كيف يقيم تمثالاً لا يتحرك . ألا تعلمون ألا تسمعون ألم تخبروا منذ البدء أما علمتم أسس الأرض . أن القابض على كرة الأرض بأسرها والسكان فيها كالجراد . الذى ينشر السماء كالقبة ويبسطها كالخيمة ليسكن فيها . الذى يجعل الأراخنة كلا شئ والأرض التى خلقها كحواء أنهم لم يغرسوا ولم يزرعوا ولم يتأصل فى الأرض ساقهم . فنفخ عليهم فيبسوا وحملهم العاصف كالقش . والآن بمن تشبهوننى فأتعالى يقول القدوس . ارفعوا عيونكم إلى العلاء وانظروا من خلق هذه كلها . الذى يخرج زينتها عدداً ويدعو كلها بأسماء كثيرة ومن كثرة مجده وعزة قوته لا ينسى شيئاً منها . فلماذا تقول يا يعقوب ولماذا تتكلم يا إسرائيل . قد اختفت طريقى عن الله وان الله قد نزع قضائى فمضى . والآن أما علمت ولم تسمع.

passed over by my God? Have you not known? have you not heard, that the everlasting God, the LORD, the Creator of the ends of the earth, faints not, neither is weary? there is no searching of his understanding. He gives power to the faint; and to them that have no might he increases strength. Even the youths shall faint and be weary, and the young men shall utterly fall: But they that wait upon the LORD shall renew their strength; they shall mount up with wings as eagles; they shall run, and not be weary; and they shall walk, and not faint. *Glory be to the Holy Trinity. Amen*

Zephaniah 3:14-20

Sing, O daughter of Zion; shout, O Israel; be glad and rejoice with all the heart, O daughter of Jerusalem. The LORD has taken away your judgments, he has cast out your enemy: the king of Israel, even the LORD, is in your midst: you shall not see harm any more. In that day it shall be said to Jerusalem, Fear not: and to Zion, Let not your hands be weak. The LORD your God in the midst of you is mighty; he will save, he will rejoice over you with joy; he will quiet you with his love, he will rejoice over you with singing. I will gather them that are sorrowful for the appointed assembly, who are among you, to whom the reproach of it was a burden. Behold, at that time I will deal with all that afflict you: and I will save her that is lame, and gather those that were driven out; and I will get them praise and fame in every land where they have been put to shame. At that time will I bring you again, even in the time that I gather you: for I will make you a name and a praise among all people of the earth, when I turn back your captivity before your eyes, says the LORD. *Glory be to the Holy Trinity. Amen.*

Zechariah 9:9-15

Rejoice greatly, O daughter of Zion! Shout, O daughter of Jerusalem! Behold, your King is coming to you; He is just and having salvation, Lowly and riding on a donkey, A colt, the foal of a donkey. I will cut off the chariot from Ephraim And the horse from Jerusalem; The battle bow shall be cut off. He shall speak peace to the nations; His dominion shall be `from sea to sea, And from the River to the ends of the earth.' As for you also, Because of the blood of your covenant, I will set your prisoners free from the waterless pit. Return to the stronghold, You prisoners of hope. Even today I declare That I will restore double to you. For I have bent Judah, My bow, Fitted the bow with Ephraim, And raised up your sons, O Zion, Against your sons, O Greece, And made you like the sword of a mighty man. Then the Lord will be seen over them, And His arrow will go forth like lightning. The Lord God will blow the trumpet, And go with whirlwinds from the south. The Lord of hosts will defend them. *Glory be to the Holy Trinity. Amen*

أن الله الأبدى الله الذى خلق أقطار الأرض لا يتعب ولا يعيا ولا حد لعلمه. الذى يهب للجياع قوتاً والمعطى وجع القلب للذين لم تحترق قلوبهم . جاعت الغلمان وتعبت الشبان . والمختارين يصيرون غير اقوياء . أما منتظروا الرب يجدون قوة وتنبت لهم أجنحة كالنسور يسرعون ولا يتعبون ويمشون ولا يجوعون . مجداً للثالوث القدوس .

(من سفر صفنيا النبى ص 3 : 14 ألخ)
افرحى يا إبنة صهيون . إهتفى يا أورشليم . افرحى وابتهجى بكل قلبك يا إبنة أورشليم فقد نزع الرب مظالمك , وخلصك من أيدى أعدائك يملك الرب فى وسطك يا إسرائيل الرب فلا ترى شراً من بعد . فى ذلك الزمان يقول الرب لأورشليم تقوى ، ويا صهيون لا تسترخى يداك ان فى وسطك الرب إلهك الجبار. فهو يخلصك ويجلب عليك فرحاً ويجددك فى محبته ويبتهج لك بترنم كما فى يوم عيد . واجمع منسحقيك ومن هو الذى يحمل عليها عاراً . هأنذا أعمل فيك ولأجلك فى ذلك الزمان قال الرب واخلص الظالعة والمنفية اقبلها إلىّ واجعلهم حمداً واسماً فى الأرض كلها. ويخزون فى ذلك الزمان إذا أحسنت إليكم وفى وقت قبولى إياكم لأنى أصيركم اسماً وحمداً فى جميع شعوب الأرض عند ما أرد سبيكم قدام أعينكم قال الرب . مجداً للثالوث الأقدس .

(من سفر زكريا النبى ص 9 : 9 - 15)
ابتهجى جداً يا إبنة صهيون واهتفى يا بنت أورشليم هوذا ملكك يأتيك عادلاً ومخلصاً وديعاً وراكباً على أتان وجحش إبن أتان . واستأصل المركبة من افرايم والخيل من أورشليم وتستأصل قوس الرب ويتكلم بالسلام للأمم يكون سلطانه من البحر إلى البحر ومن النهر إلى أقاصى الأرض وأنت بدم العهد قد أطلقت أسراك من الجب الذى لا ماء فيه . اسكنوا الحصن يا أسرى الرجاء . وعوض يوم واحد فى غربتك اعوضك ضعفين . لأنى شدّدت يهوذا لى قوساً وملأت افرايم وأنهضت بنى صهيون على بنى ياوان وأقوّيك كسيف محارب الرب عليهم بسهمه يخرج كالبرق والرب الضابط الكل ينفخ فى البوق ويسير بهيجان الغضب . رب الجنود يكون ناصراً لهم. مجداً للثالوث القدوس .

Psalms 29:3, 11

O LORD, you have brought up my soul from the grave: you have kept me alive, that I should not go down to the pit. You have turned for me my mourning into dancing: you have put off my sackcloth, and girded me with gladness; Alleluia

(باكر المزمور 29 : 3 و 11)

يارب أصعدت من الجحيم نفسى وخلصتنى من الهابطين فى الجب ، حولت نوحى إلى فرح لي ، مزقت مسحى ومنطقتنى سروراً . هلليلويا .

Luke 18:35-43

Then it happened, as He was coming near Jericho, that a certain blind man sat by the road begging. And hearing a multitude passing by, he asked what it meant. So they told him that Jesus of Nazareth was passing by. And he cried out, saying, "Jesus, Son of David, have mercy on me!" Then those who went before warned him that he should be quiet; but he cried out all the more, "Son of David, have mercy on me!" So Jesus stood still and commanded him to be brought to Him. And when he had come near, He asked him, saying, "What do you want Me to do for you?" He said, "Lord, that I may receive my sight." Then Jesus said to him, "Receive your sight; your faith has made you well." And immediately he received his sight, and followed Him, glorifying God. And all the people, when they saw it, gave praise to God.

Glory be to God forever. Amen

(الانجيل من لوقا ص 18 : 35 - 43)

ولما قرب من أريحا كان أعمى جالساً عند الطريق يستعطى فلما سمع بجمع يجتاز سأل ما هذا فأخبروه يسوع الناصرى عابراً فصاح قائلاً : يا يسوع إبن داود إرحمنى . فنهره المتقدمون ليسكت . أما هو فكان يزداد صياحاً يا إبن داود إرحمنى فوقف يسوع وأمر أن يقدم إليه.

فلما قرب منه سأله ماذا تريد أن أصنع بك فقال له : يارب أن أبصر . فقال له يسوع : أبصر إيمانك قد خلصك . فلوقته أبصر وتبعه وهو يمجد الله والشعب جميعه لما رأوا سبحوا الله . والمجد لله دائماً .

The Gospel Response
(مرد انجيل باكر)

Many are the wonders, which were performed, I believe in His might, for He is the King of Glory.	زيؤش إنتيه هان إشفيري : ني إيطافئرى إموؤو : تى ناهتى إتيفميت جورى : جيه إنثوف بيه إبؤورو إنتيه إبؤأوو .	Ϩⲉⲟϣ ⲛ̀ⲧⲉ ϩⲁⲛⲙ̀ϣⲫⲏⲣⲓ : ⲛⲏⲉⲧⲁϥⲓⲣⲓ ⲙ̀ⲙⲱⲟⲩ : ϯⲛⲁϩϯ ⲉ̀ⲧⲉϥⲙⲉⲧϫⲱⲣⲓ : ϫⲉ ⲛ̀ⲑⲟϥ ⲡⲉ ⲡ̀ⲟⲩⲣⲟ ⲛ̀ⲧⲉ ⲡ̀ⲱⲟⲩ .	كثيرة هى الأعاجيب التى صنعتها : أؤمن بجبروته لأنه هو ملك المجد .

Liturgy

(قداس سبت لعازر)

1 Corinthians 2:1-8

And I, brethren, when I came to you, did not come with excellence of speech or of wisdom declaring to you the testimony of God. For I determined not to know anything among you except Jesus Christ and Him crucified. I was with you in weakness, in fear, and in much trembling. And my speech and my preaching were not with persuasive words of human wisdom, but in demonstration of the Spirit and of power, that your faith should not be in the wisdom of men but in the power of God. However, we speak wisdom among those who are mature, yet not the wisdom of this age, nor of the rulers of this age, who are coming to nothing. But we speak the wisdom of God in a mystery, the hidden wisdom which God ordained before the ages for our glory, which none of the rulers of this age knew; for had they known, they would not have crucified the Lord of glory. The Grace of God the Father be with you all. Amen

1 Peter 1:25-2:6

Now this is the word which by the gospel was preached to you. Therefore, laying aside all malice, all deceit, hypocrisy, envy, and all evil speaking, as newborn babes, desire the pure milk of the word, that you may grow thereby, if indeed you have tasted that the Lord is gracious. Coming to Him as to a living stone, rejected indeed by men, but chosen by God and precious, you also, as living stones, are being built up a spiritual house, a holy priesthood, to offer up spiritual sacrifices acceptable to God through Jesus Christ. Therefore it is also contained in the Scripture, "BEHOLD, I LAY IN ZION A CHIEF CORNERSTONE, ELECT, PRECIOUS, AND HE WHO BELIEVES ON HIM WILL BY NO MEANS BE PUT TO SHAME. Do not love the world, …

Acts 27:38-28:10

So when they had eaten enough, they lightened the ship and threw out the wheat into the sea. When it was day, they did not recognize the land; but they observed a bay with a beach, onto which they planned to run the ship if possible. And they let go the anchors and left them in the sea, meanwhile loosing the rudder ropes; and they hoisted the mainsail to the wind and made for shore. But striking a place where two seas met, they ran the ship aground; and the prow stuck fast and remained immovable, but the stern was being broken up by the violence of the waves. And the soldiers' plan was to kill the prisoners, lest any of them should swim away and escape. But the centurion, wanting to save Paul,

(البولس من كورنثوس الأولى 2 : 1 - 8)

وأنا أيضاً لما أتيت إليكم يا اخوتى ما أتيت بسمو الكلام أو الحكمة معلماً إياكم بسر الله . لانى لم أحكم ان أعرف شيئاً بينكم إلا يسوع المسيح واياه مصلوباً . وأنا أتيت عندكم فى ضعف وخوف ورعدة كثيرة وكلامى وكرازتى لم يكونا باقناع بكلام حكمة الناس لكن ببرهان الروح والقوة . لكى لا يكون إيمانكم بحكمة الناس بل بقوة الله . لكننا نتكلم بحكمة بين الكاملين بحكمة ليست من هذا الدهر ولا بحكمة رؤساء هذا الدهر الذين يبطلون . لكن ننطق بحكمة الله فى سر الحكمة المكتومة التى سبق الله فعينها قبل الدهور لمجدنا . التى لم يعرفها أحد من رؤساء هذا العالم . لأن لو عرفوا لما صلبوا رب المجد . نعمة الله الآب …

(بطرس الأولى ص 1 : 25 - 2 : 1 - 6)

وهذه هى الكلمة التى بشرتم بها . فاطرحوا عنكم كل شر وكل خبث وكل رياء وكل حسد وكل نميمة كأطفال مولودين الآن اشتهوا اللبن الناطق العديم الغش لكى تنموا به للخلاص . إن كنتم قد ذقتم ان الرب صالح . الذى إذ تأتون إليه حجراً حياً مرذولاً من الناس ولكن مختار من الله كريم . كونوا أنتم أيضاً مبنيين كحجارة حية بيتاً روحياً كهنوتاً مقدساً لتقديم ذبائح روحية مقبولة عند الله بيسوع المسيح . لأنه مكتوب فى الكتاب هأنذا اضع فى صهيون حجر زاوية مختاراً كريماً والذى يؤمن به لن يخزى . لا تحبوا العالم …

(الابركسيس 27 : 38 - 28 : 10)

فلما شبعوا من الطعام طفقوا يخففون السفينة طارحين الحنطة فى البحر . ولما صار النهار لم يكونوا يعرفون الأرض ولكنهم أبصروا خليجاً له شاطئ . فاجمعوا أن يدفعوا السفينة إلى هناك فرفعوا المراسى تاركين إياها فى البحر وحلوا ربط الدفة ورفعوا الشراع الصغير للريح وتوجهوا نحو الشاطئ . فلما وقعوا على موضع بين بحرين دفعوا السفينة إلى هناك فثبت مقدمها ولبث لا يتحرك وأما مؤخرها فتفكك من شدة الأمواج . فتشاوروا الجند كي يقتلوا الأسرى لئلا يسبح أحد منهم

kept them from their purpose, and commanded that those who could swim should jump overboard first and get to land, and the rest, some on boards and some on parts of the ship. And so it was that they all escaped safely to land. Now when they had escaped, they then found out that the island was called Malta. And the natives showed us unusual kindness; for they kindled a fire and made us all welcome, because of the rain that was falling and because of the cold. But when Paul had gathered a bundle of sticks and laid them on the fire, a viper came out because of the heat, and fastened on his hand. So when the natives saw the creature hanging from his hand, they said to one another, "No doubt this man is a murderer, whom, though he has escaped the sea, yet justice does not allow to live." But he shook off the creature into the fire and suffered no harm. However, they were expecting that he would swell up or suddenly fall down dead. But after they had looked for a long time and saw no harm come to him, they changed their minds and said that he was a god. In that region there was an estate of the leading citizen of the island, whose name was Publius, who received us and entertained us courteously for three days. And it happened that the father of Publius lay sick of a fever and dysentery. Paul went in to him and prayed, and he laid his hands on him and healed him. So when this was done, the rest of those on the island who had diseases also came and were healed. They also honored us in many ways; and when we departed, they provided such things as were necessary. The word of the Lord shall grow, multiply, be mighty and be confirmed in the holy church of God. Amen

فيهرب . ولكن قائد المئة إذ كان يريد أن يخلص بولس منعهم عن تنفيذ مشورتهم وأمر أن القادرين على السباحة يرمون أنفسهم أولاً إلى البحر ويعومون إلى البر والباقين بعضهم على ألواح وبعضهم على قطع من السفينة وبهذه الواسطة كانت نجاتنا جميعاً إلى البر . ولما نجونا حينئذ عرفنا أن تلك الجزيرة تسمى مالطة وصنع لنا البرابرة فى ذلك المكان إحساناً عظيماً. فانهم أضرموا ناراً وقبلوا جميعنا من أجل الذى أصابنا ومن أجل البرد . فرجع بولس وجمع كثيراً من الحطب ووضعه على النار فخرجت من الحرارة أفعى ونشبت فى يده . فلما رأى البرابرة الوحش معلقاً بيده قال بعضهم لبعض لابد أن هذا الرجل قاتل فانه بعد أن نجا من البحر لم يدعه العدل يحيا . أما هو فنفض الوحش إلى النار ولم يمسه أذى . أما هم إنتظروا ان ينشق أو يسقط للحين ميتاً . فلما طال انتظارهم ورأوا انه لم يصبه ضرر تغيروا وقالوا انه إله وكان فى ذلك الموضع ضياع كثيرة لمقدم الجزيرة المسمى بوبليوس الذى قبلنا وأضافنا بلطف ثلاثة أيام . وكان أبو بوبليوس ملقى مريضاً قدامهم بحمى ووجع الامعاء فدخل إليه بولس وصلى ووضع يديه عليه فشفاه . فلما صار هذا كان الباقون الذين بهم أمراض فالجزيرة يأتون إليه ويشفون فأكرمنا هؤلاء إكراماً جزيلاً وعند اقلاعنا زودونا بما نحتاج إليه . لم تزل كلمة الرب ...

Psalms 128:8, 2

The blessing of the Lord be upon you; We bless you in the name of the Lord. Many a time they have afflicted me from my youth; Yet they have not prevailed against me. Alleluia

(المزمور 128 : 8 و 2)
بركة الرب عليكم باركناكم باسم الرب. مراراً كثيرة حاربونى منذ صباى . وانهم لم يقدروا علىّ . هلليلويا .

John 11:1-45

Now a certain man was sick, Lazarus of Bethany, the town of Mary and her sister Martha. It was that Mary who anointed the Lord with fragrant oil and wiped His feet with her hair, whose brother Lazarus was sick. Therefore the sisters sent to Him, saying, "Lord, behold, he whom You love is sick." When Jesus heard that, He said, "This sickness is not unto death, but for the glory of God, that the Son of God may be glorified through it." Now Jesus loved Martha and her sister and Lazarus. So, when He heard that he was sick, He stayed two more days in the place where He was. Then after this He said to the disciples, "Let us go to Judea again." The disciples said to Him, "Rabbi, lately the Jews sought to stone You, and are You going there again?" Jesus answered, "Are there not twelve hours in the day? If anyone

(الانجيل من يوحنا ص 11 : 1 - 45)
وكان واحد مريضاً وهو لعازر من بيت عنيا من قرية مريم ومرثا اخته . وكانت هذه هى مريم التى دهنت الرب بالطيب ومسحت قدميه بشعرها وهى التى كان لعازر المريض أخاها . فأرسلت اختاه إليه قائلتين له : يا سيد ها أن الذى تحبه مريض . فلما سمع يسوع قال هذا المرض ليس هو مرض الموت بل لأجل مجد الله ليتمجد إبن الله به . وكان يسوع يحب مرثا ومريم اختها ولعازر . فلما سمع انه مريض أقام فى الموضع الذى كان فيه يومين . وبعد ذلك قال لتلاميذه : لنذهب إلى اليهودية أيضاً . فقال له تلاميذه :   يا معلم الآن كان اليهود يطلبون أن يرجموك وتمضى أيضاً

walks in the day, he does not stumble, because he sees the light of this world. But if one walks in the night, he stumbles, because the light is not in him." These things He said, and after that He said to them, "Our friend Lazarus sleeps, but I go that I may wake him up." Then His disciples said, "Lord, if he sleeps he will get well." However, Jesus spoke of his death, but they thought that He was speaking about taking rest in sleep. Then Jesus said to them plainly, "Lazarus is dead. And I am glad for your sakes that I was not there, that you may believe. Nevertheless let us go to him." Then Thomas, who is called the Twin, said to his fellow disciples, "Let us also go, that we may die with Him." So when Jesus came, He found that he had already been in the tomb four days. Now Bethany was near Jerusalem, about two miles away. And many of the Jews had joined the women around Martha and Mary, to comfort them concerning their brother. Now Martha, as soon as she heard that Jesus was coming, went and met Him, but Mary was sitting in the house. Now Martha said to Jesus, "Lord, if You had been here, my brother would not have died. But even now I know that whatever You ask of God, God will give You." Jesus said to her, "Your brother will rise again." Martha said to Him, "I know that he will rise again in the resurrection at the last day." Jesus said to her, "I am the resurrection and the life. He who believes in Me, though he may die, he shall live. And whoever lives and believes in Me shall never die. Do you believe this?" She said to Him, "Yes, Lord, I believe that You are the Christ, the Son of God, who is to come into the world." And when she had said these things, she went her way and secretly called Mary her sister, saying, "The Teacher has come and is calling for you." As soon as she heard that, she arose quickly and came to Him. Now Jesus had not yet come into the town, but was in the place where Martha met Him. Then the Jews who were with her in the house, and comforting her, when they saw that Mary rose up quickly and went out, followed her, saying, "She is going to the tomb to weep there." Then, when Mary came where Jesus was, and saw Him, she fell down at His feet, saying to Him, "Lord, if You had been here, my brother would not have died." Therefore, when Jesus saw her weeping, and the Jews who came with her weeping, He groaned in the spirit and was troubled. And He said, "Where have you laid him?" They said to Him, "Lord, come and see." Jesus wept. Then the Jews said, "See how He loved him!" And some of them said, "Could not this Man, who opened the eyes of the blind, also have kept this man from dying?" Then Jesus, again groaning in Himself, came to the tomb. It was a cave, and a stone lay against it. Jesus said, "Take away the stone." Martha, the sister of him who was dead, said to Him, "Lord, by this time there is a stench, for he has been dead four days." Jesus said to her, "Did I not say to you that if you would believe you would see the glory

إلى هناك . أجاب يسوع : أليس النهار اثنتى عشرة ساعة فمن يمشى فى النهار لا يعثر لانه ينظر نور هذا العالم ومن يمشى فى الليل يعثر لأن النور ليس فيه . قال هذا ثم قال لهم لعازر حبيبنا قد نام لكنى أذهب لاقيمه . قال له تلاميذه: يا سيد إن كان قد نام فهو يقوم. أما يسوع فقال عن نوم موته وهم ظنوا انه قال عن رقاد النوم . حينئذ قال لهم يسوع علانية : لعازر قد مات . وأنا أفرح من اجلكم انى لم أكن هناك لتؤمنوا لكن لنذهب إليه . فقال توما الذى يدعى التوأم لرفقائه التلاميذ : لنمضى نحن أيضاً لكى نموت معه . فلما أتى يسوع وجد أنه اليوم الرابع وهو فى القبر . وكانت بيت عنيا قريبة من أورشليم نحو خمس عشرة غلوة . وكان كثيرون من اليهود قد جاءوا إلى مريم ومرثا ليعزوهما عن أخيهما . فلما سمعت مرثا أن يسوع آتٍ قامت وخرجت للقائه أما مريم فكانت جالسة فى البيت. فقالت مرثا ليسوع : يا سيد لو كنت ههنا ما كان أخى ليموت . لكنى الآن أيضاً أعلم أن كل ما تطلب من الله يعطيك الله إياه . قال لها يسوع : سيقوم أخوك . قالت له مرثا أنا أعلم انه سيقوم فى القيامة فى اليوم الأخير . قال لها يسوع : أنا هو القيامة والحياة . من يؤمن بي ولو مات فهو يحيا . وكل من هو حى ويؤمن بي فلن يموت إلى الأبد . أتؤمنين بهذا . قالت له : نعم يا سيد أنا أؤمن أنك أنت المسيح إبن الله الآتى إلى العالم . ولما قالت هذا مضت ودعت مريم اختها سراً وقالت لها : المعلم ههنا وهو يدعوكِ . فلما سمعت نهضت مسرعة وجاءت إليه لأن يسوع لم يكن قد جاء إلى القرية بل كان أيضاً فى المكان الذى لاقته فيه مرثا فاليهود الذين كانوا معها فى البيت يعزونها لما رأوا مريم قامت مسرعة وخرجت تبعوها ظانين أنها ذاهبة إلى القبر لتبكى هناك . فلما جاءت مريم إلى حيث كان يسوع ورأته خرت عند قدميه قائلة : يا سيد لو كنت ههنا ما كان أخى ليموت. فلما رآها يسوع تبكى ورأى اليهود أيضاً الذين جاءوا معها يبكون تألم بالروح واضطرب . وقال لهم : أين وضعتموه . فقالوا له : يا سيد تعال وانظر . فدمعت عينا يسوع . فقال اليهود : انظروا كيف يحبه . وقال بعض منهم : أما كان يقدر هذا الذى فتح عينى المولود أعمى أن لا يدع هذا أيضاً يموت . فتحنن يسوع فى نفسه وجاء إلى القبر وكان مغارة وكان على بابه حجر عظيم . قال لهم يسوع : ارفعوا هذا الحجر. قالت له مرثا اخت الميت : يا سيد قد أنتن لأن له أربعة ايام . قال لها يسوع : ألم أقل

of God?" Then they took away the stone from the place where the dead man was lying. And Jesus lifted up His eyes and said, "Father, I thank You that You have heard Me. And I know that You always hear Me, but because of the people who are standing by I said this, that they may believe that You sent Me." Now when He had said these things, He cried with a loud voice, "Lazarus, come forth!" And he who had died came out bound hand and foot with graveclothes, and his face was wrapped with a cloth. Jesus said to them, "Loose him, and let him go." Then many of the Jews who had come to Mary, and had seen the things Jesus did, believed in Him. *Glory be to God forever. Amen*

لكِ إنكِ إن أمنتِ ترين مجد الله . فرفعوا الحجر عن باب القبر ورفع يسوع عينيه إلى فوق وقال : يا أبتِ أشكرك لأنك سمعت لي . وأنا قد علمت انك تسمع لي في كل حين . لكن من أجل هذا الجمع المحيط بي قلت ليؤمنوا انك أنت الذى أرسلتني . ولما قال هذا صرخ بصوت عظيم لعازر هلمّ خارجاً . فخرج الميت مربوطة رجلاه ويداه بلفائف ووجهه ملفوف بمنديل . فقال لهم يسوع حلوه ودعوه يذهب . فكثيرون من اليهود الذين جاءوا إلى مريم لما رأوا ما صنع يسوع آمنوا به . والمجد لله دائماً .

The Gospel Response
مرد انجيل القداس

Hail to Lazarus, whom He raised after four days. Raise my heart my Lord Jesus, which was killed by the evil one.□	شيريه لازاروس في إيطافطوونوسف مينيصا إفطوأوو إن إيهوؤو : باهيت باتشويس إيسوس : في إيطاف خوثفيف إنجيه بى بيت هوؤو .	Ⲭⲉⲣⲉ Ⲗⲁⲍⲁⲣⲟⲥ ⲫⲏ ⲉⲧⲁϥⲧⲟⲩⲛⲟⲥϥ ⲙⲉⲛⲉⲛⲥⲁ Ⲇ̅ ⲛ̀ⲉϩⲟⲟⲩ: ⲡⲁϩⲏⲧ Ⲡⲁϭ̅ Ⲓⲏⲥ : ⲫⲏ ⲉⲧⲁϥϧⲟⲑⲃⲉϥ ⲛ̀ϫⲉ ⲡⲓⲡⲉⲧϩⲱⲟⲩ .	السلام للعازر الذى أقامه بعد أربعة أيام أقم قلبى ياربى يسوع المسيح الذى قتل الشر .

Aspasmos
الأسبسمس

Who is likened unto You? O Lord, among the gods, You are the true God, the performer of miracles.	نيم غار خين نى نووتى : إتؤنى إمموك باتشويس : إنثوك بيه إفنووتى إممي : إتئرى إنهان إشفيرى .	Ⲛⲓⲙ ⲅⲁⲣ ⲉⲛ ⲛⲓⲛⲟⲩϯ : ⲉⲧⲟⲛⲓ ⲙ̀ⲙⲟⲕ Ⲡ︦ⲟ︦ⲥ︦ : ⲛ̀ⲑⲟⲕ ⲡⲉ Ⲫϯ ⲙ̀ⲙⲏⲓ : ⲉⲧⲓⲣⲓ ⲛ̀ϩⲁⲛⲙ̀ⲫⲏⲣⲓ .	من فى الآلهة يشبهك يارب أنت هو الإله الحقيقى الصانع العجائب .
Blessed are You truly: O my Lord Jesus: with Your Good Father: and the Holy Spirit.□	إك إسماروأووت إليثوس : أو باتشويس إيسوس : نيم بيك يوت إن أغاثوس : نيم بى بنيفما إثؤواب .	Ⲕ̀ⲥⲙⲁⲣⲱⲟⲩⲧ ⲁⲗⲏⲑⲟⲥ : ⲱ̀ Ⲡ︦ⲟ︦ⲥ︦ Ⲓⲏⲥ : ⲛⲉⲙ ⲡⲉⲕⲓⲱⲧ ⲛ̀ⲁⲅⲁⲑⲟⲥ : ⲛⲉⲙ ⲡⲓⲡⲛⲉⲩⲙⲁ ⲉⲑⲩ .	مبارك أنت بالحقيقة ياربى يسوع مع أبيك الصالح والروح القدس .

أحد الشعانين

Palm Sunday

احداث هذا اليوم

ثم قبل الفصح بستة أيام و هو يوم السبت 9 نيسان أتى يسوع إلى بيت عنيا حيث كان لعازر الميت الذى أقامه يسوع من الأموات وحيث دهنت مريم قدمى يسوع بالطيب في بيت سمعان الأبرص . ثم قام فى الغد و هو يوم الأحد 10 نيسان قاصداً الدخول إلى أورشليم علانية . وهو اليوم الذى كان يأخذ فيه كل جماعة بنى إسرائيل خروف الفصح من القطيع فيحفظونه إلى اليوم الرابع عشر من هذا الشهر ثم يذبحونه فى العشية .

وكما كانت خراف الفصح تفرز وتجعل تحت الحفظ بضعة أيام فى المدينة المقدسة . هكذا بقى حمل الله الذى يرفع خطايا العالم بين جدران أورشليم مترددا بين الهيكل وبيت عنيا . ولما قرب الوقت المعين لاتمام الفداء دخل أورشليم علانية فى الوقت الذى كانت فيه مزدحمة بالزائرين الذين اتوا للاحتفال بالفصح فيها . ولما قرب المسيح من المدينة هتفت تلك الجماهير باصوات التهليل حتى بلغ هتافهم عنان السماء وهم يشيرون فى هتافهم إلى الرب يسوع بعبارات تخص المسيح المنتظر " أوصنا لإبن داود مبارك الآتى باسم الرب . اوصنا فى الأعالى . مباركة مملكة أبينا داود الآتية باسم الرب اوصنا فى الأعالى . مبارك الملك الآتى باسم الرب . سلام فى السماء ومجد فى الأعالى " .

كان يعتبر ركوب الحمير سلميا بينما كان ركوب الخيل حربيا . فاختار رئيس السلام ان يركب جحشا إبن أتان لم يركبه أحد قط . فانه كان رئيسا جديدا وامتطى حيوانا جديدا كما انه عند موته قد وضع فى قبر جديد . وبما ان الجحش لم يركبه أحد قط (العهد الجديد) يقتضى ان تصحبه أمه (العهد القديم) ليستأنس بها فتمم الرب هذه الخدمة ، ليكمل العهد القديم بالجديد .

Today's Events

Before the Passover by six days, which was Nissan 9th, the Lord came to Bethany to Simon's house where there were Lazarus whom the Lord raised from death and Mary, who anointed the feet of the Lord with ointment. On the next day, Sunday Nissan 10th, the Lord planned to enter Jerusalem publicly. Nissan 10th was the day in which the Jews used to choose the lambs for the Passover, keep them till the fourteenth of the month, then slain it in the evening.

As the lambs were supposed to be chosen and kept for few days in Jerusalem, the Lord, the Lamb of God who carries the sins of the world, stayed in Jerusalem going back and forth between the temple and Bethany. When the time came for our salvation, He entered Jerusalem publicly among the people who came to celebrate the Passover in Jerusalem. When the Lord Jesus approached the city, the multitude started to praise Him with the words specified for the coming Messiah saying "Hosanna to the Son of David. Hosanna in the Highest. This is the King of Israel. Blessed is He, Who comes in the Name of the Lord of Hosts."

Riding donkeys was considered to be for peace; while riding horses for war. The King of Peace chose to ride a colt, never ridden before. The Lord was a new King and sat on a new animal, and when He died, He was buried in a new tomb. The colt (New Testament) was ridden for the first time, and was accompanied by its mother (Old Testament) to be tamed. So, the Lord completed His service by crowning the Old Testament by the New Testament.

Palm Sunday

أحد الشعانين

The Vesper Prayer

صلاة رفع بخور عشية

+ The church and crosses are decorated with the palm leaves and olive branches. We pray the Ninth, Eleventh and Twelfth hours of the Agpeya. At the end, the psalm (116) is sang, followed by the fourth canticle, then the Psali of the Palm Sunday Ⲁⲣⲓⲥⲁⲗⲡⲓⲍⲓⲛ in Batos joyful tune, and the Theotokias and Sheris which are ended by the Batos conclusion of the Theotokia.

+ The incense is offered as usual, with the litany of the Departed, followed by this Doxology:

+ تزين الكنيسة و الصلبان بسعف النخل و أغصان الزيتون ، تصلى مزامير صلاة الساعة التاسعة والحادية عشر والثانية عشر وفى نهايتها يقال المزمور الـ (116) ⲛⲓⲉⲑⲛⲟⲥ ⲧⲏⲣⲟⲩ باللحن ثم الهوس الرابع ثم إبصالية الشعانين Ⲁⲣⲓⲥⲁⲗⲡⲓⲍⲓⲛ باللحن الواطس الفرايحى ثم يقال التداكية وتقال الشيرات بلحن الشعانين وتختم بختام الثؤطوكيات الواطس .

+ يرفع البخور كالمعتاد ، وتقال أوشية الراقدين

+ تقال ذكصولوجية الشعانين الآتية:

English	Coptic transliteration (Arabic)	Coptic	Arabic
Blow the trumpet at the new moon: with the sound of the trumpet: on your festive day: for it is an order from God.	أريصالبيزيــن خيــن أو صواى خين أو إســمي إنصالبينغـــوس : خيــن أو إهؤو إنتين شاى : جيه أوواه صاهنى إن ثيؤس .	Ⲁⲣⲓⲥⲁⲗⲡⲓⲍⲓⲛ ⲉⲛ ⲟⲩⲥⲟⲩⲁⲓ : ⲉⲛ ⲟⲩⲥⲏ ⲛⲥⲁⲗⲡⲓⲅⲅⲟⲥ : ⲉⲛ ⲟⲩⲉϩⲟⲟⲩ ⲛⲛⲉⲧⲉⲛϣⲁⲓ : ϫⲉ ⲟⲩⲁϩⲥⲁϩⲛⲓ ⲛ̀ⲑⲉⲟⲥ .	بوقوا فى رأس الشهر بصوت البوق فى يوم أعيادكم فإنه أمر الله .
He who sits upon the cherubim / riding on a colt / entered into Jerusalem / what is this great humility!	في إتهمسى هيجيــن نى شيروبيم : أف طالوف إيه أوو إيه أو : أفشيه إخوون إيروساليم أوو بيه باى نيشتى إن ثيبيو .	Ⲫⲏⲉⲧϩⲉⲙⲥⲓ ϩⲓϫⲉⲛ ⲛⲓⲭⲉⲣⲟⲩⲃⲓⲙ : ⲁϥⲧⲁⲗⲟϥ ⲉⲟⲩⲉⲱ : ⲁϥϣⲉ ⲉⲟⲩⲛⲉ̀ⲓⲗⲏⲙ : ⲟⲩ ⲡⲉ ⲡⲁⲓⲛⲓϣϯ ⲛ̀ⲑⲉⲃⲓⲟ .	الجالس على الشاروبيم ركب على جحش ووصل إلى أورشليم ما هو هذا التواضع العظيم .
According to what David said: in the Psalms: blessed is He who comes: in the name of the Lord of Hosts.	كاطا إفريتى إيطاف جوس: إنجيه دافيد خين بى بصالموس : جيه إفسمــارؤوت إنجيه في إثنيوو : خين إفران إمبتشويس إنتيه نى جُم .	Ⲕⲁⲧⲁ ⲫ̀ⲣⲏϯ ⲉⲧⲁϥϫⲟ : ⲛ̀ϫⲉ Ⲇⲁⲩⲓⲇ ⲉⲛ ⲡⲓⲯⲁⲗ : ϫⲉ ϥ̀ⲥⲙⲁⲣⲱⲟⲩⲧ ⲛ̀ϫⲉ ⲫⲏⲉⲑⲛⲏⲟⲩ : ⲉⲛ ⲫ̀ⲣⲁⲛ ⲙ̀Ⲡ̅ϭ̅ⲥ̅ ⲛ̀ⲧⲉ ⲛⲓϫⲟⲙ .	كما قال داود فى المزمور مبارك الآتى باسم رب القوات
Again, he said: out of the mouth of babes: and nursing infants: You have perfected praise.	بالين أون أفجو إمموس جيه إيفول خين روأوو إنهان كوجى إن ألوأوى نيم نى إثؤويم نشى : إنثوك أك سييتيه بى إسموو .	Ⲡⲁⲗⲓⲛ ⲟⲛ ⲁϥϫⲱ ⲙ̀ⲙⲟⲥ ϫⲉ ⲉ̀ⲃⲟⲗ ⲉⲛ ⲣⲱⲟⲩ ⲛ̀ϩⲁⲛⲕⲟⲩϫⲓ ⲛ̀ⲁⲗⲱⲟⲩⲓ ⲛⲉⲙ ⲛⲏⲉⲑⲟⲩⲉⲙϭⲓ : ⲛ̀ⲑⲟⲕ ⲁⲕⲥⲉⲃⲧⲉ ⲡⲓⲥⲙⲟⲩ .	وأيضاً قال أن من أفواه الأطفال الرضعان أنت أعددت سبحاً .
Then He completed the saying: of David the spirit-bearer: who likewise said: out of the mouth of babes.	طوتيه أف جوك إيفول إمبى صاجى : إنتيه دافيد بى بنيفماطوفورو : جيه إيفول خيـن روأوو إنهان كوجى إن ألوأوى : إمباى ريتى إفجو إمموس .	Ⲧⲟⲧⲉ ⲁϥϫⲱⲕ ⲉ̀ⲃⲟⲗ ⲙ̀ⲡⲓⲥⲁϫⲓ : ⲛ̀ⲧⲉ Ⲇⲁⲩⲓⲇ ⲡⲓⲡⲛⲉⲩⲙⲁⲧⲟⲫⲟⲣⲟ : ϫⲉ ⲉ̀ⲃⲟⲗ ⲉⲛ ⲣⲱⲟⲩ ⲛ̀ϩⲁⲛⲕⲟⲩϫⲓ ⲛ̀ⲁⲗⲱⲟⲩⲓ : ⲙ̀ⲡⲁⲓⲣⲏϯ ⲉϥϫⲱ ⲙ̀ⲙⲟⲥ .	حينئذ كمل قول داود اللابس الروح هكذا قائلاً : ان من أفواه الأطفال الصغار .

They praise Him watchfully: saying, This is Immanuel: Hosanna in the highest: this is the King of Israel.	سي هوس إيروف خين أونيهسى أف جيه فاى بيه إممانوئيـل : أوصاننا خين نى إنتشوسى : فاى بيه إبؤورو إمبى إسرائيل .	Ceϩⲱⲥ ⲉⲣⲟϥ ⲉⲛ ⲟⲩⲛⲉϩⲥⲓ ⲁⲩϫⲉ ⲫⲁⲓ ⲡⲉ Ⲉⲙⲙⲁⲛⲟⲩⲏⲗ : ⲱⲥⲁⲛⲛⲁ ⲉⲛ ⲛⲏⲉⲧϭⲟⲥⲓ : ⲫⲁⲓ ⲡⲉ ⲡ̄ⲟⲩⲣⲟ ⲙ̄Ⲡⲓⲥⲗ .	ونسبحه بتيقظ قائلين : هذا هو عمانوئيل أوصنا فى الأعالى هذا هو ملك إسرائيل .
Bring to the Lord, O sons of God: bring to the Lord glory and honor: rejoice in our God: with doxologies of blessing.	أنى أوى إمبتشويس إننى شيرى إنتى إفنوتى أنى أوى إمبتشويس إن أوأوؤو نيم أوو طايو : إشليلووى إيڤول إمبين نوتى : خين هان ذكصولوجيا إن إسمو .	Ⲁⲛⲓⲟⲩⲓ ⲙ̄ Ⲡ̄ⲟ̄ⲥ̄ ⲛ̄ⲛⲓϣⲏⲣⲓ ⲛ̄ⲧⲉ Ⲫ̄ϯ : ⲁⲛⲓⲟⲩⲓ ⲙ̄Ⲡ̄ⲟ̄ⲥ̄ ⲛ̄ⲟⲩⲱⲟⲩ ⲛⲉⲙ ⲟⲩⲧⲁⲓⲟ : ⲉ̀ϣⲗⲏⲗⲟⲩ ⲉ̀ⲃⲟⲗ ⲙ̄ⲡⲉⲛⲛⲟⲩϯ ⲉⲛ ϩⲁⲛⲇⲟⲝⲟⲗⲟⲅⲓⲁ ⲛ̄ⲥⲙⲟⲩ	قدموا للرب يا أبناء الله قدموا للرب مجداً وكرامة : ورتلوا لإلهنا بتماجيـد البركة .
Praise is due to You, O God: in Zion and Jerusalem: they send to You: prayers unto the ages.	إنثوك إفنوتى إفئرشاف ناك : إنجيه بيجو خين سيون : نيم يروساليم إف إ تى ناك : إنهان إفكى شا نى إ أون .	Ⲛ̄ⲑⲟⲕ Ⲫ̄ϯ ϥⲉⲣⲡⲣⲉ ⲛⲁⲕ : ⲛ̄ϫⲉ ⲡⲓϩⲱ ⲉⲛ Ⲥⲓⲱⲛ : ⲛⲉⲙ Ⲓⲗⲏⲙ ⲉⲩⲉ̀ϯ ⲛⲁⲕ : ⲛ̄ϩⲁⲛⲉⲩⲭⲏ ϣⲁ ⲛⲓⲉ̀ⲱⲛ .	أنت الله يليق بك : التسبيح فى صهيون وتوفى لك النذور فى أورشليم إلى الدهور .
Hosanna in the highest: this is the King of Israel: blessed is He, who comes in the name: of the Lord of Hosts.	أوصانا خين نى إنتشوسى : فاى بيه إبؤورو إمبى إسرائيل إفسمارؤووت إنجيه فى إثنيوو خيـن إفران إمبتشويس إنتيه نى جُم .	Ⲱⲥⲁⲛⲛⲁ ⲉⲛ ⲛⲏⲉⲧϭⲟⲥⲓ ⲫⲁⲓ ⲡⲉ ⲡ̄ⲟⲩⲣⲟ ⲙ̄Ⲡⲓⲥⲗ : ϥ̀ⲥⲙⲁⲣⲱⲟⲩⲧ ⲛ̄ϫⲉ ⲫⲏⲉⲑⲛⲏⲟⲩ ⲉⲛ ⲫ̀ⲣⲁⲛ ⲙ̄Ⲡ̄ⲟ̄ⲥ̄ ⲛ̄ⲧⲉ ⲛⲓϫⲟⲙ	أوصنا فى الأعالى هذا هو ملك إسرائيل مبارك الآتى باسم رب القوات .
We praise Him and glorify Him: and exalt Him above all: as the Good One and Lover of Mankind: have mercy on us according to Your great mercy.	تين هوس إيروف تين تى أوؤ ناف : تين إرهواؤ تشيبسى إمموف هوس أغاثوس أووه إمماى رومى ناى نان كاطا بيك نيشتى إن ناى .	Ⲧⲉⲛϩⲱⲥ ⲉⲣⲟϥ ⲧⲉⲛϯ ⲱⲟⲩ ⲛⲁϥ : ⲧⲉⲛⲉⲣϩⲟⲩⲟ ϭⲓⲥⲓ ⲙ̄ⲙⲟϥ : ϩⲱⲥ ⲁⲅⲁⲑⲟⲥ ⲟⲩⲟϩ ⲙ̄ⲙⲁⲓⲣⲱⲙⲓ ⲛⲁⲓ ⲛⲁⲛ ⲕⲁⲧⲁ ⲡⲉⲕⲛⲓϣ̀ϯ ⲛ̀ⲛⲁⲓ .	نسبحه ونمجده ونرفعه كثيراً كصالح ومحب البشر . ارحمنا كعظيم رحمتك .

+ **The Introduction of the Creed and the Creed.**
+ **The Priest prays Ⲫ̄ϯ ⲛⲁⲓ ⲛⲁⲛ while holding the cross decorated with the palm leaves. The Congregation chants Kirie elison, in long tune, while going around the altar three times then in the church three times then around the altar one more time. They chant Ⲉⲩⲗⲟⲅⲏⲙⲉⲛⲟⲥ, then the Exposition.**

+ نعظمك يا أم النور الحقيقى وقانون الإيمان .
+ يقول كبير الكهنة Ⲫ̄ϯ ⲛⲁⲓ ⲛⲁⲛ أللهم ارحمنا ... وهو ممسكاً بالصليب المزين بالسعف والورود والشموع وبعدها يرتل الشعب كيرى ليسون باللحن الطويل ثلاث مرات و هم يطوفون الهيكل ثلاث مرات ثم الكنيسة ثلاث مرات ثم الهيكل مرة اخرى و يقولون لحن الشعانين ايفلوجيمينوس ثم الطرح .

Ⲉⲩⲗⲟⲅⲏⲙⲉⲛⲟⲥ (Evlogeminos - أيفلوجيمينوس)

English	أيفلوجيمينوس	Ⲉⲩⲗⲟⲅⲏⲙⲉⲛⲟⲥ	مبارك
Blessed is He who comes in the name of the Lord; again, in the name of the Lord.	أوإرخومينوس : إن أونوماتى كيريــــوو : بالين إن أونوماتـــى كيريوو .	ⲟⲉⲣⲭⲟⲙⲉⲛⲟⲥ ⲉⲛⲟⲛⲟⲙⲁϯ ⲕⲩⲣⲓⲟⲩ ⲡⲁⲗⲓⲛ ⲉⲛⲟⲛⲟⲙⲁϯ ⲕⲩⲣⲓⲟⲩ .	الآتى باسم الرب. وأيضاً باسم الرب .
Hosanna to the Son of David; again, to the Son of David.	أوصاننا طــــو دافيد : إيــــو بالين طو إيو دافيد .	Ⲱⲥⲁⲛⲛⲁ ⲧⲱ ̀ⲣⲓⲱ Ⲇⲁⲩⲓⲇ . ⲡⲁⲗⲓⲛ ⲧⲱ ̀ⲣⲓⲱ Ⲇⲁⲩⲓⲇ .	اوصنا لإبن داود وأيضاً لإبن داود
Hosanna in the highest; again, in the highest.	أوصاننا إنتيس إبسيس تيس بالين إنتس إبسيس تيس .	Ⲱⲥⲁⲛⲛⲁ ⲉⲛⲧⲓⲥⲧⲯⲓⲥⲧⲓⲥ ⲡⲁⲗⲓⲛ ⲉⲛⲧⲓⲥⲧⲯⲓⲥⲧⲓⲥ .	اوصنا فى الأعالى وأيضاً فى الأعالى .
Hosanna to the King of Israel; again, to the King of Israel.	أوصاننا فاسيليطو إسرائيـــل . بالـــين فاسيليطو إسرائيل .	Ⲱⲥⲁⲛⲛⲁ ⲃⲁⲥⲓⲗⲓⲧⲟⲩ Ⲓⲥⲣⲁⲏⲗ . ⲡⲁⲗⲓⲛ ⲃⲁⲥⲓⲗⲓⲧⲟⲩ Ⲓⲥⲣⲁⲏⲗ .	اوصنا ملك إسرائيل وأيضاً ملك إسرائيل.
Let us chant saying: Alleluia, Alleluia, Alleluia. Glory be to our God; again, glory be to our God.	تين إيربصالين إنجو إمموس. ألليلويا. ألليلويا ألليلويا بى أوأوو فا بين نووتى بيه . بالـــين بى أوأوو فــا بين نووتى بيه .	Ϯⲉⲛⲉⲣⲯⲁⲗⲓⲛⲉⲛⲭⲱ ̀ⲙⲙⲟⲥ Ⲁⲗ . Ⲁⲗ . Ⲁⲗ . ⲡⲓⲱⲟⲩ ⲫⲁ ⲡⲉⲛⲛⲟⲩϯ ⲡⲉ . ⲡⲁⲗⲓⲛ ⲡⲓⲱⲟⲩ ⲫⲁ ⲡⲉⲛⲛⲟⲩϯ ⲡⲉ .	فلنرتل قائلين : هللويا هللويا هللويا المجد هو لإلهنا وأيضاً المجد هو لإلهنا.
Hosanna in the highest, this is the King of Israel, blessed is He who comes in the name, of the Lord of hosts.	أوصاننا خين نى إنتشسوسى : فاى بيه إبؤورو إمبى إسرائيل : إفسماروؤوت إنجيه فى إثيوو خين إفران إمبتشويس إنتى نى جُم .	Ⲱⲥⲁⲛⲛⲁ ϧⲉⲛ ⲛⲏⲉⲧϭⲟⲥⲓ : ⲫⲁⲓ ⲡⲉ ̀ⲡⲟⲩⲣⲟ ̀ⲙⲠⲓⲥⲗ : ϥ̀ⲥⲙⲁⲣⲱⲟⲩⲧ ̀ⲛϫⲉ ⲫⲏⲉⲑⲛⲏⲟⲩ ϧⲉⲛⲫ̀ⲣⲁⲛ ̀ⲙⲠ̅ⲟ̅ⲥ̅ ̀ⲛⲧⲉⲛⲓϫⲟⲙ .	اوصنا فى الأعالى هذا هو ملك إسرائيل مبارك الآتى باسم رب القوات .

The Exposition

Reader:

Ascend upon a high mountain, O who announces Zion. Raise your voice with strength and preach to Jerusalem. Say to the cities of Judah, "Here is your King coming, carrying his wage and handiwork before His presence, like a shepherd who shepherds his flock and with his hands gathers the lambs. Arise and decorate your gates for the Son of God is coming. With purity and peace, He will save you. Here are all your children coming to Him rejoicing while crying and saying, 'Hosanna to the Son of David.' **(Hosanna).** Now when they drew near to Jerusalem, and came to Bethphage at the Mount of Olives, Jesus sent two disciples, saying to them, "Go into the village opposite you; and as soon as you have entered it, you will find a colt tied,

ثم يقال هذا الطرح

اصعد إلى الجبال العالية يا مبشر صهيون. ارفع صوتك بقوة وبشر أورشليم وقل لمدن يهوذا هوذا ملكك يأتيك وأجرته معه وعمله قدامه . مثل الراعى الذى يرعى قطيع غنمه وبذراعه العالية يجمع الحملان . قومى زينى أبوابك لأنه سيأتى إبن الله . وهو بالطهارة والسلامة ينجيك. هوذا كل بنيك يقبلون إليه بفرح ويصرخون قائلين: أوصنا لإبن داود (أوصانا). ولما قرب من بيت فاجى عند جبل الزيتون أرسل يسوع إثنين من تلاميذه . وقال أمضيا إلى هذه القرية التى أمامكما فتجدان أتاناً وجحشاً إبن أتان . فحلاهما وأتيانى بهما . فان قال لكما أحد شيئاً فقولا له أن الرب يحتاج

on which no one has sat. Lose it and bring it. And if anyone says to you, 'Why are you doing this?' say, "The Lord has need of it, and immediately he will send it here." All this was done that it might be fulfilled which was spoken of by Zechariah, the prophet, saying, "Shout, O daughter of Jerusalem! Behold, your King is coming to you; lowly and riding on a donkey, a colt, the foal of a donkey." How great is this wonder! He, who sits on the cherubim rode on a colt according to the Economy. He sat on the earth and never left the heavens. He sits in the bosom of His Father and was present in Jerusalem. The sons of the Hebrews spread their garments in His way. The cherubim were covering their faces Mith their wings. They were worthily glorifying with unceasing lips saying, "Blessed is the glory of the Lord in Salmon, the mount of His Holiness." They were praising and saying, "Hosanna to the Son of David." Blessed is the Lord Jesus Christ, who came to save us. Glory be to Him forever. Amen. **(Hosanna).**

Second Exposition

Then, as He was now drawing near the Mount of Olives, the whole multitude began to rejoice and praise God with a loud voice for all the mighty works they had seen, saying, "Hosanna to the Son of David. Hosanna in the Highest. This is the King of Israel." **(Hosanna).** The next day, when the great multitude that had come to the feast heard that Jesus was coming to Jerusalem, they took branches of palm trees and went out to meet Him, and cried out, "Hosanna to the Son of David." **(Hosanna).** And a large crowd of Hebrews went out before him and spread their clothes on the road that the Savior would take.; others cut down branches from the trees and spread them on the road. Then the multitudes that went before Him, and those who followed Him cried out saying, "Hosanna to the Son of David." **(Hosanna).** Rejoice greatly, O daughter of Zion! Behold, your King is coming to you, lowly, and sitting on a donkey, a colt, the foal of a donkey." Then the multitudes went before and cried out, saying: "Hosanna to the Son of David! Blessed is He who comes in the name of the LORD! Hosanna in the Highest, this is the King of Israel." **(Hosanna).** Hosanna in the highest, this is the King of Israel, blessed is He who comes in the name, of the Lord of hosts. There shall come forth a Rod from the stem of Jesse, and a Branch shall grow out of his roots. The Spirit of the Lord shall rest on Him; the Spirit of wisdom and understanding, the Spirit of counsel and might, the Spirit of knowledge and of the fear of the Lord. O what a great wonder! He, who sits on the cherubim, and whom the seraphim praise, and cover their faces for His divinity, rode a colt, as planned for our salvation. They bless You in the heavens and they glorify You on the earth and

إليهما ، لما جاء التلميذان كما أمرهما وجدا الأتان والجحش مربوطين . فحلاهما وأتيا بهما إليه كى يكمل ما قاله الرب من قبل النبى : قولوا لإبنة صهيون هوذا ملكك يأتيك راكباً على أتان وجحش إبن أتان . فيا لعظم هذه الأعجوبة الجالس على الشاروبيم ركب على جحش أتان كالتدبير . هو جالس على الأرض ولم يترك عنه السموات . جالس فى حضن أبيه وحاضر فى أورشليم . أولاد العبرانيين فرشوا ثيابهم قدامه . والشاروبيم معاً يسترون وجوههم بأجنحتهم . وكانوا يمجدون باستحقاق بشفاه غير ساكتة ويقولون تبارك مجد الرب فى صهيون جبل قدسه . وكان هؤلاء يسبحون ويقولون أوصنا لإبن داود . مبارك الرب يسوع المسيح الذى أتى ليخلصنا . له المجد إلى الأبد آمين. **(أوصانا).**

(ثم هذا الطرح أيضاً)

لما قرب يسوع المسيح من منحدر جبل الزيتون صاعداً إلى أورشليم ابتدأ كل جمع التلاميذ يفرحون ويسبحون الله بصوت عظيم من أجل القوات التى رأوها صارخين قائلين: أوصنا لإبن داود . أوصنا فى الأعالى هذا هو ملك إسرائيل. **(أوصانا).** وللغد الجمع الكثير الذى جاء إلى العيد سمعوا أن يسوع سيأتى إلى أورشليم . فأخذوا سعفاً بأيديهم للقائه وهم يصرخون قائلين : أوصنا لإبن داود. **(أوصانا).** والجمع الكثير الذى من العبرانيين خرجوا قدامه وفرشوا ثيابهم فى الطريق التى سيسلكها المخلص. وآخرون منهم قطعوا أغصاناً من الشجر وجاءوا بها بفرح وفرشوها فى الطريق. والذين كانوا يسيرون أمامه والذين خلفه كانوا يصرخون قائلين: أوصنا لإبن داود. **(أوصانا).** افرحى يا إبنة صهيون فانه جاء ملكك بمجد وكرامة وعظم بهاء راكباً على جحش . والجمع يمشى أمامه صارخين قائلين: أوصنا لإبن داود . مبارك الملك الآتى باسم الرب. أوصنا فى الأعالى هذا هو ملك إسرائيل. **(أوصانا).** يزهر قضيب من أصل يسى وتصعد زهرة وتطلع من وسطه ويستريح عليه روح الله روح الحكمة وروح القوة ، روح الفهم والمشورة وروح العبادة. ويملأه الروح من مخافة الله . يا لهذه الأعجوبة العظيمة الجالس على الشاروبيم والسيرافيم تسبحه , ويغطون وجوههم من أجل لاهوته. تفضل اليوم وركب على جحش أتان كالتدبير من أجل خلاصنا. يباركونك فى السموات ويمجدونك على الأرض ويصرخون قائلين : أوصنا لإبن داود أوصنا فى الأعالى هذا هو ملك

they shout saying, "Hosanna to the Son of David. Hosanna in the Highest. This is the King of Israel. Blessed is He, who comes in the name of the Lord of Hosts. " To Him is glory, forever. Amen. **(Hosanna).**

إسرائيل مبارك الآتى باسم رب القوات . ولعظمته المجد دائماً آمين .

The Litany of Gospel, the Psalm and Gospel

+ تقال أوشية الانجيل ويقرأ الانجيل

The Psalm

Ⲯⲁⲗⲙⲟⲥ ⲣⲓⲍ : ⲕ̅ⲉ̅ ⲛⲉⲙ ⲕ̅ⲋ̅

Psalm 117:25-26

Blessed is he who comes in the name of the Lord! We have blessed you from the house of the Lord. God is the Lord, And He has given us light; Bind the sacrifice with cords to the horns of the altar. Alleluia.

Ⲧⲥⲙⲁⲣⲱⲟⲩⲧ ⲛ̀ϫⲉ ⲫⲏⲉⲑⲛⲏⲟⲩ ϧⲉⲛ ⲫ̀ⲣⲁⲛ ⲙ̀ⲡ̅ⲟ̅ⲥ̅ : ⲁⲛⲥⲙⲟⲩ ⲉⲣⲱⲧⲉⲛ ⲉⲃⲟⲗ ϧⲉⲛ ⲡ̀ⲏⲓ ⲙ̀ⲡ̅ⲟ̅ⲥ̅ .

Ⲥⲉⲙⲛⲉ ⲟⲩϣⲁⲓ ϧⲉⲛ ⲛⲉⲧⲫⲉϩ : ϣⲁ ⲛⲉⲛⲧⲁⲡ ⲛ̀ⲧⲉ ⲡⲓⲙⲁⲛⲉⲣϣⲱⲟⲩϣⲓ . ⲁⲗ

إفسماروّوت إنجيه فى إثنيوو خين إفران إمبتشويس : أن إسمو إروتين إيفول خين إبئي إمبتشويس .

سيمنيه أو شاى خين نيتفيه : شا نين طاب إنتيه بى مان إرشوؤوشى . الليلويا .

(مز 117: 25 و 26)

مبارك الآتى باسم الرب . باركناكم من بيت الرب . رتلوا عيداً فى الواصلين إلى قرون المذبح . الليلويا .

The Gospel

Ⲉⲩⲁⲅⲅⲉⲗⲓⲟⲛ Ⲕⲁⲧⲁ Ⲓⲱⲁⲛⲛⲏⲛ Ⲕⲉⲫ ⲓ̅ⲃ̅ : ⲁ̅ - ⲓ̅ⲁ̅

John 12:1-11

Then, six days before the Passover, Jesus came to Bethany, where Lazarus was who had been dead, whom He had raised from the dead. There they made Him a supper; and Martha served, but Lazarus was one of those who sat at the table with Him. Then Mary took a pound of very costly oil of spikenard, anointed the feet of Jesus, and wiped His feet with her hair. And the house was filled with the fragrance of the oil. But one of His disciples, Judas Iscariot, Simon's son, who would betray Him, said, "Why was this fragrant oil not sold for three hundred denarii and given to the poor?" This he said, not that he cared for the poor, but because he was a thief, and had the money box; and he used to take what was put in it. But Jesus said, "Let her alone; she has kept this for the day of My burial. For the poor you have with you always, but Me you do

Ⲓ̅ⲏ̅ⲥ̅ Ⲟⲩⲛ ϧⲁϫⲉⲛ ⲥⲟⲟⲩ ⲛ̀ⲉϩⲟⲟⲩ ⲛ̀ⲧⲉ ⲡⲓⲡⲁⲥⲭⲁ ⲁϥⲓ̀ ⲉ̀ⲃⲏⲑ Ⲇⲁⲛⲓⲁ : ⲡⲓⲙⲁⲉ̀ⲛⲁⲣⲉ Ⲗⲁⲍⲁⲣⲟⲥ ⲙ̀ⲙⲟϥ ⲫⲏ ⲉⲧⲁϥⲙⲟⲩ : ⲫⲏ ⲉⲧⲁ Ⲓ̅ⲏ̅ⲥ̅ ⲧⲟⲩⲛⲟⲥϥ ⲉ̀ⲃⲟⲗ ϧⲉⲛ ⲛⲏⲉⲑⲙⲱⲟⲩⲧ . ⲁⲩⲉⲣ ⲟⲩⲇⲓⲡⲛⲟⲛ ⲟⲩⲛ ⲉ̀ⲣⲟϥ ⲙ̀ⲡⲓⲙⲁ ⲉ̀ⲧⲉⲙⲙⲁⲩ : ⲟⲩⲟϩ Ⲙⲁⲣⲑⲁ ⲛⲁⲥϣⲉⲙϣⲓ ⲡⲉ : ⲟⲩⲟϩ Ⲗⲁⲍⲁⲣⲟⲥ ⲛⲉ ⲟⲩⲁⲓ ⲡⲉ ⲛ̀ⲛⲏⲉⲑⲣⲱⲧⲉⲃ ⲛⲉⲙⲁϥ . Ⲙⲁⲣⲓⲁ ⲟⲩⲛ ⲁⲥϭⲓ ⲛ̀ⲟⲩⲗⲩⲧⲣⲁ ⲛ̀ⲥⲟϫⲉⲛ ⲛ̀ⲧⲉ ⲟⲩⲛⲁⲣⲇⲟⲥ ⲙ̀ⲡⲓⲥⲧⲓⲕⲏ ⲉ̀ⲛⲁϣⲉⲛ ⲥⲟⲩⲉⲛϥ ⲟⲩⲟϩ ⲁⲥⲑⲱϩⲥ ⲛ̀ⲛⲉⲛϭⲁⲗⲁⲩϫ ⲛ̀Ⲓ̅ⲏ̅ⲥ̅ ⲙ̀ⲙⲟϥ : ⲟⲩⲟϩ ⲁⲥϥⲟⲧⲟⲩ ⲉ̀ⲃⲟⲗ ⲙ̀ⲡϥⲱⲓ ⲛ̀ⲧⲉ ⲧⲉⲥⲁⲫⲉ : ⲁ̀ⲡⲏⲓ ⲇⲉ ⲙⲟϩ ⲉ̀ⲃⲟⲗ ϧⲉⲛ ⲡⲓⲥⲑⲟⲓ ⲛ̀ⲧⲉ ⲡⲓⲥⲟϫⲉⲛ . Ⲡⲉϫⲉ ⲟⲩⲁⲓ ⲇⲉ ⲉ̀ⲃⲟⲗ ϧⲉⲛ ⲛⲉϥⲙⲁⲑⲏⲧⲏⲥ ⲉ̀ⲧⲉ Ⲓⲟⲩⲇⲁⲥ ⲡⲉ Ⲥⲓⲙⲱⲛ ⲡⲓ Ⲓⲥⲕⲁⲣⲓⲱⲧⲏⲥ : ⲫⲏⲉⲛⲁϥⲛⲁⲧⲏϥ . Ⲭⲉ ⲉⲑⲃⲉ ⲟⲩ ⲡⲁⲓⲥⲟϫⲉⲛ ⲙ̀ⲡⲟⲩⲧⲏⲓϥ ⲉ̀ⲃⲟⲗ ϧⲁ ϣⲟⲙⲧ ϣⲉ ⲛ̀ⲥⲁⲑⲉⲣⲓ ⲟⲩⲟϩ ⲛ̀ⲥⲉⲧⲏⲓⲧⲟⲩ ⲛ̀ⲛⲓϩⲏⲕⲓ . Ⲫⲁⲓ ⲇⲉ ⲉ̀ⲧⲁϥϫⲟϥ ⲟⲩⲭⲟⲧⲓ ϫⲉ ⲁⲥⲉⲣⲙⲉⲗⲓⲛ ⲛⲁϥ ϧⲁ ⲛⲓϩⲏⲕⲓ : ⲁⲗⲗⲁ ϫⲉ ⲛⲉ ⲟⲩⲣⲉϥϭⲓⲟⲩⲓ ⲡⲉ ⲟⲩⲟϩ ⲉ̀ⲣⲉ ⲡⲓⲅⲗⲟⲥⲟⲕⲟⲙⲟⲛ ⲛ̀ⲧⲟⲧϥ : ⲛⲏⲉϣⲁⲩⲥⲓⲧⲟⲩ ⲉ̀ⲣⲟϥ ⲛⲉϣⲁϥⲧⲱⲟⲩⲛ ⲙ̀ⲙⲱⲟⲩ ⲡⲉ . Ⲡⲉϫⲉ Ⲓ̅ⲏ̅ⲥ̅ Ⲟⲩⲛ ϫⲉ ⲭⲁⲥ ϩⲓⲛⲁ ⲛ̀ⲧⲉⲥⲁⲣⲉϩ ⲉ̀ⲣⲟϥ ⲉ̀ⲡⲉϩⲟⲟⲩ ⲙ̀ⲡⲁⲕⲱⲥ . Ⲛⲓϩⲏⲕⲓ ⲅⲁⲣ ⲥⲉ ⲛⲉⲙⲱⲧⲉⲛ ⲛ̀ⲥⲏⲟⲩ ⲛⲓⲃⲉⲛ ⲁⲛⲟⲕ ⲇⲉ ϯ ⲛⲉⲙⲱⲧⲉⲛ ⲁⲛ ⲛ̀ⲥⲏⲟⲩ

(يوحنا 12 : 1 - 11)

وإن يسوع قبل الفصح بستة أيام جاء إلى بيت عنيا حيث كان لعازر الميت . الذى أقامه يسوع من الأموات . فصنعوا له وليمة فى ذلك الموضع . وكانت مرثا تخدم. وأما لعازر فكان أحد المتكئين معه . فأخذت مريم رطل طيب ناردين فائق كثير الثمن ودهنت به قدمى يسوع ومسحتهما بشعر رأسها . فامتلأ البيت من رائحة الطيب . فقال واحد من تلاميذه الذى هو يهوذا سمعان الاسخريوطى الذى كان مزمعاً أن يسلمه لماذا لم يُبع هذا الطيب بثلثمائة دينار ويعطى للمساكين . وهذا قاله ليس عناية منه بالمساكين . بل لأنه كان سارقاً وكان الصندوق عنده وكان يحمل ما يلقى فيه . فقال يسوع دعوها انما حفظته ليوم دفنى. لأن المساكين معكم كل حين وأما أنا فلست معكم كل

not have always." Now a great many of the Jews knew that He was there; and they came, not for Jesus' sake only, but that they might also see Lazarus, whom He had raised from the dead. But the chief priests plotted to put Lazarus to death also, because on account of him many of the Jews went away and believed in Jesus. Glory be to God forever. Amen	ⲚⲒⲂⲈⲚ . ⲀⲩⲉⲘⲒ ⲆⲈ ⲚϪⲈ ⲞⲨⲘⲎϢ ⲈϤⲞϢ ⲚⲦⲈ ⲚⲒⲒⲞⲨⲆⲀⲒ ϪⲈ ϤⲬⲎ ⲘⲘⲀⲨ : ⲞⲨⲞ⳰Ⲅ ⲀⲨⲒ ⲈⲐⲂⲈ Ⲓⲏⲥ ⲘⲘⲀⲨⲀⲦϤ ⲀⲚ : ⲀⲖⲖⲀ ⲚⲈⲘ ⲈⲐⲂⲈ ⲠⲔⲈⲖⲀⲌⲀⲢⲞⲥ ϨⲒⲚⲀ ⲚⲦⲞⲨⲚⲀⲨ ⲈⲢⲞϤ : ⲈⲪⲎⲈⲦⲀ Ⲓⲏⲥ ⲦⲞⲨⲚⲞⲥϤ ⲈⲂⲞⲖ ϦⲈⲚ ⲚⲎⲈⲐⲘⲱⲞⲨⲦ . ⲀⲩⲈⲢⲞⲨⲤⲞⲂⲚⲒ ⲆⲈ ⲚϪⲈ ⲚⲒⲀⲢⲬⲎ ⲈⲢⲈⲨⲤ ϨⲒⲚⲀ ⲚⲤⲈϦⲰⲦⲈⲂ ⲘⲠⲔⲈⲖⲀⲌⲀⲢⲞⲥ . ϪⲈ ⲈⲐⲂⲎⲦϤ ⲚⲀⲢⲈ ⲞⲨⲘⲎϢ ϨⲎⲖ ⲠⲈ ⲈⲂⲞⲖ ϦⲈⲚ ⲚⲒⲒⲞⲨⲆⲀⲒ ⲞⲨⲞ⳰Ⲅ ⲚⲀⲨⲚⲀⲅϮ ⲠⲈ ⲈⲒⲏⲥ . Ⲡⲓⲱⲟⲩ ⲪⲀ ⲠⲈⲚⲚⲞⲨϮ ⲠⲈ .	حين . وعلم جمع كثير من اليهود أنه هناك فجاءوا ليس من أجل يسوع وحده بل لينظروا أيضاً لعازر الذى أقامه يسوع من بين الأموات. فتشاور رؤساء الكهنة أن يقتلوا لعازر أيضاً . لأن كثيرين من اليهود كانوا من أجله يمضون ويؤمنون بيسوع . والمجد لله دائماً .

The Gospel Response (مرد الانجيل)

Hail to Lazarus, whom He raised: after four days: raise my heart, O My Lord Jesus: which evil has slain.	شيريه لازاروس فى إيطاف طوونوسف : مينينصا إفتوؤو إن إهووؤو : ماطوونوس باهيت باتشويس إيسوس : فى إيطاف خوثيف إنجيه بى بيت هوؤو . Ⲭⲉⲣⲉ Ⲗⲁⲍⲁⲣⲟⲥ ⲪⲎ ⲈⲦⲀϤ ⲦⲞⲨⲚⲞⲤϤ : ⲘⲈⲚⲈⲚⲤⲀ Ⲇ̅ Ⲛ̅ ⲈϨⲞⲞⲨ : ⲘⲀⲦⲞⲨⲚⲞⲤ ⲠⲀϨⲎⲦ ⲠⲀⳆⳅ Ⲓⲏⲥ : ⲪⲎⲈⲦⲀϤϦⲞⲞⲐⲂⲈϤ ⲚϪⲈ ⲠⲒⲠⲈⲦϨⲰⲞⲨ .	السلام للعازر الذى أقامـه بعد أربعـة أيام أقم قلبى يا ربى يسوع لقد قتلتـه الشر

Concluding Hymns (ختام الصلاة)

Rejoice and be glad, O city of Zion. Exult and rejoice for, behold, your King comes riding on a colt. Before Him the children praise saying, "Hosanna in the Highest! This is the King of Israel!" **(Glory…)**	راشى أونوف سيون تى فاكى : تشى إيرؤووت أووه ثيليـل : هيبيـه غـار بيـه أوورو إفنيـو : إفطاليووت إيجين أووسيج : إفهوس خاجوف إنجيه نى ألوأوى : جيه أوصاننا خين نى إنتتشوسى : فاى بيه إبؤورو إمبى إسرائيل . **(ذوكصاباترى)** Ⲣⲁϣⲓ ⲞⲨⲚⲞϤ Ⲥⲓⲱⲛ ϮⲂⲀⲔⲒ ϬⲒⲢⲞⲨⲞⲦ ⲞⲨⲞ⳰Ⲅ ⲐⲈⲖⲎⲖ : ϨⲎⲠⲠⲈ ⲄⲀⲢ ⲠⲈⲞⲨⲢⲞ ⲈϤⲚⲎⲞⲨ ⲈϤⲦⲀⲖⲎⲞⲨⲦ ⲈϪⲈⲚ ⲞⲨⲤⲎϪ ⲈⲨϨⲰⲤ ϦⲀϪⲰϤ ⲚϪⲈ ⲚⲒⲀⲖⲰⲞⲨⲒ : ϪⲈ ⲰⲤⲀⲚⲚⲀ ϦⲈⲚ ⲚⲎⲈⲦϬⲞⲤⲒ : ⲪⲀⲒ ⲠⲈ ⲠⲞⲨⲢⲞ ⲘⲠⲒⲤⲖ̅ . **(Ⲇⲟⲝⲁⲡⲁⲧⲣⲓ..)**	يا افرحى وتهللى يا صهيون المدينة اجذلى وتهللى لأن هوذا ملكك يأتى راكباً على جحش وتسبح قدامه الأطفال قائلين أوصنا فى الأعالى هذا هو ملك إسرائيل **(المجد للآب .)**
When our Lord Jesus Christ came to the city of Jerusalem to fulfill of the scriptures of the elect prophets, then the children carried palm leaves saying, "Hosanna in the Highest! This is the King of Israel!" **(Now …)**	إيطافئي إنجى بين تشويس إيسوس بيخرستوس! تى فاكى إنتيه يروساليم : إيجوك إيفول إننى غرافى : إنتيه نى صوتب إم إبروفيتيس : أ نى ألوأوى فاى إنهان فاى : جيه أوصاننا خين نى إنتتشوسى : فاى بيه إبؤورو إمبى إسرائيل . **(كيه نين …)** Ⲉⲧⲁϥⲓ ⲚϪⲈ ⲠⲈⲚϬⲞⲒ Ⲓⲏⲥ Ⲡⲭⲥ : ⲈⲦⲂⲀⲔⲒ ⲚⲦⲈ Ⲓⲗⲏⲙ : ⲈϪⲰⲔ ⲈⲂⲞⲖ ⲚⲚⲒⲄⲢⲀⲪⲎ ⲚⲦⲈ ⲚⲒⲤⲰⲦⲠ ⲘⲠⲢⲞⲪⲎⲦⲎⲤ : Ⲁ ⲚⲒⲀⲖⲰⲞⲨⲒ ϤⲀⲒ ⲚϨⲀⲚⲂⲀⲒ : ϪⲈ ⲰⲤⲀⲚⲚⲀ ϦⲈⲚ ⲚⲎⲈⲦϬⲞⲤⲒ : ⲪⲀⲒ ⲠⲈ ⲠⲞⲨⲢⲞ ⲘⲠⲒⲤⲖ̅ . **(Ⲕⲁⲓⲛⲩⲛ..)**	فلما جاء ربنا يسوع المسيح إلى مدينةأورشليم لكمال كتب الأنبياء المختارين حمل الأطفال سعفاً قائلين أوصنا فى الأعالى هذا هو ملك إسرائيل **(الآن …)**
Some spread their vestments on the road before Him that Jesus the Nazarene may walk on them. And the little ones proclaim and say, **(Hosanna) (Now…)**	أ هان أووأون فورش إن نووإهفوس : هيجين بى مويت إمبيف إمثو : هينا إنتيف موشى إهرىى إجواؤو : إنجيه إيسوس بى نازوريؤس : إيريه هان كووجى أوش إيفول : جيه **(أوصاننا …) (كيه نين)** Ⲇ̅ ϨⲀⲚⲞⲨⲞⲚ ϤⲰⲢϢ ⲚⲚⲞⲨϨⲂⲰⲤ : ϨⲒϪⲈⲚ ⲠⲒⲘⲰⲒⲦ ⲘⲠⲈϤⲘⲐⲞϨⲒⲚⲀ ⲚⲦⲈϤⲘⲞϢⲒ ⲈϨⲢⲎⲒ ⲈϪⲰⲞⲨ : ⲚϪⲈ Ⲓⲏⲥ Ⲡⲓⲛⲁⲍⲱⲣⲉⲟⲥ : ⲈⲢⲈ ϨⲀⲚⲔⲞⲨϪⲒ ⲰϢ ⲈⲂⲞⲖ : ϪⲈ **(ⲰⲤⲀⲚⲚⲀ ..)(Ⲕⲁⲓⲛⲩⲛ ..)**	والبعض فرشوا ثيابهم على الطريق أمامه لكى يسيـر عليها يسوع الناصرى والصغار يصرخون قائلين : أوصنا . **(الآن …)**

English	Arabic (transliteration)	Coptic	Arabic
Then was fulfilled the great prophecy today, "Out of the mouth of babes, You have prepared praise." And the children proclaim and say, (Hosanna) (Now…)	طوتيه إس جوك إيفول إمفوؤو : إنجيه تى نيشتى إم إبروفيتيا : جيه إيفول خين روأوو إنهان كوجى إن ألوأوى: إنثوك أك سيبتيه بى إسموو : إف أوش إيفول إنجى نى ألوأوى جيه (أوصانا) (كيه نين)	Ϫⲟⲧⲉ ⲉⲥϫⲱⲕ ⲉⲃⲟⲗ ⲙ̀ⲫⲟⲟⲩ : ⲛ̀ϫⲉ ϯⲛⲓϣϯ ⲙ̀ⲡⲣⲟⲫⲏⲧⲓⲁ ϫⲉ ⲉⲃⲟⲗ ϧⲉⲛ ⲣⲱⲟⲩ ⲛ̀ⲥⲁⲛⲕⲟⲩϫⲓ ⲛ̀ⲁⲗⲱⲟⲩⲓ : ⲛ̀ⲑⲟⲕ ⲁⲕⲥⲉⲃⲧⲉ ⲡⲓⲥⲙⲟⲩ : ⲉⲩⲱϣ ⲉⲃⲟⲗ ⲛ̀ϫⲉ ⲛⲓⲁⲗⲱⲟⲩⲓ : ϫⲉ (ⲱⲥⲁⲛⲛⲁ ..) (Ⲕⲁⲓⲛⲩⲛ)	حينئذ كملت اليوم النبوة العظيمة من أفواه الأطفال الصغار أعددت سبحاً والأطفال يصرخون قائلين (أوصنا) (الآن)
Thence said David in the Book of the Psalms, "Blessed is He who comes in the name of the Lord God." And the children praise Him saying, (Hosanna) (Now…)	طوتيه إفجوس إنجيه دافيد : خين إبجوم إنتيه نى بصالموس : جيه إفسماروؤوت إنجيه في إثنيو : خين إفران إمبتشويس إفنوتى : إريه نى ألوأوى هوس إروف : جيه (أوصانا) (كيه نين)	Ϫⲟⲧⲉ ϥ̀ϫⲟⲥ ⲛ̀ϫⲉ Ⲇⲁⲩⲓⲇ : ϧⲉⲛ ⲡ̀ϫⲱⲙ ⲛ̀ⲧⲉ ⲛⲓⲯⲁⲗⲙⲟⲥ : ϫⲉ ϥ̀ⲥⲙⲁⲣⲱⲟⲩⲧ ⲛ̀ϫⲉ ⲫⲏⲉⲑⲛⲏⲟⲩ ϧⲉⲛ ⲫ̀ⲣⲁⲛ ⲙ̀Ⲡ̅ⲟ̅ⲥ̅ Ⲫϯ : ⲉⲣⲉ ⲛⲓⲁⲗⲱⲟⲩⲓ ⲥⲱⲥ ⲉⲣⲟϥ : ϫⲉ (ⲱⲥⲁⲛⲛⲁ..) (Ⲕⲁⲓⲛⲩⲛ..)	حينئذ قال داود فى كتاب المزامير مبارك الآتى باسم الرب الإله والأطفال تسبحه قائلين : (أوصنا) (الآن)
When Jesus entered into Jerusalem, the whole city trembled because of the multitudes surrounding Him. And the children proclaim and say, (Hosanna) (Now…)	إيطافئى إنجيه إيسوس إيخون إ يروساليم : تى فاكى تيرس إشطورتير : إثفيه نى ميش إتكوتى إروف : إريه نى ألوأوى أوش إيفول : جيه (أوصاننا) (كيه نين)	Ⲉⲧⲁϥⲓ̀ ⲛ̀ϫⲉ Ⲓⲏⲥ ⲉϧⲟⲩⲛ ⲉⲓⲗⲏⲙ : ϯⲃⲁⲕⲓ ⲧⲏⲣⲥ ϣ̀ⲑⲟⲣⲧⲉⲣ : ⲉⲑⲃⲉ ⲛⲓⲙⲏϣ ⲉⲧⲕⲱϯ ⲉⲣⲟϥ : ⲉⲣⲉ ⲛⲓⲁⲗⲱⲟⲩⲓ ⲱϣ ⲉⲃⲟⲗ : ϫⲉ (ⲱⲥⲁⲛⲛⲁ ..) (Ⲕⲁⲓⲛⲩⲛ ..)	لما دخل يسوع إلى أورشليم ارتجت المدينة كلها من أجل الجموع المحيطين به و الأطفال يصيحون (أوصنا) (الآن)
Then the lawless Jews were filled with great jealousy and said unto our Lord Jesus saying, "Let the little children stop saying, (Hosanna) (Now…)	طوتيه نى يوداى إن أنوموس أف موه خين أونيشتى إنخوس: بيجوؤو إمبينتشويس إيسوس: جيه مارو كاروأو خين ناى أوش إنجيه نى كوجى إن ألوأى : جيه (أوصاننا ...) (كيه نين)	Ϫⲟⲧⲉ ⲛⲓⲓⲟⲩⲇⲁⲓ ⲛ̀ⲁⲛⲟⲙⲟⲥ : ⲁⲩⲙⲟϩ ϧⲉⲛ ⲟⲩⲛⲓϣϯ ⲛ̀ϫⲟⲥ : ⲡⲉϫⲱⲟⲩ ⲙ̀ⲡⲉⲛⲟ̅ⲥ̅ Ⲓⲏⲥ : ϫⲉ ⲙⲁⲣⲟⲩⲭⲁⲣⲱⲟⲩ ϧⲉⲛ ⲛⲁⲓⲱϣ ⲛ̀ϫⲉ ⲛⲓⲕⲟⲩϫⲓ ⲛ̀ⲁⲗⲱⲟⲩⲓ : ϫⲉ (ⲱⲥⲁⲛⲛⲁ) (Ⲕⲁⲓⲛⲩⲛ ..)	حينئذ اليهود المخالفين امتلأوا غيرة عظيمة وقالوا للرب يسوع فليسكت هؤلاء من هذا الصياح الأطفال الصغار قائلين (أوصنا) (الآن)
Then said Jesus to the Jews, "If these little children hold their peace, the stones would cry out and praise Me saying, (Hosanna) (Now…)	بيجيه إيسوس إننى يوداى جيه إشوب أفشان كاروأوو : إنجيه نى كوجى إن ألوأوى شاف أوش إيفول إنجيه نى أونى : أووه إنطوؤوهوس إروى : جيه (أوصاننا) (كيه نين)	Ⲡⲉϫⲉ Ⲓⲏⲥ ⲛ̀ⲛⲏ ⲓⲟⲩⲇⲁⲓ ϫⲉ ⲉϣⲱⲡ ⲁⲩϣⲁⲛ ⲭⲁⲣⲱⲟⲩ ⲛ̀ϫⲉ ⲛⲓⲕⲟⲩϫⲓ ⲛ̀ⲁⲗⲱⲟⲩⲓ : ϣⲁⲩⲱϣ ⲉⲃⲟⲗ ⲛ̀ϫⲉ ⲛⲓⲱⲛⲓ : ⲟⲩⲟϩ ⲛ̀ⲧⲟⲩϩⲱⲥ ⲉⲣⲟⲓ : ϫⲉ (ⲱⲥⲁⲛⲛⲁ) (Ⲕⲁⲓⲛⲩⲛ ..)	فقال يسوع لليهود إذا سكت هؤلاء الأطفال الصغار لصرخت الحجارة وسبحتنى قائلة: (أوصنا) (الآن)

The priest ends the prayer with the blessing and dismisses congregation in peace.

ثم يختم الكاهن الصلاة بالبركة ويصرف الشعب بسلام .

The Midnight Prayer and Praise	(صلاة وتسبحة نصف الليل)

We start with the Midnight prayer from the Agpeya with the three parts. The big Psalm (Alleluia) is chanted. The Psalies of the 4 canticles are prayed as the following:

يبدأون بصلاة نصف الليل بخدماتها الثلاث ثم يقال المزمور الكبير (الليلويا) وتقال إبصاليات الهوسات الأربعة قبلها كالآتى :

1) Adam Psali for the first canticle:

Ⲁⲣⲓⲥⲁⲗⲡⲓⲍⲓⲛ : ⲙ̅ⲙⲏⲛⲓ ϧⲉⲛ ⲟⲩⲥⲟⲩⲁⲓ : ⲟⲩⲟϩ ⲁⲣⲓⲯⲁⲗⲓⲛ : ⲙ̅ⲫⲟⲟⲩ ϧⲉⲛ ⲛⲉⲧⲉⲛⲯⲁⲓ .

(1) إبصالية آدم على الهوس الأول أولها " بوقوا فى رؤوس الشهور ... " .

Ⲁⲣⲓⲥⲁⲗⲡⲓⲍⲓⲛ : ⲙ̅ⲙⲏⲛⲓ ϧⲉⲛ ⲟⲩⲥⲟⲩⲁⲓ : ⲟⲩⲟϩ ⲁⲣⲓⲯⲁⲗⲓⲛ : ⲙ̅ⲫⲟⲟⲩ ϧⲉⲛ ⲛⲉⲧⲉⲛⲯⲁⲓ .

2) Adam Psali for the second canticle:

Ⲁⲙⲱⲓⲛⲓ ⲙⲁⲣⲉⲛϩⲱⲥ : ϧⲉⲛ ⲟⲩϩⲱⲥ ⲙ̅ⲃⲉⲣⲓ : ⲉⲡⲉⲛⲛⲏⲃ Ⲡⲭ̅ⲥ̅ : ⲫⲏⲉⲧ ⲓⲣⲓ ⲛ̅ϩⲁⲛⲯ̅ⲫⲏⲣⲓ .

(2) إبصالية آدم على الهوس الثانى أولها " تعالوا نسبح تسبحة جديدة ... " .

Ⲁⲙⲱⲓⲛⲓ ⲙⲁⲣⲉⲛϩⲱⲥ : ϧⲉⲛ ⲟⲩϩⲱⲥ ⲙ̅ⲃⲉⲣⲓ : ⲉⲡⲉⲛⲛⲏⲃ Ⲡⲭ̅ⲥ̅ : ⲫⲏⲉⲧ ⲓⲣⲓ ⲛ̅ϩⲁⲛⲯ̅ⲫⲏⲣⲓ .

3) Adam Psali for the third canticle:

Ⲁⲣⲓⲥⲁⲗⲡⲓⲍⲓⲛ : ⲛ̅ⲛⲉⲟⲙⲉⲛⲓⲁ : ϧⲉⲛ ⲟⲩⲥⲁⲗⲡⲓⲅⲅⲓⲛ : ⲁⲥⲁⲧⲉ ⲁⲛⲟⲙⲓⲛⲓⲁ.

(3) إبصالية آدم على الهوس الثالث أولها " بوقوا بالبوق فى رؤوس الشهور ... " .

Ⲁⲣⲓⲥⲁⲗⲡⲓⲍⲓⲛ : ⲛ̅ⲛⲉⲟⲙⲉⲛⲓⲁ : ϧⲉⲛ ⲟⲩⲥⲁⲗⲡⲓⲅⲅⲓⲛ : ⲁⲥⲁⲧⲉ ⲁⲛⲟⲙⲓⲛⲓⲁ .

4) Batos Bsali for the commemoration:

Ⲁⲙⲱⲓⲛⲓ ⲧⲏⲣⲟⲩ ⲱ̅ ⲛⲓⲡⲓⲥⲧⲟⲥ : ⲛ̅ⲧⲉⲛ†ⲱⲟⲩ ⲛ̅Ⲓⲏ̅ⲥ̅ Ⲡⲭ̅ⲥ̅ : ⲛⲉⲙ ⲛⲓⲗⲱⲟⲩⲓ .

(4) إبصالية واطس على المجمع وأولها " تعالوا يا جميع المؤمنين ... " .

Ⲁⲙⲱⲓⲛⲓ ⲧⲏⲣⲟⲩ ⲱ̅ ⲛⲓⲡⲓⲥⲧⲟⲥ : ⲛ̅ⲧⲉⲛ†ⲱⲟⲩ ⲛ̅Ⲓⲏ̅ⲥ̅ Ⲡⲭ̅ⲥ̅ : ⲛⲉⲙ ⲛⲓⲗⲱⲟⲩⲓ

5) Adam Psali for the forth canticle:

Ⲁⲙⲱⲓⲛⲓ ⲱ̅ⲛⲓⲡⲓⲥⲧⲟⲥ : ⲛ̅ⲧⲉ†ⲱⲟⲩ ⲙ̅Ⲡⲭ̅ⲥ̅ .

(5) إبصالية آدم على الهوس الرابع أولها " تعالوا أيها المؤمنون لنمجد المسيح مع أطفال العبرانيين "

Ⲁⲙⲱⲓⲛⲓ ⲱ̅ⲛⲓⲡⲓⲥⲧⲟⲥ : ⲛ̅ⲧⲉ†ⲱⲟⲩ ⲙ̅Ⲡⲭ̅ⲥ̅ .

6) Psali of the Palm Sunday for the Theotokia:

Ⲁⲣⲓⲥⲁⲗⲗⲡⲓⲍⲓⲛ : ⲙ̅ⲫⲟⲟⲩ ϧⲉⲛ ⲟⲩⲥⲁⲗⲡⲓⲅⲅⲟⲥ.

Then we pray the Theotokia of Sunday. The praise is continued as usual.

The priest ends the prayer with the Absolution.

(6) إبصالية أحد الشعانين (بوقوا اليوم بالبوق ، ورتلوا في عيد إبن الله) .

ثم تقال تذاكية الأحد الموجودة بالإبصلمودية المقدسةالسنوية وتكمل التسبحة كالعادة

ويختمها الكاهن بتحليل الكهنة لنصف الليل.

The Offering of Morning Incense	(رفـــع بخـور بـاكـر)

The morning prayer of the Agpeya is prayed. The priest opens the curtain of the sanctuary and prays the Offering of the Morning Incense as usual.

تصلى مزامير باكر ثم يفتح الكاهن ستر الهيكل ويصلى صلاة رفع بخور باكر

After Ⲫ† ⲛⲁⲓ ⲛⲁⲛ, the deacons chant the long-tune Kirie elison, The Congregation chants Kirie elison, in long tune, while going around the altar three times then in the church three times then around the altar one more time. They chant Ⲉⲩⲗⲟⲅⲏⲙⲉⲛⲟⲥ, followed by the Exposition. They start the Procession of Palm Sunday.

يقول كبير الكهنة Ⲫ† ⲛⲁⲓ ⲛⲁⲛ أللهم ارحمنا ... وهو ممسكاً بالصليب المزين بالسعف والورود والشموع وبعدها يرتل الشعب كيرى ليسون باللحن طويل ثلاث مرات و هم يطوفون الهيكل ثلاث مرات ثم الكنيسة ثلاث مرات ثم الهيكل مرة اخرى و يقولون لحن الشعانين ايفلوجيمينوس ثم الطرح ثم دورة الشعانين.

(The Procession of Palm Sunday)	(دورة الشعانين)

The Priest offers incense in the procession before the sanctuary, and the icons of the saints. He prays the Litany of the Gospel before each Gospel.	يرفع الكاهن البخور أمام الهيكل والأيقونات ويلفون البيعة . يقول الكاهن أوشية الانجيل قبل كل إنجيل

(Before the main Sanctuary)	(قدام الهيكل الكبير)

Psalms 103:4, 137:1

Who makes His angels spirits, His ministers a flame of fire. I will praise You with my whole heart; Before the gods I will sing praises to You. I will worship toward Your holy temple. *Alleluia.*

(المزمور 103 : 4 و مز 137 : 1)

الذى صنع ملائكته أرواحاً وخدامه ناراً تلتهب . أمام الملائكة أرتل لك وأسجد قدام هيكلك المقدس . هلليلويا .

John 1:43-51

The following day Jesus wanted to go to Galilee, and He found Philip and said to him, "Follow Me." Now Philip was from Bethsaida, the city of Andrew and Peter. Philip found Nathanael and said to him, "We have found Him of whom Moses in the law, and also the prophets, wrote, Jesus of Nazareth, the son of Joseph." And Nathanael said to him, "Can anything good come out of Nazareth?" Philip said to him, "Come and see." Jesus saw Nathanael coming toward Him, and said of him, "Behold, an Israelite indeed, in whom is no deceit!" Nathanael said to Him, "How do You know me?" Jesus answered and said to him, "Before Philip called you, when you were under the fig tree, I saw you." Nathanael answered and said to Him, "Rabbi, You are the Son of God! You are the King of Israel!" Jesus answered and said to him, "Because I said to you, 'I saw you under the fig tree,' do you believe? You will see greater things than these." And He said to him, "Most assuredly, I say to you, hereafter you shall see heaven open, and the angels of God ascending and descending upon the Son of Man. *Glory be to God forever. Amen*

(الانجيل من يوحنا 1 : 43 - 52)

وللغد أراد أن يخرج إلى الجليل فوجد فيلبس وقال له يسوع : اتبعنى ، وفيلبس كان من بيت صيدا من مدينة أندراوس وبطرس . وفيلبس وجد نثنائيل وقال له : الذى كتب موسى من أجله فى الناموس والأنبياء وهو يسوع إبن يوسف الذى من الناصرة . فقال له نثنائيل : هل يمكن أن يخرج من الناصرة شئ فيه صلاح . فقال له فيلبس : تعال وانظر . فلما رأى يسوع نثنائيل مقبلاً إليه قال لأجله : هذا حقاً إسرائيلى لا غش فيه . فقال له نثنائيل من أين تعرفنى . أجاب يسوع وقال له : قبل أن يدعوك فيلبس وأنت تحت شجرة التين رأيتك . فأجاب نثنائيل وقال : يا معلم أنت هو إبن الله . أنت هو ملك إسرائيل . أجاب يسوع وقال له: لما قلت لك أننى رأيتك تحت شجرة التين آمنت سوف تعاين أعظم من هذا . وقال له : الحق الحق أقول لكم انكم تنظرون السماء مفتوحة وملائكة الله يصعدون وينزلون على إبن البشر . والمجد لله دائماً .

The Response

(يرد المرتلون بهذا الربع)

| The four incorporeal creatures / who carry the chariot of the Lord / a face of a lion, a face of an ox / a face of a man and a face of an eagle. | بى إفتوؤو إنزوؤون إن إصماتوس : إتفاى خـــــا بى هارما إنتيه إفٱوتى : أووهو إمموؤى نيم أووهو إمماسى : أووهو إنرومى نيم أووهو إن أيتوس | Ⲡⲓ ⲇ̅ ⲛ̅ ⲍⲱⲟⲛ ⲛ̅ ⲁⲥⲱⲙⲁⲧⲟⲥ : ⲉⲧϥⲁⲓ ϧⲁ ⲡⲓⲥⲁⲣⲙⲁ ⲛ̅ⲧⲉ Ⲫϯ : ⲟⲩϩⲟ ⲙ̅ⲙⲟⲩⲓ ⲛⲉⲙ ⲟⲩϩⲟ ⲙ̅ⲙⲁⲥⲓ : ⲟⲩϩⲟ ⲛ̅ⲣⲱⲙⲓ ⲛⲉⲙ ⲟⲩϩⲟ ⲛ̅ⲁ̅ϩ̅ⲧⲟⲥ . | الأربعة الحيوانات الغير المتجسدين الحاملين مركبة الله وجه أسد ووجه ثور ووجه إنسان ووجه نسر |
| Ilosanna in the highest, this is the King of Israel, blessed is | أوصاننا خين نى إنتشوسى: فاى بيه إبؤورو إمبى إسرائيل : | Ⲱⲥⲁⲛⲛⲁ ϧⲉⲛ ⲛⲏ ⲉⲧϭⲟⲥⲓ: ⲫⲁⲓ ⲡⲉ ⲡ̅ⲟⲩⲣⲟ ⲙ̅Ⲡⲓⲥⲗ̅ : | اوصانفى الأعالى هذا هو ملك إسرائيل |

| He who comes in the name, of the Lord of hosts. | إفسمارؤووت إنجيه في إثنيوو خين إفران إمبتشويس إنتيه نى جُم | Ϥⲥⲙⲁⲣⲱⲟⲩⲧ ⲛ̀ϫⲉ ⲫⲏ ⲉⲑⲛⲏⲟⲩ ϧⲉⲛ ⲫ̀ⲣⲁⲛ ⲙ̀Ⲡ̅ⲟ̅ⲥ̅ ⲛ̀ⲧⲉⲛⲓϫⲟⲙ | مبـــارك الآتى باسم رب القوات |

(Before the Icon of St. Mary)   (امام ايقونه السيدة العذراء)

Psalms 86:3, 5, 7

Glorious things have been spoken of you, O city of God. The Highest Himself has founded her. The dwelling of all within you is as the dwelling of those that rejoice. Alleluia

(المزمور 86 : 3 و 5 و 7)

أعمال مجيدة قد قيلت لأجلك يا مدينة الله ، هو العلى الذى أسسها إلى الأبد لأن سكنى الفرحين جميعهم فيك . هلليلويا

Luke 1:39-56

Now Mary arose in those days and went into the hill country with haste, to a city of Judah, and entered the house of Zacharias and greeted Elizabeth. And it happened, when Elizabeth heard the greeting of Mary, that the babe leaped in her womb; and Elizabeth was filled with the Holy Spirit. Then she spoke out with a loud voice and said, "Blessed are you among women, and blessed is the fruit of your womb! But why is this granted to me, that the mother of my Lord should come to me? For indeed, as soon as the voice of your greeting sounded in my ears, the babe leaped in my womb for joy. Blessed is she who believed, for there will be a fulfillment of those things which were told her from the Lord." And Mary said: "My soul magnifies the Lord, And my spirit has rejoiced in God my Savior. For He has regarded the lowly state of His maidservant; For behold, henceforth all generations will call me blessed. For He who is mighty has done great things for me, And holy is His name. And His mercy is on those who fear Him From generation to generation. He has shown strength with His arm; He has scattered the proud in the imagination of their hearts. He has put down the mighty from their thrones, And exalted the lowly. He has filled the hungry with good things, And the rich He has sent away empty. He has helped His servant Israel, In remembrance of His mercy, As He spoke to our fathers, To Abraham and to his seed forever." And Mary remained with her about three months, and returned to her house. Glory be to God forever. Amen.

(الانجيل من لوقا 1 : 39 - 56)

فقامت مريم فى تلك الأيام وذهبت بسرعة إلى الجبال إلى مدينة يهوذا ودخلت بيت زكريا وسلمت على اليصابات فلما سمعت اليصابات سلام مريم ارتكض الجنين فى بطنها وامتلأت اليصابات من الروح القدس وصرخت بصوت عظيم وقالت : مباركة أنت فى النساء ومباركة هى ثمرة بطنك . فمن أين لى هذا أن تأتى أم ربى إلىَّ . فهوذا حين صار صوت سلامك فى أذنى ارتكض الجنين بابتهاج فى بطنى فطوبى للتى آمنت أن يتم ما قيل لها من قبل الرب . فقالت مريم : تعظم نفسى الرب وتبتهج روحى بالله مخلصى لأنه نظر إلى اتضاع أمته فهوذا منذ الآن جميع الأجيال تطوبنى لأن القدير صنع بى عظائم واسمه قدوس ورحمته إلى جيل الأجيال للذين يتقونه . صنع قوة بذراعه شتت المستكبرين بفكر قلوبهم . أنزل الأعزاء عن الكراسى ورفع المتضعين . أشبع الجياع خيرات وصرف الأغنياء فارغين . عضد إسرائيل فتاه ليذكر رحمة كما كلم آباءنا إبراهيم ونسله إلى الأبد فمكثت مريم عندها نحو ثلاثة أشهر ثم رجعت إلى بيتها . والمجد لله دائماً .

The Response   (يرد المرتلون بهذا الربع)

| We exalt you worthily, / with Elizabeth your cousin: / saying, "Blessed are you among women, / blessed is the fruit of your womb." | تين تشيسى إممو خين أوو إم إبشا : نيم إليصابيـت تيسينجينيس : جيه تيه إسمارؤووت إنثو خين نى هيومى : إفسمارؤووت إنجيه إبؤطاه إنتيه تيه نيجى . | Ⲧⲉⲛϭⲓⲥⲓ ⲙⲙⲟ ϧⲉⲛ ⲟⲩⲉⲙⲡ̀ϣⲁ : ⲛⲉⲙ Ⲉⲗⲓⲥⲁⲃⲉⲧ ⲧⲉⲥⲩⲅⲅⲉⲛⲏⲥ : ϫⲉ ⲧⲉ ⲥⲙⲁⲣⲱⲟⲩⲧ ⲛ̀ⲑⲟ ϧⲉⲛ ⲛⲓϩⲓⲟⲙⲓ : ϥ̀ⲥⲙⲁⲣⲉⲱⲟⲩⲧ ⲛ̀ϫⲉ ⲡⲟⲩⲧⲁϩ ⲛ̀ⲧⲉ ⲧⲉ ⲛⲉϫⲓ. | نرفعك باستحقاق مع أليصابات نسيبتك قائلين : مباركة أنت فى النساء ومباركة هى ثمرة بطنك . |

Hosanna in the highest, this is the King of Israel, blessed is He who comes in the name, of the Lord of hosts.	أوصاننا خين نى ني إنتشوسى : فاى بيه إبؤورو إمبى إسرائيل : إفسمارؤووت إنجيه في إثيوو خين إفران إمبتشويس إنتيه نى جُم .	Ⲱⲥⲁⲛⲛⲁ ϧⲉⲛ ⲛⲏⲉⲧϭⲟⲥⲓ: ⲫⲁⲓ ⲡⲉ ⲡ̀ⲟⲩⲣⲟ ⲙ̀Ⲡⲓⲥⲗ : ϥ̀ⲥⲙⲁⲣⲱⲟⲩⲧ ⲛ̀ϫⲉ ⲫⲏ ⲉⲑⲛⲏⲟⲩ ϧⲉⲛ ⲫ̀ⲣⲁⲛ ⲙ̀Ⲡⲟ̅ⲥ̅ ⲛ̀ⲧⲉ ⲛⲓϫⲟⲙ.	اوصنا فى الأعالى هذا هو ملك إسرائيل مبـــارك الآتـــى باســـم رب القوات.

(Before the Icon of Archangel Gabriel)   (امام ايقونه الملاك غبريال)

Psalms 33:6-7   (المزمور 33 : 6 و 7)

The angel of the Lord encamps all around those who fear Him, And delivers them. Oh, taste and see that the Lord is good; Blessed is the man who trusts in Him!. Alleluia

يعسكر ملاك الرب حول خائفيه وينجيهم . ذوقوا وانظروا ما أطيب الرب . طوبى للإنسان المتكل عليه . هلليلويا

Luke 1:26-38   (الانجيل من لوقا ص 1 : 26 - 38)

Now in the sixth month the angel Gabriel was sent by God to a city of Galilee named Nazareth, to a virgin betrothed to a man whose name was Joseph, of the house of David. The virgin's name was Mary. And having come in, the angel said to her, "*Hail, full of grace,* the Lord is with you; blessed are you among women!" But when she saw him, she was troubled at his saying, and considered what manner of greeting this was. Then the angel said to her, "Do not be afraid, Mary, for you have *found grace with God.* And behold, you will conceive in your womb and bring forth a Son, and shall call His name JESUS. He will be great, and will be called the Son of the Highest; and the Lord God will give Him the throne of His father David. And He will reign over the house of Jacob forever, and of His kingdom there will be no end." Then Mary said to the angel, "How can this be, since I do not know a man?" And the angel answered and said to her, "The Holy Spirit will come upon you, and the power of the Highest will overshadow you; therefore, also, that Holy One who is to be born will be called the Son of God. Now indeed, Elizabeth your relative has also conceived a son in her old age; and this is now the sixth month for her who was called barren. For with God nothing will be impossible." Then Mary said, "Behold the maidservant of the Lord! Let it be to me according to your word." And the angel departed from her. Glory be to God forever, Amen.

وفى الشهر السادس أرسل جبرائيل الملاك من عند الله إلى مدينة من الجليل اسمها ناصرة إلى عذراء مخطوبة لرجل اسمه يوسف واسم العذراء مريم فدخل إليها الملاك وقال لها : سلام لكِ يا ممتلئة نعمة الرب معكِ مباركة أنت فى النساء . فلما رأته اضطربت من كلامه وفكرت ما عسى أن تكون هذه التحية . فقال لها الملاك : لا تخافى يا مريم لأنكِ قد وجدت نعمة عند الله وها أنتِ ستحبلين وتلدين إبناً وتسميه يسوع هذا يكون عظيماً وإبن العلى يدعى . ويعطيه الرب الإله كرسى داود أبيه . ويملك على بيت يعقوب إلى الأبد ولا يكون لملكه نهاية . فقالت مريم للملاك : كيف يكون لى هذا وأنا لست أعرف رجلاً فأجاب الملاك وقال لها : الروح القدس يحل عليكِ وقوة العلى تظللكِ . فلذلك أيضاً القدوس المولود منكِ يدعى إبن الله . وهوذا اليصابات نسيبتكِ هى أيضاً حبلى بإبن فى شيخوختها وهذا هو الشهر السادس لتلك المدعوة عاقراً . لأنه ليس شئ غير ممكن لدى الله . فقالت مريم للملاك : هوذا أنا أمة الرب ليكن لى كقولك فمضى من عندها الملاك . والمجد لله دائماً .

The Response   (يرد المرتلون بهذا الربع)

Gabriel the angel, / Daniel saw / standing on his feet, / by the riverbank.	غابرييل بى أنجيلوس : أفنـاف إروف إنجيه دانيـئـيل : أفؤهى إراتـف هيجين نيفات : هيجين نين إسفوطوو إم إفيارو .	Ⲅⲁⲃⲣⲓⲏⲗ ⲡⲓⲁⲅⲅⲉⲗⲟⲥ ⲁϥⲛⲁⲩ ⲉ̀ⲣⲟϥ ⲛ̀ϫⲉ Ⲇⲁⲛⲓⲏⲗ: ⲁϥⲟϩⲓⲉ̀ⲣⲁⲧϥ̀ϩⲓϫⲉⲛ ⲛⲉϥⲁⲧ ϩⲓϫⲉⲛ ⲛⲉⲛⲥ̀ⲫⲟⲧⲟⲩ ⲙ̀ⲫⲓⲁⲣⲟ	غبريل الملاك رأه دانيـــال واقفـــاً علــى قدميه على شاطئ النهر.

Hosanna in the highest, this is the King of Israel, blessed is He who comes in the name, of the Lord of hosts.	أوصاننا خين نى إتتشوسى : فاى بيه إبؤورو إمبى إسرائيل إفسمارؤووت إنجيه في إثنيوو خين إفران إمبتشويس إنتيه نى جُم.	Ⲱⲥⲁⲛⲛⲁ ϧⲉⲛ ⲛⲏ ⲉⲧϭⲟⲥⲓ: ⲫⲁⲓ ⲡⲉ ⲡⲟⲩⲣⲟ ⲙ̅Ⲡⲓⲥⲗ̅ : ϥⲥⲙⲁⲣⲱⲟⲩⲧ ⲛ̅ϫⲉ ⲫⲏ ⲉⲑⲛⲏⲟⲩ ϧⲉⲛ ⲫⲣⲁⲛ ⲙ̅Ⲡ̅ϭ̅ⲥ̅ ⲛ̅ⲧⲉ ⲛⲓϫⲟⲙ.	أوصنا فى الأعالى هذا هو ملك إسرائيل مبــارك الآتـــى باســـم رب القوات.

(Before the Icon of Archangel Michael)   (امام ايقونه الملاك ميخائيل)

Psalms 102:17, 18
Bless the Lord, you His angels, Who excel in strength, who do His word, Heeding the voice of His word. Bless the Lord, all you His hosts, You ministers of His, who do His pleasure.   *Alleluia*

(المزمور 102 : 17 و 18)
باركوا الرب يا جميع ملائكته المقتدرين بقوتهم الصانعين قوله. باركوا الرب يا جميع قواته خدامه العاملين إرادته . هلليلويا .

Matthew 13:44-52
The kingdom of heaven is like treasure hidden in a field, which a man found and hid; and for joy over it he goes and sells all that he has and buys that field. "Again, the kingdom of heaven is like a merchant seeking beautiful pearls, who, when he had found one pearl of great price, went and sold all that he had and bought it. "Again, the kingdom of heaven is like a dragnet that was cast into the sea and gathered some of every kind, which, when it was full, they drew to shore; and they sat down and gathered the good into vessels, but threw the bad away. So it will be at the end of the age. The angels will come forth, separate the wicked from among the just, and cast them into the furnace of fire. There will be wailing and gnashing of teeth." Jesus said to them, "Have you understood all these things?" They said to Him, "Yes, Lord." Then He said to them, "Therefore every scribe instructed concerning the kingdom of heaven is like a householder who brings out of his treasure things new and old. *Glory be to God forever, Amen.*

(الانجيل من متى ص 13 : 44 - 53)
يشبه ملكوت السموات كنزاً مخفياً فى حقل وجده إنسان ومن فرحه مضى وباع كل ما كان له واشترى ذلك الحقل ، أيضاً يشبه ملكوت السموات إنساناً تاجراً يطلب لآلئ حسنة فلما وجد لؤلؤة واحدة كثيرة الثمن مضى وباع كل ما له واشتراها . أيضاً يشبه ملكوت السموات شبكة مطروحة فى البحر وجامعة من كل نوع فلما إمتلأت أصعدوها على الشاطئ وجلسوا وجمعوا الجياد إلى الأوعية أما الأردياء فطرحوها خارجاً . هكذا يكون فى انقضاء الدهر يخرج الملائكة ويفرزون الأشرار من بين الأبرار ويطرحونهم فى اتون النار هناك يكون البكاء وصرير الأسنان . قال لهم يسوع أفهمتم هذا كله . فقالوا نعم يارب . فقال : من أجل هذا كل ما كاتب متعلم فى ملكوت السموات يشبه رجلاً رب بيت يخرج من كنزه جدداً وعتقاء . والمجد لله دائماً .

The Response   (يرد المرتلون بهذا الربع)

Michael, the head of the heavenly, / he is the first / among the angelic ranks / serving before the Lord.	ميخائيل إبأرخـون إننا نيفيؤوى : إنثوف إتؤى إنشورب : خين نى طاكسيس إن أنكيليكون إفشيمشى إمبى إمثو إم إبتشويس	Ⲙⲓⲭⲁⲏⲗ ⲡⲁⲣⲭⲱⲛ ⲛ̅ⲛⲁ ⲛⲓⲫⲏⲟⲩⲓ : ⲛ̅ⲑⲟϥ ⲉⲧⲟⲓ ⲛ̅ϣⲟⲣⲡ ϧⲉⲛ ⲛⲓⲧⲁⲝⲓⲥ ⲛ̅ⲁⲅⲅⲉⲗⲓⲕⲟⲛ : ⲉϥϣⲉⲙϣⲓ ⲙⲡⲉⲙⲑⲟ ⲙ̅Ⲡ̅ϭ̅ⲥ̅.	ميخائيل رئيس السمائيين هـو الأول فى الطقوس الملائكية يخدم أمام الرب .

English	Coptic transliteration (Arabic)	Coptic	Arabic
Hosanna in the highest: This is the King of Israel: Blessed is He, Who comes in the name: of the Lord of Hosts.	أوصاننا خين نى إتتشوسى : فاى بيه إبؤورو إمبى إسرائيل : إفسمارؤووت إنجيه في إثنيو خين إفران إمبتشويس إنتيه نى جم .	Ⲱⲥⲁⲛⲛⲁ ϧⲉⲛ ⲛⲏ ⲉⲧϭⲟⲥⲓ: ⲫⲁⲓ ⲡⲉ ⲡ̀ⲟⲩⲣⲟ ⲙ̀ⲡⲓⲥⲗ̅: ϥ̀ⲥ̀ⲙⲁⲣⲱⲟⲩⲧ ⲛ̀ϫⲉ ⲫⲏ ⲉⲑⲛⲏⲟⲩ ϧⲉⲛ ⲫ̀ⲣⲁⲛ ⲙ̀ⲡⲟ̅ⲥ̅ ⲛ̀ⲧⲉ ⲛⲓϫⲟⲙ.	اوصنا فى الأعالى هذا هو ملك إسرائيل مبارك الآتى باسم رب القوات.

(Before the Icon of Saint Mark)   (امام ايقونه مارمرفس الانجيلى)

Psalms 67:13

The Lord God will give a word to them that preach it in a great company. The king of the forces of the beloved, of the beloved, will even grant them for the beauty of the house to divide the spoils.

Alleluia

(المزمور 67 : 13)

الرب يعطى كلمة للمبشرين بقوة عظيمة. ملك القوات هو الحبيب، وفى بهاء بيت الحبيب أقتسموا الغنائم . هلليلويا .

Luke 10:1-12

After these things the Lord appointed seventy others also, and sent them two by two before His face into every city and place where He Himself was about to go. Then He said to them, "The harvest truly is great, but the laborers are few; therefore pray the Lord of the harvest to send out laborers into His harvest. Go your way; behold, I send you out as lambs among wolves. Carry neither money bag, knapsack, nor sandals; and greet no one along the road. But whatever house you enter, first say, 'Peace to this house.' And if a son of peace is there, your peace will rest on it; if not, it will return to you. And remain in the same house, eating and drinking such things as they give, for the laborer is worthy of his wages. Do not go from house to house. Whatever city you enter, and they receive you, eat such things as are set before you. And heal the sick there, and say to them, 'The kingdom of God has come near to you.' But whatever city you enter, and they do not receive you, go out into its streets and say, 'The very dust of your city which clings to us we wipe off against you. Nevertheless know this, that the kingdom of God has come near you.' But I say to you that it will be more tolerable in that Day for Sodom than for that city. Glory be to God forever, Amen.

(الانجيل من لوقا 10 : 1 – 12)

وبعد هذا عين الرب سبعين آخرين وأرسلهم اثنين اثنين أمام وجهه إلى كل مدينة وموضع حيث كان هو مزمعاً أن يأتى . فقال لهم إن الحصاد كثير ولكن الفعلة قليلون فاطلبوا من رب الحصاد أن يرسل فعلة إلى حصاده . اذهبوا ها أنا مرسلكم مثل حملان بين ذئاب لا تحملوا كيساً ولا مزوداً ولا أحذية ولا تسلموا على أحد فى الطريق وأى بيت دخلتموه فقولوا اولاً السلام لهذا البيت فان كان هناك إبن السلام يحل سلامكم عليه و إلا فيرجع إليكم . وأقيموا فى ذلك البيت آكلين وشاربين مما عندهم لأن الفاعل مستحق أجرته . لا تنتقلوا من بيت إلى بيت واى مدينة دخلتموها وقبلوكم فكلوا مما يقدم لكم واشفوا المرضى الذين فيها وقولوا لهم قد اقترب منكم ملكوت الله . وأية مدينة دخلتموها ولم يقبلوكم فأخرجوا إلى شوارعها وقولوا حتى الغبار الذى لصق بنا من مدينتكم ننفضه لكم . ولكن أعلموا هذا أنه قد اقترب منكم ملكوت الله . وأقول لكم إنه يكون لسدوم فى ذلك اليوم حالة أكثر إحتمالاً مما لتلك المدينة . والمجد لله دائماً.

The Response   (يرد المرتلون بهذا الربع)

English	Coptic transliteration (Arabic)	Coptic	Arabic
O Mark the Apostle / and the Evangelist, / the witness to the Passion / of the only-begotten God.□	ماركوس بى أبسطولوس : أووه بى إيف أنجيليتيس : بى ميثريه خا نى أمكافه : إنتيه بى مونوجينيس إن نووتى	Ⲙⲁⲣⲕⲟⲥ ⲡⲓⲁⲡⲟⲥⲧⲟⲗⲟⲥ: ⲟⲩⲟ̅ ⲡⲓⲉⲩⲁⲅⲅⲉⲗⲓⲧⲏⲥ: ⲡⲓⲙⲉⲑⲣⲉ ϧⲁ ⲛⲓⲙ̀ⲕⲁⲩ̅: ⲛ̀ⲧⲉ ⲡⲓⲙⲟⲛⲟⲅⲉⲛⲏⲥ ⲛ̀ⲛⲟⲩϯ	مرقس الرسول والانجيلى : الشاهد على آلام : الإله الوحيد .

| Hosanna in the highest: This is the King of Israel: Blessed is He, Who comes in the name: of the Lord of Hosts. | أوصاننا خين نى إتتشوسى : فاى بيه إبؤورو إمبى إسرائيل : إفسمارؤووت إنجيــه في إثنيوو خين إفران إمبتشويس إنتيــه نى جُم . | Ⲱⲥⲁⲛⲛⲁ ϧⲉⲛ ⲛⲏ ⲉⲧϭⲟⲥⲓ : ⲫⲁⲓ ⲡⲉ ⳿ⲡⲟⲩⲣⲟ ⳿ⲙⲠⲓⲥⲗ̅ : ⳿ϥⲥⲙⲁⲣⲱⲟⲩⲧ ⲛ̀ϫⲉ ⲫⲏ ⲉⲑⲛⲏⲟⲩ ϧⲉⲛ ⳿ⲫⲣⲁⲛ ⳿ⲙⲠⲟ̅ⲥ̅ ⲛ̀ⲧⲉ ⲛⲓϫⲟⲙ . | اوصنا فى الأعالى هذا هو ملك إسرائيل مبـارك الآتى باسم رب القوات . |

(Before the Icons of the Apostles) — (امام ايقونه سادتى الاباء الرسل)

Psalms 18:3-4

There is no speech nor language Where their voice is not heard. Their line has gone out through all the earth, And their words to the end of the world. Alleluia

(المزمور 18 : 3 و 4)

الذين لا تسمع أصواتهم فى كل الأرض خرج منطقهم وإلى أقطار المسكونة بلغت أقوالهم . هلليلويا .

Matthew 10:1-8

And when He had called His twelve disciples to Him, He gave them power over unclean spirits, to cast them out, and to heal all kinds of sickness and all kinds of disease. Now the names of the twelve apostles are these: first, Simon, who is called Peter, and Andrew his brother; James the son of Zebedee, and John his brother; Philip and Bartholomew; Thomas and Matthew the tax collector; James the son of Alphaeus, and Lebbaeus, whose surname was Thaddaeus; Simon the Cananite, and Judas Iscariot, who also betrayed Him. These twelve Jesus sent out and commanded them, saying: "Do not go into the way of the Gentiles, and do not enter a city of the Samaritans. But go rather to the lost sheep of the house of Israel. And as you go, preach, saying, 'The kingdom of heaven is at hand.' Heal the sick, cleanse the lepers, raise the dead, cast out demons. Freely you have received, freely give. Glory be to God forever, Amen.

(الانجيل من متى 10 : 1 – 8)

ثم دعا تلاميذه الاثنى عشر وأعطاهم سلطاناً على الأرواح النجسة حتى يخرجوها ويشفوا كل مرض وكل ضعف . وأما الأسماء الاثنى عشر رسولاً فهى هذه : الأول سمعان الذى يقال له بطرس وأندراوس أخوه . يعقوب بن زبدى ويوحنا أخوه . فيلبس وبرثلماوس . توما ومتى العشار . يعقوب بن حلفا وتداوس . سمعان القانوى ويهوذا الإسخريوطى الذى أسلمه . هؤلاء الاثنى عشر أرسلهم وأوصاهم قائلاً : إلى طريق الأمم لا تمضوا وإلى مدينة للسامريين لا تدخلوا بل اذهبوا بالحرى إلى خراف بين إسرائيل الضالة وفيما أنتم ذاهبون اكرزوا قائلين : إنه اقترب ملكوت السموات اشفوا مرضى طهروا برص أقيموا موتى اخرجوا شياطين مجاناً أخذتم مجاناً اعطوا . والمجد لله دائماً .

The Response — (يرد المرتلون بهذا الربع)

| Jesus Christ sent you, O twelve apostles, to preach in the nations, making them Christians. | إيسوس بيخرستوس أفؤورب إمموتين : أوبى ميت إسناف إن أبسطولوس إنتيتين هي أويش خين نى إثنوس : إريتين أيطو إن خريستيانوس . | Ⲓⲏⲥ Ⲡⲭ̅ⲥ̅ ⲁϥⲟⲩⲱⲣⲡ ⳿ⲙⲙⲱⲧⲉⲛ : ⲱⲡⲓ ⲓⲃ̅ ⲛ̀ ⲁⲡⲟⲥⲧⲟⲗⲟⲥ ⲉⲧⲉⲧⲉⲛⲥ̀ϩⲓⲱⲓϣ ϧⲉⲛ ⲛⲓⲉⲑⲛⲟⲥ ⳿ⲉⲣⲉⲧⲉⲛⲁⲓⲧⲟⲩ ⳿ⲛⲭⲣⲏⲥⲧⲓⲁⲛⲟⲥ . | أرسلكم يسوع المسيح أيها الاثنى عشر رسولاً لتبشروا فى الأمم وتصيروهم مسيحيين . |
| Hosanna in the highest: This is the King of Israel: Blessed is He, Who comes in the name: of the Lord of Hosts. | أوصاننا خين نى إتتشوسى : فاى بيه إبؤورو إمبى إسرائيل : إفسمارؤووت إنجيه في إثنيوو خين إفران إمبتشويس إنتيه نى جُم . | Ⲱⲥⲁⲛⲛⲁ ϧⲉⲛ ⲛⲏ ⲉⲧϭⲟⲥⲓ : ⲫⲁⲓ ⲡⲉ ⳿ⲡⲟⲩⲣⲟ ⳿ⲙⲠⲓⲥⲗ̅ : ⳿ϥⲥⲙⲁⲣⲱⲟⲩⲧ ⲛ̀ϫⲉ ⲫⲏ ⲉⲑⲛⲏⲟⲩ ϧⲉⲛ ⳿ⲫⲣⲁⲛ ⳿ⲙⲠⲟ̅ⲥ̅ ⲛ̀ⲧⲉ ⲛⲓϫⲟⲙ . | اوصنا فى الأعالى هذا هو ملك إسرائيل مبارك الآتى باسم رب القوات. |

(Before the Icon of St. George, or any saint of the martyrs)

(أمام أيقونة الشهيد مارجرجس أو أى شهيد من الشهداء)

Psalms 96:11

Light has sprung up for the righteous, and gladness for the upright in heart. Rejoice in the Lord, you righteous; and give thanks for a remembrance of His holiness. *Alleluia.*

(المزمور 96 : 11)

نوراً أشرق للصديقين وفرح للمستقيمين بقلبهم . افرحوا أيها الصديقون بالرب وافتخروا لذكر قدسه . هلليلويا .

Luke 21:12-19

But before all these things, they will lay their hands on you and persecute you, delivering you up to the synagogues and prisons. You will be brought before kings and rulers for My name's sake. But it will turn out for you as an occasion for testimony. Therefore settle it in your hearts not to meditate beforehand on what you will answer; for I will give you a mouth and wisdom which all your adversaries will not be able to contradict or resist. You will be betrayed even by parents and brothers, relatives and friends; and they will put some of you to death. And you will be hated by all for My name's sake. But not a hair of your head shall be lost. By your patience possess your souls. Glory be to God forever, Amen.

(الانجيل من لوقا 21 : 12 – 19)

وقبل هذا كله يلقون أيديهم عليكم ويطردونكم ويسلمونكم إلى مجامع وسجون وتساقون أمام ملوك وولاة لأجل اسمى . فيؤول ذلك لكم شهادة . فضعوا فى قلوبكم ان لا تهتموا من قبل لكى تحتجوا لأنى أنا أعطيكم فماً وحكمة لا يقدر جميع معانديكم أن يقاوموها أو يناقضوها . وسوف تسلمون من الوالدين والإخوة والأقرباء . والأصدقاء . ويقتلون منكم وتكونون مبغضين من الجميع من أجل اسمى ، ولكن شعرة من رؤوسكم لا تهلك . بصبركم اقتنوا أنفسكم . والمجد لله دائماً .

The Response (for St. George)

(يرد المرتلون بهذا الربع لمار جرجس)

English	Coptic (Arabic transliteration)	Coptic	Arabic
Saint George completed / seven whole years, / being judged daily / by seventy lawless kings.	شاشف إنرومبى أفجوكو إيفول : إنجيه فيئثؤواب جيورجيوس : إريه بى إشفه إنـــؤورو إن أنومــوس إفتــى هــاب إروف إممينـــى .	Ⲍ̄ ⲛ̅ⲣⲟⲙⲡⲓ ⲁϥϫⲟⲕⲟⲩ ⲉⲃⲟⲗ : ⲛ̅ϫⲉ ⲫⲏ ⲉⲑⲩ Ⲅⲉⲱⲣⲅⲓⲟⲥ : ⲉⲣⲉ ⲡⲓ ⲟ̄ ⲛ̅ⲟⲩⲣⲟ ⲛ̅ⲁⲛⲟⲙⲟⲥ : ⲉⲩϯϩⲁⲡ ⲉⲣⲟϥ ⲙ̅ⲙⲏⲛⲓ .	سبع سنين أكملها القديس جرجس وسبعون ملكاً منافقين يحكمون عليه دائماً

(For any Martyr)

(لأى شهيد)

English	Coptic (Arabic transliteration)	Coptic	Arabic
Hail to you O martyr: hail to the courageous hero: hail to the struggle bearer: (...)	شيرى ناك اوبى مرتيروس: شيرى بيتشويج إن جينيؤس: شيرى بى أثلوفوروس: (...)	Ⲭⲉⲣⲉ ⲛⲁⲕ ⲱ̄ ⲡⲓⲙⲁⲣⲧⲩⲣⲟⲥ: Ⲭⲉⲣⲉ ⲡⲓϣⲱⲓϫ ⲛ̅ⲧⲉⲛⲛⲉⲟⲥ: Ⲭⲉⲣⲉ ⲡⲓⲁⲑⲗⲟⲫⲟⲣⲟⲥ: (...)	السلام لك ايها الشهيد: السلام للبطل الشجاع: السلام للمجاهد: (...)

(Then they continue)

English	Coptic (Arabic transliteration)	Coptic	Arabic
Hosanna in the highest: This is the King of Israel: Blessed is He, Who comes in the name: of the Lord of Hosts.	أوصاننا خين نى إتتشوسى : فاى بيه إبؤورو أمبى إسرائيل : إفسمارؤووت إنجيه في إثنيوو خين إفران إمبتشويس إنتيـه نى جُم .	Ⲱⲥⲁⲛⲛⲁ ϧⲉⲛ ⲛⲏ ⲉⲧϭⲟⲥⲓ : ⲫⲁⲓ ⲡⲉ ⲡ̅ⲟⲩⲣⲟ ⲙ̅Ⲡⲓⲥⲗ̅ : ϥ̅ⲥⲙⲁⲣⲱⲟⲩⲧ ⲛ̅ϫⲉ ⲫⲏ ⲉⲑⲛⲏⲟⲩ ϧⲉⲛ ⲫⲣⲁⲛ ⲙ̅Ⲡϭ̅ⲥ ⲛ̅ⲧⲉⲛⲓϫⲟⲙ .	اوصنا فى الأعالى هذا هو ملك إسرائيل مبارك الآتى باسم رب القوات.

(Before the Icon of St. Abba Antony the Great, or any other saint)

(أمام أيقونة الأنبا أنطونيوس أو أى قديس من القديسين)

Psalms 68:35, 3

God is wonderful in His holy places, the God of Israel; He will give power and strength to His people; blessed be God. But let the righteous rejoice; let them exalt before God: let them be delighted with joy. Alleluia

(المزمور 68 : 35 ، 3)

عجيب هو الله فى قديسيه إله إسرائيل هو يعطى قوة وعزاً لشعبه والصديقون يفرحون ويتهللون أمام الله ويتنعمون بالسرور . هلليلويا .

Matthew 16:24-28

Then Jesus said to His disciples, "If anyone desires to come after Me, let him deny himself, and take up his cross, and follow Me. For whoever desires to save his life will lose it, but whoever loses his life for My sake will find it. For what profit is it to a man if he gains the whole world, and loses his own soul? Or what will a man give in exchange for his soul? For the Son of Man will come in the glory of His Father with His angels, and then He will reward each according to his works. Assuredly, I say to you, there are some standing here who shall not taste death till they see the Son of Man coming in His kingdom. Glory be to God forever, Amen.

(الانجيل من متى 16 : 24 – 28)

حينئذ قال يسوع لتلاميذه إن أراد أحد أن يأتى ورائى فلينكر نفسه ويحمل صليبه ويتبعنى فإن من أراد أن يخلص نفسه يهلكها ومن يهلك نفسه من أجلى يجدها لأنه ماذا ينتفع الإنسان لو ربح العالم كله وخسر نفسه أو ماذا يعطى الإنسان فداء عن نفسه فإن إبن الإنسان سوف يأتى فى مجد أبيه مع ملائكته وحينئذ يجازى كل واحد حسب عمله الحق أقول لكم إن من القيام ههنا قوماً لا يذوقون الموت حتى يرى لإبن الإنسان آتياً فى ملكوته . والمجد لله دائماً .

The Response

(يرد المرتلون بهذا الربع)

Purge from your hearts / thoughts of vice / and deceiving ideas / that darken the mind.□	فـول إيفـول خيــن نيتين هيت : إننى موكميك إنتيه تى كاكيا : نيم نى ميفى إتشيب شوب : إتنـــرى إمبى نووس إنكاكى .	Bⲱⲗ ⲉⲃⲟⲗ ϧⲉⲛ ⲛⲉⲧⲉⲛϩⲏⲧ : ⲛ̀ⲛⲓⲙⲟⲕⲙⲉⲕ ⲛ̀ⲧⲉ ϯⲕⲁⲕⲓⲁ : ⲛⲉⲙ ⲛⲓⲙⲉⲩⲓ ⲉⲧϣⲉⲃϣⲱⲃ : ⲉⲧⲓⲣⲓ ⲙ̀ⲡⲓⲛⲟⲩⲥ ⲛ̀ⲭⲁⲕⲓ .	حلـــوا مـن قلوبكم أفكـار الشر والظنون الخداعـــة التـى تظلم العقل .
Hosanna in the highest: This is the King of Israel: Blessed is He, Who comes in the name: of the Lord of Hosts.	أوصاننا خين نى إتتشوسى: فاى بيه إبؤورو إمبى إسرائيل : إفسماروؤوت إنجيه في إثنيو خين إفران إمبتشويس إنتيه نى جُم .	Ⲱⲥⲁⲛⲛⲁ ϧⲉⲛ ⲛⲏ ⲉⲧϭⲟⲥⲓ : ⲫⲁⲓ ⲡⲉ ⲡ̀ⲟⲩⲣⲟ ⲙ̀ⲡⲓⲥⲗ̅ : ϥ̀ⲥⲙⲁⲣⲱⲟⲩⲧ ⲛ̀ϫⲉ ⲫⲏ ⲉⲑⲛⲏⲟⲩ ϧⲉⲛ ⲫ̀ⲣⲁⲛ ⲙ̀Ⲡ̅ⲟ̅ⲥ̅ ⲛ̀ⲧⲉ ⲛⲓϫⲟⲙ .	اوصنا فى الأعالى هذا هو ملك إسرائيل مبارك الآتى باسم رب القوات.

(Before the Northern Door)

(أمام الباب البحرى)

Psalms 84:1-2

How lovely is Your tabernacle, O Lord of hosts! My soul longs and faints for the courts of the Lord. Alleluia.

(المزمور 84 : 1 و 2)

مساكنك محبوبة أيها الرب إله القوات تشتاق وتذوب نفسى للدخول إلى ديار الرب . هلليلويا .

Luke 13:22-30

And He went through the cities and villages, teaching, and journeying toward Jerusalem. Then one said to Him, "Lord, are there few who are saved?" And He said to them, "Strive to enter through the narrow gate, for many, I say to you, will seek to enter and will not be able. When once the Master of the house has risen up and shut the door, and you begin to stand outside and knock at the door, saying, 'Lord, Lord, open for us,' and He will answer and say to you, 'I do not know you, where you are from,' then you will begin to say, 'We ate and drank in Your presence, and You taught in our streets.' But He will say, 'I tell you I do not know you, where you are from. Depart from Me, all you workers of iniquity.' There will be weeping and gnashing of teeth, when you see Abraham and Isaac and Jacob and all the prophets in the kingdom of God, and yourselves thrust out. They will come from the east and the west, from the north and the south, and sit down in the kingdom of God. And indeed there are last who will be first, and there are first who will be last. Glory be to God forever, Amen.

(الانجيل من لوقا 13 : 23 – 30)

وكان يسير فى المدن والقرى يعلم ويسافر نحو أورشليم فقال له واحد يا سيد أقليل هم الذين يخلصون . فقال لهم إجتهدوا أن تدخلوا من الباب الضيق . فإنى أقول لكم إن كثيرين سيطلبون أن يدخلوا ولا يقدرون من بعد ما يكون رب البيت قد قام وأغلق الباب وإبتدأتم تقفون خارجاً وتقرعون الباب قائلين : يا رب يا رب افتح لنا يجيب ويقول لكم لا أعرفكم من أين أنتم . حينئذ تبتدئون تقولون أكلنا قدامك وشربنا وعلمت فى شوارعنا . فيقول لكم لا أعرفكم من أين أنتم . تباعدوا عنى يا جميع فاعلى الظلم هناك يكون البكاء وصرير الأسنان متى رأيتم إبراهيم واسحق ويعقوب وجميع الأنبياء فى ملكوت الله وأنتم مطروحون خارجاً ويأتون من المشارق و من المغارب من الشمال ومن الجنوب ويتكئون فى ملكوت الله . وهوذا آخرون يكونون أولين وأولون يكونون آخرين . والمجد لله دائماً .

The Response

(يرد المرتلون بهذا الربع)

| When You come in Your second, fearful appearance, do not let us fearfully hear, "I do not know you."☐ | أكشان إي خين تيك ماه إسنوتى : إمباروؤسيا إتؤى إنهوتى : إمبين إثرين صوتيم خين أوو إستيرتير : جيه تى صواؤون إموؤتين آن . | Ⲁⲕϣⲁⲛⲓ ϧⲉⲛ ⲧⲉⲕⲙⲁϩ Ⲃϯ : ⲙ̀ⲡⲁⲣⲟⲩⲥⲓⲁ ⲉⲧⲟⲓ ⲛ̀ϩⲟϯ : ⲙ̀ⲡⲉⲛⲑⲣⲉⲛⲥⲱⲧⲉⲙ ϧⲉⲛ ⲟⲩⲥⲑⲉⲣⲧⲉⲣ : ϫⲉ ϯⲥⲱⲟⲩⲛ ⲙ̀ⲙⲱⲧⲉⲛ ⲁⲛ .☐ | إذا أتيت فى ظهورك الثانى المخوف فلا نسمع برعدة أننى لست أعرفكم . |
| Hosanna in the highest: This is the King of Israel: Blessed is He, Who comes in the name: of the Lord of Hosts. | أوصانـنا خين نى إتتشوسى : فاى بيه إبؤورو إمبى إسرائيل : إفسمارؤوؤت إنجيه في إثيوو خين إفران إمبتشويس إنتيه نى جم . | Ⲱⲥⲁⲛⲛⲁ ϧⲉⲛ ⲛⲏ ⲉⲧϭⲟⲥⲓ: ⲫⲁⲓ ⲡⲉ ⲡ̀ⲟⲩⲣⲟ ⲙ̀Ⲡⲓⲥⲗ : ϥ̀ⲥⲙⲁⲣⲱⲟⲩⲧ ⲛ̀ϫⲉ ⲫⲏ ⲉⲑⲛⲏⲟⲩ ϧⲉⲛ ⲫ̀ⲣⲁⲛ ⲙ̀Ⲡⲟ̅ⲥ̅ ⲛ̀ⲧⲉⲛⲓϫⲟⲙ . | اوصنا فى الأعالى هذا هو ملك إسرائيل مبارك الآتى باسم رب القوات |

(Before the Baptismal Font)   (امام اللقان)

Psalms 29:3-4

The voice of the Lord is upon the waters; the God of glory has thundered; the Lord is upon many waters. The voice of the Lord is mighty; Alleluia

(المزمور 39 : 3 و 4)

صوت الرب على المياه إله المجد أرعد ، الرب على المياه الكثيرة صوت الرب بقوة . هلليلويا .

Matthew 3:13-17

Then Jesus came from Galilee to John at the Jordan to be baptized by him. And John tried to prevent Him, saying, "I need to be

(الانجيل من متى ص 3 : 13 – 17)

حينئذ جاء يسوع من الجليل إلى الأردن إلى يوحنا ليعتمد منه . ولكن يوحنا منعه قائلاً :

baptized by You, and are You coming to me?" But Jesus answered and said to him, "Permit it to be so now, for thus it is fitting for us to fulfill all righteousness." Then he allowed Him. When He had been baptized, Jesus came up immediately from the water; and behold, the heavens were opened to Him, and He saw the Spirit of God descending like a dove and alighting upon Him. And suddenly a voice came from heaven, saying, "This is My beloved Son, in whom I am well pleased. Glory be to God forever, Amen.

أنا محتاج أن أعتمد منكَ وأنت تأتى إليَّ . فأجاب يسوع وقال له : اسمح الآن لأنه هكذا يليق بنا أن نكمل كل بر . حينئذ سمح له . فلما أعتمد يسوع صعد للوقت من الماء . وإذا السموات قد انفتحت له فرأى روح الله نازلاً مثل حمامة وآتياً اليه وصوت من السموات قائلاً : هذا هو إبنى الحبيب الذى به سررت . والمجد لله دائماً .

The Response   (يرد المرتلون بهذا الربع)

| John has borne witness / in the four Gospels, / saying "I have baptized my Savior / in the waters of the Jordan." □ | أفئرميثريه إنجيه يوأنيس خين بى إفتؤو إن إف أنجيليون : جيه أيتى أوس إمباصوتير : خين نى مـؤوو إنتيــه بيوردانيس . | Ⲁϥⲉⲣⲙⲉⲑⲣⲉ ⲛ̀ϫⲉ Ⲓⲱⲁ ϧⲉⲛ ⲡⲓ Ⲇ̅ ⲛ̀ⲉⲩⲁⲅⲅⲉⲗⲓⲟⲛ : ϫⲉ ⲁⲓⲧⲱⲙⲥ ⲙ̀ⲡⲁⲥⲱⲣ : ϧⲉⲛ ⲛⲓⲙⲱⲟⲩ ⲛ̀ⲧⲉ Ⲡⲓⲓⲟⲣⲇⲁⲛⲏⲥ . | شهد يوحنا فى الأربعة الأناجيل أنى عمدت مخلصى فــى ميــاه الأردن . |
| Hosanna in the highest: This is the King of Israel: Blessed is He, Who comes in the name: of the Lord of Hosts. | أوصاننا خين نى إتتشوسى : فاى بيه إيؤورو إمبى إسرائيل : إفسمارؤووت إنجيه في إثيوو خين إفران إمبتشويس إنتيـه نى جُم . | Ⲱⲥⲁⲛⲛⲁ ϧⲉⲛ ⲛⲏ ⲉⲧϭⲟⲥⲓ: ⲫⲁⲓ ⲡⲉ ⲡ̀ⲟⲩⲣⲟ ⲙ̀Ⲡⲓⲥⲗ̅ : ϥ̀ⲥⲙⲁⲣⲱⲟⲩⲧ ⲛ̀ϫⲉ ⲫⲏ ⲉⲑⲛⲏⲟⲩ ϧⲉⲛ ⲫ̀ⲣⲁⲛ ⲙ̀Ⲡ̅ⲟ̅ⲥ̅ ⲛ̀ⲧⲉ ⲛⲓϫⲟⲙ. | اوصنا فى الأعالى هذا هو ملك إسرائيل مبارك الآتى باسم رب القوات . |

(Before the Southern Door)   (امام باب الكنيسه القبلى)

Psalms 118:19-20   (المزمور 118 : 19 ، 20)

Open to me the gates of righteousness; I will go into them, and give praise to the Lord. This is the gate of the Lord; the righteous shall enter by it. Alleluia.

افتحوا لي أبواب العدل لكى ما أدخل فيها وأعترف للرب . هذا هو باب الرب والصديقون يدخلون فيه . هلليويا .

Matthew 21:1-11   (الانجيل من متى 21 : 1 – 11)

Now when they drew near Jerusalem, and came to Bethphage, at the Mount of Olives, then Jesus sent two disciples, saying to them, "Go into the village opposite you, and immediately you will find a donkey tied, and a colt with her. Loose them and bring them to Me. And if anyone says anything to you, you shall say, 'The Lord has need of them,' and immediately he will send them." All this was done that it might be fulfilled which was spoken by the prophet, saying: "TELL THE DAUGHTER OF ZION, 'BEHOLD, YOUR KING IS COMING TO YOU, LOWLY, AND SITTING ON A DONKEY, A COLT, THE FOAL OF A DONKEY.' " So the disciples went and did as Jesus commanded them. They brought the donkey and the colt, laid their clothes on them, and set Him on them. And a very great multitude spread their clothes on the road; others cut down branches from the trees and spread them on the

ولما قربوا من أورشليم وجاءوا إلى بيت فاجى عند جبل الزيتون حينئذ أرسل يسوع تلميذين قائلاً : اذهبا إلى القرية التى أمامكما فللوقت تجدان أتاناً مربوطاً وجحشاً معه فحلاهما وأتيانى بهما . وإن قال لكم أحد شيئاً فقولا الرب محتاج إليهما . فللوقت يرسلهما . فكان هذا كله لكى يتم ما قيل بالنبى القائل : قولوا لإبنة صهيون هوذا ملكك يأتيك وديعاً راكباً على أتان وجحش إبن أتان . فذهب التلميذان وفعلا كما أمرهما يسوع وأتيا بالاتان والجحش ووضعا عليهما ثيابهما فجلس عليهما . والجميع الأكثر فرشوا ثيابهم فى الطريق وآخرون قطعوا أغصاناً من الشجر وفرشوها فى الطريق والجموع الذين تقدموا

road. Then the multitudes who went before and those who followed cried out, saying: "Hosanna to the Son of David! 'BLESSED IS HE WHO COMES IN THE NAME OF THE LORD!' Hosanna in the highest!" And when He had come into Jerusalem, all the city was moved, saying, "Who is this?" So the multitudes said, "This is Jesus, the prophet from Nazareth of Galilee. Glory be to God forever, Amen.

والذين تبعوا كانوا يصرخون قائلين : أوصنا لإبن داود . مبارك الآتى باسم الرب ولما دخل أورشليم أرتجت المدينة كلها قائلة : من هذا . فقالت الجموع هذا يسوع النبى الذى من ناصرة الجليل . والمجد لله دائماً .

The Response

(يرد المرتلون بهذا الربع)

He who sits upon the cherubim, / on the throne of His glory, / entered into Jerusalem; / what is this great humility?	فى إتهمسى هيجين نى شيروبيم : هيجين بى إثرونوس إنتيه بيف أوؤو : أفشيه إيخون إيروساليم : أو بيه باى نيشتى إنثيبيو .	Ⲫⲏⲉⲧⲥⲉⲙⲥⲓ ϧⲓⲝⲉⲛ ⲛⲓⲭⲉⲣⲟⲩⲃⲓⲙ : ϧⲓⲝⲉⲛ ⲡⲓⲑⲣⲟⲛⲟⲥ ⲛ̀ⲧⲉ ⲡⲉϥⲱⲟⲩ : ⲁϥϣⲉ ⲉ̀ϧⲟⲩⲛ ⲉ̀ⲓⲗⲏⲙ ⲟⲩ ⲡⲉ ⲡⲁⲓⲛⲓϣϯ ⲛ̀ⲑⲉⲃⲓⲟ .	الجالس على الشاروبيم على كرسى مجده دخل إلى أورشليم ما هو هذا التواضع العظيم
Hosanna in the highest: This is the King of Israel: Blessed is He, Who comes in the name: of the Lord of Hosts.	أوصاننا خين نى إنتشوسى : فاى بيه إبؤورو إمبى إسرائيل : إفسمارؤووت إنجيه في إثيوو خين إفران إمبتشويس إنتيه نى جُم .	Ⲱⲥⲁⲛⲛⲁ ϧⲉⲛ ⲛⲏ ⲉⲧϭⲟⲥⲓ: ⲫⲁⲓ ⲡⲉ ⲡ̀ⲟⲩⲣⲟ ⲙ̀Ⲡⲓⲥⲗ : ϥ̀ⲥⲙⲁⲣⲱⲟⲩⲧ ⲛ̀ϫⲉ ⲫⲏ ⲉⲑⲛⲏⲟⲩ ϧⲉⲛ ⲫ̀ⲣⲁⲛ ⲙ̀Ⲡⲟ̅ⲥ̅ ⲛ̀ⲧⲉ ⲛⲓϫⲟⲙ.	اوصنا فى الأعالى هذا هو ملك إسرائيل مبارك الآتى باسم رب القوات .

Psalms 52:8-9

(المزمور 52 : 8 و 9)

But I am as a fruitful olive in the house of God; I will wait on Your name; for it is good before the saints. Alleluia

وأنا مثل شجرة الزيتون المثمرة فى بيت الله أتمسك باسمك فأنه صالح قدام أبرارك . هلليلويا .

Luke 7:28-35

(الانجيل من لوقا 7 : 28 – 35)

For I say to you, among those born of women there is not a greater prophet than John the Baptist; but he who is least in the kingdom of God is greater than he." And when all the people heard Him, even the tax collectors justified God, having been baptized with the baptism of John. But the Pharisees and lawyers rejected the will of God for themselves, not having been baptized by him. And the Lord said, "To what then shall I liken the men of this generation, and what are they like? They are like children sitting in the marketplace and calling to one another, saying: 'We played the flute for you, And you did not dance; We mourned to you, And you did not weep.' For John the Baptist came neither eating bread nor drinking wine, and you say, 'He has a demon.' The Son of Man has come eating and drinking, and you say, 'Look, a glutton and a winebibber, a friend of tax collectors and sinners!' But wisdom is justified by all her children. Glory be to God forever, Amen.

لأنى أقول لكم أنه من بين المولودين من النساء ليس نبى أعظم من يوحنا المعمدان ولكن الأصغر فى ملكوت السموات أعظم منه. وجميع الشعب إذ سمعوا والعشارون بروا الله معتمدين بمعمودية يوحنا . وأما الفريسيون والناموسيون رفضوا مشورة الله من جهة أنفسهم غير معتمدين منه . ثم قال الرب فبمن أشبه أناس هذا الجيل وماذا يشبهون . يشبهون أولاداً جالسين فى السوق ينادون بعضهم بعضاً ويقولون زمرنا لكم فلم ترقصوا نحنا لكم فلم تبكوا . لأنه جاء يوحنا المعمدان لا يأكل خبزاً ولا يشرب خمراً فتقولون به شيطان . جاء إبن الإنسان يأكل ويشرب فتقولون هوذا إنسان أكول وشريب خمر محب للعشارين والخطاة والحكمة تبررت من جميع بنيها . والمجد لله دائماً .

The Response

(يرد المرتلون بهذا الربع)

Among those born of women / no one is like you. / You are great among all the saints, / O John the Baptist.	إمبيه أوون طونف خين نيجين ميسى : إنتيه نى هيومى إفؤنى إمموك : إنثوك أو نيشتى خين نى إثؤواب تيروو : يوأنيـس بى ريفتى أومس .	Ⲙ̀ⲡⲉⲟⲩⲟⲛ ⲧⲱⲛϥ ϧⲉⲛ ⲛⲓⲭⲓⲛⲙⲓⲥⲓ : ⲛ̀ⲧⲉ ⲛⲓⲥϩⲓⲟⲙⲓ ⲉϥⲟⲛⲓ ⲙ̀ⲙⲟⲕ : ⲛ̀ⲑⲟⲕ ⲟⲩⲛⲓϣϯ ϧⲉⲛ ⲛⲏⲉⲑⲩ ⲧⲏⲣⲟⲩ : Ⲓⲱⲁ ⲡⲓⲣⲉϥϯⲱⲙⲥ	لم يقم فى مواليد النسـاء من يشبهك أنت أعظم فى جميع القديسين يا يوحنا المعمدان .
Hosanna in the highest: This is the King of Israel: Blessed is He, Who comes in the name: of the Lord of Hosts.	أوصاننا خين نى إنتشوسى : فاى بيه إبؤورو إمبى إسرائيل : إفسمارؤووت إنجيه إنثيوو خين إفران إمبتشويس إنتيـه نى جُم .	Ⲱⲥⲁⲛⲛⲁ ϧⲉⲛ ⲛⲏ ⲉⲧϭⲟⲥⲓ : ⲫⲁⲓ ⲡⲉ ⲡ̀ⲟⲩⲣⲟ ⲙ̀Ⲡⲓⲥ̀ⲗ : ϥ̀ⲥⲙⲁⲣⲱⲟⲩⲧ ⲛ̀ϫⲉ ⲫⲏ ⲉⲑⲛⲏⲟⲩ ϧⲉⲛ ⲫ̀ⲣⲁⲛ ⲙ̀Ⲡⲟ̅ⲥ̅ ⲛ̀ⲧⲉⲛⲓϫⲟⲙ .	فى الأعالى هذا هو ملك إسرائيل مبارك الآتى باسم رب القوات.

After the end of the procession, the priest prays the Gospel litany, then the Psalm and the Gospel are read.

+ بعد إنتهاء الدورة يقول الكاهن أوشية الانجيل ويطرح المزمور قبطياً وعربياً .

The Psalm
Ⲯⲁⲗⲙⲟⲥ ⲝ̅ⲍ̅ : ⲓ̅ⲑ̅ ⲛⲉⲙ ⲗ̅ⲉ̅

Psalms 67:19, 35

(مز 67 : 19 و35)

Blessed be the Lord God, blessed be the Lord daily; and the God of our salvation shall prosper us. The God of Israel; He will give power and strength to His people; blessed be God. Alleluia	إفسمارؤوت إنجيه إبتشويس إفنوتى: إفسمارؤوت إنجيه إبتشويس إممينى إممينى إفنوتى إمبسرائيل إنثوف إفتى إنؤو جُم نيم أوو أماهى إمبيف لاؤس إفسمارؤوت إنجيه إفنوتى . ألليلويا .	Ϥ̀ⲥⲙⲁⲣⲱⲟⲩⲧ ⲛ̀ϫⲉ ⲡⲟ̅ⲥ̅ Ⲫϯ : ϥ̀ⲥⲙⲁⲣⲱⲟⲩⲧ ⲛ̀ϫⲉ ⲡ̀ⲟ̅ⲥ̅ ⲙ̀ⲙⲏⲛⲓ ⲙ̀ⲙⲏⲛⲓ . Ⲫϯ ⲙ̀Ⲡⲓⲥ̀ⲗ ⲛ̀ⲑⲟϥ ⲉϥⲉ̀ϯ ⲛ̀ⲟⲩϫⲟⲙ ⲛⲉⲙ ⲟⲩⲁⲙⲁϩⲓ ⲙ̀ⲡⲉϥⲗⲁⲟⲥ ϥ̀ⲥⲙⲁⲣⲱⲟⲩⲧ ⲛ̀ϫⲉ Ⲫϯ ⲁⲗ .	مبارك الرب الإله . مبـارك الـرب يومـاً فيوماً . إله إسرائيل هو يعطـى قـوة وعـزاً لشعبه. مبارك هو الله. هلليلويا

The Gospel
Ⲉⲩⲁⲅⲅⲉⲗⲓⲟⲛ Ⲕⲁⲧⲁ Ⲗⲟⲩⲕⲁⲛ Ⲕⲉⲫ ⲓ̅ⲑ̅ : ⲁ̅ - ⲓ̅

Luke 19:1-10

(لوقا 19 : 1 - 10)

Then Jesus entered and passed through Jericho. Now behold, there was a man named Zacchaeus who was a chief tax collector, and he was rich. And he sought to see who Jesus was, but could not because of the crowd, for he was of short stature. So he ran ahead and climbed up into a sycamore tree to see Him, for He was going to pass that way. And when Jesus came to the place, He looked up and saw him, and said to him, "Zacchaeus, make haste and come	Ⲟⲩⲟϩ ⲉⲧⲁϥϣⲉ ⲉ̀ϧⲟⲩⲛ ⲛ̀ϫⲉ Ⲓⲏⲥ ⲛⲁϥⲙⲟϣⲓ ⲡⲉ ϧⲉⲛ Ⲓⲉⲣⲓⲭⲱ . Ⲟⲩⲟϩ ⲓⲥ ⲟⲩⲣⲱⲙⲓ ⲉⲩⲙⲟⲩϯ ⲉ̀ⲡⲉϥⲣⲁⲛ ϫⲉ Ⲍⲁⲕⲭⲉⲟⲥ ⲟⲩⲟϩ ⲫⲁⲓ ⲛⲉ ⲟⲩⲁⲣⲭⲏ ⲧⲉⲗⲱⲛⲏⲥ ⲡⲉ ⲟⲩⲟϩ ⲛⲉ ⲟⲩⲣⲁⲙⲁⲟ̀ ⲡⲉ . Ⲟⲩⲟϩ ⲛⲁϥⲕⲱϯ ⲡⲉ ⲉϥⲟⲩⲱϣ ⲉ̀ⲛⲁⲩ ⲉ̀Ⲓⲏⲥ ϫⲉ ⲛⲓⲙ ⲡⲉ : ⲟⲩⲟϩ ⲛⲁϥ ϣ̀ϫⲉⲙϫⲟⲙ ⲡⲉ ⲁⲛ ϧⲉⲛ ⲧⲉϥⲙⲁⲓⲏ . Ⲟⲩⲟϩ ⲉⲧⲁϥϭⲟϫⲓ ⲉ̀ⲧϩⲏ ⲁϥϣⲉⲛⲁϥ ⲉ̀ϧ̀ⲣⲏⲓ ⲉ̀ϫⲉⲛ ⲟⲩⲥⲩⲕⲟⲙⲟⲣⲉⲁ̀ ϩⲓⲛⲁ ⲛ̀ⲧⲉϥⲛⲁⲩ ⲉ̀ⲣⲟϥ ⲟⲩⲟϩ ⲛⲁϥⲛⲁⲥⲓⲛⲓ : ⲡⲉ ⲉ̀ⲃⲟⲗ ϩⲓⲱⲧⲥ . Ⲟⲩⲟϩ ⲉⲧⲁϥⲓ̀ ⲉϫⲉⲛ ⲡⲓⲙⲁ ϥ̀ⲥⲟⲙⲥ ⲉ̀ⲣⲟϥ ⲛ̀ϫⲉ Ⲓⲏⲥ ⲡⲉϫⲁϥ ⲛⲁϥ ϫⲉ Ⲍⲁⲕⲭⲉⲟⲥ	ولما دخل يسوع مجتازاً فى أريحا . وإذا برجل اسمه زكا وهذا كان رئيساً للعشارين وكان غنياً. وكان يطلب راغباً فى أن يرى من هو يسوع ولم يقدر من أجل الجمع لأنه كان قصير القامة . فتقدم مسرعاً وصعد إلى جميزة لكى يراه . لأنه كان مزمعاً أن يجتاز بها . فلما جاء يسوع إلى الموضع نظر إليه

down, for today I must stay at your house." So he made haste and came down, and received Him joyfully. But when they saw it, they all complained, saying, "He has gone to be a guest with a man who is a sinner." Then Zacchaeus stood and said to the Lord, "Look, Lord, I give half of my goods to the poor; and if I have taken anything from anyone by false accusation, I restore fourfold." And Jesus said to him, "Today salvation has come to this house, because he also is a son of Abraham; for the Son of Man has come to seek and to save that which was lost. Glory be to God forever, Amen.	ⲭⲱⲗⲉⲙ ⲙ̅ⲙⲟⲕ ⲁⲙⲟⲩ ⲉⲡⲉⲥⲏⲧ : ⲙ̅ⲫⲟⲟⲩ ⲅⲁⲣ ϩⲱϯ ⲉⲣⲟⲓ ⲛ̅ⲧⲁϣⲱⲡⲓ ϧⲉⲛ ⲡⲉⲕⲏⲓ . ⲟⲩⲟϩ ⲁϥⲭⲱⲗⲉⲙ ⲙ̅ⲙⲟϥ ⲁϥⲓ ⲉⲡⲉⲥⲏⲧ ⲟⲩⲟϩ ⲁϥϣⲟⲡϥ ⲉⲣⲟϥ ⲉϥⲣⲁϣⲓ . Ⲟⲩⲟϩ ⲛⲏ ⲧⲏⲣⲟⲩ ⲉⲧⲁⲩⲛⲁⲩ ⲁⲩⲭⲣⲉⲙⲣⲉⲙ ⲉⲩⲭⲱ ⲙ̅ⲙⲟⲥ ϫⲉ ⲁϥϣⲉⲛⲁϥ ⲉϧⲟⲩⲛ ⲉⲡⲏⲓ ⲛ̅ⲟⲩⲣⲉϥⲉⲣⲛⲟⲃⲓ ⲛ̅ⲣⲱⲙⲓ ⲉⲉⲙⲧⲟⲛ ⲙ̅ⲙⲟϥ . Ⲁϥⲟϩⲓ ⲇⲉ ⲉⲣⲁⲧϥ ⲛ̅ϫⲉ Ⲍⲁⲕⲭⲉⲟⲥ ⲡⲉϫⲁϥ ⲙ̅ⲡⲟ̅ⲥ̅ ϫⲉ ϩⲏⲡⲡⲉ ⲡⲁⲟ̅ⲥ̅ ϯ ⲛ̅ⲧⲫⲁϣⲓ ⲛ̅ⲛⲁϩⲩ- ⲡⲁⲣⲭⲟⲛⲧⲁ ⲛ̅ⲛⲓϩⲏⲕⲓ : ⲟⲩⲟϩ ⲫⲏⲉⲧⲁⲓϭⲓⲧϥ ⲛ̅ϫⲟⲛⲥ ⲛ̅ϩⲗⲓ ϯⲛⲁⲕⲟⲃⲟⲩ ⲛⲁϥ ⲛ̅ϥⲧⲟⲩ ⲛ̅ⲕⲱⲃ . Ⲡⲉϫⲁϥ ⲇⲉ ⲛⲁϥ ⲛ̅ϫⲉ Ⲓⲏⲥ ϫⲉ ⲙ̅ⲫⲟⲟⲩ ⲁ ⲡⲓⲟⲩϫⲁⲓ ϣⲱⲡⲓ ⲙ̅ⲡⲁⲓⲏⲓ : ϫⲉ ⲛ̅ⲑⲟϥ ϩⲱϥ ⲟⲩϣⲏⲣⲓ ⲛ̅ⲧⲉ Ⲁⲃⲣⲁⲁⲙ ⲡⲉ . ⲁϥⲓ ⲅⲁⲣ ⲛ̅ϫⲉ ⲡ̅ϣⲏⲣⲓ ⲙ̅ⲫⲣⲱⲙⲓ ⲉ̅ⲕⲱϯ ⲟⲩⲟϩ ⲉ̅ⲛⲟϩⲉⲙ ⲙ̅ⲫⲏⲉⲧⲁϥⲧⲁⲕⲟ . Ⲡⲓⲱⲟⲩ ⲫⲁ ⲡⲉⲛⲛⲟⲩϯ ⲡⲉ .	وقال له : يا زكا اسرع وانزل لأنه ينبغى لي أن أكون اليوم فى بيتك . ونزل وقبله فرحاً . فلما رأى الجميع ذلك تذمروا قائلين : أنه دخل بيت رجل خاطئ ليستريح فوقف زكا وقال للرب : ها أنا يارب أعطى نصف أموالى للمساكين . ومَن أغتصبته شيئاً فأني أعوضه أربعة أضعاف فقال له يسوع : اليوم وجب الخلاص لأهل هذا البيت . إذ هو أيضاً ابن إبراهيم . لأن إبن الإنسان انما جاء لكى يطلب ويخلص ما قد هلك. والمجد لله دائماً .

The Gospel Response
(مـرد الانجيل)

English	Coptic (transliteration)	Coptic	Arabic
"The half of my goods," said Zacchaeus to his Lord, "I will give O Master, to the poor with care.	إتفاشى إننى هييارخوندا : بيجيه زاكينــــوس إمبيف أتشويس : تيناتيف أوذيسبوطا : إننى هيكى خين إشرويس .	Ⲧ̅ⲫⲁϣⲓ ⲛ̅ⲛⲓϩⲩⲡⲁⲣⲭⲱⲛⲧⲁ ⲡⲉϫⲉ Ⲍⲁⲕⲕⲉⲟⲥ ⲙ̅ⲡⲉϥⲟ̅ⲥ̅ : ϯⲛⲁⲧⲏⲓϥ ⲱ̅Ⲇⲉⲥⲡⲟⲧⲁ : ⲛ̅ⲛⲓϩⲏⲕⲓ ϧⲉⲛ ⲟⲩⲣⲱⲓⲥ .	فقال زكا لربه نصف الأموال أعطيها يا سيدى للمساكين بحرص.
"Behold salvation has come unto you today," Said the Lord God of Powers, "For you are also, a son of Abraham."	إس بى أووجاى أفشوبى ناك : بيجيه إبتشويس إفنوتى إنتى نى جُم : إمفوؤو غار جيه إنثوك هوك : أووشيرى إنتيه أبرآام .	Ⲓⲥ ⲡⲓⲟⲩϫⲁⲓ ⲁϥϣⲱⲡⲓ ⲛⲁⲕ : ⲡⲉϫⲉ Ⲡⲟ̅ⲥ̅ Ⲫ̅ϯ ⲛ̅ⲧⲉ ⲛⲓϫⲟⲙ : ⲙ̅ⲫⲟⲟⲩ ⲅⲁⲣ ϫⲉ ⲛ̅ⲑⲟⲕ ϩⲱⲕ ⲟⲩϣⲏⲣⲓ ⲛ̅ⲧⲉ Ⲁⲃⲣⲁⲁⲙ .	أجاب الرب إله القوات هوذا الخلاص قد وجب لكَ اليوم لأنك أنت أيضاً ابن إبراهيم .

(The Liturgy of Palm Sunday (قداس أحد الشعانين)

The Pauline Epistle - البولس

Ⲁⲡⲟⲥⲧⲟⲗⲟⲥ Ⲛⲓϩⲉⲃⲣⲉⲟⲥ Ⲕⲉⲫ ⲑ̄ : ⲓ̄ⲁ̄ - ⲕ̄ⲏ̄

Hebrews 9:11-28

But Christ came as High Priest of the good things to come, with the greater and more perfect tabernacle not made with hands, that is, not of this creation. Not with the blood of goats and calves, but with His own blood He entered the Most Holy Place once for all, having obtained eternal redemption. For if the blood of bulls and goats and the ashes of a heifer, sprinkling the unclean, sanctifies for the purifying of the flesh, how much more shall the blood of Christ, who through the eternal Spirit offered Himself without spot to God, cleanse your conscience from dead works to serve the living God? And for this reason He is the Mediator of the new covenant, by means of death, for the redemption of the transgressions under the first covenant, that those who are called may receive the promise of the eternal inheritance. For where there is a testament, there must also of necessity be the death of the testator. For a testament is in force after men are dead, since it has no power at all while the testator lives. Therefore not even the first covenant was dedicated without blood. For when Moses had spoken every precept to all the people according to the law, he took the blood of calves and goats, with water, scarlet wool, and hyssop, and sprinkled both the book itself and all the people, saying, "THIS IS THE BLOOD OF THE COVENANT WHICH GOD HAS COMMANDED

Ⲡⲭ̅ⲥ̅ ⲇⲉ ⲉⲧⲁϥⲓ ⲡⲓⲁⲣⲭⲏ ⲉⲣⲉⲧⲥ ⲛ̀ⲧⲉ ⲛⲓⲁⲅⲁⲑⲟⲛ ⲉⲑⲛⲁϣⲱⲡⲓ ⲉ̀ⲃⲟⲗ ϩⲓⲧⲉⲛ ϯⲛⲓϣϯ ⲛ̀ⲥⲕⲩⲛⲏ ⲟⲩⲟϩ ⲉⲧϫⲏⲕ ⲉ̀ⲃⲟⲗ : ⲛ̀ⲟⲩⲙⲟⲛⲕ ⲛ̀ϫⲓϫ ⲁⲛ ⲧⲉ : ⲉⲧⲉ ⲫⲁⲓ ⲡⲉ ϫⲉ ⲑⲁ ⲡⲁⲓⲥⲱⲛⲧ ⲁⲛ ⲧⲉ . Ⲟⲩ ⲇⲉ ⲉ̀ⲃⲟⲗ ϩⲓⲧⲉⲛ ⲡ̀ⲥⲛⲟϥ ⲛ̀ⲧⲉ ϩⲁⲛⲃⲁⲣⲏⲧ ⲁⲛ ⲧⲉ ⲛⲉⲙ ϩⲁⲛⲙⲁⲥⲓ : ⲁⲗⲗⲁ ⲉ̀ⲃⲟⲗ ϩⲓⲧⲉⲛ ⲡⲉϥⲥⲛⲟϥ ⲙ̀ⲙⲓⲛ ⲙ̀ⲙⲟϥ : ⲉ̀ⲁϥⲓ ⲉ̀ϧⲟⲩⲛ ⲉ̀ⲛⲏⲉⲑⲟⲩⲁⲃ ⲛ̀ⲟⲩⲥⲟⲡ ⲉⲁϥϫⲓⲙⲓ ⲛ̀ⲟⲩⲥⲱ̀ϯ ⲛ̀ⲉⲛⲉϩ : ⲓⲥ ϫⲉ ⲅⲁⲣ ⲡ̀ⲥⲛⲟϥ ⲛ̀ⲧⲉ ϩⲁⲛⲃⲁⲣⲏⲧ ⲛⲉⲙ ϩⲁⲛⲙⲁⲥⲓ ⲛⲉⲙ ⲟⲩⲕⲉⲣⲙⲓ ⲛ̀ⲧⲉ ⲟⲩⲃⲁϩⲥⲓ ⲉϥⲛⲟⲧϧ̀ ⲉϫⲉⲛ ⲛⲏⲉⲧϭⲁϧⲉⲙ ϣⲁϥⲧⲟⲩⲃⲱⲟⲩ ⲉ̀ⲡⲧⲟⲩⲃⲟ ⲛ̀ⲧⲉ ϯⲥⲁⲣⲝ . Ⲓⲉ ⲁⲩⲏⲣ ⲙⲁⲗⲗⲟⲛ ⲡⲉ ⲡ̀ⲥⲛⲟϥ ⲙ̀Ⲡⲭ̅ⲥ̅ : ⲫⲁⲓ ⲉⲧⲉ ⲉ̀ⲃⲟⲗ ϩⲓⲧⲉⲛ ⲡⲓⲡ̅ⲛ̅ⲁ̅ ⲉϥⲟⲩⲁⲃ ⲁϥⲉⲛϥ ⲉ̀ϧⲟⲩⲛ ⲉϥⲧⲟⲩⲃⲏⲟⲩⲧ ⲙ̀Ⲫ̀ϯ : ϥ̀ⲛⲁⲧⲟⲩⲃⲟ ⲛ̀ⲧⲉ ⲧⲉⲛⲥⲩⲛⲏⲗⲏⲥⲓⲥ ⲉ̀ⲃⲟⲗ ϩⲁ ⲛⲓϩ̀ⲃⲏⲟⲩⲓ ⲉⲑⲙⲱⲟⲩⲧ : ⲉⲣⲉⲧⲉⲛϣⲉⲙϣⲓ ⲙ̀Ⲫ̀ϯ ⲉⲧⲟⲛϧ ⲟⲩⲟϩ ⲛ̀ⲟⲩⲙⲏⲓ : Ⲟⲩⲟϩ ⲉⲑⲃⲉ ⲫⲁⲓ ⲟⲩⲙⲉⲥⲓⲧⲏⲥ ⲡⲉ ⲛ̀ⲧⲉ ⲟⲩⲇⲓⲁⲑⲏⲕⲏ ⲙ̀ⲃⲉⲣⲓ : ϩⲟⲡⲱⲥ ⲉⲁϥϣⲱⲡⲓ ⲛ̀ϫⲉ ⲟⲩⲙⲟⲩ ⲉⲩⲥⲱϯ ⲛ̀ⲧⲉ ⲛⲓⲡⲁⲣⲁⲃⲁⲥⲓⲥ ⲉⲧⲭⲏ ϩⲓϫⲉⲛ ϯⲇⲓⲁⲑⲏⲕⲏ ⲛ̀ϩⲟⲩⲓϯ : ϩⲓⲛⲁ ⲛ̀ⲥⲉϭⲓ ⲙ̀ⲡⲓⲱϣ ⲛ̀ϫⲉ ⲛⲏⲉⲧⲑⲁϩⲉⲙ ⲛ̀ⲧⲉ ϯⲕⲗⲏⲣⲟⲛⲟⲙⲓⲁ ⲛ̀ⲉⲛⲉϩ . Ⲡⲓⲙⲁ ⲅⲁⲣ ⲉ̀ⲧⲉ ⲟⲩⲟⲛ ⲟⲩⲇⲓⲁⲑⲏⲕⲏ ⲙ̀ⲙⲟϥ : ⲁⲛⲁⲅⲕⲏ ⲛ̀ⲥⲉⲉⲛ ⲫ̀ⲙⲟⲩ ⲙ̀ⲫⲏⲉⲧⲁϥⲥⲉⲙⲛⲏⲧⲥ : ϯⲇⲓⲁⲑⲏⲕⲏ ⲅⲁⲣ ⲁⲥⲧⲁϫⲣⲏⲟⲩⲧ ⲉϫⲉⲛ ϩⲁⲛⲣⲉϥⲙⲱⲟⲩⲧ ϫⲉ ⲙ̀ⲡⲁⲥ̀ϫⲉⲙϫⲟⲙ ϩⲟⲥ ⲟⲛ ⲉϥⲟⲛϧ ⲛ̀ϫⲉ ⲫⲏⲉⲧⲁϥⲥⲉⲙⲛⲏⲧⲥ . Ⲉⲑⲃⲉ ⲫⲁⲓ ⲟⲩ ⲇⲉ ϯϩⲟⲩⲓϯ ⲙ̀ⲡⲉⲥⲧⲟⲩⲃⲟ ⲁⲧϭⲛⲉ ⲥ̀ⲛⲟϥ . Ⲉⲛⲧⲟⲗⲏ ⲅⲁⲣ ⲛⲓⲃⲉⲛ ⲕⲁⲧⲁ ⲡⲓⲛⲟⲙⲟⲥ ⲉ̀ⲧⲁ Ⲙⲱⲩⲥⲏⲥ ⲥⲁϫⲓ ⲙ̀ⲙⲱⲟⲩ ⲛⲉⲙ ⲡⲓⲗⲁⲟⲥ ⲧⲏⲣϥ : ⲁϥϭⲓ ⲛ̀ⲟⲩⲥ̀ⲛⲟϥ ⲛ̀ⲧⲉ ϩⲁⲛⲙⲁⲥⲓ ⲛⲉⲙ ϩⲁⲛⲃⲁⲣⲏⲧ ⲛⲉⲙ ⲟⲩⲙⲱⲟⲩ ⲛⲉⲙ ⲟⲩⲥⲟⲣⲧ ⲛ̀ⲕⲟⲕⲕⲓⲛⲟⲛ ⲛⲉⲙ ⲟⲩϩⲩⲥⲱⲡⲟⲛ ⲡⲓⲕⲉϫⲱⲙ ⲇⲉ ϩⲱϥ ⲛⲉⲙ ⲡⲓⲗⲁⲟⲥ ⲧⲏⲣϥ ⲁϥⲛⲟϫϧⲟⲩ . Ⲉϥϫⲱ ⲙ̀ⲙⲟⲥ ϫⲉ ⲫⲁⲓ ⲡⲉ

(العبرانيين 9 : 11 - 28)

فلما جاء المسيح رئيس كهنة للخيرات الكائنة فبالمسكن الأعظم والأكمل . غير المصنوع بيد ، أى الذى ليس هو من هذه الخليقة وليس بدم تيوس وعجول بل بدمه الخصيص دخل دفعة واحدة إلى المقادس فوجد فداء أبدياً . لأنه إن كان دم التيوس والعجول ورماد العجلة إذا ما نضح على المتنجسين يقدسهم لتطهير الجسد . فكم أخرى يكون دم المسيح هذا الذى من جهة الروح القدس قدم ذاته لله نقياً ليطهر نيتكم من الأعمال الميتة . لكى تعبدوا الله الحى الحقيقى . ولأجل هذا فهو واسطة عهد جديد . حتى إذ كان موت لفداء معاصى العهد الأول . حظى المدعوون بوعد الميراث الأبدى . لأنه حيث يوجد عهد بوصية . فالضرورة داعية إلى حلول الموت بالموصى . لأن الوصية ثابتة على الأموات إذ لا قوة لها ما دام الذى قررها حياً . من أجل هذا ولا الأول لم يطهر بغير دم . ولما خاطب موسى كل الشعب بجميع الوصايا التى بحسب الناموس . أخذ دم العجول والتيوس مع ماء وصوفاً قرمزياً وزوفاً . فنضحه على المصحف نفسه وعلى كافة الشعب قائلاً : هذا هو دم العهد الذى أوصاكم الله به . كذلك أيضاً القبة وجميع آنية الخدمة نضحها هكذا بالدم .

YOU." Then likewise he sprinkled with blood both the tabernacle and all the vessels of the ministry. And according to the law almost all things are purified with blood, and without shedding of blood there is no remission. Therefore it was necessary that the copies of the things in the heavens should be purified with these, but the heavenly things themselves with better sacrifices than these. For Christ has not entered the holy places made with hands, which are copies of the true, but into heaven itself, now to appear in the presence of God for us; not that He should offer Himself often, as the high priest enters the Most Holy Place every year with blood of another—He then would have had to suffer often since the foundation of the world; but now, once at the end of the ages, He has appeared to put away sin by the sacrifice of Himself. And as it is appointed for men to die once, but after this the judgment, so Christ was offered once to bear the sins of many. To those who eagerly wait for Him He will appear a second time, apart from sin, for salvation. The Grace of God the Father be with you all. Amen

ⲡ̀ⲥⲛⲟϥ ⲛ̀ⲧⲉ ϯ̀ⲇⲓⲁⲑⲏⲕⲏ ⲑⲏⲉⲧⲁ Ⲫϯ ϧⲉⲛϧⲉⲛ ⲑⲏⲛⲟⲩ ⲉ̀ⲣⲟⲥ . Ⲟⲩⲟϩ ϯⲥⲕⲩⲛⲏ ⲛⲉⲙ ⲛⲓⲥⲕⲉⲟⲥ ⲧⲏⲣⲟⲩ ⲛ̀ⲧⲉ ⲡⲓϣⲉⲙϣⲓ ⲁϥⲛⲟϫϧⲟⲩ ⲙ̀ⲡⲁⲓⲣⲏϯ ϧⲉⲛ ⲡⲓⲥⲛⲟϥ : ⲕⲁⲧⲁ ⲟⲩⲥ̀ϧⲟⲛⲧ ϣⲁⲩⲧⲟⲩⲃⲟ ⲧⲏⲣⲟⲩ ⲕⲁⲧⲁ ⲁⲧϭ̀ⲛⲉ ⲙⲉⲛ ⲥⲛⲟϥ ⲉ̀ⲃⲟⲗ ⲙ̀ⲡⲁⲣⲉⲭⲱ ⲉ̀ⲃⲟⲗ ϣⲱⲡⲓ . Ⲁ̀ⲛⲁⲅⲕⲏ ⲙⲉⲛ ⲟⲩⲛ ⲛⲓⲥⲙⲟⲧ ⲛ̀ⲧⲉ ⲛⲏⲉⲧ ϧⲉⲛ ⲛⲓⲫⲏⲟⲩⲓ ⲛ̀ⲥⲉⲧⲟⲩⲃⲟ ϧⲉⲛ ⲛⲁⲓ : ⲛ̀ⲑⲱⲟⲩ ⲇⲉ ⲛⲁ ⲛⲓⲫⲏⲟⲩⲓ ϧⲉⲛ ϩⲁⲛϣⲟⲩϣⲱⲟⲩϣⲓ ⲉⲩⲥⲟⲧⲡ ⲉ̀ϩⲟⲧⲉ ⲛⲁⲓ : ⲛⲉ ⲧⲁ Ⲡ̅ⲭ̅ⲥ̅ ⲅⲁⲣ ⲁⲛⲓ ⲉ̀ϧⲟⲩⲛ ⲉ̀ϩⲁⲛⲙⲟⲛⲕ ⲛ̀ϫⲓϫ ⲉⲩⲟⲩⲁⲃ ⲛ̀ⲧⲩⲡⲟⲥ ⲛ̀ⲧⲉ ⲛⲓⲧⲁⲫⲙⲏⲓ : ⲁⲗⲗⲁ ⲉ̀ϧⲟⲩⲛ ⲉ̀ⲧ̀ⲫⲉ ⲉ̀ⲧⲉ ⲛ̀ⲑⲟⲥ ⲧⲉ ⲉ̀ⲟⲩⲟⲛϩϥ ⲉ̀ⲃⲟⲗ ϯⲛⲟⲩ ⲙ̀ⲡⲉ̀ⲙⲑⲟ ⲙ̀Ⲫϯ ⲉ̀ϩ̀ⲣⲏⲓ ⲉ̀ϫⲱⲛ : ϫⲉ ⲛ̀ⲧⲉϥⲉⲛϥ ⲉ̀ϩ̀ⲣⲏⲓ ⲁⲛ ⲛ̀ⲟⲩⲙⲏϣ ⲛ̀ⲥⲟⲡ ⲙ̀ⲫ̀ⲣⲏϯ ⲙ̀ⲡⲓⲁⲣⲭⲏⲉⲣⲉⲥ ⲉϣⲁϥⲓ ⲉ̀ϧⲟⲩⲛ ⲉ̀ⲛⲏⲉⲑⲟⲩⲁⲃ ⲛ̀ⲧⲣⲟⲙⲡⲓ ϧⲉⲛ ⲟⲩⲥⲛⲟϥ ⲙ̀ⲫⲱϥ ⲁⲛ ⲡⲉ . Ⲙⲙⲟⲛ ⲛⲉ ⲉⲙⲱⲧ ⲉ̀ⲣⲟϥ ⲡⲉ ⲛ̀ⲧⲉϥϭ̀ⲓ ⲉⲙⲕⲁϩ ⲛ̀ⲟⲩⲙⲏϣ ⲛ̀ⲥⲟⲡ ⲓⲥϫⲉⲛ ⲧ̀ⲕⲁⲧⲁⲃⲟⲗⲏ ⲙ̀ⲡⲓⲕⲟⲥⲙⲟⲥ : ϯⲛⲟⲩ ⲇⲉ ⲛ̀ⲟⲩⲥⲟⲡ ϣⲁ ⲡ̀ϫⲱⲕ ⲉ̀ⲃⲟⲗ ⲛ̀ⲧⲉ ⲛⲓⲉⲛⲉϩ ⲁϥⲟⲩⲟⲛϩϥ ⲉ̀ⲃⲟⲗ ϩⲓⲧⲉⲛ ⲡⲉϥϣⲟⲩϣⲱⲟⲩϣⲓ : Ⲟⲩⲟϩ ⲕⲁⲧⲁ ⲫ̀ⲣⲏϯ ⲉ̀ⲧⲉⲥⲭⲏ ⲛ̀ⲛⲓⲣⲱⲙⲓ ⲉⲑⲣⲟⲩⲙⲟⲩ ⲛ̀ⲟⲩⲥⲟⲡ ⲙⲉⲛⲉⲛⲥⲁ ϥⲁⲓ ⲇⲉ ⲟⲩϩⲁⲡ : ⲡⲁⲓⲣⲏϯ ϩⲱϥ Ⲡ̅ⲭ̅ⲥ̅ ⲁϥⲉⲛϥ ⲉ̀ϧⲟⲩⲛ ⲛ̀ⲟⲩⲥⲟⲡ ϫⲉ ⲛ̀ⲧⲉϥⲓⲛⲓ ⲛ̀ⲛⲓⲛⲟⲃⲓ ⲛ̀ⲟⲩⲙⲏϣ : ⲉ̀ϩ̀ⲣⲏⲓ ⲡⲓⲙⲁϩ ⲥⲟⲡ ⲇⲉ ⲥ̀ⲛⲁⲩ ⲉϥⲉ̀ⲟⲩⲱⲛϩϥ ⲉ̀ⲃⲟⲗ ⲁⲧϭ̀ⲛⲉ ⲛⲟⲃⲓ ⲉⲩⲛⲟϩⲉⲙ ⲛ̀ⲛⲏⲉⲧϫⲟⲩϣⲧ ⲉ̀ⲃⲟⲗ ϧⲁϫⲱϥ . Ⲡⲓϩ̀ⲙⲟⲧ ⲛⲉⲙ ϯϩⲓⲣⲏⲛⲏ .

وبالاقتراب تتطهر جميعها بالدم كالناموس . وبغير سفك دم لم تكن مغفرة . فالضرورة داعية إلى أن تتطهر أمثلة الأشياء التى فى السموات بهذه الأمور . فأما السمويات فبضحايا أجل من هذه قدراً . أن المسيح لم يدخل إلى المقادس المصنوعة بالأيادى التى هى أشباه المقادس الحقيقية . بل إلى السماء نفسها ليظهر الآن أمام الله عنا . ليس ليقرب ذاته مرات كثيرة كما يدخل رئيس الكهنة إلى المقادس فى كل سنة بدم ليس هو له . وإلا فقد كان ينبغى له أن يتألم مراراً كثيرة منذ انشاء العالم . ولكنه الآن قد ظهر مرة واحدة عند انقضاء الدهور . ليبطل الخطية بتضحيته نفسه . وكما انه موضوع للناس أن يموتوا مرة ثم بعد ذلك الدينونة . هكذا المسيح هو أيضاً قرب ذاته مرة لكى يرفع خطايا كثيرين . وأما المرة الثانية فسيظهر بغير خطية . خلاصاً للذين ينتظرونه . نعمة الله الآب ...

The Catholic Epistle - الكاثوليكون
Ⲕⲁⲑⲟⲗⲓⲕⲟⲛ Ⲡⲉⲛⲥⲁϩ Ⲡⲉⲧⲣⲟⲥ ⲁ̅ Ⲕⲉⲫ ⲇ̅ : ⲁ̅ - ⲓ̅ⲁ̅

1 Peter 4:1-11

Therefore, since Christ suffered for us in the flesh, arm yourselves also with the same mind, for he who has suffered in the flesh has ceased from sin, that he no longer should live the rest of his time in the flesh for the lusts of men, but for the will of God. For we have spent enough

Ⲡ̅ⲭ̅ⲥ̅ ⲟⲩⲛ ⲉ̀ⲧⲁϥϣⲉⲡⲙ̀ⲕⲁϩ ϧⲉⲛ ⲧ̀ⲥⲁⲣⲝ ⲉ̀ϩ̀ⲣⲏⲓ ⲉϫⲱⲛ : ⲟⲩⲟϩ ⲛ̀ⲑⲱⲧⲉⲛ ϩⲱⲧⲉⲛ ϧⲏⲕ ⲑⲏⲛⲟⲩ ⲙ̀ⲡⲁⲓⲥⲙⲟⲧ : ϫⲉ ⲫⲏⲉⲧⲁϥϭ̀ⲓ ⲙ̀ⲕⲁϩ ϧⲉⲛ ⲧ̀ⲥⲁⲣⲝ ⲁϥⲧⲁⲗϭⲟϥ ⲉ̀ⲃⲟⲗ ϩⲁ ⲫ̀ⲛⲟⲃⲓ : ⲉ̀ⲡ̀ϫⲓⲛⲧⲉϥϣ̀ⲧⲉⲙϣⲱⲡⲓ ϫⲉ ϧⲉⲛ ϩⲁⲛⲉⲡⲓⲑⲩⲙⲓⲁ ⲛ̀ⲣⲱⲙⲓ : ⲁⲗⲗⲁ ⲡ̀ⲥⲉⲡⲓ ⲛ̀ⲧⲉ ⲡⲉϥⲱⲛϧ ϧⲉⲛ ⲧ̀ⲥⲁⲣⲝ ⲛ̀ⲧⲉϥⲁⲓϥ ϧⲉⲛ ⲫ̀ⲟⲩⲱϣ ⲙ̀Ⲫϯ : ⲕⲏⲛ ⲅⲁⲣ ⲉ̀ⲣⲱⲧⲉⲛ

(بطرس الأولى 4 : 1 - 11)

فاذ قد تألم المسيح لأجلنا بالجسد فتسلحوا أنتم أيضاً بهذا المثال . لأن الذى قد تألم بالجسد فقد شفى نفسه من الخطية . لكى لا يكون بعد فى شهوات البشر . بل يقضى باقى حياته بالجسد بهوى الله . لأنه يكفيكم ذلك الزمان الذى

of our past lifetime in doing the will of the Gentiles—when we walked in lewdness, lusts, drunkenness, revelries, drinking parties, and abominable idolatries. In regard to these, they think it strange that you do not run with them in the same flood of dissipation, speaking evil of you. They will give an account to Him who is ready to judge the living and the dead. For this reason the gospel was preached also to those who are dead, that they might be judged according to men in the flesh, but live according to God in the spirit. But the end of all things is at hand; therefore be serious and watchful in your prayers. And above all things have fervent love for one another, for "LOVE WILL COVER A MULTITUDE OF SINS." Be hospitable to one another without grumbling. As each one has received a gift, minister it to one another, as good stewards of the manifold grace of God. If anyone speaks, let him speak as the oracles of God. If anyone ministers, let him do it as with the ability which God supplies, that in all things God may be glorified through Jesus Christ, to whom belong the glory and the dominion forever and ever. Amen.

Do not love the world, nor the things which are in the world.

عبر إذ كنتم تعملون بهوى الأمم . متسكعين فى الدعارة والشهوات وادمان الخمر بأنواع كثيرة . والبطر والمنادمات واللهو والدنس وعبادة الأوثان الأمر الذى فيه يستغربون إنكم لستم تركضون معهم إلى فيض هذه الخلاعة عينها لأنهم يجدفون . أولئك الذين سيعطون الجواب للمستعد أن يدين الأحياء والأموات . فإنه من أجل هذا قد بشر الأموات أيضاً كى يدانوا مثل الناس بالجسد . ويحيوا مثل الله بالروح . وانما نهاية كل شئ قد اقتربت . فتعقلوا واصحوا للصلوات . ولكن قبل كل شئ لتكن المحبة دائمة فيكم بعضكم لبعض لأن المحبة تغطى كثرة الخطايا . وكونوا محبين الضيافة بعضكم لبعض. غير متزمرين . كل واحد وواحد فبحسب النعمة التى أخذها تخدمون بها من تلقاء نفوسكم. كخدام صالحين لنعمة الله ذات الأنواع الكثيرة . ومن يتكلم فعلى حسب أقوال الله . ومن يخدم فعلى حسب القوة المهيأة من الله . لكى ما يتمجد الله فى كل شئ بيسوع المسيح . ذلك الذى له المجد والعز إلى أبد الأبدين آمين . لا تحبوا العالم.

The Praxis Response
(مـرد الابركسيس)

Hosanna in the highest: This is the King of Israel: Blessed is He, Who comes in the name: of the Lord of Hosts.

أوصاننا خين نى إنتشوسى : فاى بيه إبؤورو إمبى إسرائيل : إفسمارووؤوت إنجيه في إثنيوو خين إفران إمبشويس إنتيه نى جُم.

Ⲱⲥⲁⲛⲛⲁ ϧⲉⲛ ⲛⲏ ⲉⲧϭⲟⲥⲓ: ⲫⲁⲓ ⲡⲉ ⲡⲟⲩⲣⲟ ⲙⲡⲓⲥⲗ : ϥ̀ⲥⲙⲁⲣⲱⲟⲩⲧ ⲛ̀ϫⲉ ⲫⲏ ⲉⲑⲛⲏⲟⲩ ϧⲉⲛ ⲫⲣⲁⲛ ⲙ̀Ⲡⳓⲥ ⲛ̀ⲧⲉⲛⲓϫⲟⲙ.

اوصنا فى الأعالى هذا هو ملك إسرائيل مبارك الآتى باسم رب القوات

The Praxis - الابركسيس

Ⲡⲣⲁⲝⲓⲥ Ⲕⲉⲫ ⲕ̅ⲏ̅ : ⲓ̅ⲁ̅ - ⲗ̅ⲁ̅

Acts 28:11-31

After three months we sailed in an Alexandrian ship whose figurehead was the Twin Brothers, which had wintered at the island. And landing at Syracuse, we stayed three days. From there we circled round and reached Rhegium. And after one day the south wind blew; and the next day we came to Puteoli, where we found brethren, and were invited to stay with them seven days. And so we went toward Rome. And from there, when the brethren heard about us, they came to meet us as far as Appii Forum and Three Inns. When Paul saw them, he thanked God and took courage. Now when we came to Rome, the centurion delivered the prisoners to the captain of the guard; but Paul was permitted to dwell by himself with the soldier who guarded him. And it came to pass after three days that Paul called the leaders of the Jews together. So when they had come together, he said to them: "Men and brethren, though I have done nothing against our people or the customs of our fathers, yet I was delivered as a prisoner from Jerusalem into the hands of the Romans, who, when they had examined me, wanted to let me go, because there was no cause for putting me to death. But when the Jews spoke against it, I was compelled to appeal to Caesar, not that I had anything of which to accuse my nation. For this reason therefore I have called for you, to see you and speak with you, because for the hope of Israel I am bound with this chain." Then they said to him, "We neither received letters from Judea concerning you, nor have any of the brethren who

Ⲙⲉⲛⲉⲛⲥⲁ ϣⲟⲙⲧ ⲇⲉ ⲛ̀ⲁⲃⲟⲧ ⲁⲛ ⲓ̀ ϩⲓⲟⲩϫⲟⲓ ⲛ̀ⲧⲉ Ⲣⲁⲕⲟϯ : ⲉ̀ⲣⲉ ⲟⲩⲟⲛ ϩⲁⲛⲙⲏⲓⲛⲓ ϩⲓⲱⲧϥ ⲛ̀ⲧⲉ ϩⲁⲛⲆⲓⲟⲥⲕⲟⲣⲟⲥ : ⲉ̀ⲧⲁϥⲉⲣ ⲡⲁⲣⲁⲭⲓⲙⲁⲍⲓⲛ ϧⲉⲛ ϯⲛⲏⲥⲟⲥ : ⲟⲩⲟϩ ⲁⲛⲁⲙⲟⲛⲓ ⲉ̀Ⲥⲩⲣⲁⲕⲟⲩⲥⲁⲥ ⲁⲛϣⲱⲡⲓ ⲙ̀ⲙⲁⲩ ⲛ̀ϣⲟⲙⲧ ⲛ̀ⲉ̀ϩⲟⲟⲩ : ⲟⲩⲟϩ ⲉ̀ⲧⲁⲛ ⲓ̀ ⲉ̀ⲃⲟⲗ ⲙ̀ⲙⲁⲩ ⲁⲛⲉⲣⲕⲁⲧⲁⲛⲧⲁⲛ ⲉ̀Ⲣⲏⲅⲓⲱⲛ : ⲟⲩⲟϩ ⲙⲉⲛⲉⲛⲥⲁ ⲟⲩⲉ̀ϩⲟⲟⲩ ⲁϥⲙⲁϩⲓ ⲉ̀ϧⲟⲩⲛ ⲉ̀ϩⲣⲁⲛ ⲛ̀ϫⲉ ⲟⲩⲑⲟⲩⲣⲏⲥ ⲁⲛ ⲓ̀ ⲙ̀ⲡⲉⲛ̀ⲥⲛⲁⲩ ⲉ̀Ⲡⲟⲛⲧⲓⲗⲟⲩⲥ . Ⲟⲩⲟϩ ⲉ̀ⲧⲁⲛϫⲓⲙⲓ ⲛ̀ⲛⲓ̀ⲥⲛⲏⲟⲩ ⲙ̀ⲙⲁⲩ ⲁⲩⲑⲉⲧ ⲡⲉⲛϩⲏⲧ ⲉⲑⲣⲉⲛϣⲱⲡⲓ ϧⲁ ⲧⲟⲩⲧⲟⲩ ⲛ̀ϣⲁϣϥ ⲛ̀ⲉ̀ϩⲟⲟⲩ : ⲟⲩⲟϩ ⲡⲁⲓⲣⲏϯ ⲁⲛ ⲓ̀ ⲉ̀Ⲣⲱⲙⲏ .

Ⲉⲧⲁⲩⲥⲱⲧⲉⲙ ⲇⲉ ⲛ̀ϫⲉ ⲛⲓ̀ⲥⲛⲏⲟⲩ ⲉ̀ⲧⲉ ⲙ̀ⲙⲁⲩ ⲉⲑⲃⲏⲧⲉⲛ : ⲁⲩⲓ̀ ⲉ̀ⲃⲟⲗ ⲉ̀ϩⲣⲁⲛ ϣⲁ ⲉ̀ϩⲣⲏⲓ ⲉ̀Ⲁⲡⲡⲓⲟ̀ⲫⲟⲣⲟⲩ ⲛⲉⲙ ϣⲟⲙⲧ ⲛ̀ⲧⲁⲃⲉⲣⲛⲱⲛ : ⲉ̀ⲧⲁⲩⲛⲁⲩ ⲇⲉ ⲉ̀ⲣⲱⲟⲩ ⲛ̀ϫⲉ Ⲡⲁⲩⲗⲟⲥ ⲁϥϣⲉⲡ̀ϩⲙⲟⲧ ⲛ̀ⲧⲉⲛ Ⲫϯ ⲟⲩⲟϩ ⲁϥϭⲓ ⲛ̀ⲟⲩⲙⲉⲧϫⲁⲣϩⲏⲧ : ϩⲟⲧⲉ ⲇⲉ ⲉ̀ⲧⲁⲛϣⲉ ⲉ̀ϧⲟⲩⲛ ⲉ̀Ⲣⲱⲙⲏ : ⲁⲩⲟⲩⲁϩⲥⲁϩⲛⲓ ⲙ̀Ⲡⲁⲩⲗⲟⲥ ⲉⲑⲣⲉϥϣⲱⲡⲓ ⲙ̀ⲙⲁⲩⲁⲧϥ ⲛⲉⲙ ⲡⲓⲙⲁⲧⲟⲓ ⲉⲣⲁⲣⲉϩ ⲉ̀ⲣⲟϥ . Ⲁⲥϣⲱⲡⲓ ⲇⲉ ⲙⲉⲛⲉⲛⲥⲁ ϣⲟⲙⲧ ⲛ̀ⲉ̀ϩⲟⲟⲩ ⲁϥⲙⲟⲩϯ ⲉ̀ⲛⲓϩⲟⲩⲁϯ ⲛ̀ⲧⲉ Ⲛⲓⲟⲩⲇⲁⲓ ⲉⲧϣⲟⲡ ⲙ̀ⲙⲁⲩ : ⲉ̀ⲧⲁⲩⲓ̀ ⲇⲉ ⲉ̀ⲙⲁⲩ ⲛⲁϥϫⲱ ⲙ̀ⲙⲟⲥ ⲛⲱⲟⲩ : ⲁⲛⲟⲕ ⲛⲓⲣⲱⲙⲓ ⲛⲉⲛ̀ⲥⲛⲏⲟⲩ ⲙ̀ⲡⲓⲉⲣ ⲉ̀ϩⲗⲓ ⲉⲓϯ ⲉ̀ϧⲟⲩⲛ ⲉ̀ϩⲣⲁⲛ ⲙ̀ⲡⲓⲗⲁⲟⲥ : ⲓⲉ ⲛⲓⲥⲩⲛⲏⲑⲓⲁ ⲛ̀ⲧⲉ ⲛⲓⲓⲟϯ : ⲁⲩⲥⲟⲛϩⲧ ⲉ̀ⲃⲟⲗ ϧⲉⲛ Ⲓⲗⲏⲙ ⲁⲩⲧⲏⲓⲧ ⲉ̀ϧⲣⲏⲓ ⲉ̀ⲛⲉⲛϫⲓϫ ⲛ̀ⲛⲓⲣⲱⲙⲉⲟⲥ : ⲛⲏ ⲇⲉ ⲉ̀ⲧⲁⲩϧⲉⲧϧⲱⲧ ⲛⲁⲩⲟⲩⲱϣ ⲉ̀ⲭⲁⲧ ⲉ̀ⲃⲟⲗ ⲡⲉ ϫⲉ ⲙ̀ⲡⲓϫⲉ ⲉ̀ϩⲗⲓ ⲛ̀ⲉ̀ⲧⲓⲁ ⲛ̀ⲧⲉ ⲫ̀ⲙⲟⲩ ⲥ̀ϣⲟⲡ ⲛ̀ϧⲏⲧ : ⲉⲩⲉⲣⲁⲛⲧⲉⲗⲅⲓⲛ ⲇⲉ ⲛ̀ϫⲉ Ⲛⲓⲟⲩⲇⲁⲓ ⲁⲥⲉⲣⲁⲛⲁⲅⲕⲏ ⲉ̀ⲣⲟⲓ ⲉ̀ⲉⲣ ⲉ̀ⲡⲓⲕⲁⲗⲓⲥⲑⲉ ⲙ̀ⲡ̀ⲟⲩⲣⲟ : ⲙ̀ⲫ̀ⲣⲏϯ ⲁⲛ ϫⲉ ⲟⲩⲟⲛ ⲉ̀ϩⲗⲓ ⲛ̀ⲕⲁⲧⲏⲅⲟⲣⲓⲁ ⲙ̀ⲡⲁⲓ̀ϣⲗⲟⲗ . Ⲉⲑⲃⲉ ⲧⲁⲓⲗⲱⲓϫⲓ ⲟⲩⲛ ⲛⲁⲓⲧⲱⲃϩ ⲉ̀ⲛⲁⲩ ⲉ̀ⲣⲱⲧⲉⲛ ⲟⲩⲟϩ ⲉ̀ⲥⲁϫⲓ ⲛⲉⲙⲱⲧⲉⲛ : ⲉⲑⲃⲉ ⲧ̀ϩⲉⲗⲡⲓⲥ ⲅⲁⲣ ⲙ̀Ⲡⲓⲥ̅ⲗ̅ ϯⲥⲟⲛϩ ⲛ̀ⲧⲁⲓϩⲁⲗⲏⲥⲓⲥ : ⲛ̀ⲑⲱⲟⲩ ⲇⲉ ⲡⲉϫⲱⲟⲩ

الابركسيس 28 : 11 -31

وبعد ثلاثة أشهر اقلعنا فى سفينة اسكندرية . وكان عليها علامة الجوزاء وكانت قد شتت فى الجزيرة. ورسونا على سيراكوسا فمكثنا هناك ثلاثة أيام . ولما خرجنا من هناك درنا إلى ريغيون ومن بعد يوم واحد هبت علينا ريح الجنوب . وفى اليوم الثانى جئنا إلى بونطيلوس . ووجدنا هناك الأخوة فطيبوا قلبنا لكى نقيم عندهم سبعة أيام وهكذا جئنا إلى رومية . فلما سمع الأخوة الذين هناك بخبرنا خرجوا لاستقبالنا إلى أبيوفوروا وإلى الثلثة الحوانيت فلما رآهم بولس شكر الله وتشجع . ولما دخلنا رومية أمر بولس أن يكون وحده مع الجندى الذى كان يحرسه . ولما كان بعد ثلاثة أيام استدعى بولس وجهاء اليهود الساكنين هناك. فلما جاءوا جعل يقول لهم أيها الرجال اخوتنا . أنا لم اصنع شيئاً أناصب به الشعب أو عوائد الآباء . قُيدتْ من أورشليم وأُسلمتْ إلى أيدى الروم . هؤلاء لما فحصوا أرادوا أن يطلقونى لأنهم لم يجدوا فىَّ شيئاً يكون موجباً للموت . وفيما كان اليهود يقاومون الخطاب اضطرنى الأمر أن أستغيث بالملك . ليس كأننى أصنع شيئاً يوجب القذف على هذه الأمة فمن أجل هذه العلة كنت أطلب أن أراكم وأن أتكلم معكم . لأنى من أجل

came reported or spoken any evil of you. But we desire to hear from you what you think; for concerning this sect, we know that it is spoken against everywhere." So when they had appointed him a day, many came to him at his lodging, to whom he explained and solemnly testified of the kingdom of God, persuading them concerning Jesus from both the Law of Moses and the Prophets, from morning till evening. And some were persuaded by the things which were spoken, and some disbelieved. So when they did not agree among themselves, they departed after Paul had said one word: "The Holy Spirit spoke rightly through Isaiah the prophet to our fathers, saying, 'GO TO THIS PEOPLE AND SAY: "HEARING YOU WILL HEAR, AND SHALL NOT UNDERSTAND; AND SEEING YOU WILL SEE, AND NOT PERCEIVE; FOR THE HEARTS OF THIS PEOPLE HAVE GROWN DULL. THEIR EARS ARE HARD OF HEARING, AND THEIR EYES THEY HAVE CLOSED, LEST THEY SHOULD SEE WITH THEIR EYES AND HEAR WITH THEIR EARS, LEST THEY SHOULD UNDERSTAND WITH THEIR HEARTS AND TURN, SO THAT I SHOULD HEAL THEM." ' "Therefore let it be known to you that the salvation of God has been sent to the Gentiles, and they will hear it!" And when he had said these words, the Jews departed and had a great dispute among themselves. Then Paul dwelt two whole years in his own rented house, and received all who came to him, preaching the kingdom of God and teaching the things which concern the Lord Jesus Christ with all confidence, no one forbidding him. The word of the Lord shall grow, multiply, be mighty and be confirmed in the holy church of God. Amen

ⲛⲁϥ ϫⲉ ⲁⲛⲟⲛ ⲟⲩ Ⲇⲉ ⲙⲡⲉⲛϭⲁⲓ ⲓ ⲛⲁⲛ ⲉⲃⲟⲗ ϧⲉⲛ ϯⲓⲟⲩⲇⲉⲁ ⲉⲑⲃⲏⲧⲕ : ⲟⲩⲇⲉ ⲙⲡⲉϥⲓ ⲛϫⲉ ⲟⲩⲁⲓ ⲉⲃⲟⲗ ϧⲉⲛ ⲛⲓⲥⲛⲏⲟⲩ ⲛⲧⲉϥⲧⲁⲙⲟⲛ ⲓⲉ ⲛⲧⲉϥϫⲉ ⲟⲩⲥⲱⲃ ⲉϥϩⲱⲟⲩ ϧⲁⲣⲟⲕ : ⲧⲉⲛⲉⲣⲁⲝⲓⲟⲓⲛ Ⲇⲉ ⲉⲥⲱⲧⲉⲙ ⲉⲃⲟⲗ ϩⲓⲧⲟⲧⲕ ⲛⲛⲉⲧⲉⲛⲙⲉⲩⲓ ⲉⲣⲱⲟⲩ : ⲉⲑⲃⲉ ⲧⲁⲓϩⲉⲣⲉⲥⲓⲥ ⲅⲁⲣ ⲡⲓϩⲱⲃ ⲟⲩⲱⲛϩ ⲉⲣⲟⲛ ϫⲉ ⲥⲉⲉⲣⲁⲛⲧⲓⲗⲉⲅⲓⲛ ⲉⲑⲃⲏⲧⲥ ϧⲉⲛ ⲙⲁⲓ ⲛⲓⲃⲉⲛ . Ⲁⲩϯⲛⲉⲓ ⲉϯⲉ̀ϩⲉⲛⲓⲁ ⲉⲩⲉⲣ ⲟⲩⲱ̀ϣ ⲟⲩⲟϩ ⲛⲁϥⲥⲁϫⲓ ϧⲁⲧⲟⲧⲟⲩ ⲉϥⲉⲣ ⲙⲉⲑⲣⲉ ⲛⲱⲟⲩ ⲉⲑⲃⲉ ϯⲙⲉⲧⲟⲩⲣⲟ ⲛ̀ⲧⲉ Ⲫϯ ⲉϥϩⲱⲧ ⲙⲡⲟⲩϩⲏⲧ ⲉⲑⲃⲉ Ⲓⲏⲥ ⲉⲃⲟⲗ ϧⲉⲛ ⲫⲛⲟⲙⲟⲥ ⲙ̀Ⲙⲱⲥⲏⲥ ⲛⲉⲙ ⲛⲓⲡⲣⲟⲫⲏⲧⲏⲥ ⲓⲥϫⲉⲛ ϣⲱⲣⲡ ϣⲁ ⲣⲟⲩϩⲓ : ⲟⲩⲟϩ ϩⲁⲛⲟⲩⲟⲛ ⲙⲉⲛ Ⲇⲛⲁⲣⲉ ⲡⲟⲩϩⲏⲧ ⲑⲏⲧ ⲛⲉⲙ ⲛⲏ ⲉⲧⲁϥϫⲱ ⲙ̀ⲙⲱⲟⲩ ϩⲁⲛⲕⲉⲭⲱⲟⲩⲛⲓ Ⲇⲉ ⲛⲁⲟⲓ ⲛⲁⲑⲛⲁϩϯ . Ⲉⲩⲟⲓ Ⲇⲉ ⲛⲁⲧϯⲙⲁϯ ⲛⲉⲙ ⲛⲟⲩⲉⲣⲏⲟⲩ : ⲁϥⲭⲁⲩ ⲉⲃⲟⲗ ⲉϥϫⲱ ⲛⲟⲩⲥⲁϫⲓ ⲛⲱⲟⲩ ⲛϫⲉ Ⲡⲁⲩⲗⲟⲥ ϫⲉ ⲕⲁⲗⲱⲥ ⲁ ⲡⲓⲡ̅ⲛ̅ⲁ̅ ⲉⲑⲟⲩⲁⲃ ⲥⲁϫⲓ ⲉⲃⲟⲗ ϩⲓⲧⲟⲧϥ ⲛ̀Ⲏⲥⲁⲏⲁⲥ ⲡⲓⲡⲣⲟⲫⲏⲧⲏⲥ ⲛⲉⲙ ⲛⲉⲧⲉⲛⲓⲟϯ ⲉϥϫⲱ ⲙ̀ⲙⲟⲥ . Ϫⲉ ⲙⲟϣⲓ ϣⲁ ⲡⲁⲓⲗⲁⲟⲥ ⲁϫⲟⲥ ⲛⲱⲟⲩ : ϫⲉ ϧⲉⲛ ⲟⲩⲥⲙⲏ ⲉⲣⲉⲧⲉⲛⲉⲥⲱⲧⲉⲙ ⲟⲩⲟϩ ⲛ̀ⲛⲉⲧⲉⲛⲕⲁϯ : ⲟⲩⲟϩ ϧⲉⲛ ⲟⲩⲛⲁⲩ ⲉⲣⲉⲧⲉⲛⲉⲛⲁⲩ ⲟⲩⲟϩ ⲛ̀ⲛⲉⲧⲉⲛⲛⲁⲩ : ⲁϥⲟⲩⲙⲟⲧ ⲅⲁⲣ ⲛϫⲉ ⲡϩⲏⲧ ⲙⲡⲁⲓⲗⲁⲟⲥ ⲟⲩⲟϩ ⲁⲩⲉⲣϣ ⲉ̀ⲡⲥⲱⲧⲉⲙ ϧⲉⲛ ⲛⲟⲩⲙⲁϣϫ ⲟⲩⲟϩ ⲁⲩⲙⲁϣⲑⲁⲙ ⲛ̀ⲛⲟⲩⲃⲁⲗ : ⲙⲏ ⲡⲱⲥ ⲛ̀ⲥⲉⲛⲁⲩ ⲛ̀ⲛⲟⲩⲃⲁⲗ ⲟⲩⲟϩ ⲛ̀ⲥⲉⲥⲱⲧⲉⲙ ϧⲉⲛ ⲛⲟⲩⲙⲁϣϫ ⲟⲩⲟϩ ⲛ̀ⲥⲉⲕⲁϯ ϧⲉⲛ ⲡⲟⲩϩⲏⲧ ⲟⲩⲟϩ ⲛ̀ⲥⲉⲕⲟⲧⲟⲩ ⲛ̀ⲧⲁⲧⲟⲩⲭⲱⲟⲩ . Ⲙⲁⲣⲉ ⲡⲓϩⲱⲃ ⲟⲩⲛ ⲟⲩⲱⲛϩ ⲉⲣⲱⲧⲉⲛ ϫⲉ   ⲁ Ⲫϯ ⲧⲁⲟⲩⲟ̀ ⲙⲡⲉϥⲥⲱⲧⲏⲣ ⲉⲛⲓⲉⲑⲛⲟⲥ ⲟⲩⲟϩ ⲛ̀ⲑⲱⲟⲩ ⲟⲛ ⲉⲑⲛⲁⲥⲱⲧⲉⲙ : ⲁϥϣⲱⲡⲓ Ⲇⲉ ⲛϫⲉ Ⲡⲁⲩⲗⲟⲥ ⲛ̀ⲣⲟⲙⲡⲓ ⲥⲛⲟⲩϯ ⲧⲏⲣⲟⲩ ϧⲉⲛ ⲡⲓⲙⲁ ⲉⲧⲁϥϭⲓⲧϥ ⲉϥⲟⲧⲉϩ ⲙⲡⲉϥϣⲃⲟⲣ ⲙ̀ⲙⲓⲛ ⲙ̀ⲙⲟϥ : ⲟⲩⲟϩ ⲛⲁϥϣⲟⲡ ⲟⲩⲟⲛ ⲛⲓⲃⲉⲛ ⲉⲑⲛⲏⲟⲩ ⲉ̀ϧⲟⲩⲛ ϣⲁⲣⲟϥ : ⲉϥϩⲓⲱⲓϣ ⲛ̀ⲧⲙⲉⲧⲟⲩⲣⲟ ⲛ̀ⲧⲉ Ⲫϯ : ⲟⲩⲟϩ ⲉϥϯⲥⲃⲱ ϧⲉⲛ ⲟⲩⲱⲛϩ ⲉⲃⲟⲗ ⲛⲟⲩⲟⲛ ⲛⲓⲃⲉⲛ ⲉⲑⲃⲉ Ⲡ̅ⲟ̅ⲥ̅ Ⲓⲏⲥ Ⲡⲭ̅ⲥ̅ ⲟⲩⲟϩ ⲙ̀ⲙⲟⲛ ϩ̀ⲗⲓ ϣⲱϣⲧ ⲙ̀ⲙⲟϥ ⲡⲉ . Ⲡⲓⲥⲁϫⲓ .□

رجاء إسرائيل أنا موثق بهذه السلسلة . أما هم فقالوا له نحن لم يأتنا من اليهود كتابات لأجلك . ولم يقدم أحد من الأخوة فعرفنا أو قال عنك شيئاً رديئاً . ونحن نرغب أن نسمع منك تلك التى نحن فيها مفكرون لأن من أجل هذا الخلاف الأمر ظاهر لنا فى كل مكان يناصبون لأجله . فعينوا له يوماً فجاء إليه كثيرون إلى المنزل فجعل يقص عليهم ويشهد لهم لأجل ملكوت الله. ويقنع قلبهم لأجل يسوع من ناموس موسى والأنبياء من الصباح إلى المساء . فكان قوم منهم مقتنعين بما قيل وآخرون لم يؤمنوا فانصرفوا وهم غير متفقين بعضهم مع بعض . لما قال لهم بولس كلمة انه حسناً تكلم الروح القدس من قبل اشعياء النبى مع آبائكم قائلاً: انطلق إلى هذا الشعب وقل لهم سماعاً تسمعون ولا تفهمون. ونظراً تنظرون ولا تبصرون . لأن قلب هذا الشعب قد غلظ وثقلت إذانهم عن السماع . وطمسوا عيونهم لئلا يبصروا بعيونهم ويسمعوا بآذانهم . يفهموا بقلوبهم ويعودوا فاشفيهم . فليكن معلوماً عندكم . ان الله أرسل خلاصه إلى الأمم وهم أيضاً يطيعونه وأقام بولس سنتين كاملتين فى محل استأجره لنفسه . وكان يقبل كل من يدخل إليه كارزاً بملكوت الله . ويعلم بكل مجاهرة من أجل الرب يسوع المسيح ولم يكن أحد يمنعه . لم تزل كلمة الرب تنمو وتزداد فى هذه البيعة وكل بيعة ...

Ⲉⲩⲗⲟⲅⲓⲙⲉⲛⲟⲥ - لحن الشعانين

English	Arabic transliteration	Coptic	Arabic
Blessed is He, Who comes: in the name of the Lord: again, in the name of the Lord.	أيفلوجيمينوس أوإرخو مينوس إن أونوماتى كيريوو بالين إن أونوماتى كيريوو .	Ⲉⲩⲗⲟⲅⲓⲙⲉⲛⲟⲥ ⲟ̀ⲉⲣⲭⲟⲙⲉⲛⲟⲥ ⲉ̀ⲛⲟ̀ⲛⲟⲙⲁⲧⲓ ⲕⲩⲣⲓⲟⲩ ⲡⲁⲗⲓⲛ ⲉ̀ⲛⲟ̀ⲛⲟⲙⲁⲧⲓ ⲕⲩⲣⲓⲟⲩ .	مبارك الآتى باسم الرب . وأيضاً باسم الرب .
Hosanna to the Son of David: again, to the Son of David.	أوصاننا طو إيو دافيد . بالين طو إيو دافيد .	Ⲱⲥⲁⲛⲛⲁ ⲧⲱ ⲩ̀ⲓⲱ Ⲇⲁⲩⲓⲇ. ⲡⲁⲗⲓⲛ ⲧⲱ ⲩ̀ⲓⲱ Ⲇⲁⲩⲓⲇ .	اوصنا لإبن داود وأيضاً لإبن داود .
Hosanna in the highest: again, in the highest.	أوصاننا إنتيسيبسيستيس بالين إنتسيبسيستيس .	Ⲱⲥⲁⲛⲛⲁ ⲉⲛⲧⲓⲥⲩ̀ⲯⲓⲥⲧⲓⲥ ⲡⲁⲗⲓⲛ ⲉⲛⲧⲓⲥⲩ̀ⲯⲓⲥⲧⲓⲥ.	اوصنا فى الأعالى وأيضاً فى الأعالى .
Hosanna, to the King of Israel: again, to the King of Israel.	أوصاننا فاسيليطو إسرائيل . بالين فاسيليطو إسرائيل .	Ⲱⲥⲁⲛⲛⲁ ⲃⲁⲥⲓⲗⲓⲧⲟⲩ Ⲓⲥⲣⲁⲏⲗ ⲡⲁⲗⲓⲛ ⲃⲁⲥⲓⲗⲓⲧⲟⲩ Ⲓⲥⲣⲁⲏⲗ .	اوصنا ملك إسرائيل وأيضاً ملك إسرائيل .
Let us chant saying: Alleluia. Alleluia. Alleluia. Glory be to our God: again, Glory be to our God.	تين إيربصالين إنجو إمموس . ألليلويا. ألليلويا . ألليلويا بى أوأوو فا بين نووتى بيه . بالين بأوأوو فا بين نووتى بيه .	Ⲧⲉⲛⲉⲣⲯⲁⲗⲓⲛ ⲉⲛⲭⲱ ⲙ̀ⲙⲟⲥ Ⲁⲗ . Ⲁⲗ . Ⲁⲗ . ⲡⲓⲱ̀ⲟⲩ ⲫⲁ ⲡⲉⲛⲛⲟⲩϯ ⲡⲉ . ⲡⲁⲗⲓⲛ ⲡⲓⲱ̀ⲟⲩ ⲫⲁ ⲡⲉⲛⲛⲟⲩϯ ⲡⲉ .	فلنرتل قائلين : هلليويا هلليويا هلليويا المجد هو لإلهنا وأيضاً المجد هو لإلهنا

Then these verses - ويرتلون هذه الأرباع

English	Arabic transliteration	Coptic	Arabic
He who sits upon the cherubim / riding on a colt / entered into Jerusalem / what is this great humility!	فيى إتهمسى هيجين ننشيروبيم : أفطاليووت إ أوو إ أو : أفشيه إيخون إيروساليم أوو بيه باى نيشتى إنثيبيو .	Ⲫⲏⲉⲧϩⲉⲙⲥⲓ ϩⲓϫⲉⲛ ⲛⲓⲭⲉⲣⲟⲩⲃⲓⲙ: ⲁϥⲧⲁⲗⲏⲟⲩⲧ ⲉⲟⲩⲉ̀ⲱ̀ : ⲁϥϣⲉ ⲉ̀ϧⲟⲩⲛ ⲉ̀Ⲓⲗⲏⲙⲟⲩ ⲡⲉ ⲡⲁⲓⲛⲓϣϯ ⲛ̀ⲑⲉⲃⲓⲟ .	الجالس على الشاروبيم ركب أتان ودخل أورشليم يا لهذا التواضع العظيم .
They praise Him with alertness: saying, "This is Immanuel: Hosanna in the Highest: this is the King of Israel."	سى هوس إروف خين أونيهسى أفجيه فاى بيه إممانوئيل : أوصاننا خين نى أنتشوسى : فاى بيه إبؤرو إمبى سرائيل .	Ⲥⲉϩⲱⲥ ⲉ̀ⲣⲟϥ ϧⲉⲛ ⲟⲩⲛⲉϩⲥⲓ : ⲁϥϫⲉ ⲫⲁⲓ ⲡⲉ Ⲉⲙⲙⲁⲛⲟⲩⲏⲗ : ⲱ̀ⲥⲁⲛⲛⲁ ϧⲉⲛ ⲛⲏⲉⲧϭⲟⲥⲓ : ⲫⲁⲓ ⲡⲉ ⲡ̀ⲟⲩⲣⲟ ⲙ̀ⲡⲓⲥⲗ .	يسبحونه بتيقظ قائلين هذا هو عمانوئيل أوصنا فى الأعالى هذا هو ملك إسرائيل .
Let us say with David the chanter, "Blessed is He who comes, in the name of the Good Lord, from now and till the end of the times."	مارين جوس نيم دافيد بيهمنوطوس : جيه إفسماروؤوت إنجيه فى إثنيو : خين إفران إمبتشويس بى أغاثوس : إسجين تينوو شا إتخائه إننى سيوو .	Ⲙⲁⲣⲉⲛϫⲟⲥ ⲛⲉⲙ Ⲇⲁⲩⲓⲇ ⲡⲓⲥⲩⲙⲛⲟⲧⲟⲥ : ϫⲉ ϥ̀ⲥⲙⲁⲣⲱⲟⲩⲧ ⲛ̀ϫⲉ ⲫⲏ ⲉⲑⲛⲏⲟⲩ : ϧⲉⲛ ⲫ̀ⲣⲁⲛ ⲙ̀Ⲡ̄ⲟ̄ⲥ̄ ⲡⲓⲁ̀ⲅⲁⲑⲟⲥ : ⲓⲥϫⲉⲛ ϯⲛⲟⲩ ϣⲁ ⲧ̀ϧⲁⲉ ⲛ̀ⲛⲓⲥⲏⲟⲩ .	فنقل مع داود المرتل مبارك الآتى باسم الرب الصالح منذ الآن وإلى آخر الأزمنة .

+ Ⲛⲓⲭⲉⲣⲟⲩⲃⲓⲙ is said till the end, followed by; | + وبعد ذلك تقال نى شروبيم إلى الختام .

+ Ⲁ̅ⲅⲓⲟⲥ ⲟ̀Ⲑⲉⲟⲥ and the litany of the Gospel.

+ The Psalm is chanted. Ⲙⲁⲣⲟⲩⲃⲁⲥϥ is said if the Patriarch or the Bishop is attending. The first three Gospels are read then the priest prays the litany of the Gospel for the fourth Gospel. Each Gospel has its own response.

+ الثلاثة تقديسات و أوشية الانجيل

+ ثم يرتل المزمور وتقال Ⲙⲁⲣⲟⲩⲃⲁⲥϥ إذا كان الأب البطريرك أو الأسقف حاضراً وتقرأ الثلاثة أناجيل الأولى . ثم يقول الكاهن أوشية الانجيل للانجيل الرابع . ثم يقرأ الانجيل الرابع ولكل انجيل مرده .

The Psalm
Ⲯⲁⲗⲙⲟⲥ ⲡ̅ : ⲅ̅ ⲛⲉⲙ ⲁ̅ , ⲃ̅

Psalms 80:3, 1, 2

Blow the trumpet at the new moon, in the glorious day of your feast. Rejoice in God our helper; shout aloud to the God of Jacob. Take a psalm, and produce the timbrel, the pleasant psaltery with the harp.
Alleluia.

Ⲁ̀ⲣⲓⲥⲁⲗⲡⲓⲍⲓⲛ ϧⲉⲛ ⲟⲩⲥⲟⲩⲁⲓ ϧⲉⲛ ⲟⲩⲥⲁⲗⲡⲓⲅⲅⲟⲥ : ϧⲉⲛ ⲟⲩⲉ̀ϩⲟⲟⲩ ⲙ̄ⲙⲏⲛⲓ ⲛ̀ⲧⲉ ⲛⲉⲧⲉⲛϣⲁⲓ : (ⲗⲉⲝⲓⲥ)

Ⲑⲉⲗⲏⲗ ⲙ̄Ⲫ̄ϯ ⲡⲉⲛⲃⲟⲏⲑⲟⲥ ⲉ̀ϣⲗⲏⲗⲟⲩⲓ ⲉ̀ⲃⲟⲗ ⲙ̄Ⲫ̄ϯ ⲛ̄Ⲓⲁⲕⲱⲃ : ϭⲓ ⲛ̀ⲟⲩⲯⲁⲗⲧⲏⲣⲓⲟⲛ ⲟⲩⲟϩ ⲙⲟⲓ ⲛ̀ⲟⲩⲕⲉⲙⲕⲉⲙ ⲟⲩⲯⲁⲗⲧⲏⲣⲓⲟⲛ ⲉⲛⲉⲥⲱϥ ⲛⲉⲙ ⲕⲩⲑⲁⲣⲁ . ⲁⲗ .

أريصالبيزين خين أوو صوواى خين أوو صالبينغوس : خين أوو إيهوؤو إممينى إنتيه نيتين شاى :

ثيليل إمفنوتى بين فوثثوس إى إشليلوى إيفول إمفنوتى إنياكوب تشى إنؤو بصالتيريون أووه موى إن أووكيم كيم أوو بصالتيريون إنيصوف نيم كيثارا . اللليا .

(مز 80 : 1 - 3)

بوقوا فى رأس الشهر بالبوق . فى يوم عيدكم المشهور . ابتهجوا بالله معيننا . هللوا لاله يعقوب . خذوا مزماراً واضربوا دفاً . مزماراً مطرباً مع قيثار . الليلويا .

The First Gospel - الانجيل الأول
Ⲉⲩⲁⲅⲅⲉⲗⲓⲟⲛ Ⲕⲁⲧⲁ Ⲙⲁⲧⲑⲉⲟⲛ Ⲕⲉⲫ ⲕ̅ⲁ̅ : ⲁ̅ - ⲓ̅ⲍ̅

Matthew 21:1-17

Now when they drew near Jerusalem, and came to Bethphage, at the Mount of Olives, then Jesus sent two disciples, saying to them, "Go into the village opposite you, and immediately you will find a donkey tied, and a colt with her. Loose them and bring them to Me. And if anyone says anything to you, you shall say, 'The Lord has need of them,' and immediately he will send them." All this was done that it might be fulfilled which was spoken by the prophet, saying: "TELL THE DAUGHTER OF ZION, 'BEHOLD, YOUR KING IS COMING TO YOU, LOWLY, AND SITTING ON A DONKEY, A COLT, THE FOAL OF A DONKEY.' " So the disciples went and did as Jesus commanded them. They brought the donkey and the colt, laid their clothes on them, and set Him on

Ⲟⲩⲟϩ, ϩⲟⲧⲉ ⲉⲧⲁⲩϧⲱⲛⲧ ⲉ̀Ⲓⲗⲏ̄ⲙ ⲁⲩⲓ̀ ⲉⲃⲏⲑⲫⲁⲅⲏ ϧⲁⲧⲉⲛ ⲡⲓⲧⲱⲟⲩ ⲛ̀ⲧⲉ ⲛⲓϫⲱⲓⲧ : ⲧⲟⲧⲉ ⲁ Ⲓⲏ̄ⲥ Ⲟⲩⲱⲣⲡ ⲙ̀ⲙⲁⲑⲏⲧⲏⲥ ⲥⲛⲁⲩ : ⲉϥϫⲱ ⲙ̀ⲙⲟⲥ ⲛⲱⲟⲩ ϫⲉ ⲙⲁϣⲉⲛⲱⲧⲉⲛ ⲉ̀ⲡⲁⲓϯⲙⲓ ⲉⲧⲭⲏ ⲙ̀ⲡⲉⲧⲉⲛⲙ̀ⲑⲟ ⲟⲩⲟϩ ⲉⲣⲉⲧⲉⲛⲉ̀ϫⲓⲙⲓ ⲛ̀ⲟⲩⲉ̀ⲱ ⲉⲥⲥⲟⲛϩ ⲛⲉⲙ ⲟⲩⲥⲏϫ ⲛⲉⲙⲁⲥ ⲃⲱⲗⲟⲩ ⲁ̀ⲛⲓⲧⲟⲩ ⲛⲏⲓ : ⲁⲣⲉϣⲁⲛ ⲟⲩⲁⲓ ⲇⲉ ⲥⲁϫⲓ ⲛⲉⲙⲱⲧⲉⲛ ⲁϫⲟⲥ ϫⲉ ⲡ⳪ ⲡⲉⲧⲉⲣⲭⲣⲓⲁ ⲙ̀ⲙⲱⲟⲩ ϥⲛⲁⲟⲩⲟⲣⲡⲟⲩ ⲇⲉ ⲥⲁⲧⲟⲧϥ . Ⲫⲁⲓ ⲇⲉ ⲁϥϣⲱⲡⲓ ϩⲓⲛⲁ ⲛ̀ⲧⲉϥϫⲱⲕ ⲉ̀ⲃⲟⲗ ⲛ̀ϫⲉ ⲫⲛⲉⲧⲁϥϫⲟϥ ⲉ̀ⲃⲟⲗ ϩⲓⲧⲟⲧϥ ⲙ̀ⲡⲓⲡⲣⲟⲫⲏⲧⲏⲥ ⲉϥϫⲱ ⲙ̀ⲙⲟⲥ : ϫⲉ ⲁϫⲟⲥ ⲛ̀ⲧϣⲉⲣⲓ ⲛ̀Ⲥⲓⲱⲛ ϫⲉ ϩⲏⲡⲡⲉ ⲓⲥ ⲡⲉⲟⲩⲣⲟ ϥⲛⲏⲟⲩ ⲛⲉ ⲉ̀ⲟⲩⲣⲉⲙⲣⲁⲩϣ ⲡⲉ ⲉϥⲧⲁⲗⲏⲟⲩⲧ ⲉⲟⲩⲉ̀ⲱ ⲛⲉⲙ ⲟⲩⲥⲏϫ ⲡ̀ϣⲏⲣⲓ ⲛ̀ⲟⲩⲉ̀ⲱ : ⲉⲧⲁⲩϣⲉⲛⲱⲟⲩ ⲇⲉ ⲛ̀ϫⲉ ⲛⲓⲙⲁⲑⲏⲧⲏⲥ ⲟⲩⲟϩ ⲉⲧⲁⲩⲓⲣⲓ ⲕⲁⲧⲁ ⲫ̀ⲣⲏϯ ⲉⲧⲁ Ⲓⲏ̄ⲥ ⲟⲩⲁϩ ⲥⲁϩⲛⲓ ⲛⲱⲟⲩ . Ⲁ̀ⲩⲓⲛⲓ ⲛ̀ⲧⲉ̀ⲱ ⲛⲉⲙ ⲡⲓⲥⲏϫ ⲟⲩⲟϩ ⲁⲩⲧⲁⲗⲟ ⲛ̀ⲛⲟⲩϩⲃⲱⲥ ⲉ̀ⲣⲱⲟⲩ ⲟⲩⲟϩ ⲁⲩⲑⲣⲉϥϩⲉⲙⲥⲓ ⲥⲁⲡϣⲱⲓ ⲙ̀ⲙⲱⲟⲩ : ⲡ̀ϩⲟⲩⲟ ⲇⲉ ⲛ̀ⲛⲓⲙⲏϣ

ولما قربوا من أورشليم وجاءوا إلى بيت فاجى عند جبل الزيتون حينئذ بعث يسوع أثنين من تلاميذه . قائلاً لهما : اذهبا إلى هذه القرية التى أمامكما فستجدان أتاناً مربوطة وجحشاً معها فحلاهما وأتيانى بهما . وان قال لكما أحد شيئاً . فقولا ان الرب محتاج إليهما . فللوقت يرسلهما . فكان هذا كله لكى يتم ما قيل بالنبى القائل: قولوا لابنة صهيون هوذا ملكك يأتيك وديعاً راكباً على أتان وجحش إبن أتان . فلما ذهبا التلميذان وصنعا كما أمرهما يسوع . وأتيا بالاتان والجحش ووضعا عليهما ثيابهما وجلس

them. And a very great multitude spread their clothes on the road; others cut down branches from the trees and spread them on the road. Then the multitudes who went before and those who followed cried out, saying: "Hosanna to the Son of David! 'BLESSED IS HE WHO COMES IN THE NAME OF THE LORD!' Hosanna in the highest!" And when He had come into Jerusalem, all the city was moved, saying, "Who is this?" So the multitudes said, "This is Jesus, the prophet from Nazareth of Galilee." Then Jesus went into the temple of God and drove out all those who bought and sold in the temple, and overturned the tables of the money changers and the seats of those who sold doves. And He said to them, "It is written, 'MY HOUSE SHALL BE CALLED A HOUSE OF PRAYER,' but you have made it a 'DEN OF THIEVES.'" Then the blind and the lame came to Him in the temple, and He healed them. But when the chief priests and scribes saw the wonderful things that He did, and the children crying out in the temple and saying, "Hosanna to the Son of David!" they were indignant and said to Him, "Do You hear what these are saying?" And Jesus said to them, "Yes. Have you never read, 'OUT OF THE MOUTH OF BABES AND NURSING INFANTS YOU HAVE PERFECTED PRAISE'?" Then He left them and went out of the city to Bethany, and He lodged there. Glory be to God forever, Amen.

ⲁϥⲫⲱⲣϣ ⲛ̀ⲛⲟⲩϩⲃⲱⲥ ϩⲓ ⲡⲓⲙⲱⲓⲧ ϩⲁⲛⲕⲉⲭⲱⲟⲩⲛⲓ ⲇⲉ ⲁⲩⲕⲱⲣϫ ⲛ̀ϩⲁⲛⲕⲗⲁⲇ ⲉⲃⲟⲗ ϩⲓ ⲛⲓϣϣⲏⲛ ⲟⲩⲟϩ ⲁⲩⲫⲱⲣϣⲟⲩ ϩⲓ ⲡⲓⲙⲱⲓⲧ : ⲛⲓⲙⲏϣ ⲇⲉ ⲉ̀ⲛⲁⲩⲙⲟϣⲓ ϧⲁϫⲱϥ ⲛⲉⲙ ⲛ̀ⲏⲉⲛⲁⲩⲙⲟϣⲓ ⲛ̀ⲥⲱϥ ⲛⲁⲩⲱϣ ⲉ̀ⲃⲟⲗ ⲉⲩϫⲉ ⲙ̀ⲙⲟⲥ ϫⲉ ⲱ̀ⲥⲁⲛⲛⲁ ⲡ̀ϣⲏⲣⲓ ⲛ̀ⲇⲁⲩⲓⲇ ϥ̀ⲥⲙⲁⲣⲱⲟⲩⲧ ⲛ̀ϫⲉ ⲫⲏⲉⲑⲛⲏⲟⲩ ϧⲉⲛ ⲫ̀ⲣⲁⲛ ⲙ̀ⲡⲟ̅ⲥ̅ ⲱ̀ⲥⲁⲛⲛⲁ ϧⲉⲛ ⲛⲏⲉⲧϭⲟⲥⲓ . Ⲟⲩⲟϩ ⲉⲧⲁϥⲓ̀ ⲉ̀ϧⲟⲩⲛ ⲉ̀Ⲓⲗⲏⲙ ⲁⲥⲙⲟⲛⲙⲉⲛ ⲛ̀ϫⲉ ϯⲃⲁⲕⲓ ⲧⲏⲣⲥ ⲉⲩϫⲱ ⲙ̀ⲙⲟⲥ ϫⲉ ⲛⲓⲙ ⲡⲉ ⲫⲁⲓ : ⲛⲓⲙⲏϣ ⲇⲉ ⲛⲁⲩϫⲱ ⲙ̀ⲙⲟⲥ ϫⲉ ⲫⲁⲓ ⲡⲉ ⲡⲓⲡ̀ⲣⲟⲫⲏⲧⲏⲥ Ⲓⲏ̅ⲥ̅ ⲡⲓⲣⲉⲙⲛⲁⲍⲁⲣⲉⲑ ⲛ̀ⲧⲉ ϯⲅⲁⲗⲓⲗⲉⲁ : ⲟⲩⲟϩ ⲁϥϣⲉⲛⲁϥ ⲛ̀ϫⲉ ⲉ̀ϧⲟⲩⲛ ⲉ̀ⲡⲓⲉⲣⲫⲉⲓ ⲟⲩⲟϩ ⲁϥϩⲓⲟⲩⲓ ⲉ̀ⲃⲟⲗ ⲛ̀ⲟⲩⲟⲛ ⲛⲓⲃⲉⲛ ⲉⲧ ϯ ⲉ̀ⲃⲟⲗ ϧⲉⲛ ⲡⲓⲉⲣⲫⲉⲓ ⲛⲉⲙ ⲛⲏⲉⲧϣⲱⲡ ⲟⲩⲟϩ ⲛⲓⲧ̀ⲣⲁⲡⲉⲍⲁ ⲛ̀ⲧⲉ ⲛⲓⲣⲉϥⲉⲣⲕⲉⲣⲙⲁ ⲁϥⲫⲟⲛϧⲟⲩ ⲛⲉⲙ ⲛⲓⲕⲁⲑⲉⲇⲣⲁ ⲛ̀ⲧⲉ ⲛⲏⲉⲧϯϭⲣⲟⲙⲡⲓ ⲉ̀ⲃⲟⲗ . Ⲟⲩⲟϩ ⲡⲉϫⲁϥ ⲛⲱⲟⲩ ϫⲉ ⲥ̀ⲥϧⲏⲟⲩⲧ ϫⲉ ⲡⲁⲏⲓ ⲉⲩⲉ̀ⲙⲟⲩϯ ⲉ̀ⲣⲟϥ ϫⲉ ⲟⲩⲏⲓ ⲙ̀ⲡ̀ⲣⲟⲥⲉⲩⲭⲏ ⲛ̀ⲑⲱⲧⲉⲛ ⲇⲉ ⲧⲉⲧⲉⲛⲓⲣⲓ ⲙ̀ⲙⲟϥ ⲙ̀ⲙⲁⲛⲭⲱⲡ ⲛ̀ⲥⲟⲛⲓ : ⲟⲩⲟϩ ⲉⲧⲁⲩⲓ̀ ϩⲁⲣⲟϥ ⲛ̀ϫⲉ ϩⲁⲛⲃⲉⲗⲗⲉⲩ ⲛⲉⲙ ϩⲁⲛϭⲁⲗⲉⲩ ϧⲉⲛ ⲡⲓⲉⲣⲫⲉⲓ ⲟⲩⲟϩ ⲁϥⲉⲣⲫⲁϧⲣⲓ ⲉ̀ⲣⲱⲟⲩ : ⲉⲧⲁⲩⲛⲁⲩ ⲇⲉ ⲛ̀ϫⲉ ⲛⲓⲁⲣⲭⲏ ⲉⲣⲉⲩⲥ ⲛⲉⲙ ⲛⲓⲥⲁϧ ⲉ̀ⲛⲓϣ̀ⲫⲏⲣⲓ ⲉⲧⲁϥⲁⲓⲧⲟⲩ : ⲛⲉⲙ ⲛⲓⲁⲗⲱⲟⲩⲓ ⲉⲧⲱϣ ⲉ̀ⲃⲟⲗ ϧⲉⲛ ⲡⲓⲉⲣⲫⲉⲓ ⲉⲩϫⲱ ⲙ̀ⲙⲟⲥ ϫⲉ ⲱ̀ⲥⲁⲛⲛⲁ ⲡ̀ϣⲏⲣⲓ ⲛ̀ⲇⲁ̅ⲇ̅ ⲁⲩⲭⲣⲉⲙⲣⲉⲙ . Ⲟⲩⲟϩ ⲡⲉϫⲱⲟⲩ ⲛⲁϥ ϫⲉ ⲕ̀ⲥⲱⲧⲉⲙ ⲁⲛ ϫⲉ ⲟⲩ ⲡⲉⲧⲉ ⲛⲁⲓϫⲱ ⲙ̀ⲙⲟⲩ : Ⲓⲏ̅ⲥ̅ ⲇⲉ ⲡⲉϫⲁϥ ⲛⲱⲟⲩ ϫⲉ ⲥⲉ ⲙ̀ⲡⲉⲧⲉⲛⲱϣ ⲉⲛⲉϩ ϧⲉⲛ ⲛⲓⲅⲣⲁⲫⲏ ϫⲉ ⲉ̀ⲃⲟⲗ ϧⲉⲛ ⲣⲱⲟⲩ ⲛ̀ϩⲁⲛⲕⲟⲩϫⲓ ⲛ̀ⲁⲗⲱⲟⲩⲓ ⲛⲉⲙ ⲛⲏⲉⲑⲟⲩⲉⲙϭⲓ ⲁⲕⲥⲉⲃⲧⲉ ⲡⲓⲥ̀ⲙⲟⲩ : ⲟⲩⲟϩ ⲉⲧⲁϥⲭⲁⲩ ⲁϥⲓ̀ ⲥⲁⲃⲟⲗ ⲛ̀ϯⲃⲁⲕⲓ ⲉ̀ⲃⲏⲑ ⲁⲛⲓⲁ ⲟⲩⲟϩ ⲁϥⲉⲛⲕⲟⲧ ⲙ̀ⲙⲁⲩ . Ⲡⲓⲱⲟⲩ ⲫⲁ ⲡⲉⲛⲛⲟⲩϯ ⲡⲉ .

فوقهما . والجمع الأكثر فرشوا ثيابهم فى الطريق . وآخرون قطعوا أغصاناً من الشجر وفرشوها على الطريق . والجموع الذين تقدموا والذين تبعوا كانوا يصرخون قائلين : أوصنا لإبن داود . مبارك الآتى باسم الرب . أوصنا فى الأعالى . ولما دخل أورشليم أرتجت المدينة كلها قائلة : من هو هذا . فقالت الجموع هذا هو يسوع النبى الذى من ناصرة الجليل . ودخل يسوع إلى الهيكل وأخرج جميع الذين كانوا يبيعون ويشترون فى الهيكل وقلب موائد الصيارفة وكراسى باعة الحمام . وقال لهم مكتوب بيتى بيت الصلوة يدعى وأنتم جعلتموه مغارة للصوص . وتقدم إليه عمى وعرج فى الهيكل فشفاهم . فلما رأى رؤساء الكهنة والكتبة العجائب التى صنعها والأولاد يصيحون فى الهيكل قائلين: أوصنا لإبن داود تذمروا . وقالوا له أما تسمع ما يقولونه هؤلاء . فقال لهم يسوع نعم . أما قرأتم قط فى الكتب انه من أفواه الأطفال والرضعان هيأت سبحاً : ثم تركهم وخرج ظاهر المدينة إلى بيت عنيا وبات هناك . والمجد لله دائماً .

(The Response - يقال هذا المرد)

Hosanna in the highest: This is the King of Israel: Blessed is He, Who comes in the name: of the Lord of Hosts.	أوصاننا خين نى إنتشوسى : فاى بيه إبؤورو إمبى إسرائيل : إفسماروؤوت إنجيه في إثييو خين إفران إمبتشويس إنيتــه نى جُم .	Ⲱⲥⲁⲛⲛⲁ ϧⲉⲛ ⲛⲏ ⲉⲧϭⲟⲥⲓ: ⲫⲁⲓ ⲡⲉ ⲡ̀ⲟⲩⲣⲟ ⲙ̀Ⲡⲓⲥ̀ⲗ : ϥ̀ⲥⲙⲁⲣⲱⲟⲩⲧ ⲛ̀ϫⲉ ⲫⲏ ⲉⲑⲛⲏⲟⲩ ϧⲉⲛ ⲫ̀ⲣⲁⲛ ⲙ̀Ⲡⲟ̅ⲥ̅ ⲛ̀ⲧⲉ ⲛⲓϫⲟⲙ .	أوصنا فى الأعالى هذا هو ملك إسرائيل مبارك الآتى باسم رب القوات.

The Second Gospel - الانجيل الثانى
ⲈⲨⲀⲄⲄⲈⲖⲒⲞⲚ ⲔⲀⲦⲀ ⲘⲀⲢⲔⲞⲚ Ⲕⲉⲫ ⲓⲁ : ⲁ̅ - ⲓ̅ⲁ̅

Mark 11:1-11

Now when they drew near Jerusalem, to Bethphage and Bethany, at the Mount of Olives, He sent two of His disciples; and He said to them, "Go into the village opposite you; and as soon as you have entered it you will find a colt tied, on which no one has sat. Loose it and bring it. And if anyone says to you, 'Why are you doing this?' say, 'The Lord has need of it,' and immediately he will send it here." So they went their way, and found the colt tied by the door outside on the street, and they loosed it. But some of those who stood there said to them, "What are you doing, loosing the colt?" And they spoke to them just as Jesus had commanded. So they let them go. Then they brought the colt to Jesus and threw their clothes on it, and He sat on it. And many spread their clothes on the road, and others cut down leafy branches from the trees and spread them on the road. Then those who went before and those who followed cried out, saying: "Hosanna! 'BLESSED IS HE WHO COMES IN THE NAME OF THE LORD!' Blessed is the kingdom of our father David That comes in the name of the Lord! Hosanna in the highest!" And Jesus went into Jerusalem and into the temple. So when He had looked around at all things, as the hour was already late, He went out to Bethany with the twelve. Glory be to God forever, Amen.

ⲞⲨⲟ̅ϩ ⲉⲧⲁϥϧⲱⲛⲧ ⲉⲒⲗⲏⲙ ⲁϥⲓ ⲉⲂⲏⲑ ⲫⲀⲅⲏ ⲛⲉⲙ Ⲃⲏⲑ ⲁⲛⲓⲁ ϩⲁⲧⲉⲛ ⲡⲓⲧⲱⲟⲩ ⲛ̀ⲧⲉ ⲛⲓϫⲱⲓⲧ : ⲁϥⲟⲩⲱⲣⲡ ⲛ̀ⲥⲛⲁⲩ ⲉ̀Ⲃⲟⲗ ϧⲉⲛ ⲛⲉϥⲙⲁⲑⲏⲧⲏⲥ : ⲟⲩⲟ̅ϩ ⲡⲉϫⲁϥ ⲛⲱⲟⲩ ϫⲉ ⲙⲁϣⲉⲛⲱⲧⲉⲛ ⲉ̀ⲡⲓϯⲙⲓ ⲉⲧⲭⲏ ⲙ̀ⲡⲉⲧⲉⲛⲙ̀ⲑⲟ ⲟⲩⲟ̅ϩ ⲥⲁⲧⲉⲛ ⲑⲏⲛⲟⲩ ⲉⲣⲉⲧⲉⲛⲛⲁϣⲉ ⲉ̀ϧⲟⲩⲛ ⲉ̀ⲣⲟϥ ⲉⲣⲉⲧⲉⲛ ⲉ̀ϫⲓⲙⲓ ⲛ̀ⲟⲩⲥⲏϫ ⲉϥⲥⲟⲛϩ ⲫⲁⲓ ⲉⲧⲉ ⲙ̀ⲡⲁⲧⲉϥϩⲗⲓ ⲛ̀ⲣⲱⲙⲓ ⲁⲗⲏⲓ ⲉ̀ⲣⲟϥ ⲙⲁⲧⲟⲣⲟⲩ ⲙ̀ⲙⲟϥ ⲟⲩⲟ̅ϩ ⲁⲛⲓⲧϥ : ⲟⲩⲟ̅ϩ ⲉ̀ϣⲱⲡ ⲛ̀ⲧⲉ ⲟⲩⲓ ϫⲟⲥ ⲛⲱⲧⲉⲛ ϫⲉ ⲟⲩ ⲡⲉ ⲫⲁⲓ ⲉⲧⲉⲧⲉⲛⲓⲣⲓ ⲙ̀ⲙⲟϥ ⲁϫⲟⲥ ϫⲉ ⲡ̅ⲟ̅ⲥ̅ ⲡⲉ ⲉⲧ ⲉⲣⲭⲣⲓⲁ ⲙ̀ⲙⲟϥ : ⲟⲩⲟ̅ϩ ⲥⲁⲧⲟⲧϥ ϥⲛⲁⲟⲩⲱⲣⲡϥ ⲙ̀ⲛⲁⲓ . ⲞⲨⲟ̅ϩ ⲁⲩϣⲉⲛⲱⲟⲩ ⲟⲩⲟ̅ϩ ⲁⲩϫⲓⲙⲓ ⲛ̀ⲟⲩⲥⲏϫ ⲉϥⲥⲟⲛϩ ϩⲁⲧⲉⲛ ⲟⲩⲣⲟ ⲥⲁⲃⲟⲗ ⲙ̀ⲡⲓϣⲓⲣ ⲟⲩⲟ̅ϩ ⲁⲩⲧⲟⲣⲟⲩ ⲙ̀ⲙⲟϥ : ⲟⲩⲟ̅ϩ ϩⲁⲛⲟⲩⲟⲛ ⲉ̀Ⲃⲟⲗ ϧⲉⲛ ⲛⲏⲉⲧⲟ̅ϩⲓ ⲉⲣⲁⲧⲟⲩ ⲙ̀ⲙⲁⲩ ⲛⲁⲩⲭⲱ ⲙ̀ⲙⲟⲥ ⲛⲱⲟⲩ ϫⲉ ⲟⲩ ⲡⲉ ⲧⲉⲧⲉⲛⲓⲣⲓ ⲙ̀ⲙⲟϥ ⲉⲣⲉⲧⲉⲛϯ ⲟⲩⲱ ⲙ̀ⲡⲓⲥⲏϫ : ⲛ̀ⲑⲱⲧⲉⲛ ⲇⲉ ⲁⲩϫⲟⲥ ⲛⲱⲟⲩ ⲕⲁⲧⲁ ⲫ̀ⲣⲏϯ ⲉⲧⲁϥϫⲟⲥ ⲛⲱⲟⲩ ⲛ̀ϫⲉ Ⲓⲏⲥ ⲟⲩⲟ̅ϩ ⲁⲩⲭⲁⲩ . ⲞⲨⲟ̅ϩ ⲁⲩⲓⲛⲓ ⲙ̀ⲡⲓⲥⲏϫ ϩⲁ Ⲓⲏⲥ ⲟⲩⲟ̅ϩ ⲁⲩⲧⲁⲗⲉ ⲛⲟⲩϩⲃⲱⲥ ⲉ̀ⲣⲟϥ ⲟⲩⲟ̅ϩ ⲁϥϩⲉⲙⲥⲓ ⲉ̀ϫⲱⲟⲩ : ⲟⲩⲟ̅ϩ ϩⲁⲛⲙⲏϣ ⲁⲩⲫⲱⲣϣ ⲛ̀ⲛⲟⲩϩⲃⲱⲥ ϩⲓ ⲡⲓⲙⲱⲓⲧ : ϩⲁⲛⲕⲉⲭⲱⲟⲩⲛⲓ ⲇⲉ ⲁⲩⲕⲱⲣϫ ⲛ̀ϩⲁⲛϫⲁⲗ ⲛ̀ϣ̀ϣⲏⲛ ⲉ̀Ⲃⲟⲗ ϧⲉⲛ ⲛⲓⲓⲟ̅ϩⲓ ⲟⲩⲟ̅ϩ ⲁⲩⲫⲱⲣϣ ⲙ̀ⲙⲱⲟⲩ ϩⲓ ⲡⲓⲙⲱⲓⲧ : ⲟⲩⲟ̅ϩ ⲛⲏ ⲛⲁⲩⲙⲟϣⲓ ⲛⲉⲙ ⲛⲏⲉⲛⲁⲩⲙⲟϣⲓ ϩⲓ ⲫⲁ̅ϩⲟⲩ ⲛⲁⲩⲱϣ ⲉ̀Ⲃⲟⲗ ⲉⲩϫⲱ ⲙ̀ⲙⲟⲥ : ϫⲉ ⲱⲥⲁⲛⲛⲁ ϥ̀ⲥⲙⲁⲣⲱⲟⲩⲧ ⲛ̀ϫⲉ ⲫⲏⲉⲑⲛⲏⲟⲩ ϧⲉⲛ ⲫ̀ⲣⲁⲛ ⲙ̀ⲡ̅ⲟ̅ⲥ̅ . Ⲥ̀ⲥⲙⲁⲣⲱⲟⲩⲧ ⲛ̀ϫⲉ ϯⲙⲉⲧⲟⲩⲣⲟ ⲉⲥⲛⲏⲟⲩ ⲛ̀ⲧⲉ ⲡⲉⲛⲓⲱⲧ Ⲇⲁⲩⲓⲇ ϧⲉⲛ ⲫ̀ⲣⲁⲛ ⲙ̀ⲡ̅ⲟ̅ⲥ̅ ⲱⲥⲁⲛⲛⲁ ϧⲉⲛ ⲛⲏ ⲉⲧϭⲟⲥⲓ ⲟⲩⲟ̅ϩ ⲉⲧⲁϥ ⲓ ⲉ̀ϧⲟⲩⲛ ⲉ̀Ⲓⲗⲏⲙ ⲉ̀ϧⲟⲩⲛ ⲉ̀ⲡⲓⲉⲣⲫⲉⲓ ⲟⲩⲟ̅ϩ ⲉⲧⲁϥⲥⲟⲙⲥ ⲉ̀ⲡⲧⲏⲣϥ ⲟⲩⲟ̅ϩ ⲉⲧⲁ ⲣⲟⲩϩⲓ ϩⲏⲇⲏ ϣⲱⲡⲓ ⲛ̀ⲧⲉ ϯⲟⲩⲛⲟⲩ : ⲁϥ ⲓ ⲉ̀Ⲃⲟⲗ ⲉ̀Ⲃⲏⲑ ⲁⲛⲓⲁ ⲛⲉⲙ ⲡⲓⲙⲏⲧ̀ⲥⲛⲁⲩ .

Ⲡⲓⲱⲟⲩ ⲫⲁ ⲡⲉⲛⲛⲟⲩϯ ⲡⲉ .

(مرقس 11 : 1 – 11)

ولما قربوا من أورشليم وأتى إلى بيت فاجى وبيت عنيا عند جبل الزيتون . أرسل اثنين من تلاميذه . وقال لهما اذهبا إلى القرية التى أمامكما فللوقت تجدان جحشاً مربوطاً وهذا لم يركبه أحد من الناس فحلاه وأتيا به . وان قال لكما أحد لماذا تفعلان هذا فقولا ان الرب محتاج إليه . وللوقت يرسله إلى هنا . فمضيا ووجدا الجحش مربوطاً عند الباب خارجاً على الطريق فحلاه . فقال لهما قوم من القيام هناك ماذا تفعلان تحلان الجحش. أما هما فقالا لهم كما قال لهما يسوع فتركوهما . فأتيا بالجحش إلى يسوع والقيا عليه ثيابهما فركب عليه . وكثيرون فرشوا ثيابهم فى الطريق . وآخرون قطعوا أغصاناً من الشجر من الحقل وفرشوا فى الطريق . والذين تقدموا والذين تبعوا كانوا يصرخون قائلين : أوصنا مبارك الآتى باسم الرب . مباركة مملكة أبينا داود الآتية باسم الرب أوصنا فى الأعالى فدخل يسوع أورشليم إلى الهيكل . ولما نظر حوله إلى كل شئ. إذ كان الوقت قد أمسى. خرج إلى بيت عنيا مع الاثنى عشر . والمجد لله دائماً.

(The Response - المرد هذا يقال)

He Who sits upon the Cherubim: Today appeared in Jerusalem: Riding on a colt with great glory: surrounded by ranks of the Angelos

الجالس فـــوق الشاروبيــم : اليوم ظهر فى أورشليــم : راكباً على جحش بمجد عظيم : وحوله طقوس نى أنجيلوس

The Third Gospel - الانجيل الثالث

Ⲉⲩⲁⲅⲅⲉⲗⲓⲟⲛ Ⲕⲁⲧⲁ Ⲗⲟⲩⲕⲁⲛ Ⲕⲉⲫ̅ ⲓ̅ⲑ̅ : ⲕ̅ⲑ̅ - ⲙ̅ⲏ̅

Luke 19:29-48

And it came to pass, when He drew near to Bethphage and Bethany, at the mountain called Olivet, that He sent two of His disciples, saying, "Go into the village opposite you, where as you enter you will find a colt tied, on which no one has ever sat. Loose it and bring it here. And if anyone asks you, 'Why are you loosing it?' thus you shall say to him, 'Because the Lord has need of it.' " So those who were sent went their way and found it just as He had said to them. But as they were loosing the colt, the owners of it said to them, "Why are you loosing the colt?" And they said, "The Lord has need of him." Then they brought him to Jesus. And they threw their own clothes on the colt, and they set Jesus on him. And as He went, many spread their clothes on the road. Then, as He was now drawing near the descent of the Mount of Olives, the whole multitude of the disciples began to rejoice and praise God with a loud voice for all the mighty works they had seen, saying: " 'BLESSED IS THE KING WHO COMES IN THE NAME OF THE LORD!' Peace in heaven and glory in the highest!" And some of the Pharisees called to Him from the crowd, "Teacher, rebuke Your disciples." But He answered and said to them, "I tell you that if these should keep silent, the stones would immediately cry out." Now as He

Ⲟⲩⲟϩ ⲁⲥϣⲱⲡⲓ ⲉⲧⲁϥϧⲱⲛⲧ ⲉⲂⲏⲑ ⲫⲁⲏ ⲛⲉⲙ Ⲃⲏⲑ ⲁⲛⲓⲁ ϧⲁⲧⲉⲛ ⲡⲓⲧⲱⲟⲩ ⲉϣⲁⲩⲙⲟⲩϯ ⲉⲣⲟϥ ϫⲉ ⲫⲁ ⲛⲓϫⲱⲓⲧ ⲁϥⲟⲩⲱⲣⲡ ⲛ̀ⲥⲛⲁⲩ ⲉ̀ⲃⲟⲗ ϧⲉⲛ ⲛⲉϥⲙⲁⲑⲏⲧⲏⲥ : ⲉϥϫⲱ ⲙ̀ⲙⲟⲥ ϫⲉ ⲙⲁϣⲉⲛⲱⲧⲉⲛ ⲉ̀ⲡⲁⲓϯⲙⲓ ⲉⲧⲭⲏ ⲙ̀ⲡⲉⲧⲉⲛⲙ̀ⲑⲟ ⲉⲣⲉⲧⲉⲛⲛⲁϣⲉ ⲉ̀ϧⲟⲩⲛ ⲉⲣⲟϥ ⲧⲉⲧⲉⲛⲛⲁϫⲓⲙⲓ ⲛ̀ⲟⲩⲥⲏϫ ⲉϥⲥⲱⲛϩ ⲫⲏⲉⲧⲉ ⲙ̀ⲡⲉϩⲗⲓ ⲛ̀ⲣⲱⲙⲓ ⲁⲗⲏⲓ ⲉⲣⲟϥ ⲉⲛⲉϩ ⲃⲟⲗϥ ⲉ̀ⲃⲟⲗ ⲁⲛⲓⲧϥ ⲟⲩⲟϩ ⲉ̀ϣⲱⲡ ⲁⲣⲉϣⲁⲛⲟⲩⲁⲓ ϣⲉⲛ ⲑⲏⲛⲟⲩ ϫⲉ ⲉⲑⲃⲉ ⲟⲩ ⲧⲉⲧⲉⲛⲃⲱⲗ ⲙ̀ⲙⲟϥ ⲁϫⲟⲥ ⲙ̀ⲡⲁⲓⲣⲏϯ : ϫⲉⲡ̅ⲟ̅ⲥ̅ ⲡⲉⲧⲉⲣⲭⲣⲓⲁ ⲙ̀ⲙⲟϥ . Ⲉⲧⲁⲩϣⲉⲛⲱⲟⲩ ⲇⲉ ⲛ̀ϫⲉ ⲛⲏ ⲉⲧⲁⲩⲟⲩⲟⲣⲡⲟⲩ ⲁⲩϫⲓⲙⲓ ⲕⲁⲧⲁ ⲫⲣⲏϯ ⲉⲧⲁϥϫⲟⲥ ⲛⲱⲟⲩ : ⲉⲩⲃⲱⲗ ⲇⲉ ⲙ̀ⲡⲓⲥⲏϫ ⲉ̀ⲃⲟⲗ ⲡⲉϫⲉ ⲛⲉϥϭⲓⲥⲉⲣ ⲛⲱⲟⲩ ϫⲉ ⲉⲑⲃⲉ ⲟⲩ ⲧⲉⲧⲉⲛⲃⲱⲗ ⲙ̀ⲡⲓⲥⲏϫ : ⲛ̀ⲑⲱⲟⲩ ⲇⲉ ⲡⲉϫⲱⲟⲩ ϫⲉ ⲡ̅ⲟ̅ⲥ̅ ⲡⲉⲧⲉⲣⲭⲣⲓⲁ ⲙ̀ⲙⲟϥ .

Ⲟⲩⲟϩ ⲁⲩⲉⲛϥ ϩⲁ Ⲓⲏ̅ⲥ̅ ⲟⲩⲟϩ ⲉⲧⲁⲩⲃⲟⲣⲃⲉⲣ ⲛ̀ⲛⲟⲩϩⲃⲱⲥ ⲉ̀ϫⲉⲛ ⲡⲓⲥⲏϫ ⲁⲩⲧⲁⲗⲉ Ⲓⲏ̅ⲥ̅ ⲉⲣⲟϥ : ⲉⲩⲙⲟϣⲓ ⲇⲉ ⲛⲁⲩⲫⲱⲣϣ ⲛ̀ⲛⲟⲩϩⲃⲱⲥ ϩⲓ ⲡⲓⲙⲱⲓⲧ : ⲉϥⲛⲁϧⲱⲛⲧ ⲇⲉ ϩⲏⲇⲏ ⲉ̀ⲡⲓⲙⲁⲛ̀ⲓ ⲉ̀ⲡⲓⲥⲏⲧ ⲛ̀ⲧⲉ ⲡⲓⲧⲱⲟⲩ ⲛ̀ⲧⲉ ⲛⲓϫⲱⲓⲧ ⲁϥⲉⲣϩⲏⲧⲥ ⲛ̀ϫⲉ ⲫⲓⲙⲏϣ ⲧⲏⲣϥ ⲛ̀ⲧⲉ ⲛⲓⲙⲁⲑⲏⲧⲏⲥ ⲉⲩⲣⲁϣⲓ ⲉⲩⲥⲙⲟⲩ ⲉ̀Ⲫϯ ϧⲉⲛ ⲟⲩⲛⲓϣϯ ⲛ̀ⲥⲙⲏ ⲉⲑⲃⲉ ⲛⲓϫⲟⲙ ⲧⲏⲣⲟⲩ ⲉⲧⲁⲩⲛⲁⲩ ⲉⲣⲱⲟⲩ . Ⲉⲩϫⲱ ⲙ̀ⲙⲟⲥ ϫⲉ ϥ̀ⲥⲙⲁⲣⲱⲟⲩⲧ ⲛ̀ϫⲉ ⲡⲓⲟⲩⲣⲟ ⲫⲏⲉⲑⲛⲏⲟⲩ ϧⲉⲛ ⲫ̀ⲣⲁⲛ ⲙ̀ⲡ̅ⲟ̅ⲥ̅ : ⲟⲩϩⲓⲣⲏⲛⲏ ϧⲉⲛ ⲧ̀ⲫⲉ ⲟⲩⲟϩ ⲟⲩⲱⲟⲩ ϧⲉⲛ ⲛⲏⲉⲧϭⲟⲥⲓ : ⲟⲩⲟϩ ϩⲁⲛⲟⲩⲟⲛ ⲛ̀ⲧⲉ Ⲛⲓⲫⲁⲣⲓⲥⲉⲟⲥ ⲉ̀ⲃⲟⲗ ϧⲉⲛ ⲡⲓⲙⲏϣ ⲡⲉϫⲱⲟⲩ ⲛⲁϥ ϫⲉ ⲫ̀ⲣⲉϥⲧ̀ⲥⲃⲱ ⲁⲣⲓⲉ̀ⲡⲓⲧⲩⲙⲁⲛ ⲛ̀ⲛⲉⲕⲙⲁⲑⲏⲧⲏⲥ ϩⲓⲛⲁ ⲛ̀ⲥⲉⲭⲁⲣⲱⲟⲩ : ⲟⲩⲟϩ ⲁϥⲉⲣⲟⲩⲱ ⲡⲉϫⲁϥ ϫⲉ ϯϫⲱ ⲙ̀ⲙⲟⲥ ⲛⲱⲧⲉⲛ : ϫⲉ ⲁⲣⲉϣⲁⲛⲛⲁⲓ ⲭⲁⲣⲱⲟⲩ ⲥⲉⲛⲁϣ ⲉ̀ⲃⲟⲗ

(لوقا 19 : 29 – 48)

وإذ قرب من بيت فاجى وبيت عنيا عند الجبل الذى يدعى جبل الزيتون أرسل اثنين من تلاميذه . قائلاً اذهبا إلى هذه القرية التى أمامكما وحين تدخلانها تجدان جحشاً مربوطاً لم يركبه أحد من الناس قط . فحلاه وأتيا به . وان سألكما أحد وقال لماذا تحلانه . فقولا له هكذا : ان الرب محتاج إليه . فلما ذهب المرسلان وجدا كما قال لهما . وفيما هما يحلان الجحش قال لهما اصحابه لماذا تحلان الجحش؟ أما هما فقالا: ان الرب محتاج إليه . وأتيا به إلى يسوع وطرحا ثيابهما على الجحش واركبا يسوع . وفيما هو سائر كانوا يفرشون ثيابهم فى الطريق. وعند ما قرب من منحدر جبل الزيتون إبتدأ كل جمهور التلاميذ يفرحون ويباركون الله بصوت عظيم لأجل جميع القوات التى نظروها . قائلين : مبارك الملك الآتى باسم الرب . سلام فى السماء ومجد فى الأعالى . وان قوماً من الفريسيين من الجمع قالوا له : يا معلم انتهر تلاميذك . فأجاب وقال لهم أقول لكم : انه ان سكت هؤلاء نطقت

drew near, He saw the city and wept over it, saying, "If you had known, even you, especially in this your day, the things that make for your peace! But now they are hidden from your eyes. For days will come upon you when your enemies will build an embankment around you, surround you and close you in on every side, and level you, and your children within you, to the ground; and they will not leave in you one stone upon another, because you did not know the time of your visitation." Then He went into the temple and began to drive out those who bought and sold in it, saying to them, "It is written, 'MY HOUSE IS A HOUSE OF PRAYER,' but you have made it a 'DEN OF THIEVES.' " And He was teaching daily in the temple. But the chief priests, the scribes, and the leaders of the people sought to destroy Him, and were unable to do anything; for all the people were very attentive to hear Him. Glory be to God forever, Amen.

ⲚⲬⲈ ⲚⲀⲓⲰⲚⲒ . ⲥⲱⲥ ⲆⲈ ⲈⲦⲀϤϦⲰⲚⲦ ⲈⲦⲀϤⲚⲀⲨ ⲈϮⲂⲀⲔⲒ ⲀϤⲢⲓⲘⲒ ⲈϨⲢⲎⲒ ⲈϪⲰⲤ : ⲈϥϪⲰ ⲘⲘⲞⲤ ϪⲈ ⲈⲚⲀⲢⲈⲈⲘⲒ ϨⲰⲒ ⲡⲈ ϦⲈⲚ ⲡⲀⲓⲈϨⲞⲞⲨ ⲈⲚⲀⲦⲈ ϩⲒⲢⲎⲚⲎ ϮⲚⲞⲨ ⲆⲈ ⲀⲨϨⲰⲡ ⲈⲂⲞⲖ ϨⲀ ⲚⲈⲂⲀⲖ : ϪⲈ ⲥⲈⲚⲀⲒ ⲈϨⲢⲎⲒ ⲈϪⲰ ⲚϪⲈ ϨⲀⲚⲈϨⲞⲞⲨ ⲞⲨⲞϨ ⲥⲈⲚⲀⲦⲀⲔⲦⲈ ⲔⲀϢ ⲈⲢⲞ ⲚϪⲈ ⲚⲈⲬⲀϪⲒ ⲞⲨⲞϨ ⲥⲈⲚⲀⲔⲰϮ ⲈⲢⲞ ⲞⲨⲞϨ ⲥⲀⲚⲀϨⲈⲬϨⲰϪⲒ ⲘⲘⲞ ⲚⲥⲀⲤⲀ ⲚⲒⲂⲈⲚ . Ⲟⲩⲟϩ ⲈⲨⲈⲢⲰϦⲦ ⲘⲘⲞ ⲈⲠⲈⲤⲎⲦ ⲚⲈⲘ ⲚⲈϢⲈⲢⲒ ⲚϦⲎϮ : ⲞⲨⲞϨ ⲚⲚⲞⲨⲬⲀ ⲞⲨⲰⲚⲒ ⲈϪⲈⲚ ⲞⲨⲰⲚⲒ ⲚϦⲎϮ : ⲈⲪⲘⲀ ϪⲈ ⲘⲠⲈⲈⲘⲒ ⲈⲠⲤⲎⲞⲨ ⲚⲦⲈ ⲠⲈⲬⲈⲘ ⲠϢⲒⲚⲒ : ⲞⲨⲞϨ ⲈⲦⲀϤϢⲈ ⲈϦⲞⲨⲚ ⲈⲠⲒⲈⲢⲪⲈⲒ ⲀϤⲈⲢϨⲎⲦⲤ ⲚϨⲒⲞⲨⲒ ⲈⲂⲞⲖ ⲚⲚⲎⲦϮ ⲈⲂⲞⲖ : ⲈϥϪⲰ ⲘⲘⲞⲤ ⲚⲰⲞⲨ ϪⲈ ⲤⲤϦⲎⲞⲨⲦ ϪⲈ ⲠⲀⲎⲒ ⲈϥⲈϢⲰⲠⲒ ⲚⲞⲨⲎⲒ ⲘⲠⲢⲞⲤⲈⲨⲬⲎ ⲚⲰⲦⲈⲚ ⲆⲈ ⲀⲢⲈⲦⲈⲚⲀⲒϤ ⲘⲂⲎⲂ ⲚⲤⲞⲚⲒ .

Ⲟⲩⲟϩ ⲚⲀϤϮⲤⲂⲰ ⲘⲘⲎⲚⲒ ⲡⲈ ϦⲈⲚ ⲠⲒⲈⲢⲪⲈⲒ ⲚⲒⲀⲢⲬⲎ ⲈⲢⲈⲨⲤ ⲆⲈ ⲚⲈⲘ ⲚⲒⲤⲀϦ ⲚⲈⲘ ⲚⲒϨⲞⲨⲀϮ ⲚⲦⲈ ⲠⲒⲖⲀⲞⲤ ⲚⲀⲨⲔⲰϮ ⲡⲈ ⲚⲤⲀⲦⲀⲔⲞϤ : ⲞⲨⲞϨ ⲚⲀⲨϪⲒⲘⲒ ⲀⲚ ⲡⲈ ⲘⲪⲎⲈⲦⲞⲨⲚⲀⲀⲒϤ : ⲠⲒⲖⲀⲞⲤ ⲅⲀⲢ ⲦⲎⲢϤ ⲚⲀⲨⲀϢⲒ ⲚⲤⲰϤ ⲈⲨⲤⲰⲦⲈⲘ ⲈⲢⲞϤ.

Ⲡⲓⲱⲟⲩ ⲫⲀ ⲠⲈⲚⲚⲞⲨϮ ⲡⲈ .

الحجارة . فلما قرب ورأى المدينة بكى عليها قائلاً : لو كنت أنت تعلمين فى هذا اليوم ما هو لسلامك ولكن الآن قد أخفى عن عينيك . فأنه ستأتى أيام ويحيط بك أعداؤك ويحدقون بك ويحاصرونك من كل جهة ويهدمونك وبنيك فيك . ولا يتركون فيك حجراً على حجر . لأنك لن تعرفى زمان افتقادك . ولما دخل الهيكل إبتدأ يخرج الذين كانوا يبيعون ويشترون فيه قائلاً لهم : مكتوب أن بيتى بيت الصلوة وأنتم جعلتموه مغارة للصوص . وكان يعلم كل يوم فى الهيكل وكان رؤساء الكهنة والكتبة ومقدموا الشعب يطلبون ان يهلكوه ولم يجدوا ما يفعلون . لأن الشعب كله كان متعلقاً به يسمع منه . والمجد لله دائماً.

(The Response - المرد هذا يقال)

On the way they spread garments: and from the trees they cut branches: while proclaiming with hymns: Hosanna to the Son of David.

فى الطريق فرشوا القمصان : ومن الشجر قطعوا الأغصان : وهم يصيحون بالألحان : أوصنا إبشيرى إن دافيــــد

+ The priest prays the litany of the Gospel..

+ يقول الكاهن أوشية الانجيل

The Psalm

Ⲯⲁⲗⲙⲟⲥ ⲝ̅ⲇ̅ : ⲁ̅ ⲚⲈⲘ ⲃ̅

Psalms 64:1-2

Praise becomes You, O God, in Zion; and to You shall the vow be performed *in Jerusalem*. Hear my prayer; to You all flesh shall come. Alleluia

Ⲛ̀ⲑⲟⲕ ⲪϮ ϥⲈⲢϢⲀⲨ ⲚⲀⲔ ⲚϪⲈ ⲠⲒⲬⲰ ϦⲈⲚ Ⲥⲓⲱⲛ : ⲈⲨⲈϮ ⲚⲀⲔ ⲚⲞⲨⲈⲨⲬⲎ ϦⲈⲚ Ⲓⲉⲣⲟⲩⲥⲁⲗⲏⲙ : ⲤⲰⲦⲈⲘ ⲪϮ ⲈⲦⲀ ⲠⲢⲞⲤ ⲈⲨⲬⲎ : ϪⲈ ⲤⲈⲚⲚⲞⲨ ϨⲀⲢⲞⲔ ⲚϪⲈ ⲤⲀⲢⲜ ⲚⲒⲂⲈⲚ . ⲁ̅ⲗ̅.

إنثوك إفنوتى إفئرشاف ناك إنجيه بيجو خين سيون : إفئتى ناك إنؤو إفكى خين يروساليم : صوتيم إفنوتى إيطا إبروس إفشى : جيه سيه نيوو هاروك إنجيه صاركس نيفين . الليلويا.

(مز 64 : 1 و 2)

لك ينبغى التسبيح يا الله فى صهيون ولك توفى النذور فى أورشليم . استمع يا الله صلاتى لأنه اليك يأتى كل بشر . الليلويا .

The Fourth Gospel - الانجيل الرابع
Ⲉⲩⲁⲅⲅⲉⲗⲓⲟⲛ Ⲕⲁⲧⲁ Ⲓⲱⲁⲛⲛⲏⲛ Ⲕⲉⲫ ⲓⲃ : ⲓⲃ - ⲓⲑ

John 12:12-19

The next day a great multitude that had come to the feast, when they heard that Jesus was coming to Jerusalem, took branches of palm trees and went out to meet Him, and cried out: "Hosanna! 'BLESSED IS HE WHO COMES IN THE NAME OF THE LORD!' The King of Israel!" Then Jesus, when He had found a young donkey, sat on it; as it is written: "FEAR NOT, DAUGHTER OF ZION; BEHOLD, YOUR KING IS COMING, SITTING ON A DONKEY'S COLT." His disciples did not understand these things at first; but when Jesus was glorified, then they remembered that these things were written about Him and that they had done these things to Him. Therefore the people, who were with Him when He called Lazarus out of his tomb and raised him from the dead, bore witness. For this reason the people also met Him, because they heard that He had done this sign. The Pharisees therefore said among themselves, "You see that you are accomplishing nothing. Look, the world has gone after Him!" Glory be to God forever, Amen.

Ⲡⲉϥⲣⲁⲥϯ ⲇⲉ ⲉⲡⲓⲙⲏϣ ⲉⲧⲟϣ ⲉⲧⲁⲩ ⲓ ⲉϧⲁⲓ ⲉⲧⲁⲩⲥⲱⲧⲉⲙ ϫⲉ Ⲓⲏⲥ ⲛⲏⲟⲩ ⲉϧⲣⲏⲓ ⲉⲓⲗⲏⲙ : ⲁⲩϭⲓ ⲛ̀ϩⲁⲛⲃⲁⲓ ⲉⲃⲟⲗ ϧⲉⲛ ϩⲁⲛⲃⲉⲛⲓ ⲟⲩⲟϩ ⲁⲩⲓ ⲉⲃⲟⲗ ⲉϧⲣⲁϥ ⲟⲩⲟϩ ⲛⲁⲩⲱϣ ⲉⲃⲟⲗ ⲉⲩϫⲱ ⲙ̀ⲙⲟⲥ ϫⲉ ⲱⲥⲁⲛⲛⲁ ϥ̀ⲥⲙⲁⲣⲱⲟⲩⲧ ⲛ̀ϫⲉ ⲫⲏⲉⲑⲛⲏⲟⲩ ϧⲉⲛ ⲫ̀ⲣⲁⲛ ⲙ̀ⲡⲟⲥ ⲡ̀ⲟⲩⲣⲟ ⲙ̀ⲡⲓⲥⲗ : Ⲓⲏⲥ ⲇⲉ ⲉⲧⲁϥϫⲓⲙⲓ ⲛ̀ⲟⲩⲉⲱ ⲁϥⲁⲗⲏⲓ ⲉⲣⲟϥ ⲕⲁⲧⲁ ⲫ̀ⲣⲏϯ ⲉⲧ ⲥ̀ϧⲏⲟⲩⲧ . Ϫⲉ ⲙ̀ⲡⲉⲣⲉⲣϩⲟϯ ⲧ̀ϣⲉⲣⲓ ⲛ̀ⲥⲓⲱⲛ ϩⲏⲡⲡⲉ ⲓⲥ ⲡⲉⲟⲩⲣⲟ ⲉϥⲛⲏⲟⲩ ⲛⲉ ⲉϥⲧⲁⲗⲏⲟⲩⲧ ⲉⲟⲩⲥⲏϫ ⲡ̀ϣⲏⲣⲓ ⲛ̀ⲟⲩⲉⲱ : ⲛⲁⲓ ⲇⲉ ⲙ̀ⲡⲉ ⲛⲉϥⲙⲁⲑⲏⲧⲏⲥ ⲉⲙⲓ ⲉⲣⲱⲟⲩ ⲛ̀ϣⲟⲣⲡ : ⲁⲗⲗⲁ ϩⲟⲧⲉ ⲉⲧⲁϥϭⲓⲱⲟⲩ ⲛ̀ϫⲉ Ⲓⲏⲥ ⲧⲟⲧⲉ ⲁⲩⲉⲣⲫⲙⲉⲩⲓ ϫⲉ ⲛⲁⲓ ⲛⲉ ⲛⲏⲉⲧⲥ̀ϧⲏⲟⲩⲧ ϧⲁⲣⲟϥ ⲟⲩⲟϩ ⲛⲁⲓ ⲛⲉ ⲛⲏⲉⲧⲁϥⲁⲓⲧⲟⲩ ⲛⲁϥ : ⲛⲁϥⲉⲣⲙⲉⲑⲣⲉ ⲟⲩⲛ ⲡⲉ ⲛ̀ϫⲉ ⲡⲓⲙⲏϣ ⲉⲛⲁϥ ⲛⲉⲙⲁϥ : ϫⲉ ⲁϥⲙⲟⲩϯ ⲉⲗⲁⲍⲁⲣⲟⲥ ⲉⲃⲟⲗ ϧⲉⲛ ⲡⲓⲙ̀ϩⲁⲩ ⲟⲩⲟϩ ⲁϥⲧⲟⲩⲛⲟⲥϥ ⲉⲃⲟⲗ ϧⲉⲛ ⲛⲏⲉⲑⲙⲱⲟⲩⲧ . Ⲉⲑⲃⲉ ⲫⲁⲓ ⲛⲁⲩⲛⲏⲟⲩ ⲉⲃⲟⲗ ⲉϧⲣⲁϥ ⲡⲉ ⲛ̀ϫⲉ ⲡⲓⲙⲏϣ ϫⲉ ⲁⲩⲥⲱⲧⲉⲙ ϫⲉ ⲁϥⲉⲣ ⲡⲁⲓⲙⲏⲓⲛⲓ : ⲡⲉ ϫⲉ ⲛⲓⲫⲁⲣⲓⲥⲉⲟⲥ ⲟⲩⲛ ⲛ̀ⲟⲩⲉⲣⲏⲟⲩ ϫⲉ ⲧⲉⲧⲉⲛⲛⲁⲩ ϫⲉ ⲧⲉⲧⲉⲛⲛⲁϫⲉⲙϩⲏⲟⲩ ⲛ̀ϩⲗⲓ ⲁⲛ : ⲓⲥ ⲡⲓⲕⲟⲥⲙⲟⲥ ⲧⲏⲣϥ ⲁϥϣⲉⲛⲁϥ ⲥⲁⲙⲉⲛϩⲏⲧ. Ⲡⲓⲱⲟⲩ ⲫⲁ ⲡⲉⲛⲛⲟⲩϯ ⲡⲉ .

(19 – 12 : 12) يوحنا

وفى الغد سمع الجمع الكثير الذى جاء إلى العيد ان يسوع أت إلى أورشليم . فأخذوا سعف النخل وخرجوا للقائه وكانوا يصرخون قائلين : أوصنا مبارك الآتى باسم الرب ملك إسرائيل . ووجد يسوع جحشاً فركبه كما هو مكتوب . لا تخافى يا إبنة صهيون هوذا ملكك يأتى راكباً على جحش إبن أتان . وهذه الأمور لم يفهمها تلاميذه أولاً . ولكن لما تمجد يسوع حينئذ تذكروا ان هذه انما كتبت من أجله وصنعت له . وكان الجمع الذى معه يشهد انه دعا لعازر من القبر وأقامه من الأموات . ومن أجل هذا خرج الجمع للقائه لأنهم سمعوا أنه صنع هذه الآية . فقال الفريسيون بعضهم لبعض انظروا انكم لا تنفعون شيئاً هوذا العالم كله قد ذهب وراءه . والمجد لله دائماً .

(The Response - يقال هذا المرد)

Today the sayings are fulfilled: from the prophecies and the proverbs: as Zachariah prophesized and said: a prophecy about Jesus Christ.

اليوم تمت الأقـوال : من النبـوات والأمثـال : كما تتنبأ زكريا وقـال : نبوة عن إيسوس بخرستـوس

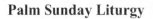

Aspasmos Adam, after Reconciliation Prayer
أسبسمس أدام بعد صلاة الصلح بطريقة (افرحى يا مريم)

English	Coptic (transliteration)	Coptic	Arabic
Christ our Savior: with great humility: entered Jerusalem: riding upon a colt.	بيخرستوس بين صوتير : خين أوو نيشتى إنثيبيو : أفشيه إيخون إيروساليـــم : أفطاليووت إ أوو إأو .	Ⲡ̅ⲭ̅ⲥ̅ ⲡⲉⲛⲥⲱⲧⲏⲣ : ϧⲉⲛ ⲟⲩⲛⲓϣϯ ⲛ̀ⲑⲉⲃⲓⲟ : ⲁϥϣⲉ ⲉ̀ϧⲟⲩⲛ ⲉ̀Ⲓ̅ⲗⲏⲙ : ⲁϥⲧⲁⲗⲏⲟⲩⲧ ⲉ̀ⲟⲩⲉ̀ⲱ .	المسيح مخلصنا بتواضع عظيم دخل إلى أورشليـــم راكباً أتاناً .
The young children: were praising and saying: Hosanna in the highest: This is the King of Israel.	إس نى كووجى : إن ألووأوى إفهوس إ إممانوئيل : جيه أوصاننا خين نى إتتشوسى : فاى بيه إبؤورو إمبى إسرائيل	Ⲧⲥ ⲛⲓⲕⲟⲩⲝⲓ ⲛ̀ⲁⲗⲱⲟⲩⲓ : ⲉⲩⲥ̀ⲱⲥ ⲉ̀Ⲉⲙⲙⲁⲛⲟⲩⲏⲗ : ϫⲉ ⲱ̀ⲥⲁⲛⲛⲁ ϧⲉⲛ ⲛⲏⲉⲧϭⲟⲥⲓ : ⲫⲁⲓ ⲡⲉ ⲡ̀ⲟⲩⲣⲟ ⲙ̀ⲡⲓⲥ̅ⲗ̅ .	والأطفال الصغار تسبح عمانوئيل قائلة : أوصنا فى الأعالى هذا هو ملك إسرائيل .

+ **The liturgy is completed till the end, and psalm 150 is said,**
then ⲭⲉ ϥ̀ⲥⲙⲁⲣⲱⲟⲩⲧ followed by Palm Sunday hymn.
+ **The readings of the General Funeral are read without Thok Teti Gom.**

150 يكمل القداس إلى آخره ويقال المزمور الـ
ثم ⲭⲉ ϥ̀ⲥⲙⲁⲣⲱⲟⲩⲧ .
ثم تقال مديحة الشعانين .
+ ثم تقرأ فصول التجنيز دون أن تقال ثوك تيه تى جُم .

The General Funeral Service

(الجناز العام)

After the liturgy of Palm Sunday and the communion, the entire congregation attends the General funeral Service at the church. This funeral is for people who depart during the Pascha week. This funeral is prayed, as the church does not raise incense during the Pashca week on Sunday, Monday, Tuesday, and Wednesday. If any one departs during this week, he or she is brought to the church to attend the Pascha prayers of that hour, without raising incense.

بعد انتهاء قداس أحد الشعانين وتوزيع الأسرار المقدسة ، يجتمع الشعب بكامله فى البيعة المقدسة لحضور التجنيز العام لجميع الراقدين فى الرب خلال اسبوع الآلام فقط ، لأنها لا تحتفل باقامة جنازات تذكارية عن أنفس المسيحيين المنتقلين فى خلال هذا الاسبوع . فهذا التجنيز يغنى عن التجنيز الأربعة أيام التى لا يجب فيها رفع البخور وهى أيام : الأحد والأثنين والثلاثاء والأربعاء . وإذا توفى أحد فى تلك الأيام ، فليحضروا به إلى البيعة وتقرأ فصول وقراءات ما يلائم ساعة دخول المتوفى إلى الكنيسة من السواعى الليلية أو النهارية بدون رفع بخور .

The reason for not holding funeral services during this week

1) This week is dedicated for the commemoration of the suffering, crucifixion and death of our Lord, God and Savior Jesus Christ.
2) Our Lord Jesus had suffered a lot in His body and soul (Matthew 26, 27, 28). That is why the church does not go to grieve other than her Bridegroom.
3) The church has dedicated this week for fasting and prayers, in sorrow for our sins and sharing the suffering of the Lord, as St. Paul said: "For godly sorrow works repentance to salvation not to be regretted: but the sorrow of the world works death." (Corinthians 7:10)

أسباب عدم إقامة جنازات فى اسبوع الآلام .

(1) لأن هذا الاسبوع قد خصص لعمل تذكار آلام وصلب وموت إبن الله المتجسد .

(2) لأن الرب يسوع قد قاسى فى هذا الاسبوع آلاماً مرة فى نفسه وجسده معاً (مت 26 و 37 و 38) لهذا رأت الكنيسة أن لا تترك فى حزن آخر حزن يسوع عريسها (3) لأن الكنيسة قد خصصت هذا الاسبوع لصرفه فى الصلاة والتسبيح والصوم ، وهى حزينة على خطايانا مشتركة فى آلام الرب عملاً بقول الكتاب على لسان بولس الرسول : " لأن الحزن الذى بحسب مشيئة الله ينشئ توبة لخلاص بلا ندامة ، أما حزن العالم فينشئ موتاً " (2كو 7 : 10) .

The reason why there are no liturgies for three days

Palm Sunday corresponds to the Sunday, which was on the tenth day of the lunar month, during which, the Israelites were supposed to buy the good lamb for the feast; and the Lord ordered them saying: " And you shall keep it up until the fourteenth day of the same month: and the whole assembly of the congregation of Israel shall kill it in the evening." Exodus 12:6

This lamb was kept alive for three days, which refer to Monday, Tuesday, and Wednesday. Then they kill Him on Thursday.

Our Lord Jesus is the true sacrifice, the lamb of God, Who was kept alive from Sunday, with His entry to Jerusalem, till Thursday, on which He offered Himself as a sacrifice without blood before they crucify Him.

السبب فى عطلة القداس ثلاثة أيام فى اسبوع الآلام

كان يوم الأحد الذى هو يوم الشعانين يوافق اليوم العاشر من الهلال يوم ابتياع الغنم للعيد حسب امر الرب فى ان يشتروا خروفاً حولياً ويكون بلا عيب ويكون ذلك فى اليوم العاشر."ويكون عندكم تحت الحفظ الى اليوم الرابع عشر من هذا الشهر. ثم يذبحه كل جمهور جماعة اسرائيل في العشية ." (خروج 12)
فصار هذا الخروف عندهم محفوظاً بغير ذبح ثلاثة أيام أى الاثنين والثلاثاء والأربعاء . ثم يذبحوه فى يوم الخميس . والسيد المسيح هو الذبيحة الحقيقية وهو حمل الله الذى يرفع خطية العالم فهو أيضاً بقى من يوم أحد الشعانين ، يوم دخوله أورشليم إلى يوم خميس العهد (ثلاثة أيام) حيث ذبح ذاته وكسر نفسه بإرادته كذبيحة غير دموية للعهد الجديد يوم الخميس الكبير قبل أن يأخذه اليهود والرومان ويقدموه لذبيحة الصليب .

The Sixth Hour of Palm Sunday - The General Funeral Service
الساعة السادسة من يوم أحد الشعانين ـ صلاة التجنيز

Ezekiel 37:1-14

(حزقيال النبى 37 : 1 - 14)

And the hand of the Lord came upon me, and the Lord brought me forth by the Spirit, and set me in the midst of the plain, and it was full of human bones. And He led me round about them every way. And behold, there were very many on the face of the plain, very dry. And He said to me, Son of man, will these bones live? And I said, O Lord God, only You know this! And He said to me, Prophesy upon these bones, and you shall say to them, You dry bones, hear the word of the Lord. Thus says the Lord to these bones: Behold, I will bring upon you the breath of life; and I will lay sinews upon you, and will bring up flesh upon you, and will spread skin upon you, and I will put My Spirit into you, and you shall live; and you shall know that I am the Lord. So I prophesied as the Lord commanded me. And it came to pass while I was prophesying, that behold, there was a rattling, and the bones approached each one to his joint. And I looked, and behold, sinews and flesh grew upon them, and skin came upon them above. But there was not breath in them. And He said to me, Prophesy to the wind, prophesy, son of man, and say to the wind, Thus says the Lord: Come from the four winds, O breath, and breathe upon these dead, that they may live. So I prophesied as He commanded me, and the breath entered into them, and they lived, and stood upon their feet, a very great congregation. And the Lord spoke to me, saying, Son of man, these bones are the whole house of Israel: and they say, Our bones have become dry, our hope has perished, we are quite spent. Therefore prophesy and say, Thus says the Lord: Behold, I will open your tombs, and will bring you up out of your tombs, and I will bring you into the land of Israel. And you shall know that I am the Lord, when I have opened your graves, that I may bring up My people from their graves. And I will put My Spirit within you, and you shall live, and I will place you upon your own land; and you shall know that I am the Lord; I have spoken, and will do it, says the Lord.

Glory be to the Holy Trinity. Amen

وكانت علىَّ يد الرب فاخرجنى بروح الرب . ووضعنى فى وسط الحقل . وهذا كان ممتلئاً عظاماً بشرية . وأَمَرتنى عليها من حولها كلها . فاذا هى كثيرة جداً على وجه الحقل ويابسة جداً . فقال لى الرب يا إبن الإنسان أترى تحيا هذه العظام؟ فقلت: أيها السيد الرب إله الجنود أنت تعلم . فقال لي: تنبأ على هذه العظام وقل لهذه العظام اليابسة اسمعى كلمة الرب . هكذا قال السيد الرب لهذه العظام: هانذا أدخــل فيــكم روحــاً فتحيون . وأضع عليكم عصباً وأكسيكم لحماً وأبسط عليكم جلداً. اجعل فيكم روحاً فتحيون . وتعلمون أنى أنا هو الرب فتنبأت كما أمرنى. فكان صوت عند تنبوّى وإذا زلزلة حدثت . فتقاربت العظام لبعضها بعضاً . ورأيت وإذا العصب والجلد بسط عليها . ولم يكن بها روح . فقال لي: تنبأ نحو الروح . تنبأ يا إبن الإنسان . وقل للروح هكذا قال السيد الرب: هلم أيها الروح من رياحك الأربع . وهب فى الأموات فيحيوا . فتنبأت كما أمرنى. فدخل فيهم الروح . وبينما أنا أتنبأ وإذ بزلزلة قد حدثت . فقاموا واقفين على أقدامهم وكانوا جيشاً عظيماً كثيراً جداً فقال لي: يا إبن الإنسان . هذه العظام كلها هى بيت إسرائيل . وهم يقولون قد سحقت عظامنا . وهلك رجاؤنا . وانقطعنا . لذلك تنبأ وقل لهم هكذا قال السيد الرب: هأنذا أفتح قبوركم وأصعدكم يا شعبى . وأجعل فيكم روح الحياة. وأتى بكم إلى أرض إسرائيل . فتعلمون أنى أنا هو الرب . حين أفتح القبور وأصعدكم منها يا شعبى . وأتى بكم إلى أرضكم . فتعلمون أنى أنا هو الرب تكلمت وفعلت قال السيد الرب . مجداً للثالوث القدوس .

The Pauline Epistle - البولس
(The Introduction - مقدمة البولس)

| For the resurrection of the dead who slept and reposed in the faith of Christ, O Lord repose all their souls. | إثيّه تي اناستاسيس : إنتيه نى ريف موؤوت نى إيطاف إنكوت : اف امطون ام موؤو خين اف ناهتى ام بخرستوس: إمبتشويس ما إمطون إننوو بسيشى تيروو . | Ⲉⲑⲃⲉ ⲧ̀ⲁⲛⲁⲥⲧⲁⲥⲓⲥ ⲛ̀ⲧⲉ ⲛⲓⲣⲉϥⲙⲱⲟⲩⲧ ⲛⲏⲉⲧⲁⲩⲉⲛⲕⲟⲧ ⲁⲩⲉⲙⲧⲟⲛⲙⲙⲱⲟⲩ ϧⲉⲛ ⲫ̀ⲛⲁϩϯ ⲙ̀Ⲡⲭ̅ⲥ̅ : Ⲡⲟ̅ⲥ̅ ⲙⲁ̀ⲙⲧⲟⲛ ⲛ̀ⲛⲟⲩⲯⲩⲭⲏ ⲧⲏⲣⲟⲩ . | من اجل قيامة الاموات الذين رقدوا و تنيحوا فى الايمان بالمسيح ، يارب نيح نفوسهم اجمعين . |

Paul, the servant of our Lord Jesus Christ, called to be an apostle, appointed to the gospel of God.	باقلوس اف فوك ام بين تشويس ايسوس بخرستوس: بى ابوسطولوس ات ثاهيم فى ايه طاف ثاثف ايه بى هى شين نوفى انثيه افنوتى.	Παⲩλος ⲫ̀ⲃⲱⲕ ⲙ̀Ⲡⲉⲛϭⲟⲓⲥ Ⲓⲏⲥ Ⲡⲭ̅ⲥ̅ : ⲡⲓⲁ̀ⲡⲟⲥⲧⲟⲗⲟⲥ ⲉⲧⲑⲁϩⲉⲙ ⲫⲏⲉⲧⲁⲩⲑⲁϣϥ ⲉ̀ⲡⲓϩⲓϣⲉⲛⲛⲟⲩϥⲓ ⲛ̀ⲧⲉ Ⲫϯ.	بولس عبد ربنا يسوع المسيح الرسول المدعو المفرز لكرازة الله.

The Pauline Epistle

Ⲁⲡⲟⲥⲧⲟⲗⲟⲥ ⲡⲣⲟⲥ Ⲛⲓⲕⲟⲣⲛⲑⲓⲟⲥ Ⲕⲉⲫ ⲓ̅ⲉ̅ : ⲁ̅ - ⲕ̅ⲃ̅

1 Corinthians 15:1-23

Moreover, brethren, I declare to you the gospel which I preached to you, which also you received and in which you stand, by which also you are saved, if you hold fast that word which I preached to you—unless you believed in vain. For I delivered to you first of all that which I also received: that Christ died for our sins according to the Scriptures, and that He was buried, and that He rose again the third day according to the Scriptures, and that He was seen by Cephas, then by the twelve. After that He was seen by over five hundred brethren at once, of whom the greater part remain to the present, but some have fallen asleep. After that He was seen by James, then by all the apostles. Then last of all He was seen by me also, as by one born out of due time. For I am the least of the apostles, who am not worthy to be called an apostle, because I persecuted the church of God. But by the grace of God I am what I am, and His grace toward me was not in vain; but I labored more abundantly than they all, yet not I, but the grace of God which was with me. Therefore, whether it was I or they, so we preach and so you believed. Now if Christ is preached that He has been raised from the dead, how do some among you say that there is no resurrection of the

Ϯⲧⲁⲙⲟ Ⲇⲉ ⲙ̀ⲙⲱⲧⲉⲛ ⲛⲁⲥⲛⲏⲟⲩ ⲉ̀ⲡⲓⲉⲩⲁⲅⲅⲉⲗⲓⲟⲛ ⲫⲏⲉⲧⲁⲓϩⲓϣⲉⲛⲛⲟⲩϥⲓ ⲙ̀ⲙⲟϥ ⲛⲱⲧⲉⲛ : ⲉⲧⲉ ⲫⲏ ⲡⲉ ⲉ̀ⲧⲁⲣⲉⲧⲉⲛ ϭⲓⲧϥ ⲫⲁⲓ ⲉⲧⲉⲛⲟ̀ϩⲓ ⲉ̀ⲣⲁⲧⲉⲛ ⲑⲏⲛⲟⲩ ⲛ̀ϧⲏⲧϥ : ⲫⲁⲓ ⲟⲛ ⲉⲧⲉⲛⲛⲁⲛⲟϩⲉⲙ ⲉ̀ⲃⲟⲗ ϩⲓⲧⲟⲧϥ ϫⲉ ϧⲉⲛ ⲟⲩⲥⲁϫⲓ ⲁⲓϩⲓϣⲉⲛⲛⲟⲩϥⲓ ⲛⲱⲧⲉⲛ ⲓⲥϫⲉ ⲧⲟⲧⲉⲛ ⲁⲙⲟⲛⲓ ⲙ̀ⲙⲟϥ ⲥⲁⲃⲟⲗ ⲓⲙⲏⲧⲓ ⲥⲓⲕⲏ ⲁⲣⲉⲧⲉⲛⲛⲁϩϯ : ⲁⲓϯ ⲅⲁⲣ ⲛ̀ⲧⲉⲛ ⲑⲏⲛⲟⲩ ⲛ̀ϣⲟⲣⲡ ⲙ̀ⲫⲏⲉⲧⲁⲓ ϭⲓⲧϥ : ϫⲉ Ⲡⲭ̅ⲥ̅ ⲁϥⲙⲟⲩ ⲉ̀ϩⲣⲏⲓ ⲉ̀ϫⲉⲛ ⲛⲉⲛⲛⲟⲃⲓ ⲕⲁⲧⲁ ⲛⲓⲅⲣⲁⲫⲏ . Ⲟⲩⲟϩ ϫⲉ ⲁⲩⲕⲟⲥϥ ⲟⲩⲟϩ ϫⲉ ⲁϥⲧⲱⲛϥ ϧⲉⲛ ⲡⲓⲉ̀ϩⲟⲟⲩ ⲙ̀ⲙⲁϩ ϣⲟⲙⲧ ⲕⲁⲧⲁ ⲛⲓⲅⲣⲁⲫⲏ : ⲟⲩⲟϩ ϫⲉ ⲁϥⲟⲩⲱⲛϩϥ ⲉ̀Ⲕⲏⲫⲁ ⲓⲧⲁ ⲁϥⲟⲩⲱⲛϩϥ ⲉ̀ⲡⲓⲙⲏⲧⲥⲛⲁⲩ ⲙⲉⲛⲉⲛⲥⲱⲥ ⲁϥⲟⲩⲱⲛϩϥ ⲥⲁ ⲡ̀ϣⲱⲓ ⲛ̀ⲧⲓⲟⲩ ϣⲉ ⲛ̀ⲥⲟⲛ ⲉⲩⲥⲟⲡ ⲛⲁⲓ ⲉ̀ⲧⲉ ⲡⲟⲩϩⲟⲩⲟ ϣⲟⲡ ϣⲁ ⲉ̀ϧⲟⲩⲛ ⲉ̀ϯⲛⲟⲩ ϩⲁⲛⲕⲉⲭⲱⲟⲩⲛⲓ Ⲇⲉ ⲁⲩⲉⲛⲕⲟⲧ . Ⲓⲧⲁ ⲁϥⲟⲩⲱⲛϩϥ ⲉ̀Ⲓⲁⲕⲱⲃⲟⲥ ⲓⲧⲁ ⲁϥⲟⲩⲱⲛϩϥ ⲉ̀ⲛⲓⲁⲡⲟⲥⲧⲟⲗⲟⲥ ⲧⲏⲣⲟⲩ : ⲉ̀ⲡϧⲁⲉ Ⲇⲉ ⲙ̀ⲙⲱⲟⲩ ⲧⲏⲣⲟⲩ ⲙ̀ⲫⲣⲏϯ ⲙ̀ⲡⲓⲟⲩϫⲉ ⲁϥⲟⲩⲱⲛϩϥ ⲉ̀ⲣⲟⲓ ϩⲱ : ⲁⲛⲟⲕ ⲅⲁⲣ ⲡⲉ ⲡⲓⲕⲟⲩϫⲓ ⲉ̀ⲃⲟⲗ ⲟⲩⲧⲉ ⲛⲓⲁⲡⲟⲥⲧⲟⲗⲟⲥ ⲧⲏⲣⲟⲩ ⲛ̀ϯⲉⲙⲡϣⲁ ⲁⲛ ⲉⲑⲣⲟⲩⲙⲟⲩϯ ⲉ̀ⲣⲟⲓ ϫⲉ ⲁⲡⲟⲥⲧⲟⲗⲟⲥ ⲉⲑⲃⲉ ⲁⲓϭⲟϫⲓ ⲛ̀ⲥⲁ ϯⲉⲕⲕⲗⲏⲥⲓⲁ ⲛ̀ⲧⲉ Ⲫϯ . Ϧⲉⲛ ⲟⲩϩⲙⲟⲧ Ⲇⲉ ⲛ̀ⲧⲉ Ⲫϯ ϯⲟⲓ ⲙ̀ⲡⲉϯⲟⲓ ⲙ̀ⲙⲟϥ ⲟⲩⲟϩ ⲡⲉϥϩⲙⲟⲧ ⲉⲧⲉ ⲛ̀ϧⲏⲧ ⲙ̀ⲡⲉϥϣⲱⲡⲓ ⲉϥϣⲟⲩⲓⲧ ⲁⲗⲗⲁ ⲁⲓϧⲓⲥⲓ ⲉ̀ϩⲟⲧⲉⲣⲱⲟⲩ ⲧⲏⲣⲟⲩ : ⲁⲛⲟⲕ Ⲇⲉ ⲁⲛ ⲁⲗⲗⲁ ⲡⲓϩⲙⲟⲧ ⲛ̀ⲧⲉ Ⲫϯ ⲉⲑ ⲛⲉⲙⲏⲓ : ⲓⲧⲉ ⲟⲩⲛ ⲁⲛⲟⲕ ⲓⲧⲉ ⲛⲏ ⲧⲉⲛϩⲓⲱⲓϣ ⲙ̀ⲡⲁⲓⲣⲏϯ ⲟⲩⲟϩ ⲡⲁⲓⲣⲏϯ ⲁⲧⲉⲧⲉⲛⲛⲁϩϯ : ⲓⲥϫⲉ Ⲇⲉ Ⲡⲭ̅ⲥ̅ ⲥⲉϩⲓⲱⲓϣ ⲙ̀ⲙⲟϥ ϫⲉ ⲁϥⲧⲱⲛϥ ⲉ̀ⲃⲟⲗ ϧⲉⲛ ⲛⲏⲉⲑⲙⲱⲟⲩⲧ ⲡⲱⲥ ⲟⲩⲟⲛ ϩⲁⲛⲟⲩⲟⲛ ϫⲉ ⲙ̀ⲙⲟⲥ ϧⲉⲛ ⲑⲏⲛⲟⲩ ϫⲉ ⲙ̀ⲙⲟⲛ ⲁⲛⲁⲥⲧⲁⲥⲓⲥ

(1 كورنثوس 15: 1-23)

وأنا أعلمكم يا أخوتى أن الانجيل الذى بشرتكم به هو الذى قبلتموه، هذا الذى أنتم فيه ثابتون . هذا الذى خلصتم من قبله . لأنى بالكلام بشرتكم به ان كنتم به تتمسكون وإلا فباطل قد أمنتم . لأنى سلمت إليكم أولاً ما قد أخذت . ان المسيح مات عن خطايانا كما فى الكتب . وأنه دفن وأنه قام فى اليوم الثالث كما فى الكتب وأنه ظهر لصفا ثم ظهر للاثنى عشر ومن بعدهم لأكثر من خمسمائة أخ معاً أكثرهم باق أحياء إلى الآن ومنهم من قد رقد . ثم ظهر ليعقوب . ثم ترأى لسائر الرسل وفى آخر جميعهم أنا الذى مثل السقط ظهر لى أيضاً وأنا أصغر جميع الرسل ولست مستحقاً أن أدعى رسولاً من أجل أنى طاردت بيعة الله وبنعمة الله صرت إلى ما أنا عليه ونعمته التى فىَّ ليست باطلة . بل وقد تعبت أكثر من جميعهم ولكن لا أنا بل نعمة الله التى معى . فأن كنت إذاً أنا أو أولئك فهكذا نبشر وهكذا آمنتم . وإن كان ينادى بالمسيح أنه قام من الأموات فكيف صار فيكم قوم يقولون أنه لا تكون قيامة للأموات . فإن لم تكن قيامة للأموات فالمسيح ما

dead? But if there is no resurrection of the dead, then Christ is not risen. And if Christ is not risen, then our preaching is empty and your faith is also empty. Yes, and we are found false witnesses of God, because we have testified of God that He raised up Christ, whom He did not raise up—if in fact the dead do not rise. For if the dead do not rise, then Christ is not risen. And if Christ is not risen, your faith is futile; you are still in your sins! Then also those who have fallen asleep in Christ have perished. If in this life only we have hope in Christ, we are of all men the most pitiable. But now Christ is risen from the dead, and has become the firstfruits of those who have fallen asleep. For since by man came death, by Man also came the resurrection of the dead. For as in Adam all die, even so in Christ all shall be made alive. But each one in his own order: Christ the firstfruits, afterward those who are Christ's at His coming. The Grace of God the Father be with you all. Amen

ⲛ̀ⲧⲉ ⲛⲓⲣⲉϥⲙⲱⲟⲩⲧ ⲛⲁϣⲱⲡⲓ · ⲓⲥϫⲉ ⲇⲉ ⲙ̀ⲙⲟⲛ ⲛ̀ⲁⲛⲁⲥⲧⲁⲥⲓⲥ ⲛ̀ⲧⲉ ⲛⲓⲣⲉϥⲙⲱⲟⲩⲧ ⲛⲁϣⲱⲡⲓ ⲓⲉ ⲟⲩ ⲇⲉ ⲙ̀ⲡⲉ Ⲡ̅ⲭ̅ⲥ̅ ⲧⲱⲛϥ: ⲓⲥϫⲉ ⲇⲉ ⲙ̀ⲡⲉ Ⲡ̅ⲭ̅ⲥ̅ ⲧⲱⲛϥ ϩⲁⲣⲁ ϥϣⲟⲩⲓⲧ ⲛ̀ϫⲉ ⲡⲉⲛϩⲓⲱⲓϣ ϥϣⲟⲩⲓⲧ ⲟⲛ ⲛ̀ϫⲉ ⲡⲉⲧⲉⲛⲕⲉⲛⲁϩϯ: ⲥⲉⲛⲁϫⲉⲙⲉⲛ ⲇⲉ ⲟⲛ ⲉⲛⲟⲓ ⲙ̀ⲙⲉⲑⲣⲉ ⲛ̀ⲛⲟⲩϫ ϧⲁ Ⲫ̀ϯ ϫⲉ ⲁⲛ ⲉⲣⲙⲉⲑⲣⲉ ϧⲁ Ⲫ̀ϯ ϫⲉ ⲁϥⲧⲟⲩⲛⲟⲥ Ⲡ̅ⲭ̅ⲥ̅ ⲫⲁⲓ ⲉⲧⲉ ⲙ̀ⲡⲉϥⲧⲟⲩⲛⲟⲥϥ ⲓⲥϫⲉ ϩⲁⲣⲁ ⲛⲓⲣⲉϥⲙⲱⲟⲩⲧ ⲛⲁ ⲧⲟⲩⲟⲩⲛⲟⲩ ⲁⲛ · Ⲓⲥϫⲉ ⲅⲁⲣ ⲛⲓⲣⲉϥⲙⲱⲟⲩⲧ ⲛⲁⲧⲟⲩⲟⲩⲛⲟⲩ ⲁⲛ ⲓⲉ ⲟⲩ ⲇⲉ ⲙ̀ⲡⲉ Ⲡ̅ⲭ̅ⲥ̅ ⲧⲱⲛϥ: ⲓⲥϫⲉ ⲇⲉ ⲙ̀ⲡⲉ Ⲡ̅ⲭ̅ⲥ̅ ⲧⲱⲛϥ ⲟⲩⲉ̀ⲫⲗⲏⲟⲩ ⲡⲉ ⲡⲉⲧⲉⲛⲛⲁϩϯ ⲉ̀ⲧⲓ ⲟⲛ ⲧⲉⲧⲉⲛⲭⲏ ⲛ̀ϧⲣⲏⲓ ϧⲉⲛ ⲛⲉⲧⲉⲛⲛⲟⲃⲓ : ⲓⲉ ϩⲁⲣⲁ ⲛⲏⲉ̀ⲧⲁⲩⲉⲛⲕⲟⲧ ϧⲉⲛ Ⲡ̅ⲭ̅ⲥ̅ ⲁⲩⲧⲁⲕⲟ : ⲓⲥϫⲉ ⲇⲉ ⲛ̀ϧⲣⲏⲓ ϧⲉⲛ ⲡⲁⲓⲱⲛϧ ⲙ̀ⲙⲁⲩⲁⲧϥ ⲁⲛⲉⲣϩⲉⲗⲡⲓⲥ ⲉ̀Ⲡ̅ⲭ̅ⲥ̅ ⲓⲉ ⲧⲉⲛⲃⲓ ⲟⲩⲛⲁⲓ ⲉ̀ⲣⲟⲛ ⲉ̀ϩⲟⲧⲉ ⲣⲱⲙⲓ ⲛⲓⲃⲉⲛ · Ϯⲛⲟⲩ ⲇⲉ ⲁ Ⲡ̅ⲭ̅ⲥ̅ ⲧⲱⲛϥ ⲉ̀ⲃⲟⲗ ϧⲉⲛ ⲛⲏⲉⲑⲙⲱⲟⲩⲧ ⲧ̀ⲁⲡⲁⲣⲭⲏ ⲛ̀ⲧⲉ ⲛⲏⲉ̀ⲧⲁⲩⲉⲛⲕⲟⲧ : ⲉⲡⲓⲇⲏ ⲅⲁⲣ ⲉ̀ⲃⲟⲗ ϩⲓⲧⲉⲛ ⲟⲩⲣⲱⲙⲓ ⲁ Ⲫⲓⲟⲧ ϣⲱⲡⲓ ⲉ̀ⲃⲟⲗ ⲟⲛ ϩⲓⲧⲉⲛ ⲕⲉⲣⲱⲙⲓ ⲧ̀ⲁⲛⲁⲥⲧⲁⲥⲓⲥ ⲛ̀ⲧⲉ ⲛⲓⲣⲉϥⲙⲱⲟⲩⲧ : ⲙ̀ⲫⲣⲏϯ ⲅⲁⲣ ⲉ̀ⲧⲉ ϧⲉⲛ Ⲁⲇⲁⲙ ⲥⲉⲛⲁⲙⲟⲩ ⲧⲏⲣⲟⲩ : ⲡⲁⲓⲣⲏϯ ⲟⲛ ϧⲉⲛ Ⲡ̅ⲭ̅ⲥ̅ ⲥⲉⲛⲁⲱⲛϧ ⲧⲏⲣⲟⲩ : ⲡⲓⲟⲩⲁⲓ ⲇⲉ ⲡⲓⲟⲩⲁⲓ ϧⲉⲛ ⲧⲉϥⲧⲁⲅⲙⲁ · Ⲡⲓϩⲙⲟⲧ ⲛⲉⲙ ϯϩⲓⲣⲏⲛⲏ

قام وإن كان المسيح لم يقم فكرازتنا باطلة وباطل أيضاً إيمانكم ونوجد نحن أيضاً شهود زور لله حيث قد شهدنا على الله أنه قد أقام المسيح وهو لم يقيمه ان كان الموتى لا يقومون. فإن كان الموتى لا يقومون فلا يكون المسيح قد قام أيضاً. وإن كان المسيح لم يقم فباطل هو إيمانكم وأنتم بعد تحت خطاياكم. أو لعل الذين ماتوا فى المسيح قد هلكوا؟ وإن كنا فى هذه الحياة فقط نرجو المسيح فنحن أشقى جميع الناس. والآن قد قام المسيح من الأموات وصار باكورة المضطجعين. وكما أنه بإنسان كان الموت كذلك بإنسان آخر تكون قيامة الأموات. وكما أنه فى آدم يموت الجميع كذلك فى المسيح أيضاً سيحيا الجميع كل واحد فى رتبته. فالمسيح هو البدء ثم الذين للمسيح عند مجيئه. نعمة الله الآب ...

+ **Then we sing Ⲁⲅⲓⲟⲥ ⲑⲉⲛ Ⲇⲟⲝⲁ Ⲡⲁⲧⲣⲓ**

+ **The priest prays the litany of the Gospel.**

+ **The psalm and Gospel are read.**

+ ثم تقال Ⲁⲅⲓⲟⲥ وبعدها Ⲇⲟⲝⲁ Ⲡⲁⲧⲣⲓ . ثم يقول الكاهن أوشية الانجيل ويرتل المزمور ويقرأ الانجيل.

The Psalm

Ⲯⲁⲗⲙⲟⲥ ⲝ̅ⲇ̅ : ⲇ̅ ⲛⲉⲙ ⲉ̅

Psalms 64:4-5

Blessed is the man You choose, And cause to approach You, That he may dwell in Your courts. We shall be satisfied with the goodness of Your house, Of Your holy temple. Alleluia

Ⲱⲟⲩⲛⲓⲁⲧϥ ⲙ̀ⲫⲏⲉⲧⲁⲕ - ⲥⲟⲧⲡϥ ⲟⲩⲟϩ ⲁⲕϣⲟⲡϥ ⲉ̀ⲣⲟⲕ : ⲉϥⲉ̀ϣⲱⲡⲓ ϧⲉⲛ ⲛⲉⲕⲁⲩⲗⲏⲟⲩ ϣⲁ ⲉ̀ⲛⲉϩ : ⲉⲛⲉ̀ⲥⲓ ⲉ̀ⲃⲟⲗ ϧⲉⲛ ⲛⲓⲁ̀ⲅⲁⲑⲟⲛ ⲛ̀ⲧⲉ ⲡⲉⲕⲏⲓ : ϥⲟⲩⲁⲃ ⲛ̀ϫⲉ ⲡⲉⲕⲉⲣⲫⲉⲓ ⲟⲩⲟϩ ϥⲟⲓ ⲛ̀ϣ̀ⲫⲏⲣⲓ ϧⲉⲛ ⲟⲩⲙⲉⲑⲙⲏⲓ . ⲁ̅ⲗ̅ .

أو أوونياتف إمفى إطاكسوتبف أوه أكشوبف إروك : إف إشوبى خين نيك أفليوو شا إنيه : إنئسى إيفول خين نى أغاثوس إنتيه بيكئي : إفؤواب إنجيه بيكئرفيى أووه إفوى إنشفيرى خين أوو ميثمى . الليلويا

(مز 64 : 4 و 5)

طوبى لمن اخترته وقبلته ليسكن فى ديارك إلى الأبد. سنشبع من خيرات بيتك. قدوس هو هيكلك وعجيب بالبر. الليلويا .

The Gospel

Ⲉⲩⲁⲅⲅⲉⲗⲓⲟⲛ Ⲕⲁⲧⲁ Ⲓⲱⲁⲛⲛⲏⲛ Ⲕⲉⲫ ⲉ̄: ⲓ̄ⲑ̄ - ⲕ̄ⲑ̄

John 5:19-29

Then Jesus answered and said to them, "Most assuredly, I say to you, the Son can do nothing of Himself, but what He sees the Father do; for whatever He does, the Son also does in like manner. For the Father loves the Son, and shows Him all things that He Himself does; and He will show Him greater works than these, that you may marvel. For as the Father raises the dead and gives life to them, even so the Son gives life to whom He will. For the Father judges no one, but has committed all judgment to the Son, that all should honor the Son just as they honor the Father. He who does not honor the Son does not honor the Father who sent Him. "Most assuredly, I say to you, he who hears My word and believes in Him who sent Me has everlasting life, and shall not come into judgment, but has passed from death into life. Most assuredly, I say to you, the hour is coming, and now is, when the dead will hear the voice of the Son of God; and those who hear will live. For as the Father has life in Himself, so He has granted the Son to have life in Himself, and has given Him authority to execute judgment also, because He is the Son of Man. Do not marvel at this; for the hour is coming in which all who are in the graves will hear His voice and come forth, those who have done good, to the resurrection of life, and those who have done evil, to the resurrection of condemnation. Glory be to God forever, Amen.

Ⲁϥⲉⲣⲟⲩⲱ ⲇⲉ ⲛ̄ϫⲉ Ⲓⲏⲥ ⲡⲉϫⲁϥ ⲛⲱⲟⲩ ϫⲉ ⲁⲙⲏⲛ ⲁⲙⲏⲛ ϯϫⲱ ⲙ̄ⲙⲟⲥ ⲛⲱⲧⲉⲛ : ϫⲉ ⲙ̄ⲙⲟⲛ ϣϫⲟⲙ ⲛ̄ⲧⲉ ⲡϣⲏⲣⲓ ⲉⲣϩ̄ⲗⲓ ⲉⲃⲟⲗ ϩⲓⲧⲟⲧϥ ⲁϥϣⲧⲉⲙⲛⲁⲩ ⲉⲫⲓⲱⲧ ⲉϥⲓⲣⲓ ⲙ̄ⲙⲟϥ : ⲛⲏ ⲅⲁⲣ ⲉⲧⲉ ⲫⲓⲱⲧ ⲣⲁ ⲙ̄ⲙⲱⲟⲩ ⲛⲁⲓⲟⲛ ⲉⲧⲉ ⲡⲓⲕⲉϣⲏⲣⲓ ⲓⲣⲓ ⲙ̄ⲙⲱⲟⲩ : ⲫⲓⲱⲧ ⲅⲁⲣ ϥⲙⲉⲓ ⲙ̄ⲡϣⲏⲣⲓ ⲟⲩⲟϩ ϩⲱⲃ ⲛⲓⲃⲉⲛ ⲧⲉϥⲓⲣⲓ ⲙ̄ⲙⲱⲟⲩ ϥⲛⲁⲧⲁⲙⲟϥ ⲉⲣⲱⲟⲩ ⲟⲩⲟϩ ϩⲁⲛ̄ϩⲃⲏⲟⲩⲓ ⲉⲧⲟⲓ ⲛ̄ⲛⲓϣⲧ̄ ⲉⲛⲁⲓ ϥⲛⲁⲧⲁⲙⲟϥ ⲉⲣⲱⲟⲩ ϩⲓⲛⲁ ⲛ̄ⲑⲱⲧⲉⲛ ⲛ̄ⲧⲉ ⲧⲉⲧⲉⲛⲉⲣϣ̄ⲫⲏⲣⲓ : ⲙ̄ⲫⲣⲏϯ ⲅⲁⲣ ⲉⲧⲉ ⲫⲓⲱⲧ ⲧⲟⲩⲛⲟⲥ ⲛⲓⲣⲉϥⲙⲱⲟⲩⲧ ⲟⲩⲟϩ ϥⲧⲁⲛϧⲟ ⲙ̄ⲙⲱⲟⲩ ⲡⲓⲣⲏϯ ⲟⲛ ⲡⲓⲕⲉϣⲏⲣⲓ ⲛⲏ ⲉⲧⲁϥⲟⲩⲁϣⲟⲩ ϥⲧⲁⲛϧⲟ ⲙ̄ⲙⲱⲟⲩ. Ⲟⲩ ⲇⲉ ⲅⲁⲣ ⲫⲓⲱⲧ ϥ̄ⲛⲁϯϩⲁⲡ ⲉϩ̄ⲗⲓ ⲁⲛ ⲁⲗⲗⲁ ⲡⲓϩⲁⲡ ⲧⲏⲣϥ ⲁϥⲧⲏⲓϥ ⲙ̄ⲡⲓϣⲏⲣⲓ : ϩⲓⲛⲁ ⲛ̄ⲧⲉ ⲟⲩⲟⲛ ⲛⲓⲃⲉⲛ ⲉⲣⲧⲓⲙⲁⲛ ⲙ̄ⲡⲓϣⲏⲣⲓ ⲙ̄ⲫⲣⲏϯ ⲉⲧⲟⲩⲉⲣⲧⲓⲙⲁⲛ ⲙ̄ⲫⲓⲱⲧ ⲫⲏⲉⲧⲉ ⲛ̄ϥⲉⲣⲧⲓⲙⲁⲛ ⲁⲛ ⲙ̄ⲡⲓϣⲏⲣⲓ ⲛ̄ϥⲉⲣⲧⲓⲙⲁⲛ ⲁⲛ ⲟⲛ ⲙ̄ⲡⲓⲕⲉⲓⲱⲧ ⲉⲧⲁϥⲧⲁⲟⲩⲟϥ : ⲁⲙⲏⲛ ⲁⲙⲏⲛ ϯϫⲱ ⲙ̄ⲙⲟⲥ ⲛⲱⲧⲉⲛ ϫⲉ ⲫⲏⲉⲧⲥⲱⲧⲉⲙ ⲉⲡⲁⲥⲁϫⲓ ⲟⲩⲟϩ ⲛ̄ⲧⲉϥⲛⲁϩϯ ⲉⲫⲏⲉⲧⲁϥⲧⲁⲟⲩⲟⲓ ⲟⲩⲟⲛⲧⲉϥ ⲛ̄ⲱⲛϧ ⲛ̄ⲉⲛⲉϩ ⲙ̄ⲙⲁⲩ ⲟⲩⲟϩ ⲛ̄ϥⲛⲁⲓ ⲁⲛ ⲉ̄ⲡⲁϩ ⲁⲗⲗⲁ ϥⲛⲁⲟⲩⲱⲧⲉⲃ ⲉⲃⲟⲗ ϧⲉⲛ ⲫⲙⲟⲩ ⲉϧⲟⲩⲛ ⲉⲡⲱⲛϧ. Ⲁⲙⲏⲛ ⲁⲙⲏⲛ ϯϫⲱ ⲙ̄ⲙⲟⲥ ⲛⲱⲧⲉⲛ ϫⲉ ⲥ̄ⲛⲏⲟⲩ ⲛ̄ϫⲉ ⲟⲩⲟⲩⲛⲟⲩ ⲉⲧⲉ ϯⲛⲟⲩ ⲧⲉ ϩⲟⲧⲉ ⲉⲣⲉ ⲛⲓⲣⲉϥⲙⲱⲟⲩⲧ ⲛⲁⲥⲱⲧⲉⲙ ⲉ̄ⲧⲥⲙⲏ ⲙ̄ⲡϣⲏⲣⲓ ⲙ̄Ⲫϯ ⲟⲩⲟϩ ⲛⲏⲉⲑⲛⲁⲥⲱⲧⲉⲙ ⲉⲩⲉⲱⲛϧ : ⲙ̄ⲫⲣⲏϯ ⲅⲁⲣ ⲉⲧⲉ ⲟⲩⲟⲛ ⲟⲩⲱⲛϧ ϣⲟⲡ ϧⲉⲛ ⲫⲓⲱⲧ ⲡⲁⲓⲣⲏϯ ⲟⲛ ⲁϥⲧⲏⲓⲥ ⲙ̄ⲡⲓⲕⲉϣⲏⲣⲓ ⲉⲑⲃⲉ ⲟⲩⲱⲛϧ ϣⲱⲡⲓ ⲛ̄ϧⲣⲏⲓ ⲛ̄ϧⲏⲧϥ : ⲟⲩⲟϩ ⲁϥϯⲉⲣϣⲓϣⲓ ⲛⲁϥ ⲉⲑⲣⲉϥⲓⲣⲓ ⲛ̄ⲟⲩϩⲁⲡ ϫⲉ ⲟⲩϣⲏⲣⲓ ⲛⲣⲱⲙⲓ ⲡⲉ. Ⲙ̄ⲡⲉⲣⲉⲣϣ̄ⲫⲏⲣⲓ ϧⲉⲛ ⲫⲁⲓ ϫⲉ ⲥ̄ⲛⲏⲟⲩ ⲛ̄ϫⲉ ⲟⲩⲟⲩⲛⲟⲩ ϩⲟⲧⲉ ⲟⲩⲟⲛ ⲛⲓⲃⲉⲛ ⲉⲧⲭⲏ ϧⲉⲛ ⲛⲓⲙ̄ϩⲁⲩ ⲉⲩⲉⲥⲱⲧⲉⲙ ⲉ̄ⲧⲉϥⲥⲙⲏ : ⲟⲩⲟϩ ⲉⲩⲉⲓ̄ ⲉⲃⲟⲗ ⲛ̄ϫⲉ ⲛⲏⲉⲧⲁⲩⲓⲣⲓ ⲛ̄ⲛⲓⲡⲉⲑⲛⲁⲛⲉⲩ ⲉⲟⲩⲁⲛⲁⲥⲧⲁⲥⲓⲥ ⲛ̄ⲱⲛϧ ⲟⲩⲟϩ ⲛⲏⲉⲧⲁⲩⲓⲣⲓ ⲛ̄ⲛⲓⲡⲉⲧϩⲱⲟⲩ ⲉⲟⲩⲁⲛⲁⲥⲧⲁⲥⲓⲥ ⲛ̄ⲕⲣⲓⲥⲓⲥ . ⲟⲩⲱϣⲧ ⲙ̄ⲡⲓⲉⲩⲁⲅⲅⲉⲗⲓⲟⲛ ⲉⲑ̄.

(يوحنا 5 : 19 - 29)

أجاب يسوع وقال لهم الحق الحق أقول لكم : ان الإبن لا يقدر أن يفعل شيئاً من ذاته وحده . إلا أن يرى الآب فاعله . لأن الأعمال التى يعملها الآب يعملها الإبن أيضاً لأن الآب يحب الإبن . وكل شئ يصنعه يريه اياه. ويريه أعمالاً أعظم من هذه لكى تتعجبوا أنتم . لأنه كما أن الآب يقيم الموتى ويحييهم ، كذلك الإبن أيضاً يحيى من يشاء. وليس الآب يدين أحداً بل قد أعطى الحكم كله للإبن لكى يكرم الإبن كما يكرمون الآب . ومن لا يكرم الإبن فليس يكرم أيضاً الآب الذى أرسله . الحق الحق أقول لكم . ان من يسمع كلامى ويؤمن بالذى أرسلنى فله الحياة الدائمة ، لا يحضر ليدان ، بل قد انتقل من الموت إلى الحياة. الحق الحق أقول لكم : انه ستأتى ساعة وهى الآن ، حين يسمع فيها الأموات صوت إبن الله والذين يسمعون يحيون. لأنه كما أن للآب الحياة فى ذاته كذلك أيضاً أعطى الإبن أن يكون له الحياة فى ذاته . وأعطاه سلطاناً أن يحكم لأنه إبن البشر . لا تتعجبوا من هذا ، فانه ستأتى ساعة حينما يسمع فيها كل من فى القبور صوته . فيخرج الذين صنعوا الحسنات إلى قيامة الحياة والذين صنعوا السيئات إلى قيامة الدينونة. والمجد لله دائماً .

Gospel Response	مرد الانجيل
For this we glorify Him, proclaiming and saying, "You are blessed, O my Lord Jesus, for You were crucified, and saved us."	فلهذا نمجده صارخين قائلين مبارك أنت ياربي يسوع لأنك صلبت وخلصتنا.

+ **The priest prays the three great litanies (Peace, Fathers, and the Congregation)**
+ **The Creed is recited. The litany of the departed is prayed. Our Father.... then the three absolutions.**
+ **Then the priest concludes the prayers and dismisses the congregation in peace.**

+ يصلى الكاهن الثلاثة أواشى الكبار : (سلامة الكنيسة والبطريرك والاجتماعات) .
+ يقال قانون الإيمان . أوشية الراقدين . أبانا الذى فى السموات ، والتحاليل الثلاثة .
+ ثم يختم الكاهن الصلاة و يصرف الشعب.

الساعة التاسعة من يوم أحد الشعانين
The Ninth Hour of Palm Sunday

Lamentations 1:1-4

And it came to pass, after Israel was taken captive, and Jerusalem made desolate, that Jeremiah sat weeping, and lamented with this lamentation over Jerusalem, and said: How does the city that was filled with people sit solitary! She has become as a widow: she that was magnified among the nations, and princess among the provinces, has become tributary. She weeps sore in the night, and her tears are on her cheeks; and there is none of all her lovers to comfort her: all that were her friends have dealt deceitfully with her, they have become her enemies. Judea is gone into captivity by reason of her affliction, and by reason of the abundance of her servitude; she dwells among the nations, she has not found rest. All her pursuers have overtaken her between her oppressors. The ways of Zion mourn, because there are none that come to the feast. All her gates are ruined. Her priests groan, her virgins are led captive, and she is in bitterness in herself. *Glory be to the Holy Trinity. Amen.*

(من مراثى أرميا النبى ص 1 : 1 - 4)

وكان بعد سبى إسرائيل وخراب أورشليم. أن أرميا جلس باكياً وناح على أورشليم بهذا النوح وقال: كيف جلست وحدها المدينة الكثيرة الشعوب؟ كيف صارت كأرملة العظيمة فى الأمم؟ رئيسة البلدان صارت تحت الجزية . تبكى فى الليل بكاء . ودموعها على خديها . ليس لها من معز من جميع محبيها . وكل أصدقائها أهانوها . وصاروا لها أعداء . قد سبيت اليهودية من المذلة وشدة العبودية . سكنت بين الامم ولم تجد راحة . قد أدركها جميع مضطهديها بين المضايق . كل طرق صهيون نائحة لعدم الآتيين إلى العيد . جميع أبوابها متهدمة . كهنتها متنهدون وعذاراها مسبية وهى مغشية بالمرارة . مجداً للثالوث القدوس.

Zephaniah 3:11-20

Says the Lord; In that day, will I take away from you your disdainful pride, and you shall no more magnify yourself upon My holy mountain. And I will leave in you a meek and lowly people; and the remnant of Israel shall fear the name of the Lord, and shall do no iniquity, neither shall they speak vanity; neither shall a deceitful tongue be found in their mouth: for they shall feed, and lie down, and there shall be none to terrify them. Rejoice, O daughter of Zion; cry aloud, O daughter of Jerusalem; rejoice and delight yourself with all your heart, O daughter of Jerusalem. The Lord has taken away your iniquities, He has ransomed you from the hand of your enemies: the Lord, the King of Israel, is in the midst of you: you shall not see evil any more. At that time the Lord shall say to Jerusalem, Be of good courage, Zion; let not your hands be slack. The Lord your God is in you; the Mighty One shall save you: He shall bring joy upon you, and shall refresh you with His love; and He shall rejoice over you with delight as in a day of feasting. And I will gather your afflicted ones. Alas! Who has taken up a reproach against her? Behold, I will work in you for your sake at that time, says the Lord: and I will save her that was oppressed, and receive her that was rejected; and I will make them a praise, and honored in all the earth. And their enemies shall be ashamed at that time, when I shall deal well with you, and at the time when I shall receive you: for I will make you honored and a praise among all the nations of the earth, when I turn back your captivity before you, says the Lord. Glory be to the Holy Trinity. Amen.

(من صفنيا النبى ص 3 : 11 - 20)

يقول الرب : فى ذلك اليوم أنزع من بيتك المرحين معك بتكبر . فلا تعودين تستعلى بكبرياء قلبك فى جبل قدسى . وأبقى فى وسطك شعباً وديعاً ومتواضعاً فيتوكلون على اسم الرب. بقية إسرائيل لا يفعلون إثماً . ولا ينطقون بالكذب . ولا يوجد فى أفواههم لسان غش . لأنهم يرعون ويضطجعون . وليس من يذعرهم. إفرحى يا إبنة صهيون تهلل يا إسرائيل. إفرحى وإبتهجى من كل قلبك يا إبنة أورشليم . لأن الرب قد رفع عنك الظلم . وخلصك من يد أعدائك . الرب يملك إسرائيل فى وسطك فلا ترين بعد شراً . فى ذلك اليوم يقول الرب لأورشليم . لا تخافى يا صهيون ولا تسترخ يداك . الرب إلهك فى وسطك جبار فهو يخلصك . ويسكب عليك الفرح . ويجددك فى محبته . ويبتهج بك متهللاً كما فى يوم عيد . وإبناؤك المتفرقين أجمعهم لئلا يكون لك عار عليهم . هأنذا فى ذلك اليوم أقتل جميع الذين أحزنوك يقول الرب . فى ذلك الوقت أنجى التى ضايقوها . وأقبل إلى التى طردوها وأجعل بنيها فى مجد . فيكون لهم اسم فى كل الأرض . ويخزى فى ذلك الحين أعداؤك . لما أحسن عليكم وأقلبكم إلى . فانى أعطيكم اسماً ومجداً فى كل شعوب الأرض . عندما أرد سبيكم أمام عيونكم يقول الرب . مجداً للثالوث القدوس.

Pascha Praise - A (12 times), Page: 6   تسبحة البصخة A (12 مرة) ، صفحة :

The Psalm

Ⲯⲁⲗⲙⲟⲥ ⲏ̄ : ⲃ̄ ⲛⲉⲙ ⲅ̄

Psalms 8:2-3

Out of the mouth of babes and infants You have perfected praise, because of Your enemies; that You might put down the enemy and avenger. For I will regard the heavens, the work of Your fingers; the moon and stars, which You have established. *Alleluia*

Ⲉⲃⲟⲗ ϧⲉⲛ ⲣⲱⲟⲩ ⲛ̀ⲥⲁⲛⲕⲟⲩϫⲓ ⲛ̀ⲁⲗⲱⲟⲩⲓ ⲛⲉⲙ ⲛⲏⲉⲑⲟⲩⲉⲙϭⲓ ⲁⲕⲥⲉⲃⲧⲉ ⲡⲓⲥⲙⲟⲩ : ⲉⲑⲃⲉ ⲛⲉⲕϫⲁϫⲓ ⲉ̀ⲡϫⲓⲛⲧⲟⲩⲣⲱ ⲛ̀ⲟⲩϫⲁϫⲓ ⲛⲉⲙ ⲟⲩⲣⲉϥϭⲓ ⲙ̀ⲡϣⲓϣ .
Ϫⲉ ϯⲛⲁⲛⲁⲩ ⲉ̀ⲛⲓⲫⲏⲟⲩⲓ ⲛⲓ̀ϩⲃⲏⲟⲩⲓ ⲛ̀ⲧⲉⲛⲉⲕⲧⲏⲃ : ⲡⲓⲓⲟϩ ⲛⲉⲙ ⲛⲓⲥⲓⲟⲩ ⲛ̀ⲑⲟⲕ ⲁⲕϩⲓⲥⲉⲛϯ ⲙ̀ⲙⲱⲟⲩ . ⲁ̅ⲗ̅

إيفول خين روأوو إنهان نسانكوجى إنألواوى نيم نى إثؤويمتشى أكسيبته بى إسموو : إثڤيه نيك كووجى إإبجين تى أوواو نيم أووريفتشى إمبشيش.
جيه تينا ناف إنيفيؤوى نى إهفيؤوى إنتين إكتيب : بى يـوه نيم نـى سـيوو إنثـوك أكهيسنتى إمموؤو . الليلويا .

(مز 8: 2، 3)
من أفواه الأطفال والرضعان هيأت سبحاً . من أجل اعدائك لتسكت عدوا ومنتقماً . لأنى أرى السموات أعمال اصابعك القمر والنجوم أنت أستها . الليلويا .

Introduction to the Gospel, Page: 8   مقدمة الأنجيل ، صفحة :

The Gospel

Ⲉⲩⲁⲅⲅⲉⲗⲓⲟⲛ Ⲕⲁⲧⲁ Ⲙⲁⲧⲑⲉⲟⲛ Ⲕⲉⲫ ⲕ̄ⲁ̄ : ⲓ̄ - ⲓ̄ⲍ̄

Matthew 21:10-17

And when He had come into Jerusalem, all the city was moved, saying, "Who is this?" So the multitudes said, "This is Jesus, the prophet from Nazareth of Galilee." Then Jesus went into the temple of God and drove out all those who bought and sold in the temple, and overturned the tables of the money changers and the seats of those who sold doves. And He said to them, "It is written, 'MY HOUSE SHALL BE CALLED A HOUSE OF PRAYER,' but you have made it a 'DEN OF THIEVES.'" Then the blind and the lame came to Him in the temple, and He healed them. But when the chief priests and scribes saw the wonderful things that He did, and the children crying out in the temple and saying, "Hosanna to the Son of David!" they

Ⲟⲩⲟϩ ⲉⲧⲁϥⲓ̀ ⲉ̀ϧⲟⲩⲛ ⲉ̀Ⲓⲗⲏⲙ ⲁⲥⲙⲟⲛⲙⲉⲛ ⲛ̀ϫⲉ ϯⲃⲁⲕⲓ ⲧⲏⲣⲥ ⲉⲩϫⲱ ⲙ̀ⲙⲟⲥ ϫⲉ ⲛⲓⲙ ⲡⲉ ⲫⲁⲓ . Ⲛⲓⲙⲏϣ ⲇⲉ ⲛⲁⲩϫⲱ ⲙ̀ⲙⲟⲥ ϫⲉ ⲫⲁⲓ ⲡⲉ ⲡⲓⲡⲣⲟⲫⲏⲧⲏⲥ Ⲓⲏⲥ ⲡⲓⲣⲉⲙⲛⲁⲍⲁⲣⲉⲑ ⲛ̀ⲧⲉ ϯⲅⲁⲗⲓⲗⲉⲁ̀ ⲟⲩⲟϩ ⲁϥϣⲉⲛⲁϥ ⲛ̀ϫⲉ Ⲓⲏⲥ ⲉ̀ϧⲟⲩⲛ ⲉ̀ⲡⲓⲉⲣⲫⲉⲓ ⲟⲩⲟϩ ⲁϥϩⲓⲟⲩⲓ ⲉ̀ⲃⲟⲗ ⲛ̀ ⲟⲩⲟⲛ ⲛⲓⲃⲉⲛ ⲉⲧϯ ⲉ̀ⲃⲟⲗ ϧⲉⲛ ⲡⲓⲉⲣⲫⲉⲓ ⲛⲉⲙ ⲛⲏⲉⲧϣⲱⲡ ⲟⲩⲟϩ ⲛⲓⲧⲣⲁⲡⲉⲍⲁ ⲛ̀ⲧⲉ ⲛⲓⲣⲉϥⲉⲣⲕⲉⲣⲙⲁ ⲁϥⲫⲟⲛϫⲟⲩ ⲛⲉⲙ ⲛⲓⲕⲁⲑⲉⲇⲣⲁ ⲛ̀ⲧⲉ ⲛⲏⲉⲧϯϭⲣⲟⲙⲡⲓ ⲉ̀ⲃⲟⲗ . Ⲟⲩⲟϩ ⲡⲉϫⲁϥ ⲛⲱⲟⲩ ϫⲉ ⲥ̀ⲥϧⲏⲟⲩⲧ ϫⲉ ⲡⲁⲏⲓ ⲉⲩⲉ̀ⲙⲟⲩϯ ⲉ̀ⲣⲟϥ ϫⲉ ⲟⲩⲏⲓ ⲙ̀ⲡⲣⲟⲥⲉⲩⲭⲏ ⲛ̀ⲑⲱⲧⲉⲛ ⲇⲉ ⲧⲉⲧⲉⲛⲓⲣⲓ ⲙ̀ⲙⲟϥ ⲙ̀ⲙⲁⲛ̀ⲭⲱⲡ ⲛ̀ⲥⲟⲛⲓ . Ⲟⲩⲟϩ ⲉⲧⲁⲩⲓ̀ ϩⲁⲣⲟϥ ⲛ̀ϫⲉ ϩⲁⲛⲃⲉⲗⲗⲉⲩ ⲛⲉⲙ ϩⲁⲛϭⲁⲗⲉⲩ ϧⲉⲛ ⲡⲓⲉⲣⲫⲉⲓ ⲟⲩⲟϩ ⲁϥⲉⲣⲫⲁϧⲣⲓ ⲉ̀ⲣⲱⲟⲩ . Ⲉⲧⲁⲩⲛⲁⲩ ⲇⲉ ⲛ̀ϫⲉ ⲛⲓⲁⲣⲭⲏ ⲉⲣⲉⲩⲥ ⲛⲉⲙ ⲛⲓⲥⲁϧ ⲉ̀ⲛⲓϣⲫⲏⲣⲓ ⲉⲧⲁϥⲁⲓⲧⲟⲩ ⲛⲉⲙ ⲛⲓⲁⲗⲱⲟⲩⲓ ⲉⲧⲱϣ ⲉ̀ⲃⲟⲗ ϧⲉⲛ ⲡⲓⲉⲣⲫⲉⲓ ⲉⲩϫⲱ ⲙ̀ⲙⲟⲥ ϫⲉ ⲱⲥⲁⲛⲛⲁ ⲡϣⲏⲣⲓ ⲛ̀Ⲇⲁⲩⲓⲇ ⲁⲩⲭⲣⲉⲙⲣⲉⲙ . Ⲟⲩⲟϩ ⲡⲉϫⲱⲟⲩ ⲛⲁϥ ϫⲉ

(متى 21 : 10 - 17)
ولما دخل أورشليم أرتجت المدينة كلها قائلة : من هذا؟ فقالت الجموع هذا هو يسوع النبى الذى من ناصرة الجليل . فدخل يسوع إلى الهيكل . وأخرج جميع الذين كانوا يبيعون ويشترون فى الهيكل وقلب موائد الصيارفة وكراسى باعة الحمام . وقال لهم مكتوب أن بيتى بيت الصلاة يدعى وأنتم جعلتموه مغارة للصوص . وتقدم إليه عمى وعرج فى الهيكل فشفاهم. فلما رأى رؤساء الكهنة والكتبة العجائب التى صنعها والأولاد يصيحون فى الهيكل ويقولون أوصنا لإبن داود ، غضبوا وقالوا له: أما تسمع ما يقول

were indignant and said to Him, "Do You hear what these are saying?" And Jesus said to them, "Yes. Have you never read, 'OUT OF THE MOUTH OF BABES AND NURSING INFANTS YOU HAVE PERFECTED PRAISE'?" Then He left them and went out of the city to Bethany, and He lodged there. Glory be to God forever, Amen.	ⲕⲱⲧⲉⲙ ⲁⲛ ϫⲉ ⲟⲩ ⲡⲉ ⲧⲉ ⲛⲁⲓ ϫⲱ ⲙ̀ⲙⲟϥ : Ⲓⲏⲥ ⲇⲉ ⲡⲉϫⲁϥ ⲛⲱⲟⲩ ϫⲉ ⲥⲉ ⲙ̀ⲡⲉⲧⲉⲛⲱϣ ⲉⲛⲉϩ ϧⲉⲛ ⲛⲓⲅⲣⲁⲫⲏ ϫⲉ ⲉ̀ⲃⲟⲗ ϧⲉⲛ ⲣⲱⲟⲩ ⲛ̀ϩⲁⲛⲕⲟⲩϫⲓ ⲛ̀ⲁⲗⲱⲟⲩⲓ ⲛⲉⲙ ⲛⲏⲉⲑⲟⲩⲉⲙϭⲓ ⲁⲕⲥⲉⲃⲧⲉ ⲡⲓⲥⲙⲟⲩ · Ⲟⲩⲟϩ ⲉⲧⲁϥⲭⲁⲩ ⲁϥⲓ̀ ⲥⲁⲃⲟⲗ ⲛ̀ϯⲃⲁⲕⲓ ⲉ̀ⲃⲏⲑ ⲁⲛⲓⲁ ⲟⲩⲟϩ ⲁϥⲉⲛⲕⲟⲧ ⲙ̀ⲙⲁⲩ · ⲟⲩⲱϣⲧ ⲙ̀ⲡⲓⲉⲩⲁⲅⲅⲉⲗⲓⲟⲛ ⲉⲑⲩ ·	هؤلاء. فقال لهم يسوع: نعم ، أما قرأتم قط فى الكتب من أفواه الأطفال والرضعان هيأت سبحاً . ثم تركهم وخرج خارج المدينة إلى بيت عنيا وبات هناك . والمجد لله دائماً.

| Introduction to the Exposition, Page: 9 | مقدمة الطرح ، صفحة : 9 |

Exposition

O come all of you today, O blessed, pious, Christian, church-loving people; Let us glorify the One God, who, in this week received the sufferings on our behalf for the salvation of our father Adam and our mother Eve, the mother of all the living. On this day, the Lord entered Jerusalem, together with His disciples. And when He entered, all the city was moved and shaken, saying, "Who is this?" And the great multitudes said, this is the great prophet from Nazareth. Then the blind and the lame came to Him, and He healed them all, and all the children cried out saying, "Hosanna to the Son of David!" But when the chief priests saw it, they murmured saying, what shall we do? And Jesus said to them, "Yes. Have you never read in the scripture, 'Out of the mouth of babes and nursing infants You have perfected praise'?" When the infidel and treacherous Jews heard this, they all took counsel to kill Him.

(North side) Christ our Savior; has come and has borne suffering; that through His Passion; He may save us.

(South side) Let us glorify Him; and exalt His Name; for He had mercy on us; according to His great mercy.

طرح

هلموا كلكم اليوم أيها الشعب المبارك، الدينين، النصارى، المحبين للكنيسة. لنمجد الله الواحد الذى قبل الآلام عنا فى هذه الجمعه، لأجل خلاص آدم أبونا وأمنا حواء أم جميع الأحياء. فى هذا اليوم دخل الرب إلى أورشليم ومعه تلاميذه، فلما دخل أرتجت وتزعزعت المدينة كلها قائلين: من هذا؟ فكان الجمع الكبير يقولون: هذا هو النبى العظيم الذى من الناصرة. وتقدم إليه العميان والعرج فشفاهم جميعا. والأطفال كلهم صرخوا قائلين: أوصنا لأبن داود. فلما رأى رؤساء الكهنة هذا ندموا وقالوا: ماذا نصنع؟ فقال لهم المخلص: نعم ما قرأتم الآن فى الكتب، أن من أفواه الأطفال والرضعان هيأت سبحاً؟! فلما سمعوا اليهود المرد هذا تشاوروا جميعا لكى يقتلوه.

(مرد بحرى) المسيح مخلصنا جاء وتألم عنا لكى بآلامه يخلصنا .

(مرد قبلى) فلنمجده ونرفع اسمه لأنه صنع معنا رحمة كعظيم رحمته .

The Conclusion of the Exposition, at both Nighttime and Daytime hours p. 9
ختام الطرح فى ساعات الليل و ساعات النهار صفحة 9

الساعة الحادية عشرة من يوم أحد الشعانين
The Eleventh Hour of Palm Sunday

Isaiah 48:12-22

Hear Me, O Jacob, and Israel whom I call; I am the first, and I endure forever. My hand also has founded the earth, and My right hand has fixed the sky; I will call them, and they shall stand together. And all shall be gathered, and shall hear; who has told them these things? Out of love to you I have fulfilled your desire on Babylon, to abolish the seed of the Chaldeans. I have spoken, I have called, I have brought him, and made his way prosperous. Draw near to Me, and hear these words; I have not spoken in secret from the beginning; when it took place, there was I, and now the Lord, *even* the Lord, and His Spirit, has sent me. Thus says the Lord that delivered you, the Holy One of Israel; I am your God, I have shown you how you should find the way in which you should walk. And if you had hearkened to My commandments, *then* would your peace have been like a river, and your righteousness as a wave of the sea. Your seed also would have been as the sand, and the offspring of your belly as the dust of the ground; neither now shall you by any means be utterly destroyed, neither shall your name perish from before Me. Go forth of Babylon, you that flee from the Chaldeans; utter aloud a voice of joy, and let this be made known, proclaim it to the end of the earth; say, The Lord has delivered His servant Jacob. And if they shall thirst, He shall lead them through the desert; He shall bring forth water to them out of the rock; the rock shall be split, and the water shall flow forth, and My people shall drink. There is no joy, says the Lord, for the ungodly. Glory be to the Holy Trinity. Amen.

Nahum 1:2-8

God is jealous, and the Lord avenges; the Lord avenges with wrath; the Lord takes vengeance on His adversaries, and He cuts off His enemies. The Lord is long suffering, and His power is great, and the Lord will not hold any guiltless: His way is in destruction and in the whirlwind, and the clouds are the dust of His feet. He threatens the sea, and dries it up, and exhausts all the rivers: the land of Bashan and Carmel are brought low, and the flourishing trees of Lebanon have come to nought. The mountains quake at Him, and the hills are shaken, and the earth recoils at His presence, even the world, and all that dwell in it. Who shall stand before His anger? And who shall withstand in the anger of His wrath? His wrath brings to nought kingdoms, and the rocks are thrown down by Him. The Lord is good to them that wait on Him in the day of affliction; and He knows them that reverence Him. But with an overrunning flood He will make an utter end: darkness shall pursue those that rise up against Him and His enemies. Glory be to the Holy Trinity. Amen.

(من إشعياء النبى ص 48 : 12-22)

اسمع لى يا يعقوب وإسرائيل الذى دعوته . أنا هو . أنا الأزلى وأنا الأبدى . ويدى التى أسست الأرض . ويمينى التى ثبتت السماء . أنا أدعوهن جميعاً فيقفن معاً . إجتمعوا كلكم وإسمعوا ما أقوله لهن هكذا اعرف ذاتك لأنى صنعت هواك ببابل . وأبدت نسل الكلدانيين. أنا تكلمت أنا دعوت وأتيت به . وقومت طريقه . إقتربوا إلى وإسمعوا هذه لأنى منذ البدء لم أتكلم فى الخفاء ولا فى الأرض المظلمة . لأنى عند كونها أنا حاضر . والآن فالرب أرسلنى مع روحه . هكذا يقول الرب مخلصك قدوس إسرائيل . أنا هو الله معلمك لتجد الطريق الذى تسير فيه ليتك اصغيت لوصاياى فكانت سلامتك كالنهر . وعدلك كأمواج البحر . ونسلك يصير كالرمل . وذرية بطنك كحصى الأرض . والآن لا أمحوك ولا يباد اسمك من قدامى . فأخرج من بابل وأهرب من الكلدانيين وبصوت الشدو أخبر ليسمعوا . ناد بهذا شيعه إلى أقطار الأرض . قل أن الرب فدى يعقوب عبده . وإذا عطشوا فى البرية أخرج لهم من الصخرة ماء . وشق الصخرة ففاضت المياه فشرب الشعب . ليس سلام للمنافقين يقول الرب . مجداً للثالوث القدوس.

(من ناحوم النبى ص 1 : 2 - 8)

الرب إله غيور ومنتقم . ينتقم الرب بغضب من المقاومين له . وهو يبيد أعداءه. الرب هو طويل الروح وعظيمة هى قوته . ولكنه لا يبرر الخاطئ . الرب فى الزوبعة وفى العاصف طريقه . والسحاب طريق أقدامه . يغضب على البحر فيبيسه وجميع الأنهار يجففها . قد ذوى بيسان والكرمل . وذبل زهر لبنان . تزلزلت منه الجبال وتحركت الآكام وإنطوت الأرض من أمام وجهه . الدنيا وكل الساكنين فيها . من يقدر أن يقف أمام سخط وجهه . ومن هو الذى يقاومه عند حنق رجزه . لأن غضبه يبيد الأراخنة ومنه تزلزلت الصخور . صالح هو الرب لمنتظريه فى يوم ضيقهم . وهو عارف لخائفيه . وبطوفان عابر يصنع هلاكاً تاماً بالقائمين عليه . وأعداؤه يطاردهم ظلام . مجداً للثالوث القدوس .

Pascha Praise - A (12 times), Page: 6   تسبحة البصخة A (12 مرة) ، صفحة :

The Psalm

Ⲯⲁⲗⲙⲟⲥ ⲕ̅ : ⲕ̅ⲃ ⲛⲉⲙ ⲅ̅

Psalms 21: 21-22

I will declare Your name to My brethren; In the midst of the assembly, I will praise You. You who fear the Lord, praise Him! All you descendants of Jacob, glorify Him, and fear Him, all you offspring of Israel! Alleluia.

Ⲥⲓⲉⲥⲁϫⲓ ⳿ⲙⲡⲉⲕⲣⲁⲛ ϧⲁⲧⲟⲧⲟⲩ ⳿ⲛⲛⲁⲥⲛⲏⲟⲩ. ⲉⲓⲉⲥⲙⲟⲩ ⳿ⲉⲣⲟⲕ ⲟⲩⲏ̀ϯ ⳿ⲛⲧⲉⲕⲕⲗⲏⲥⲓⲁ: Ⲛⲏ ⲉⲧⲉⲣϩⲟϯ ϧⲁⲧⲉⲛ ⳿ⲙⲡⲉⲛϭⲟⲓⲥ ⲥⲙⲟⲩ ⳿ⲉⲣⲟϥ: ⲙⲁⲱⲟⲩ ⲛⲁϥ ⳿ⲡⲭⲣⲟϫ ⲧⲏⲣϥ ⲛⲓⲁⲕⲱⲃ: ⲙⲁⲣⲉϥⲉⲣϩⲟϯ ϧⲁⲧⲉϥϩⲏ ⳿ⲛϫⲉ ⳿ⲡⲭⲣⲟϫ ⲧⲉⲣϥ ⳿ⲙⲡⲓⲥ̅ⲗ̅. ⲁ̅ⲗ̅.

(مز 21 : 21-22)

سي اساجي امبكران خاتوتو اناسنيو. اي ازمو ايروك اثميتي انتي اكليسيا: ني اتيرهوتي خاتهي امبينشويس ازمو ايروف: ماأو ناف بجروج تيرف اني ياكوب: ماريف انجي بجروج تيرف امبيسرائيل. الليلويا. :

أذيع اسمك بين إخوتي. وفي وسط الجماعة أسبحك. يا أيها الخائفون الرب سبحوه، ويا معشر ذرية يعقوب مجدوه. وليخشه كــل زرع إسرائيل. الليلويا. الليلويا.

Introduction to the Gospel, Page: 8   مقدمة الأنجيل ، صفحة :

The Gospel

Ⲉⲩⲁⲅⲅⲉⲗⲓⲟⲛ Ⲕⲁⲧⲁ Ⲙⲁⲧⲑⲉⲟⲥ Ⲕⲉⲫ ⲕ̅ : ⲕ̅ - ⲕ̅ⲏ

Matthew 20:20-28

Then the mother of Zebedee's sons came to Him with her sons, kneeling down and asking something from Him. And He said to her, "What do you wish?" She said to Him, "Grant that these two sons of mine may sit, one on Your right hand and the other on the left, in Your kingdom." But Jesus answered and said, "You do not know what you ask. Are you able to drink the cup that I am about to drink, and be baptized with the baptism that I am baptized with?" They said to Him, "We are able." So He said to them, "You will indeed drink My cup, and be baptized with the baptism that I am baptized with; but to sit on My right hand and on My left is not Mine to give, but it is for those for whom it is prepared by My Father." And when the ten heard it, they were greatly displeased with the two brothers. But Jesus called them to Himself and said, "You know that the rulers of the Gentiles lord it over them, and those who are great

Ⲧⲟⲧⲉ ⲁⲥ ϩⲁⲣⲟϥ ⳿ⲛϫⲉ ⳿ⲑⲙⲁⲩ ⳿ⲛⲛⲉⲛϣⲏⲣⲓ ⳿ⲛⲌⲉⲃⲉⲗⲉⲟⲥ ⲛⲉⲙ ⲛⲉⲥϣⲏⲣⲓ ⲉⲥⲟⲩⲱϣⲧ ⳿ⲙⲙⲟϥ ⲟⲩⲟϩ ⲉⲥⲉⲣⲉⲧⲓⲛ ⳿ⲙⲙⲟϥ ⳿ⲛⲟⲩϩⲱⲃ : ⳿ⲛⲑⲟϥ Ⲇⲉ ⲡⲉϫⲁϥ ⲛⲁⲥ ϫⲉ ⲟⲩ ⲡⲉ ⲉⲧⲉⲟⲩⲁϣϥ. ⲡⲉϫⲁⲥ ⲛⲁϥ ϫⲉ ⲁϫⲟⲥ ϩⲓⲛⲁ ⳿ⲛⲧⲉ ⲛⲁϣⲏⲣⲓ ⲥⲛⲁⲩ ⳿ⲛⲧⲉ ⲟⲩⲁⲓ ⳿ⲙⲙⲱⲟⲩ ϩⲉⲙⲥⲓ ⲥⲁⲧⲉⲕⲟⲩⲓⲛⲁⲙ ⲛⲉⲙ ⲟⲩⲁⲓ ⲥⲁⲧⲉⲕϫⲁϭⲏ ⳿ⲛ⳿ϧⲣⲏⲓ ϧⲉⲛ ⲧⲉⲕⲙⲉⲧⲟⲩⲣⲟ : ⲁϥⲉⲣⲟⲩⲱ ⳿ⲛϫⲉ Ⲓⲏⲥ ⲡⲉϫⲁϥ ϫⲉ ⳿ⲛⲧⲉ ⲧⲉⲛⲉ̀ⲙⲓ ⲁⲛ ϫⲉ ⲁⲣⲉⲧⲉⲛⲉⲣⲉⲧⲓⲛ ⲉⲑⲃⲉ ⲟⲩ ⲟⲩⲟⲛ ϣϫⲟⲙ ⳿ⲙⲙⲱⲧⲉⲛ ⳿ⲉⲥⲉ ⲡⲓⲁⲫⲟⲧ ⳿ⲉϯⲛⲁⲥⲟϥ ⲟⲩⲟϩ ⲡⲓⲱⲙⲥ ⳿ⲉϯⲛⲁⲱⲙⲥ ⳿ⲙⲙⲟϥ ⳿ⲉⲣⲉⲧⲉⲛⲉⲙⲥ ⳿ⲑⲛⲟⲩ ⲡⲉϫⲱⲟⲩ ⲛⲁϥ ϫⲉ ⲟⲩⲟⲛ ϣϫⲟⲙ ⳿ⲙⲙⲟⲛ. Ⲟⲩⲟϩ ⲡⲉϫⲁϥ ⲛⲱⲟⲩ ⳿ⲛϫⲉ Ⲓⲏⲥ ϫⲉ ⲡⲓⲁⲫⲟⲧ ⲙⲉⲛ ⲉⲣⲉⲧⲉⲛⲉⲥⲟϥ ⲟⲩⲟϩ ⲡⲓⲱⲙⲥ ⲧⲉⲧⲉⲛⲛⲁⲱⲙⲥ ⳿ⲙⲙⲟϥ ⳿ⲉϩⲉⲙⲥⲓ Ⲇⲉ ⲥⲁⲧⲁⲟⲩⲓⲛⲁⲙ ⲛⲉⲙ ⲧⲁϫⲁϭⲏ ⲫⲱⲓ ⲁⲛ ⲡⲉ ⳿ⲉⲧⲏⲓϥ ⲁⲗⲗⲁ ⲫⲁ ⲛⲏ ⲡⲉ ⲉⲧⲁ ⲡⲁⲓⲱⲧ ⲉⲧ ϧⲉⲛ ⲛⲓⲫⲏⲟⲩⲓ ⲥⲉⲃⲧⲱⲧϥ ⲛⲱⲟⲩ : ⲉⲧⲁⲥⲱⲧⲉⲙ Ⲇⲉ ⳿ⲛϫⲉ ⲡⲓⲕⲉⲙⲏⲧ ⳿ⲙⲙⲁⲑⲏⲧⲏⲥ ⲁⲩⲭⲣⲉⲙⲣⲉⲙ ⲉⲑⲃⲉ ⲡⲓⲥⲟⲛ ⳿ⲥⲛⲁⲩ : Ⲓⲏⲥ Ⲇⲉ ⲁϥⲙⲟⲩϯ ⳿ⲉⲣⲱⲟⲩ ⲡⲉϫⲁϥ ⲛⲱⲟⲩ ϫⲉ ⲧⲉⲧⲉⲛⲉ̀ⲙⲓ ϫⲉ ⲛⲓⲁⲣⲭⲱⲛ ⳿ⲛⲧⲉ ⲛⲓⲉⲑⲛⲟⲥ ⲡⲉⲧⲟⲓ ⳿ⲛϭⲟ̅ⲥ̅ ⳿ⲉⲣⲱⲟⲩ ⲟⲩⲟϩ

(متى 20 : 20-28)

حينئذ جاءت إليه أم إبنى زبدى مع إبنيها وسجدت له وسألته شيئاً . أما هو فقال لها: ماذا تريدين؟ قالت له: أن تقول قولاً أن يجلسا ابناى الإثنان أحدهما عن يمينك والآخر عن شمالك فى ملكوتك . فأجاب يسوع وقال: إنكما لستما تعلمان ما تطلبان . أتقدران أن تشربا من الكأس التى أنا مزمع أن أشربها والصبغة التى أصطبغها تصطبغانها . فقالا له: انا لقادران. فقال لهما يسوع : أما الكأس فتشربانها وبالصبغة التى أصطبغ بها أنا تصطبغان وأما جلوسكما عن يمينى وعن يسارى فليس لى أن أعطيه إلا للذين أعد لهم من قبل أبى الذى فى السموات. فلما سمع العشرة التلاميذ اغتاظوا من أجل الأخوين . فدعاهم يسوع وقال لهم : أما علمتم أن رؤساء الأمم يسودونهم

exercise authority over them. Yet it shall not be so among you; but whoever desires to become great among you, let him be your servant. And whoever desires to be first among you, let him be your slave, just as the Son of Man did not come to be served, but to serve, and to give His life a ransom for many. Glory be to God forever, Amen.

ⲛⲟⲩⲕⲉⲛⲓϣϯ ⲉⲧⲟⲓ ⲛ̀ⲉⲣϣⲓϣⲓ ⲉ̀ϫⲱⲟⲩ. Ⲡⲁⲓⲣⲏϯ ⲇⲉ ⲁⲛ ⲡⲉⲑⲛⲁϣⲱⲡⲓ ϧⲉⲛ ⲑⲏⲛⲟⲩ ⲁⲗⲗⲁ ⲫⲏⲉⲑⲟⲩⲱϣ ⲉ̀ⲉⲣ ⲛⲓϣϯ ϧⲉⲛ ⲑⲏⲛⲟⲩ ⲉϥⲉ̀ⲉⲣⲇⲓⲁⲕⲱⲛ ⲛⲱⲧⲉⲛ : ⲟⲩⲟϩ ⲫⲏⲉⲑⲟⲩⲱϣ ⲉ̀ⲉⲣϩⲟⲩⲓⲧ ϧⲉⲛ ⲑⲏⲛⲟⲩ ⲉϥⲉ̀ⲉⲣⲃⲱⲕ ⲛⲱⲧⲉⲛ : ⲙ̀ⲫⲣⲏϯ ϩⲱϥ ⲙ̀ⲡϣⲏⲣⲓ ⲙ̀ⲫⲣⲱⲙⲓ ⲛⲉⲧⲁϥⲓ̀ ⲁⲛ ⲉⲑⲣⲟⲩϣⲉⲙϣⲏⲧϥ ⲁⲗⲗⲁ ⲉ̀ϣⲉⲙϣⲓ ⲟⲩⲟϩ ⲉ̀ϯ ⲛ̀ⲧⲉϥⲯⲩⲭⲏ ⲛ̀ⲥⲱϯ ⲉ̀ϫⲉⲛ ⲟⲩⲙⲏϣ . ⲟⲩⲱϣⲧ ⲙ̀ⲡⲓⲉⲩⲁⲅⲅⲉⲗⲓⲟⲛ ⲉⲑⲩ .

وعظماءهم يتسلطون عليهم وأما أنتم فلا يكون فيكم هكذا، ولكن من أراد أن يكون فيكم كبيراً فليكن لكم خادماً ومن يريد أن يكون فيكم أولاً فليكن لكم عبداً . كما أن إبن البشر لم يأت لِيُخدَم بل ليخدِم ويبذل نفسه فداء عن كثيرين . والمجد لله دائماً .

Introduction to the Exposition, Page: 9 : مقدمة الطرح ، صفحة

Exposition

In the minds of the antagonizing Jews, our Lord and Savior Jesus Christ was surrounded by people, troops, soldiers and warriors, similar to the kings of this world. These were the thoughts of the mother of John and James, sons of Zebedee. She came to our Savior while He was surrounded by the people and His disciples. She worshipped Him with her sons and said, "Grant that my two sons may sit one on Your right hand, and the other on Your left, in Your kingdom." Hear then what the merciful and most compassionate Lord, who desires salvation for the whole world, said, "Are you able to drink of the cup that I shall drink of and be baptized with the baptism that I am baptized with?" They said to Him, "We are able." He answered them, "You will indeed be able to, but to sit at My right hand and at My left is not Mine to give. It shall be given to those chosen by My omnipresent Father." The two brothers were quiet when they heard these words and departed because of the magnitude of His glory.

(North side) Christ our Savior; has come and has borne suffering; that through His Passion; He may save us.

(South side) Let us glorify Him; and exalt His Name; for He had mercy on us; according to His great mercy.

طـرح

الأفكار التى كانت لليهود المخالفين بسبب مخلصنا وملكنا المسيح . أنــه مــثـل ملوك الأرض والجموع الكثيرة محيطة به . والجند والعساكر والمحاربون مثل الملوك . هكذا ظنت أم يوحنا ويعقوب إبنى زبدى . فكرت هكذا وأتت إلى مخلصنا أمام الجمع مع تلاميذه . وسجدت له مع إبنيها وسألته وطلبت منه هكذا قائلة : قل قولاً أن يجلس إبناى الإثنان معك فى ملكوتك واحد عن يمينك والآخر عن يسارك فى عز مملكتك . إسمعوا الرؤوف الكثير الرحمة الذى يريد حياة جميع العالم . قال : أتقدران أن تشربا الكأس التى أتيت بسببها لكى أشربها والصبغة التى أصطبغها . فقالا نقدر أن نصنع هذا . فلعلكما حقاً تقدران . فأما الجلوس فليس لى أن أعطيه لكما . لكنه لأبى المالئ كل موضع وهو الذى يعطيه لاصفيائه. فلما سمع الاخوان هذا سكتا . ومضيا من أجل عظيم مجده .

(مرد بحرى) المسيح مخلصنا جاء وتألم عنا لكى بآلامه يخلصنا .

(مرد قبلى) فلنمجده ونرفع اسمه لأنه صنع معنا رحمة كعظيم رحمته .

The Conclusion of the Exposition, Page: 9 : ختام الطرح ، صفحة

The Conclusion with the Daytime Litanies, Page: 10 :طلبة الصباح ، صفحة
Without Metanoia (Worships) بدون ميطانيات
Because they follow the Liturgy of Palm Sunday لأنها عقب قداس احد الشعانين

ليلة الأثنين من البصخة المقدسة

Monday Eve of the Holy Pascha

القراءات و الاحداث

الموضوع : تحدث الرب الى تلاميذه عن آلامه و موته و قيامته

الاولى : يو 12 : 20 - 36 ؛ اقتراب ساعته
الثالثه : لو 9 : 18 – 22 ؛ عنايته بتلاميذه
السادسة : مر 10 : 32 – 34 ؛ تقديم ذاته ذبيحة
التاسعة : مر 8 : 27 – 33 ؛ ارضاؤه الأب
الحادية عشرة : مت 17 : 19 – 23 ؛ قيام رؤساء الكهنة و الفريسيين عليه

كان الرب و معه التلاميذ صاعدين الى اورشليم و كان يعلم بما سيحدث له و علمهم فى مثل حبة الحنطة انه ينبغى ان يصلب و يدفن حتى يأتى بثمر كثير و يحضر كثيرين الى المجد كما قال "الحق الحق أقول لكم ان لم تقع حبة الحنطة فى الأرض وتمت فهى تبقى وحدها ولكن ان ماتت فهى تأتى بثمر كثير" (يوحنا 12 : 32)

The Readings and Events

Subject: The Lord speaks to His disciples about His suffering, death and resurrection.

First hour: John 12:20-36 ; His hour is coming.
Third hour: Luke 9:18-22 ; His care for His disciples
Sixth hour: Mark 10: 32-34 ; Offering Himself as a sacrifice.
Ninth hour: Mark 8:27-33 ; Satisfying His Father.
Eleventh hour: Matthew 17:19-23 ; The chief priests and Pharisees against Him.

The Lord and disciples were ascending to Jerusalem. He knew what would happen to Him. He taught them, in the parable of the grain of wheat, He had to be crucified and buried to bring more fruits and more people to the Glory. He said: *"Verily, verily, I say unto you, Except a grain of wheat falls into the ground and dies, it abides alone: but if it dies, it brings forth much fruit." (John 12: 32)*

الساعة الأولى من ليلة الأثنين من البصخة المقدسة
The First Hour of Monday Eve of the Holy Pascha

Zephaniah 1:2-12

Let there be an utter cutting off from the face of the land, says the Lord.   Let man and cattle be cut off; let the birds of the air and the fishes of the sea be cut off; and the ungodly shall fail, and I will take away the transgressors from the face of the land, says the Lord.   And I will stretch out My hand upon Judah, and upon all the inhabitants of Jerusalem; and I will remove the names of Baal out of this place, and the names of the priests;   and them that worship the host of heaven upon the housetops; and them that worship and swear by the Lord, and them that swear by their king;   and them that turn aside from the Lord, and them that seek not the Lord, and them that cleave not to the Lord.   Be fearful before the Lord God; for the day of the Lord is near; for the Lord has prepared His sacrifice, and has sanctified His guests.   And it shall come to pass in the day of the Lord's sacrifice, that I will take vengeance on the princes, and on the king's house, and upon all that wear strange apparel.   And I will openly take vengeance on the porches in that day, *on the men* that fill the house of the Lord their God with ungodliness and deceit.   And there shall be in that day, says the Lord, the sound of a cry from the gate of men slaying, and a howling from the second *gate*, and a great crashing from the hills.   Lament, you that inhabit the *city* that has been broken down, for all the people have become like Canaan; and all that were exalted by silver have been utterly destroyed.   And it shall come to pass in that day, that I will search Jerusalem with a candle, and I will take vengeance on the men that despise the things committed to them; but they say in their hearts, The Lord will not do any good, neither will He do any evil. Glory be to the Holy Trinity. Amen.

(من صفنيا النبى ص 1 : 2 – 12)

بالفـنـاء فلـيـفن عـن وجه الأرض يقول الرب . فليفن الإنسان والحيوان. وليفن طيـور السـمـاء وسمك البحر . ويضعف المنافقون . واستأصل المخالفين عن وجه الأرض يقول الرب . وأمد يدى على يهوذا وعلى جميع سكان أورشليم . وأبيد من هذا المكان أسماء البعل وأسماء الكهنة . والذين يسجدون على السطوح لجند السماء . والذين يحلفون بمولوخ الملك والذين يحيدون عن الرب . والذين لم يطلبوا الرب ولم يلتمسوه . خافوا الرب الإله لأنه قريب هو يوم الرب . لأن الرب قد أعد ذبيحة وقدس مدعويه . ويكون فى يوم ذبيحة الرب أنى أنتقم من الرؤساء . ومن بيت الملك. ومن جميع لابسى البرفير . وفى ذلك اليوم أنتقم من جميع الذين يتظاهرون على الأبواب الخارجية . الذين يملأون بيت الرب إلههم ظلماً وخبثاً . ويكون فى ذلك اليوم يقول الرب . صوت صراخ من باب المذبوحين وتهليل فى الباب الثانى وذبح عظيم من التلال نوحى أيتها الساكنة فى المنحوته . لأن جميع الشعب قد تشبه بكنعان وقد باد جميع المترفعين بالفضة وسيكون فى ذلك اليوم أنى أفتش أورشليم بسراج . وأعاقب الناس الذين يرفضون التحفظ القائلين فى قلوبهم أن الرب لا ينفع ولا يضر . مجداً للثالوث القدوس .

Pascha Praise - A (12 times), Page: 6	تسبحة البصخة A (12 مرة) ، صفحة :

The Psalm
Ⲯⲁⲗⲙⲟⲥ ⲕ̅ⲋ̅ : ⲓ̅ ⲛⲉⲙ ⲏ̅

Psalms 26:6-8

I will sing, even sing psalms unto the Lord. Hear, O Lord, my voice which I have uttered aloud;

Pity me, and hearken to me. My heart said to You.

Alleluia

Ⲉⲓⲉϩⲱⲥ ⲟⲩⲟϩ ⲉⲓⲉⲉⲣⲯⲁⲗⲓⲛ ⲉⲡ̅ⲟ̅ⲥ̅ : ⲥⲱⲧⲉⲙ ⲡ̅ⲟ̅ⲥ̅ ⲉⲡⲁϧⲣⲱⲟⲩ ⲉⲧⲁⲓⲱϣ ⲉⲃⲟⲗ ⲛ̀ϧⲏⲧϥ .

Ⲛⲁⲓⲛⲏⲓ ⲟⲩⲟϩ ⲥⲱⲧⲉⲙ ⲉⲣⲟⲓ : ϫⲉ ⲛ̀ⲑⲟⲕ ⲡⲉ ⲉⲧⲁ ⲡⲁϩⲏⲧ ϫⲟⲥ ⲛⲁⲕ . ⲁⲗ

أى إيهوس اووه إى إيرﭙصالين إبتشويس : صوتيم إبتشويس إباﺈخرواو إيطاى أوش إيفول إنخيتف

ناى نى أووه صوتيم إروى : جيه إنثوك ﭙيه إيطا ﭙاهيت جوس ناك .

(مز 26: 10 و11)

اسبح وأرتل للرب استمع يارب صوتى الذى به دعوتك . ارحمنى واستجب لى فان لك قال قلبى . الليلويا .

Introduction to the Gospel, Page: 8   مقدمة الأنجيل ، صفحة :

The Gospel
Ⲉⲩⲁⲅⲅⲉⲗⲓⲟⲛ Ⲕⲁⲧⲁ Ⲓⲱⲁⲛⲛⲏⲛ Ⲕⲉⲫ ⲓⲃ : ⲕ - ⲗ︤ⲋ︥

John 12:20-36

Now there were certain Greeks among those who came up to worship at the feast. Then they came to Philip, who was from Bethsaida of Galilee, and asked him, saying, "Sir, we wish to see Jesus." Philip came and told Andrew, and in turn Andrew and Philip told Jesus. But Jesus answered them, saying, "The hour has come that the Son of Man should be glorified. Most assuredly, I say to you, unless a grain of wheat falls into the ground and dies, it remains alone; but if it dies, it produces much grain. He who loves his life will lose it, and he who hates his life in this world will keep it for eternal life. If anyone serves Me, let him follow Me; and where I am, there My servant will be also. If anyone serves Me, him My Father will honor. "Now My soul is troubled, and what shall I say? 'Father, save Me from this hour'? But for this purpose I came to this hour. Father, glorify Your name." Then a voice came from heaven, saying, "I have both glorified it and will glorify it again." Therefore the people who stood by and heard it said that it had thundered. Others said, "An angel has spoken to Him." Jesus answered and said, "This voice did not come because of Me, but for your sake. Now is the judgment of this world; now the ruler of this world will be cast out. And I, if I am lifted up from the earth, will

Ⲛⲉ ⲟⲩⲟⲛ ϩⲁⲛⲟⲩⲉⲓⲛⲓⲛ ⲇⲉ ⲡⲉ ⲉ̀ⲃⲟⲗ ϧⲉⲛ ⲛⲏⲉⲑⲛⲏⲟⲩ ⲉ̀ϩ̀ⲣⲏⲓ ⲉ̀ⲡ̀ϣⲁⲓ ϩⲓⲛⲁ ⲛ̀ⲧⲟⲩⲟⲩⲱϣⲧ : ⲛⲁⲓⲟⲩⲛ ⲁⲩⲓ̀ ϩⲁ Ⲫⲓⲗⲓⲡⲡⲟⲥ ⲡⲓⲣⲉⲙ Ⲃⲏⲑ ⲥⲁⲓⲇⲁ ⲛ̀ⲧⲉ ϯⲅⲁⲗⲓⲗⲉⲁ̀ ⲟⲩⲟϩ ⲛⲁⲩϯϩⲟ ⲉⲣⲟϥ ⲡⲉ ⲉⲩϫⲱ ⲙ̀ⲙⲟⲥ ϫⲉ ⲡⲉⲛⲟ̅ⲥ̅ ⲧⲉⲛⲟⲩⲱϣ ⲉ̀ⲛⲁⲩ ⲉ̀Ⲓⲏⲥ ⲁϥⲓ̀ ⲛ̀ϫⲉ Ⲫⲓⲗⲓⲡⲡⲟⲥ ⲁϥϫⲟⲥ ⲛ̀Ⲁⲛⲇⲣⲉⲁⲥ . Ⲁⲛⲇⲣⲉⲁⲥ ⲇⲉ ⲟⲛ ⲛⲉⲙ Ⲫⲓⲗⲓⲡⲡⲟⲥ ⲁⲩⲓ̀ ⲁⲩϫⲟⲥ ⲙ̀Ⲓⲏⲥ . Ⲓⲏⲥ ⲇⲉ ⲁϥⲉⲣⲟⲩⲱ ⲡⲉϫⲁϥ ⲛⲱⲟⲩ ϫⲉ ⲁⲥⲓ̀ ⲛ̀ϫⲉ ϯⲟⲩⲛⲟⲩ ϩⲓⲛⲁ ⲛ̀ⲧⲉ ⲡ̀ϣⲏⲣⲓ ⲙ̀ⲫ̀ⲣⲱⲙⲓ ϭ̀ⲓⲱⲟⲩ : ⲁⲙⲏⲛ ⲁⲙⲏⲛ ϯϫⲱ ⲙ̀ⲙⲟⲥ ⲛⲱⲧⲉⲛ ϫⲉ ⲁⲣⲉϣⲧⲉⲙ ϯⲛⲁⲫⲣⲓ ⲛ̀ⲥⲟⲩⲟ ϭ̀ϩⲉⲓ ϩⲓϫⲉⲛ ⲡⲓⲕⲁϩⲓ ⲟⲩⲟϩ ⲛ̀ⲧⲉⲥⲙⲟⲩ ⲛ̀ⲑⲟⲥ ⲙ̀ⲙⲁⲩⲁⲧⲥ ⲉ̀ϣⲁⲥϣⲱⲡⲓ ⲉ̀ϣⲱⲡ ⲇⲉ ⲁⲥϣⲁⲛⲙⲟⲩ ϣⲁⲥⲉⲛ ⲟⲩⲙⲏϣ ⲛ̀ⲟⲩⲧⲁϩ ⲉ̀ⲃⲟⲗ : ⲫⲏⲉⲑⲙⲉⲓ ⲛ̀ⲧⲉϥⲯⲩⲭⲏ ⲉϥⲉ̀ⲧⲁⲕⲟⲥ ⲟⲩⲟϩ ⲫⲏⲉⲑⲙⲟⲥϯ ⲛ̀ⲧⲉϥⲯⲩⲭⲏ ⲛ̀ϧ̀ⲣⲏⲓ ϧⲉⲛ ⲡⲁⲓⲕⲟⲥⲙⲟⲥ ⲉϥⲉ̀ⲁⲣⲉϩ ⲉ̀ⲣⲟⲥ ⲉⲩⲱⲛϧ ⲛ̀ⲉⲛⲉϩ . Ⲫⲏⲉⲑⲛⲁϣⲉⲙϣⲓ ⲙ̀ⲙⲟⲓ ⲙⲁⲣⲉϥⲟⲩⲁϩϥ ⲛ̀ⲥⲱⲓ ⲟⲩⲟϩ ⲫ̀ⲙⲁ ⲉ̀ϯϣⲟⲡ ⲙ̀ⲙⲟϥ ⲉϥⲉ̀ϣⲱⲡⲓ ⲙ̀ⲙⲁⲩ ⲛⲉⲙⲏⲓ ⲛ̀ϫⲉ ⲡⲁⲣⲉϥϣⲉⲙϣⲓ ⲟⲩⲟϩ ⲫⲏⲉⲑⲛⲁⲉⲣ ⲣⲉϥϣⲉⲙϣⲓ ⲛⲏⲓ ϥ̀ⲛⲁⲉⲣⲧⲓⲙⲁⲛ ⲙ̀ⲙⲟϥ ⲛ̀ϫⲉ ⲡⲁⲓⲱⲧ : ϯⲛⲟⲩ ⲁ ⲧⲁⲯⲩⲭⲏ ϣ̀ⲑⲟⲣⲧⲉⲣ ⲟⲩⲟϩ ⲟⲩ ⲡⲉ ϯⲛⲁϫⲟϥ ⲡⲁⲓⲱⲧ ⲛⲁϩⲙⲉⲧ ⲉ̀ⲃⲟⲗ ϧⲉⲛ ⲧⲁⲓⲟⲩⲛⲟⲩ ⲁⲗⲗⲁ ⲉⲑⲃⲉ ⲫⲁⲓ ⲁⲓⲓ̀ ⲉ̀ⲧⲁⲓⲟⲩⲛⲟⲩ : ⲫ̀ⲓⲱⲧ ⲙⲁⲱⲟⲩ ⲙ̀ⲡⲉⲕϣⲏⲣⲓ ⲟⲩⲥⲙⲏ ⲁⲥⲓ̀ ⲉ̀ⲃⲟⲗ ϧⲉⲛ ⲧ̀ⲫⲉ ⲉⲥϫⲱ ⲙ̀ⲙⲟⲥ ϫⲉ ⲁⲓϯⲱⲟⲩ ⲡⲁⲗⲓⲛ ⲟⲛ ϯⲛⲁϯⲱⲟⲩ : ⲡⲓⲙⲏϣ ⲟⲩⲛ ⲉⲛⲁϥⲟ̀ϩⲓ ⲉ̀ⲣⲁⲧϥ ⲉⲧⲁⲩⲥⲱⲧⲉⲙ ⲛⲁⲩϫⲱ ⲙ̀ⲙⲟⲥ ϫⲉ ⲟⲩϧⲁⲣⲁⲃⲁⲓ ⲡⲉⲧⲁⲥϣⲱⲡⲓ ϩⲁⲛⲕⲉⲭⲱⲟⲩⲛⲓ ⲇⲉ ⲛⲁⲩϫⲱ ⲙ̀ⲙⲟⲥ ϫⲉ ⲟⲩⲁⲅⲅⲉⲗⲟⲥ ⲡⲉⲧⲁϥⲥⲁϫⲓ ⲛⲉⲙⲁϥ . Ⲁϥⲉⲣⲟⲩⲱ ⲛⲱⲟⲩ ⲛ̀ϫⲉ Ⲓⲏⲥ ⲟⲩⲟϩ ⲡⲉϫⲁϥ ⲉⲧⲁⲥϣⲱⲡⲓ ⲁⲛ ⲉⲑⲃⲏⲧ ⲛ̀ϫⲉ ⲧⲁⲓⲥⲙⲏ ⲁⲗⲗⲁ ⲉⲑⲃⲉ ⲑⲏⲛⲟⲩ : ϯⲛⲟⲩ ⲡ̀ϩⲁⲡ ⲡⲉ ⲛ̀ⲧⲉ ⲡⲁⲓⲕⲟⲥⲙⲟⲥ ϯⲛⲟⲩ ⲡ̀ⲁⲣⲭⲱⲛ ⲛ̀ⲧⲉ ⲡⲁⲓⲕⲟⲥⲙⲟⲥ ⲉⲩⲉ̀ϩⲓⲧϥ ⲉ̀ⲃⲟⲗ : ⲟⲩⲟϩ ⲁⲛⲟⲕ ϩⲱ ⲁⲓϣⲁⲛϭⲓⲥⲓ ⲉ̀ⲃⲟⲗ ϩⲁ ⲡ̀ⲕⲁϩⲓ ⲉⲓⲉ̀ⲥⲉⲕ ⲟⲩⲟⲛ ⲛⲓⲃⲉⲛ ϩⲁⲣⲟⲓ . Ⲫⲁⲓ

(36 - 20 :12 يوحنا)

وكان قوم من اليونانيين الذين صعدوا ليسجدوا فى العيد . فجاء هؤلاء إلى فيلبس الذى من بيت صيدا الجليل وجعلوا يسألونه قائلين: يا سيدنا نريد أن نرى يسوع . فجاء فيلبس وقال لاندراوس ، واندراوس وفيلبس قالا ليسوع . فأجابهما يسوع قائلاً: قد أتت الساعة التى يتمجد فيها إبن البشر . الحق الحق أقول لكم ان لم تقع حبة الحنطة فى الأرض وتمت فهى تبقى وحدها ولكن ان ماتت فهى تأتى بثمر كثير . من يحب نفسه يهلكها . ومن يبغض نفسه فى هذا العالم يحفظها إلى حياة أبدية . ان كان أحد يخدمنى فليتبعنى وحيث أكون أنا فهناك أيضاً يكون خادمى . ومن يخدمنى يكرمه الأب . الآن نفسى قد اضطربت . وماذا أقول؟ يا أبت نجنى من هذه الساعة . ولكن من أجل هذا أتيت إلى هذه الساعة . يا أبت مجد إبنك . فجاء صوت من السماء قائلاً: قد مجدت وأيضاً أمجد . فالجمع الذى كان واقفاً وسمع قال: قد حدث رعد . وآخرون قالوا قد كلمه ملاك . فأجاب يسوع وقال لهم: ليس من أجلى كان هذا الصوت بل من أجلكم . قد حضرت الآن دينونة هذا العالم . الآن يلقى رئيس هذا العالم خارجاً وأنا ان ارتفعت عن الأرض

draw all peoples to Myself." This He said, signifying by what death He would die. The people answered Him, "We have heard from the law that the Christ remains forever; and how can You say, 'The Son of Man must be lifted up'? Who is this Son of Man?" Then Jesus said to them, "A little while longer the light is with you. Walk while you have the light, lest darkness overtake you; he who walks in darkness does not know where he is going. While you have the light, believe in the light, that you may become sons of light." Glory be to God forever, Amen.

ⲇⲉ ⲛⲁϥ ⲭⲱ ⲙ̀ⲙⲟⲥ ⲉϥ̀ⲧⲏⲓⲛⲓ ϫⲉ ϧⲉⲛ ⲁϣ ⲙ̀ⲙⲟⲩ ϥ̀ⲛⲁⲙⲟⲩ : ⲁϥⲉⲣⲟⲩⲱ ⲛⲁϥ ⲛ̀ϫⲉ ⲡⲓⲙⲏϣ ⲉϥϫⲱ ⲙ̀ⲙⲟⲥ ϫⲉ ⲁⲛⲟⲛ ⲁⲛ ⲥⲱⲧⲉⲙ ⲉ̀ⲃⲟⲗ ϧⲉⲛ ⲡⲓⲛⲟⲙⲟⲥ ϫⲉ Ⲡⲭ̅ⲥ̅ ϣⲟⲡ ϣⲁ ⲉ̀ⲛⲉϩ : ⲟⲩⲟϩ ⲡⲱⲥ ⲉⲕϫⲱ ⲙ̀ⲙⲟⲥ ⲛ̀ⲑⲟⲕ ϫⲉ ⲥϩⲟⲩⲧ ⲡⲉ ⲛ̀ⲧⲟⲩⲣⲃⲉⲥ ⲡ̀ϣⲏⲣⲓ ⲙ̀ⲫ̀ⲣⲱⲙⲓ ⲛⲓⲙ ⲡⲉ ⲡ̀ϣⲏⲣⲓ ⲙ̀ⲫ̀ⲣⲱⲙⲓ . Ⲡⲉϫⲉ Ⲓⲏ̅ⲥ̅ ⲛⲱⲟⲩ ϫⲉ ⲉⲧⲓ ⲕⲉⲕⲟⲩϫⲓ ⲛ̀ⲥⲏⲟⲩ ⲡⲓⲟⲩⲱⲓⲛⲓ ϧⲉⲛ ⲑⲏⲛⲟⲩ ⲙⲟϣⲓ ⲟⲩⲛ ϧⲉⲛ ⲡⲓⲟⲩⲱⲓⲛⲓ ϩⲱⲥ ⲡⲓⲟⲩⲱⲓⲛⲓ ⲛ̀ⲧⲉⲛ ⲑⲏⲛⲟⲩ ϩⲓⲛⲁ ⲛ̀ⲧⲉ ϣ̀ⲧⲉⲙ ⲡⲓⲭⲁⲕⲓ ⲧⲁϩⲉ ⲑⲏⲛⲟⲩ ϫⲉ ⲫⲏⲉⲑⲙⲟϣⲓ ϧⲉⲛ ⲡⲓⲭⲁⲕⲓ ⲛ̀ϥ̀ⲉⲙⲓ ⲁⲛ ϫⲉ ⲁϥⲙⲟϣⲓ ⲉ̀ⲑⲱⲛ : ϩⲟⲥ ⲡⲓⲟⲩⲱⲓⲛⲓ ⲛ̀ⲧⲉⲛ ⲑⲏⲛⲟⲩ ⲛⲁϩϯ ⲉ̀ⲡⲓⲟⲩⲱⲓⲛⲓ ϩⲓⲛⲁ ⲛ̀ⲧⲉ ⲉⲣ̀ϣⲏⲣⲓ ⲙ̀ⲡⲓⲟⲩⲱⲓⲛⲓ . ⲟⲩⲱϣⲧ ⲙ̀ⲡⲓⲉⲩⲁⲅⲅⲉⲗⲓⲟⲛ ⲉⲑⲩ̅ .

جذبت إلىَّ كل أحد . قال هذا مشيراً إلى أية ميتة كان عتيداً أن يموتها . فأجابه الجمع قائلاً: نحن سمعنا من الناموس ان المسيح يدوم إلى الأبد ، فكيف تقول أنت أنه ينبغي أن يرتفع ابن البشر ، من هو هذا ابن البشر؟ فقال لهم يسوع: أن النور معكم زماناً يسيراً ، فسيروا فى النور ما دام لكم النور لئلا يدرككم الظلام . لأن من يمشى فى الظلام لا يدرى إلى أين يتوجه . ما دام لكم النور آمنوا بالنور لتصيروا أبناء النور . والمجد لله دائماً .

Introduction to the Exposition, Page: 9 : صفحة ، مقدمة الطرح

Exposition

If in the beginning of the month people become eager and long to see the moon's brightness, then how much more is Christ our God, the Sun of Righteousness, who shared in the walking with the people and was found in the likeness of a servant; more so when the Greeks who came to the feast and saw His great glory. They said to Philip, who was from Bethsaida: "Sir, we would like to see Jesus." Then Philip came and told Andrew, again they came and told Jesus. Then Jesus, our Lord, said: 'The hour has come, when the Son of man will be glorified." By these words He was signifying His life-giving death. When all the multitudes heard His Divine oracles, they came to Jesus, our Savior, and He taught them with parables. "Believe in the light, while you have the light, so that you may become the children of the light." We, too, believe that He is truly the Light of the Father, whom He sent into the world. His divine glory illuminated us; we who are sitting in the darkness and shadow of death. And, He raised us to the original dignity from the abyss of our sins.

طرح

إذا أزهر القمر فى أول الشهر وأشرقت أشعته على الأرض . تصير سائر الناس فى إشتياق ويشتهـون أن يروا بهاء . فكم بالحرى أعلى بزيادة المسيح إلهنا شمس البر . الذى شارك فى المشى مع الناس ووجد فى شكل العبد . لاسيما لما رأى اليونانيين الذين أتوا إلى العيد عَظم مجده قالوا لفيلبس الذى من بيت صيدا : يا سيدنا نريد أن نرى يسوع . فجاء فيلبس وقال لاندراوس واندراوس جاء وقال ليسوع . فقال ربنا يسوع: قد أتت الساعة لكى يتمجد ابن الإنسان . وإبتدأ يرمز بهذا الكلام عن موته المعطى الحياة . فلما سمع الجمع كله ، هؤلاء وأولئك ، أقواله الإلهية أجابهم المخلص وعلمهم بأمثال : آمنوا بالنور مادام هو كائن معكم لكى تصيروا إبناء النور . نحن أيضاً نؤمن أنه هو بالحقيقة نور الأب الذى أرسله إلى العالم . أضاء علينا بمجد لاهوته نحن الجلوس فى الظلمة وظلال الموت . وأصعدنا إلى العلو الأول من هوة آثامنا .

(North side) Christ our Savior; has come and has borne suffering; that through His Passion; He may save us.

(مرد بحرى) المسيح مخلصنا جاء وتألم عنا لكى بألامه يخلصنا .

(South side) Let us glorify Him; and exalt His Name; for He had mercy on us; according to His great mercy

(مرد قبلى) فلنمجده ونرفع اسمه لأنه صنع معنا رحمة كعظيم رحمته .

The Conclusion of the Exposition, Page: 9   ختام الطرح ، صفحة :

الساعة الثالثة من ليلة الاثنين من البصخة المقدسة
The Third Hour of Monday Eve of the Holy Pascha

Zephaniah 1:14-2:2

For the great day of the Lord is near, it is near, and very speedy; the sound of the day of the Lord is made bitter and harsh. A mighty day of wrath is that day, a day of affliction and distress, a day of desolation and destruction, a day of gloominess and darkness, a day of cloud and vapor, a day of the trumpet and cry against the strong cities, and against the high towers. And I will greatly afflict the men, and they shall walk as blind men, because they have sinned against the Lord; therefore He shall pour out their blood as dust, and their flesh as dung. And their silver and their gold shall by no means be able to rescue them in the day of the Lord's wrath; but the whole land shall be devoured by the fire of His jealously; for He will bring a speedy destruction on all them that inhabit the land. Be gathered and closely joined together, O unchastened nation; before you become as the flower that passes away, before the anger of the Lord come upon you, before the day of the wrath of the Lord come upon you. Glory be to the Holy Trinity. Amen.

(من صفنيا النبى 1 : 14 - 2 : 1 ، 2)

قريب هو يوم الرب العظيم . قريب هو وسريع جداً . صوت يوم الرب . مر وشديد وصعب قوى . ذلك اليوم يوم غضب يوم شدة وضيق . يوم عدم رحمة وهلاك . يوم ظلام وضباب يوم غمام وقتام . يوم صفير وصراخ على المدن الحصينة . وعلى الزوايا العالية . واضايق الناس فيمشون كالعمى لأنهم أخطأوا إلى الرب . فيسفح دمهم كالتراب ولحمهم كالجلة. لا فضتهم ولا ذهبهم بقدر أن يخلصهم فى يوم غضب الرب . وبنار غيرته تفنى الأرض كلها . لأنه يوقع قضاء سريعاً على جميع سكان الأرض . اجتمعوا وأحتشدوا يا أيها الأمم الجهلة. قبل أن تصيروا كالزهرة العابرة . قبل أن يدرككم غضب الرب . قبل أن يأتى عليكم يوم سخط الرب ؟ أطلبوا الرب يا جميع متواضعى الأرض . إصنعوا الحكم وأطلبوا العدل وجاوبوا بهما . لعلكم تستترون فى يوم رجز الرب . مجداً للثالوث القدوس .

Pascha Praise - A (12 times), Page: 6	تسبحة البصخة A (12 مرة) ، صفحة :

The Psalm
Ⲯⲁⲗⲙⲟⲥ ⲕⲍ : ⲓ̅ ⲛⲉⲙ ⲃ̅

Psalms 27:10, 2

Save Your people, and bless Your inheritance; and take care of them, and lift them up forever. Hearken to the voice of my supplication, when I pray to You. Alleluia.

Ⲛⲟϩⲉⲙ ⲙ̀ⲡⲉⲕⲗⲁⲟⲥ ⲥⲙⲟⲩ ⲉ̀ⲧⲉⲕⲕⲗⲏⲣⲟⲛⲟⲙⲉⲓⲁ : ⲁⲙⲟⲛⲓ ⲙ̀ⲙⲱⲟⲩ ϭⲁⲥⲟⲩ ϣⲁ ⲉ̀ⲛⲉϩ . ⲥⲱⲧⲉⲙ ⲡ̅ⲟ̅ⲥ̅ ⲉ̀ⲡ̀ϧ̀ⲣⲱⲟⲩ ⲛ̀ⲧⲉ ⲡⲁⲧⲱⲃϩ : ϧⲉⲛ ⲡ̀ϫⲓⲛⲧⲁⲧⲱⲃϩ ⲟⲩⲃⲏⲕ . ⲁ̅ⲗ̅ .

نوهيم إمبيك لاوس إسموو إتيك إكليرونوميا : أمونى إمموؤو تشاصو شا إينيه . صوتيم إبتشويس إبخروأوو إنتيه باطوبه : خين إبجين طاطوبه أووفيك . الليلويا .

(مز 27 : 2 و 10)

خلص شعبك بارك ميراثك ارعهم وارفعهم إلى الأبد . لتسمع يارب صوت تضرعى إذ ابتهل إليك. الليلويا.

Introduction to the Gospel, Page: 8	مقدمة الأنجيل ، صفحة :

The Gospel
Ⲉⲩⲁⲅⲅⲉⲗⲓⲟⲛ Ⲕⲁⲧⲁ Ⲗⲟⲩⲕⲁⲛ Ⲕⲉⲫ ⲑ̅ : ⲓ̅ⲏ̅ - ⲕ̅ⲃ̅

Luke 9:18-22

And it happened, as He was alone praying, that His disciples joined Him, and He asked them, saying, "Who do the crowds say that I am?" So they answered and said, "John the Baptist, but some

Ⲟⲩⲟϩ ⲁⲥϣⲱⲡⲓ ⲉϥⲭⲏ ⲥⲁ ⲡⲥⲁ ⲙ̀ⲙⲁⲩⲁⲧϥ ⲉϥⲉⲣⲡⲣⲟⲥ ⲉⲩⲭⲉⲥⲑⲉ ⲛⲁⲩⲭⲏ ⲛⲉⲙⲁϥ ⲡⲉ ⲛ̀ϫⲉ ⲛⲉϥⲙⲁⲑⲏⲧⲏⲥ ⲟⲩⲟϩ ⲁϥϣⲉⲛⲟⲩ ⲉϥϫⲱ ⲙ̀ⲙⲟⲥ ϫⲉ ⲁⲣⲉ ⲛⲓⲙⲏϣ ϫⲱ ⲙ̀ⲙⲟⲥ ϫⲉ ⲁⲛⲟⲕ ⲛⲓⲙ : ⲛ̀ⲑⲱⲟⲩ ⲇⲉ ⲉⲧⲁⲩⲉⲣⲟⲩⲱ ⲡⲉⲭⲱⲟⲩ ϫⲉ Ⲓⲱⲁⲛⲛⲏⲥ ⲡⲓⲣⲉϥϯⲱⲙⲥ ϩⲁⲛⲕⲉⲭⲱⲟⲩⲛⲓ ⲇⲉ

(لوقا 9 : 18 - 22)

وإذ كان يصلى منفرداً وحده كان تلاميذه معه فسألهم قائلاً : من تقول الجموع انى أنا؟ أما هم فأجابوا وقالوا: يوحنا المعمدان وآخرون إيليا .

say Elijah; and others say that one of the old prophets has risen again." He said to them, "But who do you say that I am?" Peter answered and said, "The Christ of God." And He strictly warned and commanded them to tell this to no one, saying, "The Son of Man must suffer many things, and be rejected by the elders and chief priests and scribes, and be killed, and be raised the third day." Glory be to God forever, Amen.	ϫⲉ Ⲏⲗⲓⲁⲥ ϩⲁⲛⲕⲉⲭⲱⲟⲩⲛⲓ ⲇⲉ ϫⲉ ⲟⲩⲡⲣⲟⲫⲏⲧⲏⲥ ⲛ̇ⲧⲉ ⲛⲓⲁⲣⲭⲉⲟⲥ ⲡⲉ ⲉⲧⲁϥⲧⲱⲛϥ. Ⲡⲉϫⲁϥ ⲇⲉ ⲛⲱⲟⲩ ⲛ̇ϫⲉ Ⲓⲏⲥ ϫⲉ ⲛ̇ⲑⲱⲧⲉⲛ ⲇⲉ ⲁⲣⲉⲧⲉⲛϫⲱ ⲙ̇ⲙⲟⲥ ϫⲉ ⲁⲛⲟⲕ ⲛⲓⲙ Ⲡⲉⲧⲣⲟⲥ ⲇⲉ ⲉⲧⲁϥⲉⲣⲟⲩⲱ ⲡⲉϫⲁϥ ϫⲉ ⲛ̇ⲑⲟⲕ Ⲡⲭ̅ⲥ̅ Ⲫϯ: ⲛ̇ⲑⲟϥ ⲇⲉ ⲉⲧⲁϥⲉⲣ ⲉ̇ⲡⲓⲧⲓⲙⲁⲛ ⲛⲱⲟⲩ ⲁϥϩⲟⲛϩⲉⲛ ⲛⲱⲟⲩ ⲉ̇ϣⲧⲉⲙ ϫⲉ ⲫⲁⲓ ⲛ̇ϩⲗⲓ: ⲉⲁϥϫⲟⲥ ϫⲉ ϩⲱϯ ⲡⲉ ⲛ̇ⲧⲉ ⲡϣⲏⲣⲓ ⲙ̇ⲫⲣⲱⲙⲓ ϭⲓ ⲟⲩⲙⲏϣ ⲛ̇ϭⲓⲥⲓ ⲟⲩⲟϩ ⲛ̇ⲧⲟⲩϣⲟϣϥ ⲛ̇ϫⲉ ⲛⲓⲡⲣⲉⲥⲃⲩⲧⲉⲣⲟⲥ ⲛⲉⲙ ⲛⲓⲁⲣⲭⲏ ⲉ̇ⲣⲉⲩⲥ ⲛⲉⲙ ⲛⲓⲥⲁϧ ⲟⲩⲟϩ ⲛ̇ⲧⲟⲩϧⲟⲑⲃⲉϥ ⲟⲩⲟϩ ⲛ̇ⲧⲉϥⲧⲱⲛϥ ϧⲉⲛ ⲡⲓⲙⲁϩϣⲟⲙⲧ ⲛ̇ⲉ̇ϩⲟⲟⲩ. ⲟⲩⲱϣⲧ ⲙ̇ⲡⲓⲉⲩⲁⲅⲅⲉⲗⲓⲟⲛ ⲉ̅ⲑ̅ⲩ̅	وآخرون يقولون ان نبياً من الأولين قد قام . فقال لهم: وأنتم من تقولون أنى أنا؟ فأجاب بطرس وقال: أنت مسيح الله. فأما هو فانتهرهم وأوصاهم أن لا يقولوا هذا لاحد . وقال: أنه ينبغي لإبن البشر أن يتألم كثيراً ويرذل من الشيوخ ورؤساء الكهنة والكتبة ويقتلونه وفى اليوم الثالث يقوم . والمجد لله دائماً.

Introduction to the Exposition, Page: 9 : مقدمة الطرح ، صفحة

Exposition

طـرح

Our Savior prayed to teach us to be always awake for prayers. After He finished, He asked his disciples "Who do the crowds say that I am?" They answered: Some say John the Baptist, but others say Elijah, or one of the old prophets. He, the Omniscient, was testing them. Then He asked, " But who do you say that I am?" Peter answered saying, "You are Christ, the Son of God, who came to the world to save us." "Blessed are you Peter, the solid rock, because flesh and blood did not reveal this to you but My Father did, so that you preach it to the world. As for the accursed Jews, they are rejecting me because of their envy, and will deliver me to death. I shall expose, and defame them; and will cause them eternal disgrace and shame."

صلى مخلصنا لكى يعلمنا أن نسهر فى كل حين للصلاة . وبعد ان فرغ سأل قائلاً : ماذا يقول الناس عنى؟ فأجابوه: ان قوماً يقولون أنك أنت القديس يوحنا المعمدان . وآخرون يقولون أنت إيليا أو واحد من الأنبياء الأولين . وأن العارف بكل شئ قبل كونه أمتحنهم ثم قال لهم : فأنتم ماذا تقولون . فأجاب بطرس وقال : أنت هو المسيح إبن الله الذى أتى إلى العالم حتى بخلصنا . طوباك أنت يا بطرس الصخرة الغير المتزعزعة لأنه ليس جسد ودم كشف لك هذا لكن أبى هو الذى أظهره لك لكى تكرز به فى المسكونة . فأما اليهود المخالفون فإنهم يجحدوننى من أجل حسدهم ويسلموننى إلى الموت . أنا أشهرهم وأفضحهم وأعطيهم عاراً وخزياً أبدياً .

(North side) Christ our Savior; has come and has borne suffering; that through His Passion; He may save us.

(مرد بحرى) المسيح مخلصنا جاء وتألم عنا لكى بألامه يخلصنا .

(South side) Let us glorify Him; and exalt His Name; for He had mercy on us; according to His great mercy.

(مرد قبلى) فلنمجده ونرفع اسمه لأنه صنع معنا رحمة كعظيم رحمته .

The Conclusion of the Exposition, Page: 9 : ختام الطرح ، صفحة

الساعة السادسة من ليلة الاثنين من البصخة المقدسة
The Sixth Hour of Monday Eve of the Holy Pascha

Joel 1:5-15

Awake, you drunkards, from your wine, and weep: mourn, all you that drink wine to drunkenness: for joy and gladness are removed from your mouth. For a strong and innumerable nation has come up against My land, their teeth are lion's teeth, and their back teeth those of a lion's whelp. He has ruined My vine, and utterly broken My fig trees: he has utterly searched My vine, and cast it down; he has peeled its branches. Lament to Me more than a virgin girded with sackcloth for the husband of her youth. The meat offering and drink offering are removed from the house of the Lord: mourn, you priests that serve at the altar of the Lord. For the plains languish: let the land mourn, for the grain languishes; the wine is dried up, the oil becomes scarce; the farmers are consumed: mourn your property on account of the wheat and barley; for the harvest has perished from off the field. The vine is dried up, and the fig trees have become few; the pomegranate, and palm tree, and apple, and all trees of the field have dried up: for the sons of men have abolished joy. Gird yourselves with sackcloth, and lament, you priests: mourn, you that serve at the altar: go in, sleep in sackcloth, you that minister to God: for the grain offering and drink offering are withheld from the house of your God. Sanctify a fast, proclaim a solemn service, gather the elders and all the inhabitants of the land into the house of your God, and cry earnestly to the Lord, Alas, Alas, Alas for the day! For the day of the Lord is near, and it will come as trouble upon trouble. Glory be to the Holy Trinity. Amen

(من يونيل النبي ص 1 : 5 – 15)

استيقظوا أيها السكارى من الخمر . وابكوا ونوحوا يا جميع شاربى الخمر المسكر . لأنه قد نزع عنكم السرور والفرح . إذ قد جاءت على الأرض أمة قوية بلا عدد . اسنانها أسنان الأسد ولها أنياب اللبوة . جعلت كرمتى للفساد وتينتى للإنحطام . وفتشتها تفتيشاً وطرحتها فابيضت قضبانها . وسيحزن الكرامون على الأرض أكثر من العروسة المشدودة على رأسها. الحزينة على بعل بكوريتها . نوحوا أيها الكهنة ويا خدام المذبح . لأنه قد رفعت الذبائح والسكيب من بيت الرب تلفت البقاع وانفسدت . ولتحزن الأرض لأنه قد عدم القمح وجف الخمر وقل الزيت ويبس . احزنوا أيها الفلاحون فى المساكن على القمح والشعير . لأنه قد تلف القطاف فى الحقل ويبست الكرمة . وذبلت شجرة التين . وشجرة الرمان مع النخلة . وشجرة التفاح وجميع أشجار الغياض يبست لأجل أن بنى البشر رذلوا الفرح . اتزروا بالمسوح ونوحوا أيها الكهنة . احزنوا يا خدام المذبح . ادخلوا بيتوا بالمسوح يا خدام الله . لأنه قد بطلت الذبيحة والسكيب من بيت الرب إلهكم. قدسوا صوماً واكرزوا بالخدمة . اجمعوا الشيوخ مع سكان الأرض وادخلوا إلي بيت واصرخوا إلى الرب إلهكم جداً . وقولوا ويل لى ويل لى . لأن يوم الرب قريب . وهو يأتى كالدمار . مجداً للثالوث القدوس

Pascha Praise - A (12 times), Page: 6	تسبحة البصخة A (12 مرة) ، صفحة :

The Psalm
Ⲯⲁⲗⲙⲟⲥ ⲕ̅ⲋ̅ : ⲁ̅ ⲛⲉⲙ ⲃ̅

Psalms 28:1-2

Bring to the Lord, you sons of God, bring to the Lord young rams; bring to the Lord glory and honor. Bring to the Lord the glory *due* to His name; worship the lord in His holy court.. Alleluia.

Ⲁⲛⲓⲟⲩⲓ ⲙ̅ⲡ̅ⲟ̅ⲥ̅ ⲛⲓϣⲏⲣⲓ ⲛ̅ⲧⲉ Ⲫ̅ϯ : ⲁⲛⲓⲟⲩⲓ ⲙ̅ⲡ̅ⲟ̅ⲥ̅ ⲛ̅ⲥⲁⲛϣⲏⲣⲓ ⲛ̅ⲱⲓⲗⲓ : ⲁⲛⲓⲟⲩⲓ ⲙ̅ⲡ̅ⲟ̅ⲥ̅ ⲛ̅ⲟⲩⲱⲟⲩ ⲛⲉⲙ ⲟⲩⲧⲁⲓⲟ : ⲁⲛⲓⲟⲩⲓ ⲙ̅ⲡ̅ⲟ̅ⲥ̅ ⲛ̅ⲟⲩⲱⲟⲩ ⲙ̅ⲡⲉϥⲣⲁⲛ ⲟⲩⲱϣⲧ ⲙ̅ⲡ̅ⲟ̅ⲥ̅ ϧⲉⲛ ⲧⲉϥⲁⲩⲗⲏ ⲉⲑⲟⲩⲁⲃ .ⲁⲗ.

أنيؤوى إمبتشويس نى شيرى إنتيه إفنوتى أنيؤوى إمبتوشيس إنهان شيرى إن أويلى أنيؤوى إمبتشويس إن أووأوأو نيم أوو طايو : أنيؤوى إمبتشويس إن أووأوأو إمبيفـران أوؤشـت إمبتشـويس خـين تيـف أفلـي إثؤواب . الليلويا .

(مز 28 : 1 ، 2)

قدموا للرب يا أبناء الله . قدموا للرب أبناء الكباش . قدموا للرب مجداً وكرامة . قدموا للرب مجداً لاسمه . اسجدوا للرب فى دار قدسه . الليلويا.

The Gospel

Ⲉⲩⲁⲅⲅⲉⲗⲓⲟⲛ Ⲕⲁⲧⲁ Ⲙⲁⲣⲕⲟⲛ Ⲕⲉⲫ ⲓ : ⲗ̄ⲃ̄ - ⲗ̄ⲇ̄

Mark 10:32-34

Now they were on the road, going up to Jerusalem, and Jesus was going before them; and they were amazed. And as they followed they were afraid. Then He took the twelve aside again and began to tell them the things that would happen to Him: "Behold, we are going up to Jerusalem, and the Son of Man will be betrayed to the chief priests and to the scribes; and they will condemn Him to death and deliver Him to the Gentiles; and they will mock Him, and scourge Him, and spit on Him, and kill Him. And the third day He will rise again." Glory be to God forever, Amen.

Ⲛⲁⲩ ⲉⲓ ⲫⲱⲓⲧ ⲇⲉ ⲡⲉ ⲉⲩⲛⲏⲟⲩ ⲉ̀ⲉ̀ϩⲣⲏⲓ ⲉ̀ⲓ̀ⲗ̅ⲏ̅ⲙ̅ ⲟⲩⲟϩ ⲛⲁϥⲙⲟϣⲓ ϧⲁϫⲱⲟⲩ ⲛ̀ϫⲉ Ⲓⲏⲥ ⲟⲩⲟϩ ⲛⲁⲩⲉⲣϩⲟϯ ⲛⲏ ⲇⲉ ⲉ̀ⲛⲁⲩⲉⲣⲁⲕⲟⲗⲟⲩⲑⲓⲛ ⲛⲁⲩⲉⲣϩⲟϯ ⲟⲩⲟϩ ⲡⲁⲗⲓⲛ ⲁϥⲓⲛⲓ ⲙ̀ⲡⲓⲙⲏⲧ ⲥ̀ⲛⲁⲩ ⲉ̀ⲧⲟⲧϥ ⲁϥⲉⲣϩⲏⲧⲥ ⲛ̀ⲉⲑⲛⲁϣⲱⲡⲓ ⲙ̀ⲙⲟϥ ⲛⲱⲟⲩ . Ⲭⲉ ϩⲏⲡⲡⲉ ⲧⲉⲛⲛⲁϣⲉⲛⲁⲛ ⲉ̀ⲉ̀ϩⲣⲏⲓ ⲉ̀ⲓ̀ⲗ̅ⲏ̅ⲙ̅ ⲟⲩⲟϩ ⲡ̀ϣⲏⲣⲓ ⲙ̀ⲫ̀ⲣⲱⲙⲓ ⲥⲉⲛⲁⲧⲏⲓϥ ⲛ̀ⲛⲓⲁⲣⲭⲏ ⲉ̀ⲣⲉⲩⲥ ⲛⲓⲙ ⲛⲓⲥⲁϧ ⲟⲩⲟϩ ⲥⲉⲛⲁϯϩⲁⲡ ⲉ̀ⲣⲟϥ ⲙ̀ⲫ̀ⲙⲟⲩ ⲟⲩⲟϩ ⲥⲉⲛⲁⲧⲏⲓϥ ⲛ̀ⲛⲓⲉⲑⲛⲟⲥ : ⲟⲩⲟϩ ⲥⲉⲛⲁⲥⲟⲃⲓ ⲙ̀ⲙⲟϥ ⲟⲩⲟϩ ⲥⲉⲛⲁϩⲓⲑⲁϥ ⲉ̀ϧⲟⲩⲛ ⲉ̀ϩⲣⲁϥ ⲟⲩⲟϩ ⲥⲉⲛⲁⲉⲣⲙⲁⲥⲧⲓⲅⲅⲟⲓⲛ ⲙ̀ⲙⲟϥ ⲟⲩⲟϩ ⲥⲉⲛⲁϧⲟⲑⲃⲉϥ ⲟⲩⲟϩ ⲙⲉⲛⲉⲛⲥⲁ ϣⲟⲙⲧ ⲛ̀ⲉϩⲟⲟⲩ ϥ̀ⲛⲁⲧⲱⲛϥ . ⲟⲩⲱϣⲧ ⲙ̀ⲡⲓⲉⲩⲁⲅⲅⲉⲗⲓⲟⲛ ⲉⲑⲟⲩ .

(34 - 32 : 10 مرقس)

وكانوا فى الطريق صاعدين إلى أورشليم وكان يسوع يسير قدامهم وكانوا يتحيرون والذين كانوا يتبعونه كانوا خائفين . فتقدم إليه أيضاً الإثنى عشر وإبتدأ يقول لهم عما يحدث له: ها نحن صاعدين إلى أورشليم وإبن الإنسان سيسلم إلى رؤساء الكهنة والكتبة فيحكمون عليه بالموت ويسلمونه إلى الأمم فيهزأون به ويتفلون عليه ويجلدونه ويقتلونه وفى اليوم الثالث يقوم . والمجد لله دائماً .

Exposition

And while Christ our Lord and his disciples were on their way to Jerusalem, the twelve apostles came to Him and He started to tell them about the sufferings that will come upon Him. He said: "Behold you that are chosen and pure; we are going up to Jerusalem. The chief priests of the Jews, their elders and scribes, will rise together against the Son of man; and they shall condemn Him to death, and shall deliver Him to the Gentiles. And they shall mock Him, and shall scourge Him, and shall spit upon Him, and crucify Him on the cross; and on the third day He shall rise again." You poor Israel, how dare you do that in your ignorance and crucify Jesus Christ, who saved you from slavery. You rewarded charity with evil, that is why your sin will remain forever.

طـرح

وفيما كان المسيح إلهنا وتلاميذه صاعدين إلى أورشليم . أتى إليه الإثنى عشر رسولاً تلاميذه القديسين . وإبتدأ يقول لهم بما سيكون له بسبب آلامه قائلاً : "اعلموا أيها الأصفياء الأطهار هذا نحن صاعدون إلى أورشليم وسوف يقوم رؤساء الكهنة اليهود ومشائخهم وكتبتهم معاً على إبن الإنسان ويحكمون عليه بحكم الموت . ويسلمونه إلى الأمم ويهزأون به ويبصقون فى وجهه . ويصلبونه على خشبة الصليب و فى اليوم الثالث يقوم" . كيف تجاسرت يا إسرائيل المسكين وفعلت هذا الأمر بجهلك و صلبت يسوع المسيح الذى أنقذك من العبودية . وجازيت الإحسان بالاساءة . من أجل ذلك خطيتك باقية إلى كمال الدهور .

(North side) Christ our Savior; has come and has borne suffering; that through His Passion; He may save us.

(مرد بحرى) المسيح مخلصنا جاء وتألم عنا لكى بألامه يخلصنا .

(South side) Let us glorify Him; and exalt His Name; for He had mercy on us; according to His great mercy

(مرد قبلى) فلنمجده ونرفع اسمه لأنه صنع معنا رحمة كعظيم رحمته .

| The Conclusion of the Exposition, Page: | 9 | ختام الطرح ، صفحة : |

الساعة التاسعة من ليلة الاثنين من البصخة المقدسة
The Ninth Hour of Monday Eve of the Holy Pascha

Micah 2:3-10

Therefore thus says the Lord; Behold, I devise evils against this family, out of which you shall not lift up your necks, neither shall you walk upright speedily: for the time is evil. In that day shall a parable be taken up against you, and a plaintive lamentation shall be uttered, saying, We are thoroughly miserable: the portion of my people has been measured out with a line, and there was none to hinder him so as to turn him back; your fields have been divided. Therefore you will have no one to cast a line for the lot. Weep not with tears in the assembly of the Lord, neither let any weep for these things; for He shall not remove the reproaches, who says, The house of Jacob has provoked the Spirit of the Lord; are not these his practices? Are not the Lord's words right with him? And have they not proceeded correctly? Even before time My people withstood him as an enemy against his peace; they have stripped off his skin to remove hope in the conflict of war. The leaders of My people shall be cast forth from their luxurious houses; they are rejected because of their evil practices; draw near to the everlasting mountains. Arise, and depart; for this is not your rest because of uncleanness: you have been utterly destroyed; you have fled, no one pursuing you. Glory be to the Holy Trinity. Amen

(من ميخا النبي ص ٢ : ٣ – ١٠)

من أجل ذلك هكذا ما يقوله الرب . هأنذا أفكر بالشرور على هذه القبيلة . ومن ثم لا تقدرون أن ترفعوا أعناقكم منها ولا تمشون متشامخين .لأنه زمان ردئ . ذلك اليوم يضربون عليكم بمثل . وينوحون نوحاً بتسبيح قائلين : لقد شقيت شقاء . ونصيب شعبى قاسوه بالحبل . ولم يكن من يحوله ليرجع . قاسوا حقولكم واقتسموا بقاعكم من أجل هذا لا يكون لك من يلقى حبلاً فى نصيب . لا تبكوا بدموع فى كنيسة الرب . ولا تسكبوا العبرات على هذا لأنه لا يترك التغيير عنه . القائل أن بيت يعقوب أغضب روح الرب . أليست هذه أعماله الكائنة معه . أليس كلامه صالحاً نحو من يسلك بالإستقامة . وقام شعبى بالعداوة قبالة سلامته . سلخوا جلده لينزع الرجاء من انكسار الحرب . من أجل ذلك مدبرو شعبى يطرحون خارجاً من بيوت نعيمهم . من أجل أعمالهم الشريرة طردوا. اقتربوا إلى الجبال الدهرية . قم انطلق لأنه ليست هذه هى راحتك. لقد هلكتم هلاكاً من أجل النجاسة وهربتم وليس من يطردكم . مجداً للثالوث القدوس .

Pascha Praise - A (12 times), Page: 6 | **تسبحة البصخة A (١٢ مرة) ، صفحة : ٦**

The Psalm
Ψⲁⲗⲙⲟⲥ ⲓ̅ⲋ̅ : ⲋ̅ ⲛⲉⲙ ⲁ̅

Psalms 16:6, 1

I have cried, for You heard me, O God: incline Your ear to me, and listen to my words. O Lord of my righteousness, attend to my petition; give ear to my prayer. Alleluia

Ⲁⲛⲟⲕ ⲁⲓⲱϣ ⲉⲃⲟⲗ ϫⲉ ⲁⲕⲥⲱⲧⲉⲙ ⲉⲣⲟⲓ : ⲣⲉⲕ ⲡⲉⲕⲙⲁϣϫ ⲉⲣⲟⲓ ⲟⲩⲟⲅ ⲥⲱⲧⲉⲙ ⲉⲛⲁⲥⲁϫⲓ . Ϭ̀ⲓⲥⲙⲏ Ⲫϯ ⲉ̀ⲧⲁⲙⲉⲑⲙⲏⲓ : ⲟⲩⲟⲅ ⲙⲁϩⲑⲏⲕ ⲉ̀ⲡⲁⲧⲅⲟ . ⲁ̅ⲗ .

أنوك أى أوش إيڤول جيه أكصوتيم إروى : ريك بيك ماشج إروى أووه صوتيم إناصاجى . تشى إسمى إفنوتى إطاميثمى : أووه ما إهثيك إباتيهو . الليلويا .

(مز ١٦ : ٦ و ١)

أنا صرخت لأنك قد سمعتنى يا الله . أمل يا رب أذنيك وانصت لكلامى . استمع يا الله عدلى واصغ إلى طلبتى . الليلويا .

Introduction to the Gospel, Page: 8 | **مقدمة الأنجيل ، صفحة : ٨**

The Gospel

Ⲉⲩⲁⲅⲅⲉⲗⲓⲟⲛ Ⲕⲁⲧⲁ Ⲙⲁⲣⲕⲟⲛ Ⲕⲉⲫ̅ : ⲕ̅ⲍ̅ - ⲗ̅ⲅ̅

Mark 8:27-33

Now Jesus and His disciples went out to the towns of Caesarea Philippi; and on the road He asked His disciples, saying to them, "Who do men say that I am?" So they answered, "John the Baptist; but some say, Elijah; and others, one of the prophets." He said to them, "But who do you say that I am?" Peter answered and said to Him, "You are the Christ." Then He strictly warned them that they should tell no one about Him. And He began to teach them that the Son of Man must suffer many things, and be rejected by the elders and chief priests and scribes, and be killed, and after three days rise again. He spoke this word openly. Then Peter took Him aside and began to rebuke Him. But when He had turned around and looked at His disciples, He rebuked Peter, saying, "Get behind Me, Satan! For you are not mindful of the things of God, but the things of men." Glory be to God forever, Amen.

Ⲟⲩⲟϩ ⲁϥⲓ ⲉⲃⲟⲗ ⲛ̀ϫⲉ Ⲓⲏ̅ⲥ̅ ⲛⲉⲙ ⲛⲉϥⲙⲁⲑⲏⲧⲏⲥ ⲉⲛⲓⲧⲱⲓ ⲛ̀ⲧⲉ Ⲕⲉⲥⲁⲣⲓⲁ ⲛ̀ⲧⲉ Ⲫⲓⲗⲡⲡⲉ ⲟⲩⲟϩ ϧⲉⲛ ⲡⲓⲙⲱⲓⲧ ⲛⲁϥϣⲓⲛⲓ ⲙ̀ⲛⲉϥⲙⲁⲑⲏⲧⲏⲥ ⲉϥϫⲱ ⲙ̀ⲙⲟⲥ ⲛⲱⲟⲩ ϫⲉ ⲁⲣⲉ ⲛⲓⲣⲱⲙⲓ ϫⲱ ⲙ̀ⲙⲟⲥ ϫⲉ ⲁⲛⲟⲕ ⲛⲓⲙ : ⲛ̀ⲑⲱⲟⲩ ⲇⲉ ⲁⲩⲭⲟⲥ ⲛⲁϥ ⲉⲩϫⲱ ⲙ̀ⲙⲟⲥ ϫⲉ Ⲓⲱⲁⲛⲛⲏⲥ ⲡⲓⲣⲉϥϯⲱ̀ⲙⲥ ϩⲁⲛⲕⲉⲭⲱⲟⲩⲛⲓ . ⲇⲉ ϫⲉ Ⲏⲗⲓⲁⲥ ϩⲁⲛⲕⲉⲭⲱⲟⲩⲛⲓ ⲇⲉ ϫⲉ ⲟⲩⲁⲓ ⲛ̀ⲧⲉ ⲛⲓⲡⲣⲟⲫⲏⲧⲏⲥ : ⲟⲩⲟϩ ⲛ̀ⲑⲟϥ ⲛⲁϥϣⲓⲛⲓ ⲙ̀ⲙⲱⲟⲩ ϫⲉ ⲛ̀ⲑⲱⲧⲉⲛ ⲧⲉⲧⲉⲛϫⲱ ⲙ̀ⲙⲟⲥ ⲉ̀ⲣⲟⲓ ϫⲉ ⲁⲛⲟⲕ ⲛⲓⲙ ⲁϥⲉⲣⲟⲩⲱ ⲛ̀ϫⲉ Ⲡⲉⲧⲟⲥ ⲡⲉϫⲁϥ ϫⲉ ⲛ̀ⲑⲟⲕ ⲡⲉ Ⲡⲭ̅ⲥ̅ . Ⲟⲩⲟϩ ⲁϥⲉⲣ ⲉ̀ⲡⲓⲧⲓⲙⲁⲛ ⲛⲱⲟⲩ ϩⲓⲛⲁ ⲛ̀ⲥⲉϣ̀ⲧⲉⲙϫⲟⲥ ⲛ̀ϩ̀ⲗⲓ ⲉⲑⲃⲏⲧϥ : ⲟⲩⲟϩ ⲁϥⲉⲣϩⲏⲧⲥ ⲛ̀ϯⲥⲃⲱ ⲛⲱⲟⲩ ϫⲉ ϩⲱϯ ⲡⲉ ⲛ̀ⲧⲉ ⲡ̀ϣⲏⲣⲓ ⲙ̀ⲫ̀ⲣⲱⲙⲓ ϭⲓ ⲟⲩⲙⲏϣ ⲛ̀ϭⲓⲥⲓ ⲟⲩⲟϩ ⲛ̀ⲧⲟⲩϣⲟϣϥ ⲉ̀ⲃⲟⲗ ϩⲓⲧⲟⲧⲟⲩ ⲛ̀ⲛⲓⲡⲣⲉⲥⲃⲩⲧⲉⲣⲟⲥ ⲛⲓⲁⲣⲭⲏ ⲉ̀ⲣⲉⲩⲥ ⲛⲉⲙ ⲛⲓⲥⲁϧ ⲟⲩⲟϩ ⲛ̀ⲧⲟⲩϧⲟⲑⲃⲉϥ ⲟⲩⲟϩ ⲙⲉⲛⲉⲛⲥⲁ ϣⲟⲙⲧ ⲛ̀ⲉϩⲟⲟⲩ ⲛ̀ⲧⲉϥⲧⲱⲛϥ : ⲟⲩⲟϩ ⲛⲁϥⲥⲁϫⲓ ⲙ̀ⲡⲓⲥⲁϫⲓ ϧⲉⲛ ⲟⲩⲡⲁⲣⲣⲏⲥⲓⲁ ⲟⲩⲟϩ ⲁϥⲁⲙⲟⲛⲓ ⲙ̀ⲙⲟϥ ⲛ̀ϫⲉ Ⲡⲉⲧⲣⲟⲥ ⲟⲩⲟϩ ⲉⲧⲁϥⲉⲣϩⲏⲧⲥ ⲛ̀ⲉⲣ ⲉ̀ⲡⲓⲧⲓⲙⲁⲛ ⲛⲁϥ . Ⲛ̀ⲑⲟϥ ⲇⲉ ⲉⲧⲁϥⲫⲟⲛϩϥ ⲟⲩⲟϩ ⲉⲧⲁϥⲛⲁⲩ ⲉ̀ⲛⲉϥⲙⲁⲑⲏⲧⲏⲥ ⲁϥⲉⲣ ⲉ̀ⲡⲓⲧⲓⲙⲁⲛ ⲙ̀Ⲡⲉⲧⲣⲟⲥ ⲟⲩⲟϩ ⲡⲉϫⲁϥ ⲛⲁϥ ϫⲉ ⲙⲁϣⲉⲛⲁⲕ ⲥⲁⲫⲁϩⲟⲩ ⲙ̀ⲙⲟⲓ ⲡⲥⲁⲧⲁⲛⲁⲥ ϫⲉ ⲭⲙⲉⲩⲓ ⲁⲛ ⲉ̀ⲛⲁ Ⲫϯ ⲁⲗⲗⲁ ⲉ̀ⲛⲁ ⲛⲓⲣⲱⲙⲓ : ⲟⲩⲱϣⲧ ⲙ̀ⲡⲓⲉⲩⲁⲅⲅⲉⲗⲓⲟⲛ ⲉⲑⲩ .

(مرقس 8 : 27 - 32)

ثم خرج يسوع وتلاميذه إلى قرى قيسارية فيلبس . وفى الطريق كان يسأل تلاميذه قائلاً : من تقول الناس انى أنا؟ أما هم فقالوا له: يقولون إنك يوحنا المعمدان وآخرون إنك إيليا وآخرون إنك أحد الأنبياء . أما هو فسألهم وقال: وأنتم من تقولون انى أنا؟ أجاب بطرس وقال أنت المسيح . فزجرهم لكيلا يقولوا لأحد شيئاً من أجله ، وإبتدأ يعلمهم أنه ينبغى لإبن الإنسان أن يتألم كثيراً من الشيوخ ورؤساء الكهنة والكتبة ويقتلونه . وبعد ثلاثة أيام يقوم . وكان يقول هذا القول علانية فامسكه بطرس وإبتدأ ينهاه . فأما هو فالتفت ونظر إلى تلاميذه وزجر بطرس وقال له اذهب عنى يا شيطان لأنك لا تفكر فيما لله بل فيما للناس. والمجد لله دائماً .

| Introduction to the Exposition, Page: | 9 | مقدمة الطرح ، صفحة : |

Exposition

طرح

While Jesus and His disciples were on the road to Caesarea Philippi, He started to talk to them overtly about what will happen to Him in Jerusalem. He must fulfill what is written: That the Son of man will have lots of pains. He will be rejected from the scribes and the elders of the Jews. And after the sufferings He will endure, He will rise on the third day. This is the stone that the builders rejected as the scriptures say: He will descend with great anger upon them, and His rage will destroy them. He will pour shame upon their faces because they

لما فرغ الرب من سؤال تلاميذه فى طريق قيصرية فيلبس ، إبتدأ يقول لهم علانية من أجل الذى سيحدث له فى أورشليم . أنه ينبغى أن يكمل المكتوب إن إبن الإنسان ينال آلاماً كثيرة. ويرذل من الكتبة وشيوخ اليهود . ومن بعد الآلام التى سيقبلها يقوم من الأموات فى اليوم الثالث. هذا هو الحجر الذى رذله البناؤون كقول الكتاب. فسيهبط عليهم غضبه العظيم ويهشمهم الرجز . وهو يصب الخزى على وجوههم لأنهم جازوا

rewarded charity with evil. And for those who obey Him, and believe in Him, He will give eternal happiness.

(North side) Christ our Savior; has come and has borne suffering; that through His Passion; He may save us.

(South side) Let us glorify Him; and exalt His Name; for He had mercy on us; according to His great mercy

الإحسان بالاساءة . والذين يسمعون ويؤمنون به سيعطيهم فرحاً لا يفنى إلى الأبد .

(مرد بحرى) المسيح مخلصنا جاء وتألم عنا لكى بألامه يخلصنا .

(مرد قبلى) فلنمجده ونرفع اسمه لأنه صنع معنا رحمة كعظيم رحمته .

The Conclusion of the Exposition, Page: 9   ختام الطرح ، صفحة :

الساعة الحادية عشر من ليلة الاثنين من البصخة المقدسة
The Eleventh Hour of Monday Eve of the Holy Pascha

Micah 3:1-4

And He shall say, Hear now these words, you heads of the house of Jacob, and you remnant of the house of Israel; is it not for you to know judgment? Who hate good, and seek evil; who tear their skins off them, and their flesh off their bones: even as they devoured the flesh of My people, and stripped their skins off them, and broke their bones, and divided them as flesh for the caldron, and as meat for the pot, thus they shall cry to the Lord, but He shall not hearken to them; and He shall turn away His face from them at that time, because they have done wickedly in their practices against themselves. Glory be to the Holy Trinity. Amen

(من ميخا النبى ص 3 : 1 - 4)

والرب يرشدهم ويقول . اسمعوا هذا يا رؤساء بيت يعقوب ومختارى بيت إسرائيل . أما ينبغى لكم أن تعرفوا الحكم أيها الباغضون الخيرات . والمبتغون الشرور . النازعون جلودهم عنهم ولحومهم عن عظامهم . وكما أكلوا لحوم شعبى وكشطوا جلودهم عن عظامهم . وكسروا عظامهم وقطعوها كلحوم المراجل . وكاللحم فى وسط القدور . حينئذ يصرخون إلى الرب فلا يجيبهم . بل يصرف وجهه عنهم فى ذلك الوقت والشر الذى صنعوه باساءتهم يأتى عليهم . مجداً للثالوث القدوس .

Pascha Praise - A (12 times), Page: 6	تسبحة البصخة A (12 مرة) ، صفحة :

The Psalm
Ψⲁⲗⲙⲟⲥ ⲓⲍ :ⲓ︤ⲋ︥ ⲛⲉⲙ ⲓⲍ

Psalms 17:16-17

He will deliver me from my mighty enemies, and from them that hate me; for they are stronger than I. They prevented me in the day of my affliction.
Alleluia

Ⲛⲁⲋⲙⲉⲧ ⲉⲃⲟⲗ ⲛ̀ⲧⲟⲧⲟⲩ ⲛ̀ⲛⲁϫⲁϫⲓ ⲉⲧϫⲟⲣ : ⲛⲉⲙ ⲉⲃⲟⲗ ⲛ̀ⲧⲟⲧⲟⲩ ⲛ̀ⲛⲏⲉⲑⲙⲟⲥϯ ⲙ̀ⲙⲟⲓ . Ϫⲉ ⲁⲩⲧⲁϫⲣⲟ ⲉ̀ϩⲟⲧ ⲉⲣⲟⲓ : ⲁⲩⲉⲣ ϣⲟⲣⲡ ⲉ̀ⲣⲟⲓ ϧⲉⲛ ⲡ̀ⲉ̀ϩⲟⲟⲩ ⲛ̀ⲧⲉ ⲡⲁⲧϩⲉⲙⲕⲟ . ⲁⲗ .

ناهميت إيفول إنطوطوو إنناجاجى إتجور : نيم إيفول إنطوطوو إننى إثموستى إمموى . جيه أفطاجرو إهوت إروى : أفئر شورب إروى خين إب إيهووؤ إنتيه باإتهيمكو . الليلويا .

(مز 16:17 و17)

نجنى من أعدائى الأقوياء ومن أيدى الذين يبغضوننى . لأنهم تقووا أكثر منى ، ادركونى فى يوم ضرى . أللليلويا .

Introduction to the Gospel, Page: 8	مقدمة الأنجيل ، صفحة :

The Gospel
Ⲉⲩⲁⲅⲅⲉⲗⲓⲟⲛ Ⲕⲁⲧⲁ Ⲙⲁⲧⲑⲉⲟⲛ Ⲕⲉⲫ ⲓⲍ :ⲓ︤ⲑ︥ - ⲕ︤ⲅ︥

Matthew 17:19-23

Then the disciples came to Jesus privately and said, "Why could we not cast it out?" So Jesus said to them, "Because of your unbelief; for assuredly, I say to you, if you have faith as a mustard seed, you will say to this mountain, 'Move from here to there,' and it will move; and nothing will be impossible for you. However, this kind does not go out except by prayer and fasting." Now while they were staying in Galilee, Jesus said

Ⲧⲟⲧⲉ ⲁϥⲓ̀ ⲛ̀ϫⲉ ⲛⲓⲙⲁⲑⲏⲧⲏⲥ ϩⲁ Ⲓⲏⲥ ⲥⲁ ⲡⲥⲁ ⲙ̀ⲙⲁⲩⲁⲧⲟⲩ ⲟⲩⲟϩ ⲡⲉϫⲱⲟⲩ ⲛⲁϥ ϫⲉ ⲉⲑⲃⲉ ⲟⲩ ⲁⲛⲟⲛ ⲙ̀ⲡⲉⲛϣϫⲉⲙϫⲟⲙ ⲉ̀ϩⲓⲧϥ ⲉ̀ⲃⲟⲗ : ⲛ̀ⲑⲟϥ ⲇⲉ ⲡⲉϫⲁϥ ⲛⲱⲟⲩ ϫⲉ ⲉⲑⲃⲉ ⲡⲉ ⲧⲉⲛⲕⲟⲩϫⲓ ⲛ̀ⲛⲁϩϯ ⲁⲙⲏⲛ ⲅⲁⲣ ϯϫⲱ ⲙ̀ⲙⲟⲥ ⲛⲱⲧⲉⲛ ϫⲉ ⲉ̀ϣⲱⲡ ⲉ̀ⲟⲩⲟⲛ ⲧⲉⲧⲉⲛⲛⲁϯ ⲙ̀ⲙⲁⲩ ⲙ̀ⲫⲣⲏϯ ⲛ̀ⲟⲩⲛⲁⲫⲣⲓ ⲛ̀ϣⲉⲗⲧⲁⲙ ⲉⲣⲉⲧⲉⲛⲉ̀ϫⲟⲥ ⲙ̀ⲡⲁⲓⲧⲱⲟⲩ ϫⲉ ⲟⲩⲱⲧⲉⲃ ⲉ̀ⲃⲟⲗ ⲧⲁⲓⲉ̀ⲙⲛⲏ ⲟⲩⲟϩ ⲉϥⲉⲟⲩⲱⲧⲉⲃ ⲟⲩⲟϩ ⲛ̀ⲛⲉ ϩ̀ⲗⲓ ⲉⲣⲁ ⲧϫⲟⲙ ⲛ̀ⲧⲉⲛ ⲑⲏⲛⲟⲩ : ⲟⲩⲟϩ ⲡⲁⲓⲅⲉⲛⲟⲥ ⲙ̀ⲡⲁϥⲓ̀ ⲉ̀ⲃⲟⲗ ϧⲉⲛ ϩ̀ⲗⲓ ⲉⲃⲏⲗ ⲛ̀ⲟⲩⲡⲣⲟⲥⲉⲩⲭⲏ ⲛⲉⲙ ⲟⲩⲛⲏⲥⲧⲓⲁ. Ⲉⲧⲁⲩⲕⲟⲧⲟⲩ ⲇⲉ ⲉ̀ϩ̀ⲣⲏⲓ ⲉ̀ϯⲄⲁⲗⲓⲗⲉ̀ⲁ ⲡⲉ ϫⲉ

(متى 17 : 19 - 23)

حينئذ جاء التلاميذ إلى يسوع منفردين وحدهم وقالوا له: لماذا لم نقدر نحن أن نخرجه؟ أما هو فقال لهم: لأجل قلة إيمانكم. الحق أقول لكم لو كان لكم إيمان مثل حبة خردل لكنتم تقولون لهذا الجبل انتقل من هنا إلى هناك فينتقل ولايكون شئ غير ممكن لديكم وأما هذا الجنس فلا يخرج إلا بالصلوة والصوم. وبينما هم

to them, "The Son of Man is about to be betrayed into the hands of men, and they will kill Him, and the third day He will be raised up." And they were exceedingly sorrowful.	Ihc nwor xe ̀pϣhpi ̀mⲫrwⲙi cenⲁthiϥ ̀eϧph ̀enenxix ̀nnirwⲙi : oroⲋ cenⲁϧoⲑⲃeϥ oroⲋ ⲙenenca ϣoⲙt ̀neϩoor eϥ'etwnϥ : oroⲋ ⲁ ̀porϩht ̀mkⲁϩ eⲙⲁϣw : orwϣt ̀mpieraggeⲗion eⲑr.	يترددون فى الجليل قال لهم يسوع: ان ابن الإنسان سيسلم إلى أيدى الناس فيقتلونه . وبعد ثلاثة أيام يقوم . فحزنت قلوبهم جداً . والمجد لله دائماً .

Glory be to God forever, Amen.

| Introduction to the Exposition, Page: 9 | مقدمة الطرح ، صفحة : ٩ |

Exposition

طـرح

Listen to the Merciful and Beneficent who is all goodness and compassion. He praises prayer and honors fasting because they are the roots for all virtues. When His disciples asked Him: "why could we not cast the demon out." He said to them, "Because of your little faith the demon would not come out. For truly I say to you, if you have faith, you will say to this mountain 'Move from here to there' and it will move; and nothing will be impossible for you;" for everything is possible to the believer. So let us cherish a great hope and a true faith free of doubt, and let us be zealous in charity that surpasses everything; for He who loves accepts everything. Let us love fasting and pray consistently so that we may gain His promises.

اسمعوا الرؤوف الصانع الخيرات ذا الصلاح والتحنن يمجد الصلاة ويكرم الصوم لأنهما أساس سائر الفضائل . فإن تلاميذه عندما سألوه قائلين : لماذا لا نقدر أن نخرج الشيطان ؟ قال لهم : لأجل قلة إيمانكم إمتنع الشيطان أن يخرج . ثم قال الرب : لو كان لكم إيمان لكنتم تقولون لهذا الجبل إنتقل إلى هنا فلوقته سريعاً كان يسمع لكم ، ولا يعسر عليكم شئ. فإن كل شئ مستطاع للمؤمن . فلنقتن لنا رجاءً عظيماً وإيماناً حقيقياً بغير شك وأنتم فى المحبة التى تفوق كل شئ ، فإن الذى يحب يصدق كل شئ . ولنواظب على الصلاة ونحب الصوم لكى نفوز بمواعيده .

(North side) Christ our Savior; has come and has borne suffering; that through His Passion; He may save us.

(مرد بحرى) المسيح مخلصنا جاء وتألم عنا لكى بألامه يخلصنا .

(South side) Let us glorify Him; and exalt His Name; for He had mercy on us; according to His great mercy

(مرد قبلى) فلنمجده ونرفع اسمه لأنه صنع معنا رحمة كعظيم رحمته .

| The Conclusion of the Exposition, Page: 9 | ختام الطرح ، صفحة : ٩ |

| The Conclusion with the Nighttime Litanies, Page: 17 | طلبة المساء ، صفحة : ١٧ |

يوم الأثنين من البصخة المقدسة

Monday of the Holy Pascha

القراءات و الاحداث

الموضوع : اهتمامه بالهيكل

الاولى : مر 11 : 12 - 24 ؛ سلطانه فى الهيكل
الثالثه : مر 11 : 11 – 19؛ تطهيره من مدنسيه
السادسة : يو 2 : 13 – 17 ؛ غيرته عليه
التاسعة : مت 21 : 23- 27 ؛ مصدر سلطانه
الحادية عشرة : يو 8 : 51- 59 ؛ قيام الرؤساء عليه

فى الطريق من بيت عنيا الى الهيكل لعن الرب يسوع شجرة التين المورقة و لكن بغير ثمار ، التى كانت ترمز للامة اليهودية التى لها مظهر خارجى و لكن بلا ثمار . و لما دخل الرب الى الهيكل طهره من كل من كان يبيع و يشترى فيه ليحفظه طاهرا من الشرور

The Readings and Events

Subject: His care about the temple

First hour: Mark 11:12-24 ; His authority in the temple
Third hour: Mark 11:11-19 ; Cleaning the temple
Sixth hour: John 2:13-17 ; His zeal
Ninth hour: Matthew 21:23-27 ; Source of His authority
Eleventh hour: John 8:51-59 ; They are against Him

On the way from Bethany to the temple, the Lord Jesus Christ cursed a fig tree that was having nothing but leaves. This was an example of the Jewish nation that had the good exterior appearance but without any fruits. When the Lord entered into the temple, He drove out those who were buying and selling in it to keep it undefiled.

الساعة الاولى من يوم الاثنين من البصخة المقدسة
The First Hour of Monday of the Holy Pascha

Genesis 1:1-2:3

In the beginning God made the heaven and the earth. But the earth was unsightly and unfurnished, and darkness was over the deep, and the Spirit of God moved over the water. And God said, Let there be light, and there was light. And God saw the light that it was good, and God divided between the light and the darkness. And God called the light Day, and the darkness He called Night, and there was evening and there was morning, the first day. And God said, Let there be a firmament in the midst of the water, and let it be a division between water and water, and it was so. And God made the firmament, and God divided between the water which was under the firmament and the water which was above the firmament. And God called the firmament Heaven, and God saw that it was good, and there was evening and there was morning, the second day. And God said, Let the water which is under the heaven be collected into one place, and let the dry land appear, and it was so. And the water which was under the heaven was collected into its places, and the dry land appeared. And God called the dry land Earth, and the gatherings of the waters He called Seas, and God saw that it was good. And God said, Let the earth bring forth the herb of grass bearing seed according to its kind and according to its likeness, and the fruit tree bearing fruit whose seed is in it, according to its kind on the earth, and it was so. And the earth brought forth the herb of grass bearing seed according to its kind and according to its likeness, and the fruit tree bearing fruit whose seed is in it, according to its kind on the earth, and God saw that it was good. And there was evening and there was morning, the third day. And God said, Let there be lights in the firmament of the heaven to give light upon the earth, to divide between day and night, and let them be for signs and for seasons and for days and for years. And let them be for light in the firmament of the heaven, so as to shine upon the earth, and it was so. And God made the two great lights, the greater light for regulating the day and the lesser light for regulating the night, the stars also. And God placed them in the firmament of the heaven, so as to shine upon the earth, and to regulate day and night, and to divide between the light and the darkness. And God saw that it was good. And there was evening and there was morning, the fourth day. And God said, Let the waters bring forth reptiles having life, and winged creatures flying above the earth in the firmament of heaven, and it was so. And God made great whales, and every living reptile, which the waters brought forth

(التكوين لموسى النبى 1 : 1 -2 : 3)

فى البدء خلق الله السماء والأرض . وكانت الأرض غير مرئية وغير مستعدة وعلى وجه الغمر ظلام وروح الله يرف على وجه المياه . وقال الله ليكن نور فكان نور . ورأى الله النور أنه حسن . وفصل الله بين النور والظلام . ودعا الله النور نهاراً والظلام دعاه ليلاً . وكان مساء وكان صباح يوماً أولاً . وقال الله ليكن جلد متوسط بين المياه . وليكن فاصل بين مياه ومياه فكان كذلك فخلق الله الجلد فى وسط المياه وفصل الله بين المياه التى تحت الجلد والمياه التى فوق الجلد . ودعا الله الجلد سماء . ورأى الله أن ذلك حسن . وكان مساء وكان صباح يوماً ثانياً . وقال الله لتجتمع المياه التى تحت السماء إلى مجمع واحد وليظهر اليبس . وكان كذلك . فاجتمعت المياه التى تحت السماء مجمعاً واحداً . وظهر اليبس ودعا الله اليبس أرضاً . ومجتمع المياه سماه بحاراً ورأى الله ذلك أنه حسن وقال الله لتنبت الأرض نباتاً عشباً يبزر بزراً كجنسه وشكله وشجراً ذا ثمر يخرج ثمراً كجنسه بزره فيه على الأرض . وكان كذلك . فأخرجت الأرض نباتاً عشباً يبزر بزراً كجنسه وشجراً مثمراً يعمل ثمراً بزره فيه كجنسه على الأرض. ورأى الله ذلك أنه حسن . وكان مساء وكان صباح يوماً ثالثاً . وقال الله لتكن أنوار فى جلد السماء لتنير على الأرض ولتفصل بين النهار والليل. وتكون لآيات وأوقات وأيام وسنين . وتكون أنوار فى جلد السماء لتضئ على الأرض . فكان كذلك . فخلق النيرين العظيمين النور الأكبر لسلطان النهار . والنور الأصغر لسلطان الليل مع النجوم وجعلها الله فى جلد السماء لتضئ على الأرض . وتتسلط على النهار والليل . ولتفصل بين النور والظلام . ورأى الله ذلك أنه حسن وكان مساء وكان صباح يوماً رابعاً . وقال الله لتفض المياه زحافات ذات أنفس حية وطيوراً تطير فوق الأرض على وجه جلد السماء . وكان كذلك . فخلق الله الحيتان العظام . وكل ذى نفس حية من الهوام التى فاضت بها المياه كأجناسها .

according to their kinds, and every creature that flies with wings according to its kind, and God saw that they were good. And God blessed them saying, Increase and multiply and fill the waters in the seas, and let the creatures that fly be multiplied on the earth. And there was evening and there was morning, the fifth day. And God said, Let the earth bring forth the living creature according to its kind, quadrupeds and reptiles and wild beasts of the earth according to their kind, and it was so. And God made the wild beasts of the earth according to their kind, and cattle according to their kind, and all the reptiles of the earth according to their kind, and God saw that they were good. And God said, Let Us make man according to Our image and likeness, and let them have dominion over the fish of the sea, and over the flying creatures of heaven, and over the cattle and all the earth, and over all the reptiles that creep on the earth. And God made man, according to the image of God He made him, male and female He made them. And God blessed them, saying, Increase and multiply, and fill the earth and subdue it, and have dominion over the fish of the seas and flying creatures of heaven, and all the cattle and all the earth, and all the reptiles that creep on the earth. And God said, Behold I have given to you every seed-bearing herb sowing seed which is upon all the earth, and every tree which has in itself the fruit of seed that is sown, to you it shall be for food. And to all the wild beasts of the earth, and to all the flying creatures of heaven, and to every reptile creeping on the earth, which has in itself the breath of life, even every green plant for food; and it was so. And God saw all the things that He had made, and, behold, they were very good. And there was evening and there was morning, the sixth day. And the heavens and the earth were finished, and the whole world of them. And God finished on the sixth day His works which He made, and He ceased on the seventh day from all His works which He made. And God blessed the seventh day and sanctified it, because in it He ceased from all His works which God began to do. Glory be to the Holy Trinity. Amen.

Isaiah 5:1-9

Now I will sing to my Beloved a song of my Beloved concerning His vineyard. My Beloved had a vineyard on a high hill in a fertile place. And I made a hedge round it, and dug a trench, and planted a choice vine, and built a tower in the midst of it, and dug a place for the wine vat in it; and I waited for it to bring forth grapes, and it brought forth thorns. And now, you dwellers in Jerusalem, and every man of Judah, judge between Me and My vineyard. What shall I do anymore to My vineyard, that I have not done to it? Whereas I expected it to bring forth grapes, but it

وكل طائر ذى جناح كجنسه . ورأى الله ذلك أنه حسن . وباركها الله قائلاً : انمى وأكثرى واملأى المياه فى البحار وليكثر الطير على الأرض . وكان مساء وكان صباح يوماً خامساً . وقال الله لتخرج الأرض أنفس حية ذوات أربع وهوام ووحوش الأرض كأجناسها وكل دبابات الأرض كأجناسها . وكان كذلك . فخلق الله جميع وحوش الأرض كأجناسها . والبهائم كأجناسها . وكل دبابات الأرض كأجناسها . ورأى الله ذلك أنه حسن . وقال الله لنخلق إنساناً على صورتنا وكمثالنا . وليتسلط على سمك البحر وطير الماء . والبهائم وعلى جميع الأرض . وكل ما يدب ويتحرك على الأرض . فخلق الله الإنسان على صورته على صورة الله خلقه . ذكراً وأنثى خلقهم. وباركهم الله قائلاً : انموا واكثروا واملأوا الأرض وسودوا عليها وتسلطوا على سمك البحر وطير السماء . وجميع البهائم وسائر الأرض . وكل الهوام التى تدب على الأض. وقال الله : ها قد أعطيتكم كل عشب مزروع يبزر بزراً على وجه الأرض كلها . وكل شجر فيه ثمر يبزر بزراً يكون لكم طعاماً . ولجميع وحوش الأرض وكل طير السماء . وكل ما يدب ويتحرك على الأرض . مما فيه نفس حية . أعطيت كل عشب أخضر طعاماً . وكان كذلك . ورأى الله جميع ما خلقه فاذا هو حسن جداً . وكان مساء وكان صباح يوماً سادساً . فأكملت السماء والأرض وكل زينتها . وأكمل الله أعماله التى خلقها فى اليوم السادس . واستراح فى اليوم السابع من جميع أعماله التى صنعها وبارك الله اليوم السابع وقدسه . لأن فيه استراح من جميع أعماله التى إبتدأ الله بخلقتها . مجداً للثالوث القدوس .

(من إشعياء النبى ص 5 : 1 - 9)
أمجد الذى أحبه بنشيد حبيب هذا الكرم. كان للحبيب كرم فى رابية . فى موضع خصب . فأحطت به سياجاً ورفعته على القصب وغرست كرماً فى سورق وبنيت فيه برجاً فى وسطه . وحفرت فيه معصرة . وانتظرت أن يخرج عنباً فاخرج شوكاً . والآن يا رجال يهوذا وسكان أورشليم . احكموا بينى وبين كرمى أى شئ يصنع لكرمى وأنا لم أصنعه به؟ لأنى رجوت أن يخرج عنباً

has brought forth thorns. And now I will tell you what I will do to My vineyard; I will take away its hedge, and it shall be for a spoil; and I will pull down its walls, and it shall be left to be trodden down. And I will forsake My vineyard; and it shall not be pruned, nor dug, and thorns shall come up upon it as on barren land; and I will command the clouds to rain no rain upon it. For the vineyard of the Lord of hosts is the house of Israel, and the men of Judah His beloved plant; I expected it to bring forth judgment, and it brought forth iniquity; and not righteousness, but a cry. Woe to them that join house to house, and add field to field, that they may take away something of their neighbor's; will you dwell alone upon the land? For these things have reached the ears of the Lord of hosts. Glory be to the Holy Trinity. Amen.

Sirach 1:1-19

All wisdom comes from the Lord and is with Him forever. Who can count the sand of the seas, the drops of rain, and the days of eternity? Who can search out the height of heaven, the breadth of the earth, the abyss, and wisdom? Wisdom was created before all things, and the insight of prudence was from eternity. To whom has the root of wisdom been revealed? And who has come to know her great deeds? There is one who is wise and is feared exceedingly, He who sits upon His throne. The Lord Himself created wisdom. He saw and numbered her and poured her out on all His works, In the midst of all flesh according to His gift; and He provided her for those who love Him. The fear of the Lord is glory and boasting, and gladness and a crown of rejoicing. The fear of the Lord will cheer the heart and will give gladness, joy, and long life. For those who fear the Lord, it shall be well to the utmost, and on the day of his death, he will be blessed. The beginning of wisdom is to fear the Lord, and she was joined with the faithful in the womb. She constructed a foundation of life among men and will be trusted among their seed. The gratification of wisdom is to fear the Lord, and she intoxicates them with her fruits. She will fill every house of theirs with objects of desire and their storehouses with her harvest. The fear of the Lord is the crown of wisdom, making peace and soundness of health to flourish. The Lord saw and numbered her, and poured out the power of comprehension; and He exalted the glory of those who hold fast to her. Glory be to the Holy Trinity. Amen.

فأخرج شوكاً . فالآن أعلمكم ماذا أفعل بكرمى. أقلع سياجه فيصير للنهب . وأهدم جدرانه فيكون مدوساً وأهمل هذا الكرم فلا يقضب ولا يفلح وينبت فيه الشوك مثل السلا . وأوصى السحاب ألا تمطر عليه مطراً . لأن كرم رب الصباؤوت هو بيت إسرائيل . ورجال يهوذا الغرس الجديد المحبوب . رجوت أن يصنع إنصافاً فصنع إثماً . وعدلاً فاذا صراخ . ويل للذين يصلون بيتاً ببيت ويقرنون حقلاً بحقل لكي يسلبوا أصحابهم . إذن أنتم تسكنون الأرض وحدكم . قد سمع هذا فى مسامع رب الصباؤوت . مجداً للثالوث القدوس .

(بدء يشوع إبن سيراخ ص 1 : 1 - 19)

كل الحكمة فهى من قبل الرب . وهى دائمة معه إلى الأبد . من يقدر أن يحصى رمل البحر . وقطرات المطر وأيام الدهور . من يستطيع أن يمسح علو السماء . ورحب الأرض . وعمق الغمر والحكمة . قبل كل شئ خيرت الحكمة . ومنذ الأزل الفهم والفطنة ينبوع الحكمة كلمة الله فى العلا . وطرقها الوصايا الأزلية . لمن استعلن أصل الحكمة؟ ومن عرف خفاياها؟ لمن تجلت معرفة الحكمة؟ ومن أدرك كثرة خبرتها؟ واحد هو حكيم عظيم المهابة جالس على عرشه . الرب هو الذى حازها ورآها وأحصاها . وأفاضها على جميع أعمالها . فهى مع كل ذى جسد على حسب عطيته . وقد منحها لمحبيه . مخافة الرب هى مجد وفخر . وسرور واكليل فرح . مخافة الرب تبهج القلب . وتعطى فرحاً وسروراً وطول أيام . المتقى الرب يكون له الخير فى آخرته . وينال حظوة فى يوم موته . رأس الحكمة مخافة الرب . إنها تولدت فى الرحم مع المؤمنين وتأسست مع البشر مدى الدهر . وهى تثبت مع نسلهم . كمال الحكمة مخافة الرب . والفرح من ثمارها . تملأ كل بيتها من المختارين . وترويهم من عصيرها . تاج الحكمة مخافة الله . وهى تنشئ زهرة ونعمة الشفاء . قد رآها وأحصاها وأفاض الفهم والمعرفة والعلم . ورفع مجد المتمسك بها . مجداً للثالوث القدوس .

A Homily of our Holy Father Abba Shenouti the Archimandrite

(عظة لأبينا القديس أنبا شنودة)

Brethren, if we want to escape God's punishment and find mercy in his eyes, let us sit every evening alone by ourselves and search our souls for what we presented to our guardian angel to offer to the Lord. Again, as the night goes by and a new day dawns and light prevails, let us search ourselves to know what we presented to our companion angel to offer to God. Let it be beyond doubt that everyone of us—male or female—young or old, who was baptized in the name of the Father, the Son and the Holy Spirit has been assigned to a designated angel until the day of his death; To report to him every day what his assigned individual has done by day or by night. Not that God is unaware of what we have done. Heaven forbids. He is more knowledgeable about it. As is written, the eyes of the Lord are watching all the time everywhere on those who commit evil and on those who do good. Rather the angels are servants installed by the Creator of the universe for those who will inherit salvation.

يا أخوة . إن كنا نريد الآن أن نفلت من يدى عقاب الله . ونجد رحمة أمامه . فلنجلس بالعشاء كل يوم منفردين وحدنا عند كمال النهار . ونفتش ذواتنا عما قدمناه للملاك الذى يخدمنا الملازم لنا ليصعده إلى الرب . وأيضاً إذا انقضى الليل وطلع النهار وأشرق النور فلنفتش ذواتنا وحدنا ونعلم ما الذى قدمناه للملاك الموكل بنا ليصعده إلى الله . ولا نشك البتة لأن كل إنسان ذكراً كان أو أنثى ، صغيراً أو كبيراً و قد اعتمد باسم الآب والابن والروح القدس قد جعل الله له ملاكاً موكلاً به إلى يوم وفاته . وليصعد إليه كل يوم أعمال الإنسان الموكل به الليلية والنهارية ليس لأن الله غير عارف بأعمالنا . حاشا . بل هو عارف بها أكثر . كما هو مكتوب: أن عينى الرب ناظرة كل حين فى كل مكان على صانعى الشر وفاعلى الخير . إنما الملائكة هم خدام قد أقامهم خالق الكل من أجل المزمعين ان يرثوا الخلاص.

We conclude the homily of our Holy Father Abba Shenouti, the Archimandrite, who enlightened our minds and our hearts. In the name of the Father, and the Son, and the Holy Spirit, one God. Amen.

فلنختم عظة أبينا القديس أنبا شنودة الذى أنار عقولنا وعيون قلوبنا باسم الآب والابن والروح القدس الإله الواحد آمين .

Pascha Praise - A (12 times), Page: 6   تسبحة البصخة A (12 مرة) ، صفحة :

The Psalm
Ⲯⲁⲗⲙⲟⲥ ⲟ̅ⲁ̅ : ⲓ̅ⲏ̅

Psalms 71:18

Blessed is the Lord God of Israel, who alone does wonders. And blessed is His glorious name forever, even forever and ever. Alleluia.

Ⲧⲥⲙⲁⲣⲱⲟⲩⲧ ⲛ̀ϫⲉ Ⲡ̅ⲟ̅ⲥ̅ Ⲫ̀ⲧ ⲙ̀ⲡⲓⲥ̅ⲗ̅ : ⲫⲏⲉⲧⲓⲣⲓ ⲛ̀ϩⲁⲛⲙⲏϣ̀ⲫⲏⲣⲓ ⲙ̀ⲙⲁⲩⲁⲧϥ : ⲥ̀ⲥⲙⲁⲣⲱⲟⲩⲧ ⲛ̀ϫⲉ ⲡⲓⲣⲁⲛ ⲉⲑⲩ ⲛ̀ⲧⲉ ⲡⲉϥⲱⲟⲩ ϣⲁ ⲉ̀ⲛⲉϩ : ⲉⲥⲉ̀ϣⲱⲡⲓ ⲉⲥⲉ̀ϣⲱⲡⲓ . ⲁ̅ⲗ̅ .

إفسماروؤوت إنجيه إبتشويس إفنوتى إمبسرائيل : فى إثرى إنهان إشفيرى إممافاتف : إفسماروؤوت إنجيه بى ران إثؤواب إنتيه بيف أوأو شا إينيه إس إشوبى إس إشوبى . ألليويا .

(مز 71 : 18)

مبارك الرب إله إسرائيل الصانع العجائب وحده . مبارك اسم مجده القدوس إلى الأبد يكون ثم يكون . الليلويا .

Introduction to the Gospel, Page: 8   مقدمة الأنجيل ، صفحة :

The Gospel

Ⲉⲩⲁⲅⲅⲉⲗⲓⲟⲛ Ⲕⲁⲧⲁ Ⲙⲁⲣⲕⲟⲛ Ⲕⲉⲫ ⲓ̅ⲁ̅ : ⲓ̅ⲃ̅ - ⲕ̅ⲇ̅

Mark 11:12-24

Now the next day, when they had come out from Bethany, He was hungry. And seeing from afar a fig tree having leaves, He went to see if perhaps He would find something on it. When He came to it, He found nothing but leaves, for it was not the season for figs. In response Jesus said to it, "Let no one eat fruit from you ever again." And His disciples heard it. So they came to Jerusalem. Then Jesus went into the temple and began to drive out those who bought and sold in the temple, and overturned the tables of the money changers and the seats of those who sold doves. And He would not allow anyone to carry wares through the temple. Then He taught, saying to them, "Is it not written, 'MY HOUSE SHALL BE CALLED A HOUSE OF PRAYER FOR ALL NATIONS' ? But you have made it a 'DEN OF THIEVES.'" And the scribes and chief priests heard it and sought how they might destroy Him; for they feared Him, because all the people were astonished at His teaching. When evening had come, He went out of the city. Now in the morning, as they passed by, they saw the fig tree dried up from the roots. And Peter, remembering, said to Him, "Rabbi, look! The fig tree which You cursed has withered away." So Jesus answered and said to them, "Have faith in God. For assuredly, I say to you, whoever says to this mountain, 'Be removed and be cast into the sea,' and does not doubt in

Ⲟⲩⲟϩ ⲉⲡⲉϥⲣⲁⲥϯ ⲉⲧⲁⲩⲓ ⲉⲃⲟⲗ ϧⲉⲛ ⲉ̄ⲃ̄ⲏ̄ⲟ̄ ⲁⲙⲓⲁ ⲁϥϩⲕⲟ : ⲟⲩⲟϩ ⲉⲧⲁϥⲛⲁⲩ ⲉⲟⲩⲃⲱ ⲛ̄ⲕⲉⲛⲧⲉ ϩⲓⲫⲟⲩⲉⲓ ⲉⲟⲩⲟⲛ ϩⲁⲛϫⲱⲃⲓ ϩⲓⲱⲧⲥ ⲁϥⲓ ⲇⲉ ϩⲁⲣⲁ ⲁϥⲛⲁϫⲉⲙ ϩⲗⲓ ϩⲓⲱⲧⲥ ⲟⲩⲟϩ ⲉⲧⲁϥⲓ ⲉϫⲱⲥ ⲙ̄ⲡⲉϥϫⲉⲙ ϩⲗⲓ ⲉⲃⲏⲗ ⲉϩⲁⲛϫⲱⲃⲓ ⲛⲉ ⲡⲥⲏⲟⲩ ⲅⲁⲣ ⲛ̄ⲕⲉⲛⲧⲉ ⲁⲛ ⲡⲉ : ⲟⲩⲟϩ ⲉⲧⲁϥⲉⲣⲟⲩⲱ ⲛ̄ϫⲉ Ⲓⲏⲥ ⲡⲉϫⲁϥ ⲛⲁⲥ ϫⲉ ⲛ̄ⲛⲉ ϩⲗⲓ ϫⲉ ⲟⲩⲉⲙ ⲟⲩⲧⲁϩ ϩⲓⲱϯ ϣⲁ ⲉⲛⲉϩ ⲟⲩⲟϩ ⲛⲁⲩⲥⲱⲧⲉⲙ ⲛ̄ϫⲉ ⲛⲉϥⲙⲁⲑⲏⲧⲏⲥ . Ⲟⲩⲟϩ ⲁⲩⲓ ⲉⲓⲗⲏⲙ ⲟⲩⲟϩ ⲉⲧⲁϥⲓ ⲉϧⲟⲩⲛ ⲛ̄ϫⲉ Ⲓⲏⲥ ⲉⲡⲓⲉⲣⲫⲉⲓ ⲁϥⲉⲣϩⲏⲧⲥ ⲛ̄ϩⲓⲟⲩⲓ ⲉⲃⲟⲗ ⲛ̄ⲛⲏ ⲧⲏⲣⲟⲩ ⲉⲧϯ ⲉⲃⲟⲗ ⲛⲉⲙ ⲛⲏⲉⲧ ϣⲱⲡ ϧⲉⲛ ⲡⲓⲉⲣⲫⲉⲓ ⲟⲩⲟϩ ⲛⲓⲧⲣⲁⲡⲉⲍⲁ ⲛ̄ⲧⲉ ⲛⲓⲕⲟⲗⲓⲃⲓⲥⲧⲏⲥ ⲛⲉⲙ ⲛⲓⲕⲁⲑⲉⲇⲣⲁ ⲛ̄ⲧⲉ ⲛⲏⲉⲧϯ ϭⲣⲟⲙⲡⲓ ⲉⲃⲟⲗ ⲁϥⲥⲟϭⲟⲩ : ⲟⲩⲟϩ ⲛⲁϥⲭⲱ ⲛ̄ϩⲗⲓ ⲁⲛ ⲡⲉ ϩⲓⲛⲁ ⲛ̄ⲧⲉϥⲉⲛ ⲟⲩⲥⲕⲉⲟⲥ ⲉⲃⲟⲗ ϩⲓⲧⲉⲛ ⲡⲓⲉⲣⲫⲉⲓ : ⲟⲩⲟϩ ⲛⲁϥϯⲥⲃⲱ ⲟⲩⲟϩ ⲛⲁϥϫⲱ ⲙ̄ⲙⲟⲥ ⲛⲱⲟⲩ ϫⲉ ⲥ̄ⲥϧⲏⲟⲩⲧ ϫⲉ ⲡⲁⲏⲓ ⲉⲩⲉⲙⲟⲩϯ ⲉⲣⲟϥ ϫⲉ ⲟⲩⲏⲓ ⲙ̄ⲡⲣⲟⲥⲉⲩⲭⲏ ⲛ̄ⲛⲓⲉⲑⲛⲟⲥ ⲧⲏⲣⲟⲩ ⲛ̄ⲑⲱⲧⲉⲛ ⲇⲉ ⲁⲣⲉⲧⲉⲛⲁⲓϥ ⲙ̄ⲃⲏⲃ ⲛ̄ⲥⲟⲛⲓ . Ⲟⲩⲟϩ ⲁⲩⲥⲱⲧⲉⲙ ⲛ̄ϫⲉ ⲛⲓⲁⲣⲭⲏⲉⲣⲉⲩⲥ ⲛⲉⲙ ⲛⲓⲥⲁϧ ⲟⲩⲟϩ ⲛⲁⲩⲕⲱϯ ϫⲉ ⲁⲩⲛⲁⲧⲁⲕⲟϥ ⲛ̄ⲁϣ ⲛ̄ⲣⲏϯ : ⲛⲁⲩⲉⲣϩⲟϯ ⲅⲁⲣ ⲡⲉ ϧⲁ ⲧⲉϥϩⲏ ⲡⲓⲙⲏϣ ⲅⲁⲣ ⲧⲏⲣϥ ⲛⲁⲩⲉⲣ ϣⲫⲏⲣⲓ ⲉϫⲉⲛ ⲧⲉϥⲥⲃⲱ : ⲟⲩⲟϩ ⲉϣⲱⲡ ⲛ̄ⲧⲉ ⲣⲟⲩϩⲓ ϣⲱⲡⲓ ⲛⲁϥϩⲏⲗ ⲥⲁⲃⲟⲗ ⲛ̄ⲧⲃⲁⲕⲓ : ⲟⲩⲟϩ ⲉⲩⲥⲓⲛⲓⲱⲟⲩ ⲛ̄ϩⲁⲛⲁⲧⲟⲟⲩⲓ ⲁϥⲛⲁⲩ ⲉϯⲃⲱ ⲛ̄ⲕⲉⲛⲧⲉ ⲉⲁⲥϣⲟⲩⲱⲓ ϩⲓ ⲧⲉⲥⲛⲟⲩⲛⲓ . Ⲟⲩⲟϩ ⲉⲧⲁϥⲉⲣ ⲫⲙⲉⲩⲓ ⲛ̄ϫⲉ Ⲡⲉⲧⲣⲟⲥ ⲡⲉϫⲁϥ ⲛⲁϥ ϫⲉ Ⲣⲁⲃⲃⲓ ⲓⲥ ϯⲃⲱ ⲛ̄ⲕⲉⲛⲧⲉ ⲉⲧⲁⲕⲥⲁϩⲟⲩⲓ ⲉⲣⲟⲥ ⲁⲥϣⲟⲩⲱⲓ : ⲟⲩⲟϩ ⲉⲧⲁϥⲉⲣⲟⲩⲱ ⲛ̄ϫⲉ Ⲓⲏⲥ ⲡⲉϫⲁϥ ⲛⲱⲟⲩ ϫⲉ ⲭⲁ ⲟⲩⲛⲁϩϯ ⲛ̄ⲧⲉ Ⲫϯ ⲛ̄ⲧⲉⲛ ⲑⲏⲛⲟⲩ : ⲁⲙⲏⲛ ⲅⲁⲣ ϯϫⲱ ⲙ̄ⲙⲟⲥ ⲛⲱⲧⲉⲛ ϫⲉ ⲫⲏⲉⲑⲛⲁϫⲟⲥ ⲙ̄ⲡⲁⲓⲧⲱⲟⲩ ϫⲉ ϥⲓⲧⲕ ⲟⲩⲟϩ ϩⲓⲧⲕ ⲉⲫⲓⲟⲙ ⲟⲩⲟϩ ⲛ̄ⲧⲉϥϣ̄ⲧⲉⲙϭⲓⲥⲁⲛⲓⲥ ϧⲉⲛ ⲡⲉϥϩⲏⲧ ⲁⲗⲗⲁ ⲛ̄ⲧⲉϥⲛⲁϩϯ ϫⲉ ⲫⲏⲉⲧⲉϥϫⲱ ⲙ̄ⲙⲟϥ

(مرقس 11 : 12 - 24)

وفى الغد لما خرجوا من بيت عنيا جاع. فرأى شجرة تين عن بعد وكان عليها ورق . فجاء إليها لعله يجد فيها شيئاً. فلما جاء إليها لم يجد شيئاً إلا ورقاً لأنه لم يكن وقت التين . فأجاب يسوع وقال لها: لا يأكل أحد منك ثمرة بعد إلى الأبد . وكان تلاميذه يسمعون وجاءوا إلى أورشليم ولما دخل يسوع الهيكل إبتدأ يخرج الذين كانوا يبيعون ويشترون فى الهيكل . وقلب موائد الصيارفة وكراسى باعة الحمام . ولم يدع أحداً يجتاز الهيكل بمتاع . وكان يعلم قائلاً لهم : أليس مكتوباً أن بيتى بيت الصلاة يدعى لجميع الأمم . وأنتم جعلتموه مغارة للصوص . وسمع رؤساء الكهنة والكتبة وكانوا يطلبون بأى نوع يهلكونه لأنهم كانوا يخافونه لأن الجمع كله كان يتعجب من تعليمه . وإذا كان المساء خرج إلى خارج المدينة . وفى الصباح إذ كانوا مجتازين رأوا التينة قد يبست من أصلها . فتذكر بطرس وقال له : ربى ها ان التينة التى لعنتها قد يبست . فأجاب يسوع وقال لهم: ليكن لكم إيمان بالله ، لأنى الحق أقول لكم ان من يقول لهذا الجبل انتقل وانطرح فى البحر وهو لا

his heart, but believes that those things he says will be done, he will have whatever he says. Therefore I say to you, whatever things you ask when you pray, believe that you receive them, and you will have them. *Glory be to God forever, Amen.*

ϥⲛⲁϣⲱⲡⲓ ⲉϥⲉϣⲱⲡⲓ ⲛⲁϥ · ⲉⲑⲃⲉ ⲫⲁⲓ ϯϫⲱ ⲙ̀ⲙⲟⲥ ⲛⲱⲧⲉⲛ ϫⲉ ϩⲱⲃ ⲛⲓⲃⲉⲛ ⲉⲧⲉⲧⲉⲛⲛⲁⲉⲣⲧⲓⲛ ⲙ̀ⲙⲟϥ ϧⲉⲛ ⲟⲩⲡⲣⲟⲥⲉⲩⲭⲏ ⲛⲁϩϯ ϫⲉ ⲁⲣⲉⲧⲉⲛϭⲓ ⲟⲩⲟϩ ⲉⲥⲉϣⲱⲡⲓ ⲛⲱⲧⲉⲛ · ⲟⲩⲱⲟⲩ ⲙ̀ⲡⲓⲉⲩⲁⲅⲅⲉⲗⲓⲟⲛ ⲉⲑ

يشك فى قلبه بل يؤمن بأن ما يقوله يكون فانه يكون له. فلأجل ذلك أقول لكم ان كل شئ تسألونه فى الصلاة آمنوا إنكم تنالونه فيكون لكم . والمجد لله دائماً .

Introduction to the Exposition, Page: 9 مقدمة الطرح ، صفحة :

Exposition

طـرح

In the beginning God created the heavens and the earth and adorned them with His spirit. He covered darkness and unveiled the light, and distinguished between them with new names. He called the light day and the darkness night. He created all these in the same day with wisdom and prudence. On the second day, God created the firmament and separated between waters and waters. God established the waters above the firmament and called them Heaven. On the third day, He gathered the waters and made the land appear over the waters. On the fourth day, God created the sun, the moon and the multitude of stars. On the fifth day, God created the birds, the big whales, the farm animals and all kinds of grass, plants and fruit yielding trees. On the sixth day, God created Adam, the great creature, the first man and a companion for him from his own flesh, male and female as designated; and gave them dominion over all the creatures He created. God rested on the seventh day from all the work, which He had done. These are the designs of the Creator and the Initiator of all creation.

(North side) Christ our Savior; has come and has borne suffering; that through His Passion; He may save us.

(South side) Let us glorify Him; and exalt His Name; for He had mercy on us; according to His great mercy

فى البدء خلق الله السماء والأرض وزينها هكذا بروح فيه . وغطى الظلمة وأخرج النور وفرق بينهما بأسماء جديدة . ودعا النور نهاراً ودعا الظلمة ليلاً . وفى ذلك اليوم خلق هذه جميعها بحكمة وفهم رفيع . وفى اليوم الثانى خلق الله جلد السماء وفصل بين مياه ومياه . وبعد هذا ثبت الله الماء العلوى وأسماه سماء . وفى اليوم الثالث جمع المياه وثبت الأرض فوق المياه ، والشمس والقمر وكثرة النجوم خلقها الله فى اليوم الرابع , الهوام والطير والحيتان الكبار وحيوانات الحقل فى اليوم الخامس . وأجناس الشجر وزرع الحقل والعشب المزروع المثمر . وفى اليوم السادس خلق الله الكائن الحى العظيم آدم أول البشر مع معينه له من جسده، ذكراً وأنثى كالتدبير . هذان جعلهما رؤساء على جميع أعماله التى خلقها الخالق و إستراح فى اليوم السابع لأن فيه أكمل جميع أعماله . هذا هو تدبير الخالق ومؤسس كل الموجودات .

(مرد بحرى) المسيح مخلصنا جاء وتألم عنا لكى بآلامه يخلصنا .

(مرد قبلى) فلنمجده ونرفع اسمه لأنه صنع معنا رحمة كعظيم رحمته .

The Conclusion of the Exposition, Page: 9 ختام الطرح ، صفحة :

الساعة الثالثة من يوم الاثنين من البصخة المقدسة
The Third Hour of Monday of the Holy Pascha

Isaiah 5:20-30

Woe to them that call evil good, and good evil; who make darkness light, and light darkness; who make bitter sweet, and sweet bitter. Woe to them that are wise in their own conceit, and knowing in their own sight. Woe to the strong of you that drink wine, and the mighty that mingle strong drink; who justify the ungodly for rewards, and take away the righteousness of the righteous. Therefore as stubble shall be burned by a coal of fire, and shall be consumed by a violent flame, their root shall be as chaff, and their flower shall go up as dust; for they rejected the law of the Lord of hosts, and insulted the word of the Holy One of Israel. Therefore the Lord of hosts was greatly angered against His people, and He reached forth His hand upon them, and struck them. And the mountains were troubled, and their carcasses were as dung in the midst of the way; yet for all this His anger has not been turned away, but His hand is yet raised. Therefore shall He lift up a signal to the nations that are afar, and shall whistle for them from the end of the earth; and behold, they are coming very quickly. They shall not hunger nor be weary, neither shall they slumber nor sleep; neither shall they loose their sashes from their loins, neither shall their sandal straps be broken. Whose arrows are sharp, and their bows bent; their horses' hoofs are counted as solid rock; their chariot wheels are as a storm. They rage as lions, and draw near as a lion's whelps; and he shall seize, and roar as a wild beast, and he shall cast them forth, and there shall be none to deliver them. And he shall roar on account of them in that day, as the sound of the swelling sea; and they shall look to the land, and behold, there shall be thick darkness in their perplexity. Glory be to the Holy Trinity. Amen.

Jeremiah 9:12-19

Who is the wise man, that he may understand this? And he that has the word of the mouth of the Lord addressed to him, let him tell you why the land has been destroyed, and has been ravaged by fire like a desert, so that no one passes through it. And the Lord said to me, Because they have forsaken My law, which I set before them, and have not hearkened to My voice; but went after the lusts of their evil heart, and after the idols which their fathers taught them to worship. Therefore thus says the Lord God of Israel: Behold, I will feed them with trouble and will cause them to drink water of gall: and I will scatter them among the nations, to them whom neither they nor their fathers knew; and I will send a sword upon them, until I have consumed them with it. Thus

(من إشعياء النبى ص 5 : 20 ألخ)

ويل للقائلين للخير شراً وللشر خيراً الجاعلين الظلام نوراً والنور ظلاماً . للقائلين عن الحلو مراً والمر حلواً . ويل للحكماء الذين هم فى أعين أنفسهم والفهماء عند ذواتهم . ويل للأقوياء الذين يشربون الخمر . وللأبطال الذين يمزجون المسكر . الذين يبررون المنافق لأجل الرشوة . وينزعون حق البار . فلذلك كما يحترق القش بجمر النار . ويلتهب بلهيبه المشتعل . فهكذا يكون أصلهم كالغبار وزهرهم كالهشيم لأنهم رذلوا شريعة الله رب الجنود . وأغضبوا واستهانوا بكلمة قدوس إسرائيل . فحمى غضب رب الصباؤوت على شعبه . ورفع يده عليهم ليضربهم . وسخط على الجبال وصارت جثث موتاهم مثل الزبل فى وسط الطريق . ومع هذا كله لم يرتد غضبه . بل يده لم تزل عالية ممدودة من أجل ذلك يرفع علامة للأمم من بعيد ويجتذبهم من أقاصى الأرض فاذا هم يأتون سريعاً بخفة . لا يجوعون ولا يتعبون ولا ينعسون . ولا ينامون . ولا يحلون مناطقهم من أوساطهم . ولا تتقطع سيور أحذيتهم . هؤلاء الذين سهامهم مسنونة وقسيهم مشدودة . حوافر خيولهم كصخرة صلبة . وبكرات مراكبهم كالعاصف . يتقدمون كالأسد . ويمسك ويصيح كوحش ويطرح وليس من يخلص . ويصرخ عليهم فى ذلك اليوم كصوت البحر الهائج وينظرون إلى علو السماء وإلى أسفل الأرض فيجدون ظلاماً شديداً . وظلمة مدلهمة . مجداً للثالوث القدوس .

(من أرميا النبى ص 9 : 12 - 19)

من هو الإنسان الحكيم فليفهم هذا . والذى عنده كلمة فم الرب فليخبركم . لماذا هلكت الأرض واحترقت وصارت كبرية بلا عابر . فقال لى الرب . لأنهم تركوا ناموسى عنهم الذى جعلته أمامهم . ولم يسمعوا لصوتى . بل ساروا وراء عناد قلوبهم الشريرة وسلكوا وراء الأصنام التى علمهم أياها آباؤهم ، لذلك قال الرب إله إسرائيل : هأنذا أطعمهم خبز الضيق وأسقيهم العلقم . وأشتتهم فى الأمم التى لم يعرفوها هم ولا آباؤهم . وأرسل عليهم سيفاً حتى أفنيهم به . هذا ما يقوله الرب : أدعوا النساء النائحات ليأتين وارسلوا إلى الحكيمات

says the Lord, Call the mourning women, and let them come; and send to the wise women, and let them utter their voice; and let them take up a lamentation for you, and let your eyes pour down tears, and your eyelids drop water. For a voice of lamentation has been heard in Zion. Glory be to the Holy Trinity. Amen

ليفتحن أفواههن بالكلام لينشدن عليكم نوحاً ولتسكب عيونكم ولتفض أجفانكم دموعاً لأنه سمع صوت النوح فى صهيون . مجداً للثالوث القدوس.

تسبحة البصخة A (12 مرة) ، صفحة :   6   Pascha Praise - A (12 times), Page:

The Psalm
Ⲯⲁⲗⲙⲟⲥ ⲣ̅ⲕ̅ⲁ̅ : ⲁ̅ ⲛⲉⲙ ⲃ̅

Psalms 121:1-2

I was glad when they said to me, Let us go into the house of the Lord. Our feet stood in your courts, O Jerusalem. Alleluia

Ⲁⲓⲟⲩⲛⲟϥ ⲉ̀ϫⲉⲛ ⲛⲏ ⲉⲧⲁⲩϫⲟⲥ ⲛⲏⲓ : ϫⲉ ⲧⲉⲛⲛⲁϣⲉⲛⲁⲛ ⲉ̀ⲡⲏⲓ ⲙ̅ⲡ̅ⲟ̅ⲥ̅ .

Ⲛⲉⲛϭⲁⲗⲁⲩϫ ⲁⲩⲟ̀ϩⲓ ⲉⲣⲁⲧⲟⲩ : ϧⲉⲛ ⲛⲓⲁⲩⲗⲏⲟⲩ ⲛ̀ⲧⲉ Ⲓⲉⲣⲟⲩⲥⲁⲗⲏⲙ. ⲁ̅ⲗ̅ .

أى أوونوف إيجين نى إيطاف جوس نى:جيه تيننا شينان إإبني إمبتشويس . نين تشالافج أفؤهى إراطو :خين نى أفليوو إنتيه يروساليم . الليلويا .

(مز 121 : 2،1)

فرحت بالقائلين لى إلى بيت الرب نذهب . وقفت أرجلنا فى ديار أورشليم . الليلويا .

مقدمة الآنجيل ، صفحة :   8   Introduction to the Gospel, Page:

The Gospel
Ⲉⲩⲁⲅⲅⲉⲗⲓⲟⲛ Ⲕⲁⲧⲁ Ⲙⲁⲣⲕⲟⲛ Ⲕⲉⲫ ⲓ̅ⲁ̅ : ⲓ̅ⲁ̅ - ⲓ̅ⲑ̅

Mark 11:11-19

And Jesus went into Jerusalem and into the temple. So when He had looked around at all things, as the hour was already late, He went out to Bethany with the twelve. Now the next day, when they had come out from Bethany, He was hungry. And seeing from afar a fig tree having leaves, He went to see if perhaps He would find something on it. When He came to it, He found nothing but leaves, for it was not the season for figs. In response Jesus said to it, "Let no one eat fruit from you ever again." And His disciples heard it. So they came to Jerusalem. Then Jesus went into the temple and began to drive out those who bought and sold in the temple, and overturned the tables of the money changers and the seats of those who sold doves. And He would not allow anyone to carry wares

Ⲟⲩⲟϩ ⲉⲧⲁϥⲓ̀ ⲛ̀ϫⲉ Ⲓⲏⲥⲟⲩⲥ ⲉ̀Ⲓⲗⲏⲙ ⲉ̀ϧⲟⲩⲛ ⲉ̀ⲡⲓⲉⲣⲫⲉⲓ ⲟⲩⲟϩ ⲉⲧⲁϥⲥⲟⲙⲥ ⲡ̀ⲧⲏⲣϥ : ⲟⲩⲟϩ ⲉⲧⲁ ⲣⲟⲩϩⲓ ϩⲏⲇⲏ ϣⲱⲡⲓ ⲛ̀ⲧⲉ ϯⲟⲩⲛⲟⲩ ⲁϥⲓ̀ ⲉ̀ⲃⲟⲗ ⲉ̀Ⲃⲏⲑⲁⲛⲓⲁ ⲛⲉⲙ ⲡⲓⲙⲏⲧ ⲥ̀ⲛⲁⲩ : ⲟⲩⲟϩ ⲉⲡⲉϥⲣⲁⲥϯ ⲉⲧⲁⲩⲓ̀ ⲉ̀ⲃⲟⲗ ϧⲉⲛ Ⲃⲏⲑⲁⲛⲓⲁ ⲁϥϩⲕⲟ : ⲟⲩⲟϩ ⲉⲧⲁϥⲛⲁⲩ ⲉ̀ⲟⲩⲃⲱ ⲛ̀ⲕⲉⲛⲧⲉ ϩⲓⲫⲟⲩⲉⲓ ⲉ̀ⲟⲩⲟⲛ ϩⲁⲛϫⲱⲃⲓ ϩⲓⲱⲧⲥ ⲁϥⲓ̀ ⲇⲉ ϩⲁⲣⲁ ⲁϥⲛⲁϫⲉⲙ ϩ̀ⲗⲓ ϩⲓⲱⲧⲥ ⲟⲩⲟϩ ⲉⲧⲁϥⲓ̀ ⲉ̀ϫⲱⲥ ⲙ̀ⲡⲉϥϫⲉⲙ ϩ̀ⲗⲓ ⲉ̀ⲃⲏⲗ ⲉ̀ϩⲁⲛϫⲱⲃⲓ ⲛⲉ ⲡⲥⲏⲟⲩ ⲅⲁⲣ ⲛ̀ⲕⲉⲛⲧⲉ ⲁⲛ ⲡⲉ . Ⲟⲩⲟϩ ⲉⲧⲁϥⲉⲣⲟⲩⲱ ⲡⲉϫⲁϥ ⲛⲁⲥ ϫⲉ ⲛ̀ⲛⲉ ϩ̀ⲗⲓ ϫⲉ ⲟⲩⲉⲙ ⲟⲩⲧⲁϩ ϩⲓⲱⲧ ϣⲁ ⲉ̀ⲛⲉϩ ⲟⲩⲟϩ ⲛⲁⲩⲥⲱⲧⲉⲙ ⲛ̀ϫⲉ ⲛⲉϥⲙⲁⲑⲏⲧⲏⲥ . Ⲟⲩⲟϩ ⲁⲩⲓ̀ ⲉ̀Ⲓⲗⲏⲙ ⲟⲩⲟϩ ⲉⲧⲁϥⲓ̀ ⲉ̀ϧⲟⲩⲛ ⲉ̀ⲡⲓⲉⲣⲫⲉⲓ ⲁϥⲉⲣϩⲏⲧⲥ ⲛ̀ϩⲓⲟⲩⲓ ⲉ̀ⲃⲟⲗ ⲛ̀ⲛⲏ ⲧⲏⲣⲟⲩ ⲉⲧ ϯ ⲉ̀ⲃⲟⲗ ⲛⲉⲙ ⲛⲏⲉⲧϣⲱⲡ ϧⲉⲛ ⲡⲓⲉⲣⲫⲉⲓ ⲟⲩⲟϩ ⲛⲓⲧⲣⲁⲡⲉⲍⲁ ⲛ̀ⲧⲉ ⲛⲓⲕⲟⲗⲓⲃⲓⲥⲧⲏⲥ ⲛⲉⲙ ⲛⲓⲕⲁⲑⲉⲇⲣⲁ ⲛ̀ⲧⲉ ⲛⲏⲉⲧ ϯ ϭⲣⲟⲙⲡⲓ ⲉ̀ⲃⲟⲗ ⲁϥⲥⲟϭⲟⲩ . Ⲟⲩⲟϩ ⲛⲁϥⲭⲱ ⲛ̀ϩ̀ⲗⲓ ⲁⲛ ⲡⲉ ϩⲓⲛⲁ ⲛ̀ⲧⲉϥⲉⲛ ⲟⲩⲥⲕⲉⲩⲟⲥ ⲉ̀ⲃⲟⲗ ϩⲓⲧⲉⲛ ⲡⲓⲉⲣⲫⲉⲓ .

(مرقس 11 : 19-11)

ولما جاء يسوع إلى أورشليم دخل الهيكل ونظر الجمع . وإذ كان المساء فى تلك الساعة خرج إلى بيت عنيا مع الإثنى عشر . وفى الغد لما خرجوا من بيت عنيا جاع. فرأى شجرة تين عن بعد . وكان عليها ورق فجاء إليها ألعله يجد فيها شيئاً . فلما جاء إليها لم يجد شيئاً إلا ورقاً لأنه لم يكن أوان التين . فأجاب وقال لها: لا يأكل أحد منك ثمرة إلى الأبد . وكان تلاميذه يسمعون . وجاءوا إلى أورشليم . ولما دخل إلى الهيكل إبتدأ يخرج جميع الذين كانوا يبيعون ويشترون فى الهيكل . وقلب موائد الصيارفة وكراسى باعة الحمام . ولم

through the temple. Then He taught, saying to them, "Is it not written, 'MY HOUSE SHALL BE CALLED A HOUSE OF PRAYER FOR ALL NATIONS' ? But you have made it a 'DEN OF THIEVES.'" And the scribes and chief priests heard it and sought how they might destroy Him; for they feared Him, because all the people were astonished at His teaching. When evening had come, He went out of the city. Glory be to God forever, Amen.

Ⲟⲩⲟϩ ⲛⲁϥϯⲥⲃⲱ ⲟⲩⲟϩ ⲛⲁϥϫⲱ ⲙⲙⲟⲥ ⲛⲱⲟⲩ ϫⲉ ⲥⲥϧⲏⲟⲩⲧ ϫⲉ ⲡⲁⲏⲓ ⲉⲩⲉⲙⲟⲩϯ ⲉⲣⲟϥ ϫⲉ ⲟⲩⲏⲓ ⲙⲡⲣⲟⲥⲉⲩⲭⲏ ⲛⲛⲓⲉⲑⲛⲟⲥ ⲧⲏⲣⲟⲩ ⲛⲑⲱⲧⲉⲛ ⲇⲉ ⲁⲣⲉⲧⲉⲛⲁⲓϥ ⲙⲃⲏⲃ ⲛⲥⲟⲛⲓ ⲟⲩⲟϩ ⲉⲧⲁⲩⲥⲱⲧⲉⲙ ⲛϫⲉ ⲛⲓⲁⲣⲭⲏ ⲉⲣⲉⲩⲥ ⲛⲉⲙ ⲛⲓⲥⲁϧ ⲟⲩⲟϩ ⲛⲁⲩⲕⲱϯ ϫⲉ ⲁⲩⲛⲁⲧⲁⲕⲟϥ ⲛⲁϣ ⲛⲣⲏϯ ⲛⲁⲩⲉⲣϩⲟⲧ ⲅⲁⲣ ⲡⲉ ϧⲁⲧⲉϥϩⲏ ⲡⲓⲙⲏϣ ⲅⲁⲣ ⲧⲏⲣϥ ⲛⲁⲩⲉⲣϣⲫⲏⲣⲓ ⲉϫⲉⲛ ⲧⲉϥⲥⲃⲱ : ⲟⲩⲟϩ ⲉϣⲱⲡ ⲛⲧⲉ ⲣⲟⲩϩⲓ ϣⲱⲡⲓ ⲛⲁϥϩⲏⲗ ⲥⲁⲃⲟⲗ ⲛϯⲃⲁⲕⲓ . ⲟⲩⲱϣⲧ ⲙⲡⲓⲉⲩⲁⲅⲅⲉⲗⲓⲟⲛ ⲉⲑⲩ .

يدع أحداً ينقل متاعاً إلى الهيكل . وكان يعلم قائلاً لهم : أليس مكتوباً أن بيتى بيت صلاة يدعى لجميع الأمم وأنتم جعلتموه مغارة لصوص . وسمع رؤساء الكهنة والكتبة الذين كانوا يطلبون بأى نوع يهلكونه ، لأنهم كانوا يخافونه ، إذ الجمع كله كان يتعجب من تعليمه. ولما صار المساء خرج إلى خارج المدينة . والمجد لله دائماً .

Introduction to the Exposition, Page: 9   مقدمة الطرح ، صفحة :

Exposition

طرح

On the evening of Hosanna Sunday our Lord and Savior Jesus Christ went with his disciples outside the city. He felt hungry and said I want something to eat. He saw a fig tree afar and went to it seeking some of its fruits. He found it fruitless. He condemned the tree and it dried from its roots. The disciples were taken by the incident and said to the Lord; the fig tree withered. Keep faith in your hearts and you shall be granted your requests. Do not be surprised that by one single word, the fig tree dried from its roots up. Because, if you have faith in your hearts, you can transfer the mountain from its location. Come all you ignorant and see what happened to the fig tree and present the Lord with good fruits to save yourselves from evil. Repent all you indolent so that you may receive forgiveness. Clean your faces with many tears because tears wipe out sins. Light your lamps with virtues so that their light may shine upon you in the day of judgment. Share the suffering with your brother and remember how the Lord suffered for our salvation.

فى عشية يوم الشعانين أتى المسيح الهنا يسوع المخلص خارج المدينة مع تلاميذه فجاع وقال : أطلب طعاماً . فرأى شجرة تين من بعيد فأتى إليها يطلب ثمراً فيها فوجد ورقاً بغير ثمر فلعنها فيبست من أصلها . فتعجب جميع تلاميذه وقالوا للرب : إن شجرة التين يبست . ضعوا الإيمان فى قلوبكم وكل شئ يُسمَع منكم ولا تتعجبوا من شجرة التين هذه إنها بكلمة واحدة يبست من أصلها . فإذا كان فى قلوبكم إيمان لنقلتم هذا الجبل من مكانه . تعالوا وأنظروا أيها الناس الجهال ما كان من شجرة التين هذه ، واصنعوا ثمراً صالحاً للرب لكى تخلصوا من الشرير ، واصنعوا توبة أيها الكسالى لكى تنالوا الغفران ، واغسلوا وجوهكم بدموع غزيرة فإن الدموع تمحى الآثام ، واوقدوا مصابيحكم بالفضائل لتضئ عليكم فى الحكم . تألم عن أخيك وانظر كيف أن الرب تألم عنا حتى خلصنا .

(North side) Christ our Savior; has come and has borne suffering; that through His Passion; He may save us.

(مرد بحرى) المسيح مخلصنا جاء وتألم عنا لكى بالامه يخلصنا .

(South side) Let us glorify Him; and exalt His Name; for He had mercy on us; according to His great mercy.

(مرد قبلى) فلنمجده ونرفع اسمه لأنه صنع معنا رحمة كعظيم رحمته .

The Conclusion of the Exposition, Page: 9   ختام الطرح ، صفحة :

الساعة السادسة من يوم الاثنين من البصخة المقدسة
The Sixth Hour of Monday of the Holy Pascha

Exodus 32:7-15

And the Lord spoke to Moses, saying, Go quickly, descend from here, for your people whom you brought out of the land of Egypt have transgressed; they have quickly gone out of the way which you commanded; they have made for themselves a calf, and worshipped it, and sacrificed to it, and said, These are your gods, O Israel, who brought you up out of the land of Egypt. Now therefore let Me alone, and I will be very angry with them and consume them, and I will make you a great nation. And Moses prayed before the Lord God, and said, Why, O Lord, are You very angry with Your people, whom You have brought out of the land of Egypt with great strength, and with Your outstretched arm? Take heed lest at any time the Egyptians speak, saying, With evil intent He brought them out to slay them in the mountains, and to consume them from off the earth; cease from Your wrathful anger, and be merciful to the sin of Your people, remembering Abraham and Isaac and Jacob Your servants, to whom You have sworn by Yourself, and have spoken to them, saying, I will greatly multiply your seed as the stars of heaven for multitude, and all this land which You spoke of to give to them, so that they shall possess it forever. And the Lord was prevailed upon to preserve His people. And Moses turned and went down from the mountain, and the two tablets of the Testimony were in his hands, tablets of stone written on both their sides: they were written within and without. Glory be to the Holy Trinity. Amen

Wisdom of Solomon 1:1-9

Love righteousness, you who judge on the earth. Think about the Lord in goodness and seek Him with sincerity of heart; because He is found by those who do not tempt Him, and He is manifest to those who do not disbelieve Him. For dishonest reasoning separates people from God, and when His power examines someone, it convicts the undiscerning; For wisdom will not enter the soul that plots evil, nor will it dwell in a body involved in sin. For a holy spirit of discipline [wisdom] flees from deceit and sends away undiscerning reasoning; it will put wrongdoing to shame when it comes near. For wisdom is a spirit that loves mankind, but she will punish a blasphemer because of his words; For God is the witness of his thoughts, the true examiner of his heart, and the hearer of his tongue; Because the Spirit of the Lord fills the world, and He who holds all things together knows what is said. Therefore no one who speaks unrighteous things will escape notice. Nor will justice, when it cross-examines, pass him by. For there shall be a close

(من سفر الخروج ص 32 : 7 - 15)

وكلم الرب موسى قائلاً : أمض مسرعاً من ههنا وانزل لأنه قد أثم شعبك الذى أخرجته من أرض مصر . وقد زاغوا سريعاً عن الطريق الذى أوصيتهم به . وصنعوا لهم عجلاً مسبوكاً وسجدوا له وذبحوا ذبائح لصنعة أيديهم قائلين : هذه هى ألهتك يا إسرائيل التى أخرجتك من أرض مصر . والآن دعنى أغضب عليهم بحنق وأبيدهم وأجعلك أمة أعظم . فتضرع موسى أمام الرب الإله قائلاً : لماذا يارب تغضب غضباً على شعبك الذى أخرجته من أرض مصر بقوتك العظيمة وذراعك الرفيعة . لئلا يقول المصريون إنك أخرجتهم بكيد لتقتلهم فى الجبال وتفنيهم عن وجه الأرض . ارجع يارب عن حمو غضبك واغفر شر شعبك . وأذكر إبراهيم واسحق ويعقوب الذين أقسمت لهم بذاتك وقلت لهم انى انى أكثر نسلكم جداً كنجوم السماء فى كثرتها . وكل هذه الأرض التى قلت عنها أن تعطيها لنسلهم فيرثوها إلى الأبد . فصفح الرب عن شر شعبه . ثم رجع موسى ونزل من الجبل ولوحا الشهادة فى يديه وهما لوحان من حجارة مكتوبان من الوجهين من هنا ومن هنا . مجداً للثالوث القدوس .

(بدء حكمة سليمان ص 1 : 1 - 9)

أحبوا العدل يا قضاة الأرض . إذكروا الرب بالصلاح . إطلبوه ببساطة قلوبكم . فانما يجده الذين لا يجربونه . ويتجلى للذين لا يكفرون به . لأن الفكر الشرير يبعدهم عن الله . وقوته الظاهرة تبكت الجبال . لأن الحكمة لا تدخل فى نفس شريرة . ولا تحل فى جسم خاطئ . لأن روح الحكمة الطاهرة يهرب من كل غش . ويبتعد عن أفكار الجهال ويبكت الظالم إذا أقبل . لأن روح الحكمة محب للبشر . فلا يبرئ المجدف بشفتيه . لأن شاهد كليتيه هو الله وهو الفاحص الحقيقى لقلبه والسامع للسانه . لأن روح الرب ملأ المسكونة وبقية الكل وهو يعرف أصواتهم فلذلك لا يستطيع أحد ان يخفى كلامه بالظلم ولا ينجو من الدينونة الآتية .

examination into the deliberations of an ungodly man, and a report of his words will come to the Lord as proof of his lawlessness. Glory be to the Holy Trinity. Amen

لأنه يفحص بمشورة المنافق . والرب لا يسمع كلامه حتى يظهر آثامه . مجداً للثالوث القدوس .

Pascha Praise - A (12 times), Page: 6   تسبحة البصخة A (12 مرة) ، صفحة :

The Psalm

Ⲯⲁⲗⲙⲟⲥ ⲣ̅ⲕ̅ⲁ̅ : ⲁ̅

Psalms 121:4

For from there the tribes went up, the tribes of the Lord, as a testimony for Israel, to give thanks unto the name of the Lord.. Alleluia.

Ⲉⲧⲁⲩϣⲉⲛⲱⲟⲩ ⲅⲁⲣ ⲉ̀ⲡϣⲱⲓ : ⲉ̀ⲙⲙⲁⲩ ⲛ̀ϫⲉ ⲛⲓⲫⲩⲗⲏ : ⲛⲓⲫⲩⲗⲏ ⲛ̀ⲧⲉ ⲡ̅ⲟ̅ⲥ̅ ⲉⲩⲙⲉⲧⲙⲉⲑⲣⲉ ⲙ̀ⲡ̀Ⲓⲥⲣⲁⲏⲗ : ⲉⲩⲟⲩⲱⲛϩ ⲉ̀ⲃⲟⲗ ⲙ̀ⲫ̀ⲣⲁⲛ ⲙ̀ⲡ̅ⲟ̅ⲥ̅ . ⲁ̅ⲗ̅ .

إيطاف شينيوؤو غار إبشوى : إمماف إنجيه نى فيلى : نى فيلى إنتيه إبتشويس إيف ميت ميثريه إمبسرائيل : إفؤوأونه إيفول إمفران إمبتشويس . الليلويا .

(مز 121 : 4)

لأنه هناك صعدت القبائل ، قبائل الرب شهادة لإسرائيل. يعترفون لاسم الرب . الليلويا.

Introduction to the Gospel, Page: 8   مقدمة الأنجيل ، صفحة :

The Gospel

Ⲉⲩⲁⲅⲅⲉⲗⲓⲟⲛ Ⲕⲁⲧⲁ Ⲓⲱⲁⲛⲛⲏⲛ Ⲕⲉⲫ Ⲃ̅ : ⲓ̅ⲅ̅ - ⲓ̅ⲍ̅

John 2:13-17

Now the Passover of the Jews was at hand, and Jesus went up to Jerusalem. And He found in the temple those who sold oxen and sheep and doves, and the money changers doing business. When He had made a whip of cords, He drove them all out of the temple, with the sheep and the oxen, and poured out the changers' money and overturned the tables. And He said to those who sold doves, "Take these things away! Do not make My Father's house a house of merchandise!" Then His disciples remembered that it was written, "ZEAL FOR YOUR HOUSE HAS EATEN ME UP." Glory be to God forever, Amen.

Ⲟⲩⲟϩ ⲉⲧⲁϥⲓ̀ ⲛ̀ϫⲉ Ⲓⲏⲥⲟⲩⲥ ⲉ̀ϩⲣⲏⲓ ⲉ̀Ⲓⲗⲏⲙ : ⲟⲩⲟϩ ⲁϥϫⲓⲙⲓ ϧⲉⲛ ⲡⲓⲉⲣⲫⲉⲓ ⲛ̀ⲛⲏⲉⲧϯ ⲉ̀ⲥⲉ ⲉ̀ⲃⲟⲗ ⲛⲉⲙ ⲉ̀ⲥⲱⲟⲩ ⲛⲉⲙ ϭⲣⲟⲙⲡⲓ ⲛⲉⲙ ⲛⲓϭⲁⲓ ⲕⲉⲣⲙⲁ ⲉⲩϩⲉⲙⲥⲓ ⲟⲩⲟϩ ⲁϥⲑⲁⲙⲓⲟ ⲛ̀ⲟⲩⲫⲣⲁⲅⲉⲗⲗⲓⲟⲛ ⲉ̀ⲃⲟⲗ ϧⲉⲛ ϩⲁⲛⲛⲟϩ ⲁϥϩⲓⲧⲟⲩ ⲧⲏⲣⲟⲩ ⲉ̀ⲃⲟⲗ ϧⲉⲛ ⲡⲓⲉⲣⲫⲉⲓ ⲛⲓⲉⲥⲱⲟⲩ ⲛⲉⲙ ⲛⲓⲉϩⲱⲟⲩ ⲟⲩⲟϩ ⲛⲓⲕⲉⲣⲙⲁ ⲛ̀ⲧⲉ ⲛⲓϭⲁⲓ ⲕⲉⲣⲙⲁ ⲁϥⲫⲟⲛⲟⲩ ⲉ̀ⲃⲟⲗ ⲟⲩⲟϩ ⲛⲟⲩ̀ⲧⲣⲁⲡⲉⲍⲁ ⲁϥⲫⲟⲛϫⲟⲩ . Ⲟⲩⲟϩ ⲡⲉϫⲁϥ ⲛ̀ⲛⲏⲉⲧϯ ϭⲣⲟⲙⲡⲓ ⲉ̀ⲃⲟⲗ ϫⲉ ⲁⲗⲓⲟⲩⲓ ⲛ̀ⲛⲁⲓ ⲉ̀ⲃⲟⲗ ⲧⲁⲓ ⲙ̀ⲡⲉⲣⲉⲣ ⲡⲏⲓ ⲙ̀ⲡⲁⲓⲱⲧ ⲛ̀ⲟⲩⲏⲓ ⲛ̀ϣⲱⲧ : ⲁⲩⲉⲣ ⲫ̀ⲙⲉⲩⲓ ⲛ̀ϫⲉ ⲛⲉϥⲙⲁⲑⲏⲧⲏⲥ ϫⲉ ⲥ̀ⲥϧⲏⲟⲩⲧ ϫⲉ ⲡⲭⲟϩ ⲙ̀ⲡⲉⲕⲏⲓ ⲡⲉⲧⲁϥⲟⲩⲟⲙⲧ . Ⲟⲩⲱϣⲧ ⲙ̀ⲡⲓⲉⲩⲁⲅⲅⲉⲗⲓⲟⲛ ⲉⲑⲩ .

(يوحنا 2 : 13 - 17)

وصعد يسوع إلى أورشليم . فوجد فى الهيكل باعة البقر والغنم والحمام والصيارفة جلوساً فصنع سوطاً من حبال وطرد الجميع من الهيكل ، الغنم والبقر، ونثر دراهم الصيارفة وقلب موائدهم . وقال لباعة الحمام: ارفعوا هذه من ههنا ولا تصيروا بيت أبى بيت تجارة. فتذكر تلاميذه أنه مكتوب: غيرة بيتك أكلتنى . والمجد لله دائماً .

Introduction to the Exposition, Page: 9   مقدمة الطرح ، صفحة :

Exposition

طرح

O Israel, God's first child; what impudence did you commit and how insensitive are your priests. The place of forgiveness became a place to sin. The house of prayer and supplication became a den of thieves and a marketplace for cattle, sheep, and pigeon merchants and for currency exchangers. What profit is that unclean and corrupt, and what injustice have you done. When the Son of God saw all this done in His Fathers House, for they have turned it in to a den for thievery, bandits, the unjust and a house of trade, He toppled the seats of pigeon merchants and the tables of the currency exchangers and scattered their funds. As they watched Him doing this, His disciples knew that it was thus written about Him; the Zeal for Your house has consumed Me. That is why He did so with impugnity. Your reign is forever in heaven and on earth and your fear O Lord has shaken the mountains. But Israel has erred and thus was denied God's help.

(North side) Christ our Savior; has come and has borne suffering; that through His Passion; He may save us.

(South side) Let us glorify Him; and exalt His Name; for He had mercy on us; according to His great mercy.

يا لهذه الجسارة التى صنعتها يا شعب إسرائيل ابن الله البكر ! وهذه البلادة التى من كهنتك ، إذ موضع الغفران صار موضع الخطية . وبيت الصلاة وموضع الطلبة صيرتموه مسكناً للصوص ومجمعاً للعجول والخراف وباعة الحمام والصيارفة . ما هو هذا الربح المملوء من كل نجاسة وهذا الظلم الذى صنعتموه؟ لما نظر ابن الله بيت أبيه وهذه كلها تصنع فيه وإنهم صيروه مسكناً للصوص الخاطفين والظلمة وبيت التجارة ، أخرج البقر والغنم معاً وكراسى باعة الحمام وموائد الصيارفة قلبها وبدد دراهمهم . فلما نظر تلاميذه إلى هذا علموا أنه هكذا هو مكتوب لأجله "أن غيرة بيتك أكلتنى" فلذا صنع هكذا بغير خوف . ان سلطانك دائم فى السماء وعلى الأرض ، وخوفك يارب زعزع الجبال . أما إسرائيل فقد صار جاهلاً ، فلذلك إستترت عنه معونته .

(مرد بحرى) المسيح مخلصنا جاء وتألم عنا لكى بألامه يخلصنا .

(مرد قبلى) فلنمجده ونرفع اسمه لأنه صنع معنا رحمة كعظيم رحمته .

الساعة التاسعة من يوم الاثنين من البصخة المقدسة
The Ninth Hour of Monday of the Holy Pascha

Genesis 2:15-3:24

And the Lord God took the man whom He had formed, and placed him in the garden of Delight, to cultivate and keep it. And the Lord God gave a charge to Adam, saying, Of every tree which is in the garden you may freely eat, but of the tree of the knowledge of good and evil, of it you shall not eat, but in whatsoever day you eat of it, you shall surely die. And the Lord God said, It is not good that the man should be alone, let Us make for him a helper suitable to him. And God formed yet farther out of the earth all the wild beasts of the field, and all the birds of the sky, and He brought them to Adam, to see what he would call them, and whatever Adam called any living creature, that was the name of it. And Adam gave names to all the cattle and to all the birds of the sky, and to all the wild beasts of the field, but for Adam there was not found a helper comparable to himself. And God brought a trance upon Adam, and he slept, and He took one of his ribs, and closed up the flesh in its place. And God formed the rib which he took from Adam into a woman, and brought her to Adam. And Adam said, This now is bone of my bones, and flesh of my flesh; she shall be called woman, because she was taken out of her husband. Therefore shall a man leave his father and his mother and shall cleave to his wife, and they two shall be one flesh. And the two were naked, both Adam and his wife, and were not ashamed. And the two were naked, both Adam and his wife, and were not ashamed. Now the serpent was the most crafty of all the brutes on the earth, which the Lord God made, and the serpent said to the woman, Has God truly said, Eat not of every tree of the garden? And the woman said to the serpent, We may eat of the fruit of the trees of the garden, but of the fruit of the tree which is in the midst of the garden, God said, You shall not eat of it, neither shall you touch it, lest you die. And the serpent said to the woman, You shall not surely die. For God knew that in whatever day you should eat of it, your eyes would be opened, and you would be as gods, knowing good and evil. And the woman saw that the tree was good for food, and that it was pleasant to the eyes to look upon and beautiful to contemplate, and having taken of its fruit she ate, and she gave to her husband also with her, and they ate. And the eyes of both were opened, and they perceived that they were naked, and they sewed fig leaves together, and made themselves coverings to go around them. And they heard the voice of the Lord God walking in the garden in the cool of the day; and both Adam and his wife hid themselves from the face of the Lord God in the midst of the trees of the garden. And the Lord God called Adam and said to

(من سفر التكوين 2 : 15 -3 : 2)

وأخذ الرب الأله الإنسان الذى خلقه . ووضعه فى فردوس النعيم ليفلحه ويحفظه . وأمر الرب الإله آدم قائلاً : من جميع الأشجار التى فى الفردوس تأكل أكلاً . وأما شجرة معرفة الخير والشر فلا تأكل منها . فأنك فى اليوم الذى تأكل منها موتاً تموت . وقال الرب الإله : لا يحسن أن يكون الإنسان وحده فلنصنع له معيناً مثله . وجبل الرب الإله من الأرض جميع وحوش البرية وجميع طيور السماء . وأحضرها إلى آدم ليرى ماذا يسميها فكل ما سماه به آدم من نفس حية فهو أسمها . وسمى آدم جميع البهائم وطيور الماء وجميع وحوش البرية . وأما آدم فلم يجد له معيناً يشبهه . فألقى الله على آدم سباتاً فنام . وأخذ ضلعاً من جنبه وملأ موضعها لحماً وبنى الرب الإله الضلع التى أخذها من آدم إمرأة وأحضرها إلى آدم . فقال آدم هذه الآن عظم من عظامى . ولحم من لحمى هذه تدعى إمرأة لأنها من إمرء أخذت . لذلك يترك الرجل أباه وأمه ويلتصق بإمرأته . ويكونان كلاهما جسداً واحداً . وكان كلاهما عريانين معاً ، آدم وإمرأته ، وهما لا يخجلان. وكانت الحية احيل جميع الوحوش التى خلقها الرب الإله على الأرض . فقالت الحية للمرأة لماذا قال الله لكما أن لا تأكلا من جميع شجر الفردوس فقالت المرأة للحية : ان من جميع ثمار شجر الفردوس نأكل وأما ثمر الشجرة التى فى وسط الفردوس فقال الله لا تأكلا منه ولا تمساه لئلا تموتا . فقالت الحية للمرأة لن تموتا موتاً . إنما الله عالم إنكما فى اليوم الذى تأكلان منه تنفتح أعينكما . وتصيران كآلهة عارفين الخير والشر . فرأت المرأة أن الشجرة جيدة للأكل ومبهجة للنظر حسنة التأمل إليها فأخذت من ثمرها وأكلت . وأعطت بعلها أيضاً معها فأكل . فأنفتحت أعينهما كلاهما وعلما إنهما عريانان فخاطا من ورق التين وصنعا لهما مآزر . فسمعا صوت الرب الإله ماشياً فى الفردوس وقت المساء . فاختفيا آدم وزوجته من وجه الرب الإله فى وسط شجر الفردوس . فنادى الرب الإله آدم وقال له : أين أنت يا آدم فقال له : سمعت صوتك ماشياً فى الفردوس فخفت .

him, Adam, where are you? And he said to Him, I heard your voice as You walked in the garden, and I feared because I was naked and I hid myself. And God said to him, Who told you that you were naked, unless you have eaten of the tree of which I commanded you not to eat? And Adam said, The woman whom You gave to be with me, she gave me of the tree and I ate. And the Lord God said to the woman, Why have you done this? And the woman said, The serpent deceived me and I ate. And the Lord God said to the serpent, Because you have done this you are cursed above all cattle and all the brutes of the earth, on your breast and belly you shall go, and you shall eat dust all the days of your life. And I will put enmity between you and the woman and between your seed and her Seed, He shall bruise your head, and you shall bruise His heel. And to the woman he said, I will greatly multiply your pains and your groanings; in pain you shall bring forth children, and your submission shall be to your husband, and he shall rule over you. And to Adam he said, Because you have listened to the voice of your wife, and eaten of the tree of which I commanded you not to eat of it, of that you have eaten, cursed is the ground in your labors, in pain shall you eat of it all the days of your life. Thorns and thistles shall it bring forth to you, and you shall eat the herb of the field. In the sweat of your face shall you eat your bread until you return to the earth out of which you were taken, for earth you are, and to earth you shall return. And Adam called the name of his wife Eve, because she was the mother of all living. And the Lord God made garments of skin for Adam and his wife, and clothed them. And God said, Behold, Adam has become as one of Us, to know good and evil, and now lest at any time he stretch forth his hand, and take of the tree of life and eat, and so he shall live forever. So the Lord God sent him forth out of the garden of Delight to cultivate the ground out of which he was taken. And he cast out Adam and caused him to dwell over against the garden of Delight, and stationed the cherubs and the fiery sword that turns about to keep the way of the tree of life. Glory be to the Holy Trinity. Amen

Isaiah 40:1-5

Comfort, yes, comfort My people, says your God. Speak, you priests, to the heart of Jerusalem; comfort her, for her humiliation is accomplished, her sin is put away; for she has received of the Lord's hand double for her sins. The voice of one crying in the wilderness, Prepare the way of the Lord, make straight the paths of our God. Every valley shall be filled, and every mountain and hill shall be brought low; and all the crooked ways shall become straight, and the rough places smooth. And the glory of the Lord shall appear, and all flesh shall see the salvation of God; for the Lord has spoken it. Glory be to the Holy Trinity. Amen.

لأنى عريان فاختبأت فقال له : من أعلمك أنك عريان إلا أنك أكلت من الشجرة التى أوصيتك أن لا تأكل منها وحدها . فأكلت منها . فقال آدم : أن المرأة التى أعطيتها لى هى التى أعطتنى من الشجرة فأكلت . فقال الرب الإله للمرأة : لماذا فعلت هذا . فقالت المرأة : الحية أغوتنى فأكلت . فقال الرب الإله للحية : لأنك فعلت هذا ، فملعونة أنت من بين جميع البهائم وجميع الوحوش التى على وجه الأرض وتسعين على صدرك وبطنك ، وتأكلين تراباً طوال أيام حياتك . وأضع عداوة بينك وبين المرأة ، وبين نسلك ونسلها . فهو يسحق رأسك وأنت ترصدين عقبه . وقال للمرأة : تكثيراً أكثر أحزان قلبك وتنهدك ، وبالاحزان تلدين البنين ، وإلى بعلك يكون رجوعك وهو يسود عليك . وقال لآدم : بما أنك أطعت إمرأتك وأكلت من الشجرة التى أوصيتك قائلاً : هذه وحدها لا تأكل منها ، فملعونة الأرض بسبب أعمالك ، بالمشقة تأكل منها كل أيام حياتك ، وشوكاً وحسكاً تنبت لك ، وتأكل عشب الأرض وبعرق وجهك تأكل خبزك ، حتى تعود إلى الأرض التى أخذت منها ، لأنك تراب وإلى التراب تعود . ودعا آدم اسم إمرأته حواء ، لأنها أم كل حي . وصنع الرب الإله لآدم وإمرأته أقمصة من جلد وكساهما وقال الرب الإله : هوذا آدم قد صار كواحد منا يعرف الخير والشر . والآن لعله يمد يده إلى شجرة الحياة فيأكل منها ويحيا إلى الأبد فأخرجه الرب الإله من فردوس النعيم . ليعمل فى الأرض التى أخذ منها . فأخرج آدم فسكن أمام فردوس النعيم . وجعل الكاروبيم وسيفاً نارياً متقلباً لحراسة طريق شجرة الحياة . مجداً للثالوث القدوس .

(من إشعياء النبى ص 40 : 1 - 5)

عزوا عزوا شعبى أيها الكهنة قال الله . تكلموا فى قلب أورشليم . عزوها لأنه قد كثر ذلها . وإنحلت خطيتها . وقبلت من يد الرب ضعفين عن خطاياها . صوت صارخ فى البرية . أعدوا طريق الرب ومهدوا سبل إلهنا . كل جبل وكل تل ينخفض . ويصير المعوج مستقيماً . والطرق الوعرة لينة . ويظهر يوم الرب . وكل ذى جسد يعاين مجد الله . لأن الرب تكلم . مجداً للثالوث القدوس .

Proverbs 1:1-9

The Proverbs of Solomon son of David, who reigned in Israel: to know wisdom and instruction, and to perceive words of understanding; to receive also hard sayings, and to understand true justice, and how to direct judgment; that he might give prudence to the simple, and to the young man discernment and understanding. For by the hearing of these a wise man will be wiser, and man of understanding will gain direction; and will understand a parable, and an enigma; the saying of the wise also, and riddles. The fear of the Lord is the beginning of wisdom; and *there is* good understanding to all that practice it: and godliness toward God is the beginning of discernment; but the ungodly will nullify wisdom and instruction. Hear, my son, the instruction of your father, and reject not the rules of your mother. For you shall receive a crown of grace for your head, and a chain of gold around your neck. Glory be to the Holy Trinity. Amen

(أمثال سليمان ص 1 : 1 - 9)

أمثال سليمان بن داود الملك الذى ملك على إسرائيل لمعرفة الحكمة والأدب . لادراك أقـوال الفطنة . لقبـول تـدرب الكلام . لتعليم العدل الحقيقى والحكم المستقيم. لكى تعطى لمن لا شر فيهم حكمة . وعملا وفهما للشباب الحدث. لأن الحكيم إذا سمع هذه فيزداد حكمة ، والفهيم يكتسب تدبيراً . فيفهم المثل والكلام العويص وأقوال الحكماء وغوامضهم . رأس الحكمة مخافة الرب والفهم صالح لكل من يعمل به . وتقوى الله هى بدء الفهم . الحكمة والأدب يحتقرهما المنافقون . اسمع يا إبنى تأديب أبيك ولا ترفض مشورة أمك . فأنهما اكليل نعمة لرأسك وقلادة ذهب لعنقك . مجداً للثالوث القدوس .

| Pascha Praise - A (12 times), Page: 6 | تسبحة البصخة A (12 مرة) ، صفحة : 6 |

The Psalm

Ψⲁⲗⲙⲟⲥ ⲝ̅ⲇ̅ : ⲇ̅ ⲛⲉⲙ ⲋ̅

Psalms 64:4, 6

Hearken to us, O God our Savior; the hope of all the ends of the earth. Blessed is he whom You have chosen and adopted; he shall dwell in Your courts *forever.* Alleluia.

Ⲥⲱⲧⲉⲙ ⲉⲣⲟⲛ Ⲫ̀ϯ ⲡⲉⲛⲥⲱⲧⲏⲣ : ϯϩⲉⲗⲡⲓⲥ ⲛ̀ⲧⲉ ⲁⲩⲣⲏϫϥ ⲙ̀ⲡⲕⲁϩⲓ ⲧⲏⲣϥ . Ⲱ̀ⲟⲩⲛⲓⲁⲧϥ ⲙ̀ⲫⲏ ⲉⲧⲁⲕⲥⲟⲧⲡϥ ⲟⲩⲟϩ ⲁⲕϣⲟⲡϥ ⲉⲣⲟⲕ : ⲉϥⲉϣⲱⲡⲓ ϧⲉⲛ ⲛⲉⲕⲁⲩⲗⲏⲟⲩ ϣⲁ ⲉ̀ⲛⲉϩ . ⲁⲗ .

صوتيم إرون إفنوتى بين بنسوتير : تى هيلبيس إنتيه أفريجف إمبكاهى تيرف. أو أوونياتف إمفى إيطاك صوتبف أووه أكشوبف إروك : إف إشوبى خين نيك أفليوو شا إينيه . الليلويا .

(مز 64 : 4 و6)

استجب لنا يا الله مخلصنا ، يا رجاء جميع أقطار الأرض . طوبى لمن اخترته وقبلته ليسكن فى ديارك إلى الأبد . الليلويا .

| Introduction to the Gospel, Page: 8 | مقدمة الأنجيل ، صفحة : 8 |

The Gospel

Ⲉⲩⲁⲅⲅⲉⲗⲓⲟⲛ Ⲕⲁⲧⲁ Ⲙⲁⲧⲑⲉⲟⲛ Ⲕⲉⲫ ⲕ̅ⲁ̅ : ⲕ̅ⲅ̅ - ⲕ̅ⲍ̅

Matthew 21:23-27

Now when He came into the temple, the chief priests and the elders of the people confronted Him as He was teaching, and said, "By what authority are You doing these things? And who gave You this authority?" But Jesus answered and said to them, "I also will ask you one thing, which if you tell Me, I likewise will tell you by what authority I do these things: The

Ⲟⲩⲟϩ ⲉⲧⲁϥⲓ̀ ⲉ̀ϧⲟⲩⲛ ⲉ̀ⲡⲓⲉⲣⲫⲉⲓ ⲁⲩⲓ̀ ϩⲁⲣⲟϥ ⲉϥϯⲥⲃⲱ ⲛ̀ϫⲉ ⲛⲓⲁⲣⲭⲏ ⲉ̀ⲣⲉⲩⲥ ⲛⲉⲙ ⲛⲓⲡⲣⲉⲥⲃⲩⲧⲉⲣⲟⲥ ⲛ̀ⲧⲉ ⲡⲓⲗⲁⲟⲥ ⲉⲩϫⲱ ⲙ̀ⲙⲟⲥ : ϫⲉ ⲁⲕⲓⲣⲓ ⲛ̀ⲛⲁⲓ ϧⲉⲛ ⲁϣ ⲛ̀ⲉⲣϣⲓϣⲓ : ⲟⲩⲟϩ ⲛⲓⲙ ⲡⲉⲧⲁϥϯ ⲙ̀ⲡⲁⲓ ⲉⲣϣⲓϣⲓ ⲛⲁⲕ . Ⲁϥⲉⲣⲟⲩⲱ ⲇⲉ ⲛ̀ϫⲉ Ⲓⲏⲥ ⲡⲉϫⲁϥ ⲛⲱⲟⲩ : ϫⲉ ϯⲛⲁϣⲉⲛ ⲑⲏⲛⲟⲩ ϩⲱ ⲉ̀ⲟⲩⲥⲁϫⲓ : ⲉϣⲱⲡ ⲁⲣⲉⲧⲉⲛϣⲁⲛⲧⲁⲙⲟⲓ ⲉ̀ⲣⲟϥ : ⲁⲛⲟⲕ ϩⲱ ϯⲛⲁⲧⲁⲙⲱⲧⲉⲛ ϫⲉ ⲁⲓⲓⲣⲓ ⲛ̀ⲛⲁⲓ ϧⲉⲛ ⲁϣ ⲛ̀ⲉⲣϣⲓϣⲓ . Ⲡⲓⲱⲙⲥ ⲛ̀ⲧⲉ Ⲓⲱⲁⲛⲛⲏⲛ ⲛⲉ ⲟⲩ ⲉ̀ⲃⲟⲗ ⲑⲱⲛ ⲡⲉ : ⲟⲩ ⲉ̀ⲃⲟⲗ ϧⲉⲛ ⲧ̀ⲫⲉ ⲡⲉ

(متى 21 : 23 - 27)

ولما دخل إلى الهيكل تقدم إليه رؤساء الكهنة وشيوخ الشعب وهو يعلم قائلين له: بأى سلطان تفعل هذا؟ ومن أعطاك هذا السلطان؟ فأجاب يسوع وقال لهم: وأنا أيضاً أسألكم كلمة ، فان أعلمتمونى عنها أعلمكم أنا أيضاً بأى سلطان فعلت هذا ، معمودية يوحنا من

baptism of John—where was it from? From heaven or from men?" And they reasoned among themselves, saying, "If we say, 'From heaven,' He will say to us, 'Why then did you not believe him?' But if we say, 'From men,' we fear the multitude, for all count John as a prophet." So they answered Jesus and said, "We do not know." And He said to them, "Neither will I tell you by what authority I do these things." Glory be to God forever, Amen.

ϢⲀⲚ ⲞⲨ ⲈⲂⲞⲖ ϦⲈⲚ ⲚⲒⲢⲰⲘⲒ ⲠⲈ : ⲚⲐⲰⲞⲨ ⲆⲈ ⲚⲀⲨⲘⲞⲔⲘⲈⲔ ⲚⲎⲢⲎⲒ ⲚϦⲎⲦⲞⲨ ⲈⲨⲬⲰ ⲘⲘⲞⲤ : ϪⲈ ⲈϢⲰⲠ ⲀⲚϢⲀⲚϪⲞⲤ ϪⲈ ⲞⲨ ⲈⲂⲞⲖ ϦⲈⲚ ⲦⲪⲈ ⲠⲈ ϤⲚⲀϪⲞⲤ ⲚⲀⲚ ϪⲈ ⲈⲐⲂⲈ ⲞⲨ ⲘⲠⲈⲦⲈⲚⲚⲀϨϮ ⲈⲢⲞϤ . ⲈϢⲰⲠ ⲆⲈ ⲀⲚϢⲀⲚϪⲞⲤ ϪⲈ ⲞⲨ ⲈⲂⲞⲖ ϦⲈⲚ ⲚⲒⲢⲰⲘⲒ ⲠⲈⲦⲈⲚⲈⲢϨⲞϮ ϦⲀ ⲦϨⲎ ⲘⲠⲒⲘⲎϢ ⲒⲰⲀⲚⲚⲎⲤ ⲄⲀⲢ ⲚⲦⲞⲦⲞⲨ ϨⲰⲤ ⲞⲨⲠⲢⲞⲪⲎⲦⲎⲤ . ⲞⲨⲞϨ ⲀⲨⲈⲢⲞⲨⲰ ⲠⲈϪⲰⲞⲨ ⲚⲒⲎⲤ ϪⲈ ⲦⲈⲚⲈⲘⲒ ⲀⲚ : ⲠⲈϪⲀϤ ⲆⲈ ⲚⲰⲞⲨ ϪⲈ ⲞⲨ ⲆⲈ ⲀⲚⲞⲔ ϨⲰ ⲚϮⲚⲀⲦⲀⲘⲰⲦⲈⲚ ⲀⲚ ϪⲈ ⲀⲒⲢⲒ ⲚⲚⲀⲒ ϦⲈⲚ ⲀϢ ⲚⲈⲢϢⲒϢⲒ . ⲞⲨⲰϢⲦ ⲘⲠⲒⲈⲨⲀⲄⲄⲈⲖⲒⲞⲚ ⲈⲐⲨ

أين كانت من السماء أم من الناس؟ أما هم فكانوا يفكرون فى أنفسهم قائلين: ان قلنا من السماء يقول لنا فلماذا لم تؤمنوا به . وان قلنا من الناس فانا نخاف من الجمع ، لأن يوحنا كان عندهم مثل نبى . فأجابوا وقالوا ليسوع: لا نعلم . فقال لهم هو أيضاً: ولا أنا أعلمكم بأى سلطان فعلت هذا . والمجد لله دائماً.

Introduction to the Exposition, Page: 9   مقدمة الطرح ، صفحة :

Exposition

طـرح

With your impeccable hands O Lord You created me and made me shine like crimson. You bestowed on me the comforts of paradise and the fruits of the trees. You awarded me the hegemony of your dominion over all creation under heaven and made all things below the animals and beasts. You did not deprive me of respect and subordinated everything to me. You gave me one commandment and I disobeyed You O my Lord and my God.

بيديك اللتين بلا عيب يارب خلقتنى وزينتنى مضيئاً كالثوب المزين . ووهبت لى نعيم الفردوس ، وثمر الأشجار أعطيته لى إنعاماً . منحتنى عزة سلطانك على كل الخليقة التى تحت السماء وجعلت سائر الأشياء دونى ، جنس الهوام والوحوش . ولم تعوزنى شيئاً من الكرامة وجعلت كل شئ يخضع لى . وأوصيتنى وصية فخالفتها يا ربى وإلهى.

I ask You, O Good One to have mercy upon me according to Your great mercy.

(المرد) أسألك أيها الصالح أن تصنع معى رحمة كعظيم رحمتك .

When I saw that you were alone O Adam when everything else was paired, I created from your bones someone modeled after you, who looks like you and found it inappropriate to have you alone by yourself. I was concerned about you and gave you power over her and on all creation to be under your dominion. You obeyed her and disregarded My instruction. You rejected My words and My commandments.

رأيتك يا آدم كائناً وحدك وكل شئ غير مفرد فجبلت لك واحدة من عظامك كشبهك ومثالك وقلت لا يحسن أن تكون وحدك ، فاهتممت بك وفعلت لك هذا . وسلطتك عليها وعلى جميع المسكونة كى تكون تحت سلطانك لكنك اطعتها وتركت أوامرى ورفضت قولى ووصاياى.

I ask You, O Good One to have mercy upon me according to Your great mercy.

(المرد) أسألك أيها الصالح أن تصنع معى رحمة كعظيم رحمتك .

Remember me O Lord. From dust I am and like the herbs of the field you gave me the prowess of Your power and diminished my humility. One tree I commanded you not to touch; why did you disobey My commandment. You implicated the woman whom I did not command as I did with you. You obeyed her, rejected My words and then hid among the trees so that I do not see you.

أذكرنى يارب اننى تراب وكمثل العشب الذى فى الحقل. أعطيتنى ياربى عزة قوتك فتناقصت حقارتى. شجرة واحدة أوصيتنى عنها فكيف صرت مخالفاً لوصيتك؟ واستظلمت المرأة هذه التى لم توصها مثلى ، فاطعتها ورفضت كلامك واختفيت فى الشجر كى لا أراك .

I ask You, O Good One to have mercy upon me according to Your great mercy.

(المرد) أسألك أيها الصالح أن تصنع معى رحمة كعظيم رحمتك .

You desired divinity and wanted to be a creator like your Lord. From the fruits of the tree, you distinguished between the good and the evil to become a God. Adam, where is the glory that was bestowed on you. You lost the cloths I dressed you with. With leaves of trees you covered your own nakedness. I created you and knew you before you were.

وفكرت يا آدم فى العلويات أعنى الألوهية وأنك تصير خالقاً مثل سيدك . وبثمرة الشجرة علمت الخير والشر لتصير إلهاً ، يا آدم أين هو المجد الذى كان لك؟ تعريت من الحلة التى ألبستك أياها ، وأخذت من ورق الشجر وسترت عورتك من وجهى . أعلمتك اننى خلقتك وعرفتك قبل أن تكون .

I ask You, O Good One to have mercy upon me according to Your great mercy.

(المرد) أسألك أيها الصالح أن تصنع معى رحمة كعظيم رحمتك .

From the beginning I informed you and instructed you with My commandments. Of all the trees in paradise I told you about this particular tree. Its fruits bear the bitterness of death and that if you ate from it, death you suffer. I did not keep you ignorant about it, but I informed you before it happened. You lent the woman your ear and obeyed her. Therefore, I shall bring the punishment upon you.

سبقت فأخبرتك من أول الأمر ، سلمت إليك كلام وصاياى . وهكذا أعلمتك عن هذه الشجرة من دون جميع الشجر الذى فى الفردوس ، هذه التى فى ثمرتها مرارة الموت وانك إن أكلت منها فموتاً تموت ، وأنا لم أدعك جاهلاً بل أعلمتك قبل أن يكون هذا ، فاملت سمعك وأطعتها كذلك سأجلب عليك العقوبة .

I ask You, O Good One to have mercy upon me according to Your great mercy.

(المرد) أسألك أيها الصالح أن تصنع معى رحمة كعظيم رحمتك .

O Adam from dust you are and to dust you shall return to cleanse you for your transgressions. And you, Eve, why did you do this and disobey My commandments. It was not that an angel or a bird talked to you about it but a serpent, beast by its nature and you listened to his advice. Many shall be your sorrows and great will be your weeping. I will create animosity between you and the serpent and between your descendants and hers. He will watch their heels and your descendant will crush his head.

يا آدم أنت تراب وساردك إلى التراب جزاء الأعمال التى تجاسرت عليها ، وأنت يا حواء لماذا صنعتِ هكذا وخالفتِ وصاياى ؟ ليس ملاك تكلم معك ولا طائر من الجو ، بل وحش ، ثعبان بطبيعته فسمعتِ منه مشورته . فكثير هى الأحزان التى تكون لكِ والتنهد والنوح العظيمان، وسأقيم عداوة بينك وبين الحية وبين نسلك ونسلها إلى إنقضاء الدهور . فهو يرصد عقب نسلك ونسلك يسحق رأسها .

I ask You, O Good One to have mercy upon me according to Your great mercy.

(المرد) أسألك أيها الصالح أن تصنع معى رحمة كعظيم رحمتك .

The Savior then summoned the serpent and cursed her and her nature saying: Cursed are you among all the beasts. On your belly you shall travel and on the dust of the earth you shall feed because of the distrust you caused. The enemy dwelt in you, and you became a shelter for the evil. And, because man listened to you, cursed shall be the whole earth with him.

ثم دعا المخلص الحية ولعنها مع طبيعتها ، وقال: ملعونة أنت من بين جميع الوحوش وعلى بطنك تسعين وتراب الأرض يكون لك طعاماً من أجل أنك صرت عثرة ، فوجد العدو مسكناً فيك وصرت بيتاً للشرير . ومن أجل أن الرجل أمال سمعه إليك فالأرض كلها ملعونة معه .

I ask You, O Good One to have mercy upon me according to Your great mercy.

(المرد) أسألك أيها الصالح أن تصنع معى رحمة كعظيم رحمتك .

As for the man who is Adam, the first to dwell in paradise He told him; because you listened to your spouse I cursed the earth for your deeds. You will live heart saddened and the earth will grow for you thistles and spines. Then He told Eve; in pain and agony you shall give births and you shall return to your spouse, and he will dominate you and you shall have no rest in your life.

وأما الرجل الذى هو آدم أول من سكن فى الفردوس ، قال له من أجل أنك سمعت لإمرأتك لعنت الأرض بأعمالك . وتعيش يا آدم حزين القلب والأرض تنبت لك حسكاً وشوكاً ، ثم قال لحواء ستلدين البنين بالأحزان والتنهد . وترجعين إلى بعلك وهو يتسلط عليك ولا تكون لك راحة فى حياتك .

I ask You, O Good One to have mercy upon me according to Your great mercy.

(المرد) أسألك أيها الصالح أن تصنع معى رحمة كعظيم رحمتك .

Then God said: behold, Adam became as one of Us; discerns between the right and the evil. I shall not leave him in paradise lest he should reach for the tree of life and eat of it. He expelled Adam and his spouse from the paradise of joy and assigned a cherub carrying a sword of fire to guard its gate.

ثم قال الرب: هوذا آدم قد صار كواحدٍ منا يعرف الخير والشر فلا أتركه فى الفردوس لئلا يمد يمينه ويأكل من شجرة الحياة . فأخرج آدم وإمرأته معه من فردوس النعيم وجعل كاروبيم وسيف نار لحراسة باب الفردوس .

I ask You, O Good One to have mercy upon me according to Your great mercy.

(المرد) أسألك أيها الصالح أن تصنع معى رحمة كعظيم رحمتك .

Where do I go from Your spirit and where do I escape from Your face. If I ascended to the heights of heaven or descended to the lowest places I find You there. And Adam went to a lower place across from the gate of paradise to till the land and eat of its fruits where he was in the grasp of the Deceiver. And Adam and Eve were condemned to the servitude of slavery, because he followed his whim, he and all his sons, until the fullness of time.

إلى أين أذهب من روحك؟ وإلى أين أهرب من وجهك؟ إن صعدت إلى أعلى السموات أو إلى الأماكن السفلية أجدك هناك . فمضى آدم إلى مكان أسفل أمام باب الفردوس ليحرث فى الأرض ويأكل ثمرتها عندما كان فى خديعة المضل . وكتب على آدم وحواء كتاب رق العبودية لأنه تبع هواه هو وبنوه كلهم إلى كمال الدهر.

(North side) Christ our Savior; has come and has borne suffering; that through His Passion; He may save us.

(مرد بحرى) المسيح مخلصنا جاء وتألم عنا لكى بآلامه يخلصنا .

(South side) Let us glorify Him; and exalt His Name; for He had mercy on us; according to His great mercy.

(مرد قبلى) فلنمجده ونرفع اسمه لأنه صنع معنا رحمة كعظيم رحمته .

الساعة الحادية عشر من يوم الاثنين من البصخة المقدسة
The Eleventh Hour of Monday of the Holy Pascha

Isaiah 50:1-3

Thus says the Lord, Of what kind is your mother's bill of divorcement, by which I put her away? Or to which debtor have I sold you? Behold, you are sold for your sins, and for your iniquities have I put your mother away. Why did I come, and there was no man? Why did I call, and there was none to hearken? Is not My hand strong to redeem? Or can I not deliver? Behold, by My rebuke I will dry up the sea, and make rivers a wilderness; and their fish shall be dried up because there is no water, and shall die of thirst. I will clothe the sky with darkness, and will make its covering as sackcloth. Glory be to the Holy Trinity. Amen

(من إشعياء النبي ص 50 : 1 – 3)

هكذا يقول الرب . أين هو كتاب طلاق أمكم الذى طلقتها به أو الى أى أى عذاب أسلمتكم؟ هوذا من أجل خطاياكم قد بعتكم . وبسبب آثامكم طلقت أمكم . لماذا أتيت ولم يكن إنسان؟ دعوت وليس من مجيب . أقصُرتْ يدى عن أن تخلص؟ أثقلت أذنى عن السماع؟ إنما خطاياكم قائمة بينكم وبين الله ، لأجل ذنوبكم صرف وجهه عنكم لكى لا يرحمكم . هل ليس لى قوة على خلاصكم؟ هوذا بغضبى أنشف البحر وأصير الأنهار قفاراً فييبس سمكها من عدم الماء ويموت من العطش. وألبس السماء ظلاماً وأجعل المسح غطاءها . مجداً للثالوث القدوس.

Sirach 1:20-30

The root of wisdom is to fear the Lord, and her branches are length of days. Unjust anger cannot be justified, for anger's decisive influence causes his fall. A patient man will hold fast until the proper time, then afterwards gladness shall burst forth for him. He shall conceal his words until the proper time, and the lips of many will tell of his understanding. In the treasures of wisdom are the parables of knowledge, but godliness is abomination to a sinner. If you desire wisdom, keep the commandments, and the Lord will supply it to you. For the fear of the Lord is wisdom and instruction, and His good pleasure is faith and gentleness. Do not disobey the fear of the Lord, and do not come to Him with a divided heart. Do not be a hypocrite in the sight of men, and be careful with your lips. Do not exalt yourself, lest you fall and bring dishonor to your soul. The Lord shall reveal your secrets, and in the midst of the assembly He will strike you down, because you did not come in the fear of the Lord And your heart was full of deceit. Glory be to the Holy Trinity. Amen.

(من يشوع بن سيراخ ص 1 : 20-30)

أصل الحكمة هى مخافة الرب . وأغصانها كثرة الأيام . الغضوب لا يمكن أن يتبرر ، لأن ميله للغضب يسقطه . الطويل الروح يصبر إلى حين ثم يعاوده السرور . يكتم كلامه إلى حين ، شفاة الكثيرين تنطق بحكمتهم . أمثال التعليم كائنة فى كنوز الحكمة . أما عند الخاطئ فعبادة الله رجس . ان اشتهيت الحكمة فاحفظ الوصايا فيهيها لك الرب . فان الحكمة والأدب هما مخافة الرب ، والذى يرضيه هو الإيمان والوداعة. لا تكن مخالفاً لمخافة الرب ولا تتقدم إليه بقلبين . لا تكن مرائياً قدام الناس واحفظ فمك وشفتيك . لا تترفع لئلا تسقط فتجلب على نفسك الهوان ويكشف الرب خفاياك ، ويصرعك فى وسط الجماعة . لأنك لم تتقدم إلى مخافة الرب ، وقلبك ممتلئ غشاً . مجداً للثالوث القدوس .

A homily of our Holy Father Abba Shenouti the Archimandrite

Occasionally there are some deeds, which we may think, they are good while in God's eyes they are bad. For example, the unqualified tolerance of sinners in holy places may lead them to be indifferent to sin. For example, the Lord did not plant good trees and bad trees in paradise but only good trees. He did not plant fruitless trees or trees with bad fruits. Even

(عظة لأبينا القديس أنبا شنودة)

قد توجد أعمال نخالها أنها صالحة ولكنها رديئة عند الله . وذلك إننا نتغاضى عن بعضنا بعضاً فنخطئ فى المواضع المقدسة . لأن الرب لم يغرس فى الفردوس الأشجار الصالحة والغير الصالحة بل غرسه من الأشجار الصالحة فقط . ولم يغرس فيه أشجاراً غير مثمرة أو

men himself when he disobeyed the commandment, he was not indifferent about men's inequity but expelled him from paradise. From this we can see, dear beloved, that the houses of the Lord should not be filled with bad and good people, as in the case of the world where the saints and sinners, the unjust and the impure mingle together. It is incumbent on us to remind those who come to the house of the Lord to behave appropriately. I know that the whole earth is God's, but if we make His house just like the rest of the earth what is going to distinguish the house of the Lord from the rest. If I as a servant of God commit the same bad deeds as the wicked, then I do not deserve to be called a servant of God. For we often sin and are unable to judge ourselves with the same standard we judge others. You see no one can fill your place with dirt unless they notice your lack of interest in it. Just like the king's pages; they can not let everyone in the king's house whether they honor the king's decree or whether they ignore them without the king's permission. If they deviate from this, they receive punishment.

رديئة الثمر . وليس هذا فقط . بل والناس أنفسهم الذين جعلهم هناك ، عند ما خالفوا لم يحتملهم بل أخرجهم منه . فمن هذا إعلموا أيها الأخوة الأحباء أنه لا يجب أن نملأ مساكن الله المقدسة من الناس الأشرار والصالحين . كما فى العالم المملوء من الخطاة والظالمين والقديسين والأنجاس . ولكن الذين يخطئون لا يتركهم فيها بل يخرجهم . أنا أعرف أن الأرض كلها هى للرب . فاذا كان بيته كباقى الأرض . فما هى ميزته إذن على غيره . فان كنت وأنا الكاهن أعمل الشر كما يعمله الأشرار على الأرض فلا يحق لى أن أدعى كاهناً لأنه مراراً كثيرة نخطئ ولا نعرف كيف ندين أنفسنا بما نقول . لا يتجرأ أحد أن يملأ بيتك قذارة إلا إذا رأى منك التهاون ولا حجاب الملك يتجرأون أن يدخلوا بكل إنسان إلى بيته من الحافظين مراسيمه أوالمخالفين لها إلا بأمره . ومتى عملوا بخلاف ذلك يعاقبون .

We conclude the homily of our Holy Father Abba Shenouti the Archimandrite, who enlightened our minds and our hearts. In the name of the Father, and the Son, and the Holy Spirit, one God. Amen.

فلنختم عظة أبينا القديس أنبا شنودة رئيس المتوحدين الذى أنار عقولنا وعيون قلوبنا بسم الآب والإبن والروح القدس الإله الواحد آمين .

Pascha Praise - A (12 times), Page: 6 | تسبحة البصخة A (12 مرة) ، صفحة :

The Psalm
Ⲯⲁⲗⲙⲟⲥ ⲓⲃ : ⲅ̄

Psalms 12:3-4			(مز 12 : 3و4)
Look on me, hearken to me, O Lord my God: lighten my eyes, lest I sleep in death; lest at any time my enemy say, I have prevailed against him: Alleluia.	Ϭⲟⲙⲥ ⲥⲱⲧⲉⲙ ⲉⲣⲟⲓ ⲡ̀ϭⲟⲓⲥ ⲡⲁⲛⲟⲩϯ : ⲙⲁ ⲫ̀ⲟⲩⲱⲓⲛⲓ ⲛ̀ⲛⲁⲃⲁⲗ ⲙⲏⲡⲱⲥ ⲛ̀ⲧⲁϩⲱⲣⲡ ϧⲉⲛ ⲫ̀ⲙⲟⲩ : ⲙⲏⲡⲟⲧⲉ ⲛ̀ⲧⲉ ⲡⲁϫⲁϫⲓ ϫⲟⲥ : ϫⲉ ⲁⲓϫⲉⲙϫⲟⲙ ⲟⲩⲃⲏϥ . ⲁ̄ⲗ̄ .	صومس صوتيم إروى إبتشويس بانووتى : ما إفوؤاوينى إننافال مى بوس إنطاهوب خين إفموو : مى بوتيه إنتيه باجاجى جوس : جيه أى جيم جُم أووفيف . الليلويا .	أنظر واستجب لى يا ربى وإلهى . انر عينى لئلا أنام فى الموت . لئلا يقول عدوى أنى قد قويت عليه . الليلويا.

Introduction to the Gospel, Page: 8 | مقدمة الأنجيل ، صفحة :

The Gospel
Ⲉⲩⲁⲅⲅⲉⲗⲓⲟⲛ Ⲕⲁⲧⲁ Ⲓⲱⲁⲛⲛⲏⲛ Ⲕⲉⲫ ⲏ̄ : ⲛ̄ⲁ̄ ϣ̀ⲃⲗ

John 8:51-59		(يوحنا ص 8 : 51-59)
Most assuredly, I say to you, if anyone keeps My word he shall never see death." Then the Jews said to Him, "Now we know that You have a demon! Abraham is dead, and the prophets; and You	Ⲁⲙⲏⲛ ⲁⲙⲏⲛ ϯϫⲱ ⲙ̀ⲙⲟⲥ ⲛⲱⲧⲉⲛ ϫⲉ ⲉϣⲱⲡ ⲁⲣⲉϣⲁⲛ ⲟⲩⲁⲓ ⲁⲣⲉϩ ⲉ̀ⲡⲁⲥⲁϫⲓ ⲛ̀ⲛⲉϥⲛⲁⲩ ⲉ̀ⲫⲙⲟⲩ ϣⲁ ⲉ̀ⲛⲉϩ : ⲡⲉϫⲉ ⲛⲓⲟⲩⲇⲁⲓ ⲛⲁϥ ϫⲉ ϯⲛⲟⲩ ⲁⲛⲉ̀ⲙⲓ ϫⲉ ⲟⲩⲟⲛ ⲟⲩⲇⲉⲙⲱⲛ ⲛⲉⲙⲁⲕ : Ⲁⲃⲣⲁⲁⲙ ⲁϥⲙⲟⲩ ⲛⲉⲙ ⲛⲓⲕⲉⲡⲣⲟⲫⲏⲧⲏⲥ ⲟⲩⲟϩ ⲛ̀ⲑⲟⲕ ⲕ̀ϫⲱ ⲙ̀ⲙⲟⲥ	الحق الحق أقول لكم ان كان أحد يحفظ كلامى فلن يرى الموت إلى الأبد . فقال له اليهود : الآن علمنا ان بك شيطاناً . قد مات إبراهيم والأنبياء . وأنت

say, 'If anyone keeps My word he shall never taste death.' Are You greater than our father Abraham, who is dead? And the prophets are dead. Who do You make Yourself out to be?" Jesus answered, "If I honor Myself, My honor is nothing. It is My Father who honors Me, of whom you say that He is your God. Yet you have not known Him, but I know Him. And if I say, 'I do not know Him,' I shall be a liar like you; but I do know Him and keep His word. Your father Abraham rejoiced to see My day, and he saw it and was glad." Then the Jews said to Him, "You are not yet fifty years old, and have You seen Abraham?" Jesus said to them, "Most assuredly, I say to you, before Abraham was, I AM." Then they took up stones to throw at Him; but Jesus hid Himself and went out of the temple, going through the midst of them, and so passed by.

Glory be to God forever, Amen.

ϫⲉ ⲫⲏⲉⲑⲛⲁⲁⲣⲉϩ ⲉⲡⲁⲥⲁϫⲓ ⲛ̅ⲛⲉϥϫⲉⲙ̅ⲧⲓ ⲙ̅ⲫⲙⲟⲩ ϣⲁ ⲉⲛⲉϩ : ⲙⲏ ⲛ̅ⲑⲟⲕ ⲟⲩⲛⲓϣϯ ⲛ̅ⲑⲟⲕ ⲉⲡⲉⲛⲓⲱⲧ ⲁⲃⲣⲁⲁⲙ ⲫⲏⲉⲧⲁϥⲙⲟⲩ ⲛⲉⲙ ⲛⲓⲕⲉⲡⲣⲟⲫⲏⲧⲏⲥ ⲁⲩⲙⲟⲩ ⲕ̅ⲣⲓ ⲙ̅ⲙⲟⲕ ⲛ̅ⲛⲓⲙ . ⲁϥⲉⲣⲟⲩⲱ ⲛ̅ϫⲉ Ⲓⲏⲥ ⲉϥϫⲱ ⲙ̅ⲙⲟⲥ ϫⲉ ⲉϣⲱⲡ ⲁⲛⲟⲕ ⲁⲓϣⲁⲛ̅ⲧⲱⲟⲩ ⲛⲏⲓ ⲙ̅ⲙⲁⲩⲁⲧ ⲡⲁⲱⲟⲩ ϩⲗⲓ ⲁⲛ ⲡⲉ . ϥϣⲟⲡ ⲛ̅ϫⲉ ⲡⲁⲓⲱⲧ ⲉⲑⲛⲁϯⲱⲟⲩ ⲛⲏⲓ : ⲫⲏ ⲛ̅ⲑⲱⲧⲉⲛ ⲉⲧⲉⲧⲉⲛ̅ϫⲱ ⲙ̅ⲙⲟⲥ ϫⲉ ⲡⲉⲧⲉⲛ̅ⲛⲟⲩϯ ⲡⲉ : ⲟⲩⲟϩ ⲙ̅ⲡⲉⲧⲉⲛ̅ⲥⲟⲩⲱⲛϥ ⲁⲛⲟⲕ ⲇⲉ ϯⲥⲱⲟⲩⲛ ⲙ̅ⲙⲟϥ ⲉϣⲱⲡ ⲇⲉ ⲁⲓϣⲁⲛ̅ϫⲟⲥ ϫⲉ ϯⲥⲱⲟⲩⲛ ⲙ̅ⲙⲟϥ ⲁⲛ ⲉⲓ̅ϣⲱⲡⲓ ⲉⲓⲟⲛⲓ ⲙ̅ⲙⲱⲧⲉⲛ ⲛ̅ⲥⲁⲙⲉⲑⲛⲟⲩϫ ⲁⲗⲗⲁ ϯⲥⲱⲟⲩⲛ ⲙ̅ⲙⲟϥ ⲟⲩⲟϩ ⲡⲉϥⲥⲁϫⲓ ϯⲁⲣⲉϩ ⲉⲣⲟϥ : ⲁⲃⲣⲁⲁⲙ ⲡⲉⲧⲉⲛⲓⲱⲧ ⲛⲁϥⲑⲉⲗⲏⲗ ⲡⲉ ⲉϥⲟⲩⲱϣ ⲉ̅ⲛⲁⲩ ⲉⲟⲩⲉϩⲟⲟⲩ ⲛ̅ⲧⲏⲓ ⲟⲩⲟϩ ⲁϥⲛⲁⲩ ⲁϥⲣⲁϣⲓ . ⲡⲉϫⲉ ⲛⲓⲓⲟⲩⲇⲁⲓ ⲟⲩⲛ ⲛⲁϥ ϫⲉ ⲙ̅ⲡⲁⲧⲉⲕⲉⲣ ⲧⲉⲃⲓ ⲛ̅ⲣⲟⲙⲡⲓ ⲟⲩⲟϩ ⲁⲕⲛⲁⲩ ⲉ̅ⲁⲃⲣⲁⲁⲙ . ⲡⲉϫⲉ Ⲓⲏⲥ ⲛⲱⲟⲩ ϫⲉ ⲁⲙⲏⲛ ⲁⲙⲏⲛ ϯϫⲱ ⲙ̅ⲙⲟⲥ ⲛⲱⲧⲉⲛ ϫⲉ ⲙ̅ⲡⲁⲧⲉ ⲁⲃⲣⲁⲁⲙ ϣⲱⲡⲓ ⲁⲛⲟⲕ ⲡⲉ : ⲁⲩⲉⲗ ⲱⲛⲓ ⲟⲩⲛ ⲛ̅ϫⲉ ⲛⲓⲓⲟⲩⲇⲁⲓ ϩⲓⲛⲁ ⲛ̅ⲥⲉϩⲓⲟⲩⲓ ⲉϫⲱϥ : Ⲓⲏⲥ ⲇⲉ ⲁϥⲭⲟⲡϥ ⲟⲩⲟϩ ⲁϥⲓ̅ ⲉ̅ⲃⲟⲗ ϧⲉⲛ ⲡⲓⲉⲣⲫⲉⲓ ⲟⲩⲟϩ ⲁϥⲥⲓⲛⲓ ⲛⲁϥⲙⲟϣⲓ ⲡⲉ ϧⲉⲛ ⲧⲟⲩⲙⲏϯ ⲟⲩⲟϩ ⲛⲁϥⲥⲓⲛⲓ ⲱⲟⲩ ⲙ̅ⲡⲁⲓⲣⲏϯ . ⲟⲩⲱϣⲧ ⲙ̅ⲡⲓⲉⲩⲁⲅⲅⲉⲗⲓⲟⲛ ⲉⲑⲟⲩ .

تقول ان كان احد يحفظ كلامى فلا يقهره الموت إلى الأبد . ألعلك أنت أعظم من أبينا إبراهيم الذى مات والأنبياء قد ماتوا أيضاً ، من تجعل نفسك ؟ أجاب يسوع قائلاً : ان كنت أنا أمجد نفسى وحدى فليس مجدى شيئاً . أبى هو الذى يمجدنى . الذى تقولون أنتم انه إلهكم . ولستم تعرفونه وأما أنا فأعرفه ، وان قلت أنى لست أعرفه صرت كاذباً مثلكم لكننى أعرفه وأحفظ كلامه . إبراهيم أبوكم تهلل مشتهياً أن يرى يومى فرأى وفرح . فقال له اليهود: ليس لك خمسون سنة بعد وقد رأيت إبراهيم . فقال لهم يسوع: الحق الحق أقول لكم قبل أن يكون إبراهيم أنا كائن . فأخذ اليهود حجارة ليرجموه فتوارى يسوع وخرج من الهيكل مجتازاً فى وسطهم ومضى هكذا . والمجد لله دائماً.

Introduction to the Exposition, Page:　9　: مقدمة الطرح ، صفحة

Exposition

O shinning True Light that fills the earth, I mean Jesus the true light that shines for all nations except the Jews for they stayed away from Him and did not look at Him.

When He revealed Himself to them and told them that those who believe in Him shall live forever, the ignorants, the breakers of the law, accuse Him that with satan He exorcises satans. They said unto Him: Abraham died and the prophets there after, how is it possible that those who believe in You never die?

- If I glorify Myself then My glory is nil. He glorifies me.

طرح

أيها النور الحقيقى الذى يضئ ، المالئ كل مكان فى المسكونة . أعنى يسوع النور الحقيقى الذى يضئ لجميع الأمم ، أما اليهود فانهم لم يقتربوا من هذا النور ليتأملوه .

أما هو فأظهر فيهم سره قائلاً: ان من يؤمن بى لن يموت إلى الأبد. اسمعوا الجهال ومخالفى الناموس و هم يقولون: أن معه شيطان ليخرج الشياطين وان إبراهيم مات والأنبياء أيضاً ، فكيف لا يموت الذى يؤمن بك؟.

- إن أنا مجدت نفسى فليس مجدى شيئاً ، لي من يمجدني.

- Do You think You are greater than our Patriarch Abraham and his descendants who all died? You are not even fifty years old how could You have seen Abraham.

- The Savior said: Verily, before Abraham was I.

We also, the community of the new nations, believe and keep His commandments in our mouths, and we acknowledge from the depth of our hearts the true Word of the Father the Pantocrator.

The Good One, who existed from the beginning with the Holy Spirit, the Comforter, continues to tell the ignorant, transgressors, and rejected children. They denied this great blessing and the many miracles that He showed in them. They did not understand that He was their Savior, as the prophets said. So, they denied Him, did not accept Him, rejected Him, and became without God.

(North side) Christ our Savior; has come and has borne suffering; that through His Passion; He may save us.

(South side) Let us glorify Him; and exalt His Name; for He had mercy on us; according to His great mercy.

ـ ألعلك أعظم من أبينا إبراهيم ومن نسله الذين ذاقوا الموت ، لك خمسون سنة من الزمان فهل رأيت إبراهيم؟ من يصدقك ؟

ـ قال المخلص بالحق: أنا كائن من قبل أن يكون إبراهيم .

نحن أيضاً نؤمن، معشر الشعوب الجديدة، ونواظب على وصاياه فى أفواهنا ونعترف من عمق قلوبنا بالكلمة الحقيقى الذى للآب الضابط الكل.

أن الصالح الكائن منذ البدء مع الروح القدس المعزى لم يزل يخبر الجهال المملوئين اثماً المخالفين، الأبناء المرذولين، فجحدوا هذه النعمة العظيمة والعجائب الجزيلة التى أظهرها فيهم ولم يفهموا أنه هو مخلصهم كما قال الأنبياء، فجحدوه ولم يقبلوه ورفضوه وصاروا بغير إله.

(مرد بحرى) المسيح مخلصنا جاء وتألم عنا لكى بإلامه يخلصنا .

(مرد قبلى) فلنمجده ونرفع اسمه لأنه صنع معنا رحمة كعظيم رحمته .

The Conclusion of the Exposition, Page: 9	ختام الطرح ، صفحة :

| The Conclusion with the Daytime Litanies, Page: 10 | طلبة الصباح ، صفحة : |

ليلة الثلاثاء من البصخة المقدسة

Tuesday Eve of the Holy Pascha

القراءات و الاحداث

الموضوع : انذار الفريسيين و رؤساء الكهنة

الاولى : لو 13 : 23 – 30؛ حثهم على الخلاص
الثالثه : لو 13 : 31 – 35 ؛ قصاصهم العتيد
السادسة : لو 21 : 34 – 38 ؛ قصاصهم المفاجئ
التاسعة : لو 11 : 37 – 52 ؛ الويلات لهم
الحادية عشرة : مر 13 : 31 – 14 : 2 ؛ خوفهم من الشعب

جاء قوم من الفريسيين الى المخلص يطلبون خروجه من المدينة لان هيرودس يريد
قتله و لكنه استمر ان يعلمهم عن الباب الضيق و وجوب السهر والاستعداد . ثم بدأ
يوبخ اورشليم و ينبئ عن خرابها

The Readings and Events

Subject: Warning of the Pharisees and chief priests

First hour: Luke 13:23-30; Encouraging them for salvation.
Third hour: Luke 13:31-35; Their coming punishment.
Sixth hour: Luke 21:34-38; Their unexpected punishment.
Ninth hour: Luke 11:37-52; The woes to them.
Eleventh hour: Mark 13: 31-14:2; Their fear of people.

Some people came to the Savior asking Him to leave the city
for Herod wanted to kill Him. The Savior continued to teach
them about the narrow door and the need for readiness. He
started to rebuke Jerusalem and to tell about its desolation.

الساعة الأولى من ليلة الثلاثاء من البصخة المقدسة
The First Hour of Tuesday Eve of the Holy Pascha

Zechariah 1:1-6

In the eighth month, in the second year of the reign of Darius, the word of the Lord came to Zacharias, the son of Barachias, the son of Iddo, the prophet, saying, The Lord has been very angry with your fathers. And you shall say to them, Thus says the Lord Almighty: Turn to Me, says the Lord of hosts, and I will turn to you, says the Lord of hosts. And be not as your fathers, whom the prophets before charged, saying, Thus says the Lord Almighty: Turn from your evil ways, and from your evil practices: but they did not hear, nor heed Me, says the Lord. Where are your fathers, and the prophets? Will they live forever? But do you receive My words and My ordinances, all that I command by My Spirit to My servants the prophets, who lived in the days of your fathers. And they answered and said, As the Lord Almighty determined to do to us, according to our ways, and according to our practices, so has He done to us. Glory be to the Holy Trinity. Amen

(من زكريا النبي ص 1 : 1 - 6)

وفى الشهر الثامن من السنة الثانية لداريوس. كانت كلمة الله إلى زكريا بن بـراشـيا بن عدو النبي قائلاً : قد غضب الرب على آبائكم قائلاً : قل لهم هكذا ما يقوله الرب الضابط الكل ارجعوا إلى وأنا أيضاً أرجع إليكم قال الرب الضابط الكل . ولا تكونوا كآبائكم الذين خاطبهم الأنبياء الاولون قائلين : هذا ما يقوله الرب الضابط الكل ارجعوا عن طرقكم الرديئة وعن أعمالكم الشريرة فلم يصغوا قال الرب الضابط الكل . فأين هم آباؤكم والأنبياء فهل يحيون إلى الأبد لكن نواميسى وأقوالى إقبلوها تلك التى أمرت بها روح عبيدى الأنبياء . الذين أدركوا آباؤكم وخاطبوهم قائلين : كما أمر الرب الضابط الكل أن يصنع بكم بحسب طرقكم . وكأعمالكم هكذا صنع بكم . مجداً للثالوث القدوس .

Pascha Praise - A (12 times), Page: 6	تسبحة البصخة A (12 مرة) ، صفحة :

The Psalm
Ⲯⲁⲗⲙⲟⲥ ⲝ̅ⲁ̅ : ⲁ̅ ⲛⲉⲙ ⲁ̅

Psalms 61:1, 4

In God is my salvation and my glory; He is the God of my help, and my hope is in God. For He is my God, and my savior; my helper, I shall not be greatly moved. Alleluia

Ⲡⲁⲟⲩⲭⲁⲓ ⲛⲉⲙ ⲡⲁⲱⲟⲩ ⲁⲩ ϧⲉⲛ ⲫⲁⲛⲟⲩϯ : Ⲫϯ ⲛ̀ⲧⲉ ⲧⲁⲃⲟⲏⲑⲓⲁ ⲟⲩⲟϩ ⲧⲁϩⲉⲗⲡⲓⲥ ⲁⲥ ϧⲉⲛ Ⲫϯ. Ⲕⲉⲅⲁⲣ ⲛ̀ⲑⲟϥ ⲡⲉ ⲡⲁⲛⲟⲩϯ ⲡⲁⲥⲱⲧⲏⲣ : ⲡⲁⲣⲉϥϣⲟⲡⲧ ___ ⲉ̀ⲣⲟϥ ⲛ̀ⲛⲁⲕⲓⲙ ⲛ̀ϩⲟⲟⲩ . ⲁ̅ⲗ̅.

با أووجاى نيم با أوأوو أف خين بانووتى . إفنوتى إنتيه طافويثيا أووه طاهيلبيس أس خين إفنوتى. كيه غار إنثوف بيه بانووتى باصوتير : باريف شوبت إروف إنناكيم إنهوأوو . الليلويا .

(مز 61 : 1 ، 4)

خلاصى ومجدى هما بالهى إله معونتى ورجائى هو بالله . لأنه إلهى و مخلصى ناصرى فلا أتزعزع أبداً . أللليلويا .

Introduction to the Gospel, Page: 8	مقدمة الأنجيل ، صفحة :

The Gospel
Ⲉⲩⲁⲅⲅⲉⲗⲓⲟⲛ Ⲕⲁⲧⲁ Ⲗⲟⲩⲕⲁⲛ Ⲕⲉⲫ ⲓ̅ⲅ̅ : ⲓ̅ⲅ̅ - ⲗ̅

Luke 13:23-30

Then one said to Him, "Lord, are there few who are saved?" And He said to them, "Strive to enter through the narrow gate, for many,

Ⲡⲉϫⲉ ⲟⲩⲁⲓ ⲇⲉ ⲛⲁϥ ϫⲉ ⲡ̅ⲟ̅ⲥ̅ ϩⲁⲛⲕⲟⲩϫⲓ ⲛⲉ ⲛⲏⲉⲑⲛⲁⲛⲟϩⲉⲙ : ⲛ̀ⲑⲟϥ ⲇⲉ ⲡⲉϫⲁϥ ⲛⲱⲟⲩ : ϫⲉ ⲁⲣⲓⲁⲅⲱⲛⲓⲍⲉⲥⲑⲉ ⲉ̀ⲓ ⲉ̀ϧⲟⲩⲛ ⲉ̀ⲃⲟⲗ ϩⲓⲧⲉⲛ ⲡⲓⲣⲟ ⲉⲧϫⲏⲟⲩ : ϫⲉ ⲛⲉ ⲟⲩⲟⲛ ⲟⲩⲙⲏϣ

(لوقا 13 : 23 - 30)

فقال له واحد: يارب أقليل هم الذين يخلصون؟ فأما هو فقال لهم: اجتهدوا أن تدخلوا

I say to you, will seek to enter and will not be able. When once the Master of the house has risen up and shut the door, and you begin to stand outside and knock at the door, saying, 'Lord, Lord, open for us,' and He will answer and say to you, 'I do not know you, where you are from,' then you will begin to say, 'We ate and drank in Your presence, and You taught in our streets.' But He will say, 'I tell you I do not know you, where you are from. Depart from Me, all you workers of iniquity.' There will be weeping and gnashing of teeth, when you see Abraham and Isaac and Jacob and all the prophets in the kingdom of God, and yourselves thrust out. They will come from the east and the west, from the north and the south, and sit down in the kingdom of God. And indeed there are last who will be first, and there are first who will be last." Glory be to God forever, Amen.

ⲧ̀ϫⲱ ⲙ̀ⲙⲟⲥ ⲛⲱⲧⲉⲛ ⲛⲁⲕⲱϯ ⲛ̀ⲥⲁ ⲓ̀ ⲉ̀ϧⲟⲩⲛ ⲟⲩⲟϩ ⲛ̀ⲛⲟⲩϣϫⲉⲙϫⲟⲙ ⲁϥϣⲁⲛϥⲟϩ ⲉ̀ⲧⲱⲛϥ ⲛ̀ϫⲉ ⲡⲓⲛⲏⲃ ϩⲓ ⲟⲩⲟϩ ⲛ̀ⲧⲉϥϣ̀ⲑⲁⲙ ⲙ̀ⲡⲓⲣⲟ : ⲟⲩⲟϩ ⲛ̀ⲧⲉ ⲧⲉⲛⲛⲁⲉⲣϩⲏⲧⲥ ⲛ̀ⲟ̀ϩⲓ ⲉⲣⲁⲧⲉⲛ ⲑⲏⲛⲟⲩ ⲥⲁⲃⲟⲗ ⲟⲩⲟϩ ⲉ̀ⲕⲱⲗϩ ⲉ̀ⲡⲓⲣⲟ ⲉⲣⲉⲧⲉⲛϫⲱ ⲙ̀ⲙⲟⲥ : ϫⲉ Ⲡ̅ⲟ̅ⲥ̅ Ⲡ̅ⲟ̅ⲥ̅ ⲁⲟⲩⲱⲛ ⲛⲁⲛ : ⲟⲩⲟϩ ⲛ̀ⲧⲉϥⲉⲣⲟⲩⲱ ⲛ̀ⲧⲉϥϫⲟⲥ ⲛⲱⲧⲉⲛ : ϫⲉ ⲛ̀ϯⲥⲱⲟⲩⲛ ⲙ̀ⲙⲱⲧⲉⲛ ⲁⲛ ϫⲉ ⲛ̀ⲑⲱⲧⲉⲛ ϩⲁⲛ ⲉ̀ⲃⲟⲗ ⲑⲱⲛ . Ⲧⲟⲧⲉ ⲉⲣⲉⲧⲉⲛⲉⲣϩⲏⲧⲥ ⲛ̀ϫⲟⲥ : ϫⲉ ⲁⲛ ⲟⲩⲱⲛ ⲙ̀ⲡⲉⲕⲙ̀ⲑⲟ ⲟⲩⲟϩ ⲁⲛⲥⲱ : ⲟⲩⲟϩ ⲁⲕϯⲥⲃⲱ ϧⲉⲛ ⲛⲉⲛⲡ̀ⲗⲁⲧⲓⲁ : ⲟⲩⲟϩ ϥ̀ⲛⲁϫⲟⲥ ⲛⲱⲧⲉⲛ ϫⲉ ⲛ̀ϯⲥⲱⲟⲩⲛ ⲙ̀ⲙⲱⲧⲉⲛ ⲁⲛ ϫⲉ ⲛ̀ⲑⲱⲧⲉⲛ ϩⲁⲛ ⲉ̀ⲃⲟⲗ ⲑⲱⲛ : ⲙⲁϣⲉⲛⲱⲧⲉⲛ ⲉ̀ⲃⲟⲗ ϩⲁⲣⲟⲓ ⲧⲏⲣⲟⲩ ⲛⲓⲉⲣⲅⲁⲧⲏⲥ ⲛ̀ⲧⲉ ϯⲁ̀ⲇⲓⲕⲓⲁ : ⲡⲓⲙⲁ ⲉⲧⲉ ⲓⲙⲁ ϥ̀ⲛⲁϣⲱⲡⲓ ⲛ̀ϫⲉ ⲫ̀ⲣⲓⲙⲓ ⲛⲉⲙ ⲡⲓⲥ̀ⲑⲉⲣⲧⲉⲣ ⲛ̀ⲧⲉ ⲛⲓⲛⲁϫϩⲓ : ϩⲟⲧⲉⲛ ⲁⲣⲉⲧⲉⲛϣⲁⲛⲛⲁⲩ ⲉ̀Ⲁⲃⲣⲁⲁⲙ ⲛⲉⲙ Ⲓⲥⲁⲁⲕ ⲛⲉⲙ Ⲓⲁⲕⲱⲃ ⲛⲉⲙ ⲛⲓⲡ̀ⲣⲟⲫⲏⲧⲏⲥ ⲧⲏⲣⲟⲩ ϧⲉⲛ ϯⲙⲉⲧⲟⲩⲣⲟ ⲛ̀ⲧⲉ Ⲫ̀ⲧ ⲛ̀ⲑⲱⲧⲉⲛ ⲇⲉ ⲉⲩⲉ̀ϩⲓⲟⲩⲓ ⲙ̀ⲙⲱⲧⲉⲛ ⲉ̀ⲃⲟⲗ . Ⲟⲩⲟϩ ⲉⲩⲉ̀ⲓ̀ ⲉ̀ⲃⲟⲗ ϧⲉⲛ ⲛⲓⲙⲁⲛ̀ϣⲁⲓ ⲛⲉⲙ ⲛⲓⲙⲁⲛ̀ϩⲱⲧⲡ ⲛⲉⲙ ⲡⲉⲙϩⲓⲧ ⲛⲉⲙ ⲥⲁⲣⲏⲥ ⲟⲩⲟϩ ⲉⲩⲉ̀ⲣⲟⲑⲃⲟⲩ ϧⲉⲛ ϯⲙⲉⲧⲟⲩⲣⲟ ⲛ̀ⲧⲉ Ⲫ̀ⲧ : ⲟⲩⲟϩ ϩⲏⲡⲡⲉ ⲟⲩⲟⲛ ϩⲁⲛ ϧⲁⲧⲉⲛ ⲉⲩⲛⲁⲉⲣϣⲟⲣⲡ ⲟⲩⲟϩ ϩⲁⲛϣⲟⲣⲡ ⲉⲩⲛⲁⲉⲣ ϧⲁⲉ . ⲟⲩⲱϣⲧ ⲙ̀ⲡⲓⲉⲩⲁⲅⲅⲉⲗⲓⲟⲛ ⲉⲑ̅ⲩ̅.

من الباب الضيق . فأنى أقول لكم أن كثيرين سيطلبون أن يدخلوا فلا يستطيعون . فاذا بلغ أن يقوم رب البيت ليغلق الباب ، فتبدأون بان تقفوا خارجاً وتقرعون الباب قائلين: يارب يارب افتح لنا . فيجيبكم قائلاً: أنى لست أعرفكم من أين أنتم . حينئذ تبتدئون ان تقولوا: أكلنا قدامك وشربنا . وعلمت فى شوارعنا . فيقول لكم: أنى لا أعرفكم من أين أنتم؟ اذهبوا عنى يا جميع فاعلى الاثم ، هناك يكون البكاء وصرير الأسنان . إذا رأيتم إبراهيم واسحق ويعقوب وجميع الأنبياء فى ملكوت الله وأنتم تطردون خارجاً . ويأتون من المشارق والمغارب والشمال والجنوب ويتكئون فى ملكوت الله . فهوذا آخرون يكونون أولين وأولون يكونون آخرين . والمجد لله دائماً .

Exposition

On His way to Jerusalem with His disciples, someone asked our Savior, "are there few who are saved?" Our Savior replied saying, "Strive to enter through the narrow gate, lest you should come and knock on the door and say, 'O Lord open (the door) unto us'; And He shall answer from inside and say unto you, 'I do not know you, where you are from. Depart away all you wrongful, peccants to the place of weeping and the gnashing of teeth. Many of the Gentiles will come from the east and the west and will nestle into the bosom of Abraham, Isaac, and Jacob in the kingdom of heaven, but you will be relegated outside, dominated by your profanity. Repent and make amends, that your sins may be taken away.

طرح

إن مخلصنا جعل مسيرته إلى أورشليم مع خواصه. فقال له واحد من الجمع يارب أقليلون هم الذين يخلصون؟ فأجابه مخلصنا قائلاً: احرصوا على الدخول من الباب الضيق لئلا تاتوا وتقرعوا الباب وتقولون يارب افتح لنا فيجيب هو من داخل قائلاً لكم : ما أعرفكم من أين أنتم إذهبوا عنى خارجاً يا جميع فاعلى الاثم حيث يكون البكاء وصرير الأسنان معاً . إن كثيرين من الأمم يأتون من المشارق والمغارب ويتكئون فى احضان إبراهيم واسحق ويعقوب فى ملكوت السموات . أما أنتم فيطردونكم خارجاً وتتسلط عليكم أثامكم . فارجعوا عن طرقكم الرديئة لكى تمحى عنكم هفواتكم .

(North side) *Christ our Savior; has come and has borne suffering; that through His Passion; He may save us.*

(مرد بحري) المسيح مخلصنا جاء وتألم عنا لكى بآلامه يخلصنا .

(South side) *Let us glorify Him; and exalt His Name; for He had mercy on us; according to His great mercy.*

(مرد قبلى) فلنمجده ونرفع اسمه لأنه صنع معنا رحمةً كعظيم رحمته .

| The Conclusion of the Exposition, Page: | 9 | ختام الطرح ، صفحة : |

الساعة الثالثة من ليلة الثلاثاء من البصخة المقدسة
The Third Hour of Tuesday Eve of the Holy Pascha

Malachi 1:1-9

The burden of the word of the Lord to Israel by the hand of his messenger. Take this to heart, I pray. I have loved you, says the Lord. And you said, How have You loved us? Was not Esau Jacob's brother? Says the Lord: yet I loved Jacob, and hated Esau and laid waste his borders, and made his heritage as dwellings of the wilderness? Because one will say, Idumea has been overthrown, but let us return and rebuild the desolate places; thus says the Lord Almighty, They shall build, but I will throw down; and they shall be called The borders of wickedness, and, The people against whom the Lord has set himself for ever. And your eyes shall see, and you shall say, The Lord has been magnified upon the borders of Israel. A son honors his father, and a servant his master: if then I am a Father, where is My honor? And if I am a Master, where is My fear? Says the Lord Almighty. You the priests are they that despise My name: yet you said, In what way have we despised Your name? In that you bring to My altar polluted bread; and you said, In what way have we polluted it? In that you say, The table of the Lord is polluted, and that which was set on it you have despised. For if you bring a blind victim for sacrifices, is it not evil? And if you bring the lame or the sick, is it not evil? Offer it now to your ruler, and see if he will receive you, if he will accept your person, says the Lord Almighty. And now entreat the face of your God, and make supplication to Him. These things have been done by your hands; shall I accept you? Says the Lord Almighty. *Glory be to the Holy Trinity. Amen*

(من ملاخى النبى ص 1 : 1 - 9)

ثقل كلام الرب لإسرائيل على يد ملاكه . ضعوا فى قلوبكم انى احببتكم يقول الرب . وقلتم بم أحببتنا ؟ ، أليس عيسو أخا ليعقوب يقول الرب ، وقد أحببت يعقوب وأبغضت عيسو ، وجعلت حدوده للفساد ونصيب ميراثه كمساكن البرية ؟ وان قال الأدوميون أننا قد إنهدمنا فنرجع ونبنى خربها هذا ما يقوله الرب الضابط الكل . هم يبنون وأنا أهدم . وادعوها تخم الاثم والشعب الذى قاومه الرب إلى الأبد . فتبصر عيونكم و تقولون : لقد تعظم الرب فوق تخوم إسرائيل . الإبن يكرم أباه والعبد سيده . فان كنت أنا أباً فاين كرامتى ؟ وان كنت سيداً فاين مهابتى ؟ ، قال الرب الضابط الكل . وأنتم أيها الكهنة تحتقرون اسمى ، وقلتم بم احتقرنا اسمك ؟ لأنكم قربتم على مذبحى خبزاً نجساً وقلتم بم نجسناه ؟ بقولكم ان مائدة الرب حقيرة وحقيرة هى الأطعمة الموضوعة عليها . إذا قربتم الأعمى ذبيحة ، أفليس ذلك شراً؟. وإذ قربتم الأعرج أو السقيم أفليس ذلك شراً؟ قربه لرئيسك أفيقبله منك ؟ أو يقبل وجهك ؟ . يقول الرب الضابط الكل . مجداً للثالوث القدوس .

Pascha Praise - A (12 times), Page: 6   تسبحة البصخة A (12 مرة) ، صفحة :

The Psalm
Ⲯⲁⲗⲙⲟⲥ ⲓⲃ̅ : ⲁ̅ ⲛⲉⲙ ⲋ̅

Psalms 12:4, 6

Look on me, hearken to me, O Lord my God: lighten my eyes, lest I sleep in death; But I have hoped in Your mercy; my heart shall rejoice in Your salvation. *Alleluia*

Ⲥⲟⲙⲥ ⲥⲱⲧⲉⲙ ⲉⲣⲟⲓ ⲡ̅ⲟ̅ⲥ̅ ⲡⲁⲛⲟⲩϯ ⲙⲁ ⲫⲟⲩⲱⲓⲛⲓ ⲛ̀ⲛⲁⲃⲁⲗ ⲙⲏⲡⲱⲥ ⲛ̀ⲧⲁϩⲱⲣⲡ ϧⲉⲛ ⲫⲙⲟⲩ.

Ⲁ̀ⲛⲟⲕ ⲇⲉ ⲁⲓⲉⲣϩⲉⲗⲡⲓⲥ ⲉ̀ⲡⲉⲕⲛⲁⲓ : ⲡⲁϩⲏⲧ ⲛⲁⲑⲉⲗⲏⲗ ⲉ̀ϩ̀ⲣⲏⲓ ⲉ̀ϫⲉⲛ ⲡⲉⲕⲛⲟϩⲉⲙ . ⲁ̅ⲗ.

صومس صوتيم إروى إبتشويس بانووتى ما إفوؤأوينى إننافال مى بوس إنطاهورب خين إفموو. أنوك ذيه إينرهيلبيس إبيك ناى : باهيت نا ثيليل إإهري إيجين بيك نوهيم . الليلويا .

(مز 12 : 4 و 6)

أنظر استجب لي يا ربى وإلهى . أنر عينى لئلا أنام فى الموت . أما أنا فعلى رحمتك توكلت. يبتهج قلبى بخلاصك . الليلويا .

Introduction to the Gospel, Page: 8 | مقدمة الأنجيل ، صفحة :

The Gospel

Ⲉⲩⲁⲅⲅⲉⲗⲓⲟⲛ Ⲕⲁⲧⲁ Ⲗⲟⲩⲕⲁⲛ Ⲕⲉⲫ ⲓ̅ⲅ̅ : ⲗ̅ⲁ̅ ⲱⲃⲗ

Luke 13:31-35

On that very day some Pharisees came, saying to Him, "Get out and depart from here, for Herod wants to kill You." And He said to them, "Go, tell that fox, 'Behold, I cast out demons and perform cures today and tomorrow, and the third day I shall be perfected.' Nevertheless I must journey today, tomorrow, and the day following; for it cannot be that a prophet should perish outside of Jerusalem. "O Jerusalem, Jerusalem, the one who kills the prophets and stones those who are sent to her! How often I wanted to gather your children together, as a hen gathers her brood under her wings, but you were not willing! See! Your house is left to you desolate; and assuredly, I say to you, you shall not see Me until the time comes when you say, 'BLESSED IS HE WHO COMES IN THE NAME OF THE LORD!' " Glory be to God forever, Amen.

Ⲛ̀ϩⲣⲏⲓ ⲇⲉ ϧⲉⲛ ⲡⲓⲉϩⲟⲟⲩ ⲉⲧⲉ ⲙ̀ⲙⲁⲩ ⲁⲩⲓ̀ ϩⲁⲣⲟϥ ⲛ̀ϫⲉ ϩⲁⲛⲫⲁⲣⲓⲥⲉⲟⲥ ⲉⲩϫⲱ ⲙ̀ⲙⲟⲥ ⲛⲁϥ : ϫⲉ ⲙⲁϣⲉ ⲛⲁⲕ ⲉ̀ⲃⲟⲗ ⲟⲩⲟϩ ϩⲱⲗ ⲉ̀ⲃⲟⲗ ⲧⲁⲓ ϫⲉ Ⲏⲣⲱⲇⲏⲥ ϥ̀ⲟⲩⲱϣ ⲉ̀ϧⲟⲑⲃⲉⲕ. Ⲟⲩⲟϩ ⲡⲉϫⲁϥ ⲛⲱⲟⲩ ϫⲉ ⲙⲁϣⲉ ⲛⲱⲧⲉⲛ ⲁ̀ϫⲟⲥ ⲛ̀ⲧⲁⲓⲃⲁϣⲟⲣ : ϫⲉ ϩⲏⲡⲡⲉ ϯϩⲓ ⲇⲉⲙⲱⲛ ⲉ̀ⲃⲟⲗ : ⲟⲩⲟϩ ϯⲧⲱⲕ ⲛ̀ϩⲁⲛⲧⲁⲗϭⲟ ⲙ̀ⲫⲟⲟⲩ ⲛⲉⲙ ⲣⲁⲥϯ ⲟⲩⲟϩ ϧⲉⲛ ⲡⲓⲙⲁϩ ϣⲟⲙⲧ ϯⲛⲁϫⲱⲕ ⲉ̀ⲃⲟⲗ. Ⲡⲗⲏⲛ ϩⲱⲧ ⲉ̀ⲣⲟⲓ ⲡⲉ ⲛ̀ⲧⲁⲉⲣ ⲫⲟⲟⲩ ⲛⲉⲙ ⲣⲁⲥϯ ⲟⲩⲟϩ ⲡⲉⲑⲛⲟⲩ ⲛ̀ⲧⲁϣⲉⲛⲏⲓ : ϫⲉ ⲛ̀ⲥ̀ⲭⲏ ⲁⲛ ⲛ̀ⲧⲉ ⲟⲩⲡⲣⲟⲫⲏⲧⲏⲥ ⲧⲁⲕⲟ ⲥⲁⲃⲟⲗ ⲛ̀Ⲓⲗⲏⲙ. Ⲓⲗⲏⲙ Ⲓⲗⲏⲙ ⲑⲏⲉⲧϧⲱⲧⲉⲃ ⲛ̀ⲛⲓⲡⲣⲟⲫⲏⲧⲏⲥ ⲟⲩⲟϩ ⲉⲧϩⲓ ⲱⲛⲓ ⲛ̀ⲛⲏ ⲉⲧⲁⲩⲟⲩⲟⲣⲡⲟⲩ ϩⲁⲣⲟⲥ : ⲟⲩⲏⲣ ⲛ̀ⲥⲟⲡ ⲁⲓⲟⲩⲱϣ ⲉ̀ⲑⲟⲩⲏⲧ ⲛⲉ ϣⲏⲣⲓ ⲙ̀ⲫⲣⲏϯ ⲛ̀ⲟⲩⲁⲗⲏⲧ ⲙ̀ⲡⲉϥⲙⲟⲥ ϧⲉⲛ ⲛⲉϥⲧⲉϩ ⲟⲩⲟϩ ⲙ̀ⲡⲉⲧⲉⲛⲟⲩⲱϣ. Ϩⲏⲡⲡⲉ ⲓⲥ ⲡⲉⲧⲉⲛⲏⲓ ⲉϥⲭⲁϥ ⲛⲱⲧⲉⲛ ⲉϥϣⲱϥ : ϯϫⲱ ⲇⲉ ⲙ̀ⲙⲟⲥ ⲛⲱⲧⲉⲛ ϫⲉ ⲛ̀ⲛⲉⲧⲉⲛⲛⲁⲩ ⲉ̀ⲣⲟⲓ ⲓⲥϫⲉⲛ ϯⲛⲟⲩ : ϣⲁⲧⲉⲧⲉⲛϫⲟⲥ ϫⲉ ϥ̀ⲥⲙⲁⲣⲱⲟⲩⲧ ⲛ̀ϫⲉ ⲫⲏⲉⲑⲛⲟⲩ ϧⲉⲛ ⲫ̀ⲣⲁⲛ ⲙ̀ⲡⲟ̅ⲥ̅. ⲟⲩⲱϣⲧ ⲙ̀ⲡⲓⲉⲩⲁⲅⲅⲉⲗⲓⲟⲛ ⲉⲑⲟⲩ.

(لوقا 13 : 31 ألخ)

وفى ذلك اليوم جاء إليه قوم من الفريسيين وقالوا له: أخرج واذهب من ههنا فأن هيرودس يريد قتلك . فقال لهم: اذهبوا وقولوا لهذا الثعلب، ها أنا أخرج الشياطين وأتمم الشفاء اليوم وغداً وفى اليوم الثالث أكمل . ولكن ينبغى لي أن أقيم اليوم وغداً وفى اليوم الآتى اذهب ، لأنه لا يهلك نبى خارج عن أورشليم . يا أورشليم يا أورشليم يا قاتلة الأنبياء وراجمة المرسلين إليها . كم من مرة أردت أن أجمع بنيك كما يجمع الطائر فراخه تحت جناحيه فلم تريدوا . هوذا بيتكم يترك لكم خراباً لا ترونني من الآن حتى تقولوا مبارك الآتى باسم الرب . والمجد لله دائماً .

Introduction to the Exposition, Page: 9 | مقدمة الطرح ، صفحة :

Exposition

On this day some people came and told Him that king Herod wants to kill him saying, "Teacher, get out of here and leave this area because this irreverent Herod wants to kill you." Jesus said to them: "Go and tell this wicked fox that I will heal many today and tomorrow and in the coming days. It is written that no prophet shall perish outside Jerusalem. O Jerusalem, Jerusalem, the one who kills the prophets and stones those that are sent to you; how often I wanted to gather your children together and you were not willing. Behold your house will be desolate forever. For those who hear Me I say, from now on you shall not see Me until you all say in one voice, Blessed is he who comes in the name of the Lord God."

طرح

فى ذلك اليوم وافاه قوم واخبروه عن هيرودس الملك ، قائلين: يا معلم أخرج من ههنا فأن هيرودس المارق يريد قتلك . فأجاب وقال للذى قال له : امض وقل لهذا الثعلب الشرير إنى أكمل شفاء كثيرين اليوم وغداً وفى اليوم الآتى . فقد كتب أنه لا يهلك نبى خارجاً عن أورشليم . يا أورشليم يا أورشليم يا قاتلة الأنبياء وراجمة المرسلين ، كم من مرة أردت أن أجمع بنيك فلم تريدى . هوذا أترك بيتكم خراباً إلى كل الأجيال. أقول لكم أيها الذين تسمعونني أنكم لا ترونني منذ هذا اليوم حتى تقولوا كلكم من فم واحد مبارك الآتى باسم الرب الإله.

(North side) Christ our Savior; has come and has borne suffering; that through His Passion; He may save us.

(مرد بحرى) المسيح مخلصنا جاء وتألم عنا لكى بألامه يخلصنا .

(South side) Let us glorify Him; and exalt His Name; for He had mercy on us; according to His great mercy.

(مرد قبلى) فلنمجده ونرفع اسمه لأنه صنع معنا رحمة كعظيم رحمته .

| The Conclusion of the Exposition, Page: 9 | ختام الطرح ، صفحة : 9 |

الساعة السادسة من ليلة الثلاثاء من البصخة المقدسة
The Sixth Hour of Tuesday Eve of the Holy Pascha

Hosea 4:15-5:7

But you, O Israel, be not ignorant, and go not to Gilgal, O men of Judah, and go not up to Beth Aven, and swear not by the living Lord. For Israel was maddened like a mad heifer; now the Lord will feed them as a lamb in a wide place. Ephraim, joined with idols, has laid stumbling blocks in his own way. He has chosen the Canaanites; they have grievously gone a-whoring; they have loved dishonor through her insolence. You are a blast of wind in her wings, and they shall be ashamed because of their altars. Hear these things, you priests, and attend, O house of Israel; and hearken, O house of the king; for the controversy is with you, because you have been a snare in Mizpah, and as a net spread on Tabor, which they that hunt the prey have fixed; but I will correct you. I know Ephraim, and Israel is not far from Me: for now Ephraim has gone grievously a-whoring, Israel is defiled. They have not framed their counsels to return to their God, for the spirit of fornication is in them, and they have not known the Lord. And the pride of Israel shall be brought low before his face, and Israel and Ephraim shall fall in their iniquities; and Judah also shall fall with them. They shall go with sheep and calves diligently to seek the Lord; but they shall not find Him, for He has withdrawn Himself from them. For they have forsaken the Lord; for strange children have been born to them. Now shall the cankerworm devour them and their heritage. Glory be to the Holy Trinity. Amen

(من هوشع النبى 4 : 15 - 5 : 1 - 7)
وأما أنت يا إسرائيل فلا تكن جاهلاً . ويا يهوذا لا تدخل الجلجال ولا تذهبوا إلى الظلم . ولا تحلفوا بالرب الحى . لأنه قد جمح إسرائيل كعجلة جامحة . فالآن يرعاهم الرب كحمل فى موضع رحب خليل الأصنام افرايم قد ترك له شكاً فاطاعوا الكنعانيين وزنوا زنى إلى الآخر وأحبوا الهوام بالتعاظم وأنت فى جناحيك هبوب ريح وسيخزون فى مذبحهم . إسمعوا لهذا أيها الكهنة وانصتوا يا بيت إسرائيل . واصغوا يا بيت الملك . لأن الحكم موضع قبالتكم . إذ قد صرتم فخاً للمحرس ، وكالشبكة المنصوبة على تابور تلك التى ينصبها الصيادون للصيد ، فأنا مؤدبكم. أنا عرفت افرايم ولم يخف عنى إسرائيل لأن الآن قد زنى افرايم وتنجس إسرائيل . ولم يوجهوا أفكار قلوبهم ليرجعوا إلى إلههم . لأن روح الزنى فيهم والرب لم يعرفوه . وسيغطى إسرائيل وجهه بذراعه من الخزى . فيتعثر إسرائيل وافرايم بالظلم ويتعثر يهوذا أيضاً معهم ويذهبون بغنم وثيران ليطلبوا الرب فلا يجدونه لأنه قد تنحى عنهم . بما أنهم قد إنصرفوا عن الرب وصارت لهم ثيران وكان لهم بنين غرباء . فالآن يأكلهم السوس مع ميراثهم . مجداً للثالوث القدوس .

Pascha Praise - A (12 times), Page: 6   : تسبحة البصخة A (12 مرة) ، صفحة

The Psalm
Ⲯⲁⲗⲙⲟⲥ ⲋ̅ : ⲁ̅ ⲛⲉⲙ ⲃ̅

Psalms 90:1-2

You are my helper and my refuge; my God; I will trust in Him. For He shall deliver you from the snare of the fowler, and from every troublesome matter. Alleluia.

Ⲡⲁⲙⲁ ⲙ̀ⲫⲱⲧ ⲡⲁⲛⲟⲩϯ ϯⲛⲉⲣϩⲉⲗⲡⲓⲥ ⲉⲣⲟϥ : ϫⲉ ⲛ̀ⲑⲟϥ ⲉϥⲉⲛⲁϩⲙⲉⲧ ⲉⲃⲟⲗ ϩⲁ ⲡⲓϥⲁϣ ⲛ̀ⲧⲉ ⲡⲓⲣⲉϥϫⲱⲣⲝ : ⲛⲉⲙ ⲉⲃⲟⲗ ϩⲁ ⲟⲩⲥⲁϫⲓ ⲛ̀ⲣⲉϥϣⲑⲟⲣⲧⲉⲣ . ⲁ̅ⲗ .

باما إمفوت بانووتى تينا إرهيلبيسس إروف : جيه أنثوف إفناهميف إيفول ها : بى فاش إنتيه بى ريف جورج : نيم إيفول ها أووصاجى إنريف إشطورتير . الليلويا .

(مز 90 : 1 و 2)
ملجأى إلهى فأتكل عليه . لأنه ينجينى من فخ الصياد . ومن كلمة مقلقلة . الليلويا .

Introduction to the Gospel, Page: 8   : مقدمة الآنجيل ، صفحة

The Gospel

Ⲉⲩⲁⲅⲅⲉⲗⲓⲟⲛ Ⲕⲁⲧⲁ Ⲗⲟⲩⲕⲁⲛ Ⲕⲉⲫ ⲕ̅ⲁ̅ : ⲗ̅ⲁ̅ ϣⲃⲗ̅

Luke 21:34-38

"But take heed to yourselves, lest your hearts be weighed down with carousing, drunkenness, and cares of this life, and that Day come on you unexpectedly. For it will come as a snare on all those who dwell on the face of the whole earth. Watch therefore, and pray always that you may be counted worthy to escape all these things that will come to pass, and to stand before the Son of Man." And in the daytime He was teaching in the temple, but at night He went out and stayed on the mountain called Olivet. Then early in the morning all the people came to Him in the temple to hear Him. Glory be to God forever, Amen.

Ⲙⲁϩⲑⲏⲧⲉⲛ ⲇⲉ ⲉⲣⲱⲧⲉⲛ ⲙⲏⲡⲟⲧⲉ ⲛ̀ⲧⲟⲩϩⲣⲟϣ ⲛ̀ϫⲉ ⲛⲉⲧⲉⲛϩⲏⲧ ϧⲉⲛ ⲟⲩⲃⲓⲏⲛ ⲛⲉⲙ ⲟⲩⲑⲓϧⲓ ⲛⲉⲙ ϩⲁⲛⲣⲱⲟⲩϣ ⲙ̀ⲃⲓⲱⲧⲓⲕⲟⲛ ⲟⲩⲟϩ ⲛ̀ⲟⲩϩⲟⲧ ϧⲉⲛ ⲟⲩϩⲟⲧ ⲛ̀ⲧⲉϥ ⲉϫⲉⲛ ⲑⲏⲛⲟⲩ ⲛ̀ϫⲉ ⲡⲓⲉϩⲟⲟⲩ ⲉⲧⲉ ⲙ̀ⲙⲁⲩ . Ⲙ̀ⲫⲣⲏϯ ⲛ̀ⲟⲩⲫⲁϣ ⲉϥⲉⲓ̀ ⲅⲁⲣ ⲉϫⲉⲛ ⲟⲩⲟⲛ ⲛⲓⲃⲉⲛ ⲉⲧϩⲉⲙⲥⲓ ϩⲓϫⲉⲛ ⲡ̀ϩⲟ ⲙ̀ⲡⲕⲁϩⲓ ⲧⲏⲣϥ : ⲣⲱⲓⲥ ⲟⲩⲛ ⲛ̀ⲥⲏⲟⲩ ⲛⲓⲃⲉⲛ ⲉⲣⲉⲧⲉⲛⲧⲱⲃϩ ϩⲓⲛⲁ ⲛ̀ⲧⲉⲧⲉⲛϣϫⲉⲙϫⲟⲙ ⲉⲉⲣ ⲥⲁⲃⲟⲗ ⲉ̀ⲛⲁⲓ ⲧⲏⲣⲟⲩ ⲉⲑⲛⲁϣⲱⲡⲓ : ⲟⲩⲟϩ ⲛ̀ⲧⲉⲧⲉⲛⲟϩⲓ ⲉ̀ⲣⲁⲧⲉⲛ ⲑⲏⲛⲟⲩ ⲙ̀ⲡⲉⲙ̀ⲑⲟ ⲙ̀ⲡ̀ϣⲏⲣⲓ ⲙ̀ⲫⲣⲱⲙⲓ . Ⲛⲁϥⲓⲣⲓ ⲇⲉ ⲛ̀ⲛⲓⲉϩⲟⲟⲩ ⲉϥϯⲥⲃⲱ ϧⲉⲛ ⲡⲓⲉⲣⲫⲉⲓ : ⲛⲓⲉϫⲱⲣϩ ⲇⲉ ⲛⲁϥⲛⲏⲟⲩ ⲉ̀ⲃⲟⲗ ⲉϥⲙ̀ⲧⲟⲛ ⲙ̀ⲙⲟϥ ϩⲓϫⲉⲛ ⲡⲓⲧⲱⲟⲩ ⲫⲏⲉⲧⲟⲩⲙⲟⲩϯ ⲉ̀ⲣⲟϥ ϫⲉ ⲫⲁ ⲛⲓϫⲱⲓⲧ : ⲟⲩⲟϩ ⲡⲓⲗⲁⲟⲥ ⲧⲏⲣϥ ⲛⲁϥϣⲱⲣⲡ ⲙ̀ⲙⲟϥ ϩⲁⲣⲟϥ ϧⲉⲛ ⲡⲓⲉⲣⲫⲉⲓ ⲉ̀ⲥⲱⲧⲉⲙ ⲉ̀ⲣⲟϥ . ⲟⲩⲱϣⲧ ⲙ̀ⲡⲓⲉⲩⲁⲅⲅⲉⲗⲓⲟⲛ ⲉⲑⲟⲩ .

(لوقا 21 : 34 ألخ)

فاحترزوا لأنفسكم لئلاً تثقل قلوبكم من الشبع والسكر والهموم الدنيوية فيقبل عليكم بغتة ذلك اليوم. لأنه يأتى كالفخ على جميع الجالسين على وجه الأرض كلها . اسهروا إذن وتضرعوا فى كل حين لكى تقووا على الهرب من هذه الأمور المزمعة أن تصير وتقفوا أمام إبن الإنسان . وكان فى النهار يعلم فى الهيكل وفى الليل يخرج ويبيت فى الجبل الذى يدعى الزيتون . وكان جميع الشعب يبكرون إليه فى الهيكل ليسمعوا منه . والمجد لله دائماً .

Introduction to the Exposition, Page: 9   : مقدمة الطرح ، صفحة

Exposition

طــرح

As an attending physician, Jesus was treating us free. He reminds us that excessive eating taxes the heart and saps the power from the body. In a parallel way, engrossment in worldly concerns could bring on us vicious passions, cause us to stray away from the fear of God, the wicked (Satan) can overwhelm us, drive us away from the path of salvation, diminish the awareness of our soul's salvation, and subject us to the dominion of death just as the prey falls in the trap. Be alert and present fruits worthy of righteousness and atonement so that you may stand in front of our Judge and Savior Jesus. He was teaching the public in the temple. By night, He rested on the Mount of Olives. By day, He went down to Jerusalem where people gathered early to listen to His teachings that are replete with righteousness. Those who heard Him, hurried to drink from the spring of His sweet water. As the Book that testifies to His coming says: "He is the healthy nourishing food for those who believe in Him."

كمثل طبيب مداو كان المسيح إلهنا يداوى مجاناً معلماً ان زيادة الأكل تثقل القلوب وتقطع القوة من الجسد والاهتمام الدنيوى أيضاً يجلب على الإنسان شروراً كثيرة ويحيد بالإنسان عن مخافة الله فيخنقه الشرير ويبعده عن طريق الخلاص ومعرفة خلاص نفسه ويوقعه فى سلطان الموت مثل الفخ الذى يخطف الفريسة . اسهروا أنتم أيضاً واصنعوا ثمرة تليق بالبر والتوبة لكى تكونوا واقفين أمام الديان يسوع المخلص . وكان يعلم الجموع فى الهيكل و فى الليل كان يستريح ، وكانت راحته فى جبل الزيتون ، وفى النهار كان يأتى إلى أورشليم . وكان جميع الشعب يبكرون إليه ليسمعوا تعاليمه المفعمة صلاحاً ، والذين سمعوا كانوا يسبقون إلى ينبوعه ويشربون منه الماء الحلو كما قال الكتاب الشاهد بمجيئه أنه الطعام الغير الفاسد المغذى لكل الذين يؤمنون به .

(North side) Christ our Savior; has come and has borne suffering; that through His Passion; He may save us.

(مرد بحرى) المسيح مخلصنا جاء وتألم عنا لكى بألامه يخلصنا .

(South side) Let us glorify Him; and exalt His Name; for He had mercy on us; according to His great mercy.

(مرد قبلى) فلنمجده ونرفه اسمه لأنه صنع معنا رحمة كعظيم رحمته .

The Conclusion of the Exposition, Page: 9   ختام الطرح ، صفحة :

الساعة التاسعة من ليلة الثلاثاء من البصخة المقدسة
The Ninth Hour of Tuesday Eve of the Holy Pascha

Hosea 10:12-11:2

Sow to yourselves for righteousness, gather in for the fruit of life; light for yourselves the light of knowledge; seek the Lord till the fruits of righteousness come upon you. For have you passed over ungodliness in silence, and reaped the sins of it? You have eaten false fruit; for you have trusted in your sins, in the abundance of your power. Therefore shall destruction rise up among your people, and all your strong places shall be ruined. As prince Shalman departed out of Beth Arbel, in the days of battle, when they dashed a mother to the ground upon the children, thus will I do to you, O house of Israel, because of the unrighteousness of your sins. Early in the morning were they cast off, the king of Israel has been cast off: for Israel is a child, and I loved him, and out of Egypt have I called his children *and my son*. As I called them, so they departed from My presence; they sacrificed to Baalam, and burnt incense to graven images. Glory be to the Holy Trinity. Amen

(من هوشع النبى ص 10 : 12 - 11 : 3)

إزرعوا لأنفسكم برأ ، أجنوا ثمرة الحياة. إستنيروا بنور المعرفة وأطلبوا الرب حتى يأتيكم ثمرة البر . لماذا سكتم على النفاق الذى فيكم وحصدتم ظلمكم وأكلتم ثمرة الكذب؟ لأنك توكلت على مركباتك وكثرة قوتك ، يقوم هلاك فى شعبك وتخرب جميع حصونك المسيحة كخروج بيت يربعام من أراخنة سليمان يوم الحرب ، إذ حطمت الأمهات مع البنين . هكذا أصنع بكم يا بيت إسرائيل أمامكم من قدام وجهى. لأن ظلمكم وشروركم طرحت ملك إسرائيل خارجاً . لأن إسرائيل صغير وأنا أحببته ودعوت إبنه و ابنى من مصر . فكما دعوتهم . هكذا ذهبوا عن وجهى فذبحوا للبعليم وبخروا للمنحوتات . مجداً للثالوث القدوس .

Pascha Praise - A (12 times), Page: 6   تسبحة البصخة A (12 مرة) ، صفحة :

The Psalm
Ψⲁⲗⲙⲟⲥ ⲗ̅ⲃ̅ : ⲓ ⲛⲉⲙ ⲓ̅ⲁ̅

Psalms 32:10-11

The Lord frustrates the counsels of the nations; He brings to nought also the reasonings of the people, and brings to nought the counsels of princes. But the counsel of the Lord endures forever, the thoughts of His heart from generation to generation. Alleluia.

Ⲡⲟ̅ⲥ̅ ⲛⲁϫⲉⲣ ⲛⲓⲥⲟϭⲛⲓ ⲛⲧⲉ ⲛⲓⲉⲑⲛⲟⲥ ⲉⲃⲟⲗ : ⲟⲩⲟⲟ ϥⲛⲁϣⲱϣϥ ⲛⲛⲓⲙⲟⲕⲙⲉⲕ ⲛⲧⲉ ⲟⲁⲛⲗⲁⲟⲥ : ⲟⲩⲟⲟ ϥⲛⲁϣⲱϣϥ ⲙ̀ⲡⲓⲥⲟϭⲛⲓ ⲛⲧⲉ ⲛⲓⲁⲣⲭⲱⲛ ⲡ̀ⲥⲟϭⲛⲓ ⲇⲉ ⲛ̀ⲑⲟϥ ⲙ̀ⲡⲟ̅ⲥ̅ ϣⲟⲡ ϣⲁ ⲉⲛⲉⲟ : ⲟⲩⲟⲟ ⲛⲓⲙⲟⲕⲙⲉⲕ ⲛⲧⲉ ⲡⲉϥⲟⲏⲧ ⲓⲥϫⲉⲛ ϫⲱⲟⲩ ϣⲁ ϫⲱⲟⲩ . ⲁ̅ⲗ̅ .

إبتشويس ناجر نى صوتشنى إنتيه نى إثنوس إيفول : أووه إفناشوشف إننى موكميك إنتيه هان نى لاؤس : أووه إفناشوشف إمبى صوتشنى إنتيه نى أرخون إبصوتشنى ذيه إنثوف إبتشويس شوب شا إينيه : أووه نى موكميك إنتيه بف هيت إسجين جوأوو شا جوأوو . الليلويا .

(مز 32 : 10 و11)

الرب يشتت أراء الأمم ويرذل أفكار الشعوب ، ويرفض مؤامرة الرؤساء . وأما مشورة الرب كائنة إلى الأبد ، وأفكار قلبه من جيل إلى جيل . الليلويا .

Introduction to the Gospel, Page: 8   مقدمة الأنجيل ، صفحة :

The Gospel
Ⲉⲩⲁⲅⲅⲉⲗⲓⲟⲛ Ⲕⲁⲧⲁ Ⲗⲟⲩⲕⲁⲛ Ⲕⲉⲫ ⲓ̅ⲁ̅ : ⲗ̅ⲍ̅ - ⲛ̅ⲃ̅

Luke 11:37-52

And as He spoke, a certain Pharisee asked Him to dine with him. So He went in and sat down to eat. When the Pharisee saw it, he marveled

Ⲉϥⲥⲁϫⲓ ⲁϥϯⲟⲟ ⲉⲣⲟϥ ⲛϫⲉ ⲟⲩⲫⲁⲣⲓⲥⲉⲟⲥ ⲟⲟⲡⲱⲥ ⲛ̀ⲧⲉϥⲟⲩⲱⲙ ⲟⲁⲧⲟⲧϥ ⲟⲩⲟⲟ ⲉⲧⲁϥϣⲉ ⲉⲟⲟⲩⲛ ⲁϥⲣⲱⲧⲉⲃ . ⲡⲓⲫⲁⲣⲓⲥⲉⲟⲥ ⲇⲉ ⲉⲧⲁϥⲛⲁⲩ ⲁϥⲉⲣ ϣⲫⲏⲣⲓ ϫⲉ ⲙ̀ⲡⲉϥϭⲓⲱⲙⲥ

(لوقا 11 : 37 - 52)

وفيما هو يتكلم سأله فريسى أن يأكل عنده . فدخل وإتكأ . وأما الفريسى فلما رأى أنه لم

that He had not first washed before dinner. Then the Lord said to him, "Now you Pharisees make the outside of the cup and dish clean, but your inward part is full of greed and wickedness. Foolish ones! Did not He who made the outside make the inside also? But rather give alms of such things as you have; then indeed all things are clean to you. "But woe to you Pharisees! For you tithe mint and rue and all manner of herbs, and pass by justice and the love of God. These you ought to have done, without leaving the others undone. Woe to you Pharisees! For you love the best seats in the synagogues and greetings in the marketplaces. Woe to you, scribes and Pharisees, hypocrites! For you are like graves which are not seen, and the men who walk over them are not aware of them." Then one of the lawyers answered and said to Him, "Teacher, by saying these things You reproach us also." And He said, "Woe to you also, lawyers! For you load men with burdens hard to bear, and you yourselves do not touch the burdens with one of your fingers. Woe to you! For you build the tombs of the prophets, and your fathers killed them. In fact, you bear witness that you approve the deeds of your fathers; for they indeed killed them, and you build their tombs. Therefore the wisdom of God also said, 'I will send them prophets and apostles, and some of them they will kill and persecute,' that the blood of all the prophets which was shed from the foundation of the world may be required of this generation, from the blood of Abel to the blood of Zechariah who perished between

ⲛ̀ϣⲟⲣⲡ ϧⲁϫⲉⲛ ⲡⲓⲟⲩⲱⲙ . Ⲡⲉϫⲁϥ ⲇⲉ ⲛⲁϥ ⲛ̀ϫⲉ ⲡⲟ̅ⲥ̅ ϫⲉ ϯⲛⲟⲩ ⲛ̀ⲑⲱⲧⲉⲛ ϧⲁ ⲛⲓⲫⲁⲣⲓⲥⲉⲟⲥ ⲧⲉⲧⲉⲛⲧⲟⲩⲃⲟ ⲥⲁⲃⲟⲗ ⲙ̀ⲡⲓⲁⲫⲟⲧ ⲛⲉⲙ ⲡⲓⲃⲓⲛⲁⲝ : ⲥⲁϧⲟⲩⲛ ⲇⲉ ⲙ̀ⲙⲱⲟⲩ ⲙⲉϩ ⲛ̀ϩⲱⲗⲉⲙ ⲛⲉⲙ ⲡⲟⲛⲏⲣⲓⲁ . Ⲛⲓⲁⲧϩⲏⲧ ⲙⲏ ⲫⲏ ⲁⲛ ⲉⲧⲁϥⲑⲁⲙⲓⲉ ⲥⲁⲃⲟⲗ ⲛ̀ⲑⲟϥ ⲟⲛ ⲁϥⲑⲁⲙⲓⲉ ⲥⲁϧⲟⲩⲛ . Ⲡⲗⲏⲛ ⲛⲏⲉⲧϣⲟⲡ ⲙⲏⲓⲧⲟⲩ ⲉ̀ⲑⲙⲉⲧⲛⲁⲏⲧ ⲟⲩⲟϩ ⲓⲥ ϩⲱⲃ ⲛⲓⲃⲉⲛ ⲥⲉⲧⲟⲩⲃⲏⲟⲩⲧ ⲛⲱⲧⲉⲛ . ⲁⲗⲗⲁ ⲟⲩⲟⲓ ⲛⲱⲧⲉⲛ ⲛⲓⲫⲁⲣⲓⲥⲉⲟⲥ ϫⲉ ⲧⲉⲧⲉⲛϯ ⲙ̀ⲫⲣⲉⲙⲏⲧ ⲙ̀ⲡⲓⲁⲃⲓⲛ ⲛ̀ⲥⲟⲓ ⲛⲉⲙ ⲡⲓⲃⲁϣⲟⲩϣ ⲛⲉⲙ ⲟⲩⲟϯ ⲛⲓⲃⲉⲛ ⲟⲩⲟϩ ⲧⲉⲧⲉⲛⲭⲱ ⲛ̀ⲥⲱⲧⲉⲛ ⲙ̀ⲡⲓϩⲁⲡ ⲛⲉⲙ ϯⲁⲅⲁⲡⲏ ⲛ̀ⲧⲉ Ⲫϯ : ⲛⲁⲓ ⲇⲉ ⲛⲁⲥⲉⲙⲡ̀ϣⲁ ⲛ̀ⲧⲉⲧⲉⲛⲁⲓⲧⲟⲩ ⲟⲩⲟϩ ⲛⲓⲕⲉⲭⲱⲟⲩⲛⲓ ⲛ̀ⲧⲉⲧⲉⲛϣ̀ⲧⲉⲙⲭⲁⲩ ⲛ̀ⲥⲁ ⲑⲏⲛⲟⲩ . Ⲟⲩⲟⲓ ⲛⲱⲧⲉⲛ ⲛⲓⲫⲁⲣⲓⲥⲟⲥ ϫⲉ ⲧⲉⲧⲉⲛⲙⲉⲓ ⲛ̀ⲛⲓϣⲟⲣⲡ ⲙ̀ⲙⲁ ⲛ̀ϩⲉⲙⲥⲓ ϧⲉⲛ ⲛⲓⲥⲩⲛⲁⲅⲱⲅⲏ ⲛⲉⲙ ⲛⲓⲁⲥⲡⲁⲥⲙⲟⲥ ϧⲉⲛ ⲛⲓⲁⲅⲱⲣⲁ . Ⲟⲩⲟⲓ ⲛⲱⲧⲉⲛ ⲛⲓⲥⲁϧ ⲛⲉⲙ ⲛⲓⲫⲁⲣⲥⲉⲟⲥ ⲛⲓϣⲟⲃⲓ ϫⲉ ⲧⲉⲧⲉⲛⲟⲓ ⲙ̀ⲫⲣⲏϯ ⲛ̀ⲛⲓⲙ̀ϩⲁⲩ ⲉ̀ⲧⲉ ⲛ̀ⲥⲉⲟⲩⲱⲛ ⲉ̀ⲃⲟⲗ ⲁⲛ ⲟⲩⲟϩ ⲛⲓⲣⲱⲙⲓ ⲉⲑⲙⲟϣⲓ ϩⲓϫⲱⲟⲩ ⲛ̀ⲥⲉⲉ̀ⲙⲓ ⲁⲛ : ⲁϥⲉⲣⲟⲩⲱ ⲇⲉ ⲛ̀ϫⲉ ⲟⲩⲁⲓ ⲛ̀ⲛⲓⲛⲟⲙⲓⲕⲟⲥ ⲡⲉϫⲁϥ ⲛⲁϥ ϫⲉ ⲡⲓⲣⲉϥϯⲥⲃⲱ ⲛⲁⲓ ⲉⲕⲭⲱ ⲙ̀ⲙⲱⲟⲩ ⲉⲕϯϣⲱϣ ⲙ̀ⲙⲟⲛ ϩⲱⲛ . Ⲛ̀ⲑⲟϥ ⲇⲉ ⲡⲉϫⲁϥ ⲛⲁϥ ϫⲉ ⲛ̀ⲑⲱⲧⲉⲛ ϩⲱⲧⲉⲛ ϧⲁ ⲛⲓⲛⲟⲙⲓⲕⲟⲥ : ⲟⲩⲟⲓ ⲛⲱⲧⲉⲛ ϫⲉ ⲧⲉⲧⲉⲛⲧⲁⲗⲟ ⲛ̀ϩⲁⲛⲉⲧⲫⲱⲟⲩⲓ ⲉⲩⲙⲟⲕϩ ⲛ̀ϥⲓⲧⲟⲩ ⲉ̀ϫⲉⲛ ⲛⲓⲣⲱⲙⲓ ⲟⲩⲟϩ ⲛ̀ⲑⲱⲧⲉⲛ ⲧⲉⲧⲉⲛϭⲓ ⲛⲉⲙ ⲛⲓⲉⲧⲫⲱⲟⲩⲓ ⲁⲛ ⲛ̀ⲟⲩⲁⲓ ⲛ̀ⲛⲉⲧⲉⲛⲧⲏⲃ ⲟⲩⲟⲓ ⲛⲱⲧⲉⲛ ϫⲉ ⲧⲉⲧⲉⲛⲕⲱⲧ ⲛ̀ⲛⲓⲙ̀ϩⲁⲩ ⲛ̀ⲧⲉ ⲛⲓⲡ̀ⲣⲟⲫⲏⲧⲏⲥ ⲛⲉⲧⲉⲛⲓⲟϯ ⲇⲉ ⲁⲩϧⲟⲑⲃⲟⲩ . Ϩⲁⲣⲁ ⲧⲉⲧⲉⲛⲉⲣⲙⲉⲑⲣⲉ ⲟⲩⲟϩ ⲧⲉⲧⲉⲛϯⲙⲁϯ ⲉ̀ϫⲉⲛ ⲛⲓϩ̀ⲃⲏⲟⲩⲓ ⲛ̀ⲧⲉ ⲛⲉⲧⲉⲛⲓⲟϯ : ϫⲉ ⲛ̀ⲑⲱⲟⲩ ⲙⲉⲛ ⲁⲩϧⲟⲑⲃⲟⲩ ⲛ̀ⲑⲱⲧⲉⲛ ⲧⲉⲧⲉⲛⲕⲱⲧ ⲛ̀ⲛⲟⲩⲙ̀ϩⲁⲩ . Ⲉⲑⲃⲉ ⲫⲁⲓ ⲁ ϯⲕⲉⲥⲟⲫⲓⲁ ⲛ̀ⲧⲉ Ⲫϯ ϫⲟⲥ : ϫⲉ ϯⲛⲁⲟⲩⲱⲣⲡ ϩⲁⲣⲱⲟⲩ ⲛ̀ϩⲁⲛⲡ̀ⲣⲟⲫⲏⲧⲏⲥ ⲛⲉⲙ ϩⲁⲛⲁⲡⲟⲥⲧⲟⲗⲟⲥ ⲟⲩⲟϩ ⲉⲩⲉ̀ϧⲱⲧⲉⲃ ⲉ̀ⲃⲟⲗ ⲛ̀ϧⲏⲧⲟⲩ ⲟⲩⲟϩ ⲉⲩⲉ̀ϭⲟϫⲓ ⲛ̀ⲥⲱⲟⲩ : ϩⲓⲛⲁ ⲛ̀ⲥⲉⲃⲓ ⲙ̀ⲡⲉⲙⲡ̀ϣⲓϣ ⲙ̀ⲡⲥ̀ⲛⲟϥ ⲛ̀ⲛⲓⲡ̀ⲣⲟⲫⲏⲧⲏⲥ ⲧⲏⲣⲟⲩ ⲉⲧⲁⲩⲫⲟⲛϥ ⲉ̀ⲃⲟⲗ ⲓⲥϫⲉⲛ ⲧ̀ⲕⲁⲧⲁⲃⲟⲗⲏ ⲙ̀ⲡⲓⲕⲟⲥⲙⲟⲥ ⲛ̀ⲧⲟⲧⲥ ⲛ̀ⲧⲁⲓⲅⲉⲛⲉⲁ̀ : ⲓⲥϫⲉⲛ ⲡ̀ⲥⲛⲟϥ ⲛ̀Ⲁⲃⲉⲗ ⲡⲓⲑⲙⲏⲓ ϣⲁ ⲡⲥ̀ⲛⲟϥ ⲛ̀Ⲍⲁⲭⲁⲣⲓⲁⲥ ⲡ̀ϣⲏⲣⲓ ⲙ̀Ⲃⲁⲣⲁⲭⲓⲁⲥ ⲫⲏⲉⲧⲁⲩⲧⲁⲕⲟϥ ⲟⲩ ⲧⲉ ⲡⲓⲙⲁⲛⲉⲣϣⲱⲟⲩϣⲓ

يغتسل أولاً قبل الأكل تعجب . فقال له الرب: أنتم الآن معشر الفريسيين تطهرون خارج الكأس والصحفة وأما داخلهما فمملوء اختطافاً وخبثاً . أيها الجهال أليس الذى صنع الخارج صنع الداخل أيضاً. بل أعطوا ما عندكم صدقة فهوذا كل شئ يتطهر لكم . ولكن ويل لكم أيها الفريسيون لأنكم تعشرون النعنع والسذاب وكل بقل وتتجاوزون حكم الله ومحبته . وكان ينبغى أن تفعلوا هذه ولا تتركوا تلك . ويل لكم أيها الفريسيون لأنكم تحبون أوائل المجالس فى المجامع والتحيات فى الأسواق . ويل لكم أيها الكتبة و الفريسيون المراؤن لأنكم مثل القبور المختفية. والناس يمشون عليها ولا يعلمون . فأجاب واحد من الناموسيين وقال له: أيها المعلم أنك بقولك هذا تشتمنا نحن أيضاً . أما هو فقال له: وأنتم أيضاً أيها الناموسيون ويل لكم لأنكم تحملون الناس أحمالاً ثقيلة وأنتم لا تمسون تلك الأحمال بأحدى أصابعكم ، ويل لكم فأنكم تشيدون قبور الأنبياء الذين قتلهم أباؤكم . فأنتم إذا تشهدون وتسرون بأعمال آباؤكم . لأنهم هم قتلوهم وأنتم تبنون قبورهم. لذلك أيضاً قالت حكمة الله: أنى أرسل إليهم أنبياء ورسلاً فيقتلون منهم ويطردون ، لكى يطلب من هذا الجيل دم جميع الأنبياء الذى سفك منذ انشاء العالم ، من دم هابيل الصديق إلى دم

the altar and the temple. Yes, I say to you, it shall be required of this generation. "Woe to you lawyers! For you have taken away the key of knowledge. You did not enter in yourselves, and those who were entering in you hindered." Glory be to God forever, Amen.

ⲛⲉⲙ ⲡⲓⲏⲓ ⲥⲉϯϫⲱ ⲙ̅ⲙⲟⲥ ⲛⲱⲧⲉⲛ ϫⲉ ⲥⲉⲛⲁⲕⲱϯ ⲛ̅ⲥⲱϥ ⲛ̅ⲧⲟⲧⲥ ⲛ̅ⲧⲁⲓⲅⲉⲛⲉⲁ . Ⲟⲩⲟⲓ ⲛⲱⲧⲉⲛ ⲛⲓⲛⲟⲙⲓⲕⲟⲥ ϫⲉ ⲁⲧⲉⲧⲉⲛⲱⲗⲓ ⲛ̅ⲛⲓϣⲟϣⲧ ⲛ̅ⲧⲉ ⲡ̅ⲥⲟⲩⲛ ⲛ̅ⲑⲱⲧⲉⲛ ⲙ̅ⲡⲉⲧⲉⲛⲓ ⲉ̇ϧⲟⲩⲛ ⲟⲩⲟϩ ⲛⲏⲉⲑⲛⲏⲟⲩ ⲉ̇ϧⲟⲩⲛ ⲉⲧⲉⲧⲉⲛⲉⲣⲕⲱⲗⲓⲛ ⲙ̅ⲙⲱⲟⲩ . ⲟⲩⲱϣⲧ ⲙ̅ⲡⲓⲉⲩⲁⲅⲅⲉⲗⲓⲟⲛ ⲉⲑⲩ .

زكريا بن براشيا الذى أهلك بين المذبح والبيت . نعم أقول لكم أنه يطلب من هذا الجيل . الويل لكم أيها الناموسيون لأنكم أخذتم مفاتيح المعرفة فما دخلتم أنتم والداخلون منعتموهم . والمجد لله دائماً .

Introduction to the Exposition, Page: 9   مقدمة الطرح ، صفحة : 9

Exposition

طرح

Listen to the merciful, compassionate, patient, who has great mercy when He catechizes us to be clean not only in our bodies but also in our hearts. The Pharisee who invited Jesus to dinner was puzzled at Him when He ate the bread without washing His hands. The Omniscient teacher said to him: "You Pharisees cleanse the outside of the cup but inside you are full of promiscuity, plunder, depredation and injustices. Give alms and just judgment and everything will be clean unto you." Let us be kind to God's creation. Thus, we may purify ourselves, bodies, and souls of all the filth of sins.

إسمعوا الرؤوف الرحوم الكثير الرحمة المتأنى ، كيف يوصينا أن نكون أطهاراً ، ليس فى أجسادنا فقط بل وفى قلوبنا أيضاً . لما تعجب منه ذلك الفريسى الذى سأله أن يأكل عنده لما رآه يأكل الخبز بغير طهر ولا غسل يد ، تكلم معه المعلم العارف بكل الأشياء قبل كونها قائلاً : أنتم يا معشر الفريسيين تطهرون خارج الكأس والطاس فأما داخلكم فإنه مملوء دعارة وإختطافاً وظلماً . اعطوا صدقة وحكماً عادلاً وكل شئ يتطهر لكم . فلنكن نحن رحومين على كل إنسان خلقه الله . وعند ذلك نطهر نفوسنا وأجسادنا وأرواحنا من كل دنس الخطية .

(North side) Christ our Savior; has come and has borne suffering; that through His Passion; He may save us.

(مرد بحرى) المسيح مخلصنا جاء وتألم عنا لكى بآلامه يخلصنا .

(South side) Let us glorify Him; and exalt His Name; for He had mercy on us; according to His great mercy.

(مرد قبلى) فلنمجده ونرفع اسمه لأنه صنع معنا رحمة كعظيم رحمته .

The Conclusion of the Exposition, Page: 9   ختام الطرح ، صفحة : 9

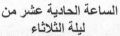

الساعة الحادية عشر من ليلة الثلاثاء من البصخة المقدسة
The Eleventh Hour of Tuesday Eve of the Holy Pascha

Amos 5:6-14

But seek the Lord, and you shall live; lest the house of Joseph blaze as fire, and it devour him, and there shall be none to quench it for the house of Israel. It is He that executes judgment in the height above, and He has established justice on the earth; who makes all things, and changes them, and turns darkness into the morning, and darkens the day into night; who calls for the water of the sea, and pours it out on the face of the earth: the Lord is His name; who dispenses ruin to strength, and brings distress upon the fortress. They hated him that reproved in the gates, and abhorred holy speech. Therefore because they have smitten the poor with their fists, and you have received of them choice gifts, you have built polished houses, but you shall not dwell in them; you have planted desirable vineyards, but you shall not drink the wine of them. For I know your many transgressions, and your sins are great, trampling on the just, taking bribes, and turning aside the judgment of the poor in the gates. Therefore the prudent shall be silent at that time; for it is a time of evils. Seek good, and not evil, that you may live; and so the Lord God Almighty shall be with you, as you have said.

Glory be to the Holy Trinity. Amen

(من عاموس النبى ص 5 : 6 - 14)

أطلبوا الرب فتحيوا ، لئلا يتقد بيت يوسف كنار فيحترق وليس من يطفئ من بيت إسرائيل . الرب يصنع حكماً فى العلى . ويجعل العدل على الأرض . هو الذى خلق كل الأشياء وينقلها. الذى يحول الظل صباحاً ويغشى النهار بالليل . الذى يدعو مياه البحر فيفيضها على وجه الأرض كلها ، الرب الإله الضابط الكل هو اسمه . المنزل الانحطام على القوة ويأتى بالدمار على الموضع الحصين . لقد أبغضوا الموبخ فى الأبواب ونجسوا الكلام الطاهر . من أجل ذلك هذا ما يقوله الرب : بما انكم ضربتم المساكين على رؤوسهم ، وأخذتم منهم هدايا فاخرة ، شيدتم بيوتاً حسنة ولا تسكنون فيها . وغرستم كروماً مختارة ولا تشربون من خمرها . فانى عالم بنفاقكم الكثير وخطاياكم المتجددة . تدوسون البار وتأخذون الرشوة وتصدون البائسين من الأبواب . لذلك يسكت العاقل فى ذلك الزمان لأنه زمان ردئ فاطلبوا الخير لا الشر لتحيوا . مجداً للثالوث القدوس .

| Pascha Praise - A (12 times), Page: 6 | تسبحة البصخة A (12 مرة) ، صفحة : |

The Psalm
Ⲯⲁⲗⲙⲟⲥ ⲣ̅ⲕ̅ⲁ̅ : ⲇ̅

Psalms 121:4
For from there the tribes went up, the tribes of the Lord, as a testimony for Israel, to give thanks unto the name of the Lord.

Alleluia

Ⲉⲧⲁⲩϣⲉⲛⲱⲟⲩ ⲅⲁⲣ ⲡ̇ϣⲱⲓ ⲙ̇ⲙⲁⲩ ⲛ̇ϫⲉ ⲛⲓⲫⲩⲗⲏ : ⲛⲓⲫⲩⲗⲏ ⲛ̇ⲧⲉ ⲡ̅ⲟ̅ⲥ̅ : ⲉⲩⲙⲉⲧⲙⲉⲑⲣⲉ ⲙ̇ⲡ̇Ⲓⲥⲗ̄ : ⲉⲟⲩⲱⲛⲋ ⲉ̇ⲃⲟⲗ ⲙ̇ⲫⲣⲁⲛ ⲙ̇ⲡ̅ⲟ̅ⲥ̅ . ⲁ̅ⲗ̅ .

إيطاف شينوؤو غار إبشوى إمماف إنجيه نى فيلي:نى فيلي إنتيه إبتشويس إفميت ميثريه إمبسرائيل:إيف أوواونه إيفول إمفران إمبتشويس . الليلويا .

(مز 121 : 4)

لأنه هناك صعدت القبائل ، قبائل الرب شهادة لإسرائيل ، يعترفون لاسم الرب . الليلويا .

| Introduction to the Gospel, Page: 8 | مقدمة الأنجيل ، صفحة : |

The Gospel
Ⲉⲩⲁⲅⲅⲉⲗⲓⲟⲛ Ⲕⲁⲧⲁ Ⲙⲁⲣⲕⲟⲛ Ⲕⲉⲫ ⲓ̅ⲅ̅ : ⲗ̅ⲃ̅ ϣⲱⲗ ⲛⲉⲙ Ⲕⲉⲫ ⲓ̅ⲇ̅ : ⲁ̅ ⲛⲙ ⲃ̅

Mark 13:32-14:2
"But of that day and hour no one knows, not even the angels in

Ⲉⲑⲃⲉ ⲡⲓⲉ̇ϩⲟⲟⲩ ⲇⲉ ⲉⲧⲉ ⲙ̇ⲙⲁⲩ ⲛⲉⲙ ϯⲟⲩⲛⲟⲩ ⲙ̇ⲙⲟⲛ ϩ̇ⲗⲓ ⲉ̇ⲙⲓ ⲉ̇ⲣⲱⲟⲩ ⲟⲩ ⲇⲉ

(مرقس 13 : 32-14: 2)

فأما ذلك اليوم وتلك الساعة فلا يعلمها

heaven, nor the Son, but only the Father. Take heed, watch and pray; for you do not know when the time is. It is like a man going to a far country, who left his house and gave authority to his servants, and to each his work, and commanded the doorkeeper to watch. Watch therefore, for you do not know when the master of the house is coming—in the evening, at midnight, at the crowing of the rooster, or in the morning— lest, coming suddenly, he find you sleeping. And what I say to you, I say to all: Watch!" After two days it was the Passover and the Feast of Unleavened Bread. And the chief priests and the scribes sought how they might take Him by trickery and put Him to death. But they said, "Not during the feast, lest there be an uproar of the people." Glory be to God forever, Amen.

ⲛⲓⲁⲅⲅⲉⲗⲟⲥ ⲛⲏ ⲉⲧ ϧⲉⲛ ⲧ̇ⲫⲉ : ⲟⲩ ⲇⲉ ⲡ̇ϣⲏⲣⲓ ⲉⲃⲟⲗ ⲉ̇ⲫⲓⲱⲧ : ⲭⲟⲩϣⲧ ⲉⲃⲟⲗ ⲣⲱⲓⲥ ⲟⲩⲟⲟ̇ ⲁⲣⲓ ⲡ̇ⲣⲟⲥⲉⲩⲭⲉⲥⲑⲉ ⲛ̇ⲧⲉⲧⲉⲛⲥⲱⲟⲩⲛ ⲅⲁⲣ ⲁⲛ ⲭⲉ ⲑ̇ⲛⲁⲩ ⲡⲉ ⲡⲓⲥⲏⲟⲩ : ⲙ̇ⲫ̇ⲣⲏϯ ⲛ̇ⲟⲩⲣⲱⲙⲓ ⲉⲁϥⲙⲟϣⲓ ⲉ̇ⲡ̇ϣⲉⲙⲙⲟ ⲟⲩⲟⲟ̇ ⲉⲁϥⲭⲱ ⲙ̇ⲡⲉϥⲏⲓ ⲟⲩⲟⲟ̇ ⲁϥϯ ⲛ̇ⲛⲉϥⲉ̇ⲃⲓⲁⲓⲕ ⲙ̇ⲡⲉⲣϣⲓϣⲓ ⲫⲟⲩⲁⲓ ⲫⲟⲩⲁⲓ ⲙ̇ⲡⲉϥⲟ̇ⲱⲃ ⲟⲩⲟⲟ̇ ⲁϥⲟⲟⲛⲟⲉⲛ ⲉ̇ⲧⲟⲧϥ ⲙ̇ⲡⲓⲙⲛⲟⲩⲧ ⲟⲓⲛⲁ ⲛ̇ⲧⲉϥⲣⲱⲓⲥ. Ⲣⲱⲓⲥ ⲟⲩⲛ ⲭⲉ ⲛ̇ⲧⲉⲧⲉⲛⲥⲱⲟⲩⲛ ⲅⲁⲣ ⲁⲛ ⲭⲉ ⲁⲣⲉ ⲡ̇ϭⲟⲓⲥ ⲙ̇ⲡⲓⲏ̇ⲓ ⲛⲏⲟⲩ ⲛ̇ⲛⲁⲩ ⲓⲉ ⲟⲁⲛⲁⲣⲟⲩⲟⲓ ⲓⲉ ϯⲫⲁϣⲓ ⲙ̇ⲡⲓⲉⲭⲱⲣⲟ ⲓⲉ ⲉⲣⲉ ⲡⲓⲁⲗⲉⲕⲧⲱⲣ ⲙⲟⲩϯ ⲓⲉ ⲟⲁⲛⲁⲧⲟⲟⲩⲓ : ⲙⲏⲡⲱⲥ ⲛ̇ⲧⲉϥⲓ̇ ⲛ̇ⲟⲩⲟⲟⲧ ϧⲉⲛ ⲟⲩⲟⲟⲧ ⲛ̇ⲧⲉϥⲭⲉⲙ ⲑⲏⲛⲟⲩ ⲉⲣⲉⲧⲉⲛⲉⲛⲕⲟⲧ : ⲡⲉ ϯⲭⲱ ⲙ̇ⲙⲟϥ ⲛⲱⲧⲉⲛ ϯⲭⲱ ⲙ̇ⲙⲟϥ ⲛ̇ⲟⲩⲟⲛ ⲛⲓⲃⲉⲛ ⲣⲱⲓⲥ. Ⲛⲉ ⲡⲓⲡⲁⲥⲭⲁ ⲡⲉ ⲛⲉⲙ ⲛⲓⲁⲧϣⲏⲣ ⲙⲉⲛⲉⲛⲥⲁ ⲉ̇ⲟⲟⲟⲩ ⲥ̇ⲛⲁⲩ ⲟⲩⲟⲟ̇ ⲛⲁⲩⲕⲱϯ ⲡⲉ ⲛ̇ⲭⲉ ⲛⲓⲁⲣⲭⲏ ⲉⲣⲉⲩⲥ ⲛⲉⲙ ⲛⲓⲥⲁϧ ⲭⲉ ⲡⲱⲥ ⲛ̇ⲧⲟⲩⲁⲙⲟⲛⲓ ⲙ̇ⲙⲟϥ ϧⲉⲛ ⲟⲩⲭⲣⲟϥ ⲛ̇ⲧⲟⲩϧⲟⲟⲃⲉϥ : ⲛⲁⲩⲭⲱ ⲅⲁⲣ ⲙ̇ⲙⲟⲥ ⲡⲉ ⲭⲉ ⲙ̇ⲡⲉⲛⲑ̇ⲣⲉⲛⲁⲓⲥ ϧⲉⲛ ⲡ̇ϣⲁⲓ ⲙⲏⲡⲟⲧⲉ ⲛ̇ⲧⲉ ⲟⲩϣ̇ⲑⲟⲣⲧⲉⲣ ϣⲱⲡⲓ ϧⲉⲛ ⲡⲓⲗⲁⲟⲥ. ⲟⲩⲱϣⲧ ⲙ̇ⲡⲓⲉⲩⲁⲅⲅⲉⲗⲓⲟⲛ ⲉⲑ̅.

أحد ولا الملائكة الذين فى السماء ولا الإبن إلا الآب ، أنظروا واسهروا وصلوا لأنكم لا تعلمون متى يكون الزمان . كمثل إنسان مسافر فترك بيته وأعطى عبيده السلطان ، كل واحد وواحد فى عمله ، وأوصى البواب بالسهر . فاسهروا إذاً لأنكم لا تعلمون متى يأتى رب البيت ، أفى المساء أم فى صياح الديك أم فى نصف الليل أم فى الصباح ، لئلا يأتى بغتة فيجدكم نياماً . وما أقوله لكم أقوله للجميع اسهروا . وكان الفصح والفطير بعد يومين وكان رؤساء الكهنة والكتبة يطلبون كيف يمسكونه بمكر ليقتلوه ولكنهم قالوا: لا نفعل هذا فى العيد لئلا يكون شغب فى الشعب . والمجد لله دائماً.

Exposition

طـرح

You alone, O Omniscient God, has the knowledge of everything before its being: the epochs, the years, the times, and the past generation. Listen to our Savior, Who with His divine mouth proclaims:

أنت وحدك أيها المدبر العالم بسائر الأشياء قبل كون جميعها. والأزمنة والسنين وكل الأوقات والأجيال الماضية أنت العالم بها . اسمعوا مخلصنا يقول علانية بفمه الإلهى هكذا قائلاً:

"But of that day and that hour no one knows, not even the angels in heaven, nor the Son, but only the Father knows it."

عن ذلك اليوم وتلك الساعة التى يأتى فيها إبن الإنسان. أنه ليس أحد من سائر البشر ولا الملائكة يعلمهما، والإبن أيضاً لا يعلمهما إلا الآب فقط العارف بكل شئ.

Watch at all times because you do not know when it shall be. Lest he makes a surprise visit and finds you asleep. Be careful and safeguard against hidden traps.

فاسهروا كل حين وصلوا فانكم لستم تعلمون متى يكون الوقت. لئلا يأتى بغتة فيجدكم نياماً. فاحترزوا واحفظوا ذواتكم لكى تخلصوا من الفخاخ المنصوبة.

(North side) Christ our Savior; has come and has borne suffering; that through His Passion; He may save us.

(مرد بحرى) المسيح مخلصنا جاء وتألم عنا لكى بألامه يخلصنا .

(South side) Let us glorify Him; and exalt His Name; for He had mercy on us; according to His great mercy.

(مرد قبلى) فلنمجده ونرفع اسمه لأنه صنع معنا رحمة كعظيم رحمته .

The Conclusion of the Exposition, Page: 9 ختام الطرح ، صفحة :

The Conclusion with the Nighttime Litanies, Page: 17 طلبة المساء ، صفحة :

يوم الثلاثاء من البصخة المقدسة

Tuesday of the Holy Pascha

القراءات و الاحداث

الموضوع : صدامه بالفريسيين و رؤساء الكهنة و تكلمه بالامثال (يوم الامثال)

الاولى : يو 8 : 21- 29 ؛ حثهم على الايمان
الثالثه : مت 23 : 37 – 24 :2 ؛ جزاؤهم لعصيانهم
السادسة : يو 8 : 12 – 20 ؛ تفنيده لأكاذيبهم
التاسعة : مت 24 : 3 – 35 ؛ جمع المختارين دونهم
الحادية عشرة : مت 25 : 14 – 26 :2 ؛ تهديدهم بجهنم

تحدث الرب يسوع مع التلاميذ عن الايمان عندما رأوا ما حدث للتينه ثم جاء الفريسيون ليحاوروه و هو فى الهيكل فكلمهم عن سلطانه الآتى من فوق ثم بدأ يحدثهم بأمثال كثيرة ومنها مثل الوزنات الذى بين فيه مصير الاشرار . و عند خروج المسيح من الهيكل اراه التلاميذ ابنية الهيكل العظيمة فبدأ ينبأهم عن خراب الهيكل و اورشليم وعلامات ذلك و علامات مجيئه الثانى و نهاية العالم

The Readings and Events

Subject: The conflict with the Pharisees and chief priests. He talks with parables (Day of the Parables)

First hour: John 8:21-29 ; encouraging their faith
Third hour: Matthew 23:37-24:2 ; Their punishment
Sixth hour: John 8:12-20 ; Disproving of their lies
Ninth hour: Matthew 24:3-35 ; Getting the selected, not them.
Eleventh hour: Threatening them with the hill.

The Lord talked with the disciples about faith when they saw what happened to the fig tree. Pharisees came to argue with Him while in the temple. He showed them His authority from above and started to speak to them with parables such as the parable of the talent, in which He showed the end of bad people. On exiting the temple, the disciples showed Him the great building of the temple. He started to prophesize about desolation of the temple and Jerusalem and the signs of that and of His second coming and the end of the world.

الساعة الاولى من يوم الثلاثاء من البصخة المقدسة
The First Hour of Tuesday of the Holy Pascha

Exodus 19:1-9

And in the third month of the departure of the children of Israel out of the land of Egypt, on the same day, they came into the Wilderness of Sinai. And they departed from Rephidim, and came into the Wilderness of Sinai, and there Israel encamped before the mountain. And Moses went up to the mount of God, and God called him out of the mountain, saying, These things shall you say to the house of Jacob, and you shall report them to the children of Israel. You have seen all that I have done to the Egyptians, and I took you up as upon eagles' wings, and I brought you near to Myself. And now if you will indeed hear My voice, and keep My covenant, you shall be to Me a peculiar people above all nations; for the whole earth is Mine. And you shall be to Me a royal priesthood and a holy nation. These words shall you speak to the children of Israel. And Moses came and called the elders of the people, and he set before them all these words, which God appointed them. And all the people answered with one accord, and said, All things that God has spoken, we will do and hearken to. And Moses reported these words to God. And the Lord said to Moses, Behold, I come to you in a pillar of a cloud, that the people may hear Me speaking to you, and may believe you forever. And Moses reported the words of the people to the Lord. Glory be to the Holy Trinity. Amen.

(من سفر الخروج ص 19 : 1 - 9)

وفى الشهر الثالث لخروج بنى إسرائيل من أرض مصر فى ذلك اليوم جاءوا إلى برية سيناء ورحلوا من رافازين ووصلوا إلى برية سيناء . ونزلوا هناك قبالة الجبل . فصعد موسى إلى جبل الله فناداه الله من الجبل قائلاً : هذا ما تقوله لبيت يعقوب وتخبر بنى إسرائيل قائلاً لهم : قد رأيتم كل الأعمال التى صنعتها بالمصريين وكيف حملتكم كأنكم على أجنحة النسور وأتيت بكم إليّ . والآن ان كنتم سمعاً تسمعون لصوتى وتحفظون عهدى ، فانكم تكونون لي شعباً مجتمعاً إلى الأبد من بين جميع الأمم . لأن لي الأرض بأسرها وأنتم تكونون لي مملكة مقدسة وأمة مطهرة . هذا هو الكلام الذى تقوله لبيت إسرائيل . فجاء موسى ودعا شيوخ الشعب وقص عليهم كل هذه الكلمات التى أمره الله بها . فاجاب جميع الشعب معاً وقالوا: كل ما تكلم به الله نسمعه ونعمل به . فرفع موسى كلام الشعب إلى الله . مجداً للثالوث القدوس.

Job 23:2-24:25

Yes, I know that pleading is out of my reach; and His hand has been made heavy upon my groaning. Oh, that I knew where I might find Him, and come to an end of the matter! And I would plead my own cause, and He would fill my mouth with arguments. And I would know the remedies which He would speak to me, and I would perceive what He would tell me. Though He should come on me in His great strength, then He would not threaten me; for truth and reproof are from Him, and He would bring forth my judgment to an end. For if I shall go first, and exist no longer, still what do I know concerning the latter end? When He worked on the left hand, then I observed it not: His right hand shall encompass me but I shall not see it. For He already knows my way, and He has tried me as gold. And I will go forth according to His commandments, for I have kept His ways; and I shall not turn aside from His commandments, neither shall I transgress; but I have hid His words in my bosom. And if He too has thus judged, who is He that has contradicted, for He has both willed a thing and done it. Therefore am I troubled at Him; and when I was reproved, I thought of Him. Therefore let me take good heed before Him: I will consider, and be terrified of Him. But the Lord has softened my heart, and the

(من أيوب الصديق 23 : 2 - 24 : 1)

أنا أعلم أن توبيخى هو منه ويده قد ثقلت على تنهدى . من الذى يعلم أنى أجده وأنهم تحابوا معى إلى التمام ولست أستطيع أن أقول حكماً أمامه . فيمتلئ فمى توبيخاً . أنا أعلم بثبات ما يقوله لي وأشعر بما يعرفنى أياه . ولا يأتى عليّ بقوة عظيمة ولا يفسح لي فى الرجز . لأن البر والتوبيخ هما منه . ويخرج حكمى إلى الانقضاء وأمضى إلى الأوائل . ولا أكون بعد . ولا أعلم ما فى الأواخر . خلق الشمال ولم أمسك ما يستر اليمين ولا أنظر . هو عارف طريقى ومحصنى مثل الذهب . فاسلك بحسب أوامره ولا أرفضها. أخفى كلامه فى حضنى . فان كان قد حكم هكذا فمن هو الذى يقاومه؟ وهو ما يريده يفعله. من أجل ذلك اسرعت إليه ، أدنى فخفت منه. لهذا أسرع قدام وجهه وأتأمل فأرتعب منه . لأن الرب قد أضعف قلبى . والضابط الكل اسرع ورائى . لأنى كنت أعلم أن الظلمة ستأتى علىّ والضباب غطى وجهى.

Almighty has troubled me. For I knew not that darkness would come upon me, and thick darkness has covered me before my face. But why have the seasons been hidden from the Lord, while the ungodly have passed over the bound, carrying off the flock with the shepherd? They have led away the donkey of the fatherless, and taken the widow's ox for a pledge. They have turned aside the weak from the right way, and the meek of the earth have hidden themselves together. And they have departed like donkeys in the field, having gone forth on my account according to their own order. His bread is sweet to His little ones. They have reaped a field that was not their own before the time; the poor have labored in the vineyards of the ungodly without pay and without food. They have caused many naked to sleep without clothes, and they have taken away the covering of their body. They are wet with the drops of the mountains: they have embraced the rock, because they had no shelter. They have snatched the fatherless from the breast, and have afflicted the outcast. And they have wrongfully caused others to sleep without clothing, and taken away the morsel of the hungry. They have unrighteously laid wait in narrow places, and have not known the righteous way. Who have cast forth the poor from the city and their own houses, and the soul of the children has groaned aloud. Why then has He not visited these? Forasmuch as they were upon the earth, and took no notice, and they knew not the way of righteousness, neither have they walked in their appointed paths? But having known their works, He delivered them into darkness; and in the night one will be as a thief: And the eye of the adulterer has watched for the darkness, saying, Eye shall not see me, and he puts a covering on his face In darkness he digs through houses; by day they conceal themselves securely; they know not the light. For the morning is to them all as the shadow of death, for each will be conscious of the terror of the shadow of death. He is swift on the face of the water; let his portion be cursed on the earth, and let their plants be laid bare. Let them be withered upon the earth, for they have plundered the sheaves of the fatherless. Then is his sin brought to remembrance, and he vanishes like a vapor of dew; but let what he has done be recompensed to him, and let every unrighteous one be crushed like rotten wood. For he has not treated the barren woman well, and has had no pity on a feeble woman. And in wrath he has overthrown the helpless; therefore when he has arisen, a man will not feel secure of his own life. When he has fallen sick, let him not hope to recover, but let him perish by disease. For his exaltation has hurt many; but he has withered as mallows in the heat, or as an ear of corn falling off of itself from the stalk. But if not, who is he that says I speak falsely, and will make my words of no account? Glory be to the Holy Trinity. Amen.

Hosea 4:1-8

Hear the word of the Lord, you children of Israel: for the Lord has a controversy with the inhabitants of the land, because there is no truth, nor mercy, nor knowledge of God in the land. Cursing, lying,

كيف خفيت هذه الساعات عن الرب . فتجاوز المنافقون حدودهم مختطفين القطيع مع راعيه . وأخذوا حمار الأيتام وارتهنوا بقرة الأرملة . وجعلوا الضعفاء يميلون عن طريق الحق وأختفى ودعاء الأرض معاً . وصاروا كالبقر فى الحقل . وطرحوا أعمالهم علىَّ واستحلفوا خبز الأطفال . وحقلا ليس لهم حصدوه قبل أوانه . يعمل الضعفاء فى كروم المنافقين بلا أجرة ولا طعام . كثيراً ما جعلوهم يبيتون عراة بغير لباس . ونزعوا كساء أنفسهم . فابتلوا من قطر الجبال . وحيث أن لا خيام لهم استتروا بالصخور . خطفوا الأيتام عن ثديهم . ومن سقط اذلوه . بظلم جعلوا قوماً ينامون عراة . وأخذوا خبز الجياع . فى المواضع الضيقة اصطادوا بالظلم . وطريق العدل لم يعرفوه . والذين طردوهم من مدنهم وبيوتهم لم يعرفوهم . فصارت نفس الأطفال فى تنهد شديد . لماذا لم يفتقد هؤلاء وهم على الأرض وهم لم يعرفوا طريق البر . ولم يمشوا فى سبله . فلما علم بأعمالهم أسلمهم للظلمة . وفى الليل يصير مثل اللص . وعين الزانى ترقب الظلام قائلاً : لا تبصرنى عين . فيجعل ستراً على وجهه . نقب بيوتاً فى الظلام وفى النهار أغلقوا على أنفسهم . فلا يعرفون النور صباحاً . لأن ظل الموت يدركهم معاً . لأنه يعرف أهوال ظل الموت. خفيف هو على وجه الماء . فليكن نصيبهم ملعوناً على الأرض . وليظهر نباتهم يابساً على وجه الأرض . لأنهم نهبوا أغمار الأيتام . وحين ذكر خطيته وصار غير ظاهر كمثل طل الندى وسيجازى بما فعل . وينسحق كل ظالم مثل الخشب الغير النافع . لأنهم لم يحسنوا إلى العاقر ولم يرحموا الأرملة . وبغضب طرحوا الضعفاء . فاذا قام لا يأمن على حياته . وإذا مـــرض لا يجعلوه يرجو أن يشفى بل يسقط بالمرض . ان كثيرين خفضهم ارتفاعه فذبلت خضرتهم بالحر مثل السنبل إذا سقط وحده من العيدان . وإلا فمن قال له أنى كذبت ويجعل كلامى كلا شئ . مجداً للثالوث القدوس.

(من هوشع النبى ص ٤ : ١ - ٨)
اسمعوا كلام الرب يا بنى إسرائيل فان للرب خصومة مع سكان الأرض لأنه لا حق ولا رحمة ولا معرفة الله على الأرض.

murder, theft, and adultery abound in the land, and they mingle blood with blood. Therefore shall the land mourn, and shall be diminished with all that dwell in it, with the wild beasts of the field, and the reptiles of the earth, and with the birds of the sky, and the fish of the sea shall fail; that neither anyone may plead, nor anyone reprove another; but My people are as a priest spoken against. Therefore they shall fall by day, and the prophet with you shall fall; I have compared your mother unto night. My people are like as if they had no knowledge. Because you have rejected knowledge, I will also reject you, that you shall not minister as priest unto Me: and as you have forgotten the law of your God, I also will forget your children. According to their multitude, so they sinned against Me; I will turn their glory into shame. They will devour the sins of My people, and will set their hearts on their iniquities. Glory be to the Holy Trinity. Amen.

A homily of our Holy Father Abba Shenouti the Archimandrite

Let me inform you about two matters. Those for whom the heavens rejoiced because they repented their sin on earth will not suffer sadness or pain in the place they are destined to inherit. As for those whom heavens did not rejoice for because they did not atone their sins and did not repent their iniquities on earth they will find neither joy nor comfort in that place. Because those who revel in pleasures and delights will enjoy neither happiness nor comfort in heavens. Have not you heard his saying Blessed are those who mourn because they shall be comforted. Also those who do not rejoice on earth shall rejoice in heavens or have not you read woe to you who laugh now for you shall weep and mourn. Isn't this the time when the meek is vested with power. And he who is not strong will say I am strong when he yields his heart to the Written Word. As the prophet says; many are those whose repeated adultery has weakened their bodies, and they shall be weakened at heart as well. As the Book says about those; "they will be devastated by their own profanity. As for those who struggle with courage it was said about them; hasten and straighten yourself to be a companion of God undisgraced worker who preaches the Word of Truth."

We conclude the homily of our Holy Father Abba Shenouti the Archimandrite, who enlightened our minds and our hearts. In the name of the Father, and the Son, and the Holy Spirit, one God. Amen.

بل لعنة وكذب وقتل وسرقة وفسق قد فاضت على الأرض ودماء تختلط بدماء . لذلك تنوح الأرض و يذبل كل من يسكن فيها مع وحوش البرية ودبابات الأرض وطيور السماء ، بل و سمك البحر أيضاً يفنى ، حتى لا يكون من يحاكم ولا من يوبخ . لأن الشعب يعاند فى عبادة الأصنام . مثل الكاهن الذى يعاند فى عبادة الاله فيتعثر بالنهار ويتعثر أيضاً النبى معك . وأمك شبهتها بالليل . وصار شعبى كمن لا معرفة له . لأنك أنت رفضت المعرفة . أنا أيضاً أرفضك فلا تكهن لى . وانسى أنا أيضاً ناموس إسرائيل وأنسى أعمالهم . هكذا أخطأوا فأبدل مجدهم هواناً . وخطايا شعبى تأكلهم . وبظلمهم تنزع نفوسهم . مجداً للثالوث القدوس .

(عظة لابينا القديس أنبا شنودة)

أنا أخبركم بأمرين . أن كل الذين فرحت بهم السماء لأجل توبتهم على الأرض سوف لا يرون حزناً ولا ألماً فى ذلك المكان ، وأما الذين لم تفرح بهم السماء لأجل الأرتداد من توبتهم على الأرض فسوف لا يرون فرحاً ولا نياحاً فى ذلك الموضع . لأن الذين سيصنعون فرحهم على الأرض لا يرون فرحاً ولا نياحاً من الآن . أما سمعتم طوبى للحزانى فأنهم يتعزون . وكذلك الآخرون الذين لا يفرحون على الأرض يفرحون أيضاً فى السموات . أما سمعتم الويل لكم أيها الضاحكون الآن فأنكم ستبكون وتحزنون . أليس هذا هو الزمان الذى فيه يلبس الضعفاء القوة ، والذى ليس بقوى يقول: أنا قوى ، عند ما يعطى قلبه للقول المكتوب . وكقول النبى: كثيرون هم الذين ضعفت أجسادهم من كثرة زناهم ، سيضعفون أيضاً فى قلوبهم ، كما يقول الكتاب عن هؤلاء هكذا أنهم يتحطمون بنجاستهم . وأما المجاهدون بشجاعة فقد قيل عنهم: اسرع وقوم ذاتك صفيا لله ، فاعلا لا يخزى ، يقطع كلمة الحق .

فلنختم عظة أبينا القديس أنبا شنودة الذى أنار عقولنا وعيون قلوبنا . باسم الآب والإبن والروح القدس إله واحد آمين.

The Psalm

Ψⲁⲗⲙⲟⲥ ⲣ̅ⲓ̅ⲑ̅ : ⲃ̅ ⲛⲉⲙ ⲉ̅

Psalms 119:2, 5

Deliver my soul, O Lord, from unjust lips, and from a deceitful tongue. I was peaceable among them that hated peace; when I spoke to them, they warred against me without a cause. Alleluia.

Ⲡ̀ϭⲟⲓⲥ ⲉⲕⲉⲛⲟϩⲉⲙ ⲛ̀ⲧⲁⲯⲩⲭⲏ ⲉⲃⲟⲗ ϧⲉⲛ ϩⲁⲛⲥ̀ⲫⲟⲧⲟⲩ ⲛ̀ⲟϫⲓ : ⲛⲉⲙ ⲉ̀ⲃⲟⲗ ϩⲁ ⲟⲩⲗⲁⲥ ⲛ̀ⲭⲣⲟϥ . Ⲛⲁⲓⲟⲓ ⲛ̀ϩⲓⲣⲏⲛⲏⲕⲟⲥ ⲡⲉ ⲛⲉⲙ ⲛⲏⲉⲑⲙⲟⲥϯ ⲛ̀ϯϩⲓⲣⲏⲛⲏ : ⲉϣⲱⲡ ⲁⲓϣⲁⲛⲥⲁϫⲓ ⲛⲉⲙⲱⲟⲩ ϣⲁⲩⲃⲱⲧⲥ ⲉ̀ⲣⲟⲓ ⲛ̀ϫⲓⲛϫⲏ . ⲁⲗ.

إبتشويس إكئنوهيم إنطا بسيشى إيفول خين هان إسفوطوو إنوَجى : نيم إيفول ها أوولاس إن إكروف . ناى أوى إنهيرينكوس بيه نيم نى إثمووستى إنتى هيرنى : إشوب إيشان صاجى نيموؤ شاف فوتس إروى إنجين جى . الليلويا.

(مز 119: 2و5)

يارب نجى نفسى من الشفاة الظالمة ومن اللسان الغاش . ومع مبغضى السلام كنت مسالماً . وحين كنت أكلمهم ، كانوا يقاتلونى مجاناً . الليلويا.

Introduction to the Gospel, Page: 8   مقدمة الأنجيل ، صفحة :

The Gospel

Ⲉⲩⲁⲅⲅⲉⲗⲓⲟⲛ Ⲕⲁⲧⲁⲓⲱⲁⲛⲛⲏⲛ Ⲕⲉⲫ ⲏ̅ : ⲕ̅ⲁ̅ - ⲕ̅ⲑ̅

John 8:21-29

Then Jesus said to them again, "I am going away, and you will seek Me, and will die in your sin. Where I go you cannot come." So the Jews said, "Will He kill Himself, because He says, 'Where I go you cannot come'?" And He said to them, "You are from beneath; I am from above. You are of this world; I am not of this world. Therefore I said to you that you will die in your sins; for if you do not believe that I am He, you will die in your sins." Then they said to Him, "Who are You?" And Jesus said to them, "Just what I have been saying to you from the beginning. I have many things to say and to judge concerning you, but He who sent Me is true; and I speak to the world those things which I heard from Him." They did not understand that He spoke to them of the Father. Then Jesus said to them, "When you lift up the Son of Man, then you will know that I am He, and that I do

Ⲡⲁⲗⲓⲛ ⲟⲛ ⲡⲉϫⲉ Ⲓⲏⲥⲟⲩⲥ ⲛⲱⲟⲩ ϫⲉ ⲁⲛⲟⲕ ϯⲛⲁϣⲉⲛⲏⲓ ⲟⲩⲟϩ ⲧⲉⲧⲉⲛⲛⲁⲕⲱϯ ⲛ̀ⲥⲱⲓ ⲟⲩⲟϩ ⲧⲉⲧⲉⲛⲛⲁϫⲉⲙⲧ ⲁⲛ ⲟⲩⲟϩ ⲧⲉⲧⲉⲛⲛⲁⲙⲟⲩ ϧⲉⲛ ⲛⲉⲧⲉⲛⲛⲟⲃⲓ ϫⲉ ⲡⲓⲙⲁ ⲁⲛⲟⲕ ⲉ̀ϯⲛⲁϣⲉⲛⲏⲓ ⲉ̀ⲣⲟϥ ⲙ̀ⲙⲟⲛ ϣ̀ϫⲟⲙ ⲙ̀ⲙⲱⲧⲉⲛ ⲉⲓ ⲉ̀ⲣⲟϥ . Ⲛⲁⲩϫⲱ ⲟⲩⲛ ⲙ̀ⲙⲟⲥ ⲡⲉ ⲛ̀ϫⲉ ⲛⲓⲓⲟⲩⲇⲁⲓ ϫⲉ ⲙⲏⲧⲓ ⲁϥⲛⲁϧⲟⲑⲃⲉϥ ⲙ̀ⲙⲁⲩⲁⲧϥ : ϫⲉ ϥ̀ϫⲱ ⲙ̀ⲙⲟⲥ ϫⲉ ⲡⲓⲙⲁ ⲁⲛⲟⲕ ⲉ̀ϯⲛⲁϣⲉⲛⲏⲓ ⲉ̀ⲣⲟϥ ⲛ̀ⲑⲱⲧⲉⲛ ⲛ̀ⲧⲉⲧⲉⲛⲛⲁϣⲓ ⲉ̀ⲣⲟϥ ⲁⲛ . Ⲟⲩⲟϩ ⲛⲁϥϫⲱ ⲙ̀ⲙⲟⲥ ⲛⲱⲟⲩ ⲡⲉ ϫⲉ ⲛ̀ⲑⲱⲧⲉⲛ ⲛ̀ⲑⲱⲧⲉⲛ ϩⲁⲛ ⲉ̀ⲃⲟⲗ ϧⲉⲛ ⲛⲏⲉⲧⲉ ⲛ̀ϧ̀ⲣⲏⲓ ⲁⲛⲟⲕ ⲇⲉ ⲁⲛⲟⲕ ⲟⲩ ⲉ̀ⲃⲟⲗ ⲙ̀ⲡ̀ϣⲱⲓ : ⲛ̀ⲑⲱⲧⲉⲛ ⲛ̀ⲑⲱⲧⲉⲛ ⲉ̀ⲃⲟⲗ ϧⲉⲛ ⲡⲁⲓⲕⲟⲥⲙⲟⲥ : ⲁⲛⲟⲕ ⲇⲉ ⲁⲛⲟⲕ ⲟⲩ ⲉ̀ⲃⲟⲗ ϧⲉⲛ ⲡⲁⲓⲕⲟⲥⲙⲟⲥ ⲁⲛ : ⲁⲓϫⲟⲥ ⲟⲩⲛ ⲛⲱⲧⲉⲛ ϫⲉ ⲧⲉⲧⲉⲛⲛⲁⲙⲟⲩ ⲛ̀ϧ̀ⲣⲏⲓ ϧⲉⲛ ⲛⲉⲧⲉⲛⲛⲟⲃⲓ : ⲉϣⲱⲡ ⲟⲩⲛ ⲁⲣⲉⲧⲉⲛϣ̀ⲧⲉⲙⲛⲁϩϯ ϫⲉ ⲁⲛⲟⲕ ⲡⲉ : ⲧⲉⲧⲉⲛⲛⲁⲙⲟⲩ ⲛ̀ϧ̀ⲣⲏⲓ ϧⲉⲛ ⲛⲉⲧⲉⲛⲛⲟⲃⲓ . Ⲛⲁⲩϫⲱ ⲟⲩⲛ ⲙ̀ⲙⲟⲥ ⲛⲁϥ ⲡⲉϫⲉ ⲛ̀ⲑⲟⲕ ⲛⲓⲙ : ⲡⲉϫⲉ Ⲓⲏⲥ ⲛⲱⲟⲩ ϫⲉ ⲛ̀ⲧⲁⲣⲭⲏ ⲁⲓⲉⲣ ⲡⲕⲉⲥⲁϫⲓ ⲛⲉⲙⲱⲧⲉⲛ : ⲟⲩⲟⲛⲧ ⲟⲩⲙⲏϣ ⲉ̀ϫⲟⲧⲟⲩ ⲉⲑⲃⲉ ⲑⲏⲛⲟⲩ ⲟⲩⲟϩ ⲉ̀ϯϩⲁⲡ : ⲁⲗⲗⲁ ⲫⲏⲉⲧⲁϥⲧⲁⲟⲩⲟⲓ ⲟⲩⲙⲏⲓ ⲡⲉ : ⲟⲩⲟϩ ⲁⲛⲟⲕ ϩⲱ ⲛⲏⲉⲧⲁⲓⲥⲟⲑⲙⲟⲩ ⲛ̀ⲧⲟⲧϥ : ⲛⲁⲓ ϯⲥⲁϫⲓ ⲙ̀ⲙⲱⲟⲩ ϧⲉⲛ ⲡⲓⲕⲟⲥⲙⲟⲥ : ⲙ̀ⲡⲟⲩⲉ̀ⲙⲓ ϫⲉ ⲛⲁϥⲥⲁϫⲓ ⲛⲉⲙⲱⲟⲩ ⲉⲑⲃⲉ ⲫ̀ⲓⲱⲧ . Ⲡⲉϫⲉ Ⲓⲏⲥ ⲛⲱⲟⲩ ϫⲉ ⲉ̀ϣⲱⲡ ⲁⲣⲉⲧⲉⲛϣⲁⲛⲃⲉⲥ ⲡ̀ϣⲏⲣⲓ ⲙ̀ⲫ̀ⲣⲱⲙⲓ : ⲧⲟⲧⲉ ⲉⲣⲉⲧⲉⲛⲉ̀ⲙⲓ ϫⲉ ⲁⲛⲟⲕ ⲡⲉ : ⲟⲩⲟϩ ⲛ̀ϯⲉⲣ ϩ̀ⲗⲓ ⲁⲛ ⲉ̀ⲃⲟⲗ ϩⲓⲧⲟⲧ ⲙ̀ⲙⲁⲩⲁⲧ

(يوحنا ص 8: 21 -29)

ثم قال لهم يسوع أيضاً: أنا أمضى وستطلوبننى فلا تجدوننى وتموتون فى خطاياكم. وحيث أمضى أنا فلا تقدرون أنتم أن تأتوا إليَّ. فقال اليهود: ألعله يقتل نفسه وحده ، حتى يقول حيث أمضى أنا لا تقدرون أنتم أن تأتوا. فقال لهم أنتم من أسفل وأما أنا فمن فوق ، أنتم من هذا العالم وأما أنا فلست من هذا العالم. قد قلت لكم انكم تموتون بخطاياكم . لأنكم ان لم تؤمنوا إنى أنا هو تموتون بخطاياكم. فقالوا له: مَن أنتَ؟ فقال لهم يسوع: أنا من البدء تكلمت معكم ولي أشياء كثيرة أقولها من أجلكم واحكم ولكن الذي أرسلني هو حق وأنا ما سمعته منه فهذا أتكلم به فى العالم . فلم يفهموا أنه كان يقول لهم عن الآب . فقال لهم يسوع: متى رفعتم إبن الإنسان فحينئذ تعلمون أنى أنا هو .

nothing of Myself; but as My Father taught Me, I speak these things. And He who sent Me is with Me. The Father has not left Me alone, for I always do those things that please Him." Glory be to God forever, Amen.	: ⲁⲗⲗⲁ ⲕⲁⲧⲁ ⲫⲣⲏϯ ⲉⲧⲁϥϯⲥⲁⲃⲟⲓ ⲛ̀ϫⲉ ⲡⲁⲓⲱⲧ ⲛⲁⲓ̀ⲧⲥⲁϫⲓ ⲙ̀ⲙⲱⲟⲩ . ⲟⲩⲟⲥ ⲫⲏⲉⲧⲁϥⲧⲁⲟⲩⲟⲓ ϥⲭⲏ ⲛⲉⲙⲏⲓ : ⲟⲩⲟⲥ ⲙ̀ⲡⲉϥⲭⲁⲧ ⲙ̀ⲙⲁⲩⲁⲧ : ϫⲉ ⲁⲛⲟⲕ ⲓⲣⲓ ⲛ̀ⲛⲏⲉⲑⲣⲁⲛⲁϥ ⲛ̀ⲥⲏⲟⲩ ⲛⲓⲃⲉⲛ . ⲟⲩⲱϣⲧ ⲙ̀ⲡⲓⲉⲩⲁⲅⲅⲉⲗⲓⲟⲛ ⲉⲑⲩ .	ولست أفعل شيئاً من ذاتى وحدى . بل أتكلم بهذا كما علمنى أبى . والذى أرسلنى هو معى . ولم يدعنى وحدى لأنى فى كل حين أفعل ما يرضيه . والمجد لله دائماً .

Introduction to the Exposition, Page: 9   مقدمة الطرح ، صفحة : ٩

Exposition	طـرح
And Israel came to Mount Rephidim after three months in the wilderness. Then the Israelites came out of Egypt and Mount Sinai to this place. Moses came and stood in the presence of God; He called and spoke to him saying: "This is what you tell the house of Israel, and report to the sons of Israel. You have seen the many deeds I have inflicted on the Egyptians and how I carried you with my soaring power as if you were on the wings of eagles. Keep my laws and commandments, take heed to my words and carry out my will, for I have chosen you from among the nations, for I have the earth and the sea as well. You will be my kingdom, a chosen people and a holy nation." And Moses came back and told the people all what God has said. The public cheered in one voice saying: "Whatever God wills, we will observe." Moses then told the Omniscient that the people adhered to his orders. But Israel turned back, Jacob retreated, and the sons of Israel strayed away. God's commandments became as if they were not, and his instructions ignored. Thus God delivered them into the hands of hateful enemies, and subjugated them to strangers once again. He humiliated them before the nations and they lived in eternal shame and disgrace.	وجاء إسرائيل إلى جبل رافازين من بعد ثلاثة أشهر وهو فى البرية . وخرج بنو إسرائيل من مصر وجبل سيناء إلى هذا المكان . فجاء موسى ووقف قدام الله فناداه وتكلم معه قائلاً : هذا ما تقوله لبيت يعقوب وتخبر به بنى إسرائيل . أنكم قد رأيتم أعمالى الكثيرة التى صنعتها أنا بالمصريين وكيف حملتكم أنا بقوتى العالية كأنكم على أجنحة النسور ، فاحفظوا ناموسى ووصاياى وانصتوا لكلامى واصنعوا إرادتى فإنى اخترتكم من بين جميع الأمم لأن ليّ الأرض كلها والبحر معاً . لتصيروا لي مملكة وشعباً مختاراً وأمة مطهرة . فجاء موسى واخبر الشعب بجميع هذا الكلام الذى قاله الرب . فصرخ جميع الشعب بصوت واحد قائلين: كل ما يأمر به الله نحن نحفظه . فقام موسى وخبر العارف أن الشعب سمع أوامره . فعاد إسرائيل ورجع يعقوب إلى خلف وحاد بنو إسرائيل . وصارت وصاياه كلا شئ وأوامره عادت باطلة. فلذلك أسلمهم إلى أعداء مبغضين واستعبدوا للغرباء مرة أخرى . ونكس رؤوسهم أمام الأمم وصاروا فى فضيحة وخزى أبدى .
(North side) Christ our Savior; has come and has borne suffering; that through His Passion; He may save us.	(مرد بحرى) المسيح مخلصنا جاء وتألم عنا لكى بآلامه يخلصنا .
(South side) Let us glorify Him; and exalt His Name; for He had mercy on us; according to His great mercy.	(مرد قبلى) فلنمجده ونرفع اسمه لأنه صنع معنا رحمة كعظيم رحمته .

The Conclusion of the Exposition, Page: 9   ختام الطرح ، صفحة : ٩

الساعة الثالثة من يوم الثلاثاء من البصخة المقدسة
The Third Hour of Tuesday of the Holy Pascha

Deuteronomy 8:11-20

Take heed to yourself that you forget not the Lord your God, so as not to keep His commands, and His judgments, and His statutes, which I command you this day, lest when you have eaten and are full, and have built nice houses, and dwelt in them; and your oxen and your sheep are multiplied to you, and your silver and your gold are multiplied to you, and all your possessions are multiplied to you, that you should be exalted in your heart, and forget the Lord your God, who brought you out of the land of Egypt, out of the house of bondage; who brought you through that great and terrible wilderness, where the biting serpent is, and scorpion, and drought, where there was no water; who brought you a fountain of water out of the flinty rock; who fed you with manna in the wilderness, which you knew not, and your fathers knew not; that He might afflict you, and thoroughly test you, and do you good in your latter days. Lest you should say in your heart, My strength, and the power of my own hand have worked for me this great wealth! But you shall remember the Lord your God, that He gives you strength to get wealth; even that He may establish His covenant, which the Lord swore to your fathers, as it is this day. And it shall come to pass, that if you do at all forget the Lord your God, and should go after other gods, and serve them, and worship them, I call heaven and earth to witness against you this day, that you shall surely perish! As also the other nations which the Lord God destroys before your face, so shall you perish, because you would not heed the voice of the Lord your God. Glory be to the Holy Trinity. Amen.

Sirach 2:1-9

My son, if you draw near to serve the Lord, prepare your soul for temptation. Set your heart right and be steadfast, and do not strive anxiously in distress. Cleave to Him and do not fall away, That you may be honored at the end of your life. Accept whatever is brought upon you, and in exchange for your humiliation, be patient; because gold is tested in fire and acceptable men in the furnace of abasement. Believe in Him, and He will help you; make your ways straight and hope in Him. You who fear the Lord, wait for His mercy, and do not turn aside, lest you fall. You who fear the Lord, believe in Him, and your reward will not fail. You who fear the Lord, hope for good things and for everlasting gladness and mercy. Glory be to the Holy Trinity. Amen.

(من سفر التثنية ص 8 : 11-20)

احترز من أن تنسى الرب إلهك ولا تحفظ وصاياه وأحكامه وحقوقه . هذه التى أنا أوصيك بها . لئلا تأكل وتشبع وتبنى بيوتاً حسنة جميلة وتسكنها . ويكثر لك الغنم والبقر . ويكثر لك الذهب والفضة. وتكثر كل مقتنياتك فتنسى الرب إلهك الذى أخرجك من أرض مصر من بيت عبوديتك ، الذى أجازك هذا القفر العظيم المخوف . حيث الحيات والعقارب اللادغة. وحيث العطش ولا يوجد ماء . الذى أخرج لك ينبوع ماء من صخرة صماء . الذى أطعمك المن فى البرية ، هذا الذى لم يعرفه آباؤك . لكى يؤدبك ويجربك ثم يحسن إليك فى آخرتك . ولا تقل فى قلبك أننى بشجاعتى وقوة يدى صنعت لى هذه الخيرات العظيمة. بل تذكر الرب إلهك فهو الذى ثبتك ليجعل لك القوة . لكى يفى بعهده الذى أقسم الرب من أجله لأبائك كما فى نهار هذا اليوم . فان أنت نسيت نسياناً الرب إلهك وذهبت وأتبعت آلهة أخرى غريبة لتعبدها وتسجد لها ، فانى أشهد عليكم اليوم السماء والأرض إنكم تهلكون هلاكاً كيفية الأمم التى أبادها الرب من أمامكم . هكذا أنتم تهلكون لأنكم لم تطيعوا لصوت الرب الهكم . مجداً للثالوث القدوس.

(من سفر يشوع بن شيراخ 2 : 1 - 9)

يا إبنى ان تقدمت لخدمة الرب هيئ نفسك للتجارب. وقَّوم قلبك واحتمل ، ولا تنحل فى زمان أتعابك. التصق به ولا تبتعد عنه لكى تنمو فى آخرتك. أقبل كل ما يأتى عليك لتكون طويل الروح فى أرض تواضعك ، فان الذهب يُمحص بالنار ، والمختارين من الناس فى أتون الذل. آمن به فينصرك. قوم سبلك وليكن عليه اتكالك. أيها المتقون الرب انتظروا رحمته ولا تحيدوا لئلا تسقطوا. يا خائفى الرب آمنوا به فلا يضيع أجركم. يا خائفى الرب ارجوا الخيرات والحياة الأبدية والرحمة. مجداً للثالوث.

Job 27:1-28:2

As God lives, who has thus judged me; and the Almighty, who has embittered my soul; verily, while my breath is yet in me, and the breath of God which remains to me is in my nostrils, my lips shall not speak evil words, neither shall my soul meditate unrighteous thoughts. Far be it from me that I should justify you till I die! For I will not let go my innocence, but keeping fast to my righteousness, I will by no means let it go: for I am not conscious to myself of having done anything amiss. But on the contrary, let my enemies be as the overthrow of the ungodly, and they that rise up against me as the destruction of transgressors. For what is the hope of the ungodly, that he holds to it? Will he indeed trust in the Lord and be saved? Will God hear his prayer? Or when distress has come upon him, has he any confidence before Him? Or will God hear him as he calls upon Him? Yet now I will tell you what is in the hand of the Lord: I will not lie concerning the things which are with the Almighty. Behold, you all know that you are adding vanity to vanity. This is the portion of an ungodly man from the Lord, and the possession of oppressors shall come upon them from the Almighty. And if their children are many, they shall be for slaughter: and if they grow up, they shall beg. And they that survive of him shall utterly perish, and no one shall pity their widows. Even if he should gather silver as dust, and prepare gold as clay, all these things shall the righteous gain, and the true-hearted shall possess His wealth. And his house is gone like moths, and like a spider's web. The rich man shall lie down, and shall not continue: he has opened his eyes, and he is no more. Pains have come upon him as water, and darkness has carried him away by night. For there is a place for the silver, where it comes, and a place for the gold, where it is refined. For iron comes out of the earth, and brass is hewn out like stone. Glory be to the Holy Trinity. Amen.

1 Kings 19:9-14

And he entered there into a cave, and rested there. And behold, the word of the Lord came to him, and He said, What are you doing here, Elijah? And Elijah said, I have been very jealous for the Lord Almighty, because the children of Israel have forsaken You; they have dug down Your altars, and have slain Your prophets with the sword; and I alone am left, and they seek my life, to take it. And He said, You shall go forth tomorrow, and shall stand before the Lord in the mount; behold, the Lord will pass by. And behold, a great and strong wind tore into the mountains, and crushed the rocks before the Lord; but the Lord was not in the wind. And after the wind there was an earthquake; but the Lord was not in the earthquake. And after the earthquake there was a fire; but the Lord was not in the fire. And after the fire there was the voice of a gentle breeze. And it came to pass when Elijah heard, that he wrapped his face in his mantle, and went forth and stood in the cave. And behold, a voice came to him and said, What are you doing here, Elijah? And Elijah said, I have

(من سفر أيوب الصديق 27 : 1- 28 : 2)

حى هو الرب الذى حكم علىّ هكذا والضابط الكل الذى مرر نفسى ، أنه ما دامت نفسى فىّ والروح القدس فى أنفى فلن تنطق شفتاى اثماً ، ولن تهذ نفسى ظلماً. حاشا لي أن أقول انكم أبراراً حتى أموت ، لأنى لن أترك وداعتى متمسكاً بالبر فلن أسقط. لست أعرف عن ذاتى أنى صنعت ظلماً. كلا فأن أعدائى يصيرون مثل انقلاب المنافقين والذين يقومون علىّ مثل هلاك مخالفى الناموس. لأن ما هو رجاء المنافق؟ و إذا توكل مؤمناً بالله هل يخلص أو يسمع طلبته؟ أو إذا حل عليه ضيق أليس له دالة أمامه حتى إذا ما صرخ إليه يستجيب له؟ ولكن هوذا أنا أعلمكم ما هو فى يد الرب ، و لا أكذب فيما هو عند ضابط الكل. هوذا كلكم تعلمون أن الأباطيل تأتى على الذين يتباطلون. هذا هو نصيب الرجل المنافق من قبل الرب ، وخزى الأقوياء يأتى عليهم من قبل ضابط الكل . إذا كثر أولاده فيكونون للذبح وإذا قووا فهم للتسول. فمن له من الصغار يموت موتاً ولا يشفق أحد على أراملهم وإذا جمع فضة مثل التراب وأعد ذهباً مثل الطين فكل هذه يأخذها الصديقون ، والمستقيمو القلوب يتسلطون على أمواله. وبيته يكون كالعث ومثل العنكبوت. الغنى يضطجع ولا يدوم وتتركه الشدائد مثل الماء وتأخذه الظلمات ليلاً . لأنه يوجد مكان للفضة تسبك فيه وموضع للذهب حيث يمحصونه والحديد يستخرج من التراب ويطرق النحاس مثل الحجر. مجداً للثالوث القدوس .

(من سفر الملوك الأول 19 : 9 - 14)

وصار كلام الرب إلى إيليا قائلاً : مالك هنا يا إيليا . فقال : غرت غيرة أيها السيد إله القوات ضابط الكل لأن بنى إسرائيل قد تركوك وهدموا مذابحك وقتلوا أنبياءك بالسيف وبقيت أنا وحدى وهم يطلبون نفسى . فقال الرب له: أخرج أنت غداً وقف أمام الرب فى الجبل. وإذ الرب عابر وريح شديدة منيعة تشقق الجبال وتحطم الصخور أمام الرب ولم يكن الرب فى الريح وبعد الريح زلزلة وبعد الزلزلة نار ولم يكن الرب فى النار. وبعد النار صوت نسيم لطيف وهدوء عظيم والرب هناك. وحدث لما سمع إيليا ، ستر وجهه بردائه وخرج ووقف أمام المغارة. وهوذا صوت الرب صار إليه قائلاً له : مالك هنا يا إيليا؟ فقال إيليا : غرت غيرة أيها السيد ضابط الكل رب القوات إله

been very jealous for the Lord Almighty; for the children of Israel have forsaken Your covenant, and they have overthrown Your altars, and have slain Your prophets with the sword! And I alone am left, and they seek my life, to take it. Glory be to the Holy Trinity. Amen

إسرائيل ، لأن بنى إسرائيل قد تركوا عهدك وهدموا مذابحك وقتلوا أنبياءك بالسيف وبقيت أنا وحدى وهم يطلبون نفسى ليأخذوها. مجداً للثالوث القدوس .

Pascha Praise - A (12 times), Page: 6	تسبحة البصخة A (12 مرة) ، صفحة :

The Psalm

Ⲯⲁⲗⲙⲟⲥ ⲣⲓ̅ⲏ̅ : ⲣ̅ⲓ̅ⲏ̅ ⲛⲉⲙ ⲣ̅ⲓ̅ⲑ̅

Psalms 118:118, 119

Plead my cause, and ransom me; revive me because of Your word. Salvation is far from sinners; for they have not searched out Your statutes. Alleluia

Ⲙⲁϩⲁⲡ ⲉ̀ⲡⲁϩⲁⲡ ⲟⲩⲟϩ ⲥⲟⲧⲧ ⲉⲑⲃⲉ ⲡⲉⲕⲥⲁϫⲓ ⲙⲁⲣⲓⲱⲛϧ.

Ϥⲟⲩⲏⲟⲩ ⲥⲁⲃⲟⲗ ⲛ̀ⲛⲓⲣⲉϥⲉⲣⲛⲟⲃⲓ ⲛ̀ϫⲉ ⲡⲓⲟⲩϫⲁⲓ : ϫⲉ ⲛⲉⲕⲙⲉⲑⲙⲏⲓ ⲙ̀ⲡⲟⲩⲕⲱϯ ⲛ̀ⲥⲱⲟⲩ. ⲁ̅ⲗ̅.

ما هاب إباهاب أووه صوتت إثفيه بيك صاجى مارى أونخ.

إف أوو إيوو صافول إننى ريفنر نوفى إنجيه بى أووجاى : جيه نيك ميثمى إمبوو كاتى إنصوأوو . الليلويا .

(مز 118: 118 و 111)

احكم حكمى ونجنى ، من أجل كلامك أحينى . بعيد الخلاص من الخطاة لأنهم لم يطلبوا حقوقك. الليلويا.

Introduction to the Gospel, Page: 8	مقدمة الأنجيل ، صفحة :

The Gospel

Ⲉⲩⲁⲅⲅⲉⲗⲓⲟⲛ Ⲕⲁⲧⲁ Ⲙⲁⲧⲑⲉⲟⲛ Ⲕⲉⲫ ⲕ̅ⲅ̅ : ⲗ̅ⲍ̅ - ⲕ̅ⲇ̅ : ⲁ̅ ⲛⲉⲙ ⲃ̅

Matthew 23:37-24:2

"O Jerusalem, Jerusalem, the one who kills the prophets and stones those who are sent to her! How often I wanted to gather your children together, as a hen gathers her chicks under her wings, but you were not willing! See! Your house is left to you desolate; for I say to you, you shall see Me no more till you say, 'BLESSED is HE WHO COMES IN THE NAME OF THE LORD!' " Then Jesus went out and departed from the temple, and His disciples came up to show Him the buildings of the temple. And Jesus said to them, "Do you not see all these things? Assuredly, I say to you, not one stone shall be left here upon another, that shall not be thrown down." Glory be to God forever, Amen.

Ⲓⲉⲣⲟⲩⲥⲁⲗⲏⲙ Ⲓⲉⲣⲟⲩⲥⲁⲗⲏⲙ ⲑⲏⲉⲧϧⲱⲧⲉⲃ ⲛ̀ⲛⲓⲡⲣⲟⲫⲏⲧⲏⲥ ⲟⲩⲟϩ ⲉⲧϩⲓⲱⲛⲓ ⲉ̀ϫⲉⲛ ⲛⲏⲉⲧⲁⲩⲟⲩⲟⲣⲡⲟⲩ ϩⲁⲣⲟⲥ : ⲟⲩⲏⲣ ⲛ̀ⲥⲟⲡ ⲁⲓⲟⲩⲱϣ ⲉ̀ⲑⲟⲩⲏⲧ ⲛⲉϣⲏⲣⲓ ⲙ̀ⲫⲣⲏϯ ⲛ̀ⲟⲩϩⲁⲗⲏⲧ ⲉ̀ϣⲁϥⲑⲱⲟⲩⲧ ⲛ̀ⲛⲉϥⲙⲁⲥ ⲉ̀ϧⲟⲩⲛ ϧⲁ ⲛⲉϥⲧⲉⲛϩ ⲟⲩⲟϩ ⲙ̀ⲡⲉⲧⲉⲛⲟⲩⲱϣ : ϩⲏⲡⲡⲉ ϯⲛⲁⲭⲱ ⲙ̀ⲡⲉⲧⲉⲛⲏⲓ ⲛⲱⲧⲉⲛ ⲉϥϣⲱϥ . ϯϫⲱ ⲅⲁⲣ ⲙ̀ⲙⲟⲥ ⲛⲱⲧⲉⲛ ϫⲉ ⲛ̀ⲛⲉⲧⲉⲛⲛⲁⲩ ⲉ̀ⲣⲟⲓ ⲓⲥϫⲉⲛ ϯⲛⲟⲩ ϣⲁⲧⲉⲧⲉⲛϫⲟⲥ ϫⲉ ϥ̀ⲥⲙⲁⲣⲱⲟⲩⲧ ⲛ̀ϫⲉ ⲫⲏⲉⲑⲛⲏⲟⲩ ϧⲉⲛ ⲫ̀ⲣⲁⲛ ⲙ̀ⲡⳓⲥ. Ⲟⲩⲟϩ ⲉⲧⲁϥⲓ̀ ⲛ̀ϫⲉ Ⲓⲏⲥ ⲉ̀ⲃⲟⲗ ϧⲉⲛ ⲡⲓⲉⲣⲫⲉⲓ ⲛⲁϥⲙⲟϣⲓ ⲡⲉ : ⲟⲩⲟϩ ⲁⲩⲓ̀ ϩⲁⲣⲟϥ ⲛ̀ϫⲉ ⲛⲉϥⲙⲁⲑⲏⲧⲏⲥ ⲉⲩⲧⲁⲙⲟ ⲙ̀ⲙⲟϥ ⲛ̀ⲛⲓⲕⲱⲧ ⲛ̀ⲧⲉ ⲡⲓⲉⲣⲫⲉⲓ : ⲛ̀ⲑⲟϥ ⲇⲉ ⲁϥⲉⲣⲟⲩⲱ ⲡⲉϫⲁϥ ⲛⲱⲟⲩ ϫⲉ ⲧⲉⲧⲉⲛⲛⲁⲩ ⲉ̀ⲛⲁⲓ ⲧⲏⲣⲟⲩ : ⲁⲙⲏⲛ ϯϫⲱ ⲙ̀ⲙⲟⲥ ⲛⲱⲧⲉⲛ ϫⲉ ⲛ̀ⲛⲟⲩⲭⲁ ⲟⲩⲱⲛⲓ ⲉ̀ϫⲉⲛ ⲟⲩⲱⲛⲓ ⲙ̀ⲡⲁⲓⲙⲁ ⲛ̀ⲥⲉⲛⲁⲃⲟⲗϥ ⲉ̀ⲃⲟⲗ ⲁⲛ . ⲟⲩⲱϣⲧ ⲙ̀ⲡⲓⲉⲩⲁⲅⲅⲉⲗⲓⲟⲛ ⲉⲑⲩ .

(متى 23: 37-34 : 2)

يا أورشليم يا أورشليم يا قاتلة الأنبياء وراجمة المرسلين إليها . كم من مرة أردت أن أجمع بنيك كما يجمع الطائر فراخه تحت جناحيه فلم تريدوا . هوذا أترك لكم بيتكم خراباً . فأنى أقول لكم انكم من الآن لا ترونى حتى تقولوا مبارك الآتى باسم الرب . ولما خرج يسوع من الهيكل ومضى . تقدم إليه تلاميذه ليروه بناء الهيكل. أما هو فأجاب وقال لهم : انظروا هذا كله . الحق أقول لكم أنه لا يترك ههنا حجر على حجر إلا وينقض . والمجد لله دائماً .

Exposition

طــرح

Several times, the Lord said "O Jerusalem, I wanted to gather your children as the hen gathers her chicks under her wings and you would not. Behold I leave your house for you desolate forever." When the disciples heard the prophecy of the prophet and of the Savior, they showed him the temple, the venerated stones, and the sanctuaries. He responded to them saying: "There will not be two stones together." Truly this happened forty years after the ascension of our Lord. The Romans came, devastated the city, and demolished the temple which remains thus to this day. One million, two hundred-thousand Jewish men were killed by the sword. They were rebuked by God's wrath and His damnation covered their faces.

كم مرة قال الرب: أردت أن أجمع بـنيك يا أورشليم كمثل الطائر الذى يجمع فراخه تحت جناحيه فلم تريدوا . ها أنا أترك لكم بيتكم خراباً ، قال الرب ، إلى الانقضاء. فلما سمع التلاميذ نبوة النبى والمخلص ، أروه بناء الهيكل والحجارة المكرمة والمحرمات. فأجابهم قائلاً : أنه لا يترك ههنا حجر على حجر إلا وينقض . فبالحقيقة صار هذا من بعد أربعين سنة لصعود مخلصنا . جاء الروم وهدموا المدينة وخربوا الهيكل إلى اليوم . مائة وعشرون ربوة من رجال من اليهود قتلوا بحد السيف وحل عليهم غضب الله واللعنة غطت وجوههم .

(North side) Christ our Savior; has come and has borne suffering; that through His Passion; He may save us.

(مرد بحرى) المسيح مخلصنا جاء وتألم عنا لكى بآلامه يخلصنا .

(South side) Let us glorify Him; and exalt His Name; for He had mercy on us; according to His great mercy.

(مرد قبلى) فلنمجده ونرفع اسمه لأنه صنع معنا رحمة كعظيم رحمته .

الساعة السادسة من يوم الثلاثاء من البصخة المقدسة
The Sixth Hour of Tuesday of the Holy Pascha

Ezekiel 21:3-13

Thus says the Lord: Behold, I am against you, and I will draw forth My sword out of its sheath, and I will destroy out of you the transgressor and the unrighteous. Because I will destroy out of you the unrighteous and the transgressor, therefore so shall My sword come forth out of its sheath against all flesh from the south to the north; and all flesh shall know that I the Lord have drawn forth My sword out of its sheath: it shall not return anymore. And you, son of man, groan with the breaking of your loins; you shall even groan heavily in their sight. And it shall come to pass, if they shall say to you, Why do you groan? That you shall say, For the report; because it comes: and every heart shall break, and all hands shall become feeble, and all flesh and every spirit shall faint, and all thighs shall be defiled with moisture: behold, it comes, says the Lord. And the word of the Lord came to me, saying, Son of man, prophesy, and you shall say, Thus says the Lord: Say, Sword, sword, be sharpened and rage, that you may slay victims; be sharpened, that you may be bright, ready for slaughter, slay, set at nought, despise every tree. And He made it ready for His hand to hold. The sword is sharpened, it is ready to put into the hand of the slayer. Cry out and howl, son of man: for this sword has come upon My people, this sword has come upon all the princes of Israel: they shall be as strangers: judgment with the sword has come upon My people; therefore clap your hands, for sentence has been passed; and what if even the tribe be rejected? It shall not be, says the Lord God. Glory be to the Holy Trinity. Amen

Sirach 4:20-5:2

Watch for a proper opportunity and keep yourself from evil; and do not bring shame upon your soul. For there is a shame that brings sin, and there is a shame which is glory and grace. Do not show partiality to someone to your own harm, and do not let your respect for another cause you to fall. Do not withhold a word in time of need; for wisdom is made known by a word, and instruction by a-word of the tongue. Do not speak against the truth, and do not be put to shame by your ignorance. Do not be ashamed to confess your sins, and do not exercise force against the current of a river. Do not subject yourself to a foolish man, and do not show partiality to a ruler. Fight to the death for the truth, and the Lord God will fight for you. Do not be rash with your tongue and sluggish and neglectful in your works. Do not be like a lion in your home and act in pretense with your servants. Do not let your hand be extended to receive and shut when you

(من سفر حزقيال النبى 21 : 3 – 13)

هذا ما يقوله السيد الرب . هأنذا ضدك وأستل سيفى من غمده وأستأصل منك الظالم و المتجاوز الناموس. هكذا يخرج سيف من غمده على كل ذى جسد. من المغرب إلى الشمال . ويعلم كل ذى جسد إنى أنا هو الرب جردت سيفى من غمده ولا يرتد بعد . أما أنت يا إبن الإنسان فتنهد بانكسار حقويك ، وبانسحاق الحزن تتأوه أمام عيونهم . ويكون إذا قالوا لك : علام تتنهد ؟ فتقول : إننى أتنهد على الخير لأنه آتٍ فينسحق كل قلب . وترتخى كل يد . ويضعف كل جسد وكل روح . ويتدنس كل صلب بالردى . ها هو آتٍ ويكون ، قال الرب. وكان إلىّ كلام الرب قائلاً : يا إبن الإنسان تنبأ وقل: هذا ما يقوله السيد الرب . قل للسيف يا سيف يا سيف احتد وأضرب لكى تذبح ذبحاً وأضرب بحدك لكى تكون لامعاً . تأهب واسحق العار . وأسقط كل الأشجار . لأنه قد أعطى ليكون مُهيئاً عندما يُمسك باليد ليَضرب بحده . سيفاً مستعداً يُعطى ليد الذى يذبح . أصرخ وولول يا إبن الإنسان لأن هذا قد صار لشعبى وعلى كل مدبرى بيت إسرائيل. وسيفاً يجول قد صار لشعبى. لذلك صفق على يدك فانه قد تذكى وهو يضرب لإخراج القبائل فلا تكون ، قال الرب . مجداً للثالوث القدوس .

(من يشوع بن سيراخ 4 : 23- 5 : 2)

تأمل الزمان وتحفظ من الشر، ولا تستحى من عدم معرفتك . فان من الحياء ما يجلب الخطية. ومنه ما هو مجد ونعمة . لا تحاب فذلك ضرر لنفسك . ولا تستحى من سقطتك . لا تمتنع عن الكلام فى وقت الخلاص . لأن بالكلام تُعرف الحكمة والفهم من نطق اللسان . لا تقاوم الحق وتستحى من جهالتك . لا تستحى أن تعترف بخطاياك ولا تغالب نهراً جارياً ولا تتزلل للرجل الأحمق . ولا تحاب المقتدر . جاهد عن الحق إلى الموت لكى يقاتل الله عنك . لا تكن سريع الكلام مكسوراً متراخياً فى أعمالك . لا تكن كأسد فى بيتك قاسياً على عبيدك . لا تكن يدك مبسوطة للأخذ مقبوضة عن العطاء. لا تتوكل على الأموال ولا تقل هى تكفينى فى

should repay. Do not set your heart on your possessions, and do not say, "I am independent." Do not follow yourself and your strength so as to walk in the desires of your heart. Glory be to the Holy Trinity. Amen.

حياتى . لا تتبع هواك وقوتك ، لتسير فى شهوات قلبك . مجداً للثالوث القدوس .

Isaiah 1:1-9

The vision which Isaiah the son of Amos saw, which he saw concerning Judah, and Jerusalem, in the reign of Uzziah, Jotham, Ahaz, and Hezekiah, who reigned over Judah. Hear, O heaven, and hearken, O earth! For the Lord has spoken, saying, I have begotten and reared up children, but they have rebelled against Me. The ox knows his owner, and the donkey his master's crib; but Israel does not know Me, and the people have not regarded Me. Alas, sinful nation, a people full of sins, an evil seed, lawless children; you have forsaken the Lord, and provoked the Holy One of Israel. Why should you be smitten anymore, transgressing more and more? The whole head is pained, and the whole heart sad. From the feet to the head, there is no soundness in them; neither wound, nor bruise, nor festering ulcer are healed; it is not possible to apply a plaister, nor oil, nor bandages. Your land is desolate, your cities are burned with fire; strangers devour your land in your presence, and it is made desolate, overthrown by strange nations. The daughter of Zion shall be deserted as a tent in a vineyard, and as a storehouse of fruits in a garden of cucumbers, as a besieged city. And if the Lord of Sabaoth had not left us a seed, we would have become like Sodom, and been made like Gomorrah. Glory be to the Holy Trinity. Amen

(من سفر إشعياء النبى 1 : 1 - 9)

رؤيا إشعياء إبن آموص التى رأها على يهوذا وأورشليم فى مملكة عزيا ويوسام واحاز وحزقيا الذين ملكوا على يهوذا . إسمعى أيتها السموات وإصغى أيتها الأرض فان الرب قد تكلم . إنى ربيت بنين ورفعتهم أما هم فتمردوا علىّ . الثور يعرف قانيه والحمار معلف صاحبه أما إسرائيل فلم يعرفنى وشعبى لم يفهمنى. ويل للأمة الخاطئة ، الشعب الممتلئ اثماً ، النسل الخبيث أولاد المخالفين . تركتم الرب عنكم وأغضبتم قدوس إسرائيل وازددتم اثماً على اثم فنزلت عليكم الضربات . كل رأس للوجع وكل قلب للحزن ، من أخمص القدم إلى قمة الرأس ليس فيه صحة بل جرح لا يوضع عليه مرهم ولا دهن ولا عصائب . أرضكم تخرب . ومدنكم تحرق بالنار . وكوركم تأكلها غرباء قدامكم . وقد خربت وانهدمت من الشعوب الغرباء . وتبقى إبنة صهيون كمظلة فى كرم وكمثل المحرس المنقطع فى المقثأة . وكالمدينة المنهوبة . ولولا أن رب الجنود أبقى لنا بقية صغيرة لصرنا مثل سدوم وشابهنا عمورة . مجداً للثالوث القدوس .

| Pascha Praise - A (12 times), Page: 6 | تسبحة البصخة A (12 مرة) ، صفحة : 6 |

The Psalm

Ⲯⲁⲗⲙⲟⲥ ⲓⲍ : ⲙ̄ⲏ ⲛⲉⲙ ⲓ̄ⲑ̄

Psalms 17:48, 19			(مز 17: 48 و19)
My deliverer from angry enemies; You shall set me on high above them that rise up against me; You shall deliver me from the unrighteous man. He will deliver me from my mighty enemies, and from them that hate me. Alleluia	Ⲡⲁⲣⲉϥⲛⲁϩⲙⲉⲧ ⲉⲃⲟⲗ ⲛ̄ⲧⲟⲧⲟⲩ ⲛ̄ⲛⲁϫⲁϫⲓ ⲛ̄ⲣⲉϥϫⲱⲛⲧ : ⲛⲉⲙ ⲉⲃⲟⲗ ⲛ̄ⲧⲟⲧⲟⲩ ⲛ̄ⲛⲏⲉⲧ ⲧⲱⲟⲩⲛ ⲙ̄ⲙⲱⲟⲩ ⲉ̀ϩⲣⲏⲓ ⲉϫⲱⲓ ⲉⲕⲉⲃⲁⲥⲧ .(ⲗⲉⲝⲓⲥ) Ⲛⲁϩⲙⲉⲧ ⲉ̀ⲃⲟⲗ ϩⲁ ⲟⲩⲣⲱⲙⲓ ⲛ̄ⲟϫⲓ ⲉϥⲉⲛⲁϩⲙⲉⲧ ⲉⲃⲟⲗ ⲛ̄ⲧⲟⲧⲟⲩ ⲛ̄ⲛⲁϫⲁϫⲓ ⲉⲧϫⲟⲣ : ⲛⲉⲙ ⲉⲃⲟⲗ ⲛ̄ⲧⲟⲧⲟⲩ ⲛ̄ⲛⲏⲉⲑⲙⲟⲥϯ ⲙ̄ⲙⲟⲓ . ⲁ̅ⲗ̅ .	باريف ناهميت إيفول إنطوطوو إنناجاجى إنريف جونت : نيم إيفول إنطوطوو إننى إتطوؤون إمموؤو إإهرى إيجوى إكتشاسى . ناهميت إيفول ها أوو رومى إنؤجى إفنناهميت إيفول إنطوطوو إنناجاجى إتجور : نيم إيفول إنطوطوو إننى إثموستى إمموى . الليلويا	منقذى من أعدائى الراجزين ومن الذين يقومون علىّ ترفعنى . (جملة) ومن الرجل الظالم تنجينى. تخلصنى من أعدائى الاشداء ومن أيدى الذين يبغضوننى. ألليلويا .

| Introduction to the Gospel, Page: 8 | مقدمة الأنجيل ، صفحة : 8 |

The Gospel

Ⲉⲩⲁⲅⲅⲉⲗⲓⲟⲛ Ⲕⲁⲧⲁ Ⲓⲱⲁⲛⲛⲏⲛ Ⲕⲉⲫ Ⲏ̄ : Ⲓ̄Ⲃ̄ - Ⲕ̄

John 8:12-20

Then Jesus spoke to them again, saying, "I am the light of the world. He who follows Me shall not walk in darkness, but have the light of life." The Pharisees therefore said to Him, "You bear witness of Yourself; Your witness is not true." Jesus answered and said to them, "Even if I bear witness of Myself, My witness is true, for I know where I came from and where I am going; but you do not know where I come from and where I am going. You judge according to the flesh; I judge no one. And yet if I do judge, My judgment is true; for I am not alone, but I am with the Father who sent Me. It is also written in your law that the testimony of two men is true. I am One who bears witness of Myself, and the Father who sent Me bears witness of Me." Then they said to Him, "Where is Your Father?" Jesus answered, "You know neither Me nor My Father. If you had known Me, you would have known My Father also." These words Jesus spoke in the treasury, as He taught in the temple; and no one laid hands on Him, for His hour had not yet come. Glory be to God forever, Amen.

Ⲡⲁⲗⲓⲛ ⲟⲛ ⲁϥⲥⲁϫⲓ ⲛⲉⲙⲱⲟⲩ ⲛ̀ϫⲉ Ⲓⲏ̅ⲥ̅ ⲉϥϫⲱ ⲙ̀ⲙⲟⲥ : ϫⲉ ⲁⲛⲟⲕ ⲡⲉ ⲫ̀ⲟⲩⲱⲓⲛⲓ ⲙ̀ⲡⲓⲕⲟⲥⲙⲟⲥ : ⲫⲏⲉⲑⲛⲁⲙⲟϣⲓ ⲛ̀ⲥⲱⲓ ⲛ̀ⲛⲉϥⲙⲟϣⲓ ϧⲉⲛ ⲡⲓⲭⲁⲕⲓ : ⲁⲗⲗⲁ ⲉϥ̀ⲉϭⲓ ⲙ̀ⲫⲟⲩⲱⲓⲛⲓ ⲛ̀ⲧⲉ ⲡⲱⲛϧ : ⲡⲉϫⲉ ⲛⲓⲫⲁⲣⲓⲥⲉⲟⲥ ⲛⲁϥ ϫⲉ ⲛ̀ⲑⲟⲕ ⲙ̀ⲙⲁⲩⲁⲧⲕ ⲉⲧⲉⲣⲙⲉⲑⲣⲉ ϧⲁⲣⲟⲕ : ⲧⲉⲕⲙⲉⲧⲙⲉⲑⲣⲉ ⲟⲩⲏⲓ ⲁⲛ ⲧⲉ : ⲁϥⲉⲣⲟⲩⲱ ⲛ̀ϫⲉ Ⲓⲏ̅ⲥ̅ ⲟⲩⲟϩ ⲡⲉϫⲁϥ ⲛⲱⲟⲩ : ϫⲉ ⲕⲁⲛ ⲉ̀ϣⲱⲡ ⲁⲛⲟⲕ ⲁⲓϣⲁⲛⲉⲣⲙⲉⲑⲣⲉ ϧⲁⲣⲟⲓ ⲧⲁⲙⲉⲧⲙⲉⲑⲣⲉ ⲟⲩⲏⲓ ⲧⲉ : ϫⲉ ϯⲉⲙⲓ ϫⲉ ⲉⲧⲁⲓⲓ̀ ⲉ̀ⲃⲟⲗ ⲑⲱⲛ ⲓⲉ ⲉⲓⲛⲁϣⲉⲛⲏⲓ ⲉ̀ⲑⲱⲛ : ⲛ̀ⲑⲱⲧⲉⲛ ⲇⲉ ⲧⲉⲧⲉⲛ̀ⲉⲙⲓ ⲁⲛ ϫⲉ ⲉⲧⲁⲓⲓ̀ ⲉ̀ⲃⲟⲗ ⲑⲱⲛ ⲓⲉ ⲉⲓⲛⲁϣⲉⲛⲏⲓ ⲉ̀ⲑⲱⲛ . Ⲛ̀ⲑⲱⲧⲉⲛ ⲇⲉ ⲁⲣⲉⲧⲉⲛϯϩⲁⲡ ⲕⲁⲧⲁ ⲥⲁⲣⲝ ⲁⲛⲟⲕ ⲇⲉ ϯϯϩⲁⲡ ⲉ̀ϩⲗⲓ ⲁⲛ : ⲟⲩⲟϩ ⲉ̀ϣⲱⲡ ⲁⲛⲟⲕ ⲁⲓϣⲁⲛϯϩⲁⲡ ⲡⲁϩⲁⲡ ⲛ̀ⲁⲟⲕ ⲟⲩⲏⲓ ⲡⲉ : ϫⲉ ⲛ̀ϯⲭⲏ ⲙ̀ⲙⲁⲩⲁⲧ ⲁⲛ ⲁⲗⲗⲁ ⲁⲛⲟⲕ ⲛⲉⲙ ⲫⲏⲉⲧⲁϥⲧⲁⲟⲩⲟⲓ ⲫ̀ⲓⲱⲧ : ⲟⲩⲟϩ ⲥ̀ⲥϧⲏⲟⲩⲧ ⲇⲉ ⲟⲛ ϧⲉⲛ ⲡⲉⲧⲉⲛⲛⲟⲙⲟⲥ ϫⲉ ⲑⲙⲉⲧⲙⲉⲑⲣⲉ ⲛ̀ⲣⲱⲙⲓ ⲥⲛⲁⲩ ⲟⲩⲏⲓ ⲧⲉ . Ⲁⲛⲟⲕ ⲇⲉ ϯⲉⲣⲙⲉⲑⲣⲉ ϧⲁⲣⲟⲓ ⲟⲩⲟϩ ϥⲉⲣⲙⲉⲑⲣⲉ ϧⲁⲣⲟⲓ ⲛ̀ϫⲉ ⲫ̀ⲓⲱⲧ ⲫⲏⲉⲧⲁϥⲧⲁⲟⲩⲟⲓ : ⲛⲁⲩϫⲱ ⲟⲩⲛ ⲙ̀ⲙⲟⲥ ⲛⲁϥ ⲡⲉ ϫⲉ ⲁϥⲑⲱⲛ ⲛⲉⲕⲓⲱⲧ ⲁϥⲉⲣⲟⲩⲱ ⲛ̀ϫⲉ Ⲓⲏ̅ⲥ̅ : ϫⲉ ⲟⲩⲇⲉ ⲁⲛⲟⲕ ⲛ̀ⲧⲉⲧⲉⲛⲥⲱⲟⲩⲛ ⲙ̀ⲙⲟⲓ ⲁⲛ ⲟⲩⲇⲉ ⲡⲁⲓⲱⲧ : ⲉ̀ⲛⲁⲣⲉⲧⲉⲛⲥⲱⲟⲩⲛ ⲙ̀ⲙⲟⲓ ⲡⲉ ⲛⲁⲣⲉⲧⲉⲛⲛⲁⲥⲟⲩⲉⲛ ⲡⲁⲓⲱⲧ : ⲛⲁⲓⲥⲁϫⲓ ⲁϥϫⲟⲧⲟⲩ ϧⲉⲛ ⲡⲓⲅⲁⲍⲟⲫⲩⲗⲁⲕⲓⲟⲛ ⲉϥϯⲥⲃⲱ ϧⲉⲛ ⲡⲓⲉⲣⲫⲉⲓ : ⲟⲩⲟϩ ⲙ̀ⲡⲉ ϩⲗⲓ ϣⲁⲙⲟⲛⲓ ⲙ̀ⲙⲟϥ ϫⲉ ⲛⲉ ⲙ̀ⲡⲁⲧⲉⲥ ⲓ̀ ⲛ̀ϫⲉ ⲧⲉϥⲟⲩⲛⲟⲩ . ⲟⲩⲱϣⲧ ⲙ̀ⲡⲓⲉⲩⲁⲅⲅⲉⲗⲓⲟⲛ ⲉⲑⲩ .

(يوحنا 8: 12 - 20)

ثم كلمهم أيضاً يسوع قائلاً : أنا هو نور العالم . ومن يتبعنى لا يمشى فى الظلمة بل يكون له نور الحياة . فقال له الفريسيون: أنت وحدك تشهد لنفسك ، فليست شهادتك حقاً . أجاب يسوع وقال لهم : أنى وان كنت أشهد لنفسى فشهادتى حق ، لأنى أعلم من أين جئت وإلى أين أذهب . وأما أنتم فلا تعلمون من أين أتيت ولا أين أمضى . أنتم انما تدينون بحسب الجسد وأنا لا أدين أحد . وان أنا دنت فدينونتى حق هى . لأنى لست وحدى بل أنا والآب الذى أرسلنى . وقد كُتب أيضاً فى ناموسكم ان شهادة رجلين حق هى . أنا أشهد لنفسى وأبى الذى أرسلنى يشهد لي . قالوا له: أين هو أبوك؟ قال يسوع: لستم تعرفوننى أنا ولا أبى أيضاً . لو كنتم تعرفوننى لعرفتم أبى أيضاً . هذه الأقوال قالها فى الخزانة وهو يعلم فى الهيكل . ولم يمسكه أحد لأن ساعته لم تكن قد أتت بعد . والمجد لله دائماً .

Introduction to the Exposition, Page: 9 : مقدمة الطرح ، صفحة

Exposition

The True God who came to the world says: "I am the light of the world", and what He says is the truth, "he who follows Me shall not walk in the darkness, but will have the light of life which will lead him to the way of the truth." Truly, You are the light of the Father and the Person from His essence, whose glory shines with great luminescence over the creation unto eternity. He drew us after Him, the estranged nation, to the

طـرح

الإله الحقيقى الذى أتى إلى العالم يقول وقوله الحق من فمه غير الكاذب: انـنى نور العالم ومن يتبعنى لن يمشى فى الظلام بل يجد نور الحياة يهديه إلى طريق الحق . أنت هو بالحق نور الآب والأقنوم الذى من جوهره . الذى مجده يشرق بلمعان عظيم على المسكونة فى آخر الدهور . جذبنا معاً نحن معشر الشعوب

knowledge of the truth in His name. He enlightened us with the light of His divinity, we who are sitting in the darkness and shadow of death. As for the contrary Jews who are His own: He relegated them to the darkness of Hell forever because they refused His words, rejected Him, and condemned Him to death. Let us praise his holy name and exalt in glorifying Him.

الغريبة إلى معرفة الحق باسمه . وأضاء علينا بنور لاهوته نحن الجلوس فى الظلمة وظلال الموت . فأما اليهود المخالفون الذين هم خواصه ، القاهم فى ظلمة الجحيم إلى الأبد ، لأنهم رفضوا أقواله ولم يقبلوه وحكموا عليه بحكم الموت . فلنعظم نحن اسمه القدوس ونمجده بغير فتور .

(North side) Christ our Savior; has come and has borne suffering; that through His Passion; He may save us.

(مرد بحرى) المسيح مخلصنا جاء وتألم عنا لكى بآلامه يخلصنا .

(South side) Let us glorify Him; and exalt His Name; for He had mercy on us; according to His great mercy.

(مرد قبلى) فلنمجده ونرفع اسمه لأنه صنع معنا رحمة كعظيم رحمته .

The Conclusion of the Exposition, Page: 9   ختام الطرح ، صفحة :

الساعة التاسعة من يوم الثلاثاء من البصخة المقدسة
The Ninth Hour of Tuesday of the Holy Pascha

Genesis 6:5-9:6

And the Lord God, having seen that the wicked actions of men were multiplied upon the earth, and that every one in his heart was intently brooding over evil continually, then God laid it to heart that He had made man upon the earth, and He pondered it deeply. And God said, I will blot out man whom I have made from the face of the earth, even man with cattle, and reptiles with flying creatures of the sky, for I am grieved that I have made them. But Noah found grace before the Lord God. And these are the generations of Noah. Noah was a just man; being perfect in his generation, Noah was well pleasing to God. And Noah begot three sons, Shem, Ham, Japheth. But the earth was corrupted before God, and the earth was filled with iniquity. And the Lord God saw the earth, and it was corrupted; because all flesh had corrupted its way upon the earth. And the Lord God said to Noah, A period of all men is come before Me; because the earth has been filled with iniquity by them, and, behold, I destroy them and the earth. Therefore make for yourself an ark of square timber; you shall make the ark in compartments, and you shall pitch it within and without with pitch. And thus shall you make the ark; three hundred cubits the length of the ark, and fifty cubits the breadth, and thirty cubits the height of it. You shall narrow the ark in making it, and in a cubit above you shall finish it, and the door of the ark you shall make on the side; with lower, second, and third stories you shall make it. And behold I bring a flood of water upon the earth, to destroy all flesh in which is the breath of life under heaven, and whatsoever things are upon the earth shall die. And I will establish My covenant with you, and you shall enter into the ark, and your sons and your wife, and your sons' wives with you. And of all cattle and of all reptiles and of all wild beasts, even of all flesh, you shall bring by pairs of all, into the ark, that you may feed them with yourself: male and female they shall be. Of all winged birds after their kind, and of all cattle after their kind, and of all reptiles creeping upon the earth after their kind, pairs of all shall come in to you, male and female to be fed with you. And you shall take to yourself of all kinds of food which you eat, and you shall gather them to yourself, and it shall be for you and them to eat. And Noah did all things whatever the Lord God commanded him, so did he. And the Lord God said to Noah, Enter therefore, you and all your family, into the ark, for I have seen that you are righteous before Me in this generation. You shall take with you seven each of every clean animal, male and female, and of the unclean animals take two each, male and female. And also seven each of the clean flying creatures of the sky, male and female, and also pairs of all

(من سفر التكوين 6 : 5- 9 : 6)

ولما رأى الرب الإله أن شرور الناس قد كثرت على الأرض ، وان كل واحد قد مال بقلبه كثيراً إلى الشر كل الأيام ففكر الرب الإله أنه خلق الإنسان على الأرض . وفكر الرب الإله فى قلبه وقال : إنى مبيد عن وجه الأرض الإنسان الذى خلقته ، من الإنسان إلى البهائم ومن الهوام إلى طيور السماء . لأنى حنقت إذ خلقتهم . وأما نوح فوجد نعمة أمام الرب الإله . وهذه مواليد نوح . كان نوح رجلاً باراً كاملاً فى جيله وأرضى نوح الله . وولد نوح ثلثة بنين ساما وحاما ويافث وتنجست الأرض أمام الله . وإمتلأت الأرض ظلماً . فنظر الرب الإله إلى الأرض فاذا هى قد فسدت لأن كل ذى جسد قد نجس طريقة على الأرض . فقال الرب الإله لنوح أن أجل كل بشر قد اقترب أمامى . لأن الأرض إمتلأت ظلماً منهم . فها أنا مهلكهم والأرض معاً فاصنع لك فلكاً من خشب السرو الذى لا يسوس وأصنع الفلك كاملاً وتطلى داخله وخارجه بالقار . وهكذا تصنع الفلك ثلاثمائة ذراعاً يكون طول الفلك . وخمسين ذراعاً عرضه . وثلاثين ذراعاً ارتفاعه . ويكون الفلك مقبباً وتصنع له كوا وتكمله إلى حد ذراع من فوق . وتصنع باب الفلك فى جانبه وطبقات سفلية ومتوسطه وعلوية تجعله . فها أنا آت بطوفان الماء على الأرض . لأهلك كل جسد فيه روح حياة تحت السماء . وكل شئ كائن على الأرض يموت . وأقرر عهدى معك فتدخل الفلك أنت وبنوك وإمرأتك ونساء بنيك معك . ومن جميع الوحوش . ومن جميع الدواب . ومن كل ذى جسد اثنين اثنين من كل تدخل إلى الفلك لكى تعولها معك . تكون ذكراً وأنثى . من الطيور الطائرة كجنسها . ومن جميع البهائم كأجناسها . ومن الهوام التى على الأرض كأجناسها اثنين اثنين تدخل إليك لتعولها معك . ويكون ذكراً وأنثى . وأنت فخذ لك من كل الأطعمة التى تأكلونها وأجمعها إليك لتكون لك وللآخرين مأكلاً . ففعل نوح كل ما أمره به الرب الإله هكذا فعل . وقال الرب الإله لنوح أمض أنت وأهل بيتك وادخل الفلك لأنك أنت هو الذى رأيتك باراً أمامى فى هذا الجيل . من جميع البهائم الطاهرة أدخل معك سبعة سبعة ذكراً وأنثى . ومن البهائم التى ليست بطاهرة اثنين اثنين ذكراً وأنثى ومن طيور السماء سبعة سبعة ذكراً وأنثى ومن طيور

unclean flying creatures, male and female, to maintain seed on all the earth. For yet seven days having passed I bring rain upon the earth forty days and forty nights, and I will blot out every offspring which I have made from the face of all the earth. And Noah did all things, whatever the Lord God commanded him. And Noah was six hundred years old when the flood of water was upon the earth. And then Noah, his sons, and his wife, and his sons' wives, went into the ark, because of the water of the flood. And of clean flying creatures and of unclean flying creatures, and of clean cattle and of unclean cattle, and of all things that creep upon the earth,   pairs went in to Noah into the ark, male and female, as God commanded Noah. And it came to pass after the seven days that the water of the flood came upon the earth. In the six hundredth year of the life of Noah, in the second month, on the twenty-seventh day of the month, on this day all the fountains of the abyss were broken up, and the flood gates of heaven were opened. And the rain was upon the earth forty days and forty nights. On that very day entered Noah, Shem, Ham, Japheth, the sons of Noah, and the wife of Noah, and the three wives of his sons with him into the ark.   And all the wild beasts after their kind, and all cattle after their kind, and every reptile moving itself on the earth after its kind, and every flying bird after its kind,   went in to Noah into the ark, pairs, male and female of all flesh in which is the breath of life. And they that entered went in male and female of all flesh, as God commanded Noah, and the Lord God shut the ark outside of him. And the flood was upon the earth forty days and forty nights, and the water abounded greatly and bore up the ark, and it was lifted on high from off the earth. And the water prevailed and abounded exceedingly upon the earth, and the ark was borne upon the water. And the water prevailed exceedingly upon the earth, and covered all the high mountains which were under heaven. Fifteen cubits upwards was the water raised, and it covered all the high mountains. And there died all flesh that moved upon the earth, of flying creatures and cattle, and of wild beasts, and every reptile moving upon the earth, and every man. And all things which have the breath of life, and whatever was on the dry land, died. And God blotted out every offspring which was upon the face of the earth, both man and beast, and reptiles, and birds of the sky, and they were blotted out from the earth, and Noah was left alone, and those with him in the ark. And the water was raised over the earth one hundred and fifty days. And God remembered Noah, and all the wild beasts, and all the cattle, and all the birds, and all the reptiles that creep, as many as were with him in the ark, and God brought a wind upon the earth, and the water stayed. And the fountains of the deep were closed up, and the flood gates of heaven, and the rain from heaven was withheld. And the water subsided, and went off the earth, and after one hundred and fifty days the water was diminished, and the ark rested in the seventh

السماء الغير الطاهرة اثنين اثنين ذكراً وأنثى . ليبقى منها نسل على الأرض كلها . لأنى بعد سبعة أيام أمطر ماء الطوفان على الأرض أربعين يوماً وأربعين ليلة . وأمحو كل الخليقة التى خلقتها عن وجه الأرض . ففعل نوح كل ما أمره به الرب الإله . وكان نوح إبن ست مئة سنة . إذ هطل ماء الطوفان على الأرض فمضى نوح وبنوه وإمرأته ونساء بنيه معه ودخلوا الفلك بسبب ماء الطوفان . ومن البهائم الطاهرة ومن البهائم التى ليست بطاهرة ومن الطيور الغير الطاهرة ومن كل الهوام التى على الأرض ، ودخل اثنان اثنان مع نوح إلى الفلك ، ذكراً وأنثى كما أمره الرب الإله . وحدث بعد سبعة أيام أن مياه الطوفان صارت على الأرض فى سنة ست مئة من حياة نوح ، فى الشهر الثانى فى اليوم السابع عشر من الشهر . فى ذلك اليوم تفجرت كل ينابيع الغمر العظيم وتفتحت ميازيب السماء وكان الطوفان على الأرض أربعين يوماً وأربعين ليلة . وفى هذا اليوم دخل نوح وبنوه إلى الفلك ، سام وحام ويافث بنو نوح وإمرأته ونساء بنيه الثلاث معه إلى الفلك . هم والوحوش كأجناسها . وكل الهوام التى تدب على الأرض كأجناسها . وكل الطيور كأجناسها دخلت الفلك اثنين اثنين . من كل جسد فيه روح حياة. والداخلات دخلت ذكراً وأنثى . من كل ذى جسد دخلت كما أمر الله نوحاً . وأغلق الرب الإله الفلك من خارج . وكان ماء الطوفان على الأرض أربعين يوماً وأربعين ليلة . وكثر الماء ورفع الفلك . فارتفع عن الأرض وتعاظم الماء وكان يتكاثر جداً على الأرض ، وكان الفلك يسير فوق الماء . وزاد الماء وكثر جداً على الأرض فتغطت جميع الجبال الشامخة التى تحت السماء . وارتفع الماء فوق الجبال خمسة عشر ذراعاً وغطى الجبال الشامخة كلها وهلك كل ذى جسد كان يدب على الأرض من الطيور والبهائم والوحوش وكل الزحافات التى كانت تزحف على الأرض وجميع الناس . كل ما كان فيه نسمة حياة وكل ما كان على اليابسة مات فمحيت كل الخليقة التى كانت على وجه الأرض كلها . من الناس والبهائم والهوام وطيور السماء ، فانمحت من على الأرض . وبقى نوح وحده ومن معه فى الفلك وارتفع الماء على الأرض مئة و خمسين يوماً .   ثم ذكر الله نوحاً وكل الوحوش وكل الدواب وكل الطيور وكل الهوام والذين كانوا معه فى الفلك . وأجاز الله ريحاً على الأرض فهبط الماء . وأنسدت ينابيع الغمر وميازيب السماء فامتنع المطر من السماء . وغاص الماء راجعاً عن الأرض متناقصاً من بعد

month, on the twenty-seventh day of the month, on the mountains of Ararat. And the water continued to decrease until the tenth month. And in the tenth month, on the first day of the month, the heads of the mountains were seen. And it came to pass after forty days Noah opened the window of the ark which he had made. And he sent forth a raven; and it went forth and returned not until the water was dried from off the earth. And he sent a dove after it to see if the water had ceased from off the earth. And the dove, not having found rest for her feet, returned to him into the ark, because the water was on all the face of the earth, and he stretched out his hand and took her, and brought her to himself into the ark. And having waited yet seven other days, he again sent forth the dove from the ark. And the dove returned to him in the evening, and had a leaf of olive, a sprig in her mouth; and Noah knew that the water had ceased from off the earth. And having waited yet seven other days, he again sent forth the dove, and she did not return to him again any more. And it came to pass in the six hundred and first year of the life of Noah, in the first month, on the first day of the month, the water subsided from off the earth, and Noah opened the covering of the ark which he had made, and he saw that the water had subsided from the face of the earth. And in the second month the earth was dried, on the twenty-seventh day of the month. And the Lord God spoke to Noah, saying, Come out from the ark, you and your wife and your sons, and your sons' wives with you. And all the wild beasts, as many as are with you, and all flesh, both of birds and beasts, and every reptile moving upon the earth, bring forth with you: and increase, and multiply upon the earth. And Noah came forth, and his wife and his sons, and his sons' wives with him. And all the wild beasts and all the cattle and every bird, and every reptile creeping upon the earth after their kind, came forth out of the ark. And Noah built an altar to the Lord, and took of all clean beasts, and of all clean birds, and offered a whole burnt offering upon the altar. And the Lord God smelled a smell of sweetness, and the Lord God having considered, said, I will not any more curse the earth, because of the works of men, because the imagination of man is intently bent upon evil things from his youth, I will not therefore any more smite all living flesh as I have done. All the days of the earth, seed and harvest, cold and heat, summer and spring, shall not cease by day or night. And God blessed Noah and his sons, and said to them, Increase and multiply, and fill the earth and have dominion over it. And the dread and the fear of you shall be upon all the wild beasts of the earth, on all the birds of the sky, and on all things moving upon the earth, and upon all the fish of the sea, I have placed them under your power. And every reptile which is living shall be to you for meat, I have given all things to you as the green herbs. But flesh with blood of life you shall not eat. For your blood of your lives will I require at the hand of all wild beasts, and I will require the

مئة وخمسين يوماً . واستقر الفلك فى الشهر السابع ، فى اليوم السابع عشر من الشهر على جبل أراراط وكانت المياه ترسب وتنقص إلى الشهر العاشر . وفى الشهر الحادى عشر فى اليوم الأول من الشهر ظهرت رؤوس الجبال . وحدث من بعد أربعين يوماً أن نوحاً فتح طاقة الفلك التى عملها وأرسل الغراب لينظر إن كان الماء انقطع . فلما خرج لم يرجع إليه حتى جف الماء من الأرض . ثم أرسل الحمامة خلفه ليرى هل انقطع الماء عن وجه الأرض. فلما لم تجد الحمامة مستقراً لرجليها رجعت إليه ودخلت الفلك ، لأن مياهاً كانت على وجه الأرض كلها . فمد يده وأخذها وأدخلها إليه فى الفلك فلبث أيضاً سبعة أيام أخر ، و عاد فأرسل الحمامة من الفلك ، فرجعت إليه عند المساء وإذا ورقة زيتون خضراء فى فمها فعلم نوح أن الماء قد انقطع عن الأرض . ثم تأنى سبعة أيام أخر وأرسل الحمامة أيضاً فلم تعد ترجع إليه. وكان فى السنة الواحدة والست مئة من حياة نوح ، فى الشهر الأول فى أول الشهر أن المياه جفت عن وجه الأرض . فكشف نوح الغطاء عن طبقات الفلك ونظر وإذا الماء قد جف عن وجه الأرض . وفى الشهر الثانى فى اليوم السابع والعشرين جفت الأرض. وكلم الرب الإله نوحاً قائلاً : أخرج من الفلك أنت وبنوك وزوجتك ونساء بنيك معك ، وكل الوحوش معك وكل ذى جسد من الطيور إلى البهائم وكل الهوام التى تدب على الأرض ، أخرجها معك . وانموا وأكثروا على الأرض . فخرج نوح وبنوه وإمرأته ونساء بنيه معه وجميع الوحوش وكل الدواب وكل الهوام التى تدب على الأرض ، وكل الطيور كأجناسها خرجت من الفلك . وبنى نوح مذبحاً لله وأخذ من كل البهائم الطاهرة ومن كل الطيور الطاهرة وأصعد محرقات على المذبح. فاشتم الرب الإله رائحة البخور فقال الرب الإله فى فكره : انى لا أعود بعد ألعن الأرض من أجل أعمال البشر . لأن قلب الإنسان مائل إلى الشر منذ حداثته . ولا أعود أيضاً أضرب كل ذى جسد حى كما فعلت كل أيام الأرض ، زرع وحصاد وبرد وحر وصيف وشتاء ونهار وليل لا يزولان. و بارك الله نوحاً و بنيه وقال لهم: انموا وأكثروا وإملأوا الأرض وتسلطوا عليها . ولتكن خشيتكم ورهبتكم على كل وحوش الأرض . وجميع طيور السماء وكل ما يدب على الأرض ، وكل أسماك البحر قد دفعتها إلى أيديكم . وكل دابة حية تكون لكم طعاماً . كالعشب الأخضر أعطيتكم جميعها ، لحماً بدم نفسه لا تأكلوه لأن دم أنفسكم أطلبه من يد جميع الوحوش ومن يد الرجل اللص

life of man at the hand of his brother man. He that sheds man's blood, instead of that blood shall his own be shed, for in the image of God I made man. But as for you, be fruitful and multiply, and fill the earth, and have dominion over it. Glory be to the Holy Trinity. Amen

أطلب نفس الرجل . ومن أهرق دم إنسان فيهرق دمه عوضاً عنه لأنى خلقت الإنسان على صورة الله. أما أنتم فانموا وأكثروا واملأوا الأرض وتكاثروا فيها . مجداً للثالوث القدوس .

Proverbs 9:1-11

Wisdom has built a house for herself, and set up seven pillars. She has killed her beasts; she has mingled her wine in a bowl, and prepared her table. She has sent forth her servants, calling with a loud proclamation to the feast, saying, Whoever is foolish, let him turn aside to me: and to them that want understanding she says, Come, eat of my bread, and drink wine which I have mingled for you. Leave folly, that you may reign forever; and seek wisdom, and improve understanding by knowledge. He that reproves evil men shall get dishonor to himself, and he that rebukes an ungodly man shall disgrace himself. Rebuke not evil men, lest they should hate you: rebuke a wise man, and he will love you. Give an opportunity to a wise man, and he will be wiser: instruct a just man, and he will receive more instruction. The fear of the Lord is the beginning of wisdom, and the counsel of saints is understanding: As for to know the law is the character of a sound mind. For in this way you shall live long, and years of your life shall be added to you. Glory be to the Holy Trinity. Amen.

(من أمثال سليمان الحكيم 9 : 1 - 11)

الحكمة بنت لها بيتاً . ونصبت فيه سبعة أعمدة . ذبحت ذبائحها ومزجت خمرها فى الأوانى وهيأت مائدتها . أرسلت عبيدها لينادوا بصوت عال على الزوايا قائلين : من كان منكم جاهلاً فيأتِ إلىَّ وناقصى الفهم قولوا لهم هلموا كلوا من خبزى واشربوا من الخمر التى مزجتها لكم ، اتركوا عنكم الجهل لتحيوا . أطلبوا الحكمة لتعمروا . وقوموا فهمكم بمعرفة . من يؤدب الأشرار يلحق بنفسه هواناً . ومن يبكت المنافق يكسب عياً لذاته . لا توبخ الأشرار لئلا يبغضوك ، وبخ حكيماً فيحبك . وبخ جاهلاً فيبغضك . أعط الحكيم سبباً فيزداد حكمة . وعلم البار فيزداد براً . رأس الحكمة مخافة الرب . ومشورة القديسين فهماً . ومعرفة الناموس هى الفكر الصالح . بهذا المثال تعيش زماناً طويلاً وتزداد لك سنو الحياة . مجداً للثالوث القدوس .

Isaiah 40:9-31

O you that brings glad tidings to Zion, go up on the high mountain; lift up your voice with strength, you that brings glad tidings to Jerusalem; lift it up, fear not; say unto the cities of Judah, Behold your God! Behold the Lord! The Lord is coming with strength, and His arm is with power; behold, His reward is with Him, and His work before Him. He shall tend His flock as a shepherd, and He shall gather the lambs with His arm, and He shall soothe them that are with young. Who has measured the water in His hand, and the heaven with a span, and all the earth in a handful? Who has weighed the mountains in scales, and the forests in a balance? Who has known the mind of the Lord? And who has been His counselor, to instruct Him? Or with whom has He taken counsel, and he has instructed Him? Or who has taught Him judgment, or who has taught Him the way of understanding; since all the nations are counted as a drop from a bucket, and as the turning of a balance, and shall be counted as spittle? And Lebanon is not enough to burn, nor all beasts enough for a whole burnt offering; and all the nations are as nothing, and counted as nothing. To whom have you compared the Lord? And with what likeness have you compared Him? Has not the artificer made an image, or the goldsmith having melted gold, guilded it over, and made it a similitude? For the artificer chooses out a wood that will not rot, and will wisely inquire how he shall set up his image, and that so

(من إشعياء النبى 40 : 9- 31)

أصعد على جبل عال يا مبشر صهيون. ارفع صوتك بقوة يا مبشر أورشليم . ارفع صوتك ولا تخف . قل لمدن يهوذا هوذا ربكم آتِ بقوة وذراعه بربوبية ، هوذا أجرته معه وعمله قدامه . كراع يرعى قطيع غنمه وبذراعه يجمع الحملان ويعزى الحبالى . من كال الماء بيده وقاس السماء بشبره والأرض كلها بقبضته؟ من وزن الجبال بالمثقال والآكام بالميزان؟ من علم قلب الرب أو من كان معه مشيراً فعلمه؟ أو من الذى أراه الحكم؟ أو طريق الفهم من عرفها له؟ أو من سبق فأعطاه حتى عوضه؟ انما الأمم كلها عنده مثل نقطة ماء تنقط من قادوس ومثل ميلان الميزان حسبوا . وجميعهم كالبصاق يعدون. وخشب لبنان لا يعد للحريق وجميع البهائم لا تعد شيئاً للمحرقة. جميع الأمم لديه كلا شئ وعنده كالعدم حسبوا . فمن شبهتم الرب وبأى مثل مثلتموه ، هل بصورة صنعها النجار وصفحة الصائغ بالذهب . وركب فيه الذهب وشبهه يتلف . انما خشبة لا تسوس اختارها النجار . وبحكمة يطلب كيف يقيم تمثالاً لا يتحرك .

that it should not be moved. Will you not know? Will you not hear? Has it not been told to you of old? Have you not known the foundations of the earth? It is He that comprehends the circle of the earth, and the inhabitants in it are as grasshoppers; He that set up the heaven as a chamber, and stretched it out as a tent to dwell in; He that appoints princes to rule as nothing, and has made the earth as nothing. For they shall not plant, neither shall they sow, neither shall their root be fixed in the ground; He has blown upon them, and they have withered, and a storm shall carry them away like sticks. Now then to whom have you compared Me, that I may be exalted? Says the Holy One. Lift up your eyes on high, and see, who has displayed all these things? Even He that brings forth His host by number; He shall call them all by name by means of His great glory, and by the power of His might; nothing has escaped you. For do not say, O Jacob, and why have you spoken, O Israel, saying, My way is hid from God, and my God has taken away my judgment, and has departed? And now, have you not known? Have you not heard? The eternal God, the God that formed the ends of the earth, shall not hunger, nor be weary, and there is no searching of His understanding. He gives strength to the hungry, and sorrow to them that are not suffering. For the young men shall hunger, and the youths shall be weary, and the choice men shall be powerless; but they that wait on God shall renew their strength; they shall put forth new feathers like eagles; they shall run, and not be weary; they shall walk, and not faint. Glory be to the Holy Trinity. Amen.

Daniel 7:9-15

I beheld until the thrones were set, and the Ancient of Days sat; and His garment was white as snow, and the hair of His head as pure wool; His throne was a flame of fire, and His wheels burning fire. A stream of fire rushed forth before Him. Thousands upon thousands ministered to Him, and ten thousand times ten thousand attended to Him. The court was seated, and the books were opened. I beheld then because of the voice of the great words which that horn spoke, until the wild beast was slain and destroyed, and his body given to be burned with fire. And the dominion of the rest of the wild beasts was taken away; but a prolonging of life was given to them for an appointed time. I beheld in the night vision, and behold, One like the Son of Man coming with the clouds of heaven, and He came to the Ancient of Days, and was brought near to Him. And to Him was given the dominion, and the honor, and the kingdom; and all nations, tribes, and languages, shall serve Him. His dominion is an everlasting dominion, which shall not pass away, and His kingdom shall not be destroyed. As for me, Daniel, my spirit in my body trembled, and the visions of my head troubled me. Glory be to the Holy Trinity. Amen.

ألا تعلمون؟ ألا تسمعون؟ ألم تخبروا من منذ البدء؟ أما فهمتم أسس الأرض؟ القابض على كل محيط الأرض والسكان فيها كالجراد . الذى رفع السماء كالقبة . وبسطها كالخيمة ليسكن فيها . الذى يجعل الأراخنة كلا شئ والأرض التى خلقها كالعدم. لأنهم لا يزرعون ولا يغرسون ولا يكون أصلهم على الأرض. لأنه نفخ عليهم فيبسوا وحملهم العاصف كالقش. والآن بمن تشبهوننى فأتعالى يقول القدوس؟ ارفعوا عيونكم إلى العلى وانظروا من خلق هذه كلها . الذى يخرج جندها عدداً . يدعوها من مياه كثيرة . ومن عزة قوته لا ينسى شيئاً منها. فلماذا تقول يا يعقوب ، وبماذا تتكلم يا إسرائيل أن طرقى خفيت عن الله وأن الله قد نزع قضائى فمضى؟ والآن ، أتعلم إنك قد سمعت أن الله الأبدى ،الله الذى خلق أقطار الأرض لا يتحرك ولا يتعب ولا حد لعلمه؟ الذى يهب للجائع قوتاً والمعطى وجع القلب للذين لا تحترق قلوبهم . جاعت الغلمان وتعب الشبان والمختارون يصيرون غير أقوياء والذين ينتظرون الله فتتجدد قوتهم وتنبت لهم أجنحة كالنسور . يسرعون ولا يتعبون يمشون ولا يعيَّون . مجداً للثالوث القدوس .

(من دانيال النبى ص 7 : 9 - 15)

أنا دانيال رأيت فى رؤى الليل ، كنت أرى أنه وُضعت عروش وجلس العتيق الآيام . لباسه أبيض كالثلج . وشعر رأسه كالصوف النقى . وعرشه لهيب نار . وعجلاته نار متقدة . ونهر نار يخرج ويجرى أمامه . والوف الوف كانت تخدمه ، وربوات ربوات وقوف قدامه. فجلس الديان وفتحت الأسفار . ورأيت فى تلك الساعة صوت الكلام العظيم الذى كان يكلم به القرن . وكنت أنظر حتى قتل الوحش وهلك ودفع جسمه ليحرق بالنار . أما باقى الوحوش فنزع عنهم سلطانهم واعطوا طول الحياة إلى زمان ووقت . ثم رأيت فى رؤى الليل وإذا مع سحب السماء مثل إبن الإنسان آتياً على سحاب السماء. فبلغ وجاء إلى العتيق الأيام فقربه أمامه . فأعطى له الرئاسة والكرامة والملك . وجميع الشعوب و الأسباط ولغات الألسن تتعبد له . وسلطانه سلطان أبدى لا يزول . وملكه ليس له إنقضاء . أما أنا دانيال فارتعدت روحى وفرائصى وافزعتنى رؤى رأسى . مجداً للثالوث القدوس.

Proverbs 8:1-12

You shall proclaim wisdom, that understanding may be obedient to you. For she is on lofty heights, and stands in the midst of the ways. For she sits by the gates of princes, and sings in the entrances, saying, You, O men, I exhort; and utter my voice to the sons of men. O you simple, understand subtlety, and you that are untaught, imbibe knowledge.

Listen to me, for I will speak solemn truths; and will produce right sayings from my lips. For my throat shall meditate truth, and false lips are an abomination before me. All the words of my mouth are in righteousness; there is nothing in them wrong or perverse.

For wisdom is better than precious stones; and no valuable substance is of equal worth with it. I, wisdom, have dwelt with counsel and knowledge, and I have called upon understanding.

Glory be to the Holy Trinity. Amen.

A homily of our Holy Father Abba Shenouti the Archimandrite

O brethren, let's do the will of God as we have time to do the service of God. Remember that death does not delay, and we are leaving the world. Where are all the people before us? Now, all of them are lying down in their tombs. Let's give fruits according to God's grace, which was given to us. We, all Christians, as human being, should live according to Jesus Christ, the true light. He is the Master, and we are His servants. He is the Shepherd, and we are the sheep, ruled under His hand. He is born of the Father, light of light, but we are His creatures. He died for us, the sinners, and gave up His life on the cross to grant us His Kingdom. The servants were not obligated to die for their Master, but the Master accepted the humiliation and died for His servants. As He died for them, they died with Him. As He is alive, they have life.

We conclude the homily of our Holy Father Abba Shenouti the Archimandrite, who enlightened our minds and our hearts. In the name of the Father, and the Son, and the Holy Spirit, one God. Amen.

(من أمثال سليمان الحكيم 8 : 1 - 12)

وأنت يا إبنى فناد بالحكمة فتعطيك الفطنة ، لأنها كائنة على الزوايا العالية وتقف فى وسط الطرق وتلازم أبواب المقتدرين وتصرخ فى المداخل قائلة: اليكم أيها الناس فهمى وتعليمى إلى بنى البشر اعطى . ايها البسطاء تفهموا الحكمة ويا أيها الجهلاء . تفطنوا فى قلوبكم ، اسمعونى فانى انطق بتعاليم وافيض من شفتى أقوالاً مستقيمة . لان حنكى يلهج بالصدق و مكرهة شفتى الكذب . كل كلمات فمي بالحق ليس فيها عوج ولا التواء. كلها واضحة لدى الفهيم و مستقيمة لدى الذين يجدون المعرفة. خذوا تاديبى لا الفضة و المعرفة اكثر من الذهب المختار. لان الحكمة خير من اللالئ و كل الجواهر لا تساويها. الحكمة أفضل من الجواهر الكريمة وكل النفائس لا تساويها. أنا الحكمة خلقت المشورة ودعوت إلى الفكر ومحبة الله والفهم . مجداً للثالوث القدوس .

(عظة لأبينا القديس الأنبا شنودة)

فلنصنع إرادة الله يا أخوتى مادام لنا وقت أن نعمل فيه أعمال الرب . تذكروا أن الموت لا يتأخر ومصيرنا أن نترك العالم . أين جميع الذين كانوا قبلنا، هوذا كلهم الآن يرقدون فى القبور. فلنصنع أثماراً تليق بنعمة الله التى أعطاها لنا. وعلينا نحن وكل المسيحيين أن نتشبه بيسوع المسيح النور الحقيقى ، لأننا نحن بشر . هو السيد ونحن عبيده ، هو الراعى ونحن غنم تحت يده ، هو مولود من الآب ولكن نحن خليقته. نور من نور مات عنا نحن الخطاة وأسلم ذاته عنا على خشبة الصليب لينعم لنا بملكوته ، ما كان العبيد ملتزمين أن يموتوا عن سيدهم أما السيد فقد استهان بالخزى ومات عن عبيده كى حسبما مات هو هم يموتون معه وكما هو حى فهم أيضاً يحيون .

فلنختم عظة أبينا القديس أنبا شنودة رئيس المتوحدين الذى أنار عقولنا وعيون قلوبنا باسم الآب والإبن والروح القدس إله واحد آمين .

The Psalm

ⲮⲀⲖⲘⲞⲤ ⲔⲆ : ⲁ ⲛⲉⲙ ⲃ̄

Psalms 24:1-2

To You, O Lord, have I lifted up my soul. O my God, I have trusted in You; let me not be confounded *forever*, neither let my enemies laugh me to scorn; let them be ashamed that transgress without cause. Alleluia.

Ⲁⲓϥⲁⲓ ⲛ̄ⲧⲁⲯⲩⲭⲏ ⲉ̀ⲡ̀ϣⲱⲓ ϩⲁⲣⲟⲕ ⲡ̅ⲟ̅ⲥ̅ ⲡⲁⲛⲟⲩϯ : ⲁⲓⲭⲁ ϩ̀ⲑⲏⲓ ⲉ̀ⲣⲟⲕ ⲛ̀ⲛⲉⲕⲑⲣⲓϭⲓϣⲓⲡⲓ ϣⲁ ⲉ̀ⲛⲉϩ . (Ⲗⲉⲍⲓⲥ)

Ⲟⲩ ⲇⲉ ⲙ̀ⲡⲉⲛⲑⲣⲟⲩⲥⲱⲃⲓ ⲛ̀ⲥⲱⲓ ⲛ̀ϫⲉ ⲛⲁϫⲁϫⲓ : ⲙⲁⲣⲟⲩϭⲓϣⲓⲡⲓ ⲛ̀ⲑⲱⲟⲩ ⲛ̀ϫⲉ ⲛⲏⲉⲧⲓⲣⲓ ⲛ̀ⲧⲁⲛⲟⲙⲓⲁ ϧⲉⲛ ⲡⲉⲧϣⲟⲩⲓⲧ . ⲁⲗ .

أيفاى إنطابسيشى إبشوى هاروك إبتشويس بانووتى : أيكا إهثى إروك إننيك إثريتشيشيى شا إينيه .

أوو ذيه إمبين إثروو صوفى إنصوى إنجيه ناجاجى : ماروو تشيشيبى إنثؤوو إنجيه نى إتترى إنتى أنوميا خين بيتشووويت . الليلويا .

(مز 24 : 1 و2)

إليك يارب رفعت نفسى ، إلهى عليك توكلت فلا تخزنى إلى الأبد .

ولا تضحك بى أعدائى . ليخز الذين يصنعون الاثم باطلاً . الليلويا .

| Introduction to the Gospel, Page: 8 | مقدمة الأنجيل ، صفحة : |

The Gospel

Ⲉⲩⲁⲅⲅⲉⲗⲓⲟⲛ Ⲕⲁⲧⲁ Ⲙⲁⲧⲑⲉⲟⲛ Ⲕⲉⲫ ⲕ̄ⲇ̄ : ⲅ̄ - ⲗ̄ⲉ̄

Matthew 24:3-35

Now as He sat on the Mount of Olives, the disciples came to Him privately, saying, "Tell us, when will these things be? And what will be the sign of Your coming, and of the end of the age?" And Jesus answered and said to them: "Take heed that no one deceives you. For many will come in My name, saying, 'I am the Christ,' and will deceive many. And you will hear of wars and rumors of wars. See that you are not troubled; for all these things must come to pass, but the end is not yet. For nation will rise against nation, and kingdom against kingdom. And there will be famines, pestilences, and earthquakes in various places. All these are the beginning of sorrows. "Then they will deliver you up to tribulation and kill you, and you will be hated by all nations for My name's sake. And then many will be offended, will betray one another, and will hate one another. Then many false prophets will rise up and deceive many. And because

Ⲉϥϩⲉⲙⲥⲓ ⲇⲉ ϩⲓϫⲉⲛ ⲡⲓⲧⲱⲟⲩ ⲛ̀ⲧⲉ ⲛⲓϫⲱⲓⲧ : ⲁⲩⲓ̀ ϩⲁⲣⲟϥ ⲛ̀ϫⲉ ⲛⲉϥⲙⲁⲑⲏⲧⲏⲥ ⲥⲁ ⲡⲥⲁ ⲙ̀ⲙⲁⲩⲁⲧⲟⲩ ⲉⲩϫⲱ ⲙ̀ⲙⲟⲥ : ϫⲉ ⲁϫⲟⲥ ⲛⲁⲛ ϫⲉ ⲁⲣⲉ ⲛⲁⲓⲛⲁϣⲱⲡⲓ ⲛ̀ⲑⲛⲁⲩ ⲟⲩⲟϩ ⲁϣ ⲡⲉ ⲡⲓⲙⲏⲓⲛⲓ ⲛ̀ⲧⲉ ⲡⲉⲕϫⲓⲛⲓ ⲛⲉⲙ ⲧ̀ϧⲁⲉ ⲛ̀ⲧⲉ ⲡⲁⲓⲉⲛⲉϩ : ⲟⲩⲟϩ ⲁϥⲉⲣⲟⲩⲱ ⲛ̀ϫⲉ Ⲓⲏⲥ ⲡⲉϫⲁϥ ⲛⲱⲟⲩ : ϫⲉ ⲁⲛⲁⲩ ⲙ̀ⲡⲉⲣⲭⲁⲥ ⲛ̀ⲧⲉ ⲟⲩⲁⲓ ⲥⲉⲣⲉⲙ ⲑⲏⲛⲟⲩ : ⲉⲣⲉ ⲟⲩⲙⲏϣ ⲅⲁⲣ ⲓ̀ ϧⲉⲛ ⲡⲁⲣⲁⲛ ⲉⲩϫⲱ ⲙ̀ⲙⲟⲥ : ϫⲉ ⲁⲛⲟⲕ ⲡⲉ Ⲡ̀ⲭ̅ⲥ̅ : ⲟⲩⲟϩ ⲉⲩⲉ̀ⲥⲉⲣⲉⲙ ⲟⲩⲙⲏϣ . Ⲉⲣⲉⲧⲉⲛⲉ̀ⲥⲱⲧⲉⲙ ⲇⲉ ⲛ̀ϩⲁⲛⲃⲱⲧⲥ ⲛⲉⲙ ϩⲁⲛⲥⲙⲏ ⲙ̀ⲃⲱⲧⲥ : ⲁⲛⲁⲩ ⲙ̀ⲡⲉⲣϣⲑⲟⲣⲧⲉⲣ ϩⲱϯ ⲅⲁⲣ ⲡⲉ ⲛ̀ⲧⲟⲩϣⲱⲡⲓ : ⲁⲗⲗⲁ ⲙ̀ⲡⲁⲧⲉⲉ̀ϯϧⲁⲉ ϣⲱⲡⲓ ⲉⲣⲉ ⲟⲩⲉⲑⲛⲟⲥ ⲅⲁⲣ ⲧⲱⲛϥ ⲉ̀ϫⲉⲛ ⲟⲩⲉⲑⲛⲟⲥ ⲟⲩⲟϩ ⲟⲩⲙⲉⲧⲟⲩⲣⲟ ⲉ̀ϫⲉⲛ ⲟⲩⲙⲉⲧⲟⲩⲣⲟ : ⲟⲩⲟϩ ⲉⲩⲉ̀ϣⲱⲡⲓ ⲛ̀ϫⲉ ϩⲁⲛⲙⲟⲛⲙⲉⲛ ⲛⲉⲙ ϩⲁⲛϩⲕⲟ ⲛⲉⲙ ϩⲁⲛⲙⲟⲩ ⲕⲁⲧⲁ ⲙⲁ : ⲛⲁⲓ ⲇⲉ ⲧⲏⲣⲟⲩ ϩⲏ ⲛ̀ⲛⲓⲛⲁⲕϩⲓ ⲛⲉ . Ⲧⲟⲧⲉ ⲉⲩⲉ̀ϯ ⲑⲏⲛⲟⲩ ⲉ̀ϧⲣⲏⲓ ⲉ̀ⲡ̀ϩⲟϫϩⲉϫ ⲟⲩⲟϩ ⲉⲩⲉ̀ϧⲱⲧⲉⲃ ⲑⲏⲛⲟⲩ : ⲟⲩⲟϩ ⲉⲣⲉⲧⲉⲛⲉ̀ϣⲱⲡⲓ ⲉⲩⲙⲟⲥϯ ⲙ̀ⲙⲱⲧⲉⲛ ⲛ̀ϫⲉ ⲛⲓⲉⲑⲛⲟⲥ ⲧⲏⲣⲟⲩ ⲉⲑⲃⲉ ⲡⲁⲣⲁⲛ : ⲧⲟⲧⲉ ⲉⲣⲉ ⲟⲩⲙⲏϣ ⲭⲁ ⲧⲟⲧⲟⲩ ⲉ̀ⲃⲟⲗ : ⲟⲩⲟϩ ⲉⲩⲉ̀ϯ ⲛ̀ⲛⲟⲩⲉⲣⲏⲟⲩ : ⲟⲩⲟϩ ⲉⲩⲉ̀ⲙⲉⲥⲧⲉ ⲛ̀ⲛⲟⲩⲉⲣⲏⲟⲩ : ⲟⲩⲟϩ ⲟⲩⲙⲏϣ ⲙ̀ⲡ̀ⲣⲟⲫⲏⲧⲏⲥ ⲛ̀ⲛⲟⲩϫ ⲉⲩⲉ̀ⲧⲱⲟⲩⲛⲟⲩ ⲟⲩⲟϩ ⲉⲩⲉ̀ⲥⲉⲣⲉⲙ ⲟⲩⲙⲏϣ . Ⲟⲩⲟϩ ⲉⲑⲃⲉ

(متى 24 : 3 - 35)

وفيما هو جالس على جبل الزيتون جاء إليه تلاميذه على انفراد وحدهم قائلين: قل لنا متى يكون هذا ، وما هى علامة مجيئك وانقضاء هذا الدهر؟ فأجاب يسوع وقال لهم: أنظروا لا يضلكم أحد ، فان كثيرين يأتون باسمى قائلين: انى أنا هو المسيح ، ويضلون كثيرين. وسوف تسمعون بحروب وأخبار حروب ، أنظروا لا تضطربوا . لأنه لابد أن تكون هذه كلها ولكن ليس المنتهى بعد . لأنه تقوم أمة على أمة ومملكة على مملكة . وتكون زلازل ومجاعات و أوبئة فى أماكن ، ولكن هذه كلها مبتدأ الأوجاع . حينئذ يسلمونكم إلى الضيق ويقتلونكم . وتكونون مبغضين من جميع الأمم لأجل اسمى . حينئذ يشك كثيرون ويسلمون بعضهم بعضاً ويبغضون بعضهم بعضاً ويقوم كثيرون من الأنبياء الكذبة ويضلون

lawlessness will abound, the love of many will grow cold. But he who endures to the end shall be saved. And this gospel of the kingdom will be preached in all the world as a witness to all the nations, and then the end will come. "Therefore when you see the 'ABOMINATION OF DESOLATION,' spoken of by Daniel the prophet, standing in the holy place" (whoever reads, let him understand), "then let those who are in Judea flee to the mountains. Let him who is on the housetop not go down to take anything out of his house. And let him who is in the field not go back to get his clothes. But woe to those who are pregnant and to those who are nursing babies in those days! And pray that your flight may not be in winter or on the Sabbath. For then there will be great tribulation, such as has not been since the beginning of the world until this time, no, nor ever shall be. And unless those days were shortened, no flesh would be saved; but for the elect's sake those days will be shortened. "Then if anyone says to you, 'Look, here is the Christ!' or 'There!' do not believe it. For false christs and false prophets will rise and show great signs and wonders to deceive, if possible, even the elect. See, I have told you beforehand. "Therefore if they say to you, 'Look, He is in the desert!' do not go out; or 'Look, He is in the inner rooms!' do not believe it. For as the lightning comes from the east and flashes to the west, so also will the coming of the Son of Man be. For wherever the carcass is, there the eagles will be gathered together. "Immediately after the tribulation of those days the sun will be darkened, and the moon will not give its light; the stars will fall from heaven, and

ⲡⲁϣⲁⲓ ⲛ̀ⲧⲉ ϯⲁⲛⲟⲙⲓⲁ ⲧⲁⲅⲡⲏ ⲛ̀ⲟⲩⲙⲏϣ ⲉⲥⲉϩⲱⲣϣ : ⲫ̀ⲏ ⲇⲉ ⲉⲑⲛⲁⲁⲙⲟⲛⲓ ⲛ̀ⲧⲟⲧϥ ϣⲁ ⲉ̀ⲃⲟⲗ ⲫⲁⲓ ⲡⲉ ⲫ̀ⲛⲉⲑⲛⲁⲛⲟϩⲉⲙ : ⲟⲩⲟϩ ⲉⲩⲉ̀ϩⲓⲱⲓϣ ⲙ̀ⲡⲁⲓⲉⲩⲁⲅⲅⲉⲗⲓⲟⲛ ⲛ̀ⲧⲉ ϯⲙⲉⲧⲟⲩⲣⲟ ϧⲉⲛ ϯⲟⲓⲕⲟⲩⲙⲉⲛⲏ ⲧⲏⲣⲥ : ⲉⲩⲙⲉⲧⲙⲉⲑⲣⲉ ⲛ̀ⲛⲓⲉⲑⲛⲟⲥ ⲧⲏⲣⲟⲩ ⲧⲟⲧⲉ ⲉⲥⲉ̀ⲓ̀ ⲛ̀ϫⲉ ϯϧⲁⲉ̀ . Ⲉϣⲱⲡ ⲇⲉ ⲛ̀ⲧⲉⲧⲉⲛⲛⲁⲩ ⲉ̀ⲡⲓⲥⲱϥ ⲛ̀ⲧⲉ ⲡ̀ϣⲁϥⲉ ⲫ̀ⲛⲉⲧⲁϥϫⲟϥ ⲉ̀ⲃⲟⲗ ϩⲓⲧⲉⲛ Ⲇⲁⲛⲓⲏⲗ ⲡⲓⲡ̀ⲣⲟⲫⲏⲧⲏⲥ ⲉϥⲟ̀ϩⲓ ⲉ̀ⲣⲁⲧϥ ϧⲉⲛ ⲡⲓⲙⲁ ⲉⲑⲟⲩⲁⲃ ⲫⲏⲉⲧⲱϣ ⲙⲁⲣⲉϥⲕⲁϯ : ⲧⲟⲧⲉ ⲛⲏⲉⲧ ϧⲉⲛ ϯⲓⲟⲩⲇⲉⲁ ⲙⲁⲣⲟⲩⲫⲱⲧ ϩⲓϫⲉⲛ ⲛⲓⲧⲱⲟⲩ : ⲟⲩⲟϩ ⲫ̀ⲛⲉⲧⲭⲏ ϩⲓϫⲉⲛ ⲡ̀ϫⲉⲛⲉⲫⲱⲣ ⲙ̀ⲡⲉⲛⲑⲣⲉϥⲓ̀ ⲉ̀ⲡⲉⲥⲏⲧ ⲉ̀ⲉⲗ ⲛⲏⲉⲧⲭⲏ ϧⲉⲛ ⲡⲉϥⲏⲓ . Ⲟⲩⲟϩ ⲫ̀ⲛⲉⲧⲭⲏ ϧⲉⲛ ⲧ̀ⲕⲟⲓ ⲙ̀ⲡⲉⲛⲑⲣⲉϥⲕⲟⲧϥ ⲉ̀ⲫⲁϩⲟⲩ ⲉⲉⲗ ⲡⲉϥϩ̀ⲃⲱⲥ : ⲟⲩⲟⲓ ⲇⲉ ⲛ̀ⲛⲏⲉⲧⲉ ⲙ̀ⲃⲟⲕⲓ ⲛⲉⲙ ⲛⲏⲉⲧ ϯϭⲓ ϧⲉⲛ ⲛⲓⲉ̀ϩⲟⲟⲩ ⲉⲧⲉ ⲙ̀ⲙⲁⲩ : ⲧⲱⲃϩ ⲇⲉ ϩⲓⲛⲁ ⲛ̀ⲧⲉ ⳙ̀ⲧⲉⲙⲡⲉⲧⲉⲛⲫⲱⲧ ϣⲱⲡⲓ ϧⲉⲛ ⲧ̀ⲫ̀ⲣⲱ ⲟⲩ ⲇⲉ ϧⲉⲛ ⲡⲥⲁⲃⲃⲟⲧⲟⲛ . Ⲉⲣⲉ ⲟⲩⲛⲓϣϯ ⲅⲁⲣ ⲛ̀ϩⲟϫϩⲉϫ ϣⲱⲡⲓ ϧⲉⲛ ⲡⲓⲥⲏⲟⲩ ⲉⲧⲉ ⲙ̀ⲙⲁⲩ : ⲙ̀ⲡⲉ ⲟⲩⲟⲛ ϣⲱⲡⲓ ⲙ̀ⲡⲉϥⲣⲏϯ ⲓⲥϫⲉⲛϩ̀ ⲙ̀ⲡⲓⲕⲟⲥⲙⲟⲥ ϣⲁ ϯⲛⲟⲩ : ⲟⲩ ⲇⲉ ⲟⲛ ⲛ̀ⲛⲉ ⲟⲩⲟⲛ ϣⲱⲡⲓ ⲙ̀ⲡⲉϥⲣⲏϯ . Ⲟⲩⲟϩ ⲉ̀ⲃⲏⲗ ϫⲉ ⲁ ⲛⲓⲉ̀ϩⲟⲟⲩ ⲉⲧⲉ ⲙ̀ⲙⲁⲩ ⲉⲣⲕⲟⲩϫⲓ : ⲛⲁⲩⲛⲛⲟϩⲉⲙ ⲁⲛ ⲡⲉ ⲛ̀ϫⲉ ⲥⲁⲣⲝ ⲛⲓⲃⲉⲛ : ⲉⲑⲃⲉ ⲛⲓⲥⲱⲧⲡ ⲇⲉ ⲉⲣⲉ ⲛⲓⲉ̀ϩⲟⲟⲩ ⲉⲧⲉ ⲙ̀ⲙⲁⲩ ⲉⲣⲕⲟⲩϫⲓ . Ⲧ̀ⲟⲧⲉ ⲁⲣⲉϣⲁⲛ ⲟⲩⲁⲓ ϫⲟⲥ ⲛⲱⲧⲉⲛ ϫⲉ ⲓⲥ Ⲡⲭ̅ⲥ̅ ⲧⲁⲓ ⲓⲉ ϥ̀ⲧⲏ ⲙ̀ⲡⲉⲣⲧⲉⲛϩⲟⲧⲟⲩ . Ⲉⲩⲉⲧⲱⲟⲩⲛⲟⲩ ⲅⲁⲣ ⲛ̀ϫⲉ ϩⲁⲛⲭ̀ⲥ ⲛ̀ⲛⲟⲩϫ ⲛⲉⲙ ϩⲁⲛⲡⲣⲟⲫⲏⲧⲏⲥ ⲛ̀ⲛⲟⲩϫ ⲟⲩⲟϩ ⲉⲩⲉ̀ϯ ⲛ̀ϩⲁⲛⲛⲓϣϯ ⲙ̀ⲙⲏⲓⲛⲓ ⲛⲉⲙ ϩⲁⲛϣ̀ⲫⲏⲣⲓ ϩⲱⲥⲧⲉ ⲉ̀ⲛⲉ ⲟⲩⲟⲛ ϣ̀ϫⲟⲙ ⲛ̀ⲥⲉⲥⲱⲣⲉⲙ ⲛ̀ⲛⲁⲕⲉⲥⲱⲧⲡ . ⲓⲥ ϩⲏⲡⲡⲉ ⲁⲓⲉⲣϣⲟⲣⲡ ⲛ̀ϫⲟⲥ ⲛⲱⲧⲉⲛ . Ⲉϣⲱⲡ ⲇⲉ ⲁⲩϣⲁⲛϫⲟⲥ ⲛⲱⲧⲉⲛ ϫⲉ ⲓⲥ ϩⲏⲡⲡⲉ ⲉϥϧⲓ ⲡ̀ϣⲁϥⲉ ⲙ̀ⲡⲉⲣⲓ̀ ⲉ̀ⲃⲟⲗ : ϩⲏⲡⲡⲉ ⲉϥ ϧⲉⲛ ⲛⲓⲧⲁⲙⲓⲟⲛ ⲙ̀ⲡⲉⲣⲧⲉⲛϩⲟⲧⲟⲩ . Ⲙ̀ⲫ̀ⲣⲏϯ ⲅⲁⲣ ⲙ̀ⲡⲓⲥⲉⲧⲉⲃⲣⲏⲝ ⲉϥϣ̀ⲓ̀ ⲉ̀ⲃⲟⲗ ⲥⲁ ⲡⲉⲓⲉⲃⲧ ⲟⲩⲟϩ ⲛ̀ⲧⲉϥⲟⲩⲟⲛϩϥ ⲥⲁ ⲡⲉⲙⲉⲛⲧ ⲫⲁⲓ ⲡⲉ ⲙ̀ⲫ̀ⲣⲏϯ ⲙ̀ⲡ̀ϫⲓⲛⲓ ⲙ̀ⲡ̀ϣⲏⲣⲓ ⲙ̀ⲫ̀ⲣⲱⲙⲓ : ⲡⲓⲙⲁ ⲉⲧⲉ ϯϣⲟⲗϩⲥ ⲙ̀ⲙⲟϥ ϣⲁⲣⲟⲩⲟⲩⲧ ⲙ̀ⲙⲁⲩ ⲛ̀ϫⲉ ⲛⲓⲁϩⲱⲙ : ⲥⲁ ⲧⲟⲧϥ ⲇⲉ ⲙⲉⲛⲉⲛⲥⲁ ⲡⲓϩⲟϫϩⲉϫ ⲛ̀ⲧⲉ ⲛⲓⲉ̀ϩⲟⲟⲩ ⲉⲧⲉ ⲙ̀ⲙⲁⲩ ⲫ̀ⲣⲏ ⲉϥⲉ̀ⲉⲣⲭⲁⲕⲓ : ⲟⲩⲟϩ ⲡⲓⲓⲟϩ ⲛ̀ⲛⲉϥϯ ⲙ̀ⲡⲉϥⲟⲩⲱⲓⲛⲓ : ⲟⲩⲟϩ ⲛⲓⲥⲓⲟⲩ ⲉⲩⲉ̀ϩⲉⲓ ⲉ̀ⲡⲉⲥⲏⲧ ⲉ̀ⲃⲟⲗ ϧⲉⲛ ⲧ̀ⲫⲉ :

كثيرين . ولكثرة الاثم تبرد المحبة من الكثيرين . ومن يصبر إلى المنتهى فهذا يخلص . ويُكرز ببشارة الملكوت هذه فى كل المسكونة شهادة لجميع الأمم . وحينئذ يأتى المنتهى . فمتى نظرتم رجسة الخراب التى قيل عنها فى دانيال النبى قائمة فى المكان المقدس فليفهم القارئ . حينئذ فليهرب الذين فى اليهودية إلى الجبال ، والذى على السطح فلا ينزل ليأخذ ما فى بيته . والذى فى الحقل فلا يرجع إلى ورائه ليأخذ ثوبه . وويل للحبالى والمرضعات فى تلك الأيام . فصلوا لكى لا يكون هربكم فى شتاء ولا فى سبت ، لأنه سيكون فى ذلك الوقت ضيق شديد لم يكن مثله منذ إبتداء العالم إلى الآن ولن يكون مثله أيضاً . ولو لم تقصَّر تلك الأيام لما كان يخلص كل ذى جسد ، لكن لأجل المختارين تقصَّر تلك الأيام . حينئذ ان قال لكم أحد هوذا المسيح هنا أو هناك فلا تصدقوا . فأنه سيقوم مسحاء كذبة وأنبياء كذبة ويعطون آيات عظيمة وعجائب حتى يضلوا لو أمكن المختارين أيضاً . ها أنا قد سبقت وقلت لكم . فان قالوا لكم ها ها هو فى البرية فلا تخرجوا ، أو ها هو فى المخادع فلا تصدقوا ، لأنه كما ان البرق يخرج من المشرق فيظهر فى المغرب هكذا يكون مجئ ابن الإنسان ، لأنه حيثما تكون الجثة فهناك تجتمع النسور . وللوقت بعد ضيق تلك الأيام تظلم الشمس والقمر لا يعطى ضوءه . والكواكب تتساقط من السماء . وقوات السموات تتزعزع . وحينئذ

the powers of the heavens will be shaken. Then the sign of the Son of Man will appear in heaven, and then all the tribes of the earth will mourn, and they will see the Son of Man coming on the clouds of heaven with power and great glory. And He will send His angels with a great sound of a trumpet, and they will gather together His elect from the four winds, from one end of heaven to the other. "Now learn this parable from the fig tree: When its branch has already become tender and puts forth leaves, you know that summer is near. So you also, when you see all these things, know that it is near—at the doors! Assuredly, I say to you, this generation will by no means pass away till all these things take place. Heaven and earth will pass away, but My words will by no means pass away. Glory be to God forever, Amen.

ⲟⲩⲟϩ ⲛⲓϫⲟⲙ ⳿ⲛⲧⲉ ⲛⲓⲫⲏⲟⲩⲓ ⲉⲩ⳿ⲉⲕⲓⲙ · Ⲧⲟⲧⲉ ⲉϥ⳿ⲉⲟⲩⲱⲛϩϥ ⳿ⲛϫⲉ ⲡⲓⲙⲏⲓⲛⲓ ⳿ⲛⲧⲉ ⳿ⲡϣⲏⲣⲓ ⳿ⲙ⳿ⲫⲣⲱⲙⲓ ϧⲉⲛ ⳿ⲧⲫⲉ : ⲧⲟⲧⲉ ⲉⲩ⳿ⲉⲛⲉϩⲡⲓ ⳿ⲛϫⲉ ⲛⲓⲫⲩⲗⲏ ⲧⲏⲣⲟⲩ ⳿ⲛⲧⲉ ⳿ⲡⲕⲁϩⲓ ⲟⲩⲟϩ ⲉⲩ⳿ⲉⲛⲁⲩ ⳿ⲉ⳿ⲡϣⲏⲣⲓ ⳿ⲙ⳿ⲫⲣⲱⲙⲓ ⲉϥⲛⲏⲟⲩ ⳿ⲉϫⲉⲛ ⲛⲓϭⲏⲡⲓ ⳿ⲛⲧⲉ ⳿ⲧⲫⲉ : ⲛⲉⲙ ⲟⲩϫⲟⲙ ⲛⲉⲙ ⲟⲩⲛⲓϣϯ ⳿ⲛⲱⲟⲩ · Ⲟⲩⲟϩ ⲉϥ⳿ⲉⲧⲁⲟⲩ⳿ⲟ ⳿ⲛⲛⲉϥⲁⲅⲅⲉⲗⲟⲥ ⲛⲉⲙ ⲟⲩⲛⲓϣϯ ⳿ⲛⲥⲁⲗⲡⲓⲅⲅⲟⲥ ⲟⲩⲟϩ ⲉⲩ⳿ⲉⲑⲱⲟⲩϯ ⳿ⲛⲛⲉϥⲥⲱⲧⲡ ϧⲉⲛ ⲡⲓϥⲧⲟⲩ ⲑⲏⲟⲩ : ⲓⲥϫⲉⲛ ⲁⲩⲣⲏϫⲟⲩ ⳿ⲛⲛⲓⲫⲏⲟⲩⲓ ϣⲁ ⲁⲩⲣⲏϫⲟⲩ : ⳿ⲉⲃⲟⲗ ϧⲉⲛ ϯⲃⲱ ⳿ⲛⲕⲉⲛⲧⲉ ⲁⲣⲓⲉⲙⲓ ⳿ⲉϯⲡⲁⲣⲁⲃⲟⲗⲏ : ϫⲉ ⳿ⲉϣⲱⲡ ϩⲏ ⲇⲏ ⳿ⲛⲧⲉ ⲛⲉⲥϫⲁⲗ ϭⲛⲟⲩⲛ ⲟⲩⲟϩ ⳿ⲛⲧⲉ ⲛⲉⲥϭⲱⲃⲓ ϯⲟⲩⲱ ⳿ⲉⲃⲟⲗ : ϣⲁⲣⲉⲧⲉⲛ⳿ⲉⲙⲓ ϫⲉ ⳿ϥϧⲉⲛⲧ ⳿ⲛϫⲉ ⲡⲓϣⲱⲙ · Ⲡⲁⲓⲣⲏϯ ⳿ⲛⲑⲱⲧⲉⲛ ϩⲱⲧⲉⲛ ⳿ⲉϣⲱⲡ ⲁⲣⲉⲧⲉⲛϣⲁⲛⲛⲁⲩ ⳿ⲉⲛⲁⲓ ⲧⲏⲣⲟⲩ : ⲁⲣⲓⲉⲙⲓ ϫⲉ ⳿ϥϧⲉⲛⲧ ϩⲓⲣⲉⲛ ⲛⲓⲣⲱⲟⲩ : ⲁⲙⲏⲛ ϯϫⲱ ⳿ⲙⲙⲟⲥ ⲛⲱⲧⲉⲛ ϫⲉ ⳿ⲛⲛⲉ ⲧⲁⲓⲅⲉⲛⲉ⳿ⲁ ⲥⲓⲛⲓ ϣⲁⲧⲉ ⲛⲁⲓ ⲧⲏⲣⲟⲩ ϣⲱⲡⲓ : ⳿ⲧⲫⲉ ⲛⲉⲙ ⳿ⲡⲕⲁϩⲓ ⲛⲁⲥⲓⲛⲓ ⲁⲗⲗⲁ ⲛⲁⲥⲁϫⲓ ⲇⲉ ⳿ⲛⲛⲟⲩⲥⲓⲛⲓ · ⲟⲩⲱϣⲧ ⳿ⲙⲡⲓⲉⲩⲁⲅⲅⲉⲗⲓⲟⲛ ⲉⲑⲩ.

تظهر علامة إبن الإنسان فى السماء . وحينئذ تنوح جميع قبائل الأرض . ويبصرون إبن الإنسان آتياً على سحاب السماء بقوة ومجد عظيم . فيرسل ملائكته ببوق عظيم الصوت ، فيجمعون مختاريه من الرياح الأربع ، من أقاصى السموات إلى أقاصيها. فمن شجرة التين تعلموا المثل . فإنها إذا لانت أغصانها و أخرجت أوراقها ، تعلمون ان الصيف قد قرب . هكذا أنتم أيضاً إذا رأيتم هذا كله ، فأعلموا أنه قريب على الأبواب . الحق أقول لكم لا يمضى هذا الجيل حتى يكون هذا كله . السماء والأرض تزولان ولكن كلامى لا يزول . والمجد لله دائماً .

Introduction to the Exposition, Page: 9   مقدمة الطرح ، صفحة :

Exposition

طرح

O come, all you people of Jerusalem, to see Jesus on the Mount of Olives, to see Jesus of Nazareth, the Son of David, and the Word of the Father, sitting there surrounded by His inquiring disciples. They reminded him of the size of the temple, the huge stone with which it was built, and how ornate it was. Our very merciful Savior who directs those who trust Him and reassures their hearts about the future with His peace and knowledge, replied saying: "Do not let anyone mislead you about any matter when you face tribulations. For nation shall rise against nation, and kingdom against kingdom; there will be earthquakes and pestilence in diverse places; there will be great afflictions and calamities on earth. Know that they will kill you and the nations will hate you. This they will inflict on you because you bear My name. Persevere so that you may be saved."

يا جميع سكان أورشليم تعالوا لنمضى إلى جبل الزيتون لننظر يسوع الناصرى إبن داود كلمة الآب جالساً هناك وتلاميذه محيطين به يسألونه . فأعلموه أولاً عن بناء الهيكل وحجارته العظيمة وكمال زينته . فأجاب مخلصنا الكثير الرحمة ، مرشد كل أحد يتوكل عليه ، بهدوء ومعرفة ليثبت قلوبهم على ما سوف يكون: انظروا لا يضلكم أحد فى شئ إذا وقعتم فى التجارب. فسوف تقوم أمة على أمة ومملكة على مملكة وتكون زلازل واوبئة فى أماكن وتكون شدائد وضيقات على الأرض. واعلموا أنهم سوف يقتلونكم والأمم سيبغضونكم. هذا سيفعلونه بكم من أجل اسمى. فاصبروا أنتم لكى تخلصوا .

(North side) Christ our Savior; has come and has borne suffering; that through His Passion; He may save us.

(مرد بحرى) المسيح مخلصنا جاء وتألم عنا لكى بألامه يخلصنا .

(South side) Let us glorify Him; and exalt His Name; for He had mercy on us; according to His great mercy.	(مرد قبلى) فلنمجده ونرفع اسمه لأنه صنع معنا رحمة كعظيم رحمته .

The Conclusion of the Exposition, Page: 9   : ختام الطرح ، صفحة

الساعة الحادية عشر من يوم الثلاثاء من البصخة المقدسة
The Eleventh Hour of Tuesday of the Holy Pascha

Isaiah 30:25-30

And there shall be upon every lofty mountain and upon every high hill, water running in that day, when many shall perish, and when the towers shall fall. And the light of the moon shall be as the light of the sun, and the light of the sun shall be sevenfold in the day when the Lord shall heal the breach of His people, and shall heal the pain of your wound. Behold, the name of the Lord comes after a long time, burning wrath; the word of His lips is with glory, a word full of anger, and the anger of His wrath shall devour like fire. And His breath, as rushing water in a valley, shall reach as far as the neck, and be divided, to confound the nations for their vain error; error also shall pursue them, and overtake them. Must you always rejoice, and go into My holy places continually, as they that keep a feast? And must you go with a flute, as those that rejoice, into the mountain of the Lord, to the God of Israel? And the Lord shall make His glorious voice to be heard, and the wrath of His outstretched arm, to make a display with wrath and anger and devouring flame; He shall lighten terribly, and His wrath shall be as water and violent hail. Glory be to the Holy Trinity. Amen.

Proverbs 6:20-7:4

My son, keep the laws of your father, and do not reject the ordinances of your mother: but bind them upon your soul continually, and hang them as a chain about your neck. Whenever you walk, lead this along and let it be with you, that it may talk with you when you wake. For the commandment of the law is a lamp and a light; a way of life; reproof also and correction: to keep you continually from a married woman, and from the flattery of a strange tongue. Let not the desire of beauty overcome you, neither be caught by her eyes, or captivated with her eyelids. For the value of a harlot is as much as of one loaf, and a woman hunts for the precious souls of men. Shall anyone bind fire in his bosom, and not burn his garments? or will anyone walk on coals of fire, and not burn his feet? So is he that goes in to a married woman; he shall not be held guiltless, neither anyone that touches her. It is not to be wondered at if one should be caught stealing, for he steals that when hungry, he may satisfy his soul: but if he should be caught, he shall repay sevenfold, and shall deliver himself by giving all his goods. But the adulterer through lack of understanding procures destruction to his soul. He endures both pain and disgrace, and his reproach shall never be wiped off. For the soul of her husband is full of jealousy: he will not spare in the day of vengeance. He will not forego his

(من إشعياء النبى ص 30 : 25- 30)

وسيكون فى ذلك اليوم على كل جبـل شامخ وعلى كل أكمة مرتفـعة ، ماء يجرى فى ذلك اليوم . عندما يهلك كثيرون ويسقط الأبراج. ويكون نور القمر كنور الشمس . ونور الشمس يصير سبعة أضعاف فى ذلك اليوم ، إذا ما جبّر الرب كسر شعبه ، وداوى ضربات جراحه . هوذا اسم الرب يأتى بعد زمن بعيد ، مشتعل غضباً و كلام شفتيه مجد وكلام مملوء حنقاً ورجز سخطه يأكل كنار . وتأتى نفخة مثل الماء الجارى فى واد إلى الأعناق . ويقسم على الأمم قلقاً لأجل الضلالة الباطلة . وستكدرهم الضلالة وتأخذهم على وجوههم . هل تتنعمون كل وقت وتدخلون مقادسى كل حين كالمعيّدين والفرحين وتدخلون بآلات اللهو إلى جبل الله ، إلى الإله القوى قدوس إسرائيل؟ فيُسمعهم الله جلال صوته ، ويظهر نزول غضب ذراعه . ويأتى عليهم بارجل غاضبة وغضب وحنق ولهيب رجز يأكل مثل الماء والبرد النازلين بعنف . مجداً للثالوث القدوس .

(من أمثال سليمان الحكيم 6 : 20- 7 : 4)

يا ابنى أحفظ شريعة أبيك ولا ترفض مشورة أمك . أربطها بثبات فى نفسك . واجعلها قلادة فى عنقك . وإذا مشيت خذها معك ولتكن لك . وإذا نمت فلتحرسك حتى إذا استيقظت فأنها تحدثك ، لأن وصية الله مصباح والناموس نور لكل السبل . لأن الأدب يكسب طريقه طول العمر . لكى يحفظك من إمرأة ليست هى لك . ومن غش لسان غريب. لا يغلبك جمال الشهوة ولا تصيدك ولا تقتنصك بحبالها . لأنه بسبب إمرأة زانية تفتقر إلى رغيف خبز واحد ، والمرأة تصطاد نفس الرجل الكريم. أيضم أحد جمر نار فى حضنه ولا تحترق ثيابه؟ أم يمشى أحد على جمر نار ولا تكتوى رجلاه؟ هكذا من يدخل على إمرأة ذات زوج لا يكون بريئاً من الخطية ، ولا من يمسها . لا عجب إذا وُجد أحد سارقاً ، فأنه يسرق ليشبع نفسه الجائعة ، وإذا أمسك يعطى سبعة أضعاف ، ويعطى كل ماله ليخلص . أما الفاسق فمن أجل جهله سيجلب على نفسه هلاكاً ويقاسى أحزاناً وخزياً ، وعاره لا يُمحى إلى الأبد . لأن حنق رجلها يلتهب ناراً ، ولن يشفق فى

enmity for any ransom: neither will he be reconciled for many gifts. My son, keep my words, and hide my commandments with you. My son, honor the Lord, and you shall be strong; and fear none but Him. Keep my commandments, and you shall live; and keep my words as the pupils of your eyes. And bind them on your fingers, and write them on the table of your heart. Say that wisdom is your sister, and gain prudence as an acquaintance for yourself. Glory be to the Holy Trinity. Amen.

A homily of our Holy Father Abba John Chrysostom

I want to remind you with what I repeatedly reiterated to you concerning our communion with the Holy Mysteries which is of Christ. I see you in a state of extreme looseness, permissiveness, and an alarming audacity and lamentable recklessness. I weep over my condition and ask myself; Do these people really know for whom do they stand? Or do these people realize the power of this Mystery? At this thought I become angry reluctantly. If I could go away, I would have left your community out of distraughtness. If I scold one of you, he disregards my words and resents the reprimand as if I were unfair to him. I am amazed that you do not get angry at those who violate you and plunder your possessions as much as you are angry at me; I who am keen over your salvation. I dread the thought that God's wrath may be inflicted upon you because of your disregard of this great Mystery. Do you really know who is He you want to partake of? This is the Holy Body of God the Word, and His blood that He offered for our salvation. Anyone who partakes in it undeservingly will suffer abominable punishment; as was the case with Judas who betrayed God when he had communion with Him without being worthy.

We conclude the homily of our Holy Father Abba John Chrysostom, who enlightened our minds and our hearts. In the name of the Father, and the Son, and the Holy Spirit, one God. Amen.

يوم المجازاة ولا يخفى عداوته نظير أى فدية ولا نظير أى هدية . يا ابنى احفظ كلامى ، وادخر وصاياى عندك . أكرم الله لتتقوى ولا تخف أحداً سواه . احفظ وصاياى فتحيا ، واحرص على كلامى كحدقة العين . اربطه على أصابعك ، اكتبه فى عمق قلبك. قل للحكمة أنتِ أختى والفهم هو قريبك . مجداً للثالوث القدوس .

(عظة لابينا القديس أنبا يوحنا فم الذهب)

أريد أن أذكركم أيها الأخوة بما قلته لكم مرات عديدة وقت تناولنا من أسرار المسيح المقدسة . إذ رأيتكم فى تراخ عظيم وعدم مخافة تستوجب النوح. فانى أبكى لنفسى وأقول فى فكرى : ألعل هؤلاء عارفون لمن هم قيام أو قوة هذا السر؟ وهكذا أغضب بغير إرادتى . وانى كنت أريد أن أخرج من وسطكم من ضيقة نفسى ، وإذا وبخت أحداً منكم لا يكترث لقولى ، بل يتذمر علىّ كأننى قد ظلمته . ياللعجب العظيم أن الذين يظلمونكم ويسلبون أمتعتكم لا تغضبون عليهم كغضبكم علىّ أنا الذى أريد خلاصكم. أنا خائف ومرتعد حين علمت بعقاب الله الذى سيحل بكم بسبب تهاونكم بهذا السر العظيم . ألعلكم تعلمون من هو هذا الذى تريدون أن تتناولوا منه؟ هو الجسد المقدس الذى لله الكلمة ، ودمه الذى بذله عن خلاصنا . هذا إذا تناول أحد منه بغير استحقاق ، يكون له عقوبة وهلاك.

فلنختم عظة أبينا القديس أنبا يوحنا فم الذهب الذى أنار عقولنا وعيون قلوبنا باسم الآب والإبن والروح القدس إله واحد آمين .

Pascha Praise - B (12 times), Page: 7	تسبحة البصخة B (12 مرة) ، صفحة :

The Psalm

Ⲯⲁⲗⲙⲟⲥ ⲙ̅ⲇ̅ : ⲑ̅ ⲛⲉⲙ Ⲯⲁⲗ ⲙ̅ : ⲁ̅

Psalms 44:9, 40:1

Your throne, O God, is forever and ever; the scepter of Your kingdom is the scepter of righteousness. Blessed is

Ⲡⲉⲕⲑⲣⲟⲛⲟⲥ Ⲫϯ ϣⲁ ⲉⲛⲉϩ ⲛ̀ⲧⲉ ⲡⲓⲉⲛⲉϩ : ⲟⲩⲟϩ ⲡ̀ϣⲃⲱⲧ ⲙ̀ⲡⲥⲱⲟⲩⲧⲉⲛ ⲡⲉ ⲡ̀ϣⲃⲱⲧ ⲛ̀ⲧⲉ ⲧⲉⲕⲙⲉⲧⲟⲩⲣⲟ .(ⲗⲉⲝⲓⲥ) Ⲱⲟⲩⲛⲓⲁⲧϥ ⲙ̀ⲫⲏⲉⲑⲛⲁⲕⲁϯ

بيك إثرونوس أفنوتى شا إينيه إنتيه بى إينيه : أووه بى إشفوت إم إبصوأووتين بيه إب إشفوت إنتيه تيك ميت أورو . أو أوونياتف إمفى إثنا كاتى

(مز 44: 9 و40 :1)
كرسيك يا الله إلى دهر الدهور . قضيب الاستقامة هو قضيب ملكك . طوبى للذى يتفهم فى أمر

| the man who thinks on the poor and needy; the Lord shall deliver him in an evil day. Alleluia. | ⲈⲀⲈⲚ ⲞⲨⲎⲔⲒ ⲚⲈⲘ ⲞⲨⲬⲰⲂ : ⳛⲈⲚ ⲠⲒⲈⲀⲞⲞⲨ ⲈⲦⲀⲰⲞⲨ ⲈϥⲚⲀⲀⲘⲈϥ Ⲛ̄ⲬⲈ ⲠϬ︦Ⲥ̄ . ⲀⲖ. | إيجين أوو هيكي نيم أووجوب : خين بي إيهووؤو إتهوأوو إيفنّاهيمِف إنجيه إبتشويس . الليلويا . | المسكين والفقير ، فى يوم السوء ينجيه الرب . هليلويا . الليلويا . |

| Introduction to the Gospel, Page: 8 : صفحة ، مقدمة الأنجيل |

The Gospel

Ⲉⲩⲁⲅⲅⲉⲗⲓⲟⲛ Ⲕⲁⲧⲁ Ⲙⲁⲧⲑⲉⲟⲛ Ⲕⲉⲫ ⲕ︦ⲉ︦ : ⲓ︦ⲇ︦ - ⲕ︦ⲋ︦ : ⲁ︦ ⲛⲉⲙ ⲃ︦

Matthew 25:14 -26:2

"For the kingdom of heaven is like a man traveling to a far country, who called his own servants and delivered his goods to them. And to one he gave five talents, to another two, and to another one, to each according to his own ability; and immediately he went on a journey. Then he who had received the five talents went and traded with them, and made another five talents. And likewise he who had received two gained two more also. But he who had received one went and dug in the ground, and hid his lord's money. After a long time the lord of those servants came and settled accounts with them. "So he who had received five talents came and brought five other talents, saying, 'Lord, you delivered to me five talents; look, I have gained five more talents besides them.' His lord said to him, 'Well done, good and faithful servant; you were faithful over a few things, I will make you ruler over many things. Enter into the joy of your lord.' He also who had received two talents came and said, 'Lord, you delivered to me two talents; look, I have gained two more talents besides them.' His lord said to him, 'Well done, good and faithful servant; you have been faithful over a few things, I will make you ruler over many things. Enter into the joy of your lord.' "Then he who had

Ⲙ̄ⲫⲣⲏϯ ⲅⲁⲣ ⲛ̄ⲟⲩⲣⲱⲙⲓ ⲉϥⲛⲁϣⲉⲛⲁϥ ⲉ̀ⲡϣⲉⲙⲙⲟ ⲁϥⲙⲟⲩϯ ⲉ̀ⲛⲉϥⲉ̀ⲃⲓⲁⲓⲕ ⲟⲩⲟⲀ ⲁϥϯ ⲙ̄ⲡⲉⲧⲉⲛⲧⲁϥ ⲉ̀ⲧⲟⲧⲟⲩ : ⲟⲩⲁⲓ ⲙⲉⲛ ⲁϥϯ ⲛⲁϥ ⲛ̄ⲧⲓⲟⲩ ⲛ̄ϫⲓⲛϭⲱⲣ : ⲕⲉ ⲟⲩⲁⲓ ⲇⲉ ⲁϥϯ ⲛⲁϥ ⲛ̄ⲥ̄ⲛⲁⲩ ⲕⲉ ⲟⲩⲁⲓ ⲇⲉ ⲁϥϯ ⲛⲁϥ ⲛ̄ⲟⲩⲁⲓ : ⲡⲓⲟⲩⲁⲓ ⲕⲁⲧⲁ ⲧⲉϥϫⲟⲙ ⲟⲩⲟⲀ ⲁϥϣⲉⲛⲁϥ ⲉ̀ⲡϣⲉⲙⲟ : ⲁϥϣⲉⲛⲁϥ ⲇⲉ ⲛ̄ϫⲉ ⲫⲏⲉⲧⲁϥϭⲓ ⲙ̄ⲡⲓ ⲧ̄ⲓⲟⲩ ⲛ̄ϫⲓⲛϭⲱⲣ ⲁϥⲉⲣⲀⲱⲃ ⲛ̄ϧⲏⲧⲟⲩ ⲟⲩⲟⲀ ⲁϥⲁϫⲫⲉ ⲕⲉ ⲧ̄ⲓⲟⲩ : ⲡⲁⲓⲣⲏϯ ⲟⲛ ⲫⲏⲉⲧⲁϥϭⲓⲙ̄ⲡⲓⲥ̄ⲛⲁⲩ ⲁϥϫⲫⲉ ⲕⲉ ⲥ̄ⲛⲁⲩ . Ⲫⲏ ⲇⲉ ⲉⲧⲁϥϭⲓ ⲙ̄ⲡⲓⲟⲩⲁⲓ ⲁϥϣⲉⲛⲁϥ ⲁϥϣⲱⲕ ⲛ̄ⲟⲩⲕⲁⲀⲓ ⲟⲩⲟⲀ ⲁϥⲭⲱⲡ ⲙ̄ⲡⲓⲀⲁⲧ ⲛ̄ⲧⲉ ⲡⲉϥϭ︦ⲥ̄ : ⲙⲉⲛⲉⲛⲥⲁ ⲟⲩⲛⲓϣϯ ⲇⲉ ⲛ̄ⲥⲏⲟⲩ ⲁϥⲓ̀ ⲛ̄ϫⲉ ⲡ︦ϭ︦ⲥ̄ ⲛ̄ⲛⲓⲉ̀ⲃⲓⲁⲓⲕ ⲉⲧⲉ ⲙ̄ⲙⲁⲩ ⲟⲩⲟⲀ ⲁϥϥⲓⲱⲡ ⲛⲉⲙⲱⲟⲩ : ⲁϥⲓ̀ ⲇⲉ ⲛ̄ϫⲉ ⲫⲏⲉⲧⲁϥϭⲓ ⲙ̄ⲡⲓ ⲧ̄ⲓⲟⲩ ⲛ̄ϫⲓⲛϭⲱⲣ ⲁϥⲉⲛ ⲕⲉ ⲧ̄ⲓⲟⲩ ⲛ̄ϫⲓⲛϭⲱⲣ ⲉϥϫⲱ ⲙ̄ⲙⲟⲥ ϫⲉ ⲡⲁϭ︦ⲥ̄ ⲧ̄ⲓⲟⲩ ⲛ̄ϫⲓⲛϭⲱⲣ ⲁⲕⲧⲏⲓⲧⲟⲩ ⲛⲏⲓ : ⲓⲥ ⲕⲉ ⲧ̄ⲓⲟⲩ ⲛ̄ϫⲓⲛϭⲱⲣ ⲁⲓϫⲫⲱⲟⲩ . Ⲡⲉϫⲉ ⲡⲉϥϭ︦ⲥ̄ ⲇⲉ ⲛⲁϥ ϫⲉ ⲕⲁⲗⲱⲥ ⲡⲓⲃⲱⲕ ⲉⲑⲛⲁⲛⲉϥ ⲟⲩⲟⲀ ⲉⲧⲉⲛⲀⲟⲧ : ⲉⲡⲓⲇⲏ ⲁⲕⲉⲛⲀⲟⲧ ϧⲉⲛ Ⲁⲁⲛⲕⲟⲩϫⲓ ⲉⲓⲉ̀ⲭⲁⲕ Ⲁⲓϫⲉⲛ Ⲁⲁⲛⲛⲓϣϯ : ⲙⲁϣⲉⲛⲁⲕ ⲉ̀ϧⲟⲩⲛ ⲉ̀ⲫⲣⲁϣⲓ ⲛ̄ⲧⲉ ⲡⲉⲕϭ︦ⲥ̄ : ⲁϥⲓ̀ ⲇⲉ ⲛ̄ϫⲉ ⲫⲏⲉⲧⲁϥϭⲓ ⲙ̄ⲡⲓϫⲓⲛϭⲱⲣ ⲥ̄ⲛⲁⲩ ⲡⲉϫⲁϥ ϫⲉ ⲡⲁϭ︦ⲥ̄ : ϫⲓⲛϭⲱⲣ ⲥ̄ⲛⲁⲩ ⲁⲕⲧⲏⲓⲧⲟⲩ ⲛⲏⲓ ⲓⲥ ⲕⲉ ⲥ̄ⲛⲁⲩ ⲁⲓϫⲫⲱⲟⲩ : ⲡⲉϫⲉ ⲡⲉϥϭ︦ⲥ̄ ⲇⲉ ⲛⲁϥ ϫⲉ ⲕⲁⲗⲱⲥ ⲡⲓⲃⲱⲕ ⲉⲑⲛⲁⲛⲉϥ ⲟⲩⲟⲀ ⲉⲧⲉⲛⲀⲟⲧ : ⲉⲡⲓⲇⲏ ⲁⲕⲉⲛⲀⲟⲧ ϧⲉⲛ Ⲁⲁⲛⲕⲟⲩϫⲓ ⲉⲓⲉ̀ⲭⲁⲕ Ⲁⲓϫⲉⲛ Ⲁⲁⲛⲛⲓϣϯ : ⲙⲁϣⲉⲛⲁⲕ ⲉ̀ϧⲟⲩⲛ ⲉ̀ⲫⲣⲁϣⲓ ⲛ̄ⲧⲉ ⲡⲉⲕϭ︦ⲥ̄ . Ⲁϥ ⲓ̀ ⲇⲉ Ⲁⲱϥ ⲛ̄ϫⲉ ⲫⲏⲉⲧⲁϥϭⲓ ⲙ̄ⲡⲓϫⲓⲛϭⲱⲣ ⲡⲉϫⲁϥ : ϫⲉ ⲡⲁϭ︦ⲥ̄ ⲁⲓⲉ̀ⲙⲓ ϫⲉ ⲛ̄ⲑⲟⲕ ⲟⲩⲣⲱⲙⲓ ⲉϥⲛⲁϣⲧ : ⲉⲕⲱⲥϧ ⲙ̄ⲫⲏⲉⲧⲉ ⲙ̄ⲡⲉⲕⲥⲁⲧϥ ⲟⲩⲟⲀ ⲉⲕⲉ̀ⲑⲱⲟⲩϯ

(متى 25 : 14 - 26 : 2)

كمثل إنسان مسافر دعا عبيده وسلمهم أمواله. فأعطى واحد خمس وزنات وآخر وزنتين وآخر وزنة . كل واحد على قدر طاقته وسافر للوقت . فمضى الذى أخذ الخمس وزنات وتاجر بها فربح خمس أخر . وهكذا الذى أخذ الوزنتين ربح وزنتين أخريين . وأما الذى أخذ الوزنة فمضى وحفر فى الأرض ودفن فضة سيده . وبعد زمان كثير جاء سيد أولئك العبيد وحاسبهم . فجاء الذى أخذ الخمس الوزنات وقدم خمس وزنات أخر قائلاً : يا سيد خمس وزنات سلمتنى وهذه خمس وزنات أخرى ربحتها . فقال سيده : نعماً أيها العبد الصالح و الأمين ، قد وُجدت أميناً فى القليل فسأقيمك على الكثير ، أدخل إلى فرح سيدك . ثم جاء الذى أخذ الوزنتين و قال : يا سيدى وزنتين سلمتنى وهاتان وزنتان أخرتان ربحتهما . فقال له سيده: نعماً أيها العبد الصالح والأمين ، قد وُجدت أميناً فى القليل فأقيمك على الكثير ، أدخل الى فرح سيدك . ثم جاء أيضاً الذى أخذ الوزنة

received the one talent came and said, 'Lord, I knew you to be a hard man, reaping where you have not sown, and gathering where you have not scattered seed. And I was afraid, and went and hid your talent in the ground. Look, there you have what is yours.' "But his lord answered and said to him, 'You wicked and lazy servant, you knew that I reap where I have sown, and gather where I have not scattered seed. So you ought to have deposited my money with the bankers, and at my coming I would have received back my own with interest. So take the talent from him, and give it to him who has ten talents. 'For to everyone who has, more will be given, and he will have abundance; but from him who does not have, even what he has will be taken away. And cast the unprofitable servant into the outer darkness. There will be weeping and gnashing of teeth.' "When the Son of Man comes in His glory, and all the holy angels with Him, then He will sit on the throne of His glory. All the nations will be gathered before Him, and He will separate them one from another, as a shepherd divides his sheep from the goats. And He will set the sheep on His right hand, but the goats on the left. Then the King will say to those on His right hand, 'Come, you blessed of My Father, inherit the kingdom prepared for you from the foundation of the world: for I was hungry and you gave Me food; I was thirsty and you gave Me drink; I was a stranger and you took Me in; I was naked and you clothed Me; I was sick and you visited Me; I was in prison and you came to Me.' "Then the righteous will answer Him, saying, 'Lord, when did we see You hungry and feed You, or thirsty and give You drink? When did we

ⲉϧⲟⲩⲛ ⲙ̀ⲫⲏⲉⲧⲉ ⲙ̀ⲡⲉⲕϫⲟⲣϥ ⲉⲃⲟⲗ : ⲟⲩⲟⲥ ⲁⲓⲉⲣϩⲟϯ ⲁⲓϣⲉⲛⲏⲓ ⲁⲓⲭⲱⲡ ⲙ̀ⲡⲉⲕϫⲓⲛϭⲱⲣ ϧⲉⲛ ⲡ̀ⲕⲁϩⲓ : ⲓⲥ ⲡⲉⲧⲉⲫⲱⲕ ⲛ̀ⲧⲟⲧ . Ⲁ̀ϥⲉⲣⲟⲩⲱ ⲇⲉ ⲛ̀ϫⲉ ⲡⲉϥϭ̅ⲥ̅ ⲡⲉϫⲁϥ ⲛⲁϥ ϫⲉ ⲡⲓⲃⲱⲕ ⲉⲧϩⲱⲟⲩ ⲟⲩⲟⲥ ⲛ̀ϭⲉⲛⲛⲉ : ⲓⲥⲭⲉ ⲁⲕⲉⲙⲓ ϫⲉ ϣⲁⲓⲱⲥϧ ⲙ̀ⲫⲏⲉⲧⲉ ⲙ̀ⲡⲓⲥⲁⲧϥ : ⲟⲩⲟⲥ ϣⲁⲓⲑⲱⲟⲩⲧ ⲉϧⲟⲩⲛ ⲙ̀ⲫⲏⲉⲧⲉ ⲙ̀ⲡⲓⲭⲟⲣϥ ⲉⲃⲟⲗ : ⲛⲁⲥⲉⲙⲡϣⲁ ⲟⲩⲛ ⲛⲁⲕ ⲡⲉ ⲉ̀ϯ ⲙ̀ⲡⲁϩⲁⲧ ⲉ̀ⲧⲟⲧⲟⲩ ⲛ̀ⲛⲓⲧⲣⲁⲡⲉⲍⲓⲧⲏⲥ : ⲟⲩⲟⲥ ⲁⲛⲟⲕ ⲁⲓϣⲁⲛⲓ ⲛⲁⲓⲛⲁⲃⲓ ⲙ̀ⲡⲉⲧⲉⲫⲱⲓ ⲛⲉⲙ ⲧⲉϥⲙⲏⲥⲓ : ⲁⲗⲓⲟⲩⲓ ⲟⲩⲛ ⲙ̀ⲡⲓϫⲓⲛϭⲱⲣ ⲛ̀ⲧⲟⲧϥ ⲙ̀ⲫⲁⲓ ⲙⲏⲓϥ ⲙ̀ⲫⲁ ⲡⲓⲙⲏⲧ ⲛ̀ϫⲓⲛϭⲱⲣ . Ⲟⲩⲟⲛ ⲅⲁⲣ ⲛⲓⲃⲉⲛ ⲉⲧⲉ ⲟⲩⲟⲛ ⲧⲁϥ ⲉⲩⲉ̀ϯ ⲛⲁϥ ⲟⲩⲟⲥ ⲉⲣⲉ ⲟⲩⲟⲛ ⲉⲣϩⲟⲩⲟ̀ ⲉⲣⲟϥ : ⲫⲏ ⲇⲉ ⲉⲧⲉ ⲙ̀ⲙⲟⲛ ⲛ̀ⲧⲁϥ ⲫⲏⲉⲧⲉ ⲛ̀ⲧⲟⲧϥ ⲉⲩⲉ̀ⲟⲗϥ ⲛ̀ⲧⲟⲧϥ ⲟⲩⲟⲥ ⲡⲓⲁⲧϣⲁⲩ ⲙ̀ⲃⲱⲕ ⲉⲧⲉ ⲙⲙⲁⲩ ⲁⲩϩⲓⲧϥ ⲉⲃⲟⲗ ⲉ̀ⲡⲓⲭⲁⲕⲓ ⲉⲧ ⲥⲁⲃⲟⲗ ⲡⲓⲙⲁ ⲉⲧⲉ ⲫ̀ⲣⲓⲙⲓ ⲛⲁϣⲱⲡⲓ ⲙ̀ⲙⲟϥ ⲛⲉⲙ ⲡⲓⲥ̀ⲑⲉⲣⲧⲉⲣ ⲛ̀ⲧⲉ ⲛⲓⲛⲁϫϩⲓ : ⲉϣⲱⲡ ⲇⲉ ⲁϥϣⲁⲛⲓ ⲛ̀ϫⲉ ⲡ̀ϣⲏⲣⲓ ⲙ̀ⲫ̀ⲣⲱⲙⲓ ϧⲉⲛ ⲡⲉϥⲱⲟⲩ ⲛⲉⲙ ⲛⲉϥⲁⲅⲅⲉⲗⲟⲥ ⲉⲑⲟⲩⲁⲃ ⲧⲏⲣⲟⲩ ⲛⲉⲙⲁϥ ⲧⲟⲧⲉ ⲉϥⲉ̀ϩⲉⲙⲥⲓ ϩⲓϫⲉⲛ ⲡ̀ⲑⲣⲟⲛⲟⲥ ⲛ̀ⲧⲉ ⲡⲉϥⲱⲟⲩ . Ⲟⲩⲟⲥ ⲉⲩⲉ̀ⲑⲱⲟⲩⲧ ⲛⲁϩⲣⲁϥ ⲛ̀ϫⲉ ⲛⲓⲉⲑⲛⲟⲥ ⲧⲏⲣⲟⲩ : ⲟⲩⲟⲥ ⲉϥⲉ̀ⲫⲟⲣϫⲟⲩ ⲉⲃⲟⲗ ⲛ̀ⲛⲟⲩⲉⲣⲏⲟⲩ : ⲙ̀ⲫⲣⲏϯ ⲙ̀ⲡⲓⲙⲁⲛⲉ̀ⲥⲱⲟⲩ ⲉϣⲁϥⲫⲱⲣϫ ⲛ̀ⲛⲓⲉⲥⲱⲟⲩ ⲉⲃⲟⲗ ϧⲉⲛ ⲛⲓⲃⲁⲉⲙⲡⲓ : ⲟⲩⲟⲥ ⲛⲓⲉⲥⲱⲟⲩ ⲙⲉⲛ ⲉϥⲉ̀ⲭⲁⲩ ⲥⲁ ⲧⲉϥⲟⲩⲓ ⲛⲁⲙ ⲛⲁⲃⲁⲉⲙⲡⲓ ⲇⲉ ⲥⲁ ⲧⲉϥϫⲁϭⲏ : ⲧⲟⲧⲉ ⲉϥⲉ̀ϫⲟⲥ ⲛ̀ϫⲉ ⲡⲓⲟⲩⲣⲟ ⲛ̀ⲛⲏⲉⲧ ⲥⲁ ⲧⲉϥⲟⲩⲓ ⲛⲁⲙ : ϫⲉ ⲁⲙⲱⲓⲛⲓ ϩⲁⲣⲟⲓ ⲛⲏⲉⲧⲥⲙⲁⲣⲱⲟⲩⲧ ⲛ̀ⲧⲉ ⲡⲁⲓⲱⲧ ⲁⲣⲓ ⲕ̀ⲗⲏⲣⲟⲛⲟⲙⲓⲛ ⲛ̀ⲧⲉ ϯⲙⲉⲧⲟⲩⲣⲟ ⲑⲏⲉⲧ ⲥⲉⲃⲧⲱⲧ ⲛⲱⲧⲉⲛ ⲓⲥϫⲉⲛ ⲧ̀ⲕⲁⲧⲁⲃⲟⲗⲏ ⲙ̀ⲡⲓⲕⲟⲥⲙⲟⲥ . Ⲁ̀ⲓ̀ϩ̀ⲕⲟ ⲅⲁⲣ ⲟⲩⲟⲥ ⲁⲧⲉⲧⲉⲛⲧⲉⲙⲙⲟⲓ ⲁⲓⲃⲓ ⲟⲩⲟⲥ ⲁⲧⲉⲧⲉⲛⲧⲥⲟⲓ : ⲛⲁⲓⲟⲓ ⲛ̀ϣⲉⲙⲙⲟ ⲟⲩⲟⲥ ⲁⲧⲉⲛϣⲟⲡⲧ ⲉⲣⲱⲧⲉⲛ : ⲛⲁⲓⲃⲏϣ ⲟⲩⲟⲥ ⲁⲧⲉⲧⲉⲛϩⲟⲃⲥⲧ : ⲛⲁⲓϣⲱⲛⲓ ⲟⲩⲟⲥ ⲁⲧⲉⲧⲉⲛ ϫⲉⲙⲡⲁϣⲓⲛⲓ : ⲛⲁⲓⲭⲏ ϧⲉⲛ ⲡⲓϣ̀ⲧⲉⲕⲟ ⲟⲩⲟⲥ ⲁⲧⲉⲧⲉⲛⲓ̀ ϣⲁⲣⲟⲓ : ⲧⲟⲧⲉ ⲉⲩⲉ̀ⲉⲣⲟⲩⲱ ⲛⲁϥ ⲛ̀ϫⲉ ⲛⲓⲑⲙⲏⲓ ⲉⲩϫⲱ ⲙⲙⲟⲥ : ϫⲉ ⲡⲉⲛϭ̅ⲥ̅ ⲉⲧⲁⲛⲛⲁⲩ ⲉⲣⲟⲕ ⲛ̀ⲑⲛⲁⲩ ⲉⲕϩⲟⲕⲉⲣ ⲟⲩⲟⲥ ⲁⲛ ⲧⲉⲙⲙⲟⲕ : ⲓⲉ ⲉⲕⲟⲃⲓ ⲟⲩⲟⲥ ⲁⲛⲧⲥⲟⲕ . ⲓⲉ ⲉⲧⲁⲛⲛⲁⲩ ⲉⲣⲟⲕ ⲛ̀ⲑⲛⲁⲩ ⲉⲕⲟⲓ ⲛ̀ϣⲉⲙⲙⲟ ⲟⲩⲟⲥ ⲁⲛϣⲟⲡⲕ ⲉⲣⲟⲛ : ⲓⲉ ⲉⲕⲃⲏϣ ⲟⲩⲟⲥ ⲁⲛϩⲟⲃⲥⲕ : ⲓⲉ

وقال: يا سيد علمت أنك إنسان قاس ، تحصد من حيث لم تزرع وتجمع من حيث لم تبذر ، فخفت ومضيت ودفنت وزنتك فى الأرض. وها هوذا ما لك عندى . فأجاب سيده وقال له : أيها العبد الشرير والكسلان . ان كنت قد علمت أنى أحصد من حيث لم أزرع وأجمع من حيث لم أبذر ، فكان ينبغى لك أن تسلم فضتى إلى الصيارفة على المائدة وكنت متى جئت استلمتها مع ربحها . خذوا منه الوزنة وأعطوها لصاحب العشر الوزنات. لأن كل من له يُعطى ويُزاد ، ومن ليس له فالذى عنده يؤخذ منه. وذلك العبد البطال ألقوه فى الظلمة الخارجية هناك يكون البكاء وصرير الأسنان . ومتى جاء ابن الإنسان فى مجده وجميع ملائكته القديسين معه ، فحينئذ يجلس على عرش مجده وتجتمع أمامه جميع الشعوب . فيميز بعضهم من بعض كما يميز الراعى الخراف من الجداء . فيقيم الخراف عن يمينه والجداء عن يساره . حينئذ يقول الملك للذين عن يمينه: تعالوا إلىَّ يا مباركى أبى رثوا الملك المعد لكم منذ إنشاء العالم. لأنى جعت فاطعمتمونى ، وعطشت فسقيتمونى وكنت غريباً فأويتمونى ، وعرياناً فكسوتمونى ، ومريضاً فزرتمونى ، ومحبوساً فأتيتم إلىَّ . حينئذ يجيبه الصديقون قائلين: يارب متى رأيناك جائعاً فأطعمناك أو عطشاناً فسقيناك؟ ومتى رأيناك غريباً فأويناك أو

see You a stranger and take You in, or naked and clothe You? Or when did we see You sick, or in prison, and come to You?' And the King will answer and say to them, 'Assuredly, I say to you, inasmuch as you did it to one of the least of these My brethren, you did it to Me.' "Then He will also say to those on the left hand, 'Depart from Me, you cursed, into the everlasting fire prepared for the devil and his angels: for I was hungry and you gave Me no food; I was thirsty and you gave Me no drink; I was a stranger and you did not take Me in, naked and you did not clothe Me, sick and in prison and you did not visit Me.' "Then they also will answer Him, saying, 'Lord, when did we see You hungry or thirsty or a stranger or naked or sick or in prison, and did not minister to You?' Then He will answer them, saying, 'Assuredly, I say to you, inasmuch as you did not do it to one of the least of these, you did not do it to Me.' And these will go away into everlasting punishment, but the righteous into eternal life." Now it came to pass, when Jesus had finished all these sayings, that He said to His disciples, "You know that after two days is the Passover, and the Son of Man will be delivered up to be crucified." Glory be to God forever, Amen.

ⲉⲧⲁⲛⲛⲁⲩ ⲉⲣⲟⲕ ⲛ̀ⲟⲩⲁⲩ ⲉⲕϣⲱⲛⲓ ⲓⲉ ⲉⲕⲭⲏ ϧⲉⲛ ⲡⲓϣⲧⲉⲕⲟ ⲟⲩⲟⲥ ⲁⲛⲓ ϣⲁⲣⲟⲕ : ⲟⲩⲟⲥ ⲉϥⲉⲉⲣⲟⲩⲱ ⲛ̀ϫⲉ ⲡⲓⲟⲩⲣⲟ ⲉϥⲉϫⲟⲥ ⲛⲱⲟⲩ : ϫⲉ ⲁⲙⲏⲛ ϯϫⲱ ⲙ̀ⲙⲟⲥ ⲛⲱⲧⲉⲛ : ϫⲉ ⲉ̀ⲫⲟⲥⲟⲛ ⲁⲣⲉⲧⲉⲛⲁⲓⲧⲟⲩ ⲛ̀ⲟⲩⲁⲓ ⲛ̀ⲛⲁⲓⲕⲟⲩϫⲓ ⲛ̀ⲥⲛⲏⲟⲩ ⲛ̀ⲧⲏⲓ ⲁⲛⲟⲕ ⲡⲉ ⲉⲧⲁⲣⲉⲧⲉⲛⲁⲓⲧⲟⲩ ⲛⲏⲓ . Ⲧⲟⲧⲉ ⲉϥⲉϫⲟⲥ ⲛ̀ⲛⲏⲉⲧϩⲱⲟⲩ ⲉⲧ ⲥⲁ ⲧⲉϥϫⲁϭⲏ : ϫⲉ ⲙⲁϣⲉⲛⲱⲧⲉⲛ ⲉ̀ⲃⲟⲗ ϩⲁⲣⲟⲓ ⲛⲏⲉⲧ ⲥ̀ϩⲟⲩⲟⲣⲧ ⲉ̀ⲡⲓⲭⲣⲱⲙ ⲛ̀ⲉⲛⲉⲥ : ⲫⲏⲉⲧⲥⲉⲃⲧⲱⲧ ⲙ̀ⲡⲓⲇⲓⲁⲃⲟⲗⲟⲥ ⲛⲉⲙ ⲛⲉϥⲁⲅⲅⲉⲗⲟⲥ : ⲁⲓϩⲕⲟ ⲅⲁⲣ ⲟⲩⲟϩ ⲙ̀ⲡⲉⲧⲉⲛⲧⲉⲙⲙⲟⲓ : ⲁⲓⲓⲃⲓ ⲟⲩⲟϩ ⲙ̀ⲡⲉⲧⲉⲛ̀ⲧⲥⲟⲓ : ⲛⲁⲓⲟⲓ ⲛ̀ϣⲉⲙⲙⲟ ⲟⲩⲟϩ ⲙ̀ⲡⲉⲧⲉⲛϣⲟⲡⲧ ⲉ̀ⲣⲱⲧⲉⲛ ⲛⲁⲓⲃⲏϣ ⲟⲩⲟϩ ⲙ̀ⲡⲉⲧⲉⲛϩⲟⲃⲥⲧ : ⲛⲁⲓϣⲱⲛⲓ ⲟⲩⲟϩ ⲙ̀ⲡⲉⲧⲉⲛϫⲉⲙⲡⲁϣⲓⲛⲓ : ⲛⲁⲓⲭⲏ ϧⲉⲛ ⲡⲓϣⲧⲉⲕⲟ ⲟⲩⲟϩ ⲙ̀ⲡⲉⲧⲉⲛⲓ̀ ϣⲁⲣⲟⲓ : ⲧⲟⲧⲉ ⲉⲩⲉⲉⲣⲟⲩⲱ ϩⲱⲟⲩ ⲉⲩϫⲱ ⲙ̀ⲙⲟⲥ : ϫⲉ ⲡⲉⲛϭⲟⲓⲥ ⲉⲧⲁⲛⲛⲁⲩ ⲉ̀ⲣⲟⲕ ⲛ̀ⲟⲩⲁⲩ ⲉⲕϩⲟⲕⲉⲣ ⲓⲉ ⲉⲕⲟ̀ⲃⲓ : ⲓⲉⲉⲕⲟⲓ ⲛ̀ϣⲉⲙⲙⲟ ⲓⲉ ⲉⲕⲃⲏϣ : ⲓⲉ ⲉⲕϣⲱⲛⲓ ⲓⲉ ⲉⲕⲭⲏ ϧⲉⲛ ⲡⲓϣⲧⲉⲕⲟ ⲟⲩⲟϩ ⲙ̀ⲡⲉⲛϣⲉⲙϣⲏⲧⲕ . Ⲧⲟⲧⲉ ⲉϥⲉⲉⲣⲟⲩⲱ ⲛⲱⲟⲩ ⲉϥϫⲱ ⲙ̀ⲙⲟⲥ : ϫⲉ ⲁⲙⲏⲛ ϯϫⲱ ⲙ̀ⲙⲟⲥ ⲛⲱⲧⲉⲛ : ϫⲉ ⲉ̀ⲫⲟⲥⲟⲛ ⲙ̀ⲡⲉⲧⲉⲛⲁⲓⲧⲟⲩ ⲛ̀ⲟⲩⲁⲓ ⲛ̀ⲛⲁⲓⲕⲟⲩϫⲓ ⲟⲩ ⲇⲉ ⲁⲛⲟⲕ ⲙ̀ⲡⲉⲧⲉⲛⲁⲓⲧⲟⲩ ⲛⲏⲓ : ⲟⲩⲟϩ ⲉⲩⲉϣⲉⲛⲱⲟⲩ ⲛ̀ϫⲉ ⲛⲁⲓ ⲉⲩⲕⲟⲗⲁⲥⲓⲥ ⲛ̀ⲉⲛⲉϩ ⲛⲓⲑⲙⲏⲓ ⲇⲉ ⲉⲩⲱⲛϧ ⲛ̀ⲉⲛⲉϩ . Ⲟⲩⲟϩ ⲁⲥϣⲱⲡⲓ ⲉⲧⲁ Ⲓⲏⲥ ϫⲉⲕ ⲛⲁⲓⲥⲁϫⲓ ⲧⲏⲣⲟⲩ ⲉ̀ⲃⲟⲗ ⲡⲉϫⲁϥ ⲛ̀ⲛⲉϥⲙⲁⲑⲏⲧⲏⲥ : ϫⲉ ⲧⲉⲧⲉⲛⲉⲙⲓ ϫⲉ ⲙⲉⲛⲉⲛⲥⲁ ⲕⲉ ⲉ̀ϩⲟⲟⲩ ⲥⲛⲁⲩ ⲡⲓⲡⲁⲥⲭⲁ ⲛⲁϣⲱⲡⲓ : ⲟⲩⲟϩ ⲡ̀ϣⲏⲣⲓ ⲙ̀ⲫⲣⲱⲙⲓ ⲥⲉⲛⲁⲧⲏⲓϥ ⲉⲑⲣⲟⲩⲁϣϥ . ⲟⲩⲱϣⲧ ⲙ̀ⲡⲓⲉⲩⲁⲅⲅⲉⲗⲓⲟⲛ ⲉⲑ︢ⲩ.

عرياناً فكسوناك؟ ومتى رأيناك مريضاً أو محبوساً فأتينا إليك؟ فيجيب الملك ويقول لهم: الحق أقول لكم ، انكم كلما فعلتم ذلك بأحد أخوتى هؤلاء الصغار فبى فعلتموه . حينئذ يقول للاشرار الذين عن يساره: اذهبوا عنى يا ملاعين إلى النار الأبدية المعدة لأبليس وملائكته . لأنى جعت فلم تطعمونى . وعطشت فلم تسقونى . وكنت غريباً فلم تأوونى . وعرياناً فلم تكسونى . ومريضاً فلم تزورونى . و محبوساً فلم تأتوا الىّ . حينئذ يجيبونه هم أيضاً ويقولون: يارب متى رأيناك جائعاً أو عطشاناً ، أو غريباً أو عرياناً ، أو مريضاً أو محبوساً ولم نخدمك؟ حينئذ يجيب ويقول لهم: الحق أقول لكم بما انكم لم تفعلوه بأحد أخوتى هؤلاء الصغار فبى لم تفعلوه . فيذهب هؤلاء إلى العذاب الدائم والصديقون إلى الحياة الأبدية . ولما أكمل يسوع هذا الكلام كله قال لتلاميذه: تعلمون أنه بعد يومين يكون الفصح وإبن الإنسان يسلم ليصلب . والمجد لله دائماً .

Introduction to the Exposition, Page: 9 مقدمة الطرح ، صفحة :

Exposition

طـرح

Against You only have I sinned. O God the Pantocrator, forgive me. In audacity, I have committed iniquities, and I was negligent in obeying Your orders. You come in the power of Your glory with hosts of angels around You. You sit on the throne of Your kingdom, O the righteous judge. All the nations from all four corners of the earth assemble in front you, yet with Your one word, they split apart to the right and to the left.

لك وحدك أخطأت أيها الرب ضابط الكل ، فأغفر لى يا ربى وإلهى . صنعت الشر بجسارة وتكاسلت فى أوامرك أيها الرب. متى جئت بقوة مجدك ويحيط بك ملائكتك فتجلس أنت أيها الديان العادل على كرسى مملكتك. وتجتمع إليك جميع الأمم من الأربع رياح زوايا الأرض ويفترقون بعضهم من بعض يميناً وشمالاً بكلمة

The sheep on your right and the goats on your left. Those on Your right will rejoice with You, as well as those virtuous who sought to please You and who observed Your commandments and fulfilled them all. Those who fed You in Your hunger and gave You a drink in Your thirst; hosted You when You were a stranger in their homes; clothed You when You were naked; visited You when You were incarcerated. In Your sickness, they served You. Then they will rejoice in their good deeds and receive their rewards to the exclusion of the goats. The righteous inherit eternal life and the goats suffer. Listen O you foolish and fathom what you lost; that mercy prides itself over justice. Be merciful before you face judgment by the Judge. After our Savior concluded his talk, He told His disciples that Passover will come after two days and that the Son of Man will fulfill the prophecies of the prophets: to be the sacrificial lamb and complete Passover to the fullness of times. O Christ our Lord, truly You have been the sacrificial lamb and complete Passover to the fullness of times. O Christ our Lord, truly You have been the unblemished lamb sacrificed for the life of mankind. He is the lamb of God, the Father, who takes away the sin of the world.

(North side) Christ our Savior; has come and has borne suffering; that through His Passion; He may save us.

(South side) Let us glorify Him; and exalt His Name; for He had mercy on us; according to His great mercy.

واحدة . وتقف الخراف عن يمينك والجداء عن يسارك . فيفرح معك الذين عن يمينك والأبرار الذين صنعوا مرضاتك المتمسكون بأوامرك وحفظوها وصنعوها جميعها . الذين أطعموك فى جوعك وسقوك أيضاً فى عطشك وفى غربتك آووك فى بيوتهم وفى عريك ستروك وعندما كنت فى السجن جاءوا لزيارتك وفى مرضك خدموك . حينئذ يفرحون بأعمالهم الحسنة ويأخذون أجرهم دون الجداء ، فيمضى الأبرار إلى الحياة الدائمة . والجداء إلى العذاب . اسمعوا أيها الجهال وافهموا أيها الضالين أن الرحمة تفتخر فى الحكم . فاصنعوا الرحمة قبل أن تأتى عليكم دينونة الديان . فلما فرغ مخلصنا من كلامه ، أخبر التلاميذ أصفياءه أنه بعد يومين يكون الفصح. فاسمعوا يا أخوتى الذين اصطفيتهم: ان ابن الإنسان سيكمل عليه المكتوب فى سفر الأنبياء لكى يكون خروفاً للذبح وفصحاً كاملاً إلى كمال الدهور . فبالحقيقة صرت أيها المسيح إلهنا حملاً بلا عيب عن حياة العالم ، الذى هو حمل الله الآب حامل خطية العالم بأسره.

(مرد بحرى) المسيح مخلصنا جاء وتألم عنا لكى بآلامه يخلصنا .

(مرد قبلى) فلنمجده ونرفع اسمه لأنه صنع معنا رحمة كعظيم رحمته .

| The Conclusion of the Exposition, Page: | 9 | ختام الطرح ، صفحة : |

| The Conclusion with the Daytime Litanies, Page: | 10 | طلبة الصباح ، صفحة : |

ليلة الأربعاء من البصخة المقدسة

Wednesday Eve of the Holy Pascha

القراءات و الاحداث

الموضوع : حكمه على رؤساء الكهنة و الفريسيين

الاولى : مت 22 : 1 - 14؛ غضبه عليهم
الثالثه : مت 24 : 36 – 51 ؛ ضمهم للمرائين
السادسة : مت 25 : 1- 13 ؛ منعهم من عرسه
التاسعة : مت 23 : 29 – 36 ؛ هلاكهم العتيد
الحادية عشرة : يو 11 : 55 – 57 ؛ بحثهم عنه

اكمل الرب امثاله متحدثاً عن مثل العرس و الكرامين و العذارى وما هى مكافئة المستعدين و جزاء الغير مستعدين . ثم ذهب يهوذا الاسخريوطى لرؤساء الكهنة ليتشاور معهم لتسليم الرب فاصدروا امراً انه ان عرف احداً اين هو فليدل عليه ليمسكوه.

The Readings and Events

Subject: His judgment regarding the chief priests and Pharisees

First hour: Matthew 22:1-14; His indignation at them.
Third hour: Matthew 24:36-51; Considering them hypocrites
Sixth hour: Matthew 25:1-13; Excluding them of His banquet
Ninth hour: Matthew 23:29-36; Their prospective perishing.
Eleventh hour: John 11:55-57; Seeking Him.

The Lord gave His parables of the marriage, the vine dressers, and the virgins. He showed the reward of the watchful people and the punishment of the unready ones. Judas Iscariot went to the chief priests to discuss how to hand the Lord Jesus to them. They had given a command, that if any one knew where He was, he should report it, that they might seize Him.

The First Hour of Wednesday Eve of the Holy Pascha

الساعة الأولى من ليلة الأربعاء من البصخة المقدسة

Ezekiel 22:17-22

And the word of the Lord came to me, saying, Son of man, behold, the house of Israel has become to Me as it were mixed with brass, and iron, and tin, and lead; they are mixed up in the midst of the silver. Therefore say, Thus says the Lord God: Because you have become one mixture, therefore I will gather you into the midst of Jerusalem. As silver, brass, iron, tin, and lead are gathered into the midst of the furnace, to blow fire into it, that they may be melted: so will I take you in My wrath, and I will gather and melt you. And I will blow upon you in the fire of My wrath, and you shall be melted in the midst thereof. As silver is melted in the midst of a furnace, so shall you be melted in the midst thereof; and you shall know that I the Lord have poured out My wrath upon you. *Glory be to the Holy Trinity. Amen*

(من حزقيال النبى ص 22 : 17 - 22)

وكانت إلىّ كلمة الرب قائلاً : يا إبن الإنسان ، هوذا قد صار لدى بيت إسرائيل جميعهم خليطاً نحاساً وقصديراً وحديداً ورصاصاً مخلوطاً مع الفضة . لأجل ذلك قل هذا ما يقوله الرب : بما انكم جميعاً قد صرتم امتزاجاً واحداً فلأجل هذا ها أنا آخذكم فى أورشليم كما آخذ الفضة والنحاس والحديد والرصاص والقصدير فى وسط الأتون . لنفخ النار عليها لسبكها ، هكذا آخذكم برجزى وأجمعكم وأذيبكم وأنفخ عليكم بنار غضبى واسبككم فى وسطها . كما تسبك الفضة فى وسط الأتون ، كذلك تسبكون فى وسطه . فتعلمون أنى أنا هو الرب صببت غضبى عليكم . مجداً للثالوث القدوس.

Ezekiel 22:23-29

And the word of the Lord came to me, saying, Son of man, say to her: You are the land that is not rained upon, neither has rain come upon you in the day of wrath; whose princes in the midst of her are as roaring lions seizing prey, devouring souls by oppression, and taking bribes; and your widows are multiplied in the midst of you. Her priests also have set at nought My law, and profaned My holy things: they have not distinguished between the holy and profane, nor have they distinguished between the unclean and the clean, and have hidden their eyes from My Sabbaths, and I was profaned in the midst of them. Her princes in the midst of her are as wolves ravening to shed blood, that they may get dishonest gain. And her prophets that daub them shall fall, that see vanities, that prophesy falsehoods, saying, Thus says the Lord, when the Lord has not spoken. *Glory be to the Holy Trinity. Amen*

(من حزقيال النبى ص 22 : 23 - 29)

وصار كلام الرب إلىّ قائلاً : يا إبن الإنسان ، قل لها أنت الأرض التى لم ترو ولم يمطر عليها فى يوم غضبى . هذه التى مدبروها فى وسطها مثل أسد يزأر . تخطف خطفاً وتأكل نفوساً بالظلم والرشوة وأراملها يكثرون فى وسطك ورذل كهنتك ناموسى ودنسوا مقادسى ولم يميزوا بين المقدس والمدنس وبين النجس والطاهر ، وحجبوا عيونهم عن سبوتى وصرت مرذولاً فى وسطك . رؤساؤك مثل ذئاب يخطفون خطفاً ويسفكون دماء كى يأخذوا ما ليس لهم. وأنبياؤها الذين مسحوهم يسقطون إذ يرون باطلاً ويسألون وهم ينطقون كذباً . مجداً للثالوث القدوس .

| Pascha Praise - B (12 times), Page: 7 | تسبحة البصخة B (12 مرة) ، صفحة : |

The Psalm

Ⲯⲁⲗⲙⲟⲥ ⲚⲎ : ⲓⲅ ⲛⲉⲙ ⲓⲇ

Psalms 58:13-14

You have been my supporter, and my refuge in the day of my affliction. You are my helper; to You, my God, shall I sing; You are my supporter, O my God, and my mercy. *Alleluia.*

Ⲁⲕϣⲱⲡⲓ ⲛⲏⲓ ⲛⲟⲩⲣⲉϥϣⲟⲡⲧ ⲉⲣⲟϥ : ⲛⲉⲙ ⲟⲩⲙⲁⲫⲱⲧ ϧⲉⲛ ⲡⲉϩⲟⲟⲩ ⲙ̀ⲡⲁϩⲟϫϩⲉϫ .

Ⲛ̀ⲑⲟⲕ ⲡⲉ ⲡⲁⲃⲟⲏⲑⲟⲥ ⲁⲓⲛⲁⲉⲣⲯⲁⲗⲓⲛ ⲉⲣⲟⲕ ⲡⲁⲛⲟⲩϯ : ϫⲉ ⲛ̀ⲑⲟⲕ ⲡⲉ ⲡⲁⲣⲉϥϣⲟⲡⲧ ⲉⲣⲟⲕ ⲡⲁⲛⲟⲩϯ ⲡⲁⲛⲁⲓ . ⲁⲗ .

أكشوبى نى إنوو ريفشوبت إروف : نيم أووما فوت خين إب إيهوؤو إمبا هوج هيج . إنتوك بيه بافوئيثوس أينا إريبصالين أروك بانوتى:جيه إنثوك بيه باريفشوبت إروك بانوتى باناى . الليلويا

(مز 58: 13 و14)

صرت ناصرى وملجائى فى يوم شدتى . أنت معينى ، لك أرتل يا إلهى لأنك أنت ناصرى وملجائى . الليلويا .

The Gospel

Ⲉⲩⲁⲅⲅⲉⲗⲓⲟⲛ Ⲕⲁⲧⲁ Ⲙⲁⲧⲑⲉⲟⲛ Ⲕⲉⲫ ⲕ̅ⲃ̅ : ⲁ̅ - ⲓ̅ⲇ̅

Matthew 22:1-14

And Jesus answered and spoke to them again by parables and said: "The kingdom of heaven is like a certain king who arranged a marriage for his son, and sent out his servants to call those who were invited to the wedding; and they were not willing to come. Again, he sent out other servants, saying, 'Tell those who are invited, "See, I have prepared my dinner; my oxen and fatted cattle are killed, and all things are ready. Come to the wedding." ' But they made light of it and went their ways, one to his own farm, another to his business. And the rest seized his servants, treated them spitefully, and killed them. But when the king heard about it, he was furious. And he sent out his armies, destroyed those murderers, and burned up their city. Then he said to his servants, 'The wedding is ready, but those who were invited were not worthy. Therefore go into the highways, and as many as you find, invite to the wedding.' So those servants went out into the highways and gathered together all whom they found, both bad and good. And the wedding hall was filled with guests. "But when the king came in to see the guests, he saw a man there who did not have on a wedding garment. So he said to him, 'Friend, how did you come in here without a wedding garment?' And he was speechless. Then the king said to the servants, 'Bind him hand and foot, take him away, and cast him into outer

Ⲟⲩⲟϩ ⲁϥⲉⲣⲟⲩⲱ ⲛ̀ⲱⲟⲩ ⲟⲛ ⲛ̀ϫⲉ Ⲓⲏⲥ ϧⲉⲛ ϩⲁⲛⲡⲁⲣⲁⲃⲟⲗⲏ ⲉϥϫⲱ ⲙ̀ⲙⲟⲥ : ϫⲉ ⲥ̀ⲟⲛⲓ ⲛ̀ϫⲉ ϯⲙⲉⲧⲟⲩⲣⲟ ⲛ̀ⲧⲉ ⲛⲓⲫⲏⲟⲩⲓ : ⲛ̀ⲟⲩⲣⲱⲙⲓ ⲛ̀ⲟⲩⲣⲟ ⲉⲁϥⲓⲣⲓ ⲛ̀ⲟⲩϩⲟⲡ ⲉⲡⲉϥϣⲏⲣⲓ : ⲟⲩⲟϩ ⲁϥⲟⲩⲱⲣⲡ ⲛ̀ⲛⲉϥⲉⲃⲓⲁⲓⲕ ⲉ̀ⲙⲟⲩϯ ⲉ̀ⲛⲏⲉⲑⲁϩⲉⲙ ⲉ̀ϧⲟⲩⲛ ⲉ̀ⲡⲓϩⲟⲡ ⲟⲩⲟϩ ⲙ̀ⲡⲟⲩⲟⲩⲱ ⲉⲓ. Ⲡⲁⲗⲓⲛ ⲟⲛ ⲁϥⲟⲩⲱⲣⲡ ⲛ̀ϩⲁⲛⲕⲉⲉⲃⲓⲁⲓⲕ ⲉϥϫⲱ ⲙ̀ⲙⲟⲥ : ϫⲉ ⲁϫⲟⲥ ⲛ̀ⲛⲏⲉⲑⲁϩⲉⲙ ϫⲉ ⲓⲥ ⲡⲁⲁⲣⲓⲥⲧⲟⲛ ⲁⲓⲥⲉⲃⲧⲱⲧϥ : ⲛⲁⲙⲁⲥⲓ ⲛⲉⲙ ⲛⲏⲉⲧϣⲁⲛⲉⲩϣ ⲥⲉϧⲱⲧ ⲟⲩⲟϩ ⲥⲉⲥⲉⲃⲧⲱⲧ ⲧⲏⲣⲟⲩ : ⲁⲙⲱⲓⲛⲓ ⲉ̀ϧⲟⲩⲛ ⲉ̀ⲡⲓϩⲟⲡ : ⲛ̀ⲑⲱⲟⲩ ⲇⲉ ⲉⲧⲁⲩⲉⲣⲁⲙⲉⲗⲏⲥ : ⲁⲩϣⲉⲛⲱⲟⲩ ⲟⲩⲁⲓ ⲙⲉⲛ ⲉⲡⲉϥⲓⲟϩⲓ : ⲕⲉⲟⲩⲁⲓ ⲇⲉ ⲉⲧⲁϥⲓⲉⲃϣⲱⲧ ⲡ̀ⲥⲉⲡⲓ ⲇⲉ ⲉⲧⲁⲩⲁⲙⲟⲛⲓ ⲛ̀ⲛⲉϥⲉⲃⲓⲁⲓⲕ ⲁⲩϣⲟϣⲟⲩ ⲟⲩⲟϩ ⲁⲩϧⲟⲑⲃⲟⲩ . Ⲡⲓⲟⲩⲣⲟ ⲇⲉ ⲉⲧⲁϥⲥⲱⲧⲉⲙ ⲁϥϫⲱⲛⲧ ⲟⲩⲟϩ ⲁϥⲧⲁⲟⲩⲟ̀ ⲛ̀ⲛⲉϥⲥⲧⲣⲁⲧⲉⲩⲙⲁ ⲟⲩⲟϩ ⲁϥⲧⲁⲕⲟ ⲛ̀ⲛⲓⲣⲉϥϧⲱⲧⲉⲃ ⲉⲧⲉ ⲙ̀ⲙⲁⲩ : ⲟⲩⲟϩ ⲧⲟⲩⲃⲁⲕⲓ ⲁϥⲣⲟⲕϩⲥ ϧⲉⲛ ⲡⲓⲭ̀ⲣⲱⲙ : ⲧⲟⲧⲉ ⲡⲉϫⲁϥ ⲛ̀ⲛⲉϥⲉⲃⲓⲁⲓⲕ : ϫⲉ ⲡⲓϩⲟⲡ ⲙⲉⲛ ⲉϥⲥⲉⲃⲧⲱⲧ : ⲛⲏⲉⲑⲁϩⲉⲙ ⲇⲉ ⲛⲁⲩⲙ̀ⲡϣⲁ ⲁⲛ ⲡⲉ : ⲙⲁϣⲉⲛⲱⲧⲉⲛ ⲇⲉ ⲉ̀ⲃⲟⲗ ⲉ̀ⲛⲓⲙⲁ ⲙ̀ⲙⲟϣⲓ ⲛ̀ⲧⲉ ⲛⲓⲙⲱⲓⲧ : ⲟⲩⲟϩ ⲛⲏⲉⲧⲉⲧⲉⲛⲛⲁϫⲉⲙⲟⲩ ⲑⲁϩⲙⲟⲩ ⲉ̀ϧⲟⲩⲛ ⲉ̀ⲡⲓϩⲟⲡ . Ⲟⲩⲟϩ ⲉⲧⲁⲩⲓ̀ ⲉ̀ⲃⲟⲗ ⲛ̀ϫⲉⲛⲉⲃⲓⲁⲓⲕ ⲉⲧⲉ ⲙ̀ⲙⲁⲩ ϩⲓ ⲛⲓⲙⲱⲓⲧ : ⲁⲩⲑⲟⲩⲱϯ ⲛ̀ⲟⲩⲟⲛ ⲛⲓⲃⲉⲛ ⲉⲧⲁⲩϫⲉⲙⲟⲩ ⲛⲏⲉⲧϩⲱⲟⲩ ⲛⲉⲙ ⲛⲏⲉⲑⲛⲁⲛⲉⲩ : ⲟⲩⲟϩ ⲁϥⲙⲟϩ ⲛ̀ϫⲉ ⲡⲓϩⲟⲡ ⲉ̀ⲃⲟⲗ ϧⲉⲛ ⲛⲏⲉⲑⲣⲱⲧⲉⲃ : ⲉⲧⲁϥⲓ̀ ⲇⲉ ⲉ̀ϧⲟⲩⲛ ⲛ̀ϫⲉ ⲡⲓⲟⲩⲣⲟ ⲉ̀ⲛⲁⲩ ⲉ̀ⲛⲏⲉⲑⲣⲱⲧⲉⲃ : ⲁϥⲛⲁⲩ ⲉ̀ⲟⲩⲣⲱⲙⲓ ⲙ̀ⲙⲁⲩ ⲛ̀ⲧⲉⲃⲥⲱ ⲙ̀ⲡⲓϩⲟⲡ ⲧⲟⲓϩⲓⲱⲧϥ ⲁⲛ : ⲟⲩⲟϩ ⲡⲉϫⲁϥ ⲛⲁϥ ϫⲉ ⲡⲁϣ̀ⲫⲏⲣ : ⲡⲱⲥ ⲁⲕⲓ ⲉ̀ϧⲟⲩⲛ ⲉ̀ⲙⲛⲁⲓ ⲛ̀ⲧⲉⲃⲥⲱ ⲙ̀ⲡⲓϩⲟⲡ ⲧⲟⲓϩⲓⲱⲧⲕ ⲁⲛ : ⲛ̀ⲑⲟϥ ⲇⲉ ⲁⲣⲱϥ ⲑⲱⲙ . Ⲧⲟⲧⲉ ⲡⲉϫⲉ ⲡ̀ⲟⲩⲣⲟ ⲛ̀ⲛⲓⲇⲓⲁⲕⲱⲛ : ϫⲉ ⲥⲟⲛϩ ⲙ̀ⲫⲁⲓ ⲛ̀ⲧⲟⲧϥ ⲛⲉⲙ ⲣⲁⲧϥ : ϩⲓⲧϥ ⲉ̀ⲡⲓⲭⲁⲕⲓ ⲉⲧ ⲥⲁⲃⲟⲗ : ⲡⲓⲙⲁ ⲉⲧⲉ ⲫ̀ⲣⲓⲙⲓ ⲛⲁϣⲱⲡⲓ ⲙ̀ⲙⲟϥ ⲛⲉⲙ ⲡⲓⲥⲑⲉⲣⲧⲉⲣ ⲛ̀ⲧⲉ ⲛⲓⲛⲁϫϩⲓ : ⲟⲩⲟⲛ

(متى 22 : 1 و 14)

ثم أجابهم يسوع بأمثالٍ قائلاً : يشبه ملكوت السموات إنساناً ملكاً صنع عرساً لإبنه . فأرسل عبيده ليدعوا المدعوين إلى العرس فلم يريدوا أن يأتوا . فأرسل أيضاً عبيداً آخرين قائلاً : قولوا للمدعوين هأنذا قد أعددت وليمتي ، وعجولي المعلوفة قد ذبحت وكل شئ معد . فتعالوا إلى العرس . أما هم فتهاونوا فذهب واحد إلى حقله . وآخر إلى تجارته . والباقون أمسكوا عبيده وأهانوهم وقتلوهم . فلما سمع الملك غضب وأرسل جنوده وأهلك أولئك القتلة وأحرق مدينتهم بالنار . حينئذ قال لعبيده : أما العرس فمستعد وأما المدعوون فغير مستحقين . فاذهبوا إلى مفارق الطرق . وكل من وجدتموه فادعوه إلى العرس. ولما خرج أولئك العبيد إلى الطرق ، جمعوا كل من وجدوا من أشرار وصالحين . فأمتلأ العرس من المتكئين . فلما دخل الملك لينظر إلى المتكئين رأى هناك رجلاً ليس عليه ثياب العرس . فقال له : يا صاحب ، كيف دخلت إلى هنا وليس عليك ثياب العرس؟ أما هو فسكت . حينئذ قال الملك للخدم: أوثقوا يديه ورجليه وأطرحوه فى الظلمة الخارجية ، هناك يكون البكاء وصرير الأسنان .

darkness; there will be weeping and gnashing of teeth.' "For many are called, but few are chosen." Glory be to God forever, Amen.	ⲟⲁⲛⲙⲏϣ ⲅⲁⲣ ⲉⲧⲑⲁⲟⲉⲙ ⲟⲁⲛⲕⲟⲩϫⲓ ⲇⲉ ⲛⲉ ⲛⲓⲥⲱⲧⲡ · ⲟⲩⲱϣⲧ ⲙ̀ⲡⲓⲉⲩⲁⲅⲅⲉⲗⲓⲟⲛ ⲉⲑⲩ ·	لأن المدعوين كثيرون والمختارين قليلون . والمجد لله دائماً .

Exposition

That king who held the marriage feast and invited the guests to the banquet, is God the Father. His Son is Jesus Christ our Savior. The feast is the world to which he came and was incarnated from the Theotokos and was among the people as one of them. The servants He commissioned to carry His message are the prophets who preceded Him preaching to the nations His imminent coming. The nations, however, neglected the matter and rejected their message; they went each one his own way: the one to his field, the other to his business, and the rest killed the messengers. The king became enraged, sent his troops, disciplined these killers, and burned their town. Who were those who were invited to the real banquet, which was for God the Word, but the contrary antipathetic Jews whose names were eliminated from the Book of Life. He, God the Father, sent others and commanded them. to go in the streets and to invite everyone they find. When they did that, they invited many who were good and many who were bad, until they had a full house. The king came in to inspect the guests; he saw someone who was not appropriately attired for the occasion. He asked him: Friend how did you get in without the proper dress. The man was speechless and embarrassed, and the servants shoved him out to the outer darkness. Who is this individual, but Judas, who lost his heavenly garment and became dressed in damnation which seeped as water into his stomach because he denied His master's blessings and dared to betray Him. He was thus estranged from his master's glory, and his priesthood was given to another.

طـــرح

الإنسان الملك الذى صنع العرس ودعا المدعوين هو الله الآب . وإبنه هو المسيح يسوع مخلصنا والعرس هو العالم الذى ظهر فيه عندما ولدته بالجسد والدة الإله وصار مع الناس كواحدٍ منهم . والعبيد الذين أرسلهم هم الأنبياء الذين سبقوه ودعوا الأمم قبل مجيئه قائلين : ان الآتى سوف يأتى ولا يبطئ . فتكاسلوا ولم يقبلوا أقوالهم ثم مضوا متهاونين واحد إلى حقله وآخر إلى تجارته والباقون امسكوا عبيده وقتلوهم . فغضب الملك وأرسل عسكره وضرب أولئك القتلة وأحرق مدينتهم . من هم الناس الذين دعوا إلى الوليمة الحقيقية التى لله الكلمة إلا اليهود المخالفين الذين محيت أسماؤهم من سفر الحياة . فعاد أيضاً وأرسل آخرين وأوصاهم هكذا قائلاً : اخرجوا إلى مسالك الطرق وادعوا كل الذين تجدونهم . فلما خرجوا دعوا كثيرين صالحين وطالحين فامتلأ العرس من المتكئين. فدخل الملك لينظر المدعوين فرأى إنساناً ليس عليه ثياب العرس فقال له : يا صاحب كيف دخلت هنا وليس عليك ثياب العرس؟ فللوقت صمت وصار فى فضيحة ثم ألقاه الخدام إلى الظلمة الخارجية . من هو هذا الإنسان إلا يهوذا الذى تعرى من الحلة السمائية ولبس اللعنة مثل الثوب ودخلت إلى أمعائه مثل الماء ، لأنه أنكر نعمة سيده وتجرأ أن يسلم معلمه . فلذلك صار غريباً من مجده ورئاسة كهنوته أخذها آخر .

(North side) Christ our Savior; has come and has borne suffering; that through His Passion; He may save us.

(مرد بحرى) المسيح مخلصنا جاء وتألم عنا لكى بآلامه يخلصنا .

(South side) Let us glorify Him; and exalt His Name; for He had mercy on us; according to His great mercy.

(مرد قبلى) فلنمجده ونرفع اسمه لأنه صنع معنا رحمة كعظيم رحمته .

الساعة الثالثة من ليلة الأربعاء من البصخة المقدسة
The Third Hour of Wednesday Eve of the Holy Pascha

Amos 5:18-27

Woe to you that desire the day of the Lord! What is this day of the Lord to you? Seeing that it is darkness, and not light. As if a man should flee from the face of a lion, and a bear should meet him; and he should spring into his house, and lean his hands upon the wall, and a serpent should bite him. Is not the day of the Lord darkness, and not light? And is not this day gloom without brightness? I hate, I reject your feasts, and I will not smell your meat offerings in your general assemblies. Wherefore if you should bring Me your whole burnt sacrifices and meat offerings, I will not accept them, neither will I have respect to your grand peace offerings. Remove from Me the sound of your songs, and I will not hear the music of your instruments. But let judgment roll down as water, and righteousness as an impassable torrent. Have you offered to Me victims and sacrifices, O house of Israel, forty years in the wilderness? Yea, you took up the tabernacle of Moloch, and the star of your god Raephan, the images of them which you made for yourselves. And I will carry you away beyond Damascus, says the Lord, the Almighty God is His name. Glory be to the Holy Trinity. Amen.

(من عاموس النبى ص 5 : 18)

ويل للذين يشتهون يوم الرب . ما بغيتكم فى يوم الرب؟ فأن هذا اليوم ظلام لا نور . كما إذا هرب إنسان من وجه أسد فصادفته لبوءة أوالتجأ إلى بيته ورفع يده على الحائط فلدغته حية. أليس يوم الرب يوم ظلام لا نور، وضباب لا ضياء له؟ لقد أبغضت أعيادكم ورذلتها ولست أشم رائحة فى أيام أعيادكم العظيمة . إنى إذا قربتم لي محرقاتكم وتقدماتكم لا أقبلها . ولست أنظر إلى فدية شكركم . ابعد عنى صوت تسابيحك. ومزمار أرغنك لست أسمعه . وليجر القضاء كالماء والعدل كالوادى الذى لا يعبر . هل قربتم لي ذبائح وتقدمات فى البرية أربعين سنة يا بيت إسرائيل ، يقول الرب . بل حملتم خيمة ملوخ ونجم إلهكم رافان ، التماثيل التى صنعتموها لكم . فأسبيكم إلى ما وراء دمشق ، قال الرب الإله ، الضابط الكل ، هو اسمه . مجداً للثالوث القدوس .

Pascha Praise - B (12 times), Page: 7   : تسبحة البصخة B (12 مرة) ، صفحة

The Psalm
Ⲯⲁⲗⲙⲟⲥ ⲝ̅ⲇ̅ : ⲇ̅ ⲛⲉⲙ ⲉ̅

Psalms 64:4, 5

Blessed is he whom You have chosen and adopted; he shall dwell in Your courts; Your temple is holy. You are wonderful in righteousness. Alleluia.

Ⲱⲟⲩⲛⲓⲁⲧϥ ⲙ̀ⲫⲏⲉⲧⲁⲕⲥⲟⲧⲡϥ ⲟⲩⲟϩ ⲁⲕϣⲟⲡϥ ⲉ̀ⲣⲟⲕ : ⲉϥⲉ̀ϣⲱⲡⲓ ϧⲉⲛ ⲛⲉⲕⲁⲩⲗⲏⲟⲩ ϣⲁ ⲉ̀ⲛⲉϩ .
Ϥ̀ⲟⲩⲁⲃ ⲛ̀ⲭⲉ ⲡⲉⲕⲉⲣⲫⲉⲓ : ⲟⲩⲟϩ ϥ̀ⲟⲓ ⲛ̀ϣ̀ⲫⲏⲣⲓ ϧⲉⲛ ⲟⲩⲙⲉⲑⲙⲏⲓ . ⲁⲗ .

أو أوونياتف إمفى إيطاكصوتبف أووه أكوشبف إروك : إيف إشوبى خين نيك أفليوو شا إينيه .
إفؤواب إنجيه بيك إرفيى : أووه إفوى إن إشفيرى خين أوو ميثمى . الليلويا .

(مز 64: 4و5)

طوبى لمن اخترته وقبلته ليسكن فى ديارك إلى الأبد . قدوس هو هيكلك وعجيب بالبر . الليلويا .

Introduction to the Gospel, Page: 8   : مقدمة الأنجيل ، صفحة

The Gospel
Ⲉⲩⲁⲅⲅⲉⲗⲓⲟⲛ Ⲕⲁⲧⲁ Ⲙⲁⲧⲑⲉⲟⲛ Ⲕⲉⲫ ⲕ̅ⲇ̅ : ⲗ̅ⲋ̅ ϣⲃⲗ

Matthew 24:36-51

"But of that day and hour no one knows, not even the angels of heaven, but My Father only. But as the days of Noah were, so also will

Ⲉⲑⲃⲉ ⲡⲓⲉ̀ϩⲟⲟⲩ ⲇⲉ ⲉⲧⲉ ⲙ̀ⲙⲁⲩ ⲛⲉⲙ ϯⲟⲩⲛⲟⲩ : ⲙ̀ⲙⲟⲛ ϩ̀ⲗⲓ ⲉⲙⲓ ⲉ̀ⲣⲱⲟⲩ : ⲟⲩⲇⲉ ⲛⲓⲁⲅⲅⲉⲗⲟⲥ ⲛ̀ⲧⲉ ⲛⲓⲫⲏⲟⲩⲓ : ⲉ̀ⲃⲏⲗ ⲉ̀ⲫⲓⲱⲧ ⲙ̀ⲙⲁⲩⲁⲧϥ : ⲙ̀ⲫⲣⲏϯ ⲅⲁⲣ ⲛ̀ⲛⲓⲉ̀ϩⲟⲟⲩ ⲛ̀ⲧⲉ

(متى ص 24 : 36 ألخ)

وأما ذلك اليوم وتلك الساعة فلا يعلمها أحد ، ولا ملائكة السموات إلا الآب وحده . وكما كان فى

the coming of the Son of Man be. For as in the days before the flood, they were eating and drinking, marrying and giving in marriage, until the day that Noah entered the ark, and did not know until the flood came and took them all away, so also will the coming of the Son of Man be. Then two men will be in the field: one will be taken and the other left. Two women will be grinding at the mill: one will be taken and the other left. Watch therefore, for you do not know what hour your Lord is coming. But know this, that if the master of the house had known what hour the thief would come, he would have watched and not allowed his house to be broken into. Therefore you also be ready, for the Son of Man is coming at an hour you do not expect. "Who then is a faithful and wise servant, whom his master made ruler over his household, to give them food in due season? Blessed is that servant whom his master, when he comes, will find so doing. Assuredly, I say to you that he will make him ruler over all his goods. But if that evil servant says in his heart, 'My master is delaying his coming,' and begins to beat his fellow servants, and to eat and drink with the drunkards, the master of that servant will come on a day when he is not looking for him and at an hour that he is not aware of, and will cut him in two and appoint him his portion with the hypocrites. There shall be weeping and gnashing of teeth." Glory be to God forever, Amen.

Ⲛⲱⲉ : ⲡⲓⲣⲏϯ ⲉⲑⲛⲁϣⲱⲡⲓ ϧⲉⲛ ⲧⲡⲁⲣⲟⲩⲥⲓⲁ ⲙⲡϣⲏⲣⲓ ⲙⲫⲣⲱⲙⲓ . Ⲙⲫⲣⲏϯ ⲅⲁⲣ ⲉⲛⲁⲩϣⲟⲡ ϧⲉⲛ ⲛⲓⲉϩⲟⲟⲩ ⲉⲧ ϧⲁϫⲱϥ ⲙⲡⲓⲕⲁⲧⲁⲕⲗⲩⲥⲙⲟⲥ ⲉⲩⲟⲩⲱⲙ ⲟⲩⲟϩ ⲉⲩⲥⲱ : ⲉⲩϭⲓⲥϩⲉⲙ ⲟⲩⲟϩ ⲉⲩϭⲓϩⲁⲓ : ϣⲁ ⲡⲓⲉϩⲟⲟⲩ ⲉⲧⲁ Ⲛⲱⲉ ϣⲉⲛⲁϥ ⲉϧⲟⲩⲛ ⲉⲧⲕⲩⲃⲱⲧⲟⲥ ⲙⲙⲟϥ . Ⲟⲩⲟϩ ⲙⲡⲟⲩⲉⲙⲓ ϣⲁⲧⲉϥⲓ ⲛϫⲉ ⲡⲓⲕⲁⲧⲁⲕⲗⲩⲥⲙⲟⲥ ⲟⲩⲟϩ ⲛⲧⲉϥⲉⲗ ⲟⲩⲟⲛ ⲛⲓⲃⲉⲛ : ⲡⲁⲓⲣⲏϯ ⲉⲑⲛⲁϣⲱⲡⲓ ϧⲉⲛ ⲡϫⲓⲛⲓ ⲙⲡϣⲏⲣⲓ ⲙⲫⲣⲱⲙⲓ : ⲧⲟⲧⲉ ⲥⲛⲁⲩ ⲉⲩⲭⲏ ϧⲉⲛ ⲧⲕⲟⲓ : ⲟⲩⲁⲓ ⲉⲩⲉⲟⲗϥ ⲟⲩⲟϩ ⲟⲩⲁⲓ ⲉⲩⲉⲭⲁϥ : ⲟⲩⲟϩ ⲥⲛⲟⲩϯ ⲉⲩⲛⲟⲩⲧ ϧⲉⲛ ⲟⲩⲉⲩⲛⲓ : ⲟⲩⲓ ⲉⲩⲉⲟⲗⲥ ⲟⲩⲟϩ ⲟⲩⲓ ⲉⲩⲉⲭⲁⲥ . Ⲣⲱⲓⲥ ⲟⲩⲛ ϫⲉ ⲧⲉⲧⲉⲛⲉⲙⲓ ⲁⲛ ϫⲉ ⲁⲣⲉ ⲡⲉⲧⲉⲛⲟ̅ⲥ̅ ⲛⲏⲟⲩ : ⲫⲁⲓ ⲇⲉ ⲁⲣⲓⲉⲙⲓ ⲉⲣⲟϥ : ϫⲉ ⲉⲛⲁⲣⲉ ⲡⲓⲛⲉⲃⲏⲓ ⲉⲙⲓ ϫⲉ ⲁⲣⲉ ⲡⲓⲥⲟⲛⲓ ⲛⲏⲟⲩ : ⲛⲁϥ ϧⲉⲛ ⲁϣ ⲛⲟⲩⲛⲟⲩ : ⲛⲁϥⲛⲁⲣⲱⲓⲥ : ϩⲓⲛⲁ ⲛⲧⲉϥϣⲧⲉⲙⲭⲁⲩ ⲉϭⲓ ⲙⲡⲉϥⲏⲓ : ⲉⲑⲃⲉ ⲫⲁⲓ ϩⲱⲧⲉⲛ ϣⲱⲡⲓ ⲉⲣⲉⲧⲉⲛⲥⲉⲃⲧⲱⲧ : ϫⲉ ϧⲉⲛ ϯⲟⲩⲛⲟⲩ ⲉⲧⲉⲧⲉⲛⲥⲉⲟⲩⲛ ⲙⲙⲟⲥ ⲁⲛ ⲉⲣⲉ ⲡϣⲏⲣⲓ ⲙⲫⲣⲱⲙⲓ ⲛⲏⲟⲩ ⲛϧⲏⲧⲥ . Ⲛⲓⲙ ϩⲁⲣⲁ ⲡⲉ ⲡⲓⲡⲓⲥⲧⲟⲥ ⲙⲃⲱⲕ ⲟⲩⲟϩ ⲛⲥⲁⲃⲉ : ⲫⲏⲉⲧⲉ ⲡⲉϥⲟ̅ⲥ̅ ⲛⲁⲭⲁϥ ⲉϩⲣⲏ ⲉϫⲉⲛ ⲛⲉϥⲉⲃⲓⲁⲓⲕ ⲉϯⲛⲱⲟⲩ ⲛⲧⲟⲩ ϧⲣⲉ ϧⲉⲛ ⲡⲥⲏⲟⲩ ⲛⲧⲏⲓⲥ : ⲱⲟⲩⲛⲓⲁⲧϥ ⲙⲡⲓⲃⲱⲕ ⲉⲧⲉ ⲙⲙⲁⲩ : ⲉϣⲱⲡ ⲁϥϣⲁⲛⲓ ⲛϫⲉ ⲡⲉϥⲟ̅ⲥ̅ ⲛⲧⲉϥϫⲉⲙϥ ⲉϥⲓⲣⲓ ⲙⲡⲁⲓⲣⲏϯ : ⲁⲙⲏⲛ ϯⲭⲱ ⲙⲙⲟⲥ ⲛⲱⲧⲉⲛ : ϫⲉ ⲉϥⲉⲭⲁϥ ϩⲓϫⲉⲛ ⲡⲉⲧⲉⲛⲧⲁϥ ⲧⲏⲣϥ . Ⲉϣⲱⲡ ⲇⲉ ⲁϥϣⲁⲛϫⲟⲥ ⲛϫⲉ ⲡⲓⲃⲱⲕ ⲉⲧϩⲱⲟⲩ ⲉⲧⲉ ⲙⲙⲁⲩ ϧⲉⲛ ⲡⲉϥϩⲏⲧ : ϫⲉ ⲡⲁⲟ̅ⲥ̅ ⲛⲁⲱⲥⲕ : ⲟⲩⲟϩ ⲛⲧⲉϥⲉⲣϩⲏⲧⲥ ⲛϩⲓⲟⲩⲓ ⲛⲛⲉϥϣⲫⲏⲣ ⲛⲉⲃⲓⲁⲓⲕ ⲛⲧⲉϥⲟⲩⲱⲙ ⲇⲉ ⲟⲩⲟϩ ⲛⲧⲉϥⲥⲱ ⲛⲉⲙ ⲛⲏⲉⲧⲑⲁϧⲓ : ⲉϥⲉⲓ ⲇⲉ ⲛϫⲉ ⲡⲟ̅ⲥ̅ ⲙⲡⲓⲃⲱⲕ ⲉⲧⲉ ⲙⲙⲁⲩ ϧⲉⲛ ⲡⲓⲉϩⲟⲟⲩ ⲉⲧⲉϥⲛⲁϫⲟⲩϣⲧ ϧⲁϫⲱϥ ⲁⲛ : ⲛⲉⲙ ϧⲉⲛ ϯⲟⲩⲛⲟⲩ ⲉⲧⲉⲛϥⲥⲱⲟⲩⲛ ⲙⲙⲟⲥ ⲁⲛ : ⲟⲩⲟϩ ⲉϥⲉⲫⲟⲣϧϥ ϧⲉⲛ ⲧⲉϥⲙⲏϯ ⲟⲩⲟϩ ⲉϥⲉⲭⲱ ⲛⲧⲉϥⲧⲟⲓ ⲛⲉⲙ ⲛⲓϣⲟⲃⲓ : ⲡⲓⲙⲁ ⲉⲧⲉ ⲫⲣⲓⲙⲓ ⲛⲁϣⲱⲡⲓ ⲙⲙⲟϥ ⲛⲉⲙ ⲡⲓⲥⲑⲉⲣⲧⲉⲣ ⲛⲧⲉ ⲛⲓⲛⲁϫϩⲓ . ⲟⲩⲱϣⲧ ⲙⲡⲓⲉⲩⲁⲅⲅⲉⲗⲓⲟⲛ ⲉⲑⲟⲩ.

أيام نوح ، كذلك يكون فى ظهور ابن الإنسان . لأنه كما كانوا قبل أيام الطوفان يأكلون ويشربون. ويتزوجون ويزوجون إلى اليوم الذى دخل فيه نوح إلى الفلك ، ولم يعلموا حتى جاء الطوفان وأخذ الجميع ، كذلك يكون أيضاً مجئ ابن الإنسان . حينئذ يكون إثنان فى الحقل فيؤخذ الواحد ويترك الآخر وإثنتان تطحنان على رحى ، فتؤخذ الواحدة وتترك الأخرى . فاسهروا إذاً لأنكم لا تعلمون فى أية ساعة يأتى ربكم . واعلموا هذا، أنه لو علم رب البيت فى أى ساعة يأتى السارق لسهر ولم يدع بيته ينقب . فلذلك كونوا أنتم أيضاً مستعدين لأن ابن الإنسان يأتى فى ساعة لا تعرفونها. فمن ترى هو العبد الأمين الحكيم الذى يقيمه سيده على عبيده ليعطيهم طعامهم فى حينه . طوبى لذلك العبد الذى إذا جاء سيده فيجده يفعل هكذا. الحق أقول لكم انه يقيمه على جميع ماله . ولكن ان قال ذلك العبد الشرير فى قلبه : أن سيدى يبطئ فى قدومه ، فيبتدئ يضرب العبيد ورفقاؤه ويأكل ويشرب مع السكيرين فيأتى سيد ذلك العبد فى يوم لا ينتظره وساعة لا يعرفها فيشقه من وسطه ويجعل نصيبه مع المرائين. هناك يكون البكاء وصرير الأسنان . والمجد لله دائماً .

Exposition

Contemplate you who exalt the Lord, the kindness of Christ our God: observe how He calls His chosen who fulfill His will, prudent and honest servants. I mean those who preserve his commandments and look forward to their awards; those who remain awake and alert, that they may receive the promised rewards. As the Bible asserts that those servants, whose master makes a surprise visit and finds them awake, are blessed. Assuredly I say: He will make His servant ruler over His property. So, for He whom He finds derelict in his duties and neglecting them often, one day, his Master will make a surprise visit, repudiate him, and make his lot with the hypocrites, in the place of darkness and suffering. Let us awake and be alert in anticipation of the day of the Lord so that we may rejoice with Him in His dwelling-place and receive His clemencies and mercies.

(North side) Christ our Savior; has come and has borne suffering; that through His Passion; He may save us.

(South side) Let us glorify Him; and exalt His Name; for He had mercy on us; according to His great mercy.

طـرح

تأملوا يا عابدى الإله إلى تحنن المسيح إلهنا . كيف يدعو أصفياءه الصانعين إرادته عبيداً حكماء وأمناء . أعنى الذين يحفظون وصاياه المتوقعين اجراً صالحاً الساهرين المتيقظين لكى ينالوا المواعيد. كما قال فى الانجيل ان ذلك العبد مغبوطاً، أعنى الذى يأتى سيده بغتة فيجده يفعل هكذا . أقول لكم أنه يقيمه وكيلاً على جميع أمواله. أما ذلك الذى يجده متغافلاً و يهمل يوماً بعد يوم ، فيجئ سيده فى ساعة لا يعرفها فيشقه من وسطه ويجعل نصيبه مع المرائين فى الظلمة وموضع العذاب. فلنتيقظ من غفلتنا وننتظر يوم الرب لنفرح معه فى دياره ونفوز بمراحمه ورأفاته .

(مرد بحرى) المسيح مخلصنا جاء وتألم عنا لكى بآلامه يخلصنا .

(مرد قبلى) فلنمجده ونرفع اسمه لأنه صنع معنا رحمة كعظيم رحمته .

The Conclusion of the Exposition, Page: 9 ختام الطرح ، صفحة :

الساعة السادسة من ليلة الأربعاء من البصخة المقدسة
The Sixth Hour of Wednesday Eve of the Holy Pascha

Jeremiah 13:9, 16: 9-13

Thus says the Lord, Thus will I ruin the pride of Judah, and the pride of Jerusalem; Behold, I will make the voice of joy to cease out of this place before your eyes, and the voice of gladness, the voice of the bridegroom, and the voice of the bride. And it shall come to pass, when you report to this people all these words, and they shall say to you, Why has the Lord pronounced all these evils against us? What is our unrighteousness? And what is our sin which we have sinned before the Lord our God? Then you shall say to them, Because your fathers forsook Me, says the Lord, and went after strange gods and served them, and worshipped them, and forsook Me, and kept not My law. And you sinned worse than your fathers, for behold, you walk every one after the lusts of your own evil heart, so as not to listen to Me. Therefore I will cast you off from this good land into a land which neither you nor your fathers have known. And you shall serve their other gods, who shall have no mercy upon you. Glory be to the Holy Trinity. Amen

(من أرميا النبى 13 : 9 ، 16 : 9 - 13)

هذا ما يقوله رب القوات إله إسرائيل: هأنذا أفسد كبرياء يهوذا أو كبرياء أورشليم العظيمة فى هذا المكان أمام عيونكم وفى أيامكم، لا يكون صوت سرور ولا صوت فرح ولا صوت عريس ولا صوت عروس . ويكون إذا عرفت الشعب بجميع هذه الأقوال ، وقالوا لك: لماذا تكلم الرب علينا بكل هذه الشرور وما الظلم أو الخطية التى صنعناها أمام الرب إلهنا؟ فتقول لهم: لأن آباءكم تركونى قال الرب، واتبعوا آلهة غريبة وعبدوها وسجدوا لها وأما أنا فتركونى ولم يحفظوا ناموسى . وقد عملتم أنتم أيضاً الشر أكثر من آبائكم . فهوذا أنتم أيضاً تسلكون كل واحد وراء شهوات قلوبكم الشريرة غير مطيعين لى ، فسأطردكم من هذه الأرض إلى أرض لا تعرفونها أنتم ولا آبائكم . وفى ذلك الموضع تتعبدون لآلهة أخرى هؤلاء الذين لا يرحمونكم . مجداً للثالوث القدوس .

| Pascha Praise - B (12 times), Page: 7 | تسبحة البصخة B (12 مرة) ، صفحة : |

The Psalm
Ψαλμος ρ̅α̅ : α̅ νεμ β̅

Psalms 101:1, 2

Hear my prayer, O Lord, and let my cry come to You. In the day when I shall call upon You, speedily hear me. Alleluia

Ⲡϭⲟⲓⲥ ⲥⲱⲧⲉⲙ ⲉ̀ⲧⲁ ⲡⲣⲟⲥⲉⲩⲭⲏ : ⲙⲁⲣⲉ ⲡⲁϧⲣⲱⲟⲩ ⲓ̀ ⲉ̀ⲡϣⲱⲓ ⲙ̀ⲡⲉⲕⲙ̀ⲑⲟ.

Ϧⲉⲛ ⲡⲓⲉ̀ϩⲟⲟⲩ ⲉ̀ⲧⲛⲁⲱϣ ⲉ̀ⲡϣⲱⲓ ⲟⲩⲃⲏⲕ ⲛ̀ϧⲏⲧϥ : ⲭⲱⲗⲉⲙ ⲥⲱⲧⲉⲙ ⲉ̀ⲣⲟⲓ . ⲁⲗ .

إبتشويس صوتيم إطا إبروس إفشى : ماريه إب أخرواوو إي إبيشوى إمبيك إمثو .

خين بى إيهوؤو إتينا أوش إبيشوى أووفيك إنخيتف : كوليم صوتيم إروى . الليلويا .

(مز 101: 1 و2)

يارب استمع صلاتى وليصعد أمامك صراخى . فى اليوم الذى أدعوك فيه استجب لى سريعاً . الليلويا .

| Introduction to the Gospel, Page: 8 | مقدمة الأنجيل ، صفحة : |

The Gospel
Ⲉⲩⲁⲅⲅⲉⲗⲓⲟⲛ Ⲕⲁⲧⲁ Ⲙⲁⲧⲑⲉⲟⲛ Ⲕⲉⲫ ⲕ̅ⲉ̅ : ⲁ̅ - ⲓ̅ⲅ̅

Matthew 25:1-13

"Then the kingdom of heaven shall be likened to ten virgins who took their lamps and went out to meet the bridegroom. Now five of them were wise, and five were foolish. Those who were foolish took their lamps

Ⲧⲟⲧⲉ ⲥ̀ⲟⲛⲓ ⲛ̀ϫⲉ ϯⲙⲉⲧⲟⲩⲣⲟ ⲛ̀ⲧⲉ ⲛⲓⲫⲏⲟⲩⲓ ⲙ̀ⲙⲏⲧ ⲙ̀ⲡⲁⲣⲑⲉⲛⲟⲥ ⲛⲁⲓ ⲉⲧⲁⲩϭⲓ ⲛ̀ⲛⲟⲩⲗⲁⲙⲡⲁⲥ ⲁⲩⲓ̀ ⲉ̀ⲃⲟⲗ ⲉ̀ϩ̀ⲣⲉⲛ ⲡⲓⲡⲁⲧϣⲉⲗⲉⲧ : ⲛⲉ ⲟⲩⲟⲛ Ϯⲟⲩ ⲇⲉ ⲛ̀ⲥⲟⲝ ⲛ̀ϧⲏⲧⲟⲩ ⲛⲉⲙ Ϯⲟⲩ ⲛ̀ⲥⲁⲃⲏ : ⲛⲓⲥⲟⲝ ⲅⲁⲣ ⲉⲧⲁⲩϭⲓ ⲛ̀ⲛⲟⲩⲗⲁⲙⲡⲁⲥ ⲟⲩⲟϩ ⲙ̀ⲡⲟⲩⲉⲗ

(متى 25 : 1 - 13)

حينئذٍ يشبه ملكوت السموات عشر عذارى أخذن مصابيحهن وخرجن للقاء العريس . وكان خمس منهن جاهلات وخمس حكيمات ، أما

and took no oil with them, but the wise took oil in their vessels with their lamps. But while the bridegroom was delayed, they all slumbered and slept. "And at midnight a cry was heard: 'Behold, the bridegroom is coming; go out to meet him!' Then all those virgins arose and trimmed their lamps. And the foolish said to the wise, 'Give us some of your oil, for our lamps are going out.' But the wise answered, saying, 'No, lest there should not be enough for us and you; but go rather to those who sell, and buy for yourselves.' And while they went to buy, the bridegroom came, and those who were ready went in with him to the wedding; and the door was shut. "Afterward the other virgins came also, saying, 'Lord, Lord, open to us!' But he answered and said, 'Assuredly, I say to you, I do not know you.' "Watch therefore, for you know neither the day nor the hour in which the Son of Man is coming." Glory be to God forever, Amen.

ⲛⲉϩ ⲛⲉⲙ ⲱⲟⲩ . Ⲛⲓⲥⲁⲃⲉⲩ ⲇⲉ ⲁⲧⲉⲗ ⲛⲉϩ ⲛ̀ϩⲣⲏⲓ ϧⲉⲛ ⲛⲟⲩⲙⲟⲕⲓ ⲛⲉⲙ ⲛⲟⲩⲗⲁⲙⲡⲁⲥ : ⲉⲧⲁϥⲱⲥⲕ ⲇⲉ ⲛ̀ϫⲉ ⲡⲓⲡⲁⲧϣⲉⲗⲉⲧ ⲁⲩϩⲓⲛⲓⲙ ⲧⲏⲣⲟⲩ ⲟⲩⲟϩ ⲁⲩⲉⲛⲕⲟⲧ : ⲉⲧⲁ ⲧ̀ⲫⲁϣⲓ ⲇⲉ ⲙ̀ⲡⲓⲉϫⲱⲣϩ ϣⲱⲡⲓ : ⲁ ⲟⲩϧ̀ⲣⲱⲟⲩ ϣⲱⲡⲓ ϫⲉ ⲓⲥ ⲡⲓⲡⲁⲧϣⲉⲗⲉⲧ ⲁϥⲓ ⲧⲉⲛ ⲑⲏⲛⲟⲩ ⲁⲙⲱⲓⲛⲓ ⲉⲃⲟⲗ ⲉ̀ϩ̀ⲣⲁϥ . Ⲧⲟⲧⲉ ⲁⲩⲧⲱⲟⲩⲛⲟⲩ ⲛ̀ϫⲉ ⲛⲓⲡⲁⲣⲑⲉⲛⲟⲥ ⲧⲏⲣⲟⲩ ⲉⲧⲉ ⲙ̀ⲙⲁⲩ ⲟⲩⲟϩ ⲁⲩⲥⲟⲗⲥⲉⲗ ⲛ̀ⲛⲟⲩⲗⲁⲙⲡⲁⲥ : ⲡⲉϫⲉ ⲛⲓⲥⲟϫ ⲇⲉ ⲛ̀ⲛⲓⲥⲁⲃⲉⲩ ϫⲉ ⲙⲟⲓ ⲛⲁⲛ ⲉⲃⲟⲗ ϧⲉⲛ ⲡⲉⲧⲉⲛⲛⲉϩ ⲙ̀ⲙⲟⲛ ⲛⲉⲛⲗⲁⲙⲡⲁⲥ ⲛⲁϭⲉⲛⲟ : ⲁⲩⲉⲣⲟⲩⲱ ⲇⲉ ⲛ̀ϫⲉ ⲛⲓⲥⲁⲃⲉⲩ ⲉⲩϫⲱ ⲙ̀ⲙⲟⲥ : ϫⲉ ⲙⲏⲡⲟⲧⲉ ⲛ̀ⲧⲉϥϣ̀ⲧⲉⲙⲣⲁϣⲧⲉⲛ ⲛⲉⲙⲱⲧⲉⲛ : ⲙⲁϣⲉⲛⲱⲧⲉⲛ ⲇⲉ ⲙⲁⲗⲗⲟⲛ ϩⲁ ⲛⲏⲉⲧ ϯ ⲉⲃⲟⲗ ⲟⲩⲟϩ ϣⲱⲡ ⲛⲱⲧⲉⲛ .

Ⲉⲧⲁⲩϣⲉⲛⲱⲟⲩ ⲇⲉ ϫⲉ ⲛ̀ⲧⲟⲩϣⲱⲡ : ⲁϥⲓ ⲛ̀ϫⲉ ⲡⲓⲡⲁⲧϣⲉⲗⲉⲧ ⲟⲩⲟϩ ⲛⲏⲉⲧ ⲥⲉⲃⲧⲱⲧ ⲁⲩϣⲉⲛⲱⲟⲩ ⲛⲉⲙⲁϥ ⲉ̀ϧⲟⲩⲛ ⲉ̀ⲡⲓϩⲟⲡ ⲟⲩⲟϩ ⲁⲩⲙⲁϣⲑⲁⲙ ⲙ̀ⲡⲓⲣⲟ : ⲉ̀ⲡ̀ϧⲁⲉ ⲇⲉ ⲁⲩⲓ ⲛ̀ϫⲉ ⲡ̀ⲥⲱϫⲡ ⲛ̀ⲛⲓⲡⲁⲣⲑⲉⲛⲟⲥ ⲉⲩϫⲱ ⲙ̀ⲙⲟⲥ : ϫⲉ ⲡⲉⲛⳆ ⲡⲉⲛⳆ ⲁⲟⲩⲱⲛ ⲛⲁⲛ : ⲛ̀ⲑⲟϥ ⲇⲉ ⲁϥⲉⲣⲟⲩⲱ ⲡⲉϫⲁϥ ϫⲉ ⲁⲙⲏⲛ ϯϫⲱ ⲙ̀ⲙⲟⲥ ⲛⲱⲧⲉⲛ ϫⲉ ϯⲥⲱⲟⲩⲛ ⲙ̀ⲙⲱⲧⲉⲛ ⲁⲛ : ⲣⲱⲓⲥ ⲟⲩⲛ ϫⲉ ⲧⲉⲧⲉⲛⲥⲱⲟⲩⲛ ⲁⲛ ⲙ̀ⲡⲓ̀ϩⲟⲟⲩ ⲟⲩ ⲇⲉ ϯⲟⲩⲛⲟⲩ . ⲟⲩⲱϣⲧ ⲙ̀ⲡⲓⲉⲩⲁⲅⲅⲉⲗⲓⲟⲛ ⲉ̀ⲑⲩ.

الجاهلات فأخذن مصابيحهن ولم يأخذن معهن زيتاً وأما الحكيمات فأخذن زيتاً فى آنيتهن مع مصابيحهن. فلما أبطأ العريس نعسن كلهن ونمن. ففى نصف الليل صار صوت: هوذا العريس قد أقبل اخرجن للقائه . حينئذ قامت أولئك العذارى وزيَّن مصابيحهن. فقالت الجاهلات للحكيمات: أعطينا من زيتكن فان مصابيحنا تنطفئ . فأجابت الحكيمات وقلن: لعله لا يكفينا واياكن . فالاحرى ان تذهبن إلى الباعة وإبتعن لكن . فلما ذهبن ليبتعن جاء العريس ودخلت معه المستعدات إلى العرس وأغلق الباب . وأخيراً جاءت بقية العذارى قائلات: يا ربنا يا ربنا افتح لنا . أما هو فأجاب وقال: الحق أقول لكن اننى لا أعرفكن. فأسهروا إذا لأنكم لا تعرفون اليوم ولا الساعة. والمجد لله دائماً .

Introduction to the Exposition, Page: 9 : مقدمة الطرح ، صفحة

Exposition

طـرح

Behold these virtues and parables that our Lord of Glory Jesus the source of every grace and good has told us; He who granted mankind to partake in His kingdom. Listen, think, and understand and know His blessed parables, for the sake of the prudent virgins who were mentioned in the Bible and were likened to his kingdom, full of joy and exultation. Ten virgins: five foolish and five wise, said the Lord. As He tells us, there was no distinction between them as virgins; but they differed in their deeds. Thus, He praised and blessed the wise five virgins because they were earnest and prudent. They filled their lanterns with oil and kept the surplus in their containers. As for the foolish virgins, they were lackadaisical and did not prepare their lanterns. When they all woke up at the given time to

يا لهذه الفضائل وهذه الأمثال التى قالها ملك المجد ، الذى هو يسوع ملك النعمة والخيرات المكمل السلام ، الذى أنعم لجنس البشر بشركة ملكوته . اسمعوا وتأملوا وافهموا واعملوا أمثاله الطوباوية . من أجل العذارى الحكيمات اللواتى نطق من أجلهن فى الأنجيل وشبههن بملكوته المملوء فرحاً وسروراً . عشر عذارى ، قال الرب ، خمس جاهلات وخمس حكيمات . قال أن هؤلاء العشرة هن كن عذارى ولكنهن أفترقن لأجل أعمالهن ، فطوب الحكيمات الفهيمات لأنهن صنعن الحكمة باجتهاد ، وملأن مصابيحهن من الزيت وأوعيتهن مما فضل عنهن . أما العذارى الجاهلات فتكاسلن ولم

proceed with their procession ahead of the bridegroom, their lanterns became useless at the wedding time and were unable to accompany the bridegroom. Those who were prepared, accompanied him to the wedding and the somnolent ones stayed outside..

يفهمن قيمة مصابيحهن ، فلما قمن جميعهن فى ساعة واحدة ليمشين قدام العريس تعطلت مصابيحهن وقت الفرح ولم يحضرن مع العريس ، والمستعدات دخلن معه إلى العرس والمتكاسلات وقفن خارجاً .

(North side) Christ our Savior; has come and has borne suffering; that through His Passion; He may save us.

(مرد بحرى) المسيح مخلصنا جاء وتألم عنا لكى بألامه يخلصنا .

(South side) Let us glorify Him; and exalt His Name; for He had mercy on us; according to His great mercy.

(مرد قبلى) فلنمجده ونرفع اسمه لأنه صنع معنا رحمة كعظيم رحمته .

The Conclusion of the Exposition, Page: 9   : ختام الطرح ، صفحة

The Ninth Hour of Wednesday Eve

الساعة التاسعة من ليلة الأربعاء

The Ninth Hour of Wednesday Eve of the Holy Pascha

الساعة التاسعة من ليلة الأربعاء من البصخة المقدسة

Hosea 9:14-10:2

(من هوشع النبى 9 : 14 - 10 : 2)

Give them, O Lord; what will You give them? A miscarrying womb, and dry breasts. All their wickedness is in Gilgal. For there I hated them; because of the wickedness of their practices, I will cast them out of My house, I will not love them anymore; all their princes are disobedient. Ephraim is sick, he is dried up at his roots, he shall by no means bear fruit any longer. For even if they should beget children, I will kill the desired fruit of their womb. God shall reject them, because they have not hearkened to Him, and they shall be wanderers among the nations. Israel is a vine with goodly branches, her fruit is abundant; according to the multitude of her fruits she has multiplied her altars; according to the wealth of his land, he has set up pillars. They have divided their hearts; now shall they be utterly destroyed. He shall dig down their altars, their pillars shall mourn. Glory be to the Holy Trinity. Amen.

اعطهم يا رب . وماذا تعطيهم؟ أعطيهم أباء بلا بنين وأثداء يابسة ، لأن جميع شرورهم فى الجلجال. لأنه فى ذلك المكان أبغضتهم من أجل سوء أعمالهم . سأطردهم من بيتى ولا أعود أحبهم . لأن جميع رؤسائهم متمردين . حزن أفرايم الذى أصله قد جف ولا يعود أن يأتى بثمرة . وإن ولدوا فانى أقتل شهوات بطونهم . يرفضهم الله لأنهم لم يسمعوا له . فيكونون تائهين بين الأمم . ان إسرائيل كرمة حسنة الأغصان وثمرتها شهية. وعلى حسب كثرة ثمره أكثر المذابح وعلى حسب خصب أرضه بنى الأنصاب. قد قسّوا قلوبهم والآن سيهلكون . هو يحطم مذابحهم ويخرب أنصابهم . مجداً للثالوث القدوس .

Pascha Praise - B (12 times), Page: 7 : تسبحة البصخة B (12 مرة) ، صفحة

The Psalm

Ⲯⲁⲗⲙⲟⲥ ⲕ̅ⲁ̅ : ⲓ̅ⲑ̅ ⲛⲉⲙ ⲕ̅

Psalms 21:19-20

(مز 21: 19 و20)

Deliver My soul from the sword; My only begotten soul from the power of the dog. Save Me from the lion's mouth; and regard My lowliness from the horns of the unicorns. Alleluia

Ⲛⲟϩⲉⲙ ⲛ̄ⲧⲁⲯⲩⲭⲏ ⲉⲃⲟⲗ ⲛ̄ⲧⲟⲧⲥ ⲛ̄ⲧⲥⲏϥⲓ : ⲛⲉⲙ ⲧⲁⲙⲉⲧϣⲏⲣⲓ ⲙ̄ⲙⲁⲩⲁⲧⲥ ⲉⲃⲟⲗ ⲛ̄ⲧⲟⲧϥ ⲛ̄ⲟⲩⲟⲩϩⲟⲣ . Ⲛⲁϩⲙⲉⲧ ⲉⲃⲟⲗ ϧⲉⲛ ⲣⲱϥ ⲛ̄ⲟⲩⲙⲟⲩⲓ : ⲟⲩⲟϩ ⲡⲁⲑⲉⲃⲓⲟ ⲉⲃⲟⲗ ϩⲁ ⲡⲓⲧⲁⲡ ⲉⲧⲉ ⲛⲁⲡⲓⲧⲁⲡ ⲛ̄ⲟⲩⲱⲧ . ⲁ̅ⲗ̅.

نوهيم إنطا إبسيشى إيفول إنطوتس إن إتسيفى : نيم طاميت شيرى إممافاتس إيفول إنطوتف إنؤو أووهور . ناهميت إيفول خين روف إنؤو مووى : أووه با ثيبيو إيفول ها بى طاب إتيه نابى طاب إنؤوأوت . الليلويا .

من السيف نفسى، ومن يد الكلب بنوتى الوحيدة. خلصنى من فم الأسد وتواضعى من قرن ذو القرن الواحد . الليلويا .

Introduction to the Gospel, Page: 8 : مقدمة الأنجيل ، صفحة

The Gospel

Ⲉⲩⲁⲅⲅⲉⲗⲓⲟⲛ Ⲕⲁⲧⲁ Ⲙⲁⲧⲑⲉⲟⲛ Ⲕⲉⲫ ⲕ̅ⲅ̅ : ⲕ̅ⲑ̅ - ⲗ̅ⲋ̅

Matthew 23:29-36

(متى 23 : 29 - 36)

Woe to you, scribes and Pharisees, hypocrites! Because you build the tombs of the prophets and adorn the monuments of the righteous, and say, 'If we had lived in the days of our fathers, we would not have been partakers with them in the blood of the prophets.' "Therefore you are witnesses against yourselves that

Ⲟⲩⲟⲓ ⲛⲱⲧⲉⲛ ⲛⲓⲥⲁϧ ⲛⲉⲙ ⲛⲓⲫⲁⲣⲓⲥⲉⲟⲥ ⲛⲓϣⲟⲃⲓ : ϫⲉ ⲧⲉⲧⲉⲛⲕⲱⲧ ⲛ̄ⲛⲓⲙϩⲁⲩ ⲛ̄ⲧⲉ ⲛⲓⲡⲣⲟⲫⲏⲧⲏⲥ ⲟⲩⲟϩ ⲛ̄ⲧⲉⲧⲉⲛⲥⲟⲗⲥⲉⲗ ⲛ̄ⲛⲓⲃⲏⲃ ⲛ̄ⲧⲉ ⲛⲓⲑⲙⲏⲓ : ⲟⲩⲟϩ ⲧⲉⲧⲉⲛϫⲱ ⲙ̄ⲙⲟⲥ ϫⲉ ⲛⲁⲛⲭⲏ ⲡⲉ ϧⲉⲛ ⲛⲓⲉϩⲟⲟⲩ ⲛ̄ⲧⲉ ⲛⲉⲛⲓⲟϯ ⲛⲁⲛⲛⲁϣⲱⲡⲓ ⲛ̄ϣⲫⲏⲣⲓ ⲉⲣⲱⲟⲩ ⲁⲛ ⲡⲉ ϧⲉⲛ ⲡ̄ⲥⲛⲟϥ ⲛ̄ⲧⲉ ⲛⲓⲡⲣⲟⲫⲏⲧⲏⲥ : ϩⲱⲥⲧⲉ ⲧⲉⲧⲉⲛⲉⲣ ⲙⲉⲑⲣⲉ ϧⲁⲣⲱⲧⲉⲛ : ϫⲉ ⲛ̄ⲑⲱⲧⲉⲛ ⲛⲉⲛϣⲏⲣⲓ ⲛ̄ⲧⲉ ⲛⲏⲉⲧⲁⲩϧⲱⲧⲉⲃ

الويل لكم أيها الكتبة و الفريسيون المراؤون . لأنكم تبنون قبور الأنبياء وتزينون مدافن الصديقين وتقولون لو كنا فى أيام آبائنا لما كنا شاركناهم فى دم الأنبياء . فأنتم تشهدون على أنفسكم أنكم بنو قتلة الأنبياء . فكملوا

you are sons of those who murdered the prophets. Fill up, then, the measure of your fathers' guilt. Serpents, brood of vipers! How can you escape the condemnation of hell? Therefore, indeed, I send you prophets, wise men, and scribes: some of them you will kill and crucify, and some of them you will scourge in your synagogues and persecute from city to city, that on you may come all the righteous blood shed on the earth, from the blood of righteous Abel to the blood of Zechariah, son of Berechiah, whom you murdered between the temple and the altar. Assuredly, I say to you, all these things will come upon this generation. Glory be to God forever, Amen.

ⲛ̅ⲛⲓⲡⲣⲟⲫⲏⲧⲏⲥ · Ⲟⲩⲟϩ ⲛ̅ⲑⲱⲧⲉⲛ ϩⲱⲧⲉⲛ ⲧⲉⲧⲉⲛϫⲉⲕ ⲡϣⲓ ⲛ̅ⲛⲉⲧⲉⲛⲓⲟϯ ⲉⲃⲟⲗ : ⲛⲓϩⲟϥ ⲙ̅ⲙⲓⲥⲓ ⲉⲃⲟⲗ ϧⲉⲛ ⲛⲓⲁϫⲱ ⲡⲱⲥ ⲧⲉⲧⲉⲛⲛⲁϣⲫⲱⲧ ⲉⲃⲟⲗ ϧⲉⲛ ϯⲕ̅ⲣⲏⲥⲓⲥ ⲛ̅ⲧⲉ ϯⲅⲉⲉⲛⲛⲁ : ⲉⲑⲃⲉ ⲫⲁⲓ ϩⲏⲡⲡⲉ ⲁⲛⲟⲕ ϯⲛⲁⲟⲩⲱⲣⲡ ϩⲁⲣⲱⲧⲉⲛ ⲛ̅ϩⲁⲛⲡⲣⲟⲫⲏⲧⲏⲥ ⲛⲉⲙ ϩⲁⲛⲥⲁⲃⲉⲩ ⲛ̅ⲥⲁϧ ⲟⲩⲟϩ ⲉⲣⲉⲧⲉⲛⲉϧⲱⲧⲉⲃ ⲉⲃⲟⲗ ⲛ̅ϧⲏⲧⲟⲩ ⲟⲩⲟϩ ⲉⲣⲉⲧⲉⲛⲉⲓϣⲓ ⲟⲩⲟϩ ⲉⲣⲉⲧⲉⲛⲉⲣⲙⲁⲥⲧⲓⲅⲅⲟⲓⲛ ⲙ̅ⲙⲱⲟⲩ ϧⲉⲛ ⲛⲉⲧⲉⲛⲥⲩⲛⲁⲅⲱⲅⲏ ⲟⲩⲟϩ ⲉⲣⲉⲧⲉⲛϭⲟϫⲓⲛⲥⲱⲟⲩ ⲓⲥϫⲉⲛ ⲃⲁⲕⲓ ⲉⲃⲁⲕⲓ · ϩⲟⲡⲱⲥ ⲛ̅ⲧⲉϥ ⲉϫⲉⲛ ⲑⲏⲛⲟⲩ ⲛ̅ϫⲉ ⲥⲛⲟϥ ⲛⲓⲃⲉⲛ ⲛ̅ⲑⲙⲏⲓ ⲉⲧⲁⲩⲫⲟⲛϥ ⲉⲃⲟⲗ ϩⲓϫⲉⲛ ⲡⲓⲕⲁϩⲓ : ⲓⲥϫⲉⲛ ⲡ̅ⲥⲛⲟϥ ⲛ̅ⲁⲃⲉⲗ ⲡⲓⲑⲙⲏⲓ ϣⲁ ⲡ̅ⲥⲛⲟϥ ⲛ̅Ⲍⲁⲭⲁⲣⲓⲁⲥ ⲡ̅ϣⲏⲣⲓ ⲙ̅Ⲃⲁⲣⲁⲭⲓⲁⲥ : ⲫⲏⲉⲧⲁⲣⲉⲧⲛ̅ϧⲟⲟⲃⲉϥ ⲟⲩⲧⲉ ⲡⲓⲉⲣⲫⲉⲓ ⲛⲉⲙ ⲡⲓⲙⲁⲛⲉⲣϣⲱⲟⲩϣⲓ : Ⲁⲙⲏⲛ ϯϫⲱ ⲙ̅ⲙⲟⲥ ⲛⲱⲧⲉⲛ ϫⲉ ⲉⲣⲉⲛⲁⲓ ⲧⲏⲣⲟⲩ ⲛⲏⲟⲩ ⲉ̀ϫⲉⲛ ⲧⲁⲓⲅⲉⲛⲉⲁ · ⲟⲩⲱϣⲧ ⲙ̅ⲡⲓⲉⲩⲁⲅⲅⲉⲗⲓⲟⲛ ⲉⲑⲩ ·

أنتم مكاييل آبائكم . أيها الحيات أولاد الأفاعى كيف تهربون من دينونة جهنم؟ من أجل ذلك ها أنا أرسل إليكم أنبياء وحكماء وكتبة فمنهم من تقتلون وتصلبون ومنهم من تجلدون فى مجامعكم وتطردونهم من مدينة إلى مدينة. لكى يأتى عليكم كل دم بار سُفك على الأرض ، من دم هابيل الصديق إلى دم زكريا بن براشيا ، الذى قتلتموه بين الهيكل والمذبح . الحق أقول لكم ان هذا كله سيأتى على هذا الجيل . والمجد لله دائماً .

Exposition

طرح

Christ paints a sad picture of the conduct and the compartment of the Pharisees. He admonishes them in an unmistakable way for carrying on the same questionable traditions of their predecessors and even surpassed them. Their predecessors slew the prophets and saints. Their successors built the tombs of these prophets. They were the snakes born of serpents. They will not escape their deeds. They will be charged with the blood of these saints; from the blood of Abel to the blood of Zechariah whom they slew between the sanctuary and the altar. All these preceding tribulations will fall on this generation because they all had conspired to kill the Son of God. That is why God scattered them all over the earth, their enemies dominated them their heritage was given to others and their dwellings became desolate.

يا لهذه الأوصاف المحزنة التى قالها المسيح على الفريسيين . إذ يعطيهم الويل بغير محاباه لأنهم تشبهوا بآبائهم وكملوا مكاييلهم . أولئك الذين قتلوا الأنبياء القديسين وهؤلاء الآخرون بنوا مقابرهم . هؤلاء هم الحيات المولودون من الأفاعى الذين لم يهربوا من جهنم ، فسينتقم منهم عن دم جميع الأبرار الذى سفك على وجه الأرض ، من دم هابيل إلى دم زكريا الذى قتلوه بين الهيكل والمذبح. كل هذه الضوائق وهذه الشدائد تسبق وتأتى على هذا الجيل لأنهم جميعهم تشاوروا مشورة واحدة على إبن الله ليقتلوه ، لذلك فرقهم الله فى الأرض واعداؤهم تسلطوا عليهم وميراثهم صار لقوم آخرين وصارت منازلهم خراباً .

(North side) Christ our Savior; has come and has borne suffering; that through His Passion; He may save us.

(مرد بحرى) المسيح مخلصنا جاء وتألم عنا لكى بآلامه يخلصنا .

(South side) Let us glorify Him; and exalt His Name; for He had mercy on us; according to His great mercy.

(مرد قبلى) فلنمجده ونرفع اسمه لأنه صنع معنا رحمة كعظيم رحمته .

The Eleventh Hour of Wednesday Eve of the Holy Pascha
الساعة الحادية عشرة من ليلة الأربعاء من البصخة المقدسة

Wisdom of Solomon 7:24-30

For wisdom moves from one place to another more easily than motion itself, and because of her purity, she penetrates all things. So, she is the exhalation of the power of God and emanation of the pure glory of the Almighty; Therefore, nothing defiled enters her. For she is the radiance of eternal light, A spotless mirror of the power of God and the image of His goodness. Though she is one, she can do all things; so while remaining in herself, she renews all things; and in every generation, she passes into holy souls and makes them friends of God and prophets. Thus, God loves nothing as much as the one who lives with wisdom. For wisdom is more beautiful than the sun and more than every constellation of stars. Compared with light she is found to be superior, for the light is followed by night, but evil cannot overcome wisdom. Glory be to the Holy Trinity. Amen

(من حكمة سليمان ص 7 : 24 - 30)

أن الحكمة تتحرك فى كل متحرك ، فهى تبلغ وتأتى على الكل من أجل طهارتها. فأنها لهب قوة الله ، وفيض من المجد المقدس الذى لضابط الكل . فلذلك لا يقدر أن يقرُبها شئ دنس لأنها ضياء النور الأزلى . ومرآة أعمال الله النقية وصورة صلاحه . تقدر على كل شئ وهى واحدة . وتجدد كل شئ . وهى ثابتة فى ذاتها وفى كل جيل تحل فى النفوس الطاهرة . وتجعلهم شركاء الله وتصيرهم أنبياء. لأن الله لا يحب أحد إلا من يساكن الحكمة ، لأنها أبهى من الشمس وأسمى من كل مركز للنجوم. وإذا قيست بالنور تقدمت عليه لأن النور يعقبه الليل وأما الحكمة فلا يقوى عليها الظلام . مجداً للثالوث القدوس .

Pascha Praise - B (12 times), Page: 7	تسبحة البصخة B (12 مرة) ، صفحة : 7

The Psalm
Ⲯⲁⲗⲙⲟⲥ ⲛ̅ⲋ̅ : ⲁ̅

Psalms 56:1

Have mercy on me, O God, have mercy on me; for my soul has trusted in You; and in the shadow of Your wings will I hope, until the iniquity has passed away. Alleluia.

Ⲛⲁⲓ ⲛⲏⲓ Ⲫ̀ⲧ ⲟⲩⲟϩ ⲛⲁⲓ ⲛⲏⲓ : ϫⲉ ⲁⲥⲭⲁϩⲑⲏⲥ ⲉ̀ⲣⲟⲕ ⲛ̀ϫⲉ ⲧⲁⲯⲩⲭⲏ : ϯⲛⲁⲉⲣ ϩⲉⲗⲡⲓⲥ ϧⲁ ⲧ̀ϧⲏⲓⲃⲓ ⲛ̀ⲧⲉ ⲛⲉⲕⲧⲉⲛϩ : ϣⲁⲧⲉⲥⲥⲓⲛⲓ ⲛ̀ϫⲉ ϯⲁⲛⲟⲙⲓⲁ . ⲁ̅ⲗ̅

ناى نى أفنووتى أووه ناى نى : جيه أسكاإهثيس إروك إنجيه طا إبسيشى : تينا إرهيليبيس خا إتخيفى إنتيه نيك تينه : شاتيس سينى إنجيه تى أنوميا . الليلويا .

(مز 56 : 1)

ارحمنى يا الله ارحمنى فأنه عليك توكلت نفسى . وبظل جناحيك اتكل إلى ان يعبر الاثم . الليلويا .

Introduction to the Gospel, Page: 8	مقدمة الأنجيل ، صفحة : 8

The Gospel
Ⲉⲩⲁⲅⲅⲉⲗⲓⲟⲛ Ⲕⲁⲧⲁ Ⲓⲱⲁⲛⲛⲏⲛ Ⲕⲉⲫ ⲓ̅ⲁ̅ : ⲛ̅ⲉ̅ ϣⲃⲗ

John 11:55-57

And the Passover of the Jews was near, and many went from the country up to Jerusalem before the Passover, to purify themselves. Then they sought Jesus, and spoke among themselves as they stood in the temple, "What do you think, that He

Ⲛⲁϥϧⲉⲛⲧ ⲇⲉ ⲡⲉ ⲛ̀ϫⲉ ⲡⲓⲡⲁⲥⲭⲁ ⲛ̀ⲧⲉ Ⲛⲓⲓⲟⲩⲇⲁⲓ : ⲟⲩⲟϩ ⲁⲩⲓ̀ ⲛ̀ϫⲉ ⲟⲩⲙⲏϣ ⲉ̀ϩ̀ⲣⲏⲓ Ⲓⲗⲏⲙ ⲉ̀ⲃⲟⲗ ϧⲉⲛ ϯⲭⲱⲣⲁ ϧⲁⲧⲉⲛ ⲡⲓⲡⲁⲥⲭⲁ ϩⲓⲛⲁ ⲛ̀ⲧⲟⲩⲧⲟⲩⲃⲱⲟⲩ : ⲛⲁⲩⲕⲱϯ ⲟⲩⲛ ⲡⲉ ⲛ̀ⲥⲁ Ⲓⲏⲥ ⲛ̀ϫⲉ Ⲛⲓⲓⲟⲩⲇⲁⲓ ⲉⲩϫⲱ ⲙ̀ⲙⲟⲥ ⲛ̀ⲛⲟⲩⲣⲏⲟⲩ ⲉ̀ⲟϩⲓ ⲉ̀ⲣⲁⲧⲟⲩ ϧⲉⲛ ⲡⲓⲉⲣⲫⲉⲓ : ϫⲉ ⲟⲩ

(يوحنا ص 11 : 55 ألخ)

وكان قد اقترب فصح اليهود ، فصعد كثيرون من الكورة إلى أورشليم قبل الفصح ليتطهروا . وكان اليهود يطلبون يسوع ويقولون فيما بينهم وهم قائمون فى

will not come to the feast?" Now both the chief priests and the Pharisees had given a command, that if anyone knew where He was, he should report it, that they might seize Him. Glory be to God forever, Amen.	ⲡⲉⲧⲉⲧⲉⲛⲙⲉⲩⲓ ⲉⲣⲟϥ ϫⲉ ϥⲛⲁⲓ ⲁⲛ ⲉⲡϣⲁⲓ : ⲛⲉ ⲁⲣϯ ⲉⲛⲧⲟⲗⲏ ⲇⲉ ⲛϫⲉ ⲛⲓⲁⲣⲭⲏⲉⲣⲉⲩⲥ ⲛⲉⲙ ⲛⲓⲫⲁⲣⲓⲥⲉⲟⲥ ⲃⲓⲛⲁ ⲁⲣⲉϣⲁⲛ ⲟⲩⲁⲓ ⲉⲙⲓ ϫⲉ ⲁϥⲑⲱⲛ ⲛⲧⲉϥⲧⲁⲙⲱⲟⲩ ⲉⲣⲟϥ ⲃⲓⲛⲁ ⲛⲥⲉⲧⲁⲃⲟϥ . ⲟⲩⲱϣⲧ ⲙⲡⲓⲉⲩⲁⲅⲅⲉⲗⲓⲟⲛ ⲉⲑⲩ .	الهيكل: ماذا تظنون ، ألعله لا يأتى إلى العيد؟ وكان رؤساء الكهنة والفريسيون قد أصدروا أمراً أنه ان عرف أحد أين هو فليدل عليه ليمسكوه . والمجد لله دائماً .

Introduction to the Exposition, Page: 9   مقدمة الطرح ، صفحة :

Exposition

It was the tradition of the Jews, that as it became near the days of the Passover, the multitudes go up the mountain from the hamlets to Jerusalem to purge themselves. When they ascended the mountain as usual, they did not see Jesus go up. They said one to the other that maybe He will not come to the feast. The hypocrites were conniving their vicious plots because the high priests, the Pharisees, and the Elders had asked the people to lead them to His location, if it were known, in order to arrest Him. O what foolishness and stupidity of these evil people who wanted to bait the Omnipotent, the source of all power. Because of their opposition, He will chain them and assign them to Hell, the place of suffering.

(North side) Christ our Savior; has come and has borne suffering; that through His Passion; He may save us.

(South side) Let us glorify Him; and exalt His Name; for He had mercy on us; according to His great mercy.

طرح

جرت عادة لسائر اليهود انه إذا اقترب عيد الفصح ، تصعد جموع كثيرة من الذكور إلى أورشليم ليتطهروا . فلما صعدوا كالعادة لم ينظروا يسوع يصعد ، فقالوا لبعضهم البعض وهم فى الهيكل: ألعله حقاً لا يأتى إلى العيد؟ وكان المنافقون يفتكرون أفكاراً مملوءة من الخبث والرياء. لأن رؤساء الكهنة والفريسيين والشيوخ كانوا قد أوصوا أنه ان علم أحداً أين هو فليدلهم عليه ليمسكوه . يا لهذا الجهل وهذه البلادة وعدم المعرفة التى لهؤلاء الأنجاس فإنهم وضعوا فخاً لصاحب القوة الشديدة ، الكلى القدرة ، لأنهم مخالفون ، فسيربطهم هو بسلاسل ويسوقهم إلى الجحيم وموضع العذاب .

(مرد بحرى) المسيح مخلصنا جاء وتألم عنا لكى بألامه يخلصنا .

(مرد قبلى) فلنمجده ونرفع اسمه لأنه صنع معنا رحمة كعظيم رحمته .

The Conclusion of the Exposition, Page: 9   ختام الطرح ، صفحة :

The Conclusion with the Nighttime Litanies, Page: 17   طلبة المساء ، صفحة :

يوم الأربعاء من البصخة المقدسة

Wednesday of the Holy Pascha

القراءات و الاحداث

الموضوع : التآمر على المسيح

الاولى : يو 11 : 45- 57 ؛ تشاورهم لقتله
الثالثه : لو 22 : 1- 6 ؛ الشعب ضدهم
السادسة : يو 12 : 1 – 8 ؛ تآمرهم عليه
التاسعة : مت 26 : 3 – 16 ؛ اتفاق يهوذا معهم
الحادية عشرة : يو 12 : 27- 36 ؛ تحذيرهم من الهلاك

بقى المسيح فى بيت عنيا استعداداً لتقديم ذاته ذبيحة عن جنس البشر و بهذا أكمل رمز خروف الفصح الذى كان يحفظ ليوم الذبح . أما يهوذا فقد اتفق معهم على اجرة الخيانة و كان يطلب فرصة لكى ما يسلمه.

The Readings and Events

Subject: The conspiracy against our Lord Jesus Christ

First hour: John 11:45-57; Their plot to kill Him.
Third hour: Luke 22:1-6; The people against them.
Sixth hour: John 12:1-8; The scheme against Him.
Ninth hour: Matthew 26:3-16; Judas' betrayal
Eleventh hour: John 12:27-36; Warning them of dooming.

Our Lord Jesus stayed at Bethany preparing to offer Himself as a sacrifice on behalf of all human kind. Through this, He completed the symbol of Passover lamb which was supposed to be kept till they slain it. Judas betrayed Jesus for some money and was watching for an opportunity to hand Him over to them.

Exodus 17:1-7

And all the congregation of the children of Israel departed from the Wilderness of Sin, according to their encampments, by the word of the Lord; and they encamped in Rephidim. And there was no water for the people to drink. And the people reviled Moses, saying, Give us water, that we may drink! And Moses said to them, Why do you revile me, and why do you tempt the Lord? And the people thirsted there for water, and there the people murmured against Moses, saying, Why is this? Have you brought us up out of Egypt to slay us and our children and our cattle with thirst? And Moses cried to the Lord, saying, what shall I do to this people? Yet a little while and they will stone me. And the Lord said to Moses, Go before this people, and take with you some of the elders of the people; and the rod with which you struck the river, take in your hand, and you shall go. Behold, I stand there before you, on the rock in Horeb, and you shall strike the rock, and water shall come out from it, and the people shall drink. And Moses did so before the sons of Israel. And he called the name of that place, Temptation and Reviling, because of the reviling of the children of Israel, and because they tempted the Lord, saying, Is the Lord among us or not? Glory be to the Holy Trinity. Amen.

Proverbs 3:5-14

Trust in God with all your heart; and be not exalted in your own wisdom. In all your ways acquaint yourself with her, that she may rightly direct your paths. Be not wise in your own conceit; but fear God, and depart from all evil. Then shall there be health to your body, and good keeping to your bones. Honor the Lord with your just labors, and give Him the firstfruits of your righteousness, that your storehouses may be completely filled with grain, and that your presses may burst forth with wine. My son, do not despise the chastening of the Lord, nor faint when you are rebuked by Him: for whom the Lord loves, He rebukes, and scourges every son whom He receives. Blessed is the man who has found wisdom, and the mortal who knows prudence. For it is better to traffic for her, than for treasures of gold and silver. Glory be to the Holy Trinity. Amen.

Hosea 5:13-6:3

And Ephraim saw his disease, and Judah his pain; then Ephraim went to the Assyrians, and sent ambassadors to King Jareb, but he could not heal you, and your pain shall by no means cease from you. For I am as a panther to Ephraim, and as a lion to the house

(سفر الخروج لموسى النبى 17 : 1 – 7)

ثم أرتحل كل جماعة بنى إسرائيل من برية سيناء بحسب مراحلهم على موجب قول الرب ونزلوا فى رافازين . ولم يكن ماء للشعب ليشرب . فخاصم الشعب موسى وقالوا له: أعطنا ماء لنشرب. فقال لهم موسى: لماذا تخاصموننى؟ ولماذا تجربون الرب؟ وعطش الشعب وتذمر على موسى قائلين: لماذا أصعدتنا من مصر لتقتلنا وأولادنا ومواشينا بالعطش؟ فصرخ موسى إلى الرب قائلاً : ماذا أفعل بهذا الشعب انهم بعد قليل يرجموننى؟ فقال الرب لموسى : انطلق قدام الشعب ، وخذ معك من شيوخ إسرائيل . وعصاك التى ضربت بها البحر خذها فى يدك وسر أمامهم إلى صخرة حوريب . ها أنا أقف هناك قدامك على صخرة حوريب وأضرب الصخرة فيخرج منها ماء ويشرب الشعب . ففعل موسى هكذا على مشهد بنى إسرائيل . وسمى ذلك المكان تجربة ومخاصمة بنى إسرائيل لأنهم جربوا الرب قائلين : أفى وسطنا الرب أم لا ؟ مجداً للثالوث القدوس .

(من أمثال سليمان الحكيم 3 : 5 - 14)

كن متكلاً على الله بكل قلبك ولا تتكبر بحكمتك . فى كل طرقك أظهرها لكى تستقيم سبلك ولا تعثر رجلك . لا تكن حكيماً فى عينى نفسك ، بل اتق الله وتجنب كل شر . حينئذ يكون شفاء لجسدك وصحة لعظامك . أكرم الله من أتعابك وقدم له البكور من أثمار برك لكى تمتلئ خزائنك من كثرة القمح ، وتفيض معاصرك من الخمر . يا إبنى لا يصغر قلبك من تأديب الرب ولا تخر عندما يوبخك. لأن من يحبه الرب يؤدبه ويجلد كل إبن يقبله . طوبى للإنسان الذى وجد حكمة والحى الذى نال أدباً . لان الاتجار فى هذه أفضل من كنوز الذهب والفضة وأكرم من الأحجار الثمينة . مجداً للثالوث القدوس .

(من هوشع النبى 5 : 13 - 6 : 1 - 3)

وذهب أفرايم مع الاشوريين وأرسل شفعاء إلى ملك ياريم . وهو لم يستطيع أن يشفيكم ولا يزيل الحزن عنكم . لأنى أنا أكون الشبل لأفرايم ، و الأسد لبيت يهوذا . وأتلقاهم فى طريق

of Judah. And I will tear, and go away; and I will take, and there shall be none to deliver. I will go and return to My place, until they are brought to naught, and then shall they seek My face. In their affliction they will seek Me early, saying, Let us go, and return to the Lord our God; for He has torn, and will heal us; He will smite, and bind us up. After two days He will heal us; in the third day we shall arise, and live before Him, and shall know Him. Let us pursue the knowledge of the Lord: we shall find Him ready as the morning, and He will come to us as the early and latter rain to the earth. Glory be to the Holy Trinity. Amen.

الاشوريين مثل اللبؤة الغضبة الجائعة . فاختطف وأمضى وأفترس وأنزع ولا يكون لكم مخلص . وأمضى وأرجع إلى هذا الموضع حتى يهلكوا . ويلتمسوا وجهى فى شدتهم . ويأتون إلىّ قائلين : فلنمضى ولنرجع إلى الرب إلهنا ، لأنه اختطف وهو يشفى . ويضرب ويداوى أيضاً . ويشفينا بعد يومين وفى اليوم الثالث نقوم ونحيا أمامه . ونعلم ونسرع إلى معرفة الرب . فنجده كالفجر المعد ويأتى إلينا كالمطر المبكر والمتأخر على الأرض. مجداً للثالوث القدوس .

Sirach 1:20-2:15

To fear the Lord is the beginning of wisdom; she is created with the faithful in the womb. He rained down knowledge and discerning comprehension, and he exalted the glory of those who held her fast. Unrighteous anger cannot be justified, for a man's anger tips the scale to his ruin. A patient man will endure until the right moment, and then joy will burst forth for him. He will hide his words until the right moment, and the lips of many will tell of his good sense. In the treasuries of wisdom are wise sayings, but godliness is an abomination to a sinner. If you desire wisdom, keep the commandments, and the Lord will supply it for you. Do not disobey the fear of the Lord; do not approach him with a divided mind. Be not a hypocrite in men's sight, and keep watch over your lips. Do not exalt yourself lest you fall, and thus bring dishonor upon yourself. The Lord will reveal your secrets. My son, if you come forward to serve the Lord, prepare yourself for temptation. For gold is tested in the fire, and acceptable men in the furnace of humiliation. You who fear the Lord, wait for his mercy; and turn not aside, lest you fall. Consider the ancient generations and see: who ever trusted in the Lord and was put to shame? Or who ever persevered in the fear of the Lord and was forsaken? Or who ever called upon him and was overlooked? Woe to timid hearts and to slack hands, and to the sinner who walks along two ways! Woe to you who have lost your endurance! What will you do when the Lord punishes you? Those who fear the Lord will not disobey his words, and those who love him will be filled with the law. O son, help your father in his old age, My son, perform your tasks in meekness; then you will be loved by those whom God accepts. Whoever loves danger will perish by it. A stubborn mind will be burdened by troubles, and the sinner will heap sin upon sin. The affliction of the proud has no healing, for a plant of wickedness has taken root in him. The mind of the intelligent man will ponder a parable, and an attentive ear is the wise man's desire. Water extinguishes a blazing fire: so almsgiving atones for sin. Glory be to the Holy Trinity. Amen.

(من يشوع بن سيراخ 1 : 16 - 2 : 23)

رأس الحكمة مخافة الرب . انها خلقت فى الرحم مع المؤمنين . انها تفيض الفهم والمعرفة والفطنة . وتعلى مجد الذين يملكونها. الغضوب لا يمكن أن يبرر لأن ميل غضبه يسقطه . طويل الأناة يصبر إلى حين ويخفى كلامه إلى حين وشفاه كثيرة تحدث بفهمه. فى ذخائر الحكمة أمثال المعرفة . أما عند الخاطئ فعبادة الله رجس . إذا رغبت فى الحكمة احفظ الوصايا والرب يهبها لك . لا تعصى مخافة الرب ولا تتقدم إليه بقلبين . كن محترساً لشفتيك . لا ترتفع لئلا تسقط فتجلب على نفسك هواناً ويكشف الرب خفاياك . يا إبنى إذا أقبلت إلى خدمة الرب فهيّئ نفسك للتجارب . فان الذهب يمحص فى النار والمرضيين من الناس يمحصون فى أتون التواضع . أيها المتقون الرب انتظروا رحمته ولا تحيدوا لئلا تسقطوا . انظروا إلى الأجيال القديمة وتأملوا: من آمن بالرب وخزى؟ أو من ثبت فى وصاياه فتركه؟ أو من صرخ إليه فأهمله قط ؟ ويل لكل قلب هياب وللأيدى المتراخية وللخاطئ الذى يمشى فى طريقين. ويل لكم أيها الذين تركوا الصبر فماذا تصنعون عندما يفتقدكم الرب؟ أن المتقين الرب لا يخالفون كلماته وأبراره يمتلئون من شرائعه . يا إبنى أعن أباك فى شيخوخته . يا إبنى أكمل أعمالك بوداعة واحفظ نفسك من أوهامهم لأن أوهامهم تقتلهم . الذى يحب الخطر يسقط فيه . القلب القاسى يتعب فى آخرته . والخاطئ يزيد خطية على خطية . ألم المتكبر لا شفاء له . وقلب العاقل يتأمل فى المثل . الماء يطفئ النار الملتهبة والصدقة تغفر كل خطية . مجداً للثالوث القدوس .

A homily of our Holy Father Abba Shenouti the archimandrite

(عظة لابينا القديس أنبا شنودة)

I will tell you this and confirm it. Do not imagine that after cutting the wheat from the chaff, that the sinners will have relief. I say to you that according to the testimony of the Books. As for the angels and archangels they will remain silent. So also will all the saints be. And the judgment of God will be decisive and final in the day where they pick out the sinners from the righteous; the time when the sinners are thrown into the hearth of burning fire. Does God need a counselor or a companion to be advised like man? What may God forget that someone else may remember? Or can you ask God about anything else other than these words. That it may be said in one voice: Your rules are just O Lord who rewards everyone according to his deeds. It is not us who would remind God of these things. It is rather He, the Father of all mercies, who remembers.

أقول هذا الكلام ولا أتركه ، وهو هذا : لا تظنوا أنه بعد عزل التبن من الحنطة يحصل الخطاة على راحة . وأقول لكم كشهادة الكتب ، أما الملائكة أو رؤساء الملائكة فانهم يصمتون جميعاً وكذلك القديسون أيضاً يصمتون جميعاً . ويكون حكم الله قولاً تاماً فاصلاً فى اليوم الذى يفرز فيه الأشرار من بين الصديقين . وقت أن يلقى الخطاة فى أتون النار المتقدة . هل الله كالبشر حتى يجعل له مشيراً أو جليساً ليسأله . ما هو الذى ينساه الله لكى يجيب به آخر؟ أو يسأله عن كلمة؟ إلا هذا القول فقط أن يقال من فم واحد: يا ديان الحق ، أحكامك عادلة ، أيها المعطى كل واحد حسب أعماله ، وليس نحن الذين نذكرك بهذا لأنك أنت الذى من عندك كل الرأفات .

We conclude the homily of our Holy Father Abba Shenouti, the Archimandrite, who enlightened our minds and our hearts. In the name of the Father, and the Son, and the Holy Spirit, one God. Amen.

فلنختم عظة أبينا القديس أنبا شنودة رئيس المتوحدين الذى أنار عقولنا وعيون قلوبنا باسم الآب والإبن والروح القدس إله واحد آمين.

| Pascha Praise - B (12 times), Page: 7 | تسبحة البصخة B (12 مرة) ، صفحة : |

The Psalm

Ⲯⲁⲗⲙⲟⲥ ⲛ̄ - ⲇ̄ ⲛⲉⲙ ⲯⲁⲗ ⲗ̄ⲃ̄ : ⲓ̄

Psalms 50:4, 32:10

(مز:50 ,4:32 10)

| That You might be justified in Your words, and might overcome when You are judged. The Lord frustrates the counsels of the nations; He brings to nought also the reasonings of the people. Alleluia. | Ϩⲟⲡⲱⲥ ⲛ̄ⲧⲉⲕⲙⲁⲓ ϧⲉⲛ ⲛⲉⲕⲥⲁϫⲓ : ⲟⲩⲟϩ ⲛ̄ⲧⲉ ⲑⲣⲟ ⲉⲕⲛⲁⲓϩⲁⲡ . Ⲡⲟ̄ⲥ̄ ⲛⲁϫⲉⲣ ⲛⲓⲥⲟϭⲛⲓ ⲛ̄ⲧⲉ ⲛⲓⲉⲑⲛⲟⲥ ⲉⲃⲟⲗ : ⲟⲩⲟϩ ϥⲛⲁϣⲟϣϥ ⲛ̄ⲛⲓⲙⲟⲕⲙⲉⲕ ⲛ̄ⲧⲉ ϩⲁⲛⲗⲁⲟⲥ . ⲁⲗ . | هوبوس إنتيكماى خين نيك صاجى : أووه إنتيه إتشرو إكناتشى هاب . إبتشويس ناجير نى صوتشنى إنتيه نى إثنوس إيفول : أووه إفناشوشف إننى موكميك إنتيه هان لاؤس . الليلويا | لكيما تتبرر فى أقوالك وتغلب إذا حوكمت . الرب يفرق مؤامرة الأمم ويرذل أفكار الشعوب . الليلويا |

| Introduction to the Gospel, Page: 8 | مقدمة الأنجيل ، صفحة : |

The Gospel

Ⲉⲩⲁⲅⲅⲉⲗⲓⲟⲛ Ⲕⲁⲧⲁ Ⲓⲱⲁⲛⲛⲏⲛ Ⲕⲉⲫ ⲓ̄ⲁ̄ : ⲱ̄ⲃ̄ⲗ̄

John 11:46-57

(يوحنا 11 : 46 ألخ)

| But some of them went away to the Pharisees and told them the things Jesus did. Then the chief priests and the Pharisees gathered a council and | Ϩⲁⲛⲟⲩⲛⲟⲩ ⲇⲉ ⲉⲃⲟⲗ ⲛ̄ϧⲏⲧⲟⲩ ⲁⲩϣⲉⲛⲱⲟⲩ ϩⲁ ⲛⲓⲫⲁⲣⲓⲥⲉⲟⲥ ⲁⲩⲧⲁⲙⲱⲟⲩ ⲉ̀ⲫⲏ ⲉⲧⲁϥⲁⲓⲧⲟⲩ ⲛ̄ϫⲉ Ⲓⲏ̄ⲥ̄ : ⲁⲩⲟⲩⲱϯ ⲟⲩⲛ ⲛ̄ϫⲉ ⲛⲓⲁⲣⲭⲏ ⲉⲣⲉⲩⲥ ⲛⲉⲙ ⲛⲓⲫⲁⲣⲓⲥⲉⲟⲥ | وذهب قوم معهم إلى الفريسيين وأخبروهم عما فعل يسوع ، فجمع رؤساء الكهنة والفريسيين |

said, "What shall we do? For this Man works many signs. If we let Him alone like this, everyone will believe in Him, and the Romans will come and take away both our place and nation." And one of them, Caiaphas, being high priest that year, said to them, "You know nothing at all, nor do you consider that it is expedient for us that one man should die for the people, and not that the whole nation should perish." Now this he did not say on his own authority; but being high priest that year he prophesied that Jesus would die for the nation, and not for that nation only, but also that He would gather together in one the children of God who were scattered abroad. Then, from that day on, they plotted to put Him to death. Therefore Jesus no longer walked openly among the Jews, but went from there into the country near the wilderness, to a city called Ephraim, and there remained with His disciples. And the Passover of the Jews was near, and many went from the country up to Jerusalem before the Passover, to purify themselves. Then they sought Jesus, and spoke among themselves as they stood in the temple, "What do you think, that He will not come to the feast?" Now both the chief priests and the Pharisees had given a command, that if anyone knew where He was, he should report it, that they might seize Him. Glory be to God forever, Amen.

ⲛ̀ⲟⲩⲑⲱⲟⲩⲧⲥ : ⲟⲩⲟϩ ⲛⲁⲩⲭⲱ ⲙ̀ⲙⲟⲥ ϫⲉ ⲟⲩ ⲡⲉⲧⲉⲛⲛⲁⲁⲓϥ ⲛⲁϣⲉ ⲛⲓⲙⲏⲓⲛⲓ ⲓ̀ⲧⲉ ⲡⲁⲓⲣⲱⲙⲓ ⲓⲣⲓ ⲙ̀ⲙⲱⲟⲩ : ⲟⲩⲟϩ ⲉ̀ϣⲱⲡ ⲁⲛϣⲁⲛⲭⲁϥ ⲙ̀ⲡⲁⲓⲣⲏϯ : ⲥⲉⲛⲁⲛⲁϩϯ ⲉ̀ⲣⲟϥ ⲧⲏⲣⲟⲩ : ⲟⲩⲟϩ ⲥⲉⲛⲁⲓ̀ ⲛ̀ϫⲉ ⲛⲓⲣⲱⲙⲉⲟⲥ ⲥⲉⲛⲁⲱⲗⲓ ⲙ̀ⲡⲉⲛⲧⲟⲡⲟⲥ ⲛⲉⲙ ⲡⲉⲛⲉ̀ϣⲗⲟⲗ . ⲁϥⲉⲣⲟⲩⲱ ⲇⲉ ⲛ̀ϫⲉ ⲟⲩⲁⲓ ⲉⲃⲟⲗ ⲛ̀ϧⲏⲧⲟⲩ ⲉ̀ⲡⲉϥⲣⲁⲛ ⲡⲉ Ⲕⲁⲓⲁⲫⲁ : ⲉϥⲟⲓ ⲛ̀ⲁⲣⲭⲏ ⲉ̀ⲣⲉⲩⲥ ⲛ̀ⲧⲉ ϯⲣⲟⲙⲡⲓ ⲉⲧⲉ ⲙ̀ⲙⲁⲩ : ⲡⲉϫⲁϥ ⲛⲱⲟⲩ : ϫⲉ ⲛ̀ⲑⲱⲧⲉⲛ ⲧⲉⲧⲉⲛⲥⲱⲟⲩⲛ ⲛ̀ϩⲗⲓ ⲁⲛ . Ⲟⲩ ⲇⲉ ⲛ̀ⲧⲉⲧⲉⲛⲙⲟⲕⲙⲉⲕ ⲙ̀ⲙⲱⲧⲉⲛ ⲁⲛ ϫⲉ ⲥⲉⲣⲛⲟϥⲣⲓ ⲛⲱⲧⲉⲛ ϩⲓⲛⲁ ⲛ̀ⲧⲉ ⲟⲩⲣⲱⲙⲓ ⲛ̀ⲟⲩⲱⲧ ⲙⲟⲩ ⲉ̀ϩⲣⲏⲓ ⲉϫⲉⲛ ⲡⲓⲗⲁⲟⲥ ⲟⲩⲟϩ ⲛ̀ⲧⲉϣⲧⲉⲙⲡⲓⲉⲑⲛⲟⲥ ⲧⲏⲣϥ ⲧⲁⲕⲟ : ⲛⲉ ⲧⲁϥϫⲉ ⲫⲁⲓ ⲁⲛ ⲉ̀ⲃⲟⲗ ϩⲓⲧⲟⲧϥ ⲙ̀ⲙⲁⲩⲁⲧϥ ⲁⲗⲗⲁ ϫⲉ ⲛⲁϥⲟⲓ ⲛ̀ⲁⲣⲭⲏ ⲉ̀ⲣⲉⲩⲥ ⲛ̀ⲧⲉ ϯⲣⲟⲙⲡⲓ ⲉⲧⲉ ⲙ̀ⲙⲁⲩ ⲁϥⲉⲣ ⲡⲣⲟⲫⲏⲧⲉⲩⲓⲛ : ϫⲉ ϩⲱⲧ ⲛ̀ⲧⲉ Ⲓⲏⲥ ⲙⲟⲩ ⲉ̀ϩⲣⲏⲓ ⲉϫⲉⲛ ⲡⲓⲉ̀ϣⲗⲟⲗ . Ⲟⲩⲟϩ ⲉϫⲉⲛ ⲡⲓⲉ̀ϣⲗⲟⲗ ⲙ̀ⲙⲁⲩⲁⲧϥ ⲁⲛ : ⲁⲗⲗⲁ ϩⲓⲛⲁ ⲛⲓⲕⲉϣⲏⲣⲓ ⲛ̀ⲧⲉ Ⲫϯ ⲉⲧⲭⲏⲣ ⲉⲃⲟⲗ ⲛ̀ⲧⲉϥⲑⲟⲩⲱⲧⲟⲩ ⲉⲩⲙⲉⲧⲟⲩⲁⲓ : ⲓⲥϫⲉⲛ ⲡⲓⲉ̀ϩⲟⲟⲩ ⲉⲧⲉ ⲙ̀ⲙⲁⲩ ⲁⲩⲥⲟϭⲛⲓ ϩⲓⲛⲁ ⲛ̀ⲥⲉϧⲟⲑⲃⲉϥ : Ⲓⲏⲥ ⲇⲉ ⲛⲁϥⲙⲟϣⲓ ⲁⲛ ϫⲉ ⲡⲉ ⲛ̀ⲟⲩⲱⲛϩ ⲉ̀ⲃⲟⲗ ϧⲉⲛ ϮⲒⲟⲩⲇⲉⲁ̀ : ⲁⲗⲗⲁ ⲁϥϣⲉⲛⲁϥ ⲉ̀ⲃⲟⲗ ⲙ̀ⲙⲁⲩ ⲉ̀ⲟⲩⲭⲱⲣⲁ ϧⲁⲧⲉⲛ ⲡⲓϣⲁϥⲉ ⲉⲟⲩⲃⲁⲕⲓ ⲉⲩⲙⲟⲩϯ ⲉ̀ⲣⲟⲥ ϫⲉ Ⲉⲫⲣⲉⲙ ⲟⲩⲟϩ ⲁϥϣⲱⲡⲓ ⲙ̀ⲙⲁⲩ ⲛⲉⲙ ⲛⲉϥⲙⲁⲑⲏⲧⲏⲥ . Ⲛⲁϥϧⲉⲛⲧ ⲇⲉ ⲡⲉ ⲛ̀ϫⲉ ⲡⲓⲡⲁⲥⲭⲁ ⲛ̀ⲧⲉ Ⲛⲓⲟⲩⲇⲁⲓ : ⲟⲩⲟϩ ⲁⲩⲓ ⲛ̀ϫⲉ ⲟⲩⲙⲏϣ ⲉ̀ϩⲣⲏⲓ Ⲓⲗⲏⲙ ⲉ̀ⲃⲟⲗ ϧⲉⲛ ϯⲭⲱⲣⲁ ϧⲁϫⲉⲛ ⲡⲓⲡⲁⲥⲭⲁ ϩⲓⲛⲁ ⲛ̀ⲧⲟⲩⲧⲟⲩⲃⲱⲟⲩ : ⲛⲁⲩⲕⲱϯ ⲟⲩⲛ ⲡⲉ ⲛ̀ⲥⲁ Ⲓⲏⲥ ⲛ̀ϫⲉ Ⲛⲓⲟⲩⲇⲁⲓ ⲉⲩⲭⲱ ⲙ̀ⲙⲟⲥ ⲛ̀ⲛⲟⲩⲉ̀ⲣⲏⲟⲩ ⲉⲩⲟϩⲓ ⲉ̀ⲣⲁⲧⲟⲩ ϧⲉⲛ ⲡⲓⲉⲣⲫⲉⲓ : ϫⲉ ⲟⲩ ⲡⲉ ⲉⲧⲉⲧⲉⲛⲙⲉⲩⲓ ⲉ̀ⲣⲟϥ : ϫⲉ ϥⲛⲁⲓ ⲁⲛ ⲉ̀ϩⲣⲏⲓ ⲉ̀ⲡⲁⲓϣⲁⲓ : ⲛⲉⲁⲩϯ ⲉⲛⲧⲟⲗⲏ ⲇⲉ ⲡⲉ ⲛ̀ϫⲉ ⲛⲓⲁⲣⲭⲏ ⲉ̀ⲣⲉⲩⲥ ⲛⲉⲙ ⲛⲓⲫⲁⲣⲓⲥⲉⲟⲥ ϩⲓⲛⲁ ⲁⲣⲉϣⲁⲛ ⲟⲩ ⲁⲩⲉ̀ⲙⲓ ϫⲉ ⲁϥϣⲟⲡ ⲛ̀ⲧⲉϥⲧⲁⲙⲱⲟⲩ ⲉ̀ⲣⲟϥ ϩⲓⲛⲁ ⲛ̀ⲥⲉⲧⲁϩⲟϥ . ⲟⲩⲱϣⲧ ⲙ̀ⲡⲓⲉⲩⲁⲅⲅⲉⲗⲓⲟⲛ ⲉⲑⲩ .

مجمعاً وقالوا: ماذا نصنع ؟ فإن هذا الرجل يعمل آيات كثيرة . وان تركناه هكذا ، يؤمن الجميع به فيأتى الرومانيون ويأخذون موضعنا وأمتنا . فأجاب واحد منهم اسمه قيافا ، كان رئيساً للكهنة فى تلك السنة وقال لهم : انكم لا تعرفون شيئاً ولا تفكرون أنه خير لكم ان يموت رجل واحد عن الشعب ولا تهلك الأمة كلها . ولم يقل هذا من تلقاء نفسه ، بل لأنه إذ كان رئيس الكهنة فى تلك السنة تنبأ أن يسوع كان مزمعاً ان يموت عن الأمة وليس عن الأمة فقط ، بل ليجمع أبناء الله المتفرقين إلى واحد . ومن ذلك اليوم تشاوروا ان يقتلوه . أما يسوع فلم يكن يمشى فى اليهودية علانية بعد ، ولكنه أنطلق من هناك إلى كورة عند البرية إلى مدينة تسمى افرايم ومكث هناك مع تلاميذه وكان قد قرب فصح اليهود . فصعد كثيرون من الكورة إلى أورشليم قبل الفصح ليتطهروا . وكان اليهود يطلبون يسوع ويقولون بعضهم لبعض فيما بينهم وهم قائمون فى الهيكل: ماذا تظنون ألعله لا يأتى إلى العيد؟ وكان رؤساء الكهنة والفريسيون قد أصدروا أمراً أنه ان عرف واحد أين هو ، فليدل عليه لكى يمسكوه . والمجد لله دائماً.

Introduction to the Exposition, Page: 9 : مقدمة الطرح ، صفحة

Exposition

As the Pharisees gathered together and said to one another: "what can we do? This man is doing many miracles and supernatural things. If we leave him alone all the people will believe in him; then the Romans will replace us." One of them, who is Caiaphas, the chief priest of the Jews said: "It is expedient for you that one man should die for the people, and that the whole nation should not perish." And from then on, they conspired to kill Jesus. Jesus went into the wilderness and stayed there with his disciples. And it was about the time of the feast of the Jews, the Jews who sought to kill Him. Verily it was a fulfillment of the prophecy of Isaiah: "Wail on a nation full of evil. A brood of evil doers. Children who are corrupt. For the ox knows its owner, and the donkey its master, but Israel does not know that I am his creator. Therefore, they shall be with their children in Hell-their home-forever."

(North side) Christ our Savior; has come and has borne suffering; that through His Passion; He may save us.

(South side) Let us glorify Him; and exalt His Name; for He had mercy on us; according to His great mercy.

طــرح

فاجتمع الفريسيون وخاطب بعضهم بعضاً قائلين : ما الذى نصنعه؟ فإن هذا الرجل يصنع آيات كثيرة وعجائب كثيرة ، وان تركناه فسيؤمن به الكل فيأتى الرومانيون ويأخذون موضعنا . فقال أحدهم الذى هو قيافا رئيس كهنة اليهود: أنه يجب أن يموت رجل واحد عن الشعب دون الامة كلها . ومن تلك الساعة تشاوروا على يسوع مشورة رديئة ليقتلوه . فمضى يسوع إلى كورة فى البرية وأقام هناك مع تلاميذه . وكان قد قرب عيد اليهود وكانوا يطلبونه لكى يقتلوه . بالحقيقة أكمل ما قاله عليهم إشعياء النبى : الويل للأمة المملوءة إثماً ، الزرع الفاسد الأبناء المخالفين. من أجل أن الثور عرف مزوده والحمار عرف قانيه وإسرائيل لم يعرفنى ولم يعلم اننى أنا خالقه . من أجل ذلك يخلدون هم وأبناؤهم فى الجحيم ، بيتهم إلى الأبد .

(مرد بحرى) المسيح مخلصنا جاء وتألم عنا لكى بألامه يخلصنا .

(مرد قبلى) فلنمجده ونرفع اسمه لأنه صنع معنا رحمة كعظيم رحمته .

The Conclusion of the Exposition, Page: 9 : ختام الطرح ، صفحة

الساعة الثالثة من يوم الأربعاء من البصحة المقدسة
The Third Hour of Wednesday of the Holy Pascha

Exodus 13:17-22

And when Pharaoh sent forth the people, God led them not by the way of the land of the Philistines, because it was near; for God said, lest at any time the people change their minds when they see war, and return to Egypt. And God led the people round by the way to the wilderness, to the Red Sea. And in the fifth generation, the children of Israel went up out of the land of Egypt. And Moses took the bones of Joseph with him, for he had solemnly adjured the children of Israel, saying, God will surely visit you, and you shall carry up my bones from here with you. And the children of Israel departed from Succoth, and encamped in Etham by the wilderness. And God led them in the day by a pillar of cloud, to show them the way, and in the night by a pillar of fire. And the pillar of cloud failed not by day, nor the pillar of fire by night, before all the people. Glory be to the Holy Trinity. Amen.

(من سفر الخروج 13 : 17 ألخ)

وعندما أطلق فرعون الشعب لم يهدهم الله إلى طريق فلسطين مع أنها كانت قريبة ، لأن الرب قال: لئلا يندم الشعب إذا رأى حرباً فيرجع إلى مصر . فأدار الله الشعب إلى الطريق الوعر إلى البحر الأحمر . فى الجيل الخامس خرج بنو إسرائيل من مصر . وحمل موسى عظام يوسف معه . لأن يوسف استحلف بنى إسرائيل بحلف قائلاً : أن الرب سيفتقدكم افتقاداً فاحملوا عظامى من هنا معكم . وارتحل بنوا إسرائيل من سكوت ونزلوا فى أثوم عند البرية . وكان الله يسير أمامهم نهاراً بعمود سحاب ليهديهم الطريق . وليلاً فى عمود نار . ولم يزل عمود السحاب نهاراً وعمود النار ليلاً من أمام الشعب بأسره . مجداً للثالوث القدوس .

Sirach 22:7-18

He who teaches a fool is like one who glues pottery together, or like trying to arouse one from a sound sleep. He who tells something to a fool tells it to a drowsy man, and at the end he will say, "What is it?" Weep for a dead man, for he left the light behind; but weep over a fool, for he left intelligence behind. Weep gladly for a dead man, because he is at rest; but the life of the fool is worse than death. Mourning for a dead man lasts seven days, but mourning for a fool or an ungodly man lasts all his life. Do not hold a conversation with a fool, and do not visit with a senseless man. Beware of him, so as to avoid trouble, and you will not be defiled when he shakes himself off. Stay away from him, and you will find rest and not be exhausted by his insanity. What will be heavier than lead? And what will be his name but "Fool"? Sand, salt, and a piece of iron are easier to bear than a senseless man. A wooden beam bound together in a building will not be broken loose in an earthquake; so a heart strengthened by reasonable counsel will not be afraid in a crisis. A heart settled on intelligent thought is like a plaster decoration on a smooth wall. As fences set on a high place will not stand firm against the wind, so a cowardly heart in the thought of a fool cannot stand firm against any kind of fear. Glory be to the Holy Trinity. Amen.

(يشوع إبن سيراخ 22 : 7 - 18)

الذى يؤدب الأحمق كمن يلصق شقفة على شقفة . وكمن ينبه مستغرقاً فى نوم ثقيل. من يكلم الأحمق كمن يكلم متناعساً وفى النهاية يقول: ماذا حدث ؟ أبك على الميت لأنه ترك النور . وأبكِ على الأحمق لأنه ترك الأدب . أفضل البكاء على الميت لأنه استراح . أما الأحمق فحياته أشقى من موته . النوح على الميت سبعة أيام . والنوح على الأحمق والمنافق جميع أيام حياته . لا تكثر الكلام مع الأحمق . ولا تخالط الجاهل . تحفظ منه لئلا تتعب وتتدنس . إذا شد الرحال اعرض عنه فتجد راحة ولا تحزن بآثامه . ما هو الاثقل من الرصاص وما اسمه أيضاً إلا الأحمق؟ الرمل والملح وقطعة الحديد أخف حملاً من الرجل الجاهل. مثل رباط الخشب مشدود فى البناء لا يتفكك فى الزلزلة كذلك القلب الثابت بالمشورة والقلب الثابت بفكر الفهم لا يجزع إلى الأبد . كزينة الجدار المشيد وكمثل قضيب على مكان مرتفع لا يهدأ أمام كل ريح كذلك القلب الضعيف وفكر الأحمق لا يهدأ أمام كل هول . مجداً للثالوث القدوس.

Job 27:16-20, 28:1-2

Even if he should gather silver as dust, and prepare gold as clay, all these things shall the righteous gain, and the true-hearted shall possess His wealth. And his house is gone like moths, and like a spider's web. The rich man shall lie down, and shall not continue:

(أيوب الصديق 27 : 16 - 28 : 2)

إذا جمع فضة كالتراب وعد ذهباً مثل الطين ، كل هذه يأخذها الصديقون ، والمستقيموا القلب يتسلطون على أموالهم . ومنزله يكون كالعث ومثل العنكبوت . الغنى

he has opened his eyes, and he is no more. Pains have come upon him as water, and darkness has carried him away by night. For there is a place for the silver, where it comes, and a place for the gold, where it is refined. Glory be to the Holy Trinity. Amen.

يضطجع ولا يعود وتدركه الآلام مثل الماء ، والظلمة تأخذه ليلاً . لأنه يوجد مكان للفضة تسبك فيه ومكان للذهب يمحص فيه . مجداً للثالوث القدوس .

Proverbs 4:4-5:4

My son, let our speech be fixed in your heart, keep our commandments, forget them not: and do not neglect the speech of my mouth. And forsake it not, and it shall cleave to you: love it, and it shall keep you. Secure it, and it shall exalt you: honor it, that it may embrace you; that it may give unto your head a crown of grace, and may cover you with a crown of delight. Hear, my son, and receive my words, and the years of your life shall be increased, that the resources of your life may be many. For I teach you the ways of wisdom; and I cause you to go in right paths. For when you go, your steps shall not be hindered; and when you run, you shall not be distressed. Take hold of my instruction; do not let it go, but keep it for yourself, for your life. Go not in the ways of the ungodly, neither covet the ways of transgressors. In whatever place they shall pitch their camp, do not go there; but turn from them, and pass away. For they cannot sleep, unless they have done evil: their sleep is taken away, and they rest not. For these live upon the bread of ungodliness and are drunken with the wine of transgression. But the ways of the righteous shine like light; they go on and shine, until the day has fully come. But the ways of the ungodly are like darkness; they know not how they stumble. My son, attend to my speech, and incline your ear to my words, that your fountains may not fail you; keep them in your heart. For they are life to those that find them, and health to all their flesh. Keep your heart with the utmost care, for out of these are the issues of life. Remove from you a deceitful mouth and put far away from you your unjust lips. Let your eyes look right on and let your eyelids assent to just things. Make straight paths for your feet and order your ways rightly. Turn not aside to the right hand, nor to the left, but turn away your foot from an evil way: A for God knows the ways on the right hand, but those on the left are crooked: B and He will make your ways straight and will guide your steps in peace. My son, attend to my wisdom, and incline your ear to my words; that you may keep good understanding, and the discretion of my lips gives you a charge. Give no heed to a worthless woman, for honey drops from the lips of a harlot, who for a season pleases your palate; but afterwards you will find her more bitter than gall, and sharper than a two-edged sword. Glory be to the Holy Trinity. Amen.

(أمثال سليمان الحكيم 4 : 4 - 5 : 4)

يا إبنى احفظ وصاياى ولا تنسها ولا تهمل كلام فمى ولا تتركه بل أقبله وأحبه ليحفظك. اقتنه فيرفعك ، كرمه فيعانقك ويعطيك أكليل نعمة على رأسك وينصرك بإكليل سرور . اسمع يا إبنى وأقبل كلامى فتكثر لك سبل الحياة. أنا أعلمك طرق الحكمة وأسيرك فى مسالك مستقيمة ، واينما ذهبت لا تضيق خطواتك وإذا أسرعت فلا تتغلب . تمسك بتعليمى ولا تتركه واحفظه لحياتك ولا تمش فى طرق المنافقين ولا تغر من طرق الخطاة . ولا تذهب معهم حينما يجتمعون. مل عنهم وابتعد لأنهم لا ينعسون حتى يعملوا الشر ، ويبعد عنهم النوم ، ولا يرتاحون لأنهم يعيشون على خبز النفاق ويسكرون من خمر الخطية. طرق الأبرار تضئ كالنور . يسيرون مضيئين حتى يكمل النهار . ولكن سبل الخطاة مظلمة ولا يعرفون كيف يتعثرون. يا إبنى اصغ إلى كلامى وأمل أذنك إلي توبيخى لكى لا تنضب ينابيعك. احفظ هذه فى داخل قلبك لانها حياة لمن يليقوا بها ، وشفاء للجسد. بكل تحفظ احفظ قلبك لأن منه مخارج الحياة. ابعد عنك الفم الخائن وابعد عنك الشفتين الخبيثتين. ولتنظر عيناك الاستقامة ودع جفونك ترمق إلى الحق . اجعل مسالك مستقيمة لرجليك وقوم طرقك ، لا تمل يمنه أو يسره. امنع قدمك عن كل طرق ردية لأن الله يعلم بالطرق التى على اليمين ، وأما التى على الشمال فهى معوجة . انه يقوم مناهجك ويرشد مواهبك فى السلام . يا إبنى اصغ إلي حكمتى وإلى كلامى أمل أذنك. لكى تحفظ رأياً صالحاً وأوصيك بفهم بشفتى. لا تلتفت إلى إمرأة ردية لأن شفتيها تقطران عسلاً وبعد ذلك تجدها أمر من العلقم وأحد من سيف ذى حدين . يا إبنى إبتعد عنها . مجداً للثالوث القدوس .

The Psalm

Ψⲁⲗⲙⲟⲥ ⲙ̄ : ⲋ̄ ⲛⲉⲙ ⲁ̄

Psalms 40:6, 1

And if he came to see me, his heart spoke vainly; he gathered iniquity to himself. Blessed is the man who thinks on the poor and needy; the Lord shall deliver him in an evil day. Alleluia

Ⲛⲁϥⲛⲏⲟⲩ ⲉϧⲟⲩⲛ ⲡⲉ ⲉⲛⲁⲩ ⲛⲁϥⲥⲁϫⲓ ⲛ̀ⲟⲩⲙⲉⲧⲉϥⲗⲏⲟⲩ : ⲟⲩⲟϩ ⲡⲉϥϩⲏⲧ ⲁϥⲑⲱⲟⲩⲧ ⲛⲁϥ ⲛ̀ⲟⲩⲁⲛⲟⲙⲓⲁ .

Ⲱⲟⲩⲛⲓⲟⲩⲛⲓⲁⲧϥ ⲙ̀ⲫⲏⲉⲑⲛⲁⲕⲁϯ ⲉϫⲉⲛ ⲟⲩϩⲏⲕⲓ ⲛⲉⲙ ⲟⲩϭⲱⲃ : ϧⲉⲛ ⲡⲓⲉϩⲟⲟⲩ ⲉⲧϩⲱⲟⲩ ⲉϥⲉⲛⲁϩⲙⲉϥ ⲛ̀ϫⲉ ⲡ̄ⲟ̄ⲥ̄ . ⲁⲗ .

ناف نيوو إيخوون بيه إناف نافصاجى إنؤو ميت إإفليوو : أووه بيف هيت أفثوأووتى ناف إنؤو أنوميا .

أوأوو نيوونياتف إمفي إثناكاتى إيجين أووهيكى نيم أووچوب : خين بى إيهوؤو إتهوأوو إفئناهميف إنجيه إبتشويس . الليلويا .

(لمز 40: 6 و1)

كان يدخل لينظر فكان يتكلم باطلاً وقلبه جمع له اثماً . طوبى لمن يتفهم فى أمر المسكين والضعيف . فى يوم السوء ينجيه الرب . الليلويا .

| Introduction to the Gospel, Page: | 8 | مقدمة الأنجيل ، صفحة : |

The Gospel

Ⲉⲩⲁⲅⲅⲉⲗⲓⲟⲛ Ⲕⲁⲧⲁ Ⲗⲟⲩⲕⲁⲛ Ⲕⲉⲫ ⲕ̄ⲃ̄ : ⲁ̄ - ⲋ̄

Luke 22:1-6

Now the Feast of Unleavened Bread drew near, which is called Passover. And the chief priests and the scribes sought how they might kill Him, for they feared the people. Then Satan entered Judas, surnamed Iscariot, who was numbered among the twelve. So he went his way and conferred with the chief priests and captains, how he might betray Him to them. And they were glad, and agreed to give him money. So he promised and sought opportunity to betray Him to them in the absence of the multitude. Glory be to God forever, Amen.

Ⲛⲁϥϧⲉⲛⲧ ⲇⲉ ⲡⲉ ⲛ̀ϫⲉ ⲡ̀ϣⲁⲓ ⲛ̀ⲧⲉ ⲛⲓⲁⲧϣⲉⲙⲏⲣ ⲫⲏⲉⲧⲟⲩⲙⲟⲩϯ ⲉⲣⲟϥ ϫⲉ ⲡⲓⲡⲁⲥⲭⲁ : ⲟⲩⲟϩ ⲛⲁⲩⲕⲱϯ ⲡⲉ ⲛ̀ϫⲉ ⲛⲓⲁⲣⲭⲏⲉⲣⲉⲩⲥ ⲛⲉⲙ ⲛⲓⲥⲁϧ ϫⲉ ⲁⲩⲛⲁⲧⲁⲕⲟϥ ⲛ̀ⲁϣ ⲛ̀ⲣⲏϯ ⲛⲁⲩⲉⲣϩⲟϯ ⲅⲁⲣ ⲡⲉ ϧⲁ ⲧ̀ϩⲏ ⲙ̀ⲡⲓⲗⲁⲟⲥ : ⲁ ⲡ̀ⲥⲁⲧⲁⲛⲁⲥ ⲇⲉ ϣⲉ ⲉϧⲟⲩⲛ ⲉⲡ̀ϩⲏⲧ ⲛ̀Ⲓⲟⲩⲇⲁⲥ ⲫⲏⲉⲧⲟⲩⲙⲟⲩϯ ⲉⲣⲟϥ ϫⲉ Ⲡⲓⲥⲕⲁⲣⲓⲱⲧⲏⲥ ⲉⲟⲩⲁⲓ ⲡⲉ ⲉ̀ⲃⲟⲗ ϧⲉⲛ ⲧ̀ⲏⲡⲓ ⲙ̀ⲡⲓⲙⲏⲧ ⲥ̀ⲛⲁⲩ. Ⲟⲩⲟϩ ⲁϥϣⲉⲛⲁϥ ⲁϥⲥⲁϫⲓ ⲛⲉⲙ ⲛⲓⲁⲣⲭⲏ ⲉⲣⲉⲩⲥ ⲛⲉⲙ ⲛⲓⲥⲁⲧⲏⲅⲟⲥ ⲉⲑⲃⲉ ⲡⲓⲣⲏϯ ⲉⲧⲉϥⲛⲁⲧⲏⲓϥ ⲉ̀ⲧⲟⲧⲟⲩ ⲟⲩⲟϩ ⲁⲩⲣⲁϣⲓ ⲟⲩⲟϩ ⲁⲩⲥⲉⲙⲛⲏⲧⲥ ⲛⲉⲙⲁϥ ⲉ̀ϯ ⲛⲁϥ ⲛ̀ⲟⲩϩⲁⲧ : ⲟⲩⲟϩ ⲁϥⲥⲉⲅⲟⲙⲟⲗⲟⲅⲓⲛ ⲟⲩⲟϩ ⲛⲁϥⲕⲱϯ ⲡⲉ ⲛ̀ⲥⲁ ⲟⲩⲉⲩⲕⲉⲣⲓⲁ ϩⲓⲛⲁ ⲛ̀ⲧⲉϥⲧⲏⲓϥ ⲧⲟⲧⲟⲩ ⲁⲧϭⲛⲉ ⲙⲏϣ. ⲟⲩⲱϣⲧ ⲙ̀ⲡⲓⲉⲩⲁⲅⲅⲉⲗⲓⲟⲛ ⲉⲑⲩ .

(لوقا ص 22 : 1 - 6)

وكان قد قرب عيد الفطر الذى يقال له الفصح . وكان رؤساء الكهنة والكتبة يطلبون كيف يهلكونه ، ولكنهم كانوا يخافون الشعب . فدخل الشيطان فى قلب يهوذا الذى يدعى الاسخريوطى ، وهو أحد الاثنى عشر . فمضى وفاوض رؤساء الكهنة وقواد الجند كيف يسلمه إليهم . ففرحوا وعاهدوه ان يعطوه فضة . فشكر وكان يتحين فرصة ليسلمه إليهم بمعزل عن الجميع . والمجد لله دائماً .

| Introduction to the Exposition, Page: | 9 | مقدمة الطرح ، صفحة : |

Exposition

طرح

When the Feast of the unleavened bread, which is the Passover of the Jews, was near, the scribes and the chief priests sought a way to kill Jesus, but they did not know what to do because they feared the public. But Satan found himself a place in the heart of his accomplice, Judas Iscariot, who was counted

ولما قرب عيد الفطير الذى هو فصح اليهود ، كان الكتبة ورؤساء الكهنة يطلبون كيف يهلكون يسوع . ولم يعلموا ماذا يصنعون. فأنهم كانوا يخافون من الجمع. فوجد الشيطان له مسكناً فى قلب رفيقه يهوذا الإسخريوطى . وكان هذا

among the disciples but was a Satan as the Lord described him. He went to the chief priests and the Sadducees to make a deal to deliver Jesus to them. The evil natured disciple discussed with his evil friends how to deliver to them the Savior of the World. They were more than pleased and paid him silver so that he may deliver him to them in absence of the people.

(North side) Christ our Savior; has come and has borne suffering; that through His Passion; He may save us.

(South side) Let us glorify Him; and exalt His Name; for He had mercy on us; according to His great mercy.

محسوباً فى عدد التلاميذ وكان شيطاناً كقول الرب. فمضى وخاطب رؤساء الكهنة والصدوقيين ليسلمه إليهم . فتكلم النجس مع أصحابه أن يسلم إليهم مخلص العالم . ففرح الأنجاس الممتلؤون غشاً فرحاً عظيماً ، وقرروا معه أن يعطوه فضة حتى يسلمه إليهم بمعزل عن الجمع .

(مرد بحرى) المسيح مخلصنا جاء وتألم عنا لكى بآلامه يخلصنا .

(مرد قبلى) فلنمجده ونرفع اسمه لأنه صنع معنا رحمة كعظيم رحمته .

The Conclusion of the Exposition, Page: 9   ختام الطرح ، صفحة :

الساعة السادسة من يوم الأربعاء من البصخة المقدسة
The Sixth Hour of Wednesday of the Holy Pascha

Exodus 14:13-15:1

And Moses said to the people, Be of good courage; stand still and see the salvation of the Lord, which He will work for us this day; for as you have seen the Egyptians today, you shall see them again no more forever. The Lord shall fight for you, and you shall hold your peace. And the Lord said to Moses, Why do you cry to Me? Speak to the children of Israel, and let them proceed. But lift up your rod, and stretch forth your hand over the sea, and divide it, and let the children of Israel enter into the midst of the sea on the dry land. And behold, I will harden the heart of Pharaoh and of all the Egyptians, and they shall go in after them; and I will be glorified upon Pharaoh, and on all his army, and on his chariots and his horses. And all the Egyptians shall know that I am the Lord, when I am glorified upon Pharaoh, and upon his chariots and his horses. And the Angel of God that went before the camp of the children of Israel moved and went behind them, and the pillar of the cloud also moved from before them and stood behind them. And it went between the camp of the Egyptians and the camp of Israel, and stood; and there was darkness and blackness; and the night passed, and they came not near to one another during the whole night. And Moses stretched forth his hand over the sea, and the Lord carried back the sea with a strong south wind all the night, and made the sea dry, and the water was divided. And the children of Israel went into the midst of the sea on the dry land, and the water of it was a wall on the right hand and on the left. And the Egyptians pursued them and went in after them, all of Pharaoh's horses, his chariots, and his horsemen, into the midst of the sea. And it came to pass in the morning watch that the Lord looked down on the camp of the Egyptians through the pillar of fire and cloud, and troubled the camp of the Egyptians, and bound the axle-trees of their chariots, and caused them to go with difficulty; and the Egyptians said, Let us flee from the face of Israel, for the Lord fights for them against the Egyptians. And the Lord said to Moses, Stretch forth your hand over the sea, and let the water be turned back to its place, and let it cover the Egyptians, coming over both their chariots and their riders. And Moses stretched forth his hand over the sea, and the water returned to its place toward day; and the Egyptians fled from the water, and the Lord shook off the Egyptians in the midst of the sea. And the water returned and covered the chariots and the riders, and all the forces of Pharaoh, who entered after them into the sea: and there was not so much as one of them left. But the children of Israel went along dry land in the midst of the sea, and the water was to them a wall on the right hand, and a wall on the left. So the Lord delivered Israel in that day from the hand of the Egyptians, and

(من سفر الخروج 14 : 13 - 15 : 1)

فقال موسى للشعب : تقووا قفوا وانظروا خلاص الرب الذى يصنعه لكم اليوم . فأنه كما رأيتم المصريين اليوم لا تعودون ترونهم إلى الأبد . الرب يقاتل عنكم وأنتم تصمتون . فقال الرب لموسى : ما بالك تصرخ إليَّ؟ قل لبنى إسرائيل أن يرجعوا إلى الوراء وخذ عصاك ومد يدك على البحر وشقه ، فيدخل بنو إسرائيل فى وسط البحر كما على اليابسة وها أنا أقسى قلب فرعون والمصريين حتى يدخلوا وراءهم فاتمجد بفرعون وكل جيشه بمركباته وفرسانه . فيعلم كل المصريين أنى أنا هو الرب أتمجد بفرعون ومراكبه وفرسانه . فقام ملاك الرب السائر أمام عسكر بنى إسرائيل وسار وراءهم. وانتقل عمود السحاب من أمامهم ودخل ما بين عسكر المصريين وعسكر إسرائيل ووقف فصار ظلاماً وضباباً . وعبر الليل ولم يختلط أحد بعضهم بعضاً الليل كله ، ومد موسى يده على البحر فجلب الرب ريحاً قبلية شديدة الليل كله فنشفت البحر وإنشق الماء . فدخل بنو إسرائيل فى وسط البحر على اليابس . وصار الماء لهم سوراً عن يمينهم وعن يسارهم . وتعقب المصريون بنى إسرائيل ودخلوا وراءهم ، جميع خيل فرعون ومركباته وفرسانه إلى وسط البحر . وكان فى هزيع الصبح ان الرب اطلع على عسكر المصريين من عمود النار والغمام . وازعج عسكر المصريين وربط بكَر مركباتهم وساقهم قسراً . فقال المصريون : فلنهرب من أمام إسرائيل لأن الرب يقاتل عنهم ضد المصريين . فقال الرب لموسى : مد يدك على البحر فيرجع الماء إلى مكانه فيغطى المصريين ومركباتهم وفرسانه. فمد موسى يده على البحر فرجع الماء إلى مكانه عند اقبال النهار والمصريون هاربون تحت الماء وغَرَّق الرب المصريين فى وسط البحر . ورجع الماء وغطى المركبات والفرسان . وكل قوة فرعون الداخلين وراءهم فى البحر . ولم يبق منهم أحد . وأما بنو إسرائيل فمشوا على اليابسة فى وسط البحر . وصار الماء سوراً لهم عن يمينهم وشمالهم . فخلص الرب فى ذلك اليوم إسرائيل من يد المصريين. ونظر إسرائيل المصريين أمواتاً

Israel saw the Egyptians dead by the shore of the sea. And Israel saw the mighty hand, the things which the Lord did to the Egyptians; and the people feared the Lord, and they believed God and Moses His servant. Then Moses and the children of Israel sang this song to God, and spoke, saying, Let us sing to the Lord, for He is very greatly glorified: horse and rider He has thrown into the sea.

Glory be to the Holy Trinity. Amen

على شاطئ البحر . وشاهد اليد القوية العظيمة التى صنعها الرب بالمصريين فخاف الشعب الرب وآمنوا بالله وبعبده موسى . حينئذ سبح موسى وبنو إسرائيل بهذه التسبحة لله وقالوا: ليقولوا فلنسبح الرب لأنه بالمجد قد تمجد . مجداً للثالوث القدوس.

Isaiah 48:1-6

Hear these words, you house of Jacob, who are called by the name of Israel, and have come forth out of Judah, who swear by the name of the Lord God of Israel, making mention of it, but not with truth, nor with righteousness; maintaining also the name of the holy city, and staying themselves on the God of Israel; the Lord of hosts is His name. The former things I have already declared; and they that have proceeded out of My mouth, and it became well known; I wrought suddenly, and the events came to pass. I know that you are stubborn, and your neck is an iron sinew, and your forehead bronze. And I told you of old what would be before it came upon you; I made it known to you, lest you should say, My idols have done it for me; and should say, My graven and molten images have commanded me. You have heard all this, but you have not known; yet I have made known to you the new things from henceforth. Glory be to the Holy Trinity. Amen

(من إشعياء النبى ص 48 : 1 - 6)

اسمعوا هذا يا بيت يعقوب المدعوين باسم اله إسرائيل ، الذين يذكرونه لا بالحق ولا بالعدل. الذين يتمسكون باسم المدينة المقدسة وينشدون باسم إله إسرائيل رب الجنود اسمه. بالأوليات أخبرت منذ زمان ومن فمى خرجت وأنبأت بها . صنعتها بغتة فحدثت . وأعلم انك أنت قاس ورقبتك عضل حديد وجبهتك نحاس وأخبرتك بما كان قبل أن يأتى عليك. أسمعتك فلا تقل: الأوثان صنعت لى هذا ، ولا تقل أن المنحوتات والمسبوكات قد أمرتنى بها. قد سمعتهم وأنتم لم تخبروا. وقد انبأتك بالحديثات منذ الآن . مجداً للثالوث القدوس .

Sirach 23:7-14

My children, hear the teaching of my mouth, for he who keeps it will not be conquered. A sinner will be overtaken by his lips, and a slanderer and arrogant man will be made to stumble by them. Do not accustom your mouth to vows, nor make a habit of using the name of the Holy One. For as a servant who is continually beaten will not lack bruises, So also he who makes a vow and continually names the Holy One will never be cleansed from sin. A man who swears many oaths will be filled with lawlessness, and that plague will not depart from his house. If he offends, his sin will be on him, and if he overlooks it, he has sinned doubly. If he swears in vain, he will not be declared righteous, for his house will be filled with trouble. There is a way of speaking comparable to death. May it not be found in the inheritance of Jacob; for all these things will be far from the godly, and they will not be involved in sins. Do not accustom your mouth to lewd expressions, for this is sinful speech. Remember your father and mother when you sit in council with great men, lest you forget yourself in their presence and by habit act foolishly. Then you will wish you had never been born, and you will curse the day of your birth. Glory be to the Holy Trinity. Amen

(من يشوع إبن سيراخ 23 : 7 - 19)

اسمع يا إبنى تعليم فمى فان من يحفظه لن يهلك . وسيوجد بشفتيه . وأما الخاطئ والشتام والمتكبر فيشكون فيه . لا تعود فمك الحلف . ولا تألف تسمية القدوس. فأنه كما أن العبد الذى يحاسب مراراً كثيرة ولا يفلت من العقاب ، كذلك من يحلف ويذكر الاسم مرات عديدة فلا يمكن أن يتبرر من خطية . الرجل الكثير الحلف يمتلئ إثماً ولا يبرح السوط بيته. فاذا ندم غفرت خطية قلبه ، وإن تغافل فخطيته مضاعفة . وإن حلف باطلاً لا يتبرر . وبيته يمتلئ نوائباً . كلام مشمول بالموت لا يوجد فى ميراثك يا يعقوب. ان هذه كلها تبتعد عن رجال الله ، فلا يوجدون فى الخطايا . لا تعلم فاك سوء الأدب . لأن كلام الخطيئة يوجد فيه . اذكر أباك وأمك إذا اجتمعت بالعظماء لئلا تنساهما أمامهم و تصير جاهلاً . فتود لو لم تولد وتلعن يوم ولدت . مجداً للثالوث القدوس.

The Psalm

Ψⲁⲗⲙⲟⲥ ⲡ̅ⲃ̅ : ⲃ̅ ⲛⲉⲙ ⲇ̅

Psalms 82:2, 4

For behold, Your enemies have made a noise; and they that hate You have lifted up the head. For they have taken counsel together with one consent; they have made a confederacy against You. Alleluia

Ⲋⲏⲡⲡⲉ ⲓⲥ ⲛⲉⲕⲭⲁϫⲓ ⲁⲧⲱϣ ⲉⲃⲟⲗ : ⲟⲩⲟ̅ⲋ ⲛ̅ⲏⲉⲑⲙⲟⲥⲧ̀ ⲙ̀ⲙⲟⲕ ⲁⲩϭ̀ⲓⲥⲓ ⲛ̀ⲧⲟⲩⲁ̀ⲫⲉ.

Ⲁⲩⲥⲟϭⲛⲓ ⲉⲩⲥⲟⲡ ϧⲉⲛ ⲟⲩ̀ⲋⲏⲧ ⲛ̀ⲟⲩⲱⲧ : ⲁⲩⲥⲉⲙⲛⲓ ⲛ̀ⲟⲩⲇⲓⲁⲑⲏ̀ⲕⲏ ϧⲁⲣⲟⲕ. ⲁⲗ.

هيببه إس نيكجاجى أفوش إيفول : أووه نى إثموستى إمموك أفتشيسى إنطوو أفيه . أفصوتشنى إفصوب خين أوهيــت إنؤوأوت : أفسيمنى إنؤو ذياثيكى خاروك . الليلويا .

(مز 82: 2و4)

هوذا أعداؤك قد صرخوا . وقد رفع مبغضوك رؤوسهم . تآمروا جميعاً بقلب واحد وتعاهدوا عليك عهداً . الليلويا .

Introduction to the Gospel, Page: 8 : مقدمة الأنجيل ، صفحة

The Gospel

Ⲉⲩⲁⲅⲅⲉⲗⲓⲟⲛ Ⲕⲁⲧⲁ Ⲓⲱⲁⲛⲛⲏⲛ Ⲕⲉⲫ ⲓ̅ⲃ̅ : ⲁ̅ - ⲏ̅

John 12:1-8

Then, six days before the Passover, Jesus came to Bethany, where Lazarus was who had been dead, whom He had raised from the dead. There they made Him a supper; and Martha served, but Lazarus was one of those who sat at the table with Him. Then Mary took a pound of very costly oil of spikenard, anointed the feet of Jesus, and wiped His feet with her hair. And the house was filled with the fragrance of the oil. But one of His disciples, Judas Iscariot, Simon's *son,* who would betray Him, said, "Why was this fragrant oil not sold for three hundred denarii and given to the poor?" This he said, not that he cared for the poor, but because he was a thief, and had the money box; and he used to take what was put in it. But Jesus said, "Let her alone; she has kept this for the day of My burial. For the poor you have with you always, but Me you do not have always."

Glory be to God forever, Amen.

Ⲓⲏⲥⲟⲩⲥ ⲟⲩⲛ ϧⲁϫⲉⲛ ⲥⲟⲟⲩ ⲛ̀ⲉ̀ⲋⲟⲟⲩ ⲛ̀ⲧⲉ ⲡⲓⲡⲁⲥⲭⲁ ⲁϥⲓ̀ ⲉ̀ⲃⲏ̀ⲑⲁⲛⲓⲁ ⲡⲓⲙⲁ ⲉ̀ⲛⲁⲣⲉ Ⲗⲁⲍⲁⲣⲟⲥ ⲙ̀ⲙⲟϥ ⲫⲏⲉⲧⲁϥⲙⲟⲩ ⲫⲏⲉⲧⲁ Ⲓⲏ̅ⲥ̅ ⲧⲟⲩⲛⲟⲥϥ ⲉ̀ⲃⲟⲗ ϧⲉⲛ ⲛⲏⲉⲑⲙⲱⲟⲩⲧ : ⲁⲩⲉⲣ ⲟⲩⲇⲓⲡⲛⲟⲛ ⲟⲩⲛ ⲉ̀ⲣⲟϥ ⲙ̀ⲡⲓⲙⲁ ⲉⲧⲉ ⲙ̀ⲙⲁⲩ : ⲟⲩⲟ̅ⲋ Ⲙⲁⲣⲑⲁ ⲛⲁⲥϣⲉⲙϣⲓ ⲡⲉ : ⲟⲩⲟ̅ⲋ Ⲗⲁⲍⲁⲣⲟⲥ ⲛⲉ ⲟⲩⲁⲓ ⲡⲉ ⲉ̀ⲃⲟⲗ ϧⲉⲛ ⲛⲏⲉⲑⲣⲱⲧⲉⲃ ⲛⲉⲙⲁϥ : Ⲙⲁⲣⲓⲁ ⲟⲩⲛ ⲁⲥϭ̀ⲓ ⲛ̀ⲟⲩⲗⲓⲧⲣⲁ ⲛ̀ⲥⲟϫⲉⲛ ⲛ̀ⲧⲉ ⲟⲩⲛⲁⲣⲇⲟⲥ ⲙ̀ⲡⲓⲥⲧⲓⲕⲏ ⲉ̀ⲛⲁϣⲉ ⲛ̀ⲥⲟⲩⲉⲛϥ : ⲟⲩⲟ̅ⲋ ⲁⲥⲑⲱⲋⲥ ⲛ̀ⲛⲉⲛϭⲁⲗⲁⲩϫ ⲛ̀Ⲓⲏ̅ⲥ̅ ⲙ̀ⲙⲟϥ : ⲟⲩⲟ̅ⲋ ⲁⲥϥⲟⲧⲟⲩ ⲙ̀ⲡⲓϥⲱⲓ ⲛ̀ⲧⲉ ⲧⲉⲥⲁ̀ⲫⲉ : ⲁ ⲡⲓⲏ̀ⲓ ⲇⲉ ⲙⲟ̅ⲋ ⲉ̀ⲃⲟⲗ ϧⲉⲛ ⲡⲓⲥ̀ⲑⲟⲓ ⲙ̀ⲡⲓⲥⲟϫⲉⲛ.

Ⲡⲉϫⲉ ⲟⲩⲁⲓ ⲇⲉ ⲉ̀ⲃⲟⲗ ϧⲉⲛ ⲛⲉϥⲙⲁⲑⲏⲧⲏⲥ ⲉⲧⲉ Ⲓⲟⲩⲇⲁⲥ ⲡⲉ Ⲥⲓⲙⲱⲛ Ⲡⲓⲥⲕⲁⲣⲓⲱⲧⲏⲥ ⲫⲏⲉ̀ⲛⲁϥⲛⲁⲧⲏⲓϥ : ϫⲉ ⲉⲑⲃⲉ ⲟⲩ ⲁ ⲡⲁⲓⲥⲟϫⲉⲛ ⲙ̀ⲡⲟⲩⲧⲏⲓϥ ⲉ̀ⲃⲟⲗ ϧⲁ ϣⲟⲙⲧ ϣⲉ ⲛ̀ⲥⲁⲑⲉⲣⲓ ⲟⲩⲟ̅ⲋ ⲑⲏⲓⲧⲟⲩ ⲛ̀ⲛⲓⲏ̀ⲕⲓ : ⲫⲁⲓ ⲇⲉ ⲁϥϫⲟϥ ⲟⲩⲭⲟⲧⲓ ϫⲉ ⲥⲉⲣ̀ⲙⲉⲗⲓⲛ ⲛⲁϥ ϧⲁ ⲛⲓⲏ̀ⲕⲓ : ⲁⲗⲗⲁ ϫⲉ ⲛⲉ ⲟⲩⲣⲉϥϭⲓⲟⲩⲓ ⲡⲉ : ⲟⲩⲟ̅ⲋ ⲉ̀ⲣⲉ ⲡⲓⲅⲗⲟⲥⲟⲕⲟⲙⲟⲛ ⲛ̀ⲧⲟⲧϥ ⲛⲉ ϣⲁⲣⲉⲋⲓⲧⲟⲩ ⲉ̀ⲣⲟϥ ϣⲁϥⲧⲱⲟⲩⲛ ⲙ̀ⲙⲱⲟⲩ.

Ⲡⲉϫⲉ Ⲓⲏ̅ⲥ̅ ⲟⲩⲛ ϫⲉ ⲭⲁⲥ ⲛ̀ⲧⲉⲥⲁ̀ⲣⲉ̅ⲋ ⲉ̀ⲣⲟϥ ⲉ̀ⲡⲓⲉ̀ⲋⲟⲟⲩ ⲙ̀ⲡⲁⲕⲱⲥ : ⲛⲓⲏ̀ⲕⲓ ⲅⲁⲣ ⲥⲉ ⲛⲉⲙⲱⲧⲉⲛ ⲛ̀ⲭⲟⲩ ⲛⲓⲃⲉⲛ : ⲁⲛⲟⲕ ⲇⲉ ϯ ⲛ̀ⲙⲱⲧⲉⲛ ⲁⲛ ⲛ̀ⲭⲟⲩ ⲛⲓⲃⲉⲛ.

Ⲟⲩⲱϣⲧ ⲙ̀ⲡⲓⲉⲩⲁⲅⲅⲉⲗⲓⲟⲛ ⲉⲑ̅ⲩ̅.

(يوحنا ص 12 : 1 - 8)

وقبل الفصح بستة أيام أتى يسوع إلى بيت عنيا حيث كان لعازر الذى مات وأقامه يسوع من بين الأموات . فصنعوا له هناك عشاء فى ذلك المكان . وكانت مرثا تخدم . وكان لعازر أحد المتكئين معه . أما مريم فأخذت رطل طيب ناردين زكى كثير الثمن . ودهنت به قدمى يسوع ومسحتهما بشعر رأسها . فأمتلأ البيت من رائحة الطيب . فقال أحد تلاميذه الذى هو يهوذا سمعان الاسخريوطى الذى كان مزمعاً أن يسلمه: لماذا لم يبع هذا الطيب بثلاث مئة دينار ويدفع للمساكين؟ وانما قال هذا ليس لأنه كان يهتم بالمساكين ، بل لأنه كان سارقاً وكان الصندوق عنده وكان يحمل ما يلقى فيه . فقال يسوع: دعوها لأنها حفظته ليوم دفنى . فان المساكين معكم فى كل حين ، وأما أنا فلست معكم فى كل حين . والمجد لله دائماً .

Exposition

Christ our Lord came to Bethany six days before Passover. They regaled him at the residence of Mary and Martha, her sister. Among those present was Lazarus whom he resurrected from the dead. Martha his sister was serving them, and Lazarus her brother was sitting with him. Mary then brought one pound of an expensive nard and she anointed his feet and wiped them with her hair. Judas Iscariot was filled with evil envy and asked cunningly; his heart full of bitterness, deceit and hypocrisy: "Would it not have been better if this oil would have been sold for 300 Denarii and given to the poor?" It was not his love and concern for the poor that prompted him to say this, but because he was a thief and as he had the money box he used to take what was put into it. The Savior responded saying: "Do not trouble the woman for she has done that for my burial. The poor you always have with you, but you do not always have me. " Let us come close to the Lord, run our tears down his feet and ask him for his forgiveness according to his abundant mercy.

(North side) Christ our Savior; has come and has borne suffering; that through His Passion; He may save us.

(South side) Let us glorify Him; and exalt His Name; for He had mercy on us; according to His great mercy.

طــرح

جاء المسيح إلهنا إلى بيت عنيا قبل الفصح بستة أيام . فصنعوا له وليمة فى بيت مريم ومرثا أختها . وكان هناك لعازر الذى أقامه من الأموات. وكانت مرثا أخت الميت واقفة تخدمهم. وكان أحد المتكئين مع ربنا يسوع لعازر أخوها . فأخذت مريم رطل طيب ناردين كثير الثمن ودهنت به رجلى يسوع ومسحتهما بشعر رأسها. فامتلأ يهوذا الإسخريوطى المخالف من الحسد الشيطانى ، وقال بمكر وقلب مملوء من كل مرارة وخبث ورياء ، قال: لماذا لم يبع هذا الطيب بثلثمائة دينار ويدفع للمساكين؟ ولم يقل هذا بفكر صالح ومحبة فى المساكين ، ولكنه كان سارقاً وكان يسرق ما يلقى فى الصندوق . فقال له المخلص : لا تتعبوها لأنها قد حفظته ليوم دفنى ، المساكين معكم فى كل حين وأما أنا فلست معكم فى كل حين . فلنقترب من الرب ولنبكِ أمامه ونبل قدميه بدموعنا ، ونسأله أن ينعم علينا بالغفران كعظيم رحمته .

(مرد بحرى) المسيح مخلصنا جاء وتألم عنا لكى بآلامه يخلصنا .

(مرد قبلى) فلنمجده ونرفع اسمع لأنه صنع معنا رحمة كعظيم رحمته .

الساعة التاسعة من يوم الأربعاء من البصخة المقدسة
The Ninth Hour of Wednesday of the Holy Pascha

Genesis 24:1-9

And Abraham was old, advanced in days, and the Lord blessed Abraham in all things. And Abraham said to his servant the elder of his house, who had rule over all his possessions, Put your hand under my thigh, and I will make you swear by the Lord the God of heaven, and the God of the earth, that you take not a wife for my son Isaac from the daughters of the Canaanites, with whom I dwell, in the midst of them. But you shall go instead to my country, where I was born, and to my tribe, and you shall take from there a wife for my son Isaac. And the servant said to him, Shall I carry back your son to the land from which you came from, if the woman should not be willing to return happily with me to this land? And Abraham said to him, See that you do not carry my son back there. The Lord the God of heaven, and the God of the earth, who took me out of my father's house, and out of the land from which I sprang, who spoke to me, and who swore to me, saying, I will give this land to you and to your seed, He shall send His angel before you, and you shall take a wife to my son from there. And if the woman should not be willing to come with you into this land, you shall be clear from my oath, only do not carry my son there again. And the servant put his hand under the thigh of his master Abraham, and swore to him concerning this matter. Glory be to the Holy Trinity. Amen

(من سفر التكوين 24 : 1 – 9)

وشاخ إبراهيم وهرم فى أيامه . وبارك الرب إبراهيم فى كل شىء. فقـال إبراهيم لعبده كبير بيته ، المولى على جميع ماله : ضع يدك تحت فخذى لاستحلفك بالرب إله السماء وإله الأرض ، أن لا تأخذ زوجة لإبنى اسحق من بنات الكنعانيين الذين أنا ساكن بينهم ، بل انطلق إلى أرضى ، الموضع الذى كنت فيه ، وإلى عشيرتى ، وتأخذ زوجة لإبنى اسحق من هناك . فقال له العبد : ربما لا تشأ المرأة أن تأتى معى لبعد هذه الأرض ، أتريد أن أرد إبنك إلى الأرض التى خرجت منها . فقال له إبراهيـم : احذر من أن ترد إبنى إلى هناك . لأن الرب إله السماء وإله الأرض ، الذى أخذنى من بيت أبى ومن الأرض التى ولدت فيها ، الذى كلمنى وأقسم لي قائلاً : أنى أعطيك هذه الأرض ولنسلك ، هو يرسل ملاكه أمامك . فتأخذ زوجة لإبنى اسحق من هناك وإن لم تشأ المرأة أن تأتى معك إلى هذه الأرض ، فتكون أنت برىء من حلفى. فقط لا ترجع إبنى إلى هناك . فوضع العبد يده تحت فخذ إبراهيم سيده وحلف له من أجل هذا الأمر . مجداً للثالوث القدوس .

Numbers 20:1-13

And the children of Israel, even the whole congregation, came into the Wilderness of Zin, in the first month, and the people stayed in Kadesh; and Miriam died there, and was buried there. And there was no water for the congregation: and they gathered themselves together against Moses and Aaron. And the people reviled Moses, saying, If only we had died in the destruction of our brethren before the Lord! And why have you brought up the congregation of the Lord into this wilderness, to kill us and our cattle? And why is this? You have brought us up out of Egypt, that we should come into this evil place; a place where there is no sowing, neither figs, nor vines, nor pomegranates, neither is there water to drink. And Moses and Aaron went from before the assembly to the door of the tabernacle of witness, and they fell upon their faces; and the glory of the Lord appeared to them. And the Lord spoke to Moses, saying, Take your rod, and call the assembly, you and Aaron your brother, and speak to the rock before them, and it shall give forth its waters; and you shall bring forth for them water out of the rock, and give drink to the congregation and their cattle. And Moses took his rod which was

(من سفر العدد 20 : 1 – 13)

وجاء بنو إسرائيل الجماعة كلها إلى جبل سيناء فى الشهر الأول وأقام الشعب بقادش . وماتت مريم ثم دفنت هناك ولم يكن ماء للجماعة . فاجتمعوا على موسى وهرون. وخاصم الشعب موسى قائلين : ليتنا متنا موت أخوتنا أمام الرب . لماذا جئتما بجماعة الرب إلى هذه البرية لتقتلانا نحن ومواشينا؟ ولماذا أخرجتمانا من أرض مصر إلى هذا الموضع الردئ ، موضع لا زرع فيه ولا تين ولا عنب ولا رمان ، وليس فيه ماء للشرب؟ فجاء موسى وهرون من أمام الجماعة إلى باب قبة الشهادة وسقطا على وجهيهما. فتجلى لهما مجد الرب. وكلم الرب موسى وهرون قائلاً : خذ العصا وأجمع الجماعة كلها أنت وهرون أخوك . وكلما الصخرة قدامهم فتعطى مياهها فتخرجا لهم ماء من الصخرة وتسقيا الجماعة ومواشيهم . فأخذ موسى العصا من أمام الرب . كما أمره الرب . وجمع موسى

before the Lord, as the Lord commanded. And Moses and Aaron assembled the congregation before the rock, and said to them, Hear me, you disobedient; must we bring you water out of this rock? And Moses lifted up his hand and struck the rock with his rod twice; and much water came forth, and the congregation drank, and their cattle. And the Lord said to Moses and Aaron, Because you have not believed Me, to sanctify Me before the children of Israel, therefore you shall not bring this congregation into the land which I have given them. This is the Water of Strife, because the children of Israel spoke insolently before the Lord, and He was sanctified in them. Glory be to the Holy Trinity. Amen

Proverbs 1:10-33

My son, let not ungodly men lead you astray, neither shall you consent to them. If they should exhort you, saying, Come with us, partake in blood, and let us unjustly hide the just man in the earth: and let us swallow him alive, as Hades would, and remove the memorial of him from the earth: let us seize on his valuable property, and let us fill our houses with spoils: but cast in your lot with us, and let us all provide a common purse, and let us have one pouch: go not in the way with them, but your foot turn aside from their paths: for nets are not spread for the birds without cause. For they that are concerned in murder store up evils for themselves; and the overthrow of transgressors is evil. These are the ways of all that perform lawless deeds; for by ungodliness they destroy their own life. Wisdom sings aloud in passages, and in the broad places speaks boldly. And she makes proclamation on the top of the walls, and sits by the gates of princes; and at the gates of the city boldly says, So long as the simple cleave to justice, they shall not be ashamed: but the foolish being lovers of haughtiness, having become ungodly have hated knowledge, and have become subject to reproofs. Behold, I will bring forth to you the utterance of my breath, and I will instruct you in my speech. Since I called, and you did not hear, and I spoke at length, and you gave no heed; but you disdained my counsels, and disregarded my reproofs; therefore I also will laugh at your destruction; and I will rejoice against you when ruin comes upon you: yea when dismay suddenly comes upon you, and your overthrow shall arrive like a tempest; and when tribulation and distress shall come upon you, or when ruin shall come upon you. For it shall be that when you call upon me, I will not listen to you: wicked men shall seek me, but shall not find me. For they hated wisdom, and did not choose the word of the Lord: neither would they attend to my counsels, but derided my reproofs. Therefore shall they eat the fruits of their own way, and shall be filled with their own ungodliness. For because they wronged the simple, they shall be slain; and an inquisition shall ruin the ungodly. But he that listens to me shall dwell in confidence, and shall rest securely from all evil.

Glory be to the Holy Trinity. Amen

وهرون الجماعة أمام الصخرة وقال لهم : اسمعوا أيها المتمردون اتخرج لكم من هذه الصخرة ماء؟ ورفع موسى يده وضرب الصخرة بالعصا مرتين . فخرج ماء غزير فشرب منه الجماعة ومواشيهم . فقال الرب لموسى وهرون لأجل انكما لم تؤمنا ، لتقدسانى أمام أعين بنى إسرائيل ، لذلك لا تدخلان هذه الجماعة إلى الأرض التى أعطيتم إياها . هذا هو ماء الخصومة . حيث اختصم بنو إسرائيل أمام الرب فتقدس فيهم . مجداً للثالوث القدوس .

(من أمثال سليمان الحكيم 1 : 10 ألخ)

يا إبنى لا يضلك الرجال المنافقون ولا تجيبهم إذا دعوك قائلين: هلم شاركنا فى الدم ، لنختف فى الأرض للرجل البار ظلماً . فلنبتلعه حياً كالجحيم ، ونبيد ذكره من الأرض . فنظفر بقنيته الثمينة . ونملأ بيوتنا غنيمة ونصيبه يقع لنا كيس فنقتنيه لنا جميعاً كيس واحد ليكن لنا . لا تمش فى الطريق معهم وامنع رجلك عن طرقهم . لأنهم نصبوا شباكهم للطيور بمكر . وشاركوا القتلة . فيدخرون لأنفسهم الشرور وسقوط الأثمة ردئ . هذه طرق كل من تناهى فى الأثم ، بالنفاق تنزع نفوسهم . الحكمة تُمدح فى الطرقات وفى الشوارع ظاهرة . وعلى زوايا الأسوار يُبشر بها. وعلى أبواب الأقوياء وأبواب المدن قد قالت بقلب قوى فى كل حين: أن عديمى الشر يتمسكون بالبر فلن يخزوا . أيها الجهال المشتهون العار الذين نافقوا وأبغضوا الفهم . وصاروا عرضة للتوبيخ . هوذا أضع أمامكم كلام من روحى وأعلمكم . قد دعوت فلم تسمعوا ، وبسطت يدى فلم تلتفتوا . بل جعلتم مشورتى كأنها ليست ثابتة . ولتوبيخى لم تصغوا . من أجل هذا أنا أيضاً أضحك عند هلاككم . وأفرح إذا لحقكم الفناء وفاجأكم الذعر وأتى الخراب كالعاصفة . إذا جاء عليكم الاستئصال وحل بكم الضيق والهلاك ، فيكون إذا دعوتمونى لا أجيب . يبكرون الاشرار فى طلبى فلا يجدوننى . بما انهم ابغضوا الحكمة . ولم يختاروا مخافة الرب . ولم يريدوا أن يتأملوا مشورتى . مستهزئين بكلامى . فلذلك يأكلون من ثمر طريقهم . ومن نفاقهم يشبعون حيث انهم ظلموا الصبيان وقتلوهم . افتقد المنافقين بالهلاك والذى يطيعنى يسكن على رجاء ويستريح بلا خوف من كل شر . مجداً للثالوث القدوس .

Isaiah 59:1-17

Has the hand of the Lord no power to save? Or has He made His ear heavy, so that He should not hear? Nay, your iniquities separate between you and God, and because of your sins has He turned away His face from you, so as not to have mercy upon you. For your hands are defiled with blood, and your fingers with sins; your lips also have spoken iniquity, and your tongue meditates unrighteousness. None speaks justly, neither is there true judgment; they trust in vanities, and speak empty words; for they conceive trouble, and bring forth iniquity. They have hatched vipers' eggs, and weave a spider's web; and he that is going to eat of their eggs, having crushed an addled egg, has found also in it a basilisk. Their web shall not become a garment, nor shall they at all clothe themselves with their works; for their works are works of iniquity. And their feet run to wickedness, and are swift to shed blood; their thoughts also are thoughts of murder; destruction and misery are in their ways; and the way of peace they know not, neither is there judgment in their ways; for their paths by which they go are crooked, and they know not peace. Therefore has judgment departed from them, and righteousness shall not overtake them; while they waited for light, darkness came upon them; while they waited for brightness, they walked in perplexity. They shall feel for the wall as blind men, and shall feel for it as if they had no eyes; and they shall feel at noon-day as at midnight; they shall groan as dying men. They shall proceed together as a bear and as a dove; we have waited for judgment, and there is no salvation, it is gone far from us. For our iniquity is great before You, and our sins have risen up against us; for our iniquities are in us, and we know our unrighteous deeds. We have sinned, and dealt falsely, and revolted from our God; we have spoken unrighteous words, and have been disobedient; we have conceived and uttered from our heart unrighteous words. And we have turned back judgment, and righteousness has departed afar off; for truth is consumed in their ways, and they could not pass by a straight path. And truth has been taken away, and they have turned aside their mind from understanding. And the Lord saw it, and it pleased Him not that there was no judgment. And He looked, and there was no man, and He observed, and there was none to help; so He defended them with His arm, and established them with His mercy. And He put on righteousness as a breastplate, and placed the helmet of salvation on His head. Glory be to the Holy Trinity. Amen.

Zechariah 11:11-14

And the Canaanites, the sheep that are kept for me, shall know that it is the word of the Lord. And I will say to them, If it is good in your eyes, give me my price, or refuse it. And they weighed for my price thirty pieces of silver. And the Lord said to me, Drop

(من إشعياء النبى ص 59 : 1 - 17)

هل يد الرب لا تقوى أن تخلص أم أذنه ثقلت عن السماع . ولكن خطاياكم قامت بينكم وبين الله . ولسبب خطاياكم صرف وجهه عنكم حتى لا يرحمكم . لأن أيديكم تلطخت بالدم وأصابعكم بالخطايا وشفاهكم نطقت بالاثم. ولسانكم يتلو ظلماً وليس من يقول الحق ولا يوجد قاض عادل . يؤمنون بالاباطيل وينطقون بالكذب. يحبلون بالتعب ويلدون بالاباطيل . فقسوا بيض الأفاعى ونسجوا خيوط العنكبوت . والمزمع أن يأكل من بيضهم لما كسره وجد فيه وحشاً وأفعى . ونسيجهم لا يكون لهم ثوباً ولا يسترون من أعمالهم . لأن أعمالهم أعمال إثم وأرجلهم تجرى إلى الشر وتسرع إلى سفك الدم . وأفكارهم أفكار شر . الكسر والشقاوة فى سبلهم وطريق السلام لم يعرفوه. وخوف الله ليس فى طريقهم لأن طرقهم التى يمشون فيها معوجة ، ولا يعرفون السلام. لهذا بعد عنهم الحكم ولا يدركهم العدل. وإذ هم يترقبون النور صار لهم الظلام ، انتظروا ضوءاً فمشوا فى عتمة ، يتلمسون الحائط مثل أعمى ويشعرون كمن ليس له أعين. ويسقطون فى الظهيرة كأنهم فى نصف الليل كمثل مائتين يتنهدون ومثل الدب ومثل الحمامة يسيرون معاً . ننتظر حكماً فلا يكون ، والخلاص بعد بعيداً. لأن إثمنا كثر أمامك وخطايانا قاومتنا. لأن آثامنا فينا . وعرفنا ظلمنا . نافقنا وكذبنا وبعدنا عن الله . تكلمنا ظلماً وخالفنا ، وحبلنا وتلونا من قلبنا أقوالاً ظالمة ، ورددنا الحكم إلى خلف ، وبعد العدل . لأن الحق باد فى أيامهم ولم يستطيعوا أن يعبروا باستقامة. والحق رُفع وتحول قلبهم عن الحق. ونظر الرب ولم يرضه لأنه لم يكن حكم. ونظر ولم يكن رجل وتأمل ولم يكن ناصر . فدفعهم بذراعه وشددهم برحمته ولبس العدل مثل درع ووضع على رأسه خوذة الخلاص . مجداً للثالوث القدوس.

(من سفر زكريا النبى 11 : 11 - 14)

ويعلم الكنعانيون ، الأغنام التى تحرس ، انها كلمة الرب وأنا أقول لهم: إذا حسن لديكم فأعطونى أجرتى التى قررتموها وإلا فامتنعوا . فقرروا أجرتى ثلاثين من الفضة . فقال لي الرب:

them into the furnace, and I will see if it is good metal, as I was proved for their sakes. And I took the thirty pieces of silver, and cast them into the furnace in the house of the Lord. And I cast away my second rod, even Line, that I might break the possession between Judah and Israel. Glory be to the Holy Trinity. Amen

القها فى المسبك وأنا أفحصها ، هل هى مختارة مثل ما جربت بها؟ فأخذت الثلاثين من الفضة وطرحتها فى المسبك فى بيت الرب ، ثم طرحت عصاى الثانية التى هى حبل القياس لانقض عهدى بين يهوذا وبنى إسرائيل . مجداً للثالوث القدوس .

A homily of our Holy Father Abba Shenouti the archimandrite

(عظة لابينا القديس أنبا شنودة رئيس المتوحدين)

Let me tell you about two things. All those for whom Heaven rejoiced, for their repentance while still on earth, they will never see sadness or suffering at that place. All those for whom Heaven never rejoiced for being not repented while still on earth, they will never see happiness or comfort at that place.

أمران أقولهما لكم ، إن جميع الذين يُفرح بهم فى السماء من أجل توبتهم وهم على الأرض لن يروا حزناً ولا وجعاً فى ذلك المكان. وأولئك الذين لم يُفرح بهم فى السماء لأجل عدم توبتهم وهم على الأرض لن يروا فرحاً ولا راحة فى ذلك المكان. فالى متى أنت تتكاسل أيضاً أيها

Till when will you be lazy you man? I urge you, shed tears for your soul as long as your tears are acceptable. Moreover, if you had done deeds requiring repentance with tears, weep for your soul by yourself, for the saints are weeping with you for the salvation of your soul. Blessed is he who sheds tears for his soul here, as he will avoid the everlasting weeping and gnashing of teeth, and he will rejoice a heavenly joy. Let us awake, my beloved, before the door of repentance is closed and when we knock, we hear that He does not know us. We will hear all that, if we keep sinning.

الإنسان؟ أطلب اليك ، ابكِ على نفسك ما دامت تقبل منك الدموع . وبالأحرى إذا كنت قد عملت أعمالاً يحق عليها البكاء ، فابك على نفسك وحدك ، ما دام جميع القديسين يبكون معك لأجل خلاص نفسك . طوبى لمن امتلأ بكاء على نفسه وحده ههنا ، فانه سينجو من البكاء وصرير الأسنان الدائم ، ويفرح فرحاً سمائياً. فلننتيظ يا أحبائى قبلما يقفل دوننا الخدر وباب التوبة ونضرع أمام الباب فنسمع: لست أعرفكم ، كل هذه وأردأ منها نسمعها إذا تمادينا فى خطايانا.

We conclude the homily of our Holy Father Abba Shenouti, the Archimandrite, who enlightened our minds and our hearts. In the name of the Father, and the Son, and the Holy Spirit, one God. Amen.

فلنختم عظة أبينا القديس أنبا شنودة رئيس المتوحدين الذى أنار عقولنا وعيون قلوبنا بسم الآب والإبن والروح القدس إله واحد آمين .

Pascha Praise - B (12 times), Page: 7 : تسبحة البصخة B (12 مرة) ، صفحة :

The Psalm
Ⲯⲁⲗⲙⲟⲥ ⲙ̄ : ⲉ̄ ⲛⲉⲙ ⲍ̄ ⲛⲉⲙ ⲍ̄

Psalms 40:5-7

My enemies have spoken evil against me, against me they devised my hurt. And if he came to see me, his heart spoke vainly; he gathered iniquity to himself. Alleluia

Ⲛⲁϫⲁϫⲓ ⲁⲩⲭⲱ ⲛ̄ϩⲁⲛⲡⲉⲧϩⲱⲟⲩ ⲛⲏⲓ : ⲁⲩⲥⲟϭⲛⲓ ϧⲁⲣⲟⲓ ⲛ̄ϩⲁⲛⲡⲉⲧϩⲱⲟⲩ . Ⲛⲁϥⲛⲏⲟⲩ ⲉ̀ϧⲟⲩⲛ ⲡⲉ ⲉ̀ⲛⲁⲩ ⲛⲁϥⲥⲁϫⲓ ⲛ̀ⲟⲩⲙⲉⲧⲉⲫⲗⲏⲟⲩ ⲟⲩⲟϩ ⲡⲉϥϩⲏⲧ ⲁϥⲑⲱⲟⲩϯ ⲛⲁϥ ⲛ̀ⲟⲩⲁⲛⲟⲙⲓⲁ . ⲁⲗ .

ناجاى أفجو إمموس إنهان بيتهوأوو ني : أفصوتشنى خاروى إنهان بيتهوأوو . نافنيوو إخوون بيه إناف نافصاجى إنؤوميت إفليوو أووه بيفهيت أفثوأووتى ناف إنؤو أنوميا . الليلويا .

(مز 40 : 5 - 7)
أعدائى تقاولوا علىّ شراً وتشاوروا علىّ بالسوء . كان يدخل لينظر ، فكان يتكلم بـاطلاً . وقلبه جمع له اثماً . الليلويا .

Introduction to the Gospel, Page: 8   مقدمة الأنجيل ، صفحة :

The Gospel

Ⲉⲩⲁⲅⲅⲉⲗⲓⲟⲛ Ⲕⲁⲧⲁ Ⲙⲁⲧⲑⲉⲟⲛ Ⲕⲉⲫ ⲕⲋ̅ : ⲅ̅ - ⲓ̅ⲋ̅

Matthew 26:3-16

Then the chief priests, the scribes, and the elders of the people assembled at the palace of the high priest, who was called Caiaphas, and plotted to take Jesus by trickery and kill Him. But they said, "Not during the feast, lest there be an uproar among the people." And when Jesus was in Bethany at the house of Simon the leper, a woman came to Him having an alabaster flask of very costly fragrant oil, and she poured it on His head as He sat at the table. But when His disciples saw it, they were indignant, saying, "Why this waste? For this fragrant oil might have been sold for much and given to the poor." But when Jesus was aware of it, He said to them, "Why do you trouble the woman? For she has done a good work for Me. For you have the poor with you always, but Me you do not have always. For in pouring this fragrant oil on My body, she did it for My burial. Assuredly, I say to you, wherever this gospel is preached in the whole world, what this woman has done will also be told as a memorial to her." Then one of the twelve, called Judas Iscariot, went to the chief priests and said, "What are you willing to give me if I deliver Him to you?" And they counted out to him thirty pieces of silver. So from that time he sought opportunity to betray Him. Glory be to God forever, Amen.

Ⲧⲟⲧⲉ ⲁⲩⲑⲱⲟⲩϯ ⲛ̀ϫⲉ ⲛⲓⲁⲣⲭⲏ ⲉ̀ⲣⲉⲩⲥ ⲛⲉⲙ ⲛⲓⲡⲣⲉⲥⲃⲩⲧⲉⲣⲟⲥ ⲛ̀ⲧⲉ ⲡⲓⲗⲁⲟⲥ ⲉ̀ϧⲟⲩⲛ ⲉ̀ⲧⲁⲩⲗⲏ ⲛ̀ⲧⲉ ⲡⲓⲁⲣⲭⲏ ⲉ̀ⲣⲉⲩⲥ ⲫⲏⲉ̀ ϣⲁⲩⲙⲟⲩϯ ⲉ̀ⲣⲟϥ ϫⲉ Ⲕⲁⲓⲁⲫⲁ : ⲟⲩⲟϩ ⲁⲩⲉⲣⲟⲩⲥⲟϭⲛⲓ ϩⲓⲛⲁ ⲛ̀ⲥⲉⲁⲙⲟⲛⲓ ⲙ̀Ⲓⲏⲥ ϧⲉⲛ ⲟⲩⲭⲣⲟϥ ⲟⲩⲟϩ ⲛ̀ⲥⲉϧⲟⲑⲃⲉϥ : ⲛⲁⲩϫⲱ ⲙ̀ⲙⲟⲥ ⲇⲉ ⲡⲉϫⲉ ⲙ̀ⲡⲉⲛ̀ⲑⲣⲉⲛⲁⲓⲥ ϧⲉⲛ ⲡ̀ϣⲁⲓ ϫⲉ ⲛ̀ⲛⲉ ⲟⲩϣⲑⲟⲣⲧⲉⲣ ϣⲱⲡⲓ ϧⲉⲛ ⲡⲓⲗⲁⲟⲥ . Ⲓⲏⲥ ⲇⲉ ⲉϥⲭⲏ ϧⲉⲛ Ⲃⲏⲑ ⲁⲛⲓⲁ ϧⲉⲛ ⲡ̀ⲏⲓ ⲛ̀Ⲥⲓⲙⲱⲛ ⲡⲓⲕⲁⲕⲥⲉϩⲧ : ⲁⲩⲓ̀ ϩⲁⲣⲟϥ ⲛ̀ϫⲉ ⲟⲩⲥϩⲓⲙⲓ ⲉ̀ⲣⲉ ⲟⲩⲟⲛ ⲟⲩⲙⲟⲕⲓ ⲛ̀ⲥⲟϫⲉⲛ ⲛ̀ⲧⲟⲧⲥ ⲉⲛⲁϣⲉ ⲛ̀ⲥⲟⲩⲉⲛϥ ⲟⲩⲟϩ ⲁⲥⲭⲟⲩⲧ ⲉ̀ϧⲣⲏⲓ ⲉϫⲉⲛ ⲧⲉϥⲁⲫⲉ ⲉϥⲣⲱⲧⲉⲃ : ⲉⲧⲁϥⲛⲁⲩ ⲇⲉ ⲛ̀ϫⲉ ⲛⲓⲙⲁⲑⲏⲧⲏⲥ ⲁⲩⲭⲣⲉⲙⲣⲉⲙ ⲉⲩϫⲱ ⲙ̀ⲙⲟⲥ ϫⲉ ⲡⲁⲓⲧⲁⲕⲟ ⲟⲩ ⲡⲉ .Ⲛⲉ ⲟⲩⲟⲛ ϣϫⲟⲙ ⲅⲁⲣ ⲡⲉⲉ̀ϯ ⲙ̀ⲫⲁⲓ ⲉ̀ⲃⲟⲗ ϧⲁ ⲟⲩⲙⲏϣ ⲟⲩⲟϩ ⲉ̀ⲧⲏⲓⲧⲟⲩ ⲛ̀ⲛⲓϩⲏⲕⲓ : ⲉⲧⲁϥⲉ̀ⲙⲓ ⲇⲉ ⲛ̀ϫⲉ Ⲓⲏⲥ ⲡⲉϫⲁϥ ⲛⲱⲟⲩ : ϫⲉ ⲉⲑⲃⲉ ⲟⲩ ⲧⲉⲧⲉⲛⲟⲩⲁϩϩⲓⲥⲓ ⲉ̀ϯⲥϩⲓⲙⲓ : ⲟⲩϩⲱⲃ ⲅⲁⲣ ⲉ̀ⲛⲁⲛⲉϥ ⲡⲉⲧⲁⲥⲁⲓϥ ⲉ̀ⲣⲟⲓ : ⲛⲓϩⲏⲕⲓ ⲅⲁⲣ ⲥⲉ ⲛⲉⲙⲱⲧⲉⲛ ⲛ̀ⲥⲏⲟⲩ ⲛⲓⲃⲉⲛ ⲁⲛⲟⲕ ⲇⲉ ϯ ⲛⲉⲙⲱⲧⲉⲛ ⲁⲛ ⲛ̀ⲥⲏⲟⲩ ⲛⲓⲃⲉⲛ . Ⲁⲥϩⲓⲟⲩⲓ ⲅⲁⲣ ⲛ̀ϫⲉ ⲑⲁⲓ ⲙ̀ⲡⲁⲓⲥⲟϫⲉⲛ ⲉ̀ϫⲉⲛ ⲡⲁⲥⲱⲙⲁ ⲉ̀ⲡϫⲓⲛⲕⲟⲥⲧ : ⲁⲙⲏⲛ ϯϫⲱ ⲙ̀ⲙⲟⲥ ⲛⲱⲧⲉⲛ : ϫⲉ ⲫⲙⲁ ⲉⲧⲟⲩⲛⲁϩⲓⲱⲓϣ ⲙ̀ⲡⲁⲓⲉⲩⲁⲅⲅⲉⲗⲓⲟⲛ ⲙ̀ⲙⲟϥ ϧⲉⲛ ⲡⲓⲕⲟⲥⲙⲟⲥ ⲧⲏⲣϥ ⲉⲩⲉ̀ⲥⲁϫⲓ ϩⲱϥ ⲙ̀ⲫⲏⲉⲧⲁ ⲧⲁⲓⲥϩⲓⲙⲓ ⲁⲓϥ ⲉⲩⲙⲉⲩⲓ ⲛⲁⲥ : ⲧⲟⲧⲉ ⲁϥϣⲉⲛⲁϥ ⲛ̀ϫⲉ ⲟⲩⲁⲓ ⲉ̀ⲃⲟⲗ ϧⲉⲛ ⲡⲓⲙⲏⲧ ⲥ̀ⲛⲁⲩ ⲫⲏⲉ̀ ϣⲁⲩⲙⲟⲩϯ ⲉ̀ⲣⲟϥ ϫⲉ Ⲓⲟⲩⲇⲁⲥ Ⲡⲓⲥⲕⲁⲣⲓⲱⲧⲏⲥ ϩⲁ ⲛⲓⲁⲣⲭⲏ ⲉ̀ⲣⲉⲩⲥ. Ⲡⲉϫⲁϥ ⲛⲱⲟⲩ ϫⲉ ⲟⲩ ⲡⲉ ⲉⲧⲉⲧⲉⲛⲛⲁⲧⲏⲓϥ ⲛⲏⲓ ⲟⲩⲟϩ ⲁⲛⲟⲕ ϩⲱ ⲛ̀ⲧⲁⲧⲏⲓϥ ⲉⲧⲉⲛ ⲑⲏⲛⲟⲩ ⲛ̀ⲑⲱⲟⲩ ⲇⲉ ⲁⲩⲥⲉⲙⲛⲏⲧⲥ ⲛⲉⲙⲁϥ ⲉ̀ϯ ⲛⲁϥ ⲙ̀ⲙⲁⲡ ⲛ̀ϩⲁⲧ : ⲟⲩⲟϩ ⲓⲥϫⲉⲛ ⲡⲓⲥⲏⲟⲩ ⲉⲧⲉ ⲙ̀ⲙⲁⲩ ⲛⲁϥⲕⲱⲧ ⲡⲉ ⲛ̀ⲥⲁ ⲟⲩⲉⲩⲕⲉⲣⲓⲁ ϩⲓⲛⲁ ⲛ̀ⲧⲉϥⲧⲏⲓϥ ⲛⲱⲟⲩ. ⲟⲩⲱϣⲧ ⲙ̀ⲡⲓⲉⲩⲁⲅⲅⲉⲗⲓⲟⲛ ⲉⲑ .

(متى 26 : 3 - 16)

حينئذ اجتمع رؤساء الكهنة وشيوخ الشعب فى دار رئيس الكهنة الذى يدعى قيافا . وتشاوروا لكى يمسكوا يسوع بمكر ويقتلوه . وكانوا يقولون: لا نفعل هذا فى العيد لئلا يحدث شغب فى الشعب . وفيما كان يسوع فى بيت عنيا فى بيت سمعان الأبرص ، جاءت إليه إمرأة معها قارورة طيب كثير الثمن ، سكبته على رأسه وهو متكئ . فلما رأى التلاميذ ذلك ، تذمروا قائلين: لماذا هذا الإتلاف ، لأنه قد كان يمكن ان يباع هذا بكثير ويعطى للمساكين. فعلم يسوع وقال لهم: لماذا تتعبون المرأة؟ فانها قد عملت بى فعلاً حسناً . لأن المساكين معكم فى كل حين ، وأما أنا فلست معكم فى كل حين . فانها انما سكبت هذا الطيب على جسدى لدفنى . الحق أقول لكم ، أنه حيثما يُكرز بهذا الانجيل فى كل العالم يخبَّر أيضاً بما فعلته هذه المرأة تذكاراً لها . حينئذ ذهب واحد من الاثنى عشر الذى يدعى يهوذا الاسخريوطى إلى رؤساء الكهنة ، وقال لهم ماذا تعطونى وأنا أسلمه إليكم؟ أما هم فتعاهدوا معه ان يعطوه ثلاثين من الفضة. ومن ذلك الوقت كان يتحين فرصة ليسلمه إليهم . والمجد لله دائماً.

Introduction to the Exposition, Page: 9   مقدمة الطرح ، صفحة :

Exposition

طـرح

The mystery of your incarnation you have concealed in our body, O Christ our God. For Abraham the great patriarch the father of all nations fathomed in great faith that God the Word shall be incarnated from his seed. When he saw that his days on earth were decreasing and that God had blessed him, he summoned his honest and loyal head servant and said to him: Put your hand under my thigh because I will ask you to swear by the Lord of heavens that you will not betroth for my Isaac a wife from this land which I dwell, But go to the land of my fathers and take for him a wife from there, from my tribe and from my fathers race. Take the matter very seriously. "The servant asked prudently: Master what if the woman refused to come with me to this land? Would you rather see me come back with your son Isaac and serve him until I can bring her back? Abraham said: Be careful not to do that. If she does not come with you then you are innocent. The servant put his hand under his master's thigh and swore to him to keep his promise. At the fullness of time God fulfilled this covenant that he pledged to our father Abraham; and Christ by whom all nations are blessed came from his descendants.

سر تأنسك أخفيته مع جسدنا أيها المسيح إلهنا ، من زرع إبراهيم الأب العظيم أب جميع الشعوب ، لما علم بإيمان أن الإله الكلمة لابد أن يتجسد من نسله ، وبالأكثر عندما رأى أيامه نقصت وأن الله بارك فى أعماله ، فدعا عبده الكبير فى بيته ، الوكيل الأمين وخاطبه قائلاً : ضع يدك على تحت فخذى لأحلفك بإله السماء انك لا تأخذ إمرأة لإبنى اسحق من هذه الأرض التى أنا ساكنها ، بل امض إلى أرض أبائى وخذ له إمرأة من ذلك المكان ، من قبيلتى وجنس آبائى. خذ له العربون بغير تهاون . فأجابه العبد بعقل هكذا قائلاً : اسمع يا سيدى أن أبت المرأة أن تأتى معى إلى هذه الأرض ، أفتريد أن أرد إبنك اسحق وأخذه معي إلى أن آتى به إلى ههنا؟ فقال له: احذر أن ترد إبنى ، فأن لم تجئ فأنت برئ . فوضع العبد يده وحلف له على ثبات هذا القول . وفى آخر الزمان أكمل الله الوعد الذى وعد به أبانا إبراهيم وظهر المسيح من صلبه الذى تتبارك به سائر الأمم .

(North side) Christ our Savior; has come and has borne suffering; that through His Passion; He may save us.

(مرد بحرى) المسيح مخلصنا جاء وتألم عنا لكى بألامه يخلصنا .

(South side) Let us glorify Him; and exalt His Name; for He had mercy on us; according to His great mercy.

(مرد قبلى) فلنمجده ونرفع اسمه لأنه صنع معنا رحمة كعظيم رحمته .

الساعة الحادية عشر من يوم الأربعاء من البصخة المقدسة
The Eleventh Hour of Wednesday of the Holy Pascha

Isaiah 28:16-29

Therefore thus says the Lord, even the Lord, Behold, I lay for the foundations of Zion a costly stone, a choice cornerstone and precious, for its foundations; and he that believes on Him shall by no means be ashamed. And I will cause judgment to be for hope, and My compassion shall be for just measures, and you that trust vainly in falsehood shall fall; for the storm shall by no means pass by you, except it also take away your covenant of death, and your trust in Hades shall by no means stand; if the rushing storm should come upon you, you shall be beaten down by it. Whenever it shall pass by, it shall overtake you; morning by morning it shall pass by in the day, and in the night there shall be an evil hope. Learn to hear, you that are distressed; we cannot fight, but we are ourselves too weak for you to be gathered. The Lord shall rise up as against a mountain of ungodly men, and shall be in the valley of Gibeon; He shall perform His works with wrath, even a work of bitterness, and His wrath shall deal strangely, and His destruction shall be strange. Therefore do not rejoice, neither let your bands be made strong; for I have heard of works finished and cut short by the Lord of hosts, which He will execute upon all the earth. Listen, and hear my voice; give ear, and hear my words. Will the plowman plow all the day? Or will he prepare the seed beforehand, before he tills the ground? Does he not, when he has leveled the surface, then sow the small black poppy, or cumin, and afterward sow wheat, barley, millet, and grain in your borders? So you shall be chastened by the judgment of your God, and shall rejoice. For the black poppy is not cleansed with harsh treatment, nor will a wagon wheel pass over the cumin; but the black poppy is threshed with a rod, and the cumin shall be eaten with bread; for I will not be angry with you forever, neither shall the voice of My anger crush you. And these signs came forth from the Lord of hosts. Take counsel, exalt vain comfort.
Glory be to the Holy Trinity. Amen.

A homily of our Holy Father Abba Severus may his blessings be with us. Amen.

Brethren, I remind you the admonition concerning the sinner, and those who reject the law and the commandments of life. Because our Lord warned them saying: Stay away from Me and into eternal fire. What comfort do they expect? There is the valley of tears; the tears that can bring no comfort. Who can intercede for the sinners on that day, when all the angels; cherubim and seraphim keep quiet and neither the righteous nor the saints

(من إشعياء النبى ص 28 : 16 - 26)

لأجل هذا هكذا يقول السيد الرب: هأنذا أطرح حجراً فى أساسات صهيون ، حجر زاوية ثميناً مختاراً كريماً فى أساساتها . فمن آمن به فلن يخزى . وأجعل الدينونة رجاء . وبرحمتى يكون الخلاص على مواضع السكن. والمتوكلون على الكذب يرجون الباطل . لأنه لا يجتازكم العاصف لئلا ينزع عهدكم مع الموت ، ورجاؤكم مع الجحيم لا ينتهى . إذا أتى عليكم العاصف الجارف تكونون له موطئاً . إذا جاء من جهتكم يأخذكم . وسوف يعبر النهار مبكراً ويرتجى السوء ليلاً . تعلموا أن تسمعوا أيها المتضايقين . أننا لا نستطيع أن نحارب ونحن ضعفاء عن أن نتجمع . وسيقوم (الرب) كالجبل للمنافقين. ويحل فى وادى جبعون . بغضب يعمل أعماله عملاً مريراً . ويصنع غضبه فى الغربة . وغريب هو حنقة. أما أنتم فلا تفرحوا ولا تدعوا قيودكم لا تقهر . لأننا قد سمعنا بأعمال القضاء والفناء من قبل رب الجنود هذه التى سيصنعها على الكل الأرض . انصتوا واسمعوا صوتى تأملوا واصغوا لأقوالى. هل يحرث الحارث اليوم كله أم يهيئ البذار قبل أن يعمل الأرض؟ أليس إذا مهد وجهها؟ حينذ يبذر قليل من الشونيز (حبة البركة) والكمون ثم يزرع الحنطة والشعير القطانى فى كل تخومها فتتعلم بحكم إلهك وتفرح. لأنه ليس بصعوبة ينتقى الشونيز ولا تدار بكرة العجلة على الكمون بل بالعصا ينتفض. الشونيز والكمون مع الخبز يؤكل لأنى لا أغضب إلى الأبد عليكم ولا يدوسكم صوت مرارتى . فهذه الآيات خرجت من رب الجنود . تشاوروا وارفعوا عزاء باطلاً. مجداً للثالوث القدوس .

(عظة لأبينا القديس أنبا ساويرس)

أيها الاخوة ها أنا أذكركم الآن من أجل الصوت الذى سيكون على الخطاة . والذين يكفرون بالناموس ووصايا الحياة . لأنه قال ابتعدوا عنى يا ملاعين إلى النار الأبدية . فأى عزاء ينتظرونه هؤلاء مرة أخرى؟ هنا هو وادى البكاء حيث تكون الدموع . هذه هى الدموع التى لا يكون بعدها عزاء. من ذا الذى يقدر أن يطلب عن الخطاة فى ذلك اليوم؟ لأن الملائكة والشاروبيم والساروفيم تصمت وجميع الأبرار

can intercede for mankind. The whole creation will be silent and the whole world will be under the judgment of God. This is the time of harvest. This is the time to pull the net ashore to sort the good fish from the bad ones. This is the day when the sinners will be told: go dwell in Hell forever.

والقديسين لا يستطيع أحد منهم أن يشفع فى البشرية فى تلك اليوم. وتقف كل الخليقة صامتة والعالم كله يكون تحت الحكم الالهى العادل . هذا هو زمان الحصاد . هذا هو وقت جذب الشبكة إلى الشاطئ حيث يعزل السمك الجيد من الردئ هذا هو اليوم الذى يقال فيه للخطاة: اذهبوا إلى الجحيم مسكنكم إلى الأبد .

We conclude the homily of our Holy Father Abba Severus, who enlightened our minds and our hearts. In the name of the Father, and the Son, and the Holy Spirit, one God. Amen.

فلنختم عظة أبينا القديس أنبا ساويرس . الذى أنار عقولنا وعيون قلوبنا باسم الآب والإبن والروح القدس إله واحد آمين .

Pascha Praise - B (12 times), Page: 7	تسبحة البصخة B (12 مرة) ، صفحة :

The Psalm

Ⲯⲁⲗⲙⲟⲥ ⲋ̄ : Ⲃ ⲛⲉⲙ ⲯⲁⲗ ⲝ̄ⲏ : ⲓ̄ⲇ̄

Psalms 6:2, 68:14

Heal me, O Lord; for my bones are vexed. My soul also is grievously vexed: And turn not away Your face from Your servant; for I am afflicted; hear me speedily. Alleluia

Ⲙⲁⲧⲁⲗϭⲟⲓ ⲡ̄ϭⲟⲓⲥ ϫⲉ ⲛⲁⲕⲁⲥ ⲁⲩⲱ̄ϣⲟⲣⲧⲉⲣ : ⲟⲩⲟⲥ ⲁ̄ⲧⲁ ⲯⲩⲭⲏ ϣⲟⲣⲧⲉⲣ ⲉⲙⲁϣⲱ . Ⲙⲡⲉⲣⲫⲱⲛⲥ ⲙ̄ⲡⲉⲕⲥⲟ ⲥⲁⲃⲟⲗ ⲙ̄ⲡⲉⲕⲁⲗⲟⲩ : ⲥⲱⲧⲉⲙ ⲉ̄ⲣⲟⲓ ⲛ̄ⲭⲱⲗⲉⲙ ϫⲉ ϯⲉϫϫⲱ . ⲁ̄ⲗ.

ما طالتشوى إبتشويس جيه ناكاس أف إشطورتير : أووه إطا بسيشى إشطورتير إماشو . إمبير فونه إمبيكهو صافول إمبيك ألوو : صوتيم إروى إنكوليم جيه تى هيج هوج . الليلويا .

(مز 6: 2، 68 :14)

اشفنى يارب فان عظامى قد أضطربت ونفسى قد انزعجت جداً . لا تصرف وجهك عن فتاك . اسمعنى سريعاً فانى فى شدة . الليلويا .

Introduction to the Gospel, Page: 8	مقدمة الأنجيل ، صفحة :

The Gospel

Ⲉⲩⲁⲅⲅⲉⲗⲓⲟⲛ Ⲕⲁⲧⲁ Ⲓⲱⲁⲛⲛⲏⲛ Ⲕⲉⲫ ⲓ̄ⲃ̄ : ⲕ̄ⲍ̄ - ⲗ̄ⲋ̄

John 12:27-36

"Now My soul is troubled, and what shall I say? 'Father, save Me from this hour'? But for this purpose I came to this hour. Father, glorify Your name." Then a voice came from heaven, saying, "I have both glorified it and will glorify it again." Therefore the people who stood by and heard it said that it had thundered. Others said, "An angel has spoken to Him." Jesus answered and said, "This voice did not come because of Me, but for your sake. Now is the judgment of this world; now the ruler of this world will be cast out. And I, if I am lifted up from the earth, will draw all peoples to Myself." This He said,

Ϯⲛⲟⲩ ⲁ ⲧⲁⲯⲩⲭⲏ ϣⲑⲟⲣⲧⲉⲣ ⲟⲩⲟⲥ ⲟⲩ ⲡⲉ ϯⲛⲁϫⲟϥ : ⲡⲁⲓⲱⲧ ⲛⲁϩⲙⲉⲧ ⲉ̄ⲃⲟⲗ ϧⲉⲛ ⲧⲁⲓⲟⲩⲛⲟⲩ : ⲁⲗⲗⲁ ⲉⲑⲃⲉ ⲫⲁⲓ ⲁⲓⲓ ⲉ̄ⲧⲁⲓⲟⲩⲛⲟⲩ : ⲫⲓⲱⲧ ⲙⲁⲱⲟⲩ ⲙ̄ⲡⲉⲕϣⲏⲣⲓ ⲟⲩⲥⲙⲏ ⲁⲥⲓ ⲉ̄ⲃⲟⲗ ϧⲉⲛ ⲧ̄ⲫⲉ ⲉⲥϫⲱ ⲙ̄ⲙⲟⲥ : ϫⲉ ⲁⲓϯⲱⲟⲩ ⲡⲁⲗⲓⲛ ϯⲛⲁϯⲱⲟⲩ : ⲡⲓⲙⲏϣ ⲟⲩⲛ ⲉ̄ⲛⲁϥⲟ̄ϩⲓ ⲉ̄ⲣⲁⲧϥ ⲉⲧⲁⲩⲥⲱⲧⲉⲙ ⲛⲁⲩϫⲱ ⲙ̄ⲙⲟⲥ ϫⲉ ⲟⲩϧⲁⲣⲁⲃⲁⲓ ⲡⲉ ⲧⲁⲥϣⲱⲡⲓ : ϩⲁⲛⲕⲉⲭⲱⲟⲩⲛⲓ ⲇⲉ ⲛⲁⲩϫⲱ ⲙ̄ⲙⲟⲥ ϫⲉ ⲟⲩⲁⲅⲅⲉⲗⲟⲥ ⲡⲉⲧⲁϥⲥⲁϫⲓ ⲛⲉⲙⲁϥ . Ⲁϥⲉⲣⲟⲩⲱ̄ ⲛ̄ϫⲉ Ⲓⲏⲥ ⲉϥϫⲱ ⲙ̄ⲙⲟⲥ ϫⲉ ⲉⲧⲁⲥϣⲱⲡⲓ ⲁⲛ ⲉⲑⲃⲏⲧ ⲛ̄ϫⲉ ⲧⲁⲓⲥⲙⲏ : ⲁⲗⲗⲁ ⲉⲑⲃⲉ ⲑⲏⲛⲟⲩ : ϯⲛⲟⲩ ⲡ̄ϩⲁⲡ ⲙ̄ⲡⲁⲓⲕⲟⲥⲙⲟⲥ : ϯⲛⲟⲩ ⲡⲁⲣⲭⲱⲛ ⲛ̄ⲧⲉ ⲡⲁⲓⲕⲟⲥⲙⲟⲥ ⲉⲩⲉ̄ϩⲓⲧϥ ⲉ̄ⲃⲟⲗ : ⲟⲩⲟⲥ ⲁⲛⲟⲕ ϩⲱ ⲁⲓϣⲁⲛϭⲓⲥⲓ ⲉ̄ⲃⲟⲗ ϩⲁ ⲡⲕⲁϩⲓ ⲉⲓⲉ̄ⲥⲉⲕ ⲟⲩⲟⲛ ⲛⲓⲃⲉⲛ ϩⲁⲣⲟⲓ : ⲫⲁⲓ ⲇⲉ ⲉϥϫⲱ ⲙ̄ⲙⲟϥ

(يوحنا 12 : 27—36)

الآن نفسى قد أضطربت وماذا أقول؟ يا أبت نجنى من هذه الساعة . ولكن لأجل هذا أتيت إلى هذه الساعة . أيها الأب مجد إبنك . فجاء صوت من السماء قائلاً . قد مجدت وسأمجد أيضاً . فلما سمع الجمع الذى كان واقفاً قالوا: انما كان رعد هو الذى حدث. وآخرون قالوا: قد كلمه ملاك . أجاب يسوع وقال: ليس من أجلى حدث هذا الصوت ، ولكن من أجلكم . الآن قد حضرت دينونة هذا العالم . الآن يلقى رئيس هذا العالم خارجاً . وأنا ان ارتفعت عن الأرض أجذب إلى كل واحد .

signifying by what death He would die. The people answered Him, "We have heard from the law that the Christ remains forever; and how can You say, 'The Son of Man must be lifted up'? Who is this Son of Man?" Then Jesus said to them, "A little while longer the light is with you. Walk while you have the light, lest darkness overtake you; he who walks in darkness does not know where he is going. While you have the light, believe in the light, that you may become sons of light." Glory be to God forever, Amen.

ⲉϥⲉⲣⲥⲩⲙⲉⲛⲓⲛ ϫⲉ ϧⲉⲛ ⲁϣ ⲙ̅ⲙⲟⲩ ϥ̅ⲛⲁⲙⲟⲩ · Ⲁϥⲉⲣⲟⲩⲱ ⲛ̅ϫⲉ ⲡⲓⲙⲏϣ ⲉϥϫⲱ ⲙ̅ⲙⲟⲥ ⲛⲁϥ : ϫⲉ ⲁⲛⲟⲛ ⲁⲛⲥⲱⲧⲉⲙ ⲉⲃⲟⲗ ϧⲉⲛ ⲡⲓⲛⲟⲙⲟⲥ ϫⲉ Ⲡⲭ̅ⲥ̅ ϣⲟⲡ ϣⲁ ⲉⲛⲉϩ ⲟⲩⲟϩ ⲡⲱⲥ ⲛ̅ⲑⲟⲕ ⲕⲱ ⲙ̅ⲙⲟⲥ : ϫⲉ ϩⲱϯ ⲡⲉ ⲛ̅ⲧⲟⲩϭⲉⲥ ⲡ̅ϣⲏⲣⲓ ⲙ̅ⲫⲣⲱⲙⲓ : ⲛⲓⲙ ⲡⲉ ⲡ̅ϣⲏⲣⲓ ⲙ̅ⲫⲣⲱⲙⲓ : ⲡⲉϫⲉ Ⲓⲏⲥ ⲛⲱⲟⲩ : ϫⲉ ⲉ̅ⲧⲓⲕⲉⲕⲟⲩϫⲓ ⲛ̅ⲥⲏⲟⲩ ⲡⲓⲟⲩⲱⲓⲛⲓ ϧⲉⲛ ⲑⲏⲛⲟⲩ : ⲙⲟϣⲓ ⲟⲩⲛ ϩⲉⲛ ⲡⲓⲟⲩⲱⲓⲛⲓ ϩⲟⲥ ⲡⲓⲟⲩⲱⲓⲛⲓ ⲛ̅ⲧⲉⲛ ⲑⲏⲛⲟⲩ : ϩⲓⲛⲁ ⲛ̅ⲧⲉϣⲧⲉⲙ ⲡⲓⲕⲁϫⲓ ⲧⲁϩⲉ ⲑⲏⲛⲟⲩ : ϫⲉ ⲫⲏⲉⲑⲙⲟϣⲓ ϧⲉⲛ ⲡⲓⲕⲁϫⲓ ⲛ̅ϥ̅ⲉⲙⲓ ⲁⲛ ϫⲉ ⲁϥⲙⲟϣⲓ ⲉ̅ⲑⲱⲛ : ϩⲟⲥ ⲡⲓⲟⲩⲱⲓⲛⲓ ⲛ̅ⲧⲉⲛ ⲑⲏⲛⲟⲩ ⲛⲁϩϯ ⲉ̅ⲡⲓⲟⲩⲱⲓⲛⲓ ϩⲓⲛⲁ ⲛ̅ⲧⲉⲧⲉⲛⲉⲣϣⲏⲣⲓ ⲙ̅ⲡⲓⲟⲩⲱⲓⲛⲓ · ⲟⲩⲱϣⲧ ⲙ̅ⲡⲓⲉⲩⲁⲅⲅⲉⲗⲓⲟⲛ ⲉⲑ̅ⲩ.

وانما قال هذا مشيراً لأية ميتة كان مزمعاً ان يموت . فأجابه الجمع قائلاً له : نحن سمعنا من الناموس ان المسيح يدوم إلى الأبد . فكيف تقول أنت أنه ينبغي ان يرتفع ابن البشر . من هو ابن الإنسان؟ فقال لهم يسوع: ان النور يبقى معكم زماناً يسيراً . فسيروا فى النور ما دام لكم النور لئلا يدرككم الظلام . لأن الذي يمشي في الظلام لا يدرى إلى أين يذهب . ما دام لكم النور آمنوا بالنور لتصيروا أبناء النور . والمجد لله دائماً .

Introduction to the Exposition, Page: 9 : مقدمة الطرح ، صفحة

Exposition

طــرح

Let us contemplate the plans of God the Word who has the power over death and the life of every one of us is from Him. However, because he was incarnated in our human form, he agonized over what had to be done and showed troubles and weakness. The Savior said: "Now is my soul troubled, and what shall I say? Father, save me from this hour? No, for this purpose I have come to this hour." Yes, truly he came to the world so that He may suffer for our salvation. To lift from Hades the first man that he created and to return the first man to his original home he and his descendants, according to his great mercies. Let us plead with him earnestly and ask him persistently to partake in the glory of his kingdom and to enforce our faith in this holy name till the last breath.

تأملوا يا أهل المعرفة تدبير الله الكلمة الذى بيده سلطان الموت وحياة كل أحد من عنده . لكن لأجل جسد البشرية الذى أخذه منا يظهر القلق والضعف . قال المخلص: الآن نفسى مضطربة وماذا أقول ، يا أبتاه نجنى من هذه الساعة لكن لأجل هذه الساعة أتيت . نعم بالحقيقة أتى إلى العالم لكى يتألم من أجل خلاصنا ، ويصعد من الجحيم الإنسان الأول الذى خلقه ، ويرده إلى وطنه الأول هو وبنيه كعظيم رحمته . فلنصرخ نحوه بغير تكاسل ونطلب إليه بغير فتور لكى يجعلنا شركاء معه فى مجد ملكوته ويثبتنا إلى النفس الأخير على الإيمان باسمه القدوس .

(North side) Christ our Savior; has come and has borne suffering; that through His Passion; He may save us.

(مرد بحرى) المسيح مخلصنا جاء وتألم عنا لكى بألامه يخلصنا .

(South side) Let us glorify Him; and exalt His Name; for He had mercy on us; according to His great mercy.

(مرد قبلى) فلنمجده ونرفع اسمه لأنه صنع معنا رحمة كعظيم رحمته .

The Conclusion of the Exposition, Page: 9 : ختام الطرح ، صفحة

The Conclusion with the Daytime Litanies, Page: 10 : طلبة الصباح ، صفحة

245

ليلة الخميس من البصخة المقدسة

Thursday Eve of the Holy Pascha

القراءات و الاحداث

الموضوع : انقلاب رؤساء الكهنة عليه

الاولى : يو 10 : 17 – 21 ؛ اختلافهم على سلطانه
الثالثه : مر 14 : 3 – 11 ؛ خيانة يهوذا له
السادسة : يو 12 : 36 – 43 ؛ عدم اعترافهم به
التاسعة : يو 10 : 29- 38 ؛ تفنيده لتهمتهم بانه يجدف
الحادية عشرة : يو 12 : 44 – 50 ؛ ادانتهم بكلامه

الايام تمضى و رب المجد يعد نفسه ليقدمها ذبيحة عن العالم كله بارادته و اختياره وحده و اخفى مخلصنا عن الجميع اين سياكل الفصح حتى لا يتمكن يهوذا من تسليمه قبل ان تاتى ساعته و قبل ان يؤسس الفصح الجديد

The Readings and Events

Subject: The opposition by the chief priests

First hour: John 10:17-21; Splitting up regarding His authority
Third hour: Mark 14:3-11; Betrayal by Judas
Sixth hour: John 12:36-43; Their unbelief in Him
Ninth hour: John 10:29-38; Refuting their accusation
Eleventh hour: John 12:44-50; Condemning them by His speech

Days are passing, and the Lord of glory is preparing to offer Himself a sacrifice on behalf of the whole world by His own will and His choice. Our Savior concealed where He would eat the Passover so that Judas would not betray Him before His hour and before establishing the new Passover.

الساعة الأولى من ليلة الخميس من البصخة المقدسة
The First Hour of Thursday Eve of the Holy Pascha

Ezekiel 43:5-11

And the Spirit took me up, and brought me into the inner court. And behold, the house of the Lord was full of glory. And I stood, and behold, there was a voice out of the house of one speaking to me, and a man stood near me, and he said to me, Son of man, you have seen the place of My throne, and the place of the soles of My feet, in which My name shall dwell in the midst of the house of Israel forever; and the house of Israel shall no more profane My holy name, they and their princes, by their fornication, or by the murders of their princes in the midst of them; when they set My doorway by their doorway, and My thresholds near to their thresholds; and they made My wall as it were joining myMself and them, and they profaned My holy name with their iniquities which they wrought; and I destroyed them in My wrath and with slaughter. And now let them put away from Me their fornication, and the murders of their princes, and I will dwell in the midst of them forever. And you, son of man, show the house to the house of Israel, that they may cease from their sins; and show its aspect and the arrangement of it. And they shall bear their punishment for all the things that they have done. And you shall describe the house, and its entrances, and the plan thereof, and all its ordinances, and you shall make known to them all the regulations of it, and describe them before them. And they shall keep all My commandments, and all My ordinances, and do them. Glory be to the Holy Trinity. Amen

(من حزقيال النبى 3 : 5 - 11)

فحملنى الروح وأدخلنى إلى الدار الداخلية . وإذا البيت ممتلئ من مجد الرب . فوقفت وإذا بصوت يتكلم معى من البيت وكان الرجل واقفاً بجانبى . وقال لي: أترى يا إبن الإنسان مكان عرشى ، وموضع باطن قدمى هؤلاء الذين يكون فيهم اسمى في وسط بيت إسرائيل إلى الأبد؟ ولن ينجس بعد بيت إسرائيل اسمى القدوس ، هم ومدبريهم ، في الاثم أوقتل مدبريهم فى وسطهم . عندما جعلوا بابى عند أبوابهم . وأعتابى بجانب أعتابهم . وجعلوا سياجهم كما لو كانت تمسكنى معهم . فنجسوا اسمى القدوس بآثامهم التى يفعلونها . فسحقتهم بغضبى قتلاً. والآن فيتركوا شرورهم وقتل مدبريهم أمامى . فأحل فى وسطهم إلى الأبد . وأنت أيضاً يا إبن الإنسان أخبر بيت إسرائيل عن البيت وشكله ورسمه . فيكفون عن خطاياهم . وهؤلاء ينالون عقابهم من أجل كل ما صنعوه. وترسم البيت وهيئته ومخارجه ومداخله ونظامه . وكل أوامره أخبرهم بها . وأكتب ذلك أمامهم فيحفظون جميع حقوقى وجميع وصاياى ويعملون بها . مجداً للثالوث القدوس.

Pascha Praise - B (12 times), Page: 7	تسبحة البصخة B (12 مرة) ، صفحة :

The Psalm
Ⲯⲁⲗⲙⲟⲥ ⲍ̅ⲏ̅ : ⲁ̅ ⲛⲉⲙ ⲓ̅ⲅ̅

Psalms 68:1, 13			(مز 68: 1و13)
Save me, O God; for the waters have come in to my soul. According to the multitude of Your compassions look upon me. Alleluia	Ⲙⲁⲧⲁⲛϧⲟⲓ Ⲫϯ ϫⲉ ⲁ ϩⲁⲛⲙⲱⲟⲩ : ϣⲉ ⲉ̀ϧⲟⲩⲛ ϣⲁ ⲧⲁⲯⲩⲭⲏ : ⲕⲁⲧⲁ ⲡ̀ⲁϣⲁⲓ ⲛ̀ⲧⲉ ⲛⲉⲕⲙⲉⲧϣⲉⲛϩⲏⲧ : ϫⲟⲩϣⲧ ⲉ̀ϧⲣⲏⲓ ⲉ̀ϫⲱⲓ.ⲁ̅ⲗ̅.	ماطانخوى إفنوتى جيه أ هان موؤو : شيه إيخون شا طابشى : كاطا إب أشاى إنتيه نيكميت شيتهيت : جووشت إخرى إيجوى . الليلويا .	احينى يا الله فان المياه قد بلغت إلى نفسي . أنظر إليَّ ككثرة رأفتك . الليلويا.

Introduction to the Gospel, Page: 8	مقدمة الأنجيل ، صفحة :

The Gospel

Ⲉⲩⲁⲅⲅⲉⲗⲓⲟⲛ Ⲕⲁⲧⲁ Ⲓⲱⲁⲛⲛⲏⲛ Ⲕⲉⲫ ⲓ̄ : ⲓ̅ⲍ̅ - ⲕ̅ⲁ̅

John 10:17-21

"Therefore My Father loves Me, because I lay down My life that I may take it again. No one takes it from Me, but I lay it down of Myself. I have power to lay it down, and I have power to take it again. This command I have received from My Father." Therefore there was a division again among the Jews because of these sayings. And many of them said, "He has a demon and is mad. Why do you listen to Him?" Others said, "These are not the words of one who has a demon. Can a demon open the eyes of the blind? Glory be to God forever, Amen.

Ⲉⲑⲃⲉ ⲫⲁⲓ ϥⲙⲉⲓ ⲙ̀ⲙⲟⲓ ⲛ̀ϫⲉ ⲡⲁⲓⲱⲧ : ϫⲉ ⲁⲛⲟⲕ ϯⲛⲁⲭⲱ ⲛ̀ⲧⲁⲯⲩⲭⲏ ϩⲓⲛⲁ ⲟⲛ ⲛ̀ⲧⲁϭⲓⲧⲥ : ⲙ̀ⲙⲟⲛ ϩⲗⲓ ⲱⲗⲓ ⲙ̀ⲙⲟⲥ ⲛ̀ⲧⲟⲧ : ⲁⲗⲗⲁ ⲁⲛⲟⲕ ⲉ̀ϯⲭⲱ ⲙ̀ⲙⲟⲥ ⲉ̀ϧⲣⲏⲓ ⲉⲃⲟⲗ ϩⲓⲧⲟⲧ ⲙ̀ⲙⲁⲩⲁⲧ : ⲟⲩⲟⲛ ⲉ̀ⲣϣⲓϣⲓ ⲙ̀ⲙⲁⲩ ⲉⲭⲁⲥ ⲟⲩⲟⲛ ϯⲉⲣϣⲓϣⲓ ⲙ̀ⲙⲁⲩ ⲟⲛ ⲉ̀ϭⲓⲧⲥ : ⲑⲁⲓ ⲧⲉ ϯⲉⲛⲧⲟⲗⲏ ⲉ̀ⲧⲁⲓϭⲓⲧⲥ ⲉⲃⲟⲗ ϩⲓⲧⲉⲛ ⲡⲁⲓⲱⲧ .

Ⲟⲩⲥⲭⲓⲥⲙⲁ ⲟⲛ ⲁϥϣⲱⲡⲓ ϧⲉⲛ Ⲛⲓⲓⲟⲩⲇⲁⲓ ⲉⲑⲃⲉ ⲡⲁⲓⲥⲁϫⲓ : ϩⲁⲛⲙⲏϣ ⲇⲉ ⲉ̀ⲃⲟⲗ ⲛ̀ϧⲏⲧⲟⲩ ⲛⲁⲩⲭⲱ ⲙ̀ⲙⲟⲥ ϫⲉ ⲟⲩⲟⲛ ⲟⲩⲇⲉⲙⲱⲛ ⲛⲉⲙⲁϥ ⲟⲩⲟϩ ϥⲗⲟⲃⲓ : ⲉⲑⲃⲉ ⲟⲩ ⲧⲉⲧⲉⲛⲥⲱⲧⲉⲙ ⲉ̀ⲣⲟϥ .

Ϩⲁⲛⲕⲉⲭⲱⲟⲩⲛⲓ ⲇⲉ ⲛⲁⲩⲭⲱ ⲙ̀ⲙⲟⲥ ϫⲉ ⲛⲁⲓⲥⲁϫⲓ ⲛⲁⲟⲩⲣⲱⲙⲓ ⲁⲛ ⲡⲉ ⲉ̀ⲟⲩⲟⲛ ⲟⲩⲇⲉⲙⲱⲛ ⲛⲉⲙⲁϥ ⲙⲏ ⲟⲩⲟⲛ ϣϫⲟⲙ ⲛ̀ⲟⲩⲇⲉⲙⲱⲛ ⲉ̀ⲁⲟⲩⲱⲛ ⲛ̀ⲛⲓⲃⲁⲗ ⲛ̀ⲟⲩⲃⲉⲗⲗⲉ . ⲟⲩⲱϣⲧ ⲙ̀ⲡⲓⲉⲩⲁⲅⲅⲉⲗⲓⲟⲛ ⲉⲑⲩ .

(21 - 17 : 10 يوحنا)

من أجل هذا يحبنى أبي لأنى أضع نفسى لآخذها أيضاً . ليس أحد يأخذهــا منى . ولكنى اضعها أنا من ذاتي وحدى . ولي سلطان أن أضعها . ولى سلطان أن آخذها أيضاً . وهذه هى الوصية التى قبلتها من أبى . فحدث أيضاً انشقاق بين اليهود لأجل هذا الكلام . فقال كثيرون منهم: أنه به شيطان وقد جن ، فلماذا تسمعون له . وآخرون قالوا: ان هذا الكلام ليس كلام من به شيطان ، هل شيطاناً يقدر أن يفتح أعين العميان ؟ والمجد لله دائماً .

Introduction to the Exposition, Page: 9	مقدمة الطرح ، صفحة :

Exposition

Christ our Lord, master and king reveals his divinity and dominion. The God who prevails over all hegemony and power in heavens and on earth. That is why He tells us: My Father loves Me and I humble Myself to earn it. No one can force the cross on Me, but only through My own will that I humble Myself and that I have the power to take it away. There developed a schism among the Jews because of these words that He told them. The hypocrites among them said He is crazy, do not listen to Him. Others said, these are not the words of a possessed man. Crazy people cannot open the eyes of someone born blind. Truly He is the light for the faithful hearts—except for the contrary Jews whom he blinded the vision of their hearts and their eyes—so that they may not see with their eyes and that they may not understand with their hearts and return to Him with true love, great hope and total honesty and that He may forgive their sins so as to save them of their transgressions.

طـرح

ربنا وسيدنا وملكنا المسيح يظهر لاهوته وسلطانه . أنه هو الإله المتعالى على كل رئاسة وكل سلطان فى السماء وعلى الأرض . فلذلك قال: أن الآب يحبنى ، فانى أضع نفسى لكى آخذها . وليس أحد ينزعها منى لكن أنا الذى اضعها بإرادتى ، فإن لى سلطان أن اضعها ولى سلطان أن آخذها . فصار إنشقاق بين اليهود من أجل هذا الكلام الذى قاله لهم ، وقال قوم من المنافقين: أنه مجنون لماذا تسمعون منه ، وقال آخرون: هذا الكلام ليس هو كلام إنسان به شيطان ، لا يقدر مجنون أن يفتح عينى أعمى مولود . هو بالحقيقة الذى يضىء أعين قلوب المؤمنون به ما خلا اليهود المخالفين ، طمس عيون قلوبهم وأجسادهم كيلا ينظروا بعيونهم ويفهموا بقلوبهم ويرجعوا إليه بمحبة حقيقية ورجاء عظيم وأمانة كاملة ويغفر لهم كثرة خطاياهم ويسامحهم بزلاتهم .

(North side) Christ our Savior; has come and has borne suffering; that through His Passion; He may save us.

(South side) Let us glorify Him; and exalt His Name; for He had mercy on us; according to His great mercy.

(مرد بحرى) المسيح مخلصنا جاء وتألم عنا لكى بألامه يخلصنا .

(مرد قبلى) فلنمجده ونرفع إسمه لأنه صنع معنا رحمة كعظيم رحمته .

| The Conclusion of the Exposition, Page: | 9 | ختام الطرح ، صفحة : |

الساعة الثالثة من ليلة الخميس من البصخة المقدسة
The Third Hour of Thursday Eve of the Holy Pascha

Amos 4:4-13

You went into Bethel and sinned, and you multiplied sin at Gilgal; and you brought your meat offerings in the morning, and your tithes every third day. And they read the law outdoors, and called for public professions: proclaim aloud that the children of Israel have loved these things, says the Lord. And your teeth shall be idle in all your cities, and lack of bread in all your places; yet you did not return to Me, says the Lord. Also I withheld from you the rain three months before the harvest, and I will rain upon one city, and on another city I will not rain; one part shall be rained upon, and the part on which I shall not rain shall be dried up. And the inhabitants of two or three cities shall be gathered to one city to drink water, and they shall not be satisfied; yet you have not returned to Me, says the Lord. I blasted you with parching, and with blight; you multiplied your gardens, your vineyards, and your fig trees, and the cankerworm devoured your olive trees; yet still you did not return to Me, says the Lord. I sent pestilence among you by the way of Egypt, and slew your young men with the sword, together with your horses that were taken captive; and in My wrath against you I set fire to your camps; yet not even thus did you return to Me, says the Lord. I overthrew you, as God overthrew Sodom and Gomorrah, and you became as a brand plucked out of the fire; yet not even thus did you return to Me, says the Lord. Therefore thus will I do to you, O Israel: because I will do thus to you, prepare to call on your God, O Israel. For behold, I am He that strengthens the thunder, and creates the wind, and proclaims His Christ to men, forming the morning and the darkness, and mounting on the high places of the earth; The Lord God Almighty is His name. Glory be to the Holy Trinity. Amen

(من عاموس النبى ص 4 : 4 ألخ)

هذا ما يقولـه الرب الإلـه: انكم دخلتم إلى بيـت فأثمتم ، وفى جلجـال جلعـاد أكثرتم النفاق . وفى كل صباح قدمتم ذبائحكم . وفى اليوم الثالث عشوركم . وقرأتم ناموساً خارجاً . طلبوا الإعتراف والانذار لأن بنى إسرائيل أحبوا هذه ، قال الرب الإله . فأنى أنا سأعطيكم ضرس الأسنان فى جميع مدنكم . وعوز الخبز فى جميع مدنكم. فلم ترجعوا إليّ ، يقول الرب . وأنا أيضاً منعت عنكم المطر قبل الحصاد بثلاثة أشهر. سأمطر على مدينة واحدة وعلى مدينة أخرى لا أمطر. جزء واحد يشرب ، والجزء الآخر لا أمطر عليه فيجف . فتجتمع مدينتان أو ثلاث إلى مدينة واحدة ليشربوا ماء ولا يرتووا. وكذلك لم ترجعوا إليّ ، قال الرب . ضربتكم الحمى والبرد فأكثرتم نجاساتكم . وأكل القَ○مُص (أبناء الجراد) جناتكم وكرومكم وتينكم وزيتونكم . وكذلك أيضاً لم ترجعوا إليّ ، قال الرب . فأرسلت عليكم وباء فى طرق مصر . قتلت بالسيف شبانكم مع سلب خيلكم . وأتيت بالنار على عساكركم بغضب . وهكذا أيضاً لم ترجعوا إليّ قال الرب . فهدمتكم كما هدم الله سدوم وعمورة فصرتم كعشب قد أحرق بالنار ولم ترجعوا إليّ ، يقول الرب . لذلك أصنع بك هكذا يا إسرائيل . وبما أنى اصنع هذا ، فاستعد لتدعو إلهك يا إسرائيل. فها أنا المثبت الرعد والخالق الريح والمبشر بمسيحه فى البشر. الخالق الصبح والنسمة والراكب على أعالى الأرض ، الرب الإله ضابط الكل هو إسمه . مجداً للثالوث القدوس .

Pascha Praise - B (12 times), Page: 7	تسبحة البصخة B (12 مرة) ، صفحة :

The Psalm

Ψⲁⲗⲙⲟⲥ ⲛ̅ⲅ̅ : ⲓⲏ ⲛⲉⲙ ⲁ̅

Psalms 54:18, 1

His words were smoother than oil, yet are they darts. Hearken, O God, to my prayer; and disregard not my supplication. Alleluia

Ⲁⲩϭⲛⲟⲛ ⲛ̀ϫⲉ ⲛⲉϥⲥⲁϫⲓ ⲉ̀ϩⲟⲧⲉ ⲟⲩⲛⲉϩ : ⲟⲩⲟϩ ⲛ̀ⲑⲱⲟⲩ ϩⲁⲛⲥⲟⲑⲛⲉϥ ⲛⲉ : ϭⲓⲥⲙⲏ Ⲫϯ ⲉ̀ⲧⲁⲡⲣⲟⲥⲉⲩⲭⲏ : ⲟⲩⲟϩ ⲙ̀ⲡⲉⲣϩⲓ ⲛ̀ϩⲟ ⲙ̀ⲡⲁⲧⲱⲃϩ.ⲁⲗ .

أفتشنون إنجيه نيف صاجى إهوتيه أوونيه : أووه إنثوؤو هان صوثنيف نيه : تشى إسمى إفنوتى إطا إبروس إفشى : أووه إمبير هى إبهو إمبا طوبه . الليلويا .

(مز 54: 18 و1)

كلامه الين من الدهن وهو نصال . انصت يا الله لصلاتى . ولا تغفل عن تضرعي . الليلويا الليلويا .

The Gospel

Ⲉⲩⲁⲅⲅⲉⲗⲓⲟⲛ Ⲕⲁⲧⲁ Ⲙⲁⲣⲕⲟⲛ Ⲕⲉⲫ ⲓⲇ̅ : ⲅ̅ - ⲓⲁ̅

Mark 14:3-11

And being in Bethany at the house of Simon the leper, as He sat at the table, a woman came having an alabaster flask of very costly oil of spikenard. Then she broke the flask and poured it on His head. But there were some who were indignant among themselves, and said, "Why was this fragrant oil wasted? For it might have been sold for more than three hundred denarii and given to the poor." And they criticized her sharply. But Jesus said, "Let her alone. Why do you trouble her? She has done a good work for Me. For you have the poor with you always, and whenever you wish you may do them good; but Me you do not have always. She has done what she could. She has come beforehand to anoint My body for burial. Assuredly, I say to you, wherever this gospel is preached in the whole world, what this woman has done will also be told as a memorial to her." Then Judas Iscariot, one of the twelve, went to the chief priests to betray Him to them. And when they heard it, they were glad, and promised to give him money. So he sought how he might conveniently betray Him. Glory be to God forever, Amen.

Ⲟⲩⲟϩ ⲉϥⲭⲏ ϧⲉⲛ Ⲃⲏⲑ ⲁⲛⲓⲁ ϧⲉⲛ ⲡ̅ⲏⲓ ⲛ̅Ⲥⲓⲙⲱⲛ ⲡⲓⲕⲁⲕⲥⲉϩⲧ ⲉϥⲣⲱⲧⲉⲃ : ⲁⲥⲓ ⲛ̅ϫⲉ ⲟⲩⲥϩⲓⲙⲓ ⲉⲣⲉ ⲟⲩⲟⲛ ⲟⲩⲙⲟⲕⲓ ⲛ̅ⲥⲟϫⲉⲛ ⲛ̅ⲧⲟⲧⲥ ⲛⲁⲣⲇⲟⲥ ⲙ̅ⲡⲓⲥⲧⲓⲕⲏ ⲉⲛⲁϣⲉ ⲛ̅ⲥⲟⲩⲉⲛϥ : ⲉⲁⲥϭⲟⲩϧⲉⲙ ⲙ̅ⲡⲓⲙⲟⲕⲓ ⲁⲥϧⲟϫⲧ ⲉϫⲉⲛ ⲧⲉϥⲁⲫⲉ . Ⲛⲁⲣⲉ ϩⲁⲛⲟⲩⲟⲛ ⲭⲣⲉⲙⲣⲉⲙ ⲛⲉⲙ ⲛⲟⲩⲉⲣⲏⲟⲩ : ϫⲉ ⲉⲑⲃⲉ ⲟⲩ ⲁ ⲡⲁⲓⲧⲁⲕⲟ ⲛ̅ⲧⲉ ⲡⲁⲓⲥⲟϫⲉⲛ ϣⲱⲡⲓ . Ⲛⲉ ⲟⲩⲟⲛ ϣ̅ϫⲟⲙ ⲅⲁⲣ ⲉ̅ϯ ⲙ̅ⲫⲁⲓ ⲉⲃⲟⲗ ⲥⲁ ⲡ̅ϣⲱⲓ ⲛ̅ϣⲟⲙⲧ ϣⲉ ⲛ̅ⲥⲁⲑⲉⲣⲓ ⲟⲩⲟϩ ⲉ̅ⲧⲏⲓⲧⲟⲩ ⲛ̅ⲛⲓϩⲏⲕⲓ : ⲟⲩⲟϩ ⲛⲁⲩⲙ̅ⲃⲟⲛ ⲉ̅ⲣⲟⲥ .

Ⲡⲉϫⲉ Ⲓⲏⲥ ⲛⲱⲟⲩ ϫⲉ ⲭⲁⲥ : ⲁ ϭⲱⲧⲉⲛ ⲧⲉⲧⲉⲛϯϭⲓⲥⲓ ⲛⲁⲥ : ⲟⲩϩⲱⲃ ⲉⲛⲁⲛⲉϥ ⲡⲉⲧⲁⲥⲉⲣϩⲱⲃ ⲉ̅ⲣⲟϥ ⲛ̅ϧⲏⲧ . Ⲛ̅ⲥⲟⲩ ⲛⲓⲃⲉⲛ ⲛⲓϩⲏⲕⲓ ⲥⲉ ⲛⲉⲙⲱⲧⲉⲛ : ⲟⲩⲟϩ ⲉϣⲱⲡ ⲛ̅ⲧⲉⲧⲉⲛⲟⲩⲱϣ ⲟⲩⲟⲛ ϣ̅ϫⲟⲙ ⲙ̅ⲙⲱⲧⲉⲛ ⲉ̅ⲉⲣⲡⲉⲑⲛⲁⲛⲉϥ ⲛⲉⲙⲱⲟⲩ ⲛ̅ⲥⲟⲩ ⲛⲓⲃⲉⲛ : ⲁⲛⲟⲕ ⲇⲉ ϯ ⲛⲉⲙⲱⲧⲉⲛ ⲁⲛ ⲛ̅ⲥⲟⲩ ⲛⲓⲃⲉⲛ . Ⲫⲏ ⲉⲧⲁⲥϭⲓⲧⲥ ⲁⲥⲁⲓϥ : ⲁⲥⲉⲣϣⲟⲣⲡ ⲅⲁⲣ ⲛ̅ⲑⲁϩⲥ ⲙ̅ⲡⲁⲥⲱⲙⲁ ⲙ̅ⲡⲁⲓⲥⲟϫⲉⲛ ⲉ̅ⲡ̅ϫⲓⲛⲕⲟⲥⲧ . Ⲁⲙⲏⲛ ϯϫⲱ ⲙ̅ⲙⲟⲥ ⲛⲱⲧⲉⲛ : ϫⲉ ⲡⲓⲙⲁ ⲉ̅ⲧⲟⲩⲛⲁϩⲓⲱⲓϣ ⲙ̅ⲡⲁⲓⲉⲩⲁⲅⲅⲉⲗⲓⲟⲛ ⲙ̅ⲙⲟϥ ϧⲉⲛ ⲡⲓⲕⲟⲥⲙⲟⲥ ⲧⲏⲣϥ : ⲫⲏϩⲱϥ ⲉⲧⲁ ⲑⲁⲓⲁⲓϥ ⲉ̅ⲧⲉⲥⲁϫⲓ ⲙ̅ⲙⲟϥ ⲉⲩⲙⲉⲩⲓ ⲛⲁⲥ . Ⲟⲩⲟϩ Ⲓⲟⲩⲇⲁⲥ Ⲡⲓⲥⲕⲁⲣⲓⲱⲧⲏⲥ ⲡⲓⲟⲩⲁⲓ ⲛ̅ⲧⲉ ⲡⲓⲙⲏⲧ ⲥⲛⲁⲩ : ⲁϥϣⲉⲛⲁϥ ϩⲁ ⲛⲓⲁⲣⲭⲏ ⲉⲣⲉⲩⲥ ϩⲓⲛⲁ ⲛ̅ⲧⲉϥⲧⲏⲓϥ ⲛⲱⲟⲩ . Ⲛ̅ⲑⲱⲟⲩ ⲇⲉ ⲉⲧⲁⲩⲥⲱⲧⲉⲙ ⲁⲩⲣⲁϣⲓ ⲟⲩⲟϩ ⲁⲩϯ ⲛⲁϥ ⲛ̅ⲟⲩϩⲁⲧ : ⲟⲩⲟϩ ⲛⲁϥⲕⲱϯ ϫⲉ ⲡⲱⲥ ϥⲛⲁⲧⲏⲓϥ ϧⲉⲛ ⲟⲩⲉⲩⲕⲉⲣⲓⲁ . ⲟⲩⲱϣⲧ ⲙ̅ⲡⲓⲉⲩⲁⲅⲅⲉⲗⲓⲟⲛ ⲉⲑ .

(مرقس 14 : 3 - 11)

وفيما هو فى بيت عنيا فى منزل سمعان الأبرص وهو متكئ . جاءت إمرأة معها قارورة طيب من ناردين خالص كثير الثمن. فكسرت القارورة وسكبته على رأسه . وان قوماً تذمروا فيما بينهم قائلين : لما كان إتلاف هذا الطيب ، فإنه كان يمكن أن يُباع هذا بأكثر من ثلاثمئة دينار ويعطى للمساكين. وكانوا يؤنبونها . فقال لهم يسوع: دعوها ، ما بالكم تعنفونها؟ عملاً حسناً عملته بي . لأن المساكين عندكم فى كل حين . وإن أردتم أن تحسنوا إليهم متى شئتم فى كل حين . وأما أنا فلست عندكم فى كل حين . وانها قد صنعت ما فى وسعها وقد سبقت فطيبت جسدى لدفنى . الحق أقول لكم . أنه حيثما يكرز بهذا الانجيل فى العالم كله . يخبر أيضاً بما صنعته هذه تذكاراً لها. وان يهوذا الاسخريوطى أحد الاثنى عشر ، ذهب إلى رؤساء الكهنة ليسلمه إليهم . اما هم فلما سمعوا ، فرحوا وأعطوه فضة . وكان يطلب كيف يجد فرصة ليسلمه . والمجد لله دائماً .

Exposition

The woman poured the precious spikenard over the Lord's feet and who wiped them with her hair because of her loyalty and great love. Thus, she earned for herself good dividends and her name filled the earth. The disciples spread the word about her deed in all corners of the earth. Her name is honored in all generations and mentioned by all the faithful. Behold these spiritual gifts and the high esteem she gained. Let us be filled with zeal over her virtue and love of the Lord with all our hearts. Not like Judas who became infuriated by her good deed. This cost him his evil thoughts that led him to betray his master. And the silver he received as a price of the precious blood (of Jesus Christ) will perish with him in hell. His name disappeared in a single generation, and he was denied descendants on earth.

(North side) Christ our Savior; has come and has borne suffering; that through His Passion; He may save us.

(South side) Let us glorify Him; and exalt His Name; for He had mercy on us; according to His great mercy.

طـرح

المرأة التى دهنت رجلى الرب بالطيب الفائق ، ومسحتهما بشعر رأسها من أجل ثبات أمانتها وحبها الكثير ، هذه اقتنت لها نصيباً صالحاً وصيتاً عالياً فى جميع العالم ، وبشر الرسل بما فعلته فى جميع زوايا الأرض . فدام إسمها فى جميع الأجيال يتلوه سائر المؤمنين. يا لهذه المواهب الروحانية وهذه الكرامات العالية التى فازت بها . فلنمتلئ غيرة على فضيلتها ونحب الرب من كل قلوبنا ، وليس مثل يهوذا الذى حنق عليها من أجل انها صنعت الخير . فكلفته أفكاره الشريرة أن يبيع سيده ، والفضة التى أخذها ثمن الذكى ، ستهبط معه إلى الجحيم. ليفنى إسمه فى جيل واحد ولا يكون له خلف على الأرض .

(مرد بحرى) المسيح مخلصنا جاء وتألم عنا لكى بألامه يخلصنا .

(مرد قبلى) فلنمجده ونرفع إسمه لأنه صنع معنا رحمة كعظيم رحمته .

The Conclusion of the Exposition, Page: 9   : ختام الطرح ، صفحة

الساعة السادسة من ليلة الخميس من البصخة المقدسة
The Sixth Hour of Thursday Eve of the Holy Pascha

Amos 3:1-11

Hear this word, O house of Israel, which the Lord has spoken concerning you, and against the whole family whom I brought up out of the land of Egypt, saying, You especially have I known out of all the families of the earth: therefore will I take vengeance upon you for all your sins. Shall two walk together at all, if they do not know one another? Will a lion roar out of his thicket if he has no prey? Will a young lion utter his voice at all out of his lair, if he has taken nothing? Will a bird fall on the earth without a fowler? Will a snare be taken up from the earth without having taken anything? Shall the trumpet sound in the city, and the people not be alarmed? Shall there be evil in a city which the Lord has not wrought? For the Lord God will do nothing without revealing instruction to His servants the prophets. A lion shall roar, and who will not be alarmed? The Lord God has spoken, and who will not prophesy? Proclaim it to the regions among the Assyrians, and to the regions of Egypt, and say, Gather yourselves to the mountain of Samaria, and behold many wonderful things in the midst of it, and the oppression that is in it. And she knew not what things would come against her, says the Lord, even those that store up wrong and misery in their countries. Therefore thus says the Lord God; O Tyre, your land shall be made desolate round about you; and he shall bring down your strength out of you. Glory be to the Holy Trinity. Amen

(من عاموس النبى 3 : 1 - 11)

إسمعوا هذا القول الذى تكلمت به عليكم يا بيت إسرائيل ، وعلى كل القبائل التى أخرجتها من أرض مصر ، قائلاً : أياكم عرفت من بين جميع قبائل الأرض . فلذلك أنتقم منكم عن جميع خطاياكم. أيسير إثنان معاً ولا يعرف بعضهما البعض قط؟ أيزمجر الأسد فى الغابة وليس له فريسة؟ أيطلق الشبل صوته من عرينه قط إلا إذا خطف شيئاً؟ أيسقط طير على الأرض من غير قانص؟ أيكون فخ على الأرض من غير أن يصيد شيئاً؟ أيصوت بوق فى مدينة ولا يهلع الشعب؟ هل تحدث بلية فى مدينة والرب لم يصنعها؟ أن الرب الإله لا يصنع أمراً إلا ويعلن تأديبه لعبيده الأنبياء . أسد قد زمجر فمن لا يخاف . الرب الإله تكلم فمن لا يتنبأ . اخبروا كور الأشوريين وكور مصر وقولوا. اجتمعوا على جبل السامرة . وانظروا الغرائب الكثيرة التى فى وسطها والجور الذى فى داخلها . ولم تعلم ما يكون أمامها. يقول الرب: بما أنهم يكنزون ظلماً وشقاء فى كورهم ، فلذلك ما يقوله الرب الإله لصور: أن أرضك التى حولك تخرب ، وقوتك تسقط منك . مجداً للثالوث القدوس .

Pascha Praise - B (12 times), Page: 7   تسبحة البصخة B (12 مرة) ، صفحة : 7

The Psalm

Ⲯⲁⲗⲙⲟⲥ ⲣ̅ⲗ̅ⲑ̅ : ⲁ̅ ⲛⲉⲙ ⲃ̅

Psalms 139:1-2			(مز 139: 1 و2)
Rescue me, O Lord, from the evil man; deliver me from the unjust man. Who have devised injustice in their hearts; all the day they prepared war. Alleluia	Ⲛⲁϩⲙⲉⲧ ⲡ̀ϭⲟⲓⲥ ⲥⲁⲃⲟⲗ ⲛ̀ⲟⲩⲣⲱⲙⲓ ⲉϥϩⲱⲟⲩ : ⲉ̀ⲃⲟⲗ ϩⲁ ⲟⲩⲣⲱⲙⲓ ⲛ̀ⲣⲉϥϭⲓ ⲛ̀ϫⲟⲛⲥ ⲙⲁⲧⲟⲩⲃⲟⲓ. Ⲛⲏⲉⲧⲁⲩⲥⲟϭⲛⲓ ⲛ̀ϩⲁⲛϭⲓ ⲛ̀ϫⲟⲛⲥ ϧⲉⲛ ⲡⲟⲩϩⲏⲧ : ⲙ̀ⲡⲓⲉ̀ϩⲟⲟⲩ ⲧⲏⲣϥ ⲁⲩⲥⲟⲃϯ ⲛ̀ϩⲁⲛⲃⲱⲧⲥ.ⲁⲗ.	ناهميت إبتشويس صافول إنؤورومى إفهوأوو : إيفول ها أوورومى إنريفتشى إنجونس ماطوؤفوى . ني إيطاف صوتشنى إنهانتشى إنجونس خين بووهيت : إمبى إيهوؤو تيرف أفصوبتى إنهان فوتس . الليلويا.	نجنى يارب من إنسان شرير ومن رجل ظالم انقذنى . الذين تفكروا بالظلم فى قلبهم النهار كله كانوا يستعدون للقتال . الليلويا .

Introduction to the Gospel, Page: 8   مقدمة الأنجيل ، صفحة : 8

The Gospel

Ⲉⲩⲁⲅⲅⲉⲗⲓⲟⲛ Ⲕⲁⲧⲁ Ⲓⲱⲁⲛⲛⲏⲛ Ⲕⲉⲫ ⲓ̅ⲃ̅ : ⲗ̅ⲋ̅ - ⲙ̅ⲅ̅

John 12:36-43

These things Jesus spoke, and departed, and was hidden from them. But although He had done so many signs before them, they did not believe in Him, that the word of Isaiah the prophet might be fulfilled, which he spoke: "LORD, WHO HAS BELIEVED OUR REPORT? AND TO WHOM HAS THE ARM OF THE LORD BEEN REVEALED?" Therefore they could not believe, because Isaiah said again: "HE HAS BLINDED THEIR EYES AND HARDENED THEIR HEARTS, LEST THEY SHOULD SEE WITH THEIR EYES, LEST THEY SHOULD UNDERSTAND WITH THEIR HEARTS AND TURN, SO THAT I SHOULD HEAL THEM." These things Isaiah said when he saw His glory and spoke of Him. Nevertheless even among the rulers many believed in Him, but because of the Pharisees they did not confess Him, lest they should be put out of the synagogue; for they loved the praise of men more than the praise of God. Glory be to God forever, Amen.

Ⲛⲁⲓ ⲉⲧⲁϥϫⲟⲧⲟⲩ ⲛ̀ϫⲉ Ⲓⲏ̅ⲥ̅ ⲁϥϣⲉⲛⲁϥ ⲁϥⲭⲟⲡϥ ⲉ̀ⲃⲟⲗ ⲥⲁⲣⲱⲟⲩ . Ⲛⲁⲓⲙⲏⲱ ⲇⲉ ⲙ̀ⲙⲏⲓⲛⲓ ⲁϥⲁⲓⲧⲟⲩ ⲙ̀ⲡⲟⲩⲙ̀ⲑⲟ ⲉ̀ⲃⲟⲗ ⲙ̀ⲡⲟⲩⲛⲁⲥϯ ⲉ̀ⲣⲟϥ : ⲥⲓⲛⲁ ⲛ̀ⲧⲉϥϫⲱⲕ ⲉ̀ⲃⲟⲗ ⲛ̀ϫⲉ ⲡⲥⲁϫⲓ ⲛ̀Ⲏⲥⲁⲏⲁⲥ ⲡⲓⲡⲣⲟⲫⲏⲧⲏⲥ ⲫⲏⲉⲧⲁϥϫⲟϥ : ϫⲉ ⲡⲟ̅ⲥ̅ ⲛⲓⲙ ⲡⲉ ⲉⲧⲁϥⲛⲁⲥϯ ⲉ̀ⲧⲉⲛⲥⲙⲏ : ⲟⲩⲟⲥ ⲡ̀ϣⲱⲃϣ ⲙ̀ⲡⲟ̅ⲥ̅ ⲉⲧⲁϥϭⲱⲣⲡ ⲉ̀ⲛⲓⲙ . Ⲉⲑⲃⲉ ⲫⲁⲓ ⲛⲉ ⲙ̀ⲙⲟⲛ ⲩ̀ϫⲟⲙ ⲙ̀ⲙⲱⲟⲩ ⲉ̀ⲛⲁⲥϯ : ϫⲉ ⲁϥϫⲟⲥ ⲟⲛ ⲛ̀ϫⲉ Ⲏⲥⲁⲏⲁⲥ : ϫⲉ ⲁϥⲑⲱⲙ ⲛ̀ⲛⲟⲩⲃⲁⲗ : ⲟⲩⲟⲥ ⲁϥⲑⲱⲙ ⲙ̀ⲡⲟⲩⲥⲏⲧ : ⲥⲓⲛⲁ ⲛ̀ⲧⲟⲩϣ̀ⲧⲉⲙⲛⲁⲩ ⲛ̀ⲛⲟⲩⲃⲁⲗ : ⲟⲩⲟⲥ ⲛ̀ⲧⲟⲩϣ̀ⲧⲉⲙⲕⲁϯ ϧⲉⲛ ⲡⲟⲩⲥⲏⲧ : ⲟⲩⲟⲥ ⲛ̀ⲧⲟⲩⲕⲟⲧⲟⲩ ⲥⲁⲣⲟⲓ ⲛ̀ⲧⲁ ⲧⲟⲩϫⲱⲟⲩ : ⲛⲁⲓ ⲁϥϫⲟⲧⲟⲩ ⲛ̀ϫⲉ Ⲏⲥⲁⲏⲁⲥ ϫⲉ ⲁϥⲛⲁⲩ ⲉ̀ⲡⲱⲟⲩ ⲙ̀Ⲫϯ ⲟⲩⲟⲥ ⲁϥⲥⲁϫⲓ ⲉⲑⲃⲏⲧϥ . Ⲟⲙⲱⲥ ⲙⲉⲛⲧⲟⲓ ⲟⲩⲙⲏϣ ⲉ̀ⲃⲟⲗ ϧⲉⲛ ⲛⲓⲕⲉⲁⲣⲭⲱⲛ ⲁⲩⲛⲁⲥϯ ⲉ̀ⲣⲟϥ : ⲁⲗⲗⲁ ⲛⲁⲩⲟⲩⲱⲛⲥ ⲙ̀ⲙⲟϥ ⲉ̀ⲃⲟⲗ ⲁⲛ ⲡⲉ ⲉⲑⲃⲉ ⲛⲓⲫⲁⲣⲓⲥⲉⲟⲥ : ϫⲉ ⲛ̀ⲛⲟⲩⲁⲓⲧⲟⲩ ⲙ̀ⲁⲡⲟⲩⲥⲩⲛⲁⲅⲱⲅⲟⲥ : ⲁⲩⲙⲉⲛⲣⲉ ⲡ̀ⲱⲟⲩ ⲅⲁⲣ ⲛ̀ⲛⲓⲣⲱⲙⲓ ⲙⲁⲗⲗⲟⲛ ⲉ̀ⲥⲟⲧⲉ ⲡ̀ⲱⲟⲩ ⲙ̀Ⲫϯ . ⲟⲩⲱϣⲧ ⲙ̀ⲡⲓⲉⲩⲁⲅⲅⲉⲗⲓⲟⲛ ⲉⲑⲩ.

(يوحنا 12 : 36 - 43)

قال يسوع هذا ثم مضى وتوارى عنهم . ومع هذه الآيات الكثيرة التى صنعها أمامهم لم يؤمنوا به . ليتم القول الذى قاله إشعياء النبى: يارب من صدق خبرنا؟ ولمن استعلنت ذراع الرب؟ ومن أجل هذا لم يقدروا ان يؤمنوا لأن إشعياء قال أيضاً: قد طمس عيونهم . وقفل قلوبهم . لئلا يبصروا بعيونهم ويفهموا بقلوبهم ويرجعوا إلىَّ لاشفيهم . قال إشعياء هذا لما رأى مجد الله وتكلم عنه . ومع هذا أن كثيراً من الرؤساء أيضاً آمنوا به . ولكنهم لسبب الفريسيين لم يعترفوا به لئلا يصيروا خارج المجمع لأنهم احبوا مجد الناس أكثر من مجد الله . والمجد لله دائماً .

Introduction to the Exposition, Page:	9	مقدمة الطرح ، صفحة :

Exposition

Isaiah the prophet—by the Spirit— chastizes the sons of Israel for their foolishness and rebukes them outright because of the vileness of their deeds and their sins. They rejected the miracles that Immanuel made, rejected His words full of grace and leaned towards myths and vagaries and rejected the glory of His divinity. O great prophet (Isaiah), chastise these disobedient children and fruitless trees for they have emulated their fathers and followed on their heels: O Lord who believes our word? And Your arm, O Lord, to whom has it been announced? The voice of the Lord is His only-begotten Son who appeared in the flesh to the sons of Israel. He showed in them His mercy and His justice and nevertheless they did not obey Him and did not believe in Him. How could they believe: Isaiah prophesied about them and said: I blind their eyes,

طـرح

إشعياء النبى يصرخ بالروح نحو الشعب الجاهل بنى إسرائيل. يبكتهم بغير محاباة من أجل دنس أعمالهم و آثامهم . لما ظهر عمانوئيل وصنع أعمالاً تبهر العقول ، تعدوا أقواله المملوءة نعمة ومالوا إلى الخرافات والأعمال الباطلة ، وجحدوا مجد لاهوته هؤلاء الأبناء المرذولين والزرع الغير المثمر . بكت رأيهم أيها النبى العظيم لأنهم تشبهوا بأبائهم وأكملوا مكاييلهم ، فيقول (إشعياء): يارب من صدق خبرنا؟ وذراعك يارب لمن أعلنت؟ ان صوت الرب هو إبنه الوحيد الذى تراءى بالجسد لبنى إسرائيل. عدله ورحمته أظهرهما فيهم ومع هذا لم يطيعوا ولم يؤمنوا به . كيف يؤمنون وإشعياء سبق فنطق من أجلهم هكذا

harden their hearts, deafen their ears and their understanding altogether. Listen O Israel; no one else will save you from God's wrath but Jesus the Savior of the world, He who made the two into one by His Incarnation. The light has come to His own and His own loved the darkness and the Gentiles accepted His commandments and became His nation everywhere. They experience His mercy and His immeasurable grace that He bestowed on them.

قائلاً : أنه أطمس عيونهم وبلد قلوبهم ونقل آذانهم وأفهامهم معاً . اسمع يا إسرائيل: ليس آخر يقوم يخلص شعبك من قبله إلا يسوع مخلص العالم الذى جعل الإثنين واحداً . بتجسده جاء النور إلى خاصته وخاصته لم تقبله. بل أحبوا الظلمة . والشعوب الغريبة قبلت وصاياه وصارت له شعباً مجتمعاً فى كل مكان . وعرفوا رحمته وغزير نعمته التى أفاضها عليهم كصلاحه .

(North side) Christ our Savior; has come and has borne suffering; that through His Passion; He may save us.

(مرد بحرى) المسيح مخلصنا جاء وتألم عنا لكى بآلامه يخلصنا .

(South side) Let us glorify Him; and exalt His Name; for He had mercy on us; according to His great mercy.

(مرد قبلى) فلنمجده ونرفع إسمه لأنه صنع معنا رحمة كعظيم رحمته .

The Conclusion of the Exposition, Page: 9 : ختام الطرح ، صفحة

الساعة التاسعة من ليلة الخميس من البصخة المقدسة
The Ninth Hour of Thursday Eve of the Holy Pascha

Ezekiel 20:27-33

Therefore, son of man, speak to the house of Israel, and you shall say to them, Thus says the Lord: In this too have your fathers provoked Me in their trespasses in which they transgressed against Me. Whereas I brought them into the land concerning which I lifted up My hand to give it to them; and they looked upon every high hill, and every shady tree, and they sacrificed there to their gods, and offered there sweet-smelling savors, and there they poured out their drink offerings. And I said to them, What is Bamah, that you go in there? And they called its name Bamah, until this day. Therefore say to the house of Israel, Thus says the Lord: Do you pollute yourselves with the iniquities of your fathers, and do you go a-whoring after their abominations, and do you pollute yourselves with the first-fruits of your gifts, in the offerings wherewith you pollute yourselves in all your imaginations, until this day; and shall I answer you, O house of Israel? As I live, says the Lord, I will not answer you, neither shall this thing come upon your spirit. And it shall not be as you say, We will be as the nations, and as the tribes of the earth, to worship stocks and stones. Therefore, as I live, says the Lord, I will reign over you with a strong hand, and with a high arm, and with outpoured wrath. Glory be to the Holy Trinity. Amen

(من حزقيال النبي ص 20 : 27 - 33)

لأجل ذلك كلم بيت إسرائيل يا إبن آدم وقل لهم ، هذا ما يقوله أدوناى الرب: إلى هذه الساعة أغضبونى أباؤكم بآثامهم التى سقطوا فيها أمامى. وأدخلتهم إلى الأرض التى بسطت يدى عليها ، لأعطيهم أياها. فرأوا كل تل عال . وإلى أسفل كل الأشجار المورقة ، وذبحوا هناك الذبائح للآلهة وقربوا البخور فى ذلك الموضع . وسكبوا هناك سكائبهم. فقلت لهم: ما هذه الأبانا المرتفعة التى تدخلون إليها ؟ فدعى إسمها أبانا إلى هذا اليوم. لذلك قل لبيت إسرائيل: هذا ما يقوله السيد الرب ، إذا كنتم ستتنجسون بأثام الآباء وتتبعون أرجاسهم بتقديم باكورات تقدماتكم واجازة ابنائكم فى النار ، تنجسون جميع أفكاركم إلى هذا اليوم . وأنا أيضاً هل أجاوبكم يا بيت إسرائيل؟ حى أنا ، يقول أدوناى الرب . أننى لا أجاوبكم . سوف لا يخطر هذا على بالكم ولن يكون هكذا . إذ تقولون: اننا سنصير مثل الأمم . وكقبائل الأرض وكنفوس البشر فنعبد الخشب والحجر. فلذلك حى أنا ، يقول أدوناى الرب: أننى بيد عزيزة وبذراع عالية ، وبغضب مسكوب أملك عليكم . مجداً للثالوث القدوس .

| Pascha Praise - B (12 times), Page: 7 | تسبحة البصخة B (12 مرة) ، صفحة : 7 |

The Psalm

Ψⲁⲗⲙⲟⲥ ⲍ̅ : ⲁ̅ ⲛⲉⲙ ⲃ̅

Psalms 7:1-2

O Lord my God, in You have I trusted: save me from all them that persecute me, and deliver me. Lest at any time the enemy seize my soul as a lion. Alleluia

Ⲡϭⲟⲓⲥ Ⲡⲁⲛⲟⲩϯ ⲁⲓⲭⲁ ⲉ̇ϩⲏⲓ ⲉ̇ⲣⲟⲕ : ⲛⲁϩⲙⲉⲧ ⲟⲩⲟϩ ⲙⲁⲧⲟⲩϫⲟⲓ : ⲉ̇ⲃⲟⲗ ⲛ̇ⲧⲟⲧⲟⲩ ⲛ̇ⲛⲏⲉⲧϭⲟϫⲓ ⲛ̇ⲥⲱⲓ : ⲙⲏⲡⲟⲧⲉ ⲛ̇ⲧⲟⲩϩⲱⲗⲉⲙ ⲛ̇ⲧⲁⲯⲩⲭⲏ ⲙ̇ⲫⲣⲏϯ ⲛⲟⲩⲙⲟⲩⲓ . ⲁⲗ.

إبتشويس بانووتى أيكا أهثي إروك : ناهميت أووه ماطووجوى : إيفول إنطوطو إنني إتتشوجى إنصوى : مي بوتيه إنطو هوليم إنطا بسيشى إمفريتي إنؤومووى . الليلويا .

(مز 7 : 1 و 2)

أيها الرب إلهى عليك توكلت فخلصنى ، ومن أيدى جميع الطاردين لى نجنى . لئلا يخطفوا نفسى مثل الأسد. الليلويا .

| Introduction to the Gospel, Page: 8 | مقدمة الأنجيل ، صفحة : 8 |

The Gospel

Ⲉⲩⲁⲅⲅⲉⲗⲓⲟⲛ Ⲕⲁⲧⲁ Ⲓⲱⲁⲛⲛⲏⲛ Ⲕⲉⲫ ⲓ: ⲕ̅ⲑ̅ - ⲗ̅ⲏ̅

John 10:29-38

(يوحنا 10 : 29 - 38)

My Father, who has given them to Me, is greater than all; and no one is able to snatch them out of My Father's hand. I and My Father are one." Then the Jews took up stones again to stone Him. Jesus answered them, "Many good works I have shown you from My Father. For which of those works do you stone Me?" The Jews answered Him, saying, "For a good work we do not stone You, but for blasphemy, and because You, being a Man, make Yourself God." Jesus answered them, "Is it not written in your law, 'I SAID, "YOU ARE GODS" '? If He called them gods, to whom the word of God came (and the Scripture cannot be broken), do you say of Him whom the Father sanctified and sent into the world, 'You are blaspheming,' because I said, 'I am the Son of God'? If I do not do the works of My Father, do not believe Me; but if I do, though you do not believe Me, believe the works, that you may know and believe that the Father is in Me, and I in Him." Glory be to God forever, Amen.

Ⲫⲏⲉⲧⲁ ⲡⲁⲓⲱⲧ ⲧⲏⲓϥ ⲛⲏⲓ ⲟⲩⲛⲓϣϯ ⲡⲉ ⲉⲟⲩⲟⲛ ⲛⲓⲃⲉⲛ : ⲟⲩⲟϩ ⲙⲙⲟⲛ ϩⲗⲓ ⲛⲁϣϩⲟⲗⲙⲟⲩ ⲉⲃⲟⲗ ϧⲉⲛ ⲧⲭⲓϫ ⲙⲡⲁⲓⲱⲧ : ⲁⲛⲟⲕ ⲛⲉⲙ ⲡⲁⲓⲱⲧ ⲁⲛⲟⲛ ⲟⲩⲁⲓ : ⲁⲩⲉⲗⲱⲛⲓ ⲟⲩⲛ ⲛϫⲉ Ⲛⲓⲟⲩⲇⲁⲓ ϩⲓⲛⲁ ⲛⲥⲉϩⲓⲟⲩⲓ ⲉϫⲱϥ . Ⲁϥⲉⲣⲟⲩⲱ ⲛⲱⲟⲩ ⲛϫⲉ Ⲓⲏⲥ ⲉϥϫⲱ ⲙⲙⲟⲥ : ϫⲉ ⲟⲩⲙⲏϣ ⲛϩⲱⲃ ⲉⲛⲁⲛⲉⲩ ⲁⲓⲧⲁⲙⲱⲧⲉⲛ ⲉⲣⲱⲟⲩ ⲉⲃⲟⲗ ϩⲓⲧⲉⲛ ⲡⲁⲓⲱⲧ : ⲉⲑⲃⲉ ⲁϣ ⲟⲩⲛ ⲛϩⲱⲃ ⲧⲉⲧⲉⲛⲛⲁϩⲓⲱⲛⲓ ⲉϫⲱⲓ : ⲁⲩⲉⲣⲟⲩⲱ ⲛⲁϥ ⲛϫⲉ Ⲛⲓⲟⲩⲇⲁⲓ ⲟⲩⲟϩ ⲡⲉϫⲱⲟⲩ ϫⲉ : ⲉⲑⲃⲉ ⲟⲩϩⲱⲃ ⲉⲛⲁⲛⲉϥ ⲧⲉⲛⲛⲁϩⲓⲱⲛⲓ ⲉϫⲱⲕ ⲁⲛ ⲁⲗⲗⲁ ⲉⲑⲃⲉ ⲟⲩϫⲉⲟⲩⲁ̀ : ϫⲉ ⲛ̀ⲑⲟⲕ ⲟⲩⲣⲱⲙⲓ ϩⲱⲕ ⲕⲓⲣⲓ ⲙⲙⲟⲕ ⲛ̀ⲛⲟⲩϯ : ⲁϥⲉⲣⲟⲩⲱ ⲛⲱⲟⲩ ⲛϫⲉ Ⲓⲏⲥ ⲟⲩⲟϩ ⲡⲉϫⲁϥ : ϫⲉ ⲙⲏ ⲥ̀ⲥϧⲏⲟⲩⲧ ⲁⲛ ϧⲉⲛ ⲡⲉⲧⲉⲛⲛⲟⲙⲟⲥ ϫⲉ ⲁⲛⲟⲕ ⲁⲓϫⲟⲥ ϫⲉ ⲛ̀ⲑⲱⲧⲉⲛ ϩⲁⲛⲛⲟⲩϯ .

Ⲓⲥϫⲉ ⲁϥϫⲟⲥ ⲛ̀ⲛⲏ ϫⲉ ⲛⲟⲩϯ ⲛⲏⲉⲧⲁ ⲡⲥⲁϫⲓ ⲙ̀Ⲫϯ ϣⲱⲡⲓ ϩⲁⲣⲱⲟⲩ ⲟⲩⲟϩ ⲙⲙⲟⲛ ϣϫⲟⲙ ⲛⲧⲉ ϯⲅⲣⲁⲫⲏ ⲃⲱⲗ ⲉⲃⲟⲗ : ⲫⲏⲉⲧⲁ ⲫⲓⲱⲧ ⲧⲟⲩⲃⲟϥ ⲟⲩⲟϩ ⲁϥⲟⲩⲟⲣⲡϥ ⲉⲡⲓⲕⲟⲥⲙⲟⲥ ⲛ̀ⲑⲱⲧⲉⲛ ⲧⲉⲧⲉⲛϫⲱ ⲙⲙⲟⲥ ϫⲉ ⲁⲕⲕⲉⲟⲩⲁ̀ ϫⲉ ⲁⲓϫⲟⲥ ϫⲉ ⲁⲛⲟⲕ ⲡⲉ ⲡ̀ϣⲏⲣⲓ ⲙ̀Ⲫϯ ⲓⲥϫⲉ ϯⲓⲣⲓ ⲁⲛ ⲛ̀ⲛⲓϩⲃⲏⲟⲩⲓ ⲛⲧⲉ ⲡⲁⲓⲱⲧ ⲙ̀ⲡⲉⲣⲛⲁϩϯ ⲉⲣⲟⲓ : ⲓⲥϫⲉ ⲇⲉ ϯⲓⲣⲓ ⲙⲙⲱⲟⲩ ⲕⲁⲛ ϣⲱⲡ ⲁⲣⲉⲧⲉⲛϣⲧⲉⲙⲛⲁϩϯ ⲉⲣⲟⲓ ⲛⲁϩϯ ⲉⲛⲓϩⲃⲏⲟⲩⲓ : ϩⲓⲛⲁ ⲛ̀ⲧⲉⲧⲉⲛⲉⲙⲓ ⲟⲩⲟϩ ⲛ̀ⲧⲉⲧⲉⲛⲥⲱⲟⲩⲛ ϫⲉ ⲁⲛⲟⲕ ϯ ϧⲉⲛ ⲡⲁⲓⲱⲧ ⲟⲩⲟϩ ⲡⲁⲓⲱⲧ ⲛ̀ϧⲏⲧ . ⲟⲩⲱϣⲧ ⲙ̀ⲡⲓⲉⲩⲁⲅⲅⲉⲗⲓⲟⲛ ⲉⲑⲟⲩ .

أبى الذى أعطانى اياها هو أعظم من الكل . فلا يقدر أحد أن يخطفها من يد أبى . أنا وأبى واحد . فتناول اليهود حجارة ليرجموه . فأجابهم يسوع قائلاً : أعمالاً كثيرة حسنة أريتكم من عند أبى فمن أجل أي عمل ترجمونى . فأجابه اليهود قائلين : لسنا من أجل عمل حسن نرجمك بل لأجل تجديف . لأنك وأنت إنسان تجعل نفسك آلهاً . فأجابهم يسوع وقال: أليس مكتوباً فى ناموسكم أنا قلت انكم آلهة؟ فان كان قال لاولئك آلهة الذين صارت إليهم كلمة الله ، ولا يمكن أن ينقض المكتوب ، فالذى قدسه الآب وأرسله إلى العالم أتقولون له أنتم: أنك تجدف ، لأنى قلت أنا إبن الله . ان كنت لا أعمل أعمال أبى فلا تؤمنوا بى . وان كنت أعملها ولا تؤمنوا بى ، فامنوا بالأعمال لتعلموا وتعرفوا أنى فى أبي وأبي فيّ . والمجد لله دائماً.

| Introduction to the Exposition, Page: | 9 | مقدمة الطرح ، صفحة : |

Exposition

طرح

O you foolish obstinate, corrupt and contrary people, listen to the Merciful with His divine mouth praise the faithful saying; what the Father has given me is more precious than all the things on earth, and no one can take them away from my Father's hand. I and the Father are one with the Holy Spirit without separation. When the Jews in their envy picked the rocks to stone Him, He responded to them in modesty saying: I did among you good deeds from My

أيها الناس الجهلة المعاندين ، الشعب النجس المخالف. إسمعوا الرحوم بفمه الإلهى يمدح المؤمنين به قائلاً : الذى أعطانى الآب أعظم من كل من على الأرض ، وليس أحد يقدر أن يخطفهم ولا يسلبهم من يد أبى ، وأنا والآب واحد مع الروح القدس بغير إفتراق ، وللوقت تناول اليهود حجارة بحسد عظيم ليرجموه. فأجابهم المخلص بوداعة ليعلمهم: أظهرت لكم أعمالاً حسنة مكرمة جداً من عند أبى .

Father. What do you stone Me for when I seek your salvation? Know and be certain you foolish Jews that I am in My Father and My Father is in Me.

من أجل أى شئ ترجمونني وأنا أريد خلاصكم ؟ إعلموا وتيقنوا أيها اليهود الجهال إننى فى أبى وأبى فيّ .

(North side) Christ our Savior; has come and has borne suffering; that through His Passion; He may save us.

(مرد بحرى) المسيح مخلصنا جاء وتألم عنا لكى بآلامه يخلصنا .

(South side) Let us glorify Him; and exalt His Name; for He had mercy on us; according to His great mercy.

(مرد قبلى) فلنمجده ونرفع إسمه لأنه صنع معنا رحمة كعظيم رحمته .

The Conclusion of the Exposition, Page: 9 : ختام الطرح ، صفحة

الساعة الحادية عشر من ليلة الخميس من البصخة المقدسة
The Eleventh Hour of Thursday Eve of the Holy Pascha

Jeremiah 8:4-10

For thus says the Lord, Shall not he that falls arise? Or he that turns away, shall he not turn back again? Why have My people turned away with a shameless revolting, and strengthened themselves in their willfulness, and refused to return? Hearken, I pray, and hear: will they not speak thus, There is no man that repents of his wickedness, saying, What have I done? The runner has failed from his course, as a tired horse in his neighing. Even the stork in the heaven knows her time, also the turtledove and wild swallow; the sparrows observe the times of their coming in; but this My people knows not the judgments of the Lord. How will you say, We are wise, and the law of the Lord is with us? In vain have the scribes used a false pen. The wise men are ashamed, and alarmed, and taken; because they have rejected the word of the Lord; what wisdom is there in them? Glory be to the Holy Trinity. Amen

(من أرميا النبى ص 8 : 4 - 10)

هذا ما يقوله الرب: هل من يسقط لا يقوم؟ ومن يرتد هل لا يـرجـع؟ . لـماذا ارتـد هذا الـشـعـب ارتداداً وقحاً وتمسكوا بهواهم وأبوا أن يرجعوا؟ انصتوا الآن وإسمعوا كلاماً ، لأنه هكذا ، ليس أحد من الناس يتوب عن شره قائلاً: ماذا صنعت؟ . الذى يجرى قد كف عن موضع جريه . كحصان عرقان من صهيله . عرف اللقلق فى السماء ميعاده . واليمامه والسنونة وعصفور الحقل عرفت أوقات دخولها . أما شعبى فلم يعرف حكم الرب . كيف تقولون: أننا نحن حكماء وناموس الرب لنا . والناموس الذى كان محسوباً للكتبة صار باطلاً وليس حقاً . خزى الحكماء وتملكهم الفزع لأنهم رفضوا كلمة الرب ، بعيدة هى الحكمة عنهم . مجداً للثالوث القدوس .

Pascha Praise - B (12 times), Page: 7	تسبحة البصخة B (12 مرة) ، صفحة :

The Psalm
Ⲯⲁⲗⲙⲟⲥ ⲝ̅ⲁ̅ : ⲁ̅ ⲛⲉⲙ ⲁ̅

Psalms 61: 4, 1

In God is my salvation and my glory; He is the God of my help, and my hope is in God. For He is my God, and my savior; my helper, I shall not be greatly moved. Alleluia

Ⲡⲁⲟⲩϫⲁⲓ ⲛⲉⲙ ⲡⲁⲱⲟⲩ ⲁⲩ ϧⲉⲛ ⲫⲁⲛⲟⲩϯ : Ⲫϯ ⲛ̀ⲧⲉ ⲧⲁⲃⲟⲏⲑⲓⲁ ⲟⲩⲟⲅ ⲧⲁⲅⲉⲗⲡⲓⲥ ⲁⲥ ϧⲉⲛ Ⲫϯ : ⲕⲉ ⲅⲁⲣ ⲛ̀ⲑⲟϥ ⲡⲉ ⲡⲁⲛⲟⲩϯ ⲡⲁⲥⲱⲧⲏⲣ : ⲡⲁⲣⲉϥϣⲟⲡⲧ ⲉ̀ⲣⲟϥ ⲛ̀ⲛⲁⲕⲓⲙ ⲛ̀ⲅⲟⲩⲟ . ⲁ̅ⲗ .

با أوجاى نيم با أوأوو أف خين بانووتى : إفنووتى إنتيه طافوئيثيا أووه طاهيلبيس أس خين إفنووتى كيه غار إنثوف بيه بانووتى باصوتير : باريفشوبت إروف إننا كيم إنهووأو . أللـيلـويا .

(مز 61: 4و1)

خلاصى ومجدى بالهى . إله معونتى . رجائى هو بالله . لأنه إلهى ومخلصى ، ناصرى فلا أتزعزع أبداً . أللـيلـويا .

Introduction to the Gospel, Page: 8	مقدمة الأنجيل ، صفحة :

The Gospel
Ⲉⲩⲁⲅⲅⲉⲗⲓⲟⲛ Ⲕⲁⲧⲁ Ⲓⲱⲁⲛⲛⲏⲛ Ⲕⲉⲫ ⲓⲃ̅ : ⲙ̅ⲁ̅ - ⲛ̅

John 12:44-50

Then Jesus cried out and said, "He who believes in Me, believes not in Me but in Him who sent Me. And he who sees Me sees Him who sent Me. I have come as a

Ⲓⲏⲥⲟⲩⲥ ⲇⲉ ⲁϥⲱϣ ⲉ̀ⲃⲟⲗ ⲟⲩⲟⲅ ⲡⲉϫⲁϥ : ϫⲉ ⲫⲏⲉⲑⲛⲁϯ ⲉ̀ⲣⲟⲓ ⲁϥⲛⲁⲅϯ ⲉ̀ⲣⲟⲓ ⲁⲛ : ⲁⲗⲗⲁ ⲁϥⲛⲁⲅϯ ⲉ̀ⲫⲏⲉⲧⲁϥⲧⲁⲟⲩⲓ . Ⲟⲩⲟⲅ ⲫⲏⲉⲑⲛⲁⲩ ⲉ̀ⲣⲟⲓ ⲁϥⲛⲁⲩ ⲉ̀ⲫⲏⲉⲧⲁϥⲧⲁⲟⲩⲓ . Ⲁ̀ⲛⲟⲕ ⲁⲓⲓ ⲉ̀ⲟⲩⲱⲓⲛⲓ ⲉ̀ⲡⲓⲕⲟⲥⲙⲟⲥ : ⲅⲓⲛⲁ

(يوحنا 12 : 44 - 50)

فصاح يسوع وقال: الذى يؤمن بى فليس بى يؤمن بل آمن بالذى أرسلنى ومن يرانى فقد رأى الذى أرسلنى . أنا قد

light into the world, that whoever believes in Me should not abide in darkness. And if anyone hears My words and does not believe, I do not judge him; for I did not come to judge the world but to save the world. He who rejects Me, and does not receive My words, has that which judges him, the word that I have spoken will judge him in the last day. For I have not spoken on My own authority; but the Father who sent Me gave Me a command, what I should say and what I should speak. And I know that His command is everlasting life. Therefore, whatever I speak, just as the Father has told Me, so I speak." Glory be to God forever, Amen.

ⲟⲩⲟⲛ ⲛⲓⲃⲉⲛ ⲉⲑⲛⲁⲥⲱⲧ ⲉⲣⲟⲓ ⲛ̀ⲧⲉϥϣ̀ⲧⲉⲙⲟϩⲓ ϧⲉⲛ ⲡⲓⲭⲁⲕⲓ.

Ⲟⲩⲟϩ ⲫⲏⲉⲑⲛⲁⲥⲱⲧⲉⲙ ⲉⲛⲁⲥⲁϫⲓ ⲟⲩⲟϩ ⲛ̀ⲧⲉϥϣ̀ⲧⲉⲙⲁⲣⲉϩ ⲉⲣⲱⲟⲩ ⲁⲛⲟⲕ ⲉⲑⲛⲁϯ ϩⲁⲡ ⲉⲣⲟⲓ ⲁⲛ : ⲛⲉ ⲉⲧⲁⲓⲓ ⲅⲁⲣ ⲁⲛ ϩⲓⲛⲁ ⲛ̀ⲧⲁϯϩⲁⲡ ⲉⲡⲓⲕⲟⲥⲙⲟⲥ ⲁⲗⲗⲁ ϩⲓⲛⲁ ⲛ̀ⲧⲁⲛⲟϩⲉⲙ ⲙ̀ⲡⲓⲕⲟⲥⲙⲟⲥ. Ⲫⲏⲉⲧⲭⲱ ⲙ̀ⲙⲟⲓ ⲉ̀ⲃⲟⲗ ⲟⲩⲟϩ ⲉⲧⲉ ⲛ̀ϥ̀ⲛⲁϭⲓ ⲛ̀ⲛⲁⲥⲁϫⲓ ⲁⲛ : ⲟⲩⲟⲛ ⲛ̀ⲧⲁϥ ⲙ̀ⲫⲏⲉⲑⲛⲁϯϩⲁⲡ ⲉⲣⲟϥ : ⲡⲓⲥⲁϫⲓ ⲉⲧⲁⲓⲥⲁϫⲓ ⲙ̀ⲙⲟϥ ⲫⲏⲉⲧⲉ ⲙ̀ⲙⲁⲩ ⲉⲑⲛⲁϯϩⲁⲡ ⲉⲣⲟϥ ϧⲉⲛ ⲡⲓⲉ̀ϩⲟⲟⲩ ⲛ̀ϧⲁⲉ. Ϫⲉ ⲁⲛⲟⲕ ⲙ̀ⲡⲓⲥⲁϫⲓ ⲉ̀ⲃⲟⲗ ϩⲓⲧⲟⲧ ⲙ̀ⲙⲁⲩⲁⲧ : ⲁⲗⲗⲁ ⲫ̀ⲓⲱⲧ ⲫⲏ ⲉⲧⲁϥⲧⲁⲟⲩⲟⲓ ⲛ̀ⲑⲟϥ ⲡⲉ ⲉⲧⲁϥϯ ⲉⲛⲧⲟⲗⲏ ⲛⲏⲓ : ⲟⲩ ⲡⲉ ϯⲛⲁϫⲟϥ ⲓⲉ ⲟⲩ ⲡⲉ ϯⲛⲁⲥⲁϫⲓ ⲙ̀ⲙⲟϥ.

Ⲟⲩⲟϩ ϯⲉ̀ⲙⲓ ϫⲉ ⲧⲉϥⲉⲛⲧⲟⲗⲏ ⲟⲩⲱⲛϧ ⲛ̀ⲉⲛⲉϩ ⲧⲉ : ⲛⲏ ⲟⲩⲛ ⲁⲛⲟⲕ ⲉ̀ϯϫⲱ ⲙ̀ⲙⲱⲟⲩ ⲕⲁⲧⲁ ⲫ̀ⲣⲏϯ ⲉⲧⲁϥϫⲟⲥ ⲛⲏⲓ ⲛ̀ϫⲉ ⲡⲁⲓⲱⲧ ⲡⲁⲓⲣⲏϯ ϯⲥⲁϫⲓ. ⲟⲩⲱϣⲧ ⲙ̀ⲡⲓⲉⲩⲁⲅⲅⲉⲗⲓⲟⲛ ⲉⲑⲩ.

جئت نوراً للعالم . حتى كل من يؤمن بى لا يمكث فى الظلمة . وان كان أحد يسمع كلامى ولا يحفظه فأنا لا أدينه . لأنى لم آتِ لادين العالم بل لأخلص العالم. ومن ينكرني ولم يقبل كلامى فله من يدينه . الكلام الذى تكلمت به هو الذى يدينه فى اليوم الأخير . لأنى لم أتكلم من ذاتى وحدى . بل الأب الذى أرسلنى هو الذى أعطانى الوصية ماذا أقول وبماذا أتكلم . أعلم ان وصيته هى حياة أبدية . والذى أتكلم أنا به فكما قال لى أبى هكذا أتكلم . والمجد لله دائماً .

Introduction to the Exposition, Page: 9   مقدمة الطرح ، صفحة : 9

Exposition

طــرح

Our Savior the Son of the living God said: I am the light of the world. He who believes in Me and accepts My words will not be in the darkness. He who denies Me and does not want to listen to My words nor to obey them, I will not judge him, but the words I said will. Because what I say is from the Father who sent Me. He gave me the commandment of what to say and what to tell. We believe in you that you are the omnipotent Word of God, the benevolent Father and that You have power over all, and nothing is impossible with You.

قال المخلص إبن الله الحى: أنا هو نور العالم بأسره. ومن يؤمن بى ويقبل كلامى لا يمكن أن يلبث فى الظلام . ومن يجحدنى ولم يرد أن يسمع لقولى ولم يطعه ، فانا لا أدينه ، لكن القول الذى قلته أنا هو يدينه. فإن القول الذى نطقت به ليس هو لى بل للاب الذى أرسلنى . وهو أعطانى الوصية بماذا أقول وأنطق . نحن نؤمن إنك أنت بالحقيقة كلمة الله الأب الصالح وان لك القدرة على كل شئ وليس شئ يعسر عليك.

(North side) Christ our Savior; has come and has borne suffering; that through His Passion; He may save us.

(مرد بحرى) المسيح مخلصنا جاء وتألم عنا لكى بآلامه يخلصنا .

(South side) Let us glorify Him; and exalt His Name; for He had mercy on us; according to His great mercy.

(مرد قبلى) فلنمجده ونرفع إسمه لأنه صنع معنا رحمة كعظيم رحمته .

The Conclusion of the Exposition, Page: 9   ختام الطرح ، صفحة : 9

The Conclusion with the Nighttime Litanies, Page: 17   طلبة المساء ، صفحة : 17

خميس العهد من البصخة المقدسة

Covenant Thursday of the Holy Pascha

القراءات و الاحداث

الموضوع : الفصح الكبير

الاولى : لو 22 : 7 – 13 ؛ امره باعداده
الثالثه : مت 26 : 17 – 19 ؛ اقتراب وقته
السادسة : مر 14 : 12 – 16 ؛ مكان اعداده
التاسعة : مت 26 : 17 – 19 ؛ اعداده
قداس اللقان : يو 13 : 1 – 17 ؛ التوبة و الانكسار قبل الفصح الجديد
قداس الخميس الكبير : مت 26 : 20 – 29 ؛ جسده المقدس و دمه الكريم
الحادية عشرة : يو 13 : 21 – 30 ؛ خروج يهوذا

فى هذا اليوم اكل الرب الفصح القديم مع التلاميذ لينهى فصح العهد القديم الذى كان رمزاً
للفصح الجديد حمل الله الذى ذبح عن حياة العالم كله و ليس عن حياة الابكار فقط . وقبل تاسيس
الرب للسر الجديد الذى هو جسده الطاهر و دمه الكريم ، غسل ارجل التلاميذ ليعلمنا ان تناولنا
من الفصح الجديد لابد و ان يسبقه غسيل التوبه مع الانكسار و لذلك وضعت الكنيسة فى هذه
الساعة من المزمور الخمسين : "تنضح على بزوفاك فاطهر ، تغسلنى فابيض اكثر من الثلج ".

The Readings and Events

Subject: The Great Passover

First hour: Luke 22:7-13; His command to be prepared.
Third hour: Matthew 26:17-19; His appointed time is near.
Sixth hour: Mark 14:12-16; The place of the Passover.
Ninth hour: Matthew 26:17-19; It is prepared.
    Liturgy of the Water: John 13:1-17;
        The Repentance and humbleness before the new Passover.
    Liturgy of the Great Thursday: Matthew 26:20-29;
        Establishment of the Eucharist.
Eleventh hour: John 13:21-30; Judas went out.

In this day, the Lord ate the old Passover with the disciples to stop the Passover of the Old Testament, which was a symbol of the new Passover, the Lamb of God, Who was slain for the life of everyone, not only for the firstborn. Before establishing the new sacrament, the Eucharist, the Lord washed the feet of the disciples to teach us that partaking of the Eucharist should be preceded by washing of the repentance and humbleness. That is why the selected psalm of this hour is from psalm 50: "You shall sprinkle me with hyssop, and I shall be purified. You shall wash me and I shall be made whiter than snow."

The First Hour of Thursday of the Holy Pascha
الساعة الاولى من يوم الخميس من البصخة المقدسة

Exodus 17:8-16

And Amalek came and fought with Israel in Rephidim. And Moses said to Joshua, Choose out for yourself mighty men, and go forth and set the army in array against Amalek tomorrow; and behold, I shall stand on the top of the hill, and the rod of God will be in my hand. And Joshua did as Moses said to him, and he went out and set the army in array against Amalek, and Moses and Aaron and Hur went up to the top of the hill. And it came to pass, when Moses lifted up his hands, Israel prevailed; and when he let down his hands, Amalek prevailed. But the hands of Moses were heavy, and they took a stone and put it under him, and he sat upon it; and Aaron and Hur supported his hands, one on this side and the other on that, and the hands of Moses were supported till the going down of the sun. And Joshua routed Amalek and all his people with the edge of the sword. And the Lord said to Moses, Write this for a memorial in a book, and speak in the ears of Joshua; for I will utterly blot out the memorial of Amalek from under heaven. And Moses built an altar to the Lord, and called the name of it, The Lord my Refuge. For with a secret hand the Lord wages war upon Amalek to all generations. Glory be to the Holy Trinity. Amen.

Exodus 15:23-16:3

So Moses brought up the children of Israel from the Red Sea, and brought them into the wilderness of Shur; and they went three days in the wilderness, and found no water to drink. And they came to Marah, and they could not drink the water of Marah, for it was bitter; therefore he named the name of that place, Bitterness. And the people murmured against Moses, saying, What shall we drink? And Moses cried to the Lord, and the Lord showed him a tree, and he cast it into the water, and the water was sweetened. There He established to him ordinances and judgments, and there He tested him, and said, If you will indeed hear the voice of the Lord your God, and do the things pleasing before Him, and will heed His commands, and keep all His ordinances, no disease which I have brought upon the Egyptians will I bring upon you, for I am the Lord your God that heals you. And they came to Elim, where there were twelve fountains of water and seventy stems of palm trees; and they camped there by the waters. And they departed from Elim, and all the congregation of the children of Israel came to the Wilderness of Sin, which is between Elim and Sinai; and on the fifteenth day, in the second month after their departure from the land of Egypt, all the congregation of the children of Israel murmured against Moses and Aaron. And the children of Israel said to them, Would we had died smitten by the Lord in the land of Egypt, when we sat by the fleshpots, and ate bread to the full! For

(من سفر الخروج 17 : 8 ألخ)

وأتى عماليق وحارب إسرائيل فى رافازين . فقال موسى ليشوع : اختر لك رجالاً وأخرج حارب عماليق غداً . وهوذا أنا أقف على رأس الجبل . وعصا الله فى يدى .ففعل يشوع كما قال له موسى . وخرج فحارب عماليق . وصعد موسى وهرون وحور على قمة الجبل . فكان إذا رفع موسى يديه يغلب بنو إسرائيل ، وإذا خفض يديه يغلب عماليق . فلما كلت يدا موسى أخذا حجراً ووضعاه تحته وجلس عليه. ودعم هرون وحور يديه ، أحدهما من هنا والآخر من هناك . فكانت يدا موسى ثابتتين إلى غروب الشمس فقتل يشوع عماليق وكل جمعه قتلا بحد السيف. فقال الرب لموسى أكتب هذا فى سفر للذكرى وسلمه ليدىّ يشوع لأنى سأمحو ذكرى عماليق محوا من تحت السماء. فبنى موسى مذبحاً ودعا اسمه الرب ملجأى . لأنه بيد خفية يحارب الرب عماليق من جيل إلى جيل. مجداً للثالوث القدوس .

(من سفر الخروج 15 : 23- 16 : 3)

ثم إرتحل موسى ببنى إسرائيل من البحر الأحمر وجاء بهم إلى برية شور وساروا ثلاثة أيام فى البرية ولم يجدوا ماء للشرب . فجاءوا إلى مامرة ولم يقدروا أن يشربوا ماء من ماره لأنه مر ولذلك دعى ذلك المكان مر فتذمر الشعب على موسى قائلين : ماذا نشرب فصرخ موسى إلى الرب فأراه الرب عوداً فطرحه فى الماء فصار الماء عذباً فى ذلك المكان قرر له الفرائض والأحكام وفى ذلك المكان جربه وقال له ان أنت سمعت وأطعت صوت الرب إلهك وعملت ما يرضيه أمامه وحفظت كل وصاياه وأوامره فكل مرض أتيت به على المصريين لا أجلبه عليك لأنى أنا الرب الذى يشفيك . وجاءوا إلى إيليم وكان هناك إثنتا عشرة عين ماء وسبعون نخلة فنزلوا هناك عند الماء ثم ارتحلوا من إيليم وأتى كل جماعة بنى إسرائيل إلى برية سيناء التى بين إيليم وبين سيناء فى اليوم الخامس عشر من الشهر الثانى لخروجهم من أرض مصر . فتذمر جماعة بنى إسرائيل على موسى وهارون وقال لهما بنو إسرائيل ليتنا متنا فى أرض مصر إذ كنا جالسين عند قدور اللحم ونأكل خبزاً وشبعنا وأخرجتمونا إلى

you have brought us out into this wilderness, to slay all this congregation with hunger. Glory be to the Holy Trinity. Amen

البرية لكى تميتونا مع كل الجماعة بالجوع . مجداً للثالوث القدوس .

Isaiah 58:1-11

Cry aloud, and spare not; lift up your voice as with a trumpet, and declare to My people their sins, and to the house of Jacob their iniquities. They seek Me day by day, and desire to know My ways, as a people that had done righteousness, and had not forsaken the judgment of their God; they now ask of Me righteous judgment, and desire to draw near to God, saying, Why have we fasted, and You did not see? Why have we afflicted our souls, and you did not know it? Nay, in the days of your fasts you find your pleasures, and all them that are under your power you wound. If you fast for quarrels and strife, and strike the lowly with your fists, why do you fast to Me as you do this day, so that your voice may be heard in crying? I have not chosen this fast, nor such a day for a man to afflict his soul; although you should bend down your neck as a ring, and spread under you sackcloth and ashes, neither thus shall you call a fast acceptable. I have not chosen such a fast, says the Lord; but do you loose every burden of iniquity, do you untie the knots of hard bargains, set the bruised free, and cancel every unjust account? Break your bread to the hungry, and lead the unsheltered poor to your house; if you see one naked, clothe him, and you shall not disregard the relations of your own seed. Then shall your light break forth as the morning, and your health shall speedily spring forth; and your righteousness shall go before you, and the glory of God shall surround you. Then shall you cry, and God shall hearken to you; while you are yet speaking He will say, Behold, I am here. If you remove from you the band, and the stretching forth of the hands, and murmuring speech; and if you give bread to the hungry from your heart, and satisfy the afflicted soul; then shall your light spring up in darkness, and your darkness shall be as noon day; and your God shall be with you continually, and you shall be satisfied according as your soul desires; and your bones shall be made fat, and shall be as a well-watered garden, and as a fountain from which the water has not failed. Glory be to the Holy Trinity. Amen

(من إشعياء النبى ص 58 : 1 - 9)

اصرخ بقوة ولا تشفق ارفع صوتك مثل بوق . أخبر شعبى بخطاياهم وبيت يعقوب بذنوبهم. يطلبوننى يوماً فيوماً ويشتهون أن يعرفوا طرقى مثل شعب يصنع العدل ولم يترك حكم إلهه . يسألونى الآن حكماً عادلاً ويشتهون أن يقتربوا إلى الله قائلين : لماذا صمنا ولم تنظرنا وإذللنا أنفسنا ولم تعلم؟ لأن فى أيام صومكم تجدون مسرتكم وتعنتون من هم تحت سلطانكم ، وتصومون للمنازعات والمخاصمات وتضربون الذليل. لماذا تصومون لى مثل اليوم ، لاسمع صوتكم بصراخ؟ لست اختار أنا هذا الصوم ولا يوماً يذل الإنسان نفسه. ولو انك احنيت عنقك مثل الطوق وتفرش مسحاً ورماداً تحتك ، فليس هكذا تدعون صوماً مقبولاً. ليس هذا الصوم أنا اخترته قال الرب. لكن حل كل رباط الظلم . فك كل عقد المعاملات الاقتسارية (النير) . ارسل للمنكسرين بالتخلية وخزق كل مكتوب ظالم. اكسر خبزك للجائع . ادخل المساكين الذين لا مأوى لهم إلى بيتك . ان رأيت عرياناً أكسوه. وخواص زرعك لا تتغافل عنه . حينئذ ينفجر نورك مثل الصبح . وأشفيتك تشرق سريعاً . ويتقدم عدلك قدامك. ومجد الله يجللك. حينئذ تصرخ والله يسمعك. وإذ تتكلم يقول هأنذا . وأن نزعت عنك الرباط والمشورة الردية وكلمة التمرد ، وتعطى للجائع خبزك من كل قلبك وتشبع النفس الذليلة ، حينئذ يشرق نورك فى الظلمة وتصير ظلمتك مثل الظهيرة . ويكون الهك معك كل حين وتمتلئ كما تشتهى نفسك. مجداً للثالوث القدوس .

Ezekiel 18:20-32

But the soul that sins shall die; and the son shall not bear the iniquity of the father, nor shall the father bear the iniquity of the son; the righteousness of the righteous shall be upon him, and the iniquity of the transgressor shall be upon him. And if the transgressor shall turn away from all his iniquities which he has committed, and keep all My commandments, and do justice and mercy, he shall surely live, and shall no means die. None of his trespasses which he has committed shall be remembered; in his righteousness which he has done he shall live. Shall I at all desire the death of the sinner, says he Lord, as I desire that he should turn

(من حزقيال النبى ص 18 : 20 - 32)

هذا ما يقوله الرب: النفس التى تخطئ هى التى تموت . الإبن لا يحمل ظلم أبيه ولا الأب ظلم إبنه . بر البار عليه يعود ونفاق المنافق عليه يعود . والمنافق إذا تاب عن جميع خطاياه وحفظ وصاياى كلها وأجرى العدل والرحمة فأنه يحيا حياة ولا يموت. وكل خطاياه لا تذكر وبرره الذى صنعه يحيا. لأننى لا أريد موت الخاطئ يقول الرب . مثل ما يرجع عن طريقه

from his evil way, and live? But when the righteous man turns away from his righteousness, and commits iniquity, according to all the transgressions which the transgressor has wrought, none of his righteousness which he has wrought shall be at all remembered; in his trespass in which he has trespassed, and in his sins in which he has sinned, in them shall he die. Yet you have said, The way of the Lord is not straight. Hear now, all the house of Israel: will not My way be straight? Is your way straight? When the righteous turns away from his righteousness and commits a trespass, and dies in the trespass he has committed, he shall even die in it. And when the wicked man turns away from his wickedness that he has committed, and shall do judgment and justice, he has kept his soul, and has turned away from all his ungodliness which he has committed: he shall surely live, he shall not die. Yet the house of Israel says, The way of the Lord is not right. Is not My way right, O house of Israel? Is not your way wrong? I will judge you, O house of Israel, says the Lord, each one according to his way: be converted, and turn from all your ungodliness, and it shall not become to you the punishment of iniquity. Cast away from yourselves all your ungodliness in which you have sinned against Me; and make to yourselves a new heart and a new spirit: for why should you die, O house of Israel? For I desire not the death of him that dies, says the Lord. Glory be to the Holy Trinity. Amen

الردية ويحيا . وإذا أرتد البار عن بره وصنع كل الآثام التى يصنعها المنافق ، فكل بره الذى صنعه فى زلاته التى صنعها لا يذكر له. ولكنه يموت بالخطية التى أخطأ بها . فاسمعوا الآن يا بيت إسرائيل لأنكم تقولون أن طريقى غير مستقيم وطرقنا مستقيمة ، فطرقكم غير مستقيمة . عندما يرتد البار عن بره ويفعل الآثم فأنه باثمه الذى صنعه يموت. وعندما يرجع المنافق من طريق نفاقه الذى صنعه وأجرى حكماً وعدلاً ويحفظ نفسه ويرجع عن كل نفاقه الذى صنعه ، يحيا حياة ولا يموت. لأن بيت إسرائيل يقول ان طريقى ليست مستقيمة. أليست طرقكم هى الغير مستقيمة؟ لهذا أدينكم ، كل واحد عن طرقه يا بيت إسرائيل يقول الرب . والآن ارجعوا وابتعدوا عن معاصيكم فلا يكون عذاب ظلم وانبذوا عنكم جميع معاصيكم التى صنعتموها ضدى . واقتنوا قلباً جديداً فلماذا تموتون يا بيت إسرائيل؟ إنى لا أريد موت من يموت يقول الرب ضابط الكل . مجداً للثالوث القدوس.

A homily of our Holy Father St. John Chrysostom

(عظة لابينا القديس يوحنا فم الذهب)

This is the day to approach the awesome table. Let us proceed in purity. No body should be as wicked as Judas, since it is written: as soon as he took the bread, satan entered into him, and he betrayed the Lord of Glory. Everybody should examine himself before approaching the Body and Blood of Christ in order not to be judged, because it is not a human being who gives the bread and blood; He is the Christ, Who was crucified on our behalf, and He is mysteriously standing by this table. He, to Whom belongs the power and grace, says "This is My Body". As the word He uttered once, since the beginning, saying "Be fruitful, and multiply in the earth.." is always working in our nature to multiply, similarly, the Word Christ said about this table, is still working in the churches fulfilling the purpose of the sacrifice till this day and unto His coming.

هذا هو يوم التقدم إلى المائدة الرهيبة فلنتقدم كلنا إليها بطهارة ولا يكن أحدنا شريراً مثل يهوذا. لأنه مكتوب لما تناول الخبز دخله الشيطان فسلم رب المجد . وليفحص كل واحد منا ذاته قبل أن يتقدم إلى جسد ودم المسيح لكى لا يكون له دينونة. لأنه ليس إنسان الذى يناول الخبز والدم ، ولكن هو المسيح الذى صلب عنا وهو القائم على هذه المائدة بسر. هذا الذى له القوة والنعمة يقول: هذا هو جسدى . وكما أن الكلمة التى نطق بها مرة واحدة منذ البدء قائلاً: اكثروا وانموا واملأوا الأرض ، هى دائمة فى كل حين تفعل فى طبيعتنا زيادة التناسل ، كذلك الكلمة التى قالها المسيح عن تلك المائدة باقية فى الكنائس إلى هذا اليوم وإلى مجيئه مكملة كل عمل الذبيحة .

We conclude the homily of our Holy Father St. John Chrysostom, who enlightened our minds and our hearts. In the name of the Father, and the Son, and the Holy Spirit, one God. Amen.

فلنختم عظة أبينا القديس أنبا يوحنا فم الذهب الذى أنار عقولنا وعيون قلوبنا باسم الآب والإبن والروح القدس إله واحد آمين.

رفع بخور باكر
Offering of the Morning Incense

+ The curtain of the sanctuary is opened.	+ يفتح باب الهيكل.
+ Thanksgiving prayer.	+ صلاة الشكر
+ The verses of Cymbals	+ ارباع الناقوس
+ Psalm 50	+ المزمور الخمسون
+ The Litany of the Sick, page 22	+ أوشية المرضى ، صفحة 22
+ The Litany of the Oblations, page 37	+ أوشية القرابين ، صفحة 37
+ The Gloria and the Doxologies	+ تسبحة الملائكة و الذكصولوجيات
+ The Priest offers incense in the church without kissing for the kiss of Judas.	+ يطوف الكاهن البيعة بالبخور من غير تقبيل لأجل قبلة يهوذا.
+ The Creed is recited till " ..was incarnate .. and became man." then concluded by "Yes we believe in the Holy Spirit.."	+ تقال الأمانة لغاية " تجسد وتأنس " ويكمل من أول " نعم نؤمن بالروح القدس إلى آخرها.
+ The Priest prays "Ⲫϯ ⲛⲁⲓ ⲛⲁⲛ"	+ يرفع الكاهن الصليب ويقول Ⲫϯ ⲛⲁⲓ ⲛⲁⲛ
+ Lord have mercy (3 times) in the long tune.	+ ويجاوبه الشعب Ⲕⲉ Ⲕⲉ Ⲕⲉ باللحن الطويل
+ The following is prayed	+ وبعدها يقال بلحن الحزن :

This is He Who presented Himself up on the Cross, an acceptable sacrifice for the salvation of our race.	Ⲫⲁⲓ ⲉ̀ⲧⲁϥⲉⲛϥ ⲉ̀ ϣ̀ϣⲱⲓ : ⲛ̀ⲟⲩⲑⲩⲥⲓⲁ ⲉⲥϣⲏⲡ : ϩⲓϫⲉⲛ ⲡⲓ ⳨ : ϧⲁ ⲡ̀ⲟⲩϫⲁⲓ ⲙ̀ⲡⲉⲛⲅⲉⲛⲟⲥ .	فاى إيطاف إنف إ إشوى إن أوو ثيسيا إسشيب هيجين بسطافروس خا إبؤووجاى إم ببين جينوس .	هذا الذى أصعد ذاته ذبيحة مقبولة على الصليب عن خلاص جنسنا .
And His Good Father smelled His sweet aroma on Golgotha in the evening.	Ⲁϥϣⲱⲗⲉⲙ ⲉⲣⲟϥ : ⲛ̀ϫⲉ ⲡⲉϥⲓⲱⲧ ⲛ̀ⲁ̀ⲅⲁⲑⲟⲥ : ⲙ̀ⲫ̀ⲛⲁⲩ ⲛ̀ⲧⲉ ϩⲁⲛⲁⲣⲟⲩϩⲓ : ϩⲓϫⲉⲛ ϯⲅⲟⲗⲅⲟⲑⲁ .	أف شوليم إيروف : إنجيه بيفيوت إن أغاثوس : إم إفناف إنته هان رووهى : هيجين تى غولغوثا .	فأشتمه أبوه الصالح وقت المساء على الجلجثة .
For You are indeed...	Ⲕ̀ⲥⲙⲁⲣⲱⲟⲩⲧ ⲁ̀ⲗⲏⲑⲱⲥ : ..	إك إسمارؤووت أليثوس...	مبارك ....

Introduction to the Acts
(مقدمة الابركسيس)

A reading from the Acts of our Holy Fathers, the Apostles, may their blessings be with us, Amen.	Ⲡⲣⲁⲍⲉⲱⲛ ⲧⲱⲛ ⲁ̀ⲅⲓⲱⲛ ⲛ̀ⲁⲡⲟⲥⲧⲟⲗⲱⲛ ⲧⲟⲁⲛⲁⲅⲛⲱⲥⲙⲁ : ⲡ̀ⲣⲁⲝⲓⲥ ⲡ̀ⲣⲁⲝⲓⲥ ⲛ̀ⲧⲉ ⲛⲉⲛⲓⲟϯ ⲛ̀ⲁⲡⲟⲥⲧⲟⲗⲟⲥ ⲉⲣⲉⲡⲟⲩⲥⲙⲟⲩ ⲉⲑⲩ ϣⲱⲡⲓ ⲛⲉⲙⲁⲛ ⲁⲙⲏⲛ .	إيراكسيون طون أجيون إن أبوسطولون طو أناغنوزما : إيراكسيس إيراكسيس إنتى نينيوتى إن أبوسطولوس إريبو إسموو إؤواب شوبى نيمان آمين.	الفصل من أعمال الرسل القديسين . قصص آبائنا الرسل بركتهم المقدسة تكون معنا آمين

The Praxis
Ⲡⲣⲁⲍⲓⲥ Ⲕⲉⲫ ⲁ̅ : ⲓⲉ̅ - ⲕ̅

Acts 1:15-20			(اع 1 : 15 - 20)
And in those days Peter stood up in the midst of the disciples (altogether the number of names	Ⲟⲩⲟϩ ⲛ̀ϩ̀ⲣⲏⲓ ⲇⲉ ϧⲉⲛ ⲛⲁⲓⲉ̀ϩⲟⲟⲩ ⲁϥⲧⲱⲛϥ ⲛ̀ϫⲉ Ⲡⲉⲧⲣⲟⲥ ϧⲉⲛ ⲑ̀ⲙⲏϯ ⲛ̀ⲛⲓⲥⲛⲏⲟⲩ : ⲛⲉ ⲟⲩⲟⲛ ⲟⲩⲙⲏϣ ⲇⲉ		وفى تلك الأيام قام بطرس فى وسط الأخوة وكان عدد الاسماء جميعاً

was about a hundred and twenty), and said, "Men and brethren, this Scripture had to be fulfilled, which the Holy Spirit spoke before by the mouth of David concerning Judas, who became a guide to those who arrested Jesus; for he was numbered with us and obtained a part in this ministry." (Now this man purchased a field with the wages of iniquity; and falling headlong, he burst open in the middle and all his entrails gushed out. And it became known to all those dwelling in Jerusalem; so that field is called in their own language, Akel Dama, that is, Field of Blood.) "For it is written in the Book of Psalms: 'LET HIS DWELLING PLACE BE DESOLATE, AND LET NO ONE LIVE IN IT'; and, 'LET ANOTHER TAKE HIS OFFICE.' The word of the Lord shall grow, multiply, be mighty and be confirmed in the holy church of God. Amen

ⲉⲩⲑⲟⲩⲏⲧ ϩⲓ ⲫⲁⲓ ⲉⲫⲁⲓ ⲉⲧⲛⲁⲉⲣ ⳉⲉⲭⲟⲩⲧ ⲛ̀ⲣⲁⲛ ⲟⲩⲟϩ ⲡⲉϫⲁϥ . Ⲛⲓⲣⲱⲙⲓ ⲛⲉⲛⲥⲛⲏⲟⲩ : ϩⲱϯ ⲛ̀ⲧⲉⲥϫⲱⲕ ⲉⲃⲟⲗ ⲛ̀ϫⲉ ϯⲅⲣⲁⲫⲏ : ⲑⲏⲉⲧⲁϥⲉⲣϣⲟⲣⲡ ⲛ̀ϫⲟⲥ ⲛ̀ϫⲉ ⲡⲓⲡⲛⲁ ⲉⲑⲟⲩⲁⲃ ⲉⲃⲟⲗ ϧⲉⲛ ⲣⲱϥ ⲛ̀Ⲇⲁⲩⲓⲇ : ⲉⲑⲃⲉ Ⲓⲟⲩⲇⲁⲥ ⲫⲏⲉⲧⲁϥⲉⲣ ϭⲁⲩⲙⲱⲓⲧ ⲛ̀ⲛⲏⲉⲧⲁⲙⲟⲛⲓ ⲛ̀Ⲓⲏⲥ . Ⲭⲉ ⲛⲁϥⲏⲡ ⲛ̀ϧⲣⲏⲓ ⲛ̀ϧⲏⲧⲉⲛ ⲡⲉ ⲟⲩⲟϩ ⲁ ⲡⲓⲱⲡ ⲓ̀ ⲉⲣⲟϥ ⲙ̀ⲡⲓⲕⲗⲏⲣⲟⲥ ⲛ̀ⲧⲉ ⲧⲁⲓⲇⲓⲁⲕⲟⲛⲓⲁ . Ⲫⲁⲓ ⲙⲉⲛ ⲟⲩⲛ ⲁϥϣⲱⲡ ⲛ̀ⲟⲩⲓⲟϩⲓ ⲉⲃⲟⲗ ϧⲉⲛ ⲫ̀ⲃⲉⲭⲉ ⲛ̀ⲧⲉ ϯⲁⲇⲓⲕⲓⲁ : ⲟⲩⲟϩ ⲁϥϩⲉⲓ ϩⲓϫⲉⲛ ⲡⲉϥϩⲟ : ⲁϥⲕⲱϣ ϧⲉⲛ ⲧⲉϥⲙⲏϯ : ⲛⲏⲉⲧ ⲥⲁϧⲟⲩⲛ ⲙ̀ⲙⲟϥ ⲧⲏⲣⲟⲩ ⲁⲩⲫⲱⲛ ⲉ̀ⲃⲟⲗ . Ⲟⲩⲟϩ ⲁϥⲟⲩⲱⲛϩ ⲉ̀ⲃⲟⲗ ⲛ̀ⲟⲩⲟⲛ ⲛⲓⲃⲉⲛ ⲉⲧϣⲟⲡ ϧⲉⲛ Ⲓⲗⲏⲙ : ϩⲱⲥⲧⲉ ⲛ̀ⲥⲉⲙⲟⲩϯ ⲉ̀ⲫ̀ⲣⲁⲛ ⲙ̀ⲡⲓⲓⲟϩⲓ ⲉⲧⲉ ⲙⲙⲁⲩ ϧⲉⲛ ⲧⲟⲩⲁⲥⲡⲓ ϫⲉ ⲁⲭⲉⲗⲇⲁⲙⲁ : ⲉⲧⲉ ⲡⲓⲓⲟϩⲓ ⲛ̀ⲧⲉ ⲡⲓⲥⲛⲟϥ ⲡⲉ . Ⲋ̀ⲥϧⲏⲟⲩⲧ ⲅⲁⲣ ϩⲓ ⲡⲭⲱⲙ ⲛ̀ⲧⲉ ⲛⲓⲯⲁⲗⲙⲟⲥ : ϫⲉ ⲧⲉϥⲉⲣⲃⲓ ⲙⲁⲣⲉⲥϣⲱϥ : ⲟⲩⲟϩ ⲙ̀ⲡⲉⲛⲑⲣⲉϥϣⲱⲡⲓ ⲛ̀ϫⲉ ⲫⲏⲉⲧϣⲟⲡ ⲛ̀ϧⲏⲧⲥ : ⲛ̀ⲧⲉϥ ⲙⲉⲧⲉ̀ⲡⲓⲥⲕⲟⲡⲟⲥ ⲙⲁⲣⲉ ⲕⲉⲟⲩⲁⲓ ϭⲓⲧⲥ . Ⲡⲓⲥⲁϫⲓ ⲇⲉ ⲛ̀ⲧⲉ Ⲡⳓⲥ .

نحو مئة وعشرين اسماً ، فقال أيها الرجال الأخوة ، ينبغى أن يتم هذا المكتوب ، الذى سبق الروح القدس فقاله بفم داود عن يهوذا ، الذى صار دليلاً للذين قبضوا على يسوع . لأنه كان معدوداً بيننا وصار له نصيب فى هذه الخدمة . فاقتنى هذا حقلاً من أجرة الظلم . وإذ سقط على وجهه وإنشق من وسطه فأنسكبت أحشاؤه كلها . وصار ذلك معلوماً عند جميع سكان أورشليم . حتى سمى ذلك الحقل بلغتهم (أيكيل داماغ) الذى تفسيره حقل دما أى حقل الدم . لأنه مكتوب فى سفر المزامير: لتصر داره خراباً ، ولا يكن فيها ساكن . وليأخذ أسقفيته آخر . لم تزل كلمة الرب ...

Chanting, while proceeding the church in the opposite direction, starting towards the south

تقال هذه القطعة تبكيتاً ليهوذا الاسخريوطى وهم يطوفون البيعة يساراً

Judas (6) who has broken the law.	Ⲓⲟⲩⲇⲁⲥ ⲟ̀ⲡⲁⲣⲁⲛⲟⲙⲟⲥ : ⲁⲣⲅⲩⲣⲓⲱ ⲉⲡⲁⲣⲁⲑⲉⲥ ⲁⲥⲭⲟ ⲧⲓⲥ ⲓⲟⲩⲇⲉⲓⲥ ⲡⲁⲣⲁⲛⲟⲙⲓⲥ : ⲓⲇⲉ ⲡⲁⲣⲁⲛⲟⲙⲓ ⲉ̀ⲡⲓⲗⲁⲃⲟⲛ ⲙⲉⲛⲓ ⲧⲟⲛ ⲭⲟ : ⲥⲧⲁⲩⲣⲱ ⲡⲣⲟⲥ ⲏ̀ⲗⲱⲥⲁⲛ ⲉⲛⲧⲱ ⲕⲣⲁⲛⲓⲱ ⲧⲟⲡⲱ.	يووداس أو بارانوموس : أرجيريو إباراثيس أسخريستوس تيس يوذيس بارانوميس : بارانومى إبى لافو مين طون خرستوس : إسطافرو إبروس إيلوصان إندو إكرانيو طوبو .	يا يهوذا يا مخالف الناموس . بالفضة بعت سيدك المسيح لليهود مخالفى الناموس فأما مخالفى الناموس فقد أخذوا المسيح وسمروه على الصليب فى موضع الأقرانيون .

With silver, you have sold Christ to the Jews, who have broken the law. The law breakers took Christ and nailed Him on the Cross at the place of Cranium.

Judas (6)	(Ⲓⲟⲩⲇⲁⲥ ..)	(يووداس)	(يا يهوذا ...)

Barabbas the condemned thief was set free and the Master, the Judge they crucified. They thrust a spear in Your side, and as a thief they nailed You on the Cross. They laid You in a

Ⲃⲁⲣⲁⲃⲃⲁⲛ ⲧⲟⲛ ⲕⲁⲧⲁⲕⲣⲓⲧⲟⲛ: ⲁⲡⲉⲗⲩⲥⲁⲛⲁⲩ ⲧⲟⲛ ⲕⲣⲓⲧⲏⲛ : ⲕⲉⲇⲉⲥⲡⲟⲧⲏⲛ ⲉⲥⲧⲁⲩⲣⲱⲥⲁⲛ . Ⲓⲥ ⲧⲏⲛ ⲛⲗⲉⲩⲣⲁⲛ ⲗⲟⲅⲭⲏⲛ ⲉⲡⲓⲑⲉⲛⲧⲏⲥ : ⲕⲉⲱⲥ ⲧⲏⲥⲧⲏⲥ ⲍⲩⲗⲱ ⲡⲣⲟⲥ ⲏ̀ⲗⲱⲛⲁⲥ ⲉ̀ⲑⲕⲁⲛ : ⲉⲛ

طون بارابان كاطاكريطون : أبيليصاناف طون إكريتين : كيه نيسبوتين إسطافروصان : إس تين إنليفران لونشين إبثينديس : كيؤس تيستيس : زيلو إبروس إيلوناس إنكان

باراباس اللص المسجون أطلقوه والسيد الديان صلبوه فى جنبك وضعوا حربة ومثل لص سمروك على خشبة ووضعوك فى قبر يا

tomb, O You, who raised Lazarus from the tomb.	ⲙ̀ⲛⲏⲙⲓ̀ⲱⲟ ⲉⲕⲧⲟⲧ ⲧⲁⲫⲟⲧ : ⲉ̀ⲅⲓⲣⲁⲥⲧⲟⲛ Ⲗⲁⲍⲁⲣⲟⲛ	إن إمنيم إأوأو : إغراسطون لازارون .	من أقام لعازر من القبر .

Judas (6) — (Ⲓⲟⲩⲇⲁⲥ..) — (يووداس) — (يا يهوذا ...)

For as Jonah stayed three days inside the whale's belly, also our Savior stayed three days. After He died, they sealed the tomb.	Ⲱⲥⲡⲉⲣ ⲅⲁⲣ Ⲓⲱⲛⲁⲥ ⲧ̀ⲣⲓⲥ ⲛ̀ⲉ̀ⲙⲉⲣⲁⲥ ⲉ̀ⲙⲓⲛⲉⲛ : ⲉⲛⲕⲓⲗⲓⲁ ⲧⲟⲩⲕⲏ ⲧⲟⲩⲟⲩⲧⲱⲥ ⲕⲉ ⲥⲱⲧⲏⲣ ⲏ̀ⲙⲱⲛ : ⲧ̀ⲣⲓⲥ ⲛ̀ⲉ̀ⲙⲉⲣⲁⲥ ⲉ̀ⲙⲓⲛⲉⲛ : ⲙⲉⲧⲁⲧⲟⲩ ⲧⲉⲑⲛⲏⲕⲟⲧⲟⲩⲧⲟⲛ ⲧⲁⲫⲟⲛ : ⲉⲥⲫⲁⲣⲅⲓⲥⲁⲛⲧⲟ.	أوسبير غار يوناس إتريس إيمراس إيمنين : إنكيليا طووكى طوو أووطوس كيه صوتير إيمون : إتريس إيميراس إيمينين : ميطاطوو تيثنيكو طووطون طافون: إسفارجيصاندو .	لأنه كما مكث يونان ثلاثة أيام فى بطن الحوت هكذا مخلصنا أقام ثلاثة أيام وبعد أن مات ختموا القبر .

Judas (6) — (Ⲓⲟⲩⲇⲁⲥ ..) — (يووداس) — (يا يهوذا ...)

Truly He rose but the soldiers were not aware that truly the Savior of the world has risen. He who suffered and died for our sake, O Lord, glory be to You. Amen.	Ⲟⲛⲧⲱⲥ ⲁⲛⲉⲥⲧⲏ ⲕⲉ ⲟⲩⲕⲉⲩⲛⲱⲥ ⲁⲛⲥⲧⲣⲁⲧⲓⲁⲱⲧⲉ : ⲟⲩⲛⲧⲱⲥⲅⲉⲣⲑⲓⲥ ⲟ̀ⲃⲱⲧⲏⲣ ⲧⲟⲩⲕⲟⲥⲙⲟⲩ : ⲟ̀ⲡⲁⲑⲱⲛ ⲕⲉ ⲁⲛⲁⲥ ⲧⲁⲥⲇⲓⲁⲧⲟⲩ : ⲅⲉⲛⲟⲥ ⲏ̀ⲙⲱⲛ Ⲕⲩⲣⲓⲉ Ⲇⲟⲝⲁⲥⲓ : ⲁ̀ⲙⲏⲛ.	أوندوس أنيستى كيه أووكيغنوس أنستراتياوتيه : أووندوسجيرثيس أوفوتير طوو كوزمو : أو باثون كيه أناس طاسدياطوو : جينوس إيمون كيريه ذوكصاسى : آمين .	بالحقيقة قام والجند لم يعلموا . أنه حقاً نهض مخلص العالم الذى تألم وقام لأجل جنسنا يارب لك المجد إلى الأبد آمين .

Ⲁ̀ⲅⲓⲟⲥ is prayed in the Paschal tune
ويقال أجيوس بلحن الصلبوت

Holy God, Holy Mighty, Holy Immortal, Who was crucified for us, Have mercy upon us.	Ⲁ̀ⲅⲓⲟⲥ ⲟ̀ Ⲑⲉⲟⲥ : ⲁ̀ⲅⲓⲟⲥ Ⲓⲥⲭⲩⲣⲟⲥ : ⲁ̀ⲅⲓⲟⲥ Ⲁ̀ⲑⲁⲛⲁⲧⲟⲥ : ⲟ̀ ⲥⲧⲁⲩⲣⲱⲑⲓⲥ Ⲇⲓ Ⲏ̀ⲙⲁⲥ Ⲉ̀ⲗⲉ̀ⲏⲥⲟⲛ ⲏ̀ⲙⲁⲥ.	قدوس الله . قدوس القوى . قدوس الحى الذى لا يموت ، الذى صلب عنا ، أرحمنا .
Holy God, Holy Mighty, Holy Immortal, Who was crucified for us, Have mercy upon us.	Ⲁ̀ⲅⲓⲟⲥ ⲟ̀ Ⲑⲉⲟⲥ : ⲁ̀ⲅⲓⲟⲥ Ⲓⲥⲭⲩⲣⲟⲥ : ⲁ̀ⲅⲓⲟⲥ Ⲁ̀ⲑⲁⲛⲁⲧⲟⲥ : ⲟ̀ ⲥⲧⲁⲩⲣⲱⲑⲓⲥ Ⲇⲓ Ⲏ̀ⲙⲁⲥ Ⲉ̀ⲗⲉ̀ⲏⲥⲟⲛ ⲏ̀ⲙⲁⲥ.	قدوس الله . قدوس القوى . قدوس الحى الذى لا يموت ، الذى صلب عنا ، أرحمنا .
Holy God, Holy Mighty, Holy Immortal, Who was crucified for us, Have mercy upon us.	Ⲁ̀ⲅⲓⲟⲥ ⲟ̀ Ⲑⲉⲟⲥ : ⲁ̀ⲅⲓⲟⲥ Ⲓⲥⲭⲩⲣⲟⲥ : ⲁ̀ⲅⲓⲟⲥ Ⲁ̀ⲑⲁⲛⲁⲧⲟⲥ : ⲟ̀ ⲥⲧⲁⲩⲣⲱⲑⲓⲥ Ⲇⲓ Ⲏ̀ⲙⲁⲥ Ⲉ̀ⲗⲉ̀ⲏⲥⲟⲛ ⲏ̀ⲙⲁⲥ.	قدوس الله . قدوس القوى . قدوس الحى الذى لا يموت ، الذى صلب عنا ، أرحمنا .
Glory be to the Father and to the Son, and to the Holy Spirit, both now, and ever, and unto the ages of ages, Amen.	Ⲇⲟⲝⲁ Ⲡⲁⲧⲣⲓ ⲕⲉ Ⲩ̀ⲓⲱ : ⲕⲉ ⲁ̀ⲅⲓⲱ ⲡ̀ⲛⲁⲧⲓ . Ⲕⲉ ⲛⲩⲛ ⲕⲉ ⲁ̀ⲓ ⲕⲉ ⲓⲥ ⲧⲟⲩⲥ ⲉ̀ⲱ̀ⲛⲁⲥ ⲧⲱⲛ ⲉ̀ⲱ̀ⲛⲱⲛ ⲁ̀ⲙⲉⲛ.	المجد للآب و الإبن و الروح القدس . الآن و كل أوان و الى دهر الدهور ، آمين .

The priest prays the Litany of the Gospel

ثم يقول الكاهن أوشية الانجيل

The Psalm

Ψⲁⲗⲙⲟⲥ ⲛ̅ⲇ̅ : ⲓ̅ⲏ̅ ⲛⲉⲙ ⲓ̅

Psalms 54:18, 10

His words were softer than oil, Yet they were drawn swords. For it is not an enemy who reproaches me; Then I could bear it. Nor is it one who hates me who has exalted himself against me; Then I could hide from him. Alleluia

Ⲁⲩϭⲛⲟⲛ ⲛ̀ϫⲉ ⲛⲉϥⲥⲁϫⲓ ⲉ̀ⲥⲟⲧⲉ ⲟⲩⲛⲉϩ : ⲛ̀ⲑⲱⲟⲩ ϩⲁⲛⲥⲟⲑⲛⲉϥ ⲛⲉ : ϫⲉ ⲉ̀ⲛⲉ ⲟⲩϫⲁϫⲓ ⲡⲉⲧⲁϥϯϣⲱϣ ⲛⲏⲓ ⲛⲁⲓⲛⲁϥⲁⲓ ⲉ̀ⲣⲟϥ ⲡⲉ : ⲟⲩⲟϩ ⲉ̀ⲛⲉ ⲡⲉⲑⲙⲟⲥϯ ⲙ̀ⲙⲟⲓ ⲁϥϫⲱ ⲛ̀ϩⲁⲛⲛⲓϣϯ ⲛ̀ⲥⲁϫⲓ ⲉ̀ϩⲣⲏⲓ ⲉ̀ϫⲱⲓ ⲛⲁⲓⲛⲁⲭⲟⲡⲧ ⲉ̀ⲃⲟⲗ ϩⲁⲣⲟϥ . ⲁⲗ.

أفتشنون إنجيه نيف صاجى إهوتيه أوو نيه : إنثوأوو هان صوثنيف نيه : جيه إنيه أووجاى بيطافتى شوش نى ناينافاى إروف بيه : أووه إنيه بيثموستى إمموى أڤجو إنهان نيشتى إنصاجى إهرى إجوى نايناكوبت إيفول هاروف . الليلويا .

(مز 54: 18 و 10)

كلامه ألين من الدهن وهو نصال . فلو كان العدو عيرنى إذا لاحتملت . ولو ان مبغضى عظّم علىّ الكلام لاختفيت منه . الليلويا .

Introduction to the Gospel, Page: 8 : مقدمة الأنجيل ، صفحة

The Gospel

Ⲉⲩⲁⲅⲅⲉⲗⲓⲟⲛ Ⲕⲁⲧⲁ Ⲗⲟⲩⲕⲁⲛ Ⲕⲉ̅ⲫ ⲕ̅ⲃ̅ : ⲍ̅ - ⲓⲅ̅

Luke 22:7-13

Then came the Day of Unleavened Bread, when the Passover must be killed. And He sent Peter and John, saying, "Go and prepare the Passover for us, that we may eat." So they said to Him, "Where do You want us to prepare?" And He said to them, "Behold, when you have entered the city, a man will meet you carrying a pitcher of water; follow him into the house which he enters. Then you shall say to the master of the house, 'The Teacher says to you, "Where is the guest room where I may eat the Passover with My disciples?" ' Then he will show you a large, furnished upper room; there make ready." So they went and found it just as He had said to them, and they prepared the Passover. Glory be to God forever, Amen.

Ⲁϥⲓ̀ ⲇⲉ ⲛ̀ϫⲉ ⲡⲓⲉ̀ϩⲟⲟⲩ ⲛ̀ⲧⲉ ⲛⲓⲁⲧϣⲉⲙⲏⲣ ⲫⲏⲉⲧⲉ ⲥ̀ϣⲉ ⲉ̀ϣⲁⲧ ⲙ̀ⲡⲓⲡⲁⲥⲭⲁ ⲛ̀ϧⲏⲧϥ . Ⲟⲩⲟϩ ⲁϥⲟⲩⲱⲣⲡ ⲙ̀Ⲡⲉⲧⲣⲟⲥ ⲛⲉⲙ Ⲓⲱⲁⲛⲛⲏⲥ ⲉⲁϥϫⲟⲥ : ϫⲉ ⲙⲁϣⲉⲛⲱⲧⲉⲛ ⲥⲉⲃⲧⲉ ⲡⲓⲡⲁⲥⲭⲁ ⲛⲁⲛ ϩⲓⲛⲁ ⲛ̀ⲧⲉⲛⲟⲩⲟⲙϥ . Ⲛ̀ⲑⲱⲟⲩ ⲇⲉ ⲡⲉϫⲱⲟⲩ ⲛⲁϥ ϫⲉ ⲭ̀ⲟⲩⲱϣ ⲉ̀ⲧⲉⲛⲥⲉⲃⲧⲱⲧϥ ⲑⲱⲛ . Ⲛ̀ⲑⲟϥ ⲇⲉ ⲡⲉϫⲁϥ ⲛⲱⲟⲩ : ϫⲉ ϩⲏⲡⲡⲉ ⲉ̀ⲣⲉⲧⲉⲛⲛⲁϣⲉⲛⲱⲧⲉⲛ ⲉ̀ϧⲟⲩⲛ ⲉ̀ϯⲃⲁⲕⲓ : ϥⲛⲁⲓ̀ ⲉ̀ⲃⲟⲗ ⲉ̀ϩⲣⲏⲓ ⲑⲏⲛⲟⲩ ⲛ̀ϫⲉ ⲟⲩⲣⲱⲙⲓ ⲉϥϥⲁⲓ ⲛ̀ⲟⲩϣⲟϣⲟⲩ ⲙ̀ⲙⲱⲟⲩ : ⲙⲟϣⲓ ⲛ̀ⲥⲱϥ ⲉ̀ⲡⲓⲏⲓ ⲉ̀ⲧⲉϥⲛⲁϣⲉ ⲉ̀ϧⲟⲩⲛ ⲉ̀ⲣⲟϥ . Ⲟⲩⲟϩ ⲁϫⲟⲥ ⲙ̀ⲡⲓⲛⲉⲃ̀ⲏⲓ ⲛ̀ⲧⲉ ⲡⲓⲏⲓ : ϫⲉ ⲡⲉϫⲉ ⲡⲓⲣⲉϥϯⲥⲃⲱ ⲛⲁⲕ ϫⲉ ⲁⲩ ⲡⲉ ⲡⲁⲙⲁ ⲛ̀ⲉⲙⲧⲟⲛ : ⲫⲙⲁ ⲉ̀ϯⲛⲁⲟⲩⲱⲙ ⲙ̀ⲡⲁⲡⲁⲥⲭⲁ ⲙ̀ⲙⲟϥ ⲛⲉⲙ ⲛⲁⲙⲁⲑⲏⲧⲏⲥ . Ⲟⲩⲟϩ ⲫⲏⲉⲧⲉ ⲙ̀ⲙⲁⲩ ϥⲛⲁⲧⲁⲙⲱⲧⲉⲛ ⲉ̀ⲟⲩⲛⲓϣϯ ⲙ̀ⲙⲁ ⲉϥⲥⲁⲡϣⲱⲓ ⲉϥⲫⲱⲣϣ : ⲥⲉⲃⲧⲱⲧ ⲙ̀ⲙⲁⲩ . Ⲉⲧⲁⲩϣⲉⲛⲱⲟⲩ ⲇⲉ ⲁⲩϫⲓⲙⲓ ⲕⲁⲧⲁ ⲫ̀ⲣⲏϯ ⲉⲧⲁϥϫⲟⲥ ⲛⲱⲟⲩ : ⲟⲩⲟϩ ⲁⲩⲥⲉⲃⲧⲉ ⲡⲓⲡⲁⲥⲭⲁ . ⲟⲩⲱϣⲧ ⲙ̀ⲡⲓⲉⲩⲁⲅⲅⲉⲗⲓⲟⲛ ⲉ̅ⲑ̅ⲩ̅ .

(لوقا 22: 7 - 13)

جاء يوم الفطير الذى ينبغى أن يُذبح فيه الفصح . فأرسل بطرس ويوحنا قائلاً : أمضيا وأعدا لنا الفصح لنأكله . فقالا له : أين تريد أن نعده . فقال لهما: إذا دخلتما المدينة يلقاكما رجل حامل جرة ماء ، فاتبعاه إلى البيت الذى يدخله وقولا لرب البيت ، المعلم يقول لكَ أين موضع راحتى الذى آكل فيه الفصح مع تلاميذى؟ فهو يريكما علية كبيرة مفروشة فاعدا هناك . فانطلقا ووجدا كما قال لهما . فاعدا الفصح . والمجد لله دائماً .

Introduction to the Exposition, Page: 9 : مقدمة الطرح ، صفحة

Exposition

طـرح

"Passover is drawing near O Lord. Tell us where to prepare for You. You are our Passover, O Jesus Christ.", said the disciples. He sent two of his disciples, Peter and John, and he told them: go to this town and you will find a man carrying a jar of water. Follow his footsteps to the place where he goes in. Go see the owner of the house and tell him, the Lord says: where is the place where I celebrate Passover? He will show you an upper room, which is vacant but furnished. Make preparations for Passover there. They did as the Lord said. Come along all you nations and rejoice, God the Word is our Passover. The First Passover lamb delivered the people from the servitude of Pharaoh. The new Passover is the Son of God Who saves the World from corruption. In so many forms He prepared the world, from sunrise to sunset, for eternal salvation. He lifted us to the heights of his mercy and compassion. He manifested the greatness of His grace that He bestowed on all the creation. He took what is ours and gave us what is His, and granted us His righteousness.

(North side) Christ our Savior; has come and has borne suffering; that through His Passion; He may save us.

(South side) Let us glorify Him; and exalt His Name; for He had mercy on us; according to His great mercy.

يوم الفصح قد إقترب يا سيدنا عرفنا المكان الذى نعده لك. قال التلاميذ للمعلم: أنت هو فصحنا يا يسوع المسيح . فأرسل إثنين من تلاميذه الصفا ويوحنا وقال لهما: قوما وامضيا إلى هذه المدينة فتجدان رجلاً حاملاً جرة ماء. إذا مشى سيرا أنتما خلفه إلى الموضع الذى يدخل إليه . فقولا لصاحب البيت: يقول المعلم أين المكان الذى آكل فيه الفصح؟ فذاك يريكما غليةً فوقانية خالية مفروشة . اعدا الفصح فى ذلك الموضع . وهكذا صنعا كقول الرب . تعالوا أيها الأمم افرحوا وتهللوا أن الإله الكلمة صار لكم فصحاً . الفصح الأول الذى بالخروف خلص الشعب من عبودية فرعون . والفصح الجديد هو ابن الله الذى خلص العالم من الفساد . بأنواع كثيرة وأشياء شتى اعد الخلاص والنجاة الأبدية . لكن هذا الخلاص هو لكل العالم من مشارق الشمس إلى مغاربها. جذب كل أحد إلى علو رحمته وللرأفة التى كان يصنعها ، وأظهر لهم كثرة نعمته التى افاضها على كل موضع من المسكونة . اخذ الذى لنا وجعله مع الذى له وتفضل علينا بصلاحه .

(مرد بحرى) المسيح مخلصنا جاء وتألم عنا لكى بآلامه يخلصنا .

(مرد قبلى) فلنمجده ونرفع إسمه لأنه صنع معنا رحمة كعظيم رحمته .

| The Conclusion of the Exposition, Page: | 9 | : ختام الطرح ، صفحة |

| The Conclusion with the Daytime Litanies, Page: | 10 | : طلبة الصباح ، صفحة |

The Third, Sixth and Ninth hours are prayed at the second section of the church as usual in the Pascha.

ثم تصلى ساعات الثالثة و السادسة و التاسعة فى الخورس الثانى كالمعتاد فى البصخة

The Third Hour of Thursday of the Holy Pascha
الساعة الثالثة من يوم الخميس من البصخة المقدسة

Exodus 32:30-33:5

And it came to pass on the next day that Moses said to the people, You have sinned a great sin; and now I will go up to God, that I may make atonement for your sin. And Moses returned to the Lord and said, I pray, O Lord, this people have sinned a great sin, and they have made for themselves golden gods. And now if You will forgive their sin, forgive; and if not, blot me out of Your book, which You have written. And the Lord said to Moses, If anyone has sinned against Me, I will blot them out of My book. And now go, descend from here, and lead this people into the place of which I spoke to you. Behold, My angel shall go before your face; and in the day when I shall visit I will bring upon them their sin. And the Lord struck the people for the making of the calf, which Aaron had made. And the Lord said to Moses, Go forward, go up from here, you and your people, whom you brought out of the land of Egypt, into the land which I swore to Abraham, Isaac, and Jacob, saying, I will give it to your seed. And I will send at the same time My angel before your face, and he shall cast out the Amorite and the Hittite and the Perizzite and the Girgashite and the Hivite and the Jebusite and the Canaanite. And I will bring you into a land flowing with milk and honey; for I will not go up with you, because you are a stiff-necked people, lest I consume you by the way. And the people, having heard this grievous saying, mourned in mourning apparel. For the Lord said to the children of Israel, You are a stiff-necked people; take heed lest I bring on you another plague and destroy you. Glory be to the Holy Trinity. Amen

Sirach 24:1-15

A reading from the Wisdom of Joshua, son of Sirach, the prophet. May his holy blessings be with us. Amen. Wisdom will praise herself, and in the midst of her people she will boast. In the assembly of the Most High, she will open her mouth and boast in the presence of His host. "I came forth from the mouth of the Most High And covered the earth like a mist. I pitched my tent in the high places and my throne on the pillar of cloud. I alone encircle the ring of heaven, And I walk in the depth of the abyss. In the waves of the sea, in all the earth, and in every people and nation, I have gained a possession. With all these, I have sought a place to rest; In what inheritance will I lodge? "Then the Creator of all things commanded me, And He who created me gave me a place to live. He said, 'Pitch your tent in Jacob and receive an inheritance in Israel.' Before the age, He created me from the beginning, And in the age to come I will not cease. I serve before Him in His holy tabernacle; Therefore, I am established in Zion. In the beloved city

(الخروج ص 22 : 30 - 33 : 5)

وكان بعد الغد ان قال موسى للشعب: أنتم قد أخطأتم خطية عظيمة ، فأصعد الآن إلى الله لعلى أكفر عن خطيتكم . فرجع موسى إلى الرب وقال : اتضرع إليك يارب قد خطئ هذا الشعب خطية عظيمة . وصنعوا لهم آلهة من ذهب والآن ان كنت تغفر لهم خطيتهم فأغفر وإلا فامحنى من سفرك الذى كتبتنى فيه . فقال الرب لموسى : من أخطأ أمامى أمحوه من سفرى . والآن امض لتنزل وتقود هذا الشعب إلى حيث قلت لك . هوذا ملاكى يسير أمامك . وفى يوم افتقادى أجلب عليهم خطيتهم . فضرب الرب الشعب بسبب صنع العجل الذى صنعه هرون . وقال الرب لموسى اذهب وانطلق من ههنا . أنت وشعبك هؤلاء الذين أخرجتهم من أرض مصر . إلى الأرض التى اقسمت لإبراهيم واسحق ويعقوب قائلاً : لنسلك أعطيها . وأنا أرسل أمامك ملاكى . ويطرد الآمورى والكلدانى والفرزانى واليبوسانى والكنعانى وادخلك إلى الأرض التى تفيض لبناً وعسلاً . وأما أنا فلا أصعد معك . لانك شعب صلب الرقبة لئلا افنيك فى الطريق . فلما سمع الشعب هذا الكلام القاسى ناحوا . فقال الرب لبنى إسرائيل: أنتم شعب صلب الرقبة . انظروا لئلا أتى عليكم بضربة أخرى فابيدكم . مجداً للثالوث القدوس .

(من يشوع بن سيراخ 24 : 1 - 15)

الحكمة تمدح نفسها . وتقبل طالبيها. وتفتخر وسط الجماعات . وتفتح فاها فى جماعة العلى . وتفتخر أمام قوته قائلة : انى خرجت من فم العلى . وغشيت الأرض مثل الضباب وسكنت فى الأعالى . وعرشى فى عامود سحاب وطفت حول السماء وحدى وسلكت فى عمق الغمر وفى أمواج البحر والأرض باسرها . وهبطت فى كل الشعوب وكل الأمم . فى هذه كلها التمست مسكناً ، فبأى ميراث أحل حينئذ؟ أوصانى خالق الجميع ، والذى خلقنى عين مسكنى وقال: اسكنى فى يعقوب ، ورثى فى إسرائيل . قبل الدهور ومن البدء خلقتنى وإلى الأبد لا أزول. وقد خدمت أمامه فى الخيمة المقدسة وهكذا فى صهيون ثبتنى لاسكن فى مدينته المحبوبة وسلطانى فى أورشليم . مجداً للثالوث القدوس .

likewise He gives me rest, and my authority is in Jerusalem. Glory be to the Holy Trinity. Amen.

Zechariah 9:11-14

And you, by the blood of your covenant, have sent forth your prisoners out of the waterless pit.You shall dwell in strongholds, you prisoners of the congregation: and for one day of your captivity I will recompense you double.   For I have bent you, O Judah, for Myself as a bow, I have filled Ephraim; and I will raise up your children, O Zion, against the children of the Greeks, and I will handle you as the sword of a warrior. And the Lord shall be over them, and His arrow shall go forth as lightning: and the Lord Almighty shall blow with the trumpet. Glory be to the Holy Trinity. Amen

(من سفر زكريا النبى 9 : 11 - 14)

وبدم عهدك أنت أيضاً أطلق أسراك من الجب الذى ليس فيه ماء . إرجعوا إلى الحصن يا أسرى الرجاء. وبدل يوم واحد من سبيك سأرد عليك ضعفين. لأنى أوترت يهوذا لنفسى ، ومثل قوس ملأت أفرايم وأقيم أولادك يا صهيون على بنى ياوان وأقويك كسيف محارب. والرب يكون عليهم وقوسه يخرج مثل البرق. والرب الضابط الكل يبوق فى بوق عظيم . مجداً للثالوث القدوس .

Proverbs 29:27 – 30:1

My son, fear and accept my words, and repent. These things says the man to them that trust in God; and I cease. For I am the most wise of all men, and there is not in me the wisdom of men. God has taught me wisdom, and I know the knowledge of the Holy One. Who has gone up to heaven, and come down? Who has gathered the winds in His bosom? Who has wrapped up the waters in a garment? Who has dominion of all the ends of the earth? What is His name? Or what is the name of His Son? For all the words of God are tried in the fire, and He defends those that reverence Him. Add not unto His words, lest He reprove you, and you be made a liar. Glory be to the Holy Trinity. Amen.

(من أمثال سليمان 29 : 27 - 30 : 1)

يا إبنى هب كلامى واقبله وتب. هذه الأشياء التى يقولها الإنسان للذين يؤمنون بالله . وأنا أسكت لأنى أعقل من كل إنسان وليس لى حكمة البشر . الله هو الذى علمنى الحكمة. وأنا أعرف معرفة القدوس. من الذى جمع الرياح فى حضنه؟ ومن الذى صَر المياه فى ثوبه؟ من الذى تسلط على أقطار الأرض؟ ما هو اسمه واسم إبنه؟ لأن قول الله مختار وممحص، ومعرفة الناموس هى ذكر حسن. وهو ذاته ينصر الذين يخافونه. لا تزد على كلماته لئلا يوبخك فتكذب . مجداً للثالوث القدوس .

Pascha Praise – B (12 times), Page: 7   : صفحة ، تسبحة البصخة B (12 مرة)

The Psalm

Ⲯⲁⲗⲙⲟⲥ ϙⲅ̅ : ⲓ̅ⲅ̅ ⲛⲉⲙ ⲓ̅ⲉ̅

Psalms 93:13, 15

They will hunt for the soul of the righteous, and condemn innocent blood. And He will recompense to them their iniquity and their wickedness; the Lord our God shall utterly destroy them. Alleluia

Ⲥⲉⲛⲁϫⲱⲣⲝ ⲉ̀ϫⲉⲛ ⲧ̀ⲯⲩⲭⲏ ⲛ̀ⲟⲩⲑⲙⲏⲓ : ⲟⲩⲟϩ ⲟⲩⲥ̀ⲛⲟϥ ⲛ̀ⲁⲑⲛⲟⲃⲓ ⲥⲉⲛⲁϩⲓⲧϥ̀ ⲉ̀ⲡ̀ϩⲁⲡ . Ⲟⲩⲟϩ ⲉϥⲉ̀ⲧⲱⲃ ⲛⲱⲟⲩ ⲛ̀ⲧⲟⲩⲁⲛⲟⲙⲓⲁ ⲛⲉⲙ ⲡⲟⲩⲡⲉⲧϩⲟⲩ : ⲟⲩⲟϩ ⲉϥⲉ̀ⲧⲁⲕⲱⲟⲩ ⲛ̀ϫⲉ Ⲡ̅ⲟ̅ⲥ̅ Ⲡⲁⲛⲟⲩϯ . ⲁⲗ .

سينا جورج إيجين إتبيسيشى إنؤو إثمي : أووه أوو إسنوف إن أثنوفى سيناهيتف إإبهاب . أووه إفئطوب نوأوو إنطوو أنوميا نيم بوو بيتهوو : أووه إفئطاكوأوو إنجيه إبتشويس بانووتى . الليلويا

(مز 93: 13 و15)

يتصيدون على نفس الصديق . ويلقون إلى الحكم دماً زكياً. وسيكافئهم بآثمهم وشرهم ويبيدهم الرب إلهى . الليلويا .

Introduction to the Gospel, Page: 8   : صفحة ، مقدمة الأنجيل

The Gospel

Ⲉⲩⲁⲅⲅⲉⲗⲓⲟⲛ Ⲕⲁⲧⲁ Ⲙⲁⲧⲑⲉⲟⲛ Ⲕⲉⲫ ⲕ̅ⲋ̅ : ⲓ̅ⲍ̅ - ⲓ̅ⲑ̅

Matthew 26:17-19

Now on the first day of the Feast of Unleavened Bread the disciples came to Jesus, saying to Him, "Where do You want us to prepare for You to eat the Passover?" And He said, "Go into the city to a certain man, and say to him, 'The Teacher says, "My time is at hand; I will keep the Passover at your house with My disciples." ' " So the disciples did as Jesus had directed them; and they prepared the Passover. Glory be to God forever, Amen.

Ⲛ̀ϩⲣⲏⲓ ⲇⲉ ϧⲉⲛ ⲡⲓ̀ϩⲟⲟⲩ ⲛ̀ϩⲟⲩⲓⲧ ⲛ̀ⲧⲉ ⲛⲓⲁⲧⲕⲱⲃ : ⲁⲩⲓ̀ ⲛ̀ϫⲉ ⲛⲓⲙⲁⲑⲏⲧⲏⲥ ϩⲁ Ⲓⲏⲥ ⲉⲩⲭⲱ ⲙ̀ⲙⲟⲥ : ϫⲉ ⲁⲕⲟⲩⲱϣ ⲉ̀ⲥⲉⲃⲧⲉ ⲡⲓⲡⲁⲥⲭⲁ ⲛⲁⲕ ⲑⲱⲛ ⲉ̀ⲟⲩⲟⲙϥ . Ⲛ̀ⲑⲟϥ ⲇⲉ ⲡⲉϫⲁϥ ⲛⲱⲟⲩ : ϫⲉ ⲙⲁϣⲉⲛⲱⲧⲉⲛ ⲉ̀ⲧⲁⲓⲃⲁⲕⲓ ϩⲁ ⲡⲁⲫⲙⲁⲛ ⲛ̀ⲣⲱⲙⲓ ⲟⲩⲟϩ ⲁϫⲟⲥ ⲛⲁϥ : ϫⲉ ⲡⲉϫⲉ ⲡⲓⲣⲉϥϯⲥⲃⲱ ϫⲉ ⲡⲁⲥⲛⲟⲩ ⲁϥϧⲱⲛⲧ : ⲉⲓⲛⲁⲓⲣⲓ ⲙ̀ⲡⲁⲡⲁⲥⲭⲁ ϧⲁⲧⲟⲧⲕ ⲛⲉⲙ ⲛⲁⲙⲁⲑⲏⲧⲏⲥ : ⲟⲩⲟϩ ⲁⲩⲓⲣⲓ ⲛ̀ϫⲉ ⲛⲓⲙⲁⲑⲏⲧⲏⲥ ⲙ̀ⲫⲣⲏϯ ⲉ̀ⲧⲁ Ⲓⲏⲥ ϫⲟⲥ ⲛⲱⲟⲩ ⲟⲩⲟϩ ⲁⲩⲥⲉⲃⲧⲉ ⲡⲓⲡⲁⲥⲭⲁ . ⲟⲩⲱϣⲧ ⲙ̀ⲡⲓⲉⲩⲁⲅⲅⲉⲗⲓⲟⲛ ⲉⲑ .

(متى 26 : 17 - 19)

وفى أول يوم من الفطير جاء التلاميذ إلى يسوع قائلين: أين تريد أن نعد لكَ الفصح لتأكله؟ أما هو فقال لهم : اذهبوا إلى هذه المدينة إلى فلان الرجل وقولوا له: المعلم يقول ان زمانى قد اقترب ، وعندك اصنع الفصح مع تلاميذى . ففعل التلاميذ كما أمرهم يسوع وأعدوا الفصح . والمجد لله دائماً .

| Introduction to the Exposition, Page: 9 | مقدمة الطرح ، صفحة : 9 |

Exposition

And on the next day, Moses said to the whole group of the sons of Israel: You have sinned before the Lord and made an ox to worship. Now I will go to intercede on your behalf so that He may grant you His mercy and forgive your sins. The prophet went back to God and bowed down before Him saying: O Merciful and patient Lord forgive your people's sin. If you elect not to forgive them, please blot me out of Your book of Life. The Lord said to him: If anyone has sinned against Me, I will blot them out of My book. And the people, having heard this grievous saying, mourned in mourning apparel. For the Lord said: You are a stiff-necked people; take heed lest I bring on you another plague and destroy you.

(North side) Christ our Savior; has come and has borne suffering; that through His Passion; He may save us.

(South side) Let us glorify Him; and exalt His Name; for He had mercy on us; according to His great mercy.

طرح

وفى الغد أجاب موسى وقال لكل جماعة بنى إسرائيل: انكم أخطأتم أمام الرب وصنعتم لكم عجلاً . والآن سأمضى وأسأل فيكم لعله يرحمكم ويغفر خطاياكم . فعاد النبى إلى الرب وسجد أمامه قائلاً : أيها الرب الرؤوف الطويل الروح اغفر خطايا شعبك . وان كنت لا تشاء ان تغفر لهم فامح اسمى من سفر الحياة . فقال له الرب: ان الذى أخطأ هو الذى يُمحى من سفرى . فلما سمع الشعب هذا القول الصعب ، ناحوا بنحيب عظيم . فقال الرب: انك أنت شعب قاسى غليظ الرقبة أثيم ، فانظر وتيقن فاننى مُنزل عليك ضربة عظيمة وأمحوك .

(مرد بحرى) المسيح مخلصنا جاء وتألم عنا لكى بآلامه يخلصنا .

(مرد قبلى) فلنمجده ونرفع اسمه لأنه صنع معنا رحمة كعظيم رحمته .

| The Conclusion of the Exposition, Page: 9 | ختام الطرح ، صفحة : 9 |

الساعة السادسة من يوم الخميس من البصخة المقدسة
The Sixth Hour of Thursday of the Holy Pascha

Jeremiah 7:2-15

Hear the word of the Lord, all Judea. Thus says the Lord God of Israel: Correct your ways and your devices, and I will cause you to dwell in this place. Trust not in yourselves with lying words, for they shall not profit you at all, saying, It is the temple of the Lord, the temple of the Lord. For if you thoroughly correct your ways and your practices, and do indeed execute judgment between a man and his neighbor; and oppress not the stranger, and the orphan, and the widow, and shed not innocent blood in this place, and go not after strange gods to your hurt; then will I cause you to dwell in this place, in the land which I gave to your fathers of old, and forever. But seeing you have trusted in lying words, whereby you shall not be profited; and you murder, and commit adultery, and steal, and swear falsely, and burn incense to Baal, and have gone after strange gods whom you know not, so that it is evil with you; yet have you come, and stood before Me in the house which is called by My name, and you have said, We have refrained from doing all these abominations. Is My house, which is called by My name, a den of robbers in your eyes? And behold, I have seen it, says the Lord. For go to My place with is in Shiloh, where I caused My name to dwell before, and see what I did to it because of the wickedness of My people Israel. And now, because you have done all these deeds, and I spoke to you, but you hearkened not to Me; and I called you, but you answered not. Therefore I also will do to the house which is called by My name, in which you trust, and to the place which I gave to you and to your fathers, as I did to Shiloh. And I will cast you out of My sight, as I cast away your brethren, all the seed of Ephraim. Glory be to the Holy Trinity. Amen

Ezekiel 20:39-44

And as for you, O house of Israel, thus says the Lord, even the Lord: Put away each one his evil practices, and hereafter if you hearken to Me, then shall you no more profane My holy name by your gifts and by devices. For upon My holy mountain, on the high mountain, says the Lord, even the Lord, there shall all the house of Israel serve Me forever. And there will I accept you, and there will I have respect to your first-fruits, and the firstfruits of your offerings, in all your holy things. I will accept you with a sweet-smelling savor, when I bring you out from the nations, and take you out of the countries in which you have been dispersed; and I will be sanctified among you in the sight of the nations. And you shall know that I am the Lord, when I have brought you into the land of Israel, into the land concerning which I lifted up My hand to give it to your fathers.

(من سفر أرميا النبى ص 7 : 2 - 15)

اسمعوا كلمة الرب يا جميع اليهودية . هذا ما يقوله رب القوات إله إسرائيل: قوِّموا طرقكم وأعمالكم فاسكنكم فى هذا الموضع . لا تتكلوا على نفوسكم ولا على كلام الكذب . لأنه لا ينفعكم البتة قائلين : هذا هيكل الرب . لأنكم إذا قوّمتم طرقكم وأعمالكم ، وأجريتم الحكم بين الرجل وصاحبه ولم تظلموا الغريب واليتيم والأرملة ولم تسفكوا دماً زكياً فى هذا الموضع . ولم تتبعوا آلهة غريبة هى شر لكم فانى أسكنكم فى هذا الموضع . فى الأرض التى أعطيتها لكم ولآبائكم من الأبد وإلى الدهر . فان توكلتم على كلام الكذب الذى لا تستفيدون منه وتسرقون وتقتلون وتزنون وتحلفون بالكذب على الظلم وتبخرون للبعل وتتبعون آلهة غريبة لم تعرفوها فانه سيكون شر لكم . ثم تأتون وتقفون أمامى فى البيت الذى دعى اسمى عليه وتقولون إننا قد فرغنا من ان نعمل الخطايا جميعها. هل بيتى مغارة لصوص هذا الذى دُعى اسمى عليه أمامكم هانذا قد رأيت ذلك يقول الرب . انكم قد دخلتم موضعى فى شيلوه المكان الذى جعلت اسمى فيه أولاً . ورأيتم ما قد صنعت به بسبب شر شعبى إسرائيل . والآن بما انكم عملتم هذه الأعمال كلها وقد كلمتكم فلم تسمعوا لى ودعوتكم فلم تجيبونى فالآن سأصنع بيتى هذا الذى دعى اسمى عليه . هذا الذى أنتم تترجونه . وبالموضع الذى أعطيته لكم ولآبائكم كما صنعت بشيلوه واخرجكم كما أخرجت جميع أخوتكم كل نسل افرايم . مجداً للثالوث القدوس .

(من سفر حزقيال النبى 20 : 39 - 44)

وأنتم يا بيت إسرائيل . اسمعوا قول الرب . هذا ما يقوله أدوناى الرب . ليقلع كل واحد وواحد منكم عن شروره . وبعد ذلك تطيعونى ولا تنجسوا اسمى القدوس بأصنامكم وأعمالكم لأنى أتيت على جبل قدسى . على جبل إسرائيل العالى يقول الرب . هناك يتعبد لى كل بيت إسرائيل. وهناك أقبلكم إلىّ . وهناك أطلب قرابينكم وباكورات مرفوعاتكم مع جميع مقدساتكم . وبرائحة البخور أقبلكم إلىّ إذا اخترتكم من بين الشعوب وقبلتكم إلىّ من الكور التى تشتم فيها . وأتقدس فيكم أمام أعين الأمم فتعلمون انى أنا هو الرب . حينما ادخلتكم إلى أرض إسرائيل . إلى الأرض التى مددت يدى عليها لأعطيها لآبائكم . وفى ذلك الموضع

And you shall there remember your ways, and your devices in which you defiled yourselves; and you shall bewail yourselves for all your wickedness. And you shall know that I am the Lord, when I have done thus to you, that My name may not be profaned in your evil ways, and in your corrupt devices, says the Lord. *Glory be to the Holy Trinity. Amen*

تذكرون طرقكم النجسة وأعمالكم الشريرة التى تنجستم بها . وترون وتنظرون وجوهكم فى كل ظلمكم وتعلمون أنى أنا هو الرب حين ما أصنع لكم هكذا . لكيلا يتدنس اسمى كطرقكم الرديئة وأعمالكم الفاسدة يقول أدوناى الرب . مجداً للثالوث القدوس .

Sirach 12:13-13:1

Who will pity a snake charmer when he is bitten, or those who go near wild animals? So, no one will pity one who approaches a sinful man and gets involved in his sins. He will stay with you for a while, but if you turn aside from him, he will not put up with you. An enemy speaks sweetly with his lips, but in his heart, he will plan to throw you into a pit. An enemy will shed tears, but if he finds an opportunity, he will not be satisfied apart from shedding your blood. If evil comes upon you, you will find your enemy there ahead of you, and as he pretends to help you, he will pull your feet from under you. He will shake his head and applaud with his hands; and he will whisper many things and alter his expression. Whoever touches pitch will be stained, and whoever associates with an arrogant man will become like him. *Glory be to the Holy Trinity. Amen*

(من يشوع بن سيراخ 12 : 13 - 13 : 1)

من يرحم راقياً قد لدغته الحية؟ أو يشفق على الذين يدنون من الوحوش؟ هكذا الذى يساير الرجل الخاطئ النشوان بخطاياه أنه يلبث معك ساعة وان ملت لا يثبت . العدو يتملق بشفتيه ويفكر فى قلبه يأتمر ليسقطك فى الحفرة . العدو تدمع عيناه وان وجد فرصة لا يشبع من دمك . ان لحقك شر وجدته قريباً منك ويوهمك أنه سيعينك وهو يعطيك مرارة ويحرك رأسه ليضرب بيديه ويتأسف جداً ويعبس وجهه . من يلمس القار يتلوث به . ومن يمشى مع المتكبر يشبهه . مجداً للثالوث القدوس .

Pascha Praise - B (12 times), Page: 7   : تسبحة البصخة B (12 مرة) ، صفحة

The Psalm

Ⲯⲁⲗⲙⲟⲥ ⲗ̅ : ⲓ̅ⲏ ⲛⲉⲙ ⲓ̅ⲅ̅

Psalms 30:18, 13

Let the deceitful lips become dumb, which speak iniquity against the righteous with pride and scorn. For I heard the slander of many that dwelt round about; when they were gathered together against me, they took counsel to take my life. *Alleluia*

Ⲙⲁⲣⲟⲩⲉⲣⲁⲧⲥⲁϫⲓ ⲛϫⲉ ⲛⲓⲥⲫⲟⲧⲟⲩ ⲛⲟϫⲓ : ⲛⲏⲉⲧⲥⲁϫⲓ ⲛⲟⲩⲁⲛⲟⲙⲓⲁ ϧⲁ ⲡⲓⲑⲙⲏⲓ .

Ϫⲉ ⲁⲓⲥⲱⲧⲉⲙ ⲉ̀ⲡϣⲱϣ ⲛⲟⲩⲙⲏϣ ⲉⲩϣⲟⲡ ⲙ̀ⲡⲁⲕⲱⲧ : ϧⲉⲛ ⲡϫⲓⲛ ⲑⲣⲟⲩⲟⲩⲱϯ ⲉⲩⲥⲟⲡ ⲉ̀ϩⲣⲏⲓ ⲉ̀ϫⲱⲓ ⲁⲩⲥⲟϭⲛⲓ ⲉ̀ϭⲓ ⲛ̀ⲧⲁⲯⲩⲭⲏ . ⲁ̅ⲗ̅ .

ماروو إر اتصاجى إنجيه نى إسفوطوو إنؤجى : نى إتصاجى إنؤو أنوميا خا بى إثمى .

جيه أيصوتيم إ̀بشوش إنؤو ميش إفشوب إمباكوتى : خين إبجين إثروو ثؤاووتى إفصوب إ̀هرى إجوى أفصوتشنى إنتشى إنطابسيشى . الليلويا.

(مز 30: 18 و13)

ولتنصر خرساء الشفاه الغاشة. المتكلمة على الصديق بالاثم . لأنى سمعت المذمة من كثيرين يسكنون حولى حين اجتمعوا علىّ جميعاً تآمروا على أخذ نفسى . الليلويا .

Introduction to the Gospel, Page: 8   : مقدمة الأنجيل ، صفحة

The Gospel

Ⲉⲩⲁⲅⲅⲉⲗⲓⲟⲛ Ⲕⲁⲧⲁ Ⲙⲁⲣⲕⲟⲛ Ⲕⲉⲫ ⲓ̅ⲇ̅ : ⲓ̅ⲃ̅ - ⲓ̅ⲋ̅

Mark 14:12-16

Now on the first day of Unleavened Bread, when they killed the Passover lamb, His disciples said to Him,

Ⲟⲩⲟϩ ϧⲉⲛ ⲡⲓ̀ⲉϩⲟⲟⲩ ⲛ̀ϩⲟⲩⲓⲧ ⲛ̀ⲧⲉ ⲛⲓⲁⲧϣⲉⲙⲏⲣ : ϩⲟⲧⲉ ⲉⲩϣⲱⲧ ⲙ̀ⲡⲓⲡⲁⲥⲭⲁ : ⲡⲉϫⲱⲟⲩ ⲛⲁϥ ⲛϫⲉ ⲛⲉϥⲙⲁⲑⲏⲧⲏⲥ : ϫⲉ

(مرقس 14: 12 - 16)

وفى اليوم الأول من الفطير إذ كانوا يذبحون الفصح قال له تلاميذه:

"Where do You want us to go and prepare, that You may eat the Passover?" And He sent out two of His disciples and said to them, "Go into the city, and a man will meet you carrying a pitcher of water; follow him. Wherever he goes in, say to the master of the house, 'The Teacher says, "Where is the guest room in which I may eat the Passover with My disciples?" ' Then he will show you a large upper room, furnished and prepared; there make ready for us." So His disciples went out, and came into the city, and found it just as He had said to them; and they prepared the Passover. Glory be to God forever, Amen..

ⲁⲕⲟⲩⲱϣ ⲛ̀ⲧⲉ ϣⲉⲛⲁⲛ ⲉ̀ⲑⲱⲛ ⲛ̀ⲧⲉⲛⲥⲟⲃϯ ϩⲓⲛⲁ ⲛ̀ⲧⲉⲕⲟⲩⲱⲙ ⲙ̀ⲡⲓⲡⲁⲥⲭⲁ. Ⲟⲩⲟϩ ⲁϥⲟⲩⲱⲣⲡ ⲛ̀ⲥⲛⲁⲩ ⲛ̀ⲧⲉ ⲛⲉϥⲙⲁⲑⲏⲧⲏⲥ ⲟⲩⲟϩ ⲡⲉϫⲁϥ ⲛⲱⲟⲩ : ϫⲉ ⲙⲁϣⲉⲛⲱⲧⲉⲛ ⲉ̀ϯⲃⲁⲕⲓ ⲟⲩⲟϩ ϥ̀ⲛⲁⲉⲣⲁⲡⲁⲛⲧⲁⲛ ⲉ̀ⲣⲱⲧⲉⲛ ⲛ̀ϫⲉ ⲟⲩⲣⲱⲙⲓ ⲉϥϥⲁⲓ ⲛ̀ⲟⲩϣⲟϣⲟⲩ ⲙ̀ⲙⲱⲟⲩ : ⲙⲟϣⲓ ⲛ̀ⲥⲱϥ. Ⲟⲩⲟϩ ⲡⲓⲙⲁ ⲉ̀ⲧⲉ ϥ̀ⲛⲁϣⲉⲛⲁϥ ⲉ̀ϧⲟⲩⲛ ⲉ̀ⲣⲟϥ ⲁϫⲟⲥ ⲙ̀ⲡⲓⲛⲏⲃ ϩⲓ ϫⲉ ⲡⲉϫⲉ ⲡⲓⲣⲉϥϯⲥⲃⲱ ϫⲉ ⲁϥⲑⲱⲛ ⲡⲓⲙⲁ ⲛ̀ⲉⲙⲧⲟⲛ ⲡⲓⲙⲁ ⲉ̀ϯⲛⲁⲟⲩⲱⲙ ⲙ̀ⲡⲓⲡⲁⲥⲭⲁ ⲛ̀ϧⲏⲧϥ ⲛⲉⲙ ⲛⲁⲙⲁⲑⲏⲧⲏⲥ. Ⲟⲩⲟϩ ⲛ̀ⲑⲟϥ ϥ̀ⲛⲁⲧⲁⲙⲱⲧⲉⲛ ⲉ̀ⲟⲩⲛⲓϣϯ ⲙ̀ⲙⲁ ⲉϥϭⲟⲥⲓ ⲉϥⲫⲟⲣϣ ⲉϥⲥⲉⲃⲧⲱⲧ : ⲥⲉⲃⲧⲱⲧ ⲛⲁⲛ ⲙ̀ⲙⲁⲩ. Ⲟⲩⲟϩ ⲁⲩⲓ ⲉ̀ⲃⲟⲗ ⲛ̀ϫⲉ ⲡⲓⲙⲁⲑⲏⲧⲏⲥ ⲥⲛⲁⲩ ⲁⲩⲓ ⲉ̀ϯⲃⲁⲕⲓ ⲟⲩⲟϩ ⲁⲩϫⲓⲙⲓ ⲕⲁⲧⲁ ⲫ̀ⲣⲏϯ ⲉⲧⲁϥϫⲟⲥ ⲛⲱⲟⲩ : ⲟⲩⲟϩ ⲁⲩⲥⲉⲃⲧⲉ ⲡⲓⲡⲁⲥⲭⲁ. ⲟⲩⲱϣⲧ ⲙ̀ⲡⲓⲉⲩⲁⲅⲅⲉⲗⲓⲟⲛ ⲉⲑⲟⲩ.

أين تريد أن نمضى ونعد لتأكل الفصح؟ فأرسل اثنين من تلاميذه و قال لهما: اذهبا إلى المدينة فسيلقاكما رجل حامل جرة ماء فاتبعاه . وحيثما يدخل فقولا لرب البيت: أن المعلم يقول أين موضع الراحة الذى آكل فيه الفصح مع تلاميذى . فهو يريكما علية كبيرة مفروشة معدة . فهناك أعدا لنا . فخرج التلميذان وأتيا إلى المدينة فوجدا كما قال لهما وأعدا الفصح . والمجد لله دائماً.

Introduction to the Exposition, Page: 9 : مقدمة الطرح ، صفحة

Exposition

طــرح

Listen O Israel to the voice of the Lord, Adonai God the Pantocrator said: let everyone purge himself of his sins and iniquities for you have maculated My Holy Name with your idol and your perfid deeds. Then I will accept you on my holy mountain and you shall worship Me in that place. I will be sanctified in you and will raise you above all nations. And you will know that I am the Lord God and that there is no god other than Me. The heavenly and earthly, the seas and all that is therein, worship Me. All are under My dominion and seek My mercy.

اسمعوا قول الرب يا آل إسرائيل ، قال أدوناى الرب ضابط الكل: ليبتعد كل واحد منكم عن شروره وآثامه ، فإنكم نجستم اسمى القدوس بأوثانكم وأعمالكم الخبيثة . وأنا أقبلكم على جبل قدسى وتعبدوننى فى ذلك الموضع . وأتقدس فيكم وأرفعكم عند جميع الأمم . وتعلمون إننى أنا هو الرب وليس إله آخر غيرى. والسمائيون والأرضيون والبحار وسائر ما فيها تتعبد لى وهى كلها تحت سلطانى تتوقع الرحمة التى من قبلى .

(North side) Christ our Savior; has come and has borne suffering; that through His Passion; He may save us.

(مرد بحرى) المسيح مخلصنا جاء وتألم عنا لكى بآلامه يخلصنا .

(South side) Let us glorify Him; and exalt His Name; for He had mercy on us; according to His great mercy.

(مرد قبلى) فلنمجده ونرفع اسمه لأنه صنع معنا رحمة كعظيم رحمته .

The Conclusion of the Exposition, Page: 9 : ختام الطرح ، صفحة

الساعة التاسعة من يوم الخميس من البصخة المقدسة
The Ninth Hour of Thursday of the Holy Pascha

Genesis 22:1-19

And it came to pass after these things that God tempted Abraham, and said to him, Abraham, Abraham; and he said, Behold! I am here. And He said, Take your son, the beloved one, whom you have loved, Isaac, and go into the high land, and offer him there for a whole burnt offering on one of the mountains which I will tell you of. And Abraham rose up in the morning and saddled his donkey, and he took with him two servants, and Isaac his son, and having split wood for a whole burnt offering, he arose and departed, and came to the place of which God spoke to him, on the third day; and Abraham, having lifted up his eyes, saw the place afar off. And Abraham said to his servants, Sit here with the donkey, and I and the lad will proceed thus far, and having worshipped, we will return to you. And Abraham took the wood of the whole burnt offering, and laid it on Isaac his son, and he took into his hands both the fire and the knife, and the two went together. And Isaac said to Abraham his father, Father. And he said, What is it, son? And he said, Behold the fire and the wood, but where is the sheep for a whole burnt offering? And Abraham said, God will provide for Himself a sheep for a whole burnt offering, my son. And both, having gone together, came to the place which God spoke of to him; and there Abraham built the altar, and laid the wood on it, and having bound the feet of Isaac his son together, he laid him on the altar upon the wood. And Abraham stretched forth his hand to take the knife to kill his son. But the Angel of the Lord called him out of heaven, and said, Abraham, Abraham. And he said, Behold, I am here. And He said, Lay not your hand upon the child, neither do anything to him, for now I know that you fear God, and for My sake you have not spared your beloved son. And Abraham lifted up his eyes and beheld, and lo! A ram caught by his horns in a plant of Sabek; and Abraham went and took the ram, and offered him up for a whole burnt offering in the place of Isaac his son. And Abraham called the name of that place, The Lord has seen; that they might say today, In the mount the Lord was seen. Then the Angel of the Lord called Abraham the second time out of heaven, saying, I have sworn by Myself, says the Lord, because you have done this thing, and on My account have not spared your beloved son, surely blessing I will bless you, and multiplying I will multiply your seed as the stars of heaven, and as the sand which is by the shore of the sea, and your seed shall inherit the cities of their enemies. And in your seed shall all the nations of the earth be blessed, because you have obeyed My voice. And Abraham returned to his servants, and they arose and went together to the well of the oath; and Abraham dwelt at the well of the oath. Glory be to the Holy Trinity. Amen

(من سفر التكوين ص 23 : 1 - 19)

وحدث بعد هذه الأمور أن الله امتحن إبراهيم وقال له: يا إبراهيم يا إبراهيم . فقال: هانذا . قال له: خذ إبنك الحبيب الذى تحبه اسحق وامض إلى الأرض المرتفعة واصعده لى هناك محرقة على أحد الجبال التى أريك. فقام إبراهيم مبكراً واسرج أتانه . وأخذ إثنين من غلمانه معه ، واسحق إبنه وشقق حطب المحرقة . وقام ومضى إلى الموضع الذى قال له الله . وفى اليوم الثالث رفع إبراهيم عينيه فأبصر المكان من بعيد . فقال إبراهيم لغلاميه: إجلسا أنتما ههنا مع الأتان وأنا والغلام نمضى إلى هناك فنسجد ونرجع إليكما . فأخذ إبراهيم حطب المحرقة وحمله اسحق إبنه . وأخذ بيده النار والسكين وذهبا كلاهما معاً . وقال اسحق لإبراهيم أبيه: يا أبى . فقال: ماذا تقول يا إبنى . قال: هوذا النار والحطب فأين الحمل الذى يقدم للمحرقة؟ فقال إبراهيم: ان الله يأتى له بحمل للمحرقة يا إبنى . ومضيا كلاهما معاً . فلما وصلا إلى المكان الذى قال له الله عنه ، بنى هناك إبراهيم مذبحاً ورفع عليه الحطب وأوثق اسحق إبنه ووضعه على المذبح فوق الحطب . ومد إبراهيم يده ليأخذ السكين ليذبح اسحق إبنه . فناداه ملاك الرب من السماء قائلاً : إبراهيم إبراهيم . فقال: هانذا. فقال : لا تمد يدك إلى الغلام ولا تفعل به شيئاً ، لانى الآن علمت إنك تخاف الله ، ولم تشفق على إبنك الحبيب لاجلى . فرفع إبراهيم عينيه ونظر وإذا بكبش موثق بقرنيه فى شجرة صاباك (بلوط). فمضى إبراهيم وأخذ الكبش واصعده محرقة عوضاً عن اسحق إبنه . وسمى إبراهيم اسم ذلك الموضع ، الرب تراءى لى على هذا الجبل . ونادى ملاك الرب إبراهيم مرة ثانية من السماء قائلاً : انى أقسمت بذاتى يقول الرب . بما انك عملت كلامى ولم تشفق على إبنك الحبيب من أجلى ، لاباركنك تبريكاً وأكثرن نسلك تكثيراً كنجوم السماء . وكالرمل الذى على شاطئ البحر . ويرث نسلك مدن مضايقيك وتتبارك بك جميع قبائل الأرض من أجل إنك سمعت لقولى . ثم رجع إبراهيم إلى غلاميه . فقاموا وانصرفوا معاً إلى بئر الحلف (بئر سبع) . مجداً للثالوث القدوس .

Isaiah 61:1-6

The Spirit of the Lord is upon Me, because He has anointed Me; He has sent Me to preach the gospel to the poor, to heal the brokenhearted, to proclaim liberty to the captives, and recovery of sight to the blind; to declare the acceptable year of the Lord, and the day of recompense; to comfort all that mourn; that there should be given to them that mourn in Zion glory instead of ashes, the oil of joy to the mourners, the garment of glory for the spirit of heaviness; and they shall be called generations of righteousness, the planting of the Lord for glory. And they shall build the old waste places, they shall raise up those that were before made desolate, and shall renew the desert cities, even those that had been desolate for many generations. And strangers shall come and feed your flocks, and aliens shall be your plowmen and vinedressers. But you shall be called priests of the Lord, the ministers of God; you shall eat the strength of nations, and shall be admired because of their wealth. Thus shall they inherit the land a second time, and everlasting joy shall be upon their head. *Glory be to the Holy Trinity. Amen*

Genesis 14:17-20

And the king of Sodom went out to meet him, after he returned from the slaughter of Chedorlaomer, and the kings with him, to the valley of Shaveh; this was the plain of the kings. And Melchizedek king of Salem brought forth loaves and wine, and he was the priest of the Most High God. And he blessed Abram, and said, Blessed be Abram of the Most High God, who made heaven and earth, and blessed be the Most High God, who delivered your enemies into your power. And Abram gave him a tithe of all. *Glory be to the Holy Trinity. Amen*

Job 27:1-28:13

As God lives, who has thus judged me; and the Almighty, who has embittered my soul; verily, while my breath is yet in me, and the breath of God which remains to me is in my nostrils, my lips shall not speak evil words, neither shall my soul meditate unrighteous thoughts. Far be it from me that I should justify you till I die! For I will not let go my innocence, but keeping fast to my righteousness, I will by no means let it go: for I am not conscious to myself of having done anything amiss. But on the contrary, let my enemies be as the overthrow of the ungodly, and they that rise up against me as the destruction of transgressors. For what is the hope of the ungodly, that he holds to it? Will he indeed trust in the Lord and be saved? Will God hear his prayer? Or when distress has come upon him, has he any confidence before Him? Or will God hear him as he calls upon Him? Yet now I will tell you what is in the hand of the Lord: I will not lie concerning the things which are with the Almighty. Behold, you all know that you are adding vanity to vanity. This is the portion of an ungodly man from the Lord, and the possession of oppressors shall

(من سفر إشعياء النبى ص 61 : 1 - 6)

روح الرب علىَّ . لذلك مسحنى لأبشر المساكين . وأرسلنى لأشفى المنكسرى القلوب وأبشر المسبيين بالعتق والعمى بالبصر. لانادى بسنة مقبولة للرب وبيوم المجازاة. وأعزى جميع النائحين . وأعطى مجداً لنائحى صهيون عوضاً عن الرماد . ودهن فرح للنائحين . وحلة مجد بدل روح كآبة القلب . فيدعون جيل الأبرار وغرس الرب الممجد . ويبنون خرب الدهر ويشيدون ما دمر منذ القدم ويجددون المدن الموحشة التى خربت منذ أجيال ويأتى الغرباء ويرعون غنمهم . والقبائل الغريبة يكونون لهم حراثين وكرامين. أما أنتم فتدعون كهنة الرب وخدام الله . وتأكلون قوة الأمم ومن الغنى يتعجبون منكم ويتلاشى حزنكم وخزيكم وتنالون وترثون دائماً فى أرضهم . وتأخذون نصيبهم . ويكون لكم فرح . مجداً للثالوث القدوس .

(من سفر التكوين 14 : 17 - 20)

ثم خرج ملك سدوم فتلقاه ابرام بعد رجوعه من حرب كدرلعومر والملوك الذين معه إلى مرج شَوَى الذى هو مرج الملك. وأخرج ملكى صادق ملك ساليم خبزاً وخمراً لأنه كان كاهن الله العلى . وبارك ابرام وقال مبارك ابرام من الله العلى الذى خلق السماء والأرض ومبارك الله العلى هذا الذى أسلم أعداءك فى يديك. واعطاه العشر من كل شئ . مجداً للثالوث القدوس .

(أيوب الصديق 27 : 1- 28 : 1 - 13)

حى هو الرب الذى حكم علىَّ هكذا والضابط الكل الذى أحزن نفسى أنه ما دامت نسمتى فىَّ والروح القدس فى أنفى لن تنطق شفتاى إثماً ولاتتلو نفسى ظلماً . حاشاى أن أقول أنكم أبرار إلى الآن ، ولن أقلع عن كمالى . وقد تمسكت بالحق فلا أتركه عنى . ولست أعرف إنى فعلت شيئاً من الشر أو الظلم . بل أعدائى يصيرون مثل سقوط المنافقين والقائمون علىَّ مثل هلاك مخالفى الناموس. فأنه ما هو رجاء المنافق إذا صبر وتوكل على الرب . أتراه يخلص؟ أو يسمع الرب صلاته؟ أو إذا أتى عليه ضيق ، هل يجد أى دالة أمامه؟ أو إذا صرخ إليه الرب هل يسمعه؟ بل إنى أعرفكم بما فى يدئ الرب ولا أكذب بما هو عند الضابط الكل . هوذا كلكم تعلمون أنه باطل هو نصيب الرجل المنافق من قبل الرب ،

come upon them from the Almighty. And if their children are many, they shall be for slaughter: and if they grow up, they shall beg. And they that survive of him shall utterly perish, and no one shall pity their widows. Even if he should gather silver as dust, and prepare gold as clay, all these things shall the righteous gain, and the true-hearted shall possess His wealth. And his house is gone like moths, and like a spider's web. The rich man shall lie down, and shall not continue: he has opened his eyes, and he is no more. Pains have come upon him as water, and darkness has carried him away by night. And a burning wind shall catch him, and he shall depart, and it shall utterly drive him out of his place. And God shall cast trouble upon him, and not spare: he flees desperately from out of His hand. He shall cause men to clap their hands against them, and shall hiss him out of his place. For there is a place for the silver, where it comes, and a place for the gold, where it is refined. For iron comes out of the earth, and brass is hewn out like stone. He has set a bound to darkness, and he searches out every limit: a stone is darkness, and the shadow of death. There is a cutting off the torrent by reason of dust, so they that forget the right way are weakened; they are removed from among men. As for the earth, out of it shall come bread; under it has been turned up as it were fire. Her stones are the place of the sapphire, and her dust supplies man with gold. There is a path, the fowl has not known it, neither has the eye of the vulture seen it. Neither have the sons of the proud trodden it, a lion has not passed upon it. He has stretched forth his hand on the sharp rock, and turned up mountains by the roots; and he has interrupted the whirlpools of rivers, and my eye has seen every precious thing. And he has laid bare the depths of rivers, and has brought his power to light. But where has wisdom been discovered? And where is the place of understanding? A mortal has not known its way, neither indeed has it been discovered among men. Glory be to the Holy Trinity. Amen

A homily of our Holy Father Abba Shenouti the Archimandrite

There may be deeds that we think are right while they are evil in God's eyes. That is we do accept some of them, and therefore sinning in the holy places. For God did not plant good and bad trees in the paradise. He planted all from the good trees only. He did not plant unfruitful trees or trees with bad fruits. Moreover, those whom He had put in the paradise were not accepted and driven out when they disobeyed Him. Therefore, beloved brethren, you have to know that God's places should not be full of evil people as well as good people. Unlike the world which is full of sinners, unjust, saints, and unclean people. Those that sin, He does not leave but takes away. I know that the whole earth is for the Lord. If this is the condition in His house and on the entire earth, then those who dwell on it, shall live with Him. Therefore, we should fear Him and keep

وخزى الأقوياء يأتى عليه من قبل الضابط الكل . إن كثر بنوه فيكونون للذبح وإذا إعتزوا يتسولون . والباقون له موتاً يموتون . وأراملهم لا يرحمهم أحد . جمعوا الفضة كالتراب . وأعدوا الذهب كالطين . هذه جميعها يأخذها الصديقون . ويرث أهل البيت أمواله . بيته صار مثل العث ومثل خيوط العنكبوت . يضطجع الغنى ولا يعود . يفتح عينيه فلا يوجد . دخلت عليه الأحزان كالمياه فى الليل فيحمله الضباب . ويأخذه العاصف فيذهب . ويقتلعه من مقره مهاناً منبوذاً ولا يشفق عليه . وهروباً يهرب من يديه ، فيرفع يديه عليه ويستأصله من مكانه . الموضع الذى استخرجوا منه الفضة لا يوجد . واستخرجوا الحديد من الأرض ومن الحجر يشغل النحاس . وضع للظلمة حداً . وهو يفحص فى كل طرف . على الحجر الذى فى الظلمة وظلال الموت ، ويقطع جيراً من الوادى . والذين ينسون البر مرضوا من البشر . والأرض تأتى بالخبز . ينقلب أسفلها كما بالنار . حجارتها هى موضع الياقوت وترابها ذهب . سبيل لم يعرفه طير . ولم تنظره عين نسر . ولم يطأه بنو المتكبرين . ولم يعبره الأسد . إلى الزاوية يمد يده ويهدم الجبال من أساساتها . ويقلب قوة الأنهار. أظهر لهم كل فعل جليل رأته أعينهم . وكشف قوته نوراً . أما الحكمة فاين توجد؟ وأين مقر الفهم؟ لا يعرف الإنسان طريقها ولا وجود لها فى البشر . مجداً للثالوث القدوس .

(عظة لأبينا القديس أنبا شنودة)

قد توجد أعمال نخالها أنها صالحة ولكنها رديئة عند الله . وذلك اننا نتغاضى عن بعضها بعضاً فنخطئ فى المواضع المقدسة . لأن الرب لم يغرس فى الفردوس الأشجار الصالحة والغير الصالحة بل غرسه من الأشجار الصالحة فقط . ولم يغرس فيه أشجار غير مثمرة أو رديئة الثمر . وليس هذا فقط ، بل والناس أنفسهم الذين جعلهم هناك عندما خالفوا ، لم يحتملهم بل أخرجهم منه . فمن هذا أعلموا أيها الأخوة الأحباء انه لا يجب أن تملأ مساكن الله المقدسة من الناس الأشرار والصالحين . كما فى العالم المملوء من الخطاة والظالمين والقديسين والأنجاس. ولكن الذين يخطئون لا يتركهم فيها بل يخرجهم. أنا أعرف أن الأرض كلها هى للرب. فان كان هكذا بيته وكذا

His commandments. If we fall in one of them, we should cry and mourn before Him. So, when He sees our mourning and strive, as the woman who washed His feet with her tear, He may be worthy to hear His sweet voice calling us and saying: Your sins are forgiven, your faith has healed you, go in peace. My brethren, you have seen that faith works in heart for salvation and shows its desire for it. Those who do not have the desire to keep God's commandments and do not have zeal to follow the spiritual men whom He witnessed that they knew the truth and accepted His commands through their deeds; also those with no faith, shall fall in every awful deed and shall destroy their souls. As it is written that the wise hears advise but the foolish shall fall on their faces.

الأرض كلها ، فالذين يسكنون فيها يحيون به. لهذا يجب علينا أن نخافه ونحفظ وصاياه. فاذا ما سقطنا فى واحدة منها فلنبك وننتحب أمامه. حتى إذا ما رأى تنهد وشوق أنفسنا مثل المرأة التى بلت قدميه بدموعها ، نكون حقاً مستحقين صوته الحلو القائل: مغفورة لك خطاياك اذهب بسلام ، إيمانك قد خلصك. وقد رأيتم يا اخوتى ان الإيمان يعمل فى القلب للخلاص ويعلن شوقه فيه. فاذن كل من ليس له شوق فى حفظ وصايا الله وغيرة فى الاقتداء بالممتلئين بالروح الذين شهد لهم انهم عرفوا الحق وقبلوا نصيحته بأعمالهم ، وكذلك الذين ليس لهم إيمان ، يسقطون فى كل عمل ردئ ويهلكون النفس ، كما هو مكتوب: أن الرجل العاقل يقبل النصيحة ويعمل والجاهل يسقط على وجهه.

We conclude the homily of our Holy Father Abba Shenouti the Archimandrite, who enlightened our minds and our hearts. In the name of the Father, and the Son, and the Holy Spirit, one God. Amen.

فلنختم عظة أبينا القديس أنبا شنودة رئيس المتوحدين الذى أنار عقولنا وعيون قلوبنا باسم الآب والإبن والروح القدس إله واحد آمين .

Pascha Praise - B (12 times), Page: 7   تسبحة البصخة B (12 مرة) ، صفحة :

The Psalm

Ѱⲁⲗⲙⲟⲥ ⲕⲃ̄ : ⲁ̄

Psalms 22:1

The Lord is my shepherd, I shall not want. In a place of green grass, there He has made me dwell; He has nourished me by the water of rest.

Alleluia

Ⲡϭⲟⲓⲥ ⲡⲉⲑⲛⲁⲁⲙⲟⲛⲓ ⲙ̄ⲙⲟⲓ : ⲛ̄ⲛⲉϥϧⲣⲓⲉⲣ ϧⲁⲉ ⲛ̄ϩⲗⲓ : ⲁϥⲑⲣⲓϣⲱⲡⲓ ϧⲉⲛ ⲟⲩⲙⲁ ⲉϥⲟⲩⲉⲧⲟⲩⲱⲧ : ⲁϥϣⲁⲛⲟⲩϣⲧ ϩⲓϫⲉⲛ ⲫ̄ⲙⲱⲟⲩ ⲛ̄ⲧⲉ ⲡⲉⲙⲧⲟⲛ . ⲁⲗ .

إبتشويس بيثنا أمونى إمموى : إننيف إثرى إر خايبه إن إهلى : أفثثرى شوبى خين أووما إفئوؤ إتؤوأوت : أفشان أووشت هيجين إفموؤو إنتيه إبئمطون . الليلويا .

(مز 22 : 1)
الرب يرعانى فلا يعوزنى شئ . فى مكان خضرة أسكننى . على ماء الراحة ربانى . الليلويا.

Introduction to the Gospel, Page: 8   مقدمة الأنجيل ، صفحة :

The Gospel

Ⲉⲩⲁⲅⲅⲉⲗⲓⲟⲛ Ⲕⲁⲧⲁ Ⲙⲁⲧⲑⲉⲟⲛ Ⲕⲉ̄ⲫ ⲕⲋ̄ : ⲓⲍ̄ - ⲓ̄ⲑ̄

Matthew 26:17-19

Now on the first day of the Feast of Unleavened Bread the disciples came to Jesus, saying to Him, "Where do You want us to prepare for You to eat the Passover?" And He said, "Go into

Ⲛ̄ϩⲣⲏⲓ ⲇⲉ ϧⲉⲛ ⲡⲓϩⲟⲩⲟⲩ ⲛ̄ϩⲟⲩⲓⲧ ⲛ̄ⲧⲉ ⲛⲓⲁⲧⲕⲱⲃ : ⲁⲩⲓ̀ ϩⲁ Ⲓⲏ̄ⲥ ⲛ̄ϫⲉ ⲛⲉϥⲙⲁⲑⲏⲧⲏⲥ ⲉⲩϫⲱ ⲙ̄ⲙⲟⲥ : ϫⲉ ⲁⲕⲟⲩⲱϣ ⲉ̀ⲥⲉⲃⲧⲉ ⲡⲓⲡⲁⲥⲭⲁ ⲛⲁⲕ ⲑⲱⲛ ⲉ̀ⲟⲩⲟⲙϥ . Ⲛ̄ⲑⲟϥ ⲇⲉ ⲡⲉϫⲁϥ ⲛⲱⲟⲩ : ϫⲉ ⲙⲁϣⲉⲛⲱⲧⲉⲛ

(متى 16 : 17 - 19)
وفى اليوم الأول من الفطير تقدم إلى يسوع تلاميذه قائلين: أين تريد أن نعد لك الفصح لتأكله؟ أما هو فقال لهم : اذهبوا إلى

the city to a certain man, and say to him, 'The Teacher says, "My time is at hand; I will keep the Passover at your house with My disciples." So the disciples did as Jesus had directed them; and they prepared the Passover.	ⲉⲧⲁⲓⲃⲁⲕⲓ ϧⲁ ⲡⲁⲫⲙⲁⲛ ⲛ̀ⲣⲱⲙⲓ ⲟⲩⲟϩ ⲁϫⲟⲥ ⲛⲁϥ ϫⲉ : ⲡⲉϫⲉ ⲡⲓⲣⲉϥϯⲥⲃⲱ ϫⲉ ⲡⲁⲥⲏⲟⲩ ⲁϥϧⲱⲛⲧ : ⲁⲓⲛⲁⲓⲣⲓ ⲙ̀ⲡⲁⲡⲁⲥⲭⲁ ϧⲁⲧⲟⲧⲕ ⲛⲉⲙ ⲛⲁⲙⲁⲑⲏⲧⲏⲥ : ⲟⲩⲟϩ ⲁⲩⲓⲣⲓ ⲛ̀ϫⲉ ⲛⲓⲙⲁⲑⲏⲧⲏⲥ ⲙ̀ⲫⲣⲏϯ ⲉⲧⲁ Ⲓⲏⲥ ϫⲟⲥ ⲛⲱⲟⲩ ⲟⲩⲟϩ ⲁⲩⲥⲉⲃⲧⲉ ⲡⲓⲡⲁⲥⲭⲁ . ⲟⲩⲱϣⲧ ⲙ̀ⲡⲓⲉⲩⲁⲅⲅⲉⲗⲓⲟⲛ ⲉⲑ .	المدينة إلى فلان الرجل وقولوا له: المعلم يقول ان وقتى قد قرب ، وعندك اصنع فصحي مع تلاميذى . ففعل التلاميذ كما قال لهم يسوع وأعدوا الفصح . والمجد لله دائماً .
Glory be to God forever, Amen.		

Introduction to the Exposition, Page: 9 مقدمة الطرح ، صفحة :

Exposition

And when Abraham had loftiness in God's eyes more than all other people, the Lord appeared to him and said: Abraham, Abraham whom I love, obey my words and do my will. Take your dear son Isaac and offer him as a sacrifice to me on a mountain. Abraham did as the Lord commanded. He took his beloved son, two of his servants, and a donkey, and went forth. When he saw the mountain afar, he left the two servants and the donkey with them and said: my son and I shall go there to worship and come back. He loaded the wood of the burnt offering on his only son and carried the knife and the fire. They went up the mountain to the place that the Lord the Pantocrator showed him. Isaac said to his father Abraham: Here is the fire where is the lamb? Abraham said to him: My son, the Lord will provide for Himself an acceptable lamb that pleases Him. Then he gathered stones, and built an altar, and stacked the firewood on the altar before he lit it. He bound the boy's hands and feet and put him on the wood. The boy said: Today, I am your sacrifice that you offer, father. When Abraham stretched out his hand and took the knife to fulfill the offering, the Lord called him and said: Abraham, hold your hand and do not do anything to him for I have known your love to me. Blessing I will bless and multiplying I will multiply your beloved son Isaac. And as you did not hesitate to offer your first-born, I shall bless you and your descendants. Your descendants shall become as the stars and will be as numerous as the sand. Abraham looked behind him and saw a sheep tied with its horns to a tree of Safak. He unbound Isaac and slew the sheep instead of him. And the Lord the Pantocrator blessed Abraham because He found him acceptable in all his deeds. And the old man (Abraham) returned and went back with the two servants and his son.

طرح

فلما ازداد إبراهيم رفعة أمام الرب أكثر من جميع الناس ، ظهر له الرب وخاطبه هكذا قائلاً: يا إبراهيم يا إبراهيم الذى أحبه ، اسمع كلامى وافعل إرادتى ، خذ اسحق إبنك حبيبك وقدمه لى محرقة على أحد الجبال. فقام إبراهيم كقول الرب وأخذ إبنه حبيبه وغلامين من عبيده وأسرج دابته وسار هكذا . فلما رأى الجبل من بعيد ترك الغلامين والدابة معهما وقال : أنا وإبنى ننطلق إلى هناك لنسجد ثم نعود إليكما . وحمل الحطب على وحيده والسكين والنار كان مع إبراهيم ، وصعد الإثنان على الجبل المقدس الموضع الذى أعلمه به الضابط الكل . فقال اسحق لأبيه إبراهيم: هوذا الحطب فأين هو الحمل؟ فقال: يا إبنى الله يعد حملاً للذبح مقبولاً يرضيه . ثم جمع احجاراً وبنى مذبحاً و جعل الحطب عليه قبل أن يوقد النار ، وشد يدى الصبى وساقيه وجعله على الحطب . فقال الصبى: هأنذا اليوم قربانك يا أبتاه الذى تصنعه. فمد يده وأخذ السكين لكى يكمل القضية . وإذا بصوت كان من الرب نحو إبراهيم هكذا قائلاً : إمسك يدك ولا تصنع به شراً فقد عرفت محبتك لى . بالنمو ينمو وبالكثرة يكثر اسحق إبنك الحبيب . وكما إنك لم تشفق على إبنك بكرك أنا سأباركك وزرعك معاً وبنوك يكونون مثل النجوم ويكثر عددهم مثل الرمل . ثم إلتفت إبراهيم فنظر خروفاً مربوطاً بقرنيه فى شجرة صافاك . فحل اسحق من وثاقه وذبح الخروف عوضاً عنه ، وبارك الرب ضابط الكل إبراهيم لأنه وجده مرضياً له فى سائر أعماله . وهكذا رجع الشيخ وأخذ الغلامين وإبنه ومضوا .

(North side) Christ our Savior; has come and has borne suffering; that through His Passion; He may save us.	(مرد بحرى) المسيح مخلصنا جاء وتألم عنا لكى بآلامه يخلصنا .
(South side) Let us glorify Him; and exalt His Name; for He had mercy on us; according to His great mercy.	(مرد قبلى) فلنمجده ونرفع اسمه لأنه صنع معنا رحمةً كعظيم رحمته .

The Conclusion of the Exposition, Page: 9	ختام الطرح ، صفحة : ٩

The Conclusion with the Daytime Litanies, Page: 10	طلبة الصباح ، صفحة : ١٠

قداس لقان خميس العهد

Liturgy of Blessing the Water

**Liturgy of
Blessing the Water**

قداس لقان
خميس العهد

القراءات و الاحداث

الموضوع : الرب يسوع يغسل ارجل التلاميذ .

يو 13 : 1 - 17

قبل العشاء إذ علم يسوع أن ساعته قد جاءت ، لكى ينتقل من هذا العالم ذاهباً إلى الآب . وقد أحب خاصته اللذين فى العالم وأحبهم إلى النهاية ، قام عن العشاء وخلع ثيابه وأخذ منديلاً وإئتزر به ثم صب ماء فى مغسل وإبتدأ يغسل أرجل تلاميذه ويمسحهما بالمنشفة التى كان مؤتزراً بها .

يا لهذا الاتضاع العجيب الذى يريدنا ان نعيش به لانه قال فإن كنت وأنا ربكم ومعلمكم قد غسلت أرجلكم فأنتم أيضاً يجب أن يغسل بعضكم أرجل بعض . الآن ما صنعته لكم هو مثالاً حتى كما صنعت أنا بكم تصنعون أنتم بعضكم ببعض .

و هذا الامر له ضرورة اخرى تعليمية و هى ان الرب يأمرنا بضرورة التوبة و تطهير النفس قبل التناول اذ يقول الرب : الذى قد أغتسل ليس له حاجة إلا إلى غسل رجليه بل هو طاهر كله و لذلك اوضحت الكنيسة هذاالتعليم باختيار مزمور هذا الانجيل و هو من مزمور 50 " تنضح على بزوفك فأطهر وتغسلنى بأبيض أكثر من الثلج . قلباً نقياً تخلق في يا الله ، وروحاً مستقيماً جدد فى أحشائى ."

The Readings and Events

Subject: Our Lord Jesus Christ washes the feet of the disciples

John 13:1-17

Now before the feast of the Passover, when Jesus knew that his hour had come that he should depart out of this world unto the Father, having loved his own who were in the world, he loved them unto the end. He rose from supper, and laid aside his garments; and took a towel, and girded himself. After that he poured water into a basin, and began to wash the disciples' feet, and to wipe them with the towel with which he was girded.

This is the great humbleness He wants us to practice. He said If I then, your Lord and Teacher, have washed your feet; you also ought to wash one another's feet. For I have given you an example, that you should do as I have done to you.

This command has another essential teaching. The Lord commands us to practice repentance and purification of the soul before partaking of the communion. The Lord said: He that is washed needs not except to wash his feet, but is clean completely. To emphasize this teaching, the church has chosen verses from psalm 50 to accompany this Gospel reading; Purge me with hyssop, and I shall be clean; Wash me, and I shall be whiter than snow. Create in me a clean heart, O God, And renew a steadfast spirit within me.

قداس لقان خميس العهد
Liturgy of Blessing the Water

The basin (Lakkan) and another vessel are filled with water. The priests and deacons put on their liturgical garments. While holding candles, they chant: Ek-Ezmaroout (annual tune) The Priest starts with:	يملأ اللقان و اناء آخر ماء عذباً . يرتدى الكهنة و الشمامسة ملابس الخدمة ، و يتوجهون و بأيديهم الشموع مرتلين باللحن السنوى: اك ازماروؤوت ... ثم يبدأ الكاهن الصلاة ...

Have mercy on us...	Ελεнcoн ..	اليسون ...
Our Father Who art...	Πєниωτ ετδεн ниφнoϊ ..	أبانا الذى فى السموات ...
Thanksgiving prayer	Uαρεнщεπ ..	صلاة الشكر
Verses of Cymbals	Ϫεноϯωщτ ..	أرباع الناقوس
Psalm 50, Have mercy on me...	Nαι ннι Φϯ .. Φαλuoc ..	ارحمنى يا الله ألخ (مز 50)

Genesis 18:1-23

And God appeared to him by the oak of Mamre, as he sat by the door of his tent in the heat of the day. And he lifted up his eyes and looked, and behold, three men stood before him; and having seen them, he ran to meet them from the door of his tent, and bowed himself to the ground. And he said, Lord, if indeed I have found grace in Your sight, pass not by Your servant. Let water now be brought, and let them wash Your feet, and refresh yourselves under the tree. And I will bring bread, and you shall eat, and after this you shall depart on your journey, on account of which refreshment you have turned aside to your servant. And he said, So do, as you have said. And Abraham hastened to the tent to Sarah, and said to her, Quickly, knead three measures of fine flour, and make cakes. And Abraham ran to the herd, and took a young calf, tender and good, and gave it to his servant, and he hastened to prepare it. And he took butter and milk, and the calf which he had prepared; and he set them before them, and they did eat, and he stood by them under the tree. And He said to him, Where is Sarah your wife? And he answered and said, Behold, in the tent. And He said, I will return and come to you according to this period seasonably, and Sarah your wife shall have a son; and Sarah heard at the door of the tent, being behind him. And Abraham and Sarah were old, advanced in days, and the custom of women ceased with Sarah. And Sarah laughed in herself, saying, The thing has not as yet happened to me, even until now, and my lord is old. And the Lord said to Abraham, Why is it that Sarah has laughed in herself, saying, Shall I then indeed bear? But I am grown old. Shall anything be impossible with the Lord? At this time I will return to you seasonably, and Sarah shall have a son. But Sarah denied, saying, I did not laugh, for she was afraid. And He said to her, No, but you did laugh! And the men, having risen up from there, looked towards Sodom and Gomorrah. And Abraham went with them, attending them on their journey. And the Lord said,

(من سفر التكوين 18 : 1 - 22)

وظهر الرب لإبراهيم عند شجرة ممرا وهو جالس على باب خيمته وقت الظهيرة ، فرفع عينيه ونظر ، وإذا ثلاثة رجال واقفون لديه . فلما نظرهم ركض لإستقبالهم من باب الخيمة وسجد على الأرض وقال : يا سيدى إن كنت قد وجدت نعمة لديك فلا تتجاوز عبدك ، فليؤخذ قليل ماء واغسلوا أرجلكم ثم استريحوا تحت الشجرة . فنأخذ خبزاً وتأكلون ، وبعد هذا تمضوا لأنكم قد مررتم على عبدكم . فقالوا : افعل هكذا كما قلت . فأسرع إبراهيم إلى الخيمة ، إلى سارة وقال لها : اسرعى واعجنى ثلاث مكاييل واصنعيها خبز ملة . ثم ركض إبراهيم إلى ابقاره وأخذ عجلاً رخصاً حسناً وأعطاه لغلمانه ليعمله طعاماً ، ثم أخذ زبداً ولبناً ، والعجل الذى عمله ووضعه قدامهم وأكلوا بينما كان هو واقفاً تحت الشجرة . وقالوا له : أين سارة إمرأتك؟ أما هو فأجاب قائلاً : ها هى داخل الخباء . فقال : إنى أرجع إليك فى هذا الزمن من العام المقبل ويكون لسارة إمرأتك إبن . فسمعت سارة وهى عند باب الخيمة من خلفه ، وكان إبراهيم وسارة شيخين متقدمين فى أيامهما وقد انقطع ان يكون لسارة كما للنساء ، فضحكت سارة فى نفسها قائلة : أيكون لى هذا الآن وقد شاخ سيدى؟ فقال الرب لإبراهيم: لماذا ضحكت سارة فى نفسها قائلة أترى بالحقيقة ألد وأنا قد شخت؟. هل يستحيل على الله شىء؟ فى مثل هذا الزمان ارجع إليك فى العام المقبل ويكون لسارة إبن ، فأنكرت سارة قائلة : لم أضحك ، لأنها خافت . فقال : لا بل ضحكت . ثم قام الرجال من هناك وتطلعوا نحو سدوم وعامورة ، وكان إبراهيم

Shall I hide from Abraham My servant what things I intend to do? But Abraham shall become a great and populous nation, and in him shall all the nations of the earth be blessed. For I know that he will order his sons, and his house after him, and they will keep the ways of the Lord, to do justice and judgment, that the Lord may bring upon Abraham all things whatsoever He has spoken to him. And the Lord said, The cry of Sodom and Gomorrah has been increased towards Me, and their sins are very great. I will therefore go down and see, if they completely correspond with the cry which comes to Me, and if not, that I may know. And the men, having departed from there, came to Sodom; and the Lord stood before Abraham. And Abraham drew near and said, Would You destroy the righteous with the wicked, and shall the righteous be as the wicked? Glory be to the Holy Trinity. Amen

Proverbs 9:1-11

Wisdom has built a house for herself, and set up seven pillars. She has killed her beasts; she has mingled her wine in a bowl, and prepared her table. She has sent forth her servants, calling with a loud proclamation to the feast, saying, Whoever is foolish, let him turn aside to me: and to them that want understanding she says, Come, eat of my bread, and drink wine which I have mingled for you. Leave folly, that you may reign forever; and seek wisdom, and improve understanding by knowledge. He that reproves evil men shall get dishonor to himself, and he that rebukes an ungodly man shall disgrace himself. Rebuke not evil men, lest they should hate you: rebuke a wise man, and he will love you. Give an opportunity to a wise man, and he will be wiser: instruct a just man, and he will receive more instruction. The fear of the Lord is the beginning of wisdom, and the counsel of saints is understanding: A for to know the law is the character of a sound mind. For in this way you shall live long, and years of your life shall be added to you. Glory be to the Holy Trinity. Amen

Exodus 14, 15

When Israel crossed the Red Sea, they walked through dry land in the midst of the sea, and their enemies went into the sea; and the Lord brought upon them the water of the sea. Israel and all the house of Jacob were saved. They danced and sang this song: Let us sing to the Lord, for He is very greatly glorified. Glory be to the Holy Trinity. Amen.

Joshua 1, 2

Joshua and all the people went over Jordan, they treaded on stones that were immersed in the water. Their feet strengthened and they defeated their enemies. Glory be to the Holy Trinity. Amen.

ماشياً معهم ليشيعهم . فقال الرب: هل أخفى ما أنا فاعله عن عبدى إبراهيم ، وإبراهيم يكون أمة عظيمة وكثيرة وتتبارك به جميع أمم الأرض . لأنى علمت أنه يوصى بنيه وبيته من بعده فيحفظوا طرق الرب ، ليعملوا براً وعدلاً لكى يعمل الرب لإبراهيم بما تكلم به معه . فقال الرب: إن صراخ سدوم وعاموره قد كثر وخطاياهم عظيمة جداً . إنى أنزل لأعرف هل صراخها الآتى إلىّ قد كمل أم لا؟ وأنصرف الرجال من هناك وذهبوا نحو سدوم ، وأما إبراهيم فكان لم يزل واقفاً أمام الرب . فاقترب إبراهيم وقال للرب: لا تهلك البار مع الأثيم ، فيكون الصديق مثل المنافق . مجداً للثالوث القدوس .

(من سفر أمثال سليمان 9 : 1 - 11)

الحكمة بنت لها بيتاً ودعمته بسبعة أعمدة ، وذبحت ذبائحها ومزجت خمرها فى البواطى ، وهيأت مائدتها ، وأرسلت عبيدها لتدعو بصوت عال على الزوايا قائلة : من كان جاهل فيكم فليأت إلىّ ، والناقص علماً فليقبل نحوى. فأقول لهم: تعالوا إلىّ ، وكلوا من خبزى وإشربوا من خمرى التى مزجتها لكم. اتركوا الجهل فتحيوا . أطلبوا الحكمة فتعمروا . وانهضوا الفهم بالعلم . من يوبخ مستهزئاً يكسب لنفسه هواناً ، ومن يُنذر شريراً يكسب عياً . لا توبخ مستهزئاً لئلا يبغضك ، وبخ حكيماً فيحبك . وبخ الجاهل فيمقتك . أعط الحكيم سبباً فيزداد حكمة ، علم صديقاً فيزداد قبولاً . بدء الحكمة مخافة الرب ، ومشورة الأبرار فهم . معرفة الناموس للفطنة الجيدة وبهذا النوع تعيش زمناً كثيراً وتزداد سنو حياتك . مجداً للثالوث القدوس .

(من سفر الخروج 14 و 15)

حينما عبر إسرائيل البحر الأحمر ، وداست أرجلهم البحر ، انطمس اعداءهم فى العمق ، وانغمست أرجل العساكر فى الماء قسراً ، وأما أرجل إسرائيل وجميع بيت يعقوب رفعت ونجوا من الهلاك . وقالوا هذه التسبحة : فلنسبح الرب لأنه بالمجد قد تمجد . مجداً للثالوث القدوس .

(من سفر يشوع بن نون ص 1 و 3)

يشوع وكافة الشعب عبروا الأردن ووطئت أرجلهم الحجارة التى فى المياه فتوثقت أمامهم وأهلكوا أعدائهم . مجداً للثالوث القدوس .

Isaiah 4:1-4

And in that day God shall shine gloriously in counsel on the earth, to exalt and glorify the remnant of Israel. And it shall be, that the remnant left in Zion, and the remnant left in Jerusalem, even all that are appointed to life in Jerusalem, shall be called holy. For the Lord shall wash away the filth of the sons and daughters of Zion, and shall purge out the blood from the midst of them, with the spirit of judgment, and the spirit of burning. Glory be to the Holy Trinity. Amen

(من سفر إشعياء ص 4: 1 - 4)

فى ذلك اليوم ينير الله بالمشورة والمجد على الأرض ليرتفع ويتمجد كل من يبقى من إسرائيل ، ويكون كل من يبقى فى صهيون ، وبقية أورشليم يدعون أطهاراً . يكتب للحياة كل من فى أورشليم لأن الرب يغسل أعمال بنى البشر وأولاد صهيون . مجداً للثالوث القدوس .

Isaiah 55:1-56:1

You that thirst, go to the water, and all that have no money, go and buy; and eat and drink wine and milk without money or price. Why do you value at the price of money, and give your labor for that which will not satisfy? Hearken to Me, and you shall eat that which is good, and your soul shall feast itself on good things. Give heed with your ears, and follow My ways; hearken to Me, and your soul shall live in prosperity; and I will make with you an everlasting covenant, the sure mercies of David. Behold I have made him a testimony among the Gentiles, a prince and commander to the Gentiles. Nations which know you not shall call upon you, and peoples which are not acquainted with you shall flee to you for refuge, for the sake of the Lord your God, the Holy One of Israel; for He has glorified you. Seek the Lord, and when you find Him, call upon Him; and when He draws near to you, let the ungodly leave his ways, and the transgressor his counsels; and let him return to the Lord, and he shall find mercy; for He shall abundantly pardon your sins. For My counsels are not as your counsels, nor are My ways as your ways, says the Lord. But as the heaven is distant from the earth, so is My way distant from your ways, and your thoughts from My mind. For as the rain shall come down, or snow from heaven, and shall not return until it has saturated the earth, and it bring forth and bud, and give seed to the sower, and bread for food; so shall My word be, whatever shall proceed out of My mouth, it shall by no means return to Me void, until all the things which I willed have been accomplished; and I will make your ways prosperous, and will effect My commands. For you shall go forth with joy, and shall be taught with gladness; for the mountains and the hills shall exalt to welcome you with joy, and all the trees of the field shall applaud with their branches. And instead of the bramble shall come up the cypress, and instead of the nettle shall come up the myrtle; and the Lord shall be for a name, and for an everlasting sign, and shall not fail.Thus says the Lord: Keep justice, and do righteousness; for My salvation is about to come, and My mercy to be revealed. Glory be to the Holy Trinity. Amen

(من إشعياء 55 : 1 - 13 و 56 : 1)

أيها العطاش اذهبوا إلى المياه ، ويا من ليس لهم فضة اذهبوا واشتروا لتأكلوا وتشربوا بلا فضة ولا ثمن خبزاً ولبناً وشحماً . لماذا تشترون بفضة وتعبكم لغير شبع؟ اسمعوا لي فتأكلوا الخيرات ولتتلذذ بالدسم نفوسكم . أميلوا آذانكم وهلموا إليّ ، أطيعونى فتحيا نفوسكم بالخيرات واقطع لكم عهداً أبدياً ، مراحم داود الصادقة . هوذا قد جعلته شاهداً فى الأمم ورئيساً وموصياً للشعوب . ها أمة لا تعرفها تدعوها وأمة لا تعرفك تركض إليك . من أجل إلهك قدوس إسرائيل لأنه قد مجدك . إطلبوا الرب وحين تجدوه ادعوه ما دام قريب منكم . ليترك الشرير طريقه ، ورجل الإثم أفكاره وليتب إلى الرب فيخلصه لأنه بكثرة يغفر لكم خطاياكم . لأن أفكاركم ليست كأفكارى ، ولا طرقكم كطرقى ، يقول الرب. لأنه كما ناءت السموات عن الأرض هكذا ناءت طرقى عن طرقكم ، وأفكارى عن أفكاركم . لأنه كما إذا نزل المطر أو الثلج من السماء لا يرجع حتى يروى الأرض ويجعلها تلد وتنبت وتعطى زرعاً للزارع ، وخبزاً للأكل ، هكذا تكون الكلمة التى تخرج من فمى لا ترجع إليّ حتى تكمل ما أريده وتقوم طرقى وأوامرى . لأنكم بفرح تخرجون وترجعون لأن الجبال والآكام تنشد أمامكم ترنماً ، وكل شجر الحقل تصفق بأغصانها. عوضاً عن الشوك ينبت سرو وعوضاً عن القريس (السوكران) يصعد آس . ويكون للرب إسماً علامة أبدية لا تنقطع . هكذا قال الرب : إحفظوا الحكم ، واجروا العدل ، لأنه قريب مجئ خلاصى ، واستعلان برى . مجداً للثالوث القدوس .

Ezekiel 36:25-29

And I will sprinkle clean water upon you, and you shall be purged from all your uncleannesses, and from all your idols, and I will cleanse you. And I will give you a new heart, and will put a new spirit in you: and I will take away the heart of stone out of your flesh, and will give you a heart of flesh. And I will put My Spirit in you, and will cause you to walk in My ordinances, and to keep My judgments, and do them. And you shall dwell upon the land which I gave to your fathers; and you shall be to Me a people, and I will be to you a God. And I will save you from all your uncleannesses. Glory be to the Holy Trinity. Amen

Ezekiel 47:1-9

And he brought me to the entrance of the house. And behold, water issued from under the porch eastward, for the front of the house looked eastward; and the water came down from the right side, from the south to the altar. And he brought me out by the way of the northern gate, and he led me round by the way outside to the gate of the court that looks eastward. And behold, water came down from the right side, in the direction in which a man went forth opposite; and there was a measuring line in his hand, and he measured a thousand cubits with the measure; and he passed through the water; it was water of a fountain. And again he measured a thousand, and passed through the water; and the water was up to his thighs. And again he measured a thousand; and he passed through water up to the loins. And again he measured a thousand; and he could not pass through, for the water rose as of a torrent which men cannot pass over. And he said to me, Have you seen this, son of man? Then he brought me, and led me back to the brink of the river as I returned. And behold, on the brink of the river there were so many trees on this side and on that side. And he said to me, This is the water that goes forth to Galilee that lies eastward, and it is gone down to Arabia, and has reached as far as to the sea to the outlet of the water; and it shall heal the waters. And it shall come to pass, that every animal of living and moving creatures, all on which the river shall come, shall live; and there shall be there very many fish; for this water shall go there, and it shall heal them, and they shall live: everything on which the river shall come shall live. Glory be to the Holy Trinity. Amen.

A homily of our Holy Father Abba Shenouti the archimandrite

Brethren, we ought to be humbled in front of Him who suffered on our behalf. We ought to fear Him who poured the water in a bowl and washed the feet of His disciples with His impeccable hands. Let us present Him with good deeds that deserve this great modesty which He carried out for our sake. Let us repent

(من سفر حزقيال 36 : 25 - 28)

هذا ما يقوله الرب الإله ، إنى سأنضح عليكم ماءً مختاراً فتطهرون من جميع خطاياكم ، ومن سائر آثامكم ، وأعطيكم قلباً جديداً وأجعل فى داخلكم روحاً جديداً ، وانزع القلب الحجرى من أجسادكم ، وأصير روحى داخلكم وأصنع بكم كمثل الأبناء الأحياء . وأجعلكم تسلكون فى فرائضى وتحفظون أحكامى وتعملون بها ، لكى تسكنوا على الأرض التى أعطيتها لآبائكم وتكونون لى شعباً ، وأنا أيضاً أكون لكم إلهاً ، وأطهركم من آثامكم . مجداً للثالوث القدوس .

(من سفر حزقيال 47 : 1 - 9)

ثم حملنى الروح وأدخلنى من باب البيت وإذا ماء خارج من المشرق من تحت أسقفة الباب الشرقى لأن وجه البيت كان نحو المشرق وكان الماء منحدراً من الجانب الأيمن للبيت عن جنوبى المذبح . ثم أخرجنى من طريق باب الشمال ، وطاف بى الباب الخارجى من الباب الذى يتجه نحو المشرق . وإذا ماء كان يجرى تحت الجانب الأيمن ، و كمثل إنسان قدامه وقصبة فى يده . فقاس ألفاً بالمقياس وعبر فى الماء وكان الماء إلى الركبة ، ثم قاس ألفاً أخرى بالقياس وعبر فى الماء ، فكان الماء إلى الحقوين ، ثم قاس ألفاً أيضاً فى وادى لم يستطع عبوره لأن الماء طمت كمياه فى واد منحدر لا يُعبر . وقال لى أرأيت يا إبن الإنسان؟ ثم ذهب بى وارجعنى إلى شاطئ النهر . وإذا عند رجوعى أشجار كثيرة جداً على شاطئ النهر من هنا ومن هناك . وقال لى : هذه المياه خارجة من الجليل الذى بالدائرة الشرقية وتنحدر إلى بلاد العرب وتذهب إلى البحر على الماء الجارى فتطهر سائر المياه ويصير أن كل نفس حية تدب حيثما يتبدد ماء هذا النهر عليها تتطهر من كل شئ وكل ما يأتى عليه ماء هذا النهر يطهر ويحيا . مجداً للثالوث القدوس .

عظة لأبينا القديس أنبا شنودة رئيس المتوحدين

فلنستح الآن يا أخوتى من الذى تألم عنا ، ولنخف من الذى اشتد بمنديل وصب الماء فى المغسل وغسل أرجل تلاميذه بيديه الطاهرتين ، ولنصنع ثماراً تستحق هذا الإتضاع العظيم الذى صار فيه من أجلنا . لكى نتوب سريعاً من

for our sins that we committed. Because, if we do not repent, we will be called in heaven as lovers of sins. What will be our hope if we are cast out of heaven, forced to face the judgment and are rejected for our sins? We will be judged twice; not because we have sinned without knowledge but because of what we did with knowledge was worse than what we did without knowledge and not because we have sinned, but because we did not repent. Why can't the sheep know the voice of the real shepherd, the life giver, and take refuge in Him? He who purchased it with His blood, took care of it, and gave Himself up for it. He who gave us His Body to eat and His Blood to drink; Jesus Christ our Lord and Savior, the Son of God, who dwells in the highest forever.

خطايانا التى ارتكبناها . لأننا إن لم نتب فسيقال عنا فى السموات إننا محبون للخطايا . فماذا يكون رجاؤنا بعد إذ طردنا من السماء وطرحنا إلى الحكم ورُفضنا لأجل خطايانا؟ فندان دينونة مضاعفة لا لأننا أخطأنا بغير معرفة فقط ، بل لأن ما عملناه بمعرفة كان أردأ مما عملناه بغير معرفة . ولا لكوننا أخطأنا فقط بل لكوننا لم نتب. لماذا لم تعرف الخراف صوت الراعى الحقيقى المحيي وتلتجئ إليه ؟ ذلك الذى اشتراها بدمه وأعالها وأسلم ذاته فداء عنا . الذى أعطانا جسده لنأكله ودمه لنشربه . يسوع المسيح ربنا ومخلصنا ، الإله إبن الإله العلى الكائن فى الأعالى إلى الأبد .

We conclude the homily of our Holy Father Shenouti the archimandrite, who enlightened our minds and our hearts. In the name of the Father, and the Son, and the Holy Spirit, one God. Amen.

فلنختم عظة أبينا القديس أنبا شنودة رئيس المتوحدين الذى أنار عقولنا وعيون قلوبنا باسم الآب والإبن والروح القدس الإله الواحد آمين .

The Congregation:
We worship You O Christ..
Ⲧⲉⲛⲟⲩⲱϣⲧ ⲙ̀ⲙⲟⲕ ⲱ̀ Ⲡⲭ̅ⲥ̅...

يرد الشعب قائلاً :
نسجد لكَ أيها المسيح ...
Ⲧⲉⲛⲟⲩⲱϣⲧ ⲙ̀ⲙⲟⲕ ⲱ̀ Ⲡⲭ̅ⲥ̅...

The priest offers incense without kissing and the deacon reads the Pauline Epistle in the Annual tune

يرفع الكاهن بخور البولس و يطوف بالبخور بدون تقبيل و يقرأ الشماس البولس باللحن السنوى

The Pauline Epistle - البولس

1 Timothy 4:9-5:10
This is a faithful saying and worthy of all acceptance. For to this end we both labor and suffer reproach, because we trust in the living God, who is the Savior of all men, especially of those who believe. These things command and teach. Let no one despise your youth, but be an example to the believers in word, in conduct, in love, in spirit, in faith, in purity. Till I come, give attention to reading, to exhortation, to doctrine. Do not neglect the gift that is in you, which was given to you by prophecy with the laying on of the hands of the eldership. Meditate on these things; give yourself entirely to them, that your progress may be evident to all. Take heed to yourself and to the doctrine. Continue in them, for in doing this you will save both yourself and those who hear you. Do not rebuke an older man, but exhort him as a father, younger men as brothers, older women as mothers, younger women as sisters, with all purity. Honor widows who are really widows. But if any widow has children or grandchildren, let them first learn to show piety at home and to repay their parents; for this is good and acceptable before God. Now she who

(تيموثاوس الأولى 4 : 9 - 5 : 10)
صادقة هى الكلمة ومستحقة أن نقبلها بكل القبول ، لأننا من أجل هذا نتعب ونعير لأننا توكلنا على الإله الحى ، الذى هو مخلص كافة الناس ، ولاسيما المؤمنين. أوص بهذه وعلم . لا يستهن أحد بحداثتك بل كن مثالاً للمؤمنين فى الكلام ، فى التصرف ، فى المحبة ، فى الإيمان ، فى الطهارة . إلى أن أجئ اعكف على القراءة والصلاة والتعليم . لا تتوان فى الموهبة التى فيك ، فهذه أعطيتها بالنبوة ، وبوضع أيدى القسوسية ، إدرس هذه المناقب وكن فيها لكى يكون تقدمك ظاهراً لكل أحد . إحتفظ بنفسك وبالتعليم وداوم عليهما . لأنك إن فعلت هذا تخلص نفسك والذين يسمعونك . لا تنتهر شيخاً بل عظه كأب . والأحداث كإخوة ، والعجائز كأمهات . والحدثات كإخوات بكل طهارة . أكرم الأرامل اللواتى هن بالحقيقة أرامل . ولكن إن كانت أرملة لها أولاد أو أحفاد فليتعلموا أولاً العبادة فى بيتهم ويكرموا آباءهم الأولين لأن هذا صالح

is really a widow, and left alone, trusts in God and continues in supplications and prayers night and day. But she who lives in pleasure is dead while she lives. And these things command, that they may be blameless. But if anyone does not provide for his own, and especially for those of his household, he has denied the faith and is worse than an unbeliever. Do not let a widow under sixty years old be taken into the number, and not unless she has been the wife of one man, well reported for good works: if she has brought up children, if she has lodged strangers, if she has washed the saints' feet, if she has relieved the afflicted, if she has diligently followed every good work. The Grace of God the Father be with you all. Amen

ومقبول أمام الله . لكن التى هى بالحقيقة أرملة وبقيت وحيدة فقد ألقت رجاءها على الله وهى تواظب على الطلبات والصلوات ليلاً ونهاراً وأما المتنعمة فقد ماتت وهى حية . فأوص هؤلاء الأخريات لكى يكنَّ بغير حجة . وإن كان أحد لا يهتم خصوصاً بأهل بيته فقد أنكر الإيمان وهو أشر من غير المؤمن ولا تدعى أرملة إن لم تكن أقل من ستين سنة إمرأة رجل واحد ويكون مشهوداً لها فى أعمال صالحة وتكون قد ربت الأولاد وأضافت الغرباء وغسلت أرجل القديسين وساعدت المتضايقين واتبعت كل عمل صالح . نعمة الله الآب ...

In Annual Tune

باللحن السنوى

Holy God, Holy Mighty, Holy Immortal, Who was crucified for us, Have mercy upon us.	Ⲁ̀ⲅⲓⲟⲥ ⲟ̀ Ⲑⲉⲟⲥ : ⲁ̀ⲅⲓⲟⲥ Ⲓⲥⲭⲩⲣⲟⲥ : ⲁ̀ⲅⲓⲟⲥ Ⲁ̀ⲑⲁⲛⲁⲧⲟⲥ : ⲟ̀ ⲥⲧⲁⲩⲣⲱⲑⲉⲓⲥ Ⲇⲓ Ⲏⲙⲁⲥ Ⲉ̀ⲗⲉⲏⲥⲟⲛ ⲏ̀ⲙⲁⲥ.	قدوس الله . قدوس القوى قدوس الحى الذى لا يموت ، الذى صلب عنا ، أرحمنا .
Holy God, Holy Mighty, Holy Immortal, Who was crucified for us, Have mercy upon us.	Ⲁ̀ⲅⲓⲟⲥ ⲟ̀ Ⲑⲉⲟⲥ : ⲁ̀ⲅⲓⲟⲥ Ⲓⲥⲭⲩⲣⲟⲥ : ⲁ̀ⲅⲓⲟⲥ Ⲁ̀ⲑⲁⲛⲁⲧⲟⲥ : ⲟ̀ ⲥⲧⲁⲩⲣⲱⲑⲉⲓⲥ Ⲇⲓ Ⲏⲙⲁⲥ Ⲉ̀ⲗⲉⲏⲥⲟⲛ ⲏ̀ⲙⲁⲥ.	قدوس الله . قدوس القوى قدوس الحى الذى لا يموت ، الذى صلب عنا ، أرحمنا .
Holy God, Holy Mighty, Holy Immortal, Who was crucified for us, Have mercy upon us.	Ⲁ̀ⲅⲓⲟⲥ ⲟ̀ Ⲑⲉⲟⲥ : ⲁ̀ⲅⲓⲟⲥ Ⲓⲥⲭⲩⲣⲟⲥ : ⲁ̀ⲅⲓⲟⲥ Ⲁ̀ⲑⲁⲛⲁⲧⲟⲥ : ⲟ̀ ⲥⲧⲁⲩⲣⲱⲑⲉⲓⲥ Ⲇⲓ Ⲏⲙⲁⲥ Ⲉ̀ⲗⲉⲏⲥⲟⲛ ⲏ̀ⲙⲁⲥ.	قدوس الله . قدوس القوى قدوس الحى الذى لا يموت ، الذى صلب عنا ، أرحمنا .
Glory be to the Father and to the Son, and to the Holy Spirit, both now, and ever, and unto the ages of ages, Amen.	Ⲇⲟⲝⲁ Ⲡⲁⲧⲣⲓ ⲕⲉ Ⲩⲓⲱ : ⲕⲉ ⲁ̀ⲅⲓⲱ ⲡⲛⲁ̀ⲧⲓ. Ⲕⲉ ⲛⲩⲛ ⲕⲉ ⲁ̀ⲓ ⲕⲉ ⲓⲥ ⲧⲟⲩⲥ ⲉ̀ⲱⲛⲁⲥ ⲧⲱⲛ ⲉ̀ⲱⲛⲱⲛ ⲁ̀ⲙⲉⲛ.	المجد للآب و الإبن و الروح القدس . الآن و كل آوان و الى دهر الدهور ، آمين .

The priest prays the litany of the Gospel. The Psalm and Gospel are read in the annual tune.
When it is read "...took a towel and girded Himself" the priest does the same.

ثم يقول الكاهن أوشية الإنجيل ويطرح المزمور ويقرأ الإنجيل باللحن السنوى .
و عندما ثُقرأ ".. وأخذ منديلاً وإنتزر به" يفعل الكاهن هكذا ايضاً .

The Psalm
Ⲯⲁⲗⲙⲟⲥ Ⲛ̅ : ⲍ̅ - ⲓ̅

Psalms 50:7, 10			(مز 50: 7 - 10)
Purge me with hyssop, and I shall be clean; Wash me, and I shall be whiter than snow. Create in me a clean heart, O God, And renew a steadfast spirit within me. Alleluia.	Ⲉ̀ⲕⲉⲛⲟⲩⲭϧ ⲉϫⲱⲓ ⲙ̀ⲡⲉⲕϣⲉⲛⲥⲩⲥⲱⲡⲟⲛ ⲉⲓ ⲉ̀ⲧⲟⲩⲃⲟ : ⲉⲕⲉⲣⲁϧⲧ ⲉⲓ ⲉ̀ⲟⲩⲃⲁϣ ⲉ̀ϩⲟⲧⲉ ⲟⲩⲭⲓⲱⲛ : ⲟⲩϩⲏⲧ ⲉϥⲟⲩⲁⲃ ⲉⲕⲉ̀ⲥⲟⲛⲧϥ ⲛ̀ϧⲏⲧ Ⲫϯ : ⲟⲩⲡⲛ̅ⲁ̅ ⲉϥⲥⲟⲩⲧⲱⲛ ⲁⲣⲓⲧϥ ⲙ̀ⲃⲉⲣⲓ ϧⲉⲛ ⲛⲏⲉⲧⲥⲁϧⲟⲩⲛ ⲙ̀ⲙⲟⲓ .ⲁ̅ⲗ̅.	إكنووجخ إيجوى إمبيك شيتهيصوبون يه إطوفو : إكئراخت يه إ أووفاش إ هوتيه أووشيون : أووهيت إفؤواب إكئصونتف إنخيت إفنووتى : أوو بنيمفا إفصووطون أريتف إمفيرى خين نى إتصاخوون إمموى . الليلويا.	تنضح علىّ بزوفك فأطهر وتغسلنى بأبيض أكثر من الثلج . قلباً نقياً تخلق فيّ يا الله، وروحاً مستقيماً جدد فى أحشائى. الليلويا.

John 13:1-17

(الإنجيل من يوحنا ص 13 : 1 - 17)

Now before the Feast of the Passover, when Jesus knew that His hour had come that He should depart from this world to the Father, having loved His own who were in the world, He loved them to the end. And supper being ended, the devil having already put it into the heart of Judas Iscariot, Simon's son, to betray Him, Jesus, knowing that the Father had given all things into His hands, and that He had come from God and was going to God, rose from supper and laid aside His garments, took a towel and girded Himself. After that, He poured water into a basin and began to wash the disciples' feet, and to wipe them with the towel with which He was girded. Then He came to Simon Peter. And Peter said to Him, "Lord, are You washing my feet?" Jesus answered and said to him, "What I am doing you do not understand now, but you will know after this." Peter said to Him, "You shall never wash my feet!" Jesus answered him, "If I do not wash you, you have no part with Me." Simon Peter said to Him, "Lord, not my feet only, but also my hands and my head!" Jesus said to him, "He who is bathed needs only to wash his feet, but is completely clean; and you are clean, but not all of you." For He knew who would betray Him; therefore He said, "You are not all clean." So when He had washed their feet, taken His garments, and sat down again, He said to them, "Do you know what I have done to you? You call Me Teacher and Lord, and you say well, for so I am. If I then, your Lord and Teacher, have washed your feet, you also ought to wash one another's feet. For I have given you an example, that you should do as I have done to you. Most assuredly, I say to you, a servant is not greater than his master; nor is he who is sent greater than he who sent him. If you know these things, blessed are you if you do them. Glory be to God forever, Amen.

وقبل عيد الفصح إذ علم يسوع أن ساعته قد جاءت ، لكى ينتقل من هذا العالم ذاهباً إلى الآب. وقد أحب خاصته الذين فى العالم وأحبهم إلى النهاية ، وبعد العشاء إذ بابليس كان قد فرغ مما القى فى قلب الذى يسلمه الذى هو يهوذا سمعان الإسخريوطى . فلما رأى يسوع أن الآب قد دفع كل شئ إلى يديه وأنه من عند الله خرج وإلى الله يمضى ، قام عن العشاء وخلع ثيابه وأخذ منديلاً وإتزر به ثم صب ماء فى مغسل وإبتدأ يغسل أرجل تلاميذه ويمسحهما بالمنشفة التى كان مؤتزراً بها . فلما جاء إلى سمعان بطرس ليغسل رجليه . قال له بطرس : يا سيدى أنت تغسل رجلى؟ أجاب يسوع وقال له : إن الذى أصنعه أنا لا تعرفه أنت الآن . ولكنك تعرفه بعد ذلك . قال له بطرس : لن تغسل رجلى أبداً . فأجابه يسوع وقال: الحق الحق أقول لك إن لم أغسل قدميك فليس لك معى نصيب . قال له سمعان بطرس : يا سيد ليس رجلى فقط بل يدىّ ورأسى أيضاً . قال له يسوع : الذى قد أغتسل ليس له حاجة إلا إلى غسل رجليه بل هو طاهر كله وأنتم طاهرون ولكن ليس كلكم. لأنه عرف مسلمه لذلك قال لستم كلكم طاهرين . فلما غسل أرجلهم وأخذ ثيابه و إتكأ أيضاً ، قال لهم : أتفهمون ما قد صنعته بكم؟ أنتم تدعوننى المعلم والرب وحسناً تقولون لأنى أنا هو . فإن كنت وأنا ربكم ومعلمكم قد غسلت أرجلكم ، فأنتم أيضاً يجب أن يغسل بعضكم أرجل بعض . الآن ما صنعته لكم هو مثالاً حتى كما صنعت أنا بكم ، تصنعون أنتم بعضكم ببعض . الحق الحق أقول لكم أنه ليس عبد أعظم من سيده ، ولا رسول أعظم من مرسله . إن علمتم هذا فطوباكم إن عملتموه . والمجد لله دائماً .

+ **The priest, holding the cross with three candles, prayes:**

+ يرفع الكاهن الصليب وثلاثة شمعات ويقول:

God, have mercy upon us..

ⲪϮ ⲛⲁⲓ ⲛⲁⲛ ⲑⲉⲱⲟⲩⲛⲁⲓ ⲉ̀ⲣⲟⲛ..

أللهم ارحمنا وقرر لنا رحمتك ..

ⲪϮ ⲛⲁⲓ ⲛⲁⲛ ⲑⲉⲱⲟⲩⲛⲁⲓ ⲉ̀ⲣⲟⲛ..

+ **Congregation prays "Lord have mercy" in the long tune ten times.**

+ يجاوبه الشعب قائلاً : Ⲕⲩⲣⲓⲉⲉ̀ⲗⲉⲏⲥⲟⲛ بالكبير عشر مرات .

Then the Gospel response:

ثم مرد الإنجيل

Jesus Christ is the same yesterday, today, and forever. In one hypostasis, we worship and glorify Him.

Ⲓⲏⲥ Ⲡⲭⲥ ⲛ̀ⲥⲁϥ ⲛⲉⲙ ⲫⲟⲟⲩ ⲛ̀ⲑⲟϥ ⲛ̀ⲑⲟϥ ⲡⲉ ⲛⲉⲙ ϣⲁ ⲉ̀ⲛⲉⲏ : ϧⲉⲛ ⲟⲩⲅⲩⲡⲟⲥⲧⲁⲥⲓⲥ ⲛ̀ⲟⲩⲱⲧ : ⲧⲉⲛⲟⲩⲱϣⲧ ⲙ̀ⲙⲟϥ ⲧⲉⲛϯⲱⲟⲩ ⲛⲁϥ.

يسوع المسيح هو هو أمساً و اليوم و الى الابد . بأقنوم واحد ، نسجد له و نمجده .

(The priest prays these litanies)

(يقول الكاهن الطلبة)

O You who girded Yourself with a towel and covered up Adam's nakedness. You, who gave us the garment of Divine Sonship, we ask You, O Christ our God, hear us and have mercy upon us.
Lord have mercy.

يا من إشتد بمنديل وستر كل عراء آدم . وأنعم علينا بلباس البنوة الإلهية . نطلب إليك أيها المسيح إلهنا إسمعنا وإرحمنا .
(يارب ارحم)

O You who for the love of mankind became Man; You girded Yourself with a towel to cleanse us from the stains of our sins; we ask You, O Christ our God, hear us and have mercy upon us.
Lord have mercy.

يا من أجل محبته للبشر صار إنساناً وبمحبته لنا إشتد بمنديل وغسل أدناس خطايانا ، نسألك أيها المسيح إلهنا أن تسمعنا وترحمنا .
(يارب ارحم)

O You who prepared for us the way of life through the washing of the chosen holy disciples' feet; we ask You, O Christ our God, hear us and have mercy upon us.
Lord have mercy.

يا من أعد لنا طريق الحياة بواسطة غسل أرجل رسله المختارين الأطهار نسألك أيها المسيح إلهنا اسمعنا وارحمنا.
(يارب ارحم)

O Christ our God who walked on the waters and through Your love of mankind, washed the disciples' feet; we ask You, O Christ our God, hear us and have mercy upon us.
Lord have mercy.

أيها المسيح إلهنا يا من جعل مشيه على المياه وبمحبته للبشر غسل أرجل تلاميذه . نطلب إليك أيها المسيح إلهنا اسمعنا وارحمنا .
(يارب ارحم)

O You who clothed Yourself in light like a garment, girded Yourself and washed the disciples' feet and wiped them; we ask You, O Christ our God, hear us and have mercy upon us.
Lord have mercy.

يا من التحف بالنور كالثوب واشتد بمئزرة وغسل أرجل تلاميذه ومسحها . نسألك أيها المسيح إلهنا اسمعنا وارحمنا .
(يارب ارحم)

O our God, have mercy upon us all, according to the multitude of Your mercy. We entreat Your goodness O Lord our God, hear us and have mercy upon us.
Lord have mercy.

اللهم ارحمنا جميعاً كعظيم رحمتك . ونطلب من صلاحك أيها الرب إلهنا تستجيب لنا وترحمنا .
(يارب ارحم)

O Christ our God, the Pantocrator, the Provider of divine gifts to those who serve Your holy name, who sustains and supports all. You who feed them through Your love; we ask You, O Christ our God, hear us and have mercy upon us.
Lord have mercy.

أيها المسيح الرب إلهنا الضابط الكل الرازق المواهب الإلهية للذين يخدمون إسمك القدوس الذى ينمى ويربى ويعول الكل ويقوتهم بمحبته . نطلب إليك أيها المسيح إلهنا استجب لنا وارحمنا .
(يارب ارحم)

O You who gathered the water to one source, and made a limit for it above the sky; we ask You, O Christ our God, hear us and have mercy upon us.
Lord have mercy.

يا من جمع المياه إلى مجمع واحد ، وجعل لها حداً فوق السموات . نطلب إليك أيها المسيح إلهنا استجب لنا وارحمنا .
(يارب ارحم)

O You who weighed the water with Your hands, and measured the heaven with the span of Your hand, and held all the earth with the palm of Your hand; we ask You, O Christ our God, hear us and have mercy upon us.
Lord have mercy.

الذى كال الماء بيده ، وقاس السماء بشبره ، والأرض كلها بقبضته . نسألك أيها المسيح إلهنا استجب لنا وارحمنا .
(يارب ارحم)

O You who through Your will made the springs into rivers and through Your indefinable love to mankind had prepared all things and created everything out of nothing for our services; we ask You, O Christ our God, hear us and have mercy upon us.
Lord have mercy.

الذى صيَّر ينابيع الأودية أنهاراً بإرادته المقدسة وبمحبتك الغير مدركة للبشر أعددت لنا كل شئ لخدمتنا ، وخلق الكل من لا شئ . نطلب إليك أيها المسيح إلهنا استجب لنا وارحمنا .
(يارب ارحم)

Again, O You the giver of truth and infinite richness, Lover of Mankind, O Lord of mercy; visit the earth and water it by the rising of the rivers, to bring forth good fruits; we ask You, O Christ our God, hear us and have mercy upon us.
Lord have mercy.

هكذا أيضاً أيها المعطى الحق وعظم الغنى ومحبة البشر يا إله الرحمة إفتقد الأرض واروها بصعود النهر فتثمر حسناً . نطلب إليك أيها المسيح إلهنا استجب لنا وارحمنا .
(يارب ارحم)

May its furrows be watered and its fruits be plentiful through Your Goodness; we ask You, O Christ our God, hear us and have mercy upon us.
Lord have mercy.

ليروى حرثها ، ليكثر ثمارها بصلاحك . نسألك أيها المسيح إلهنا إستجب لنا وإرحمنا .
(يارب ارحم)

Give joy to the face of the earth and renew it. Raise the waters of the rivers according to their measure; we ask You, O Christ our God, hear us and have mercy upon us.
Lord have mercy.

فرح وجه الأرض ، جددها دفعة أخرى ، أصعد نهر النيل كمقداره . نطلب إليك أيها المسيح إلهنا إستجب لنا وإرحمنا .
(يارب ارحم)

Bless the crown of the year with Your Goodness. Fill the land of our country with fatness to increase its furrows, and bless its fruits; we ask You, O Christ our God, hear us and have mercy upon us.
Lord have mercy.

بارك إكليل السنة بصلاحك ، وبقاع بلدنا (مصر) إملأها من الدسم ليكثر حرثها وتتبارك أثمارها . نطلب إليك أيها المسيح إلهنا إستجب لنا وإرحمنا .
(يارب ارحم)

Give joy to the land of our country, may its hills rejoice with gladness, through Your Goodness; we ask You, O Christ our God, hear us and have mercy upon us.
Lord have mercy.

لتفرح حدود كورة بلدنا (مصر) ولتهلل الأكام بفرح من قبل صلاحك . نطلب إليك أيها المسيح إلهنا استجب لنا وارحمنا .

(يارب ارحم)

O Lord, save Your people, bless Your inheritance and visit the whole world with Your loving kindness and mercy. Exalt the horn of the Christians with the power of Your Life-Giving Cross; we ask You, O Christ our God, hear us and have mercy upon us.
Lord have mercy.

اللهم خلص شعبك . بارك ميراثك . افتقد العالم أجمع بالمراحم والرأفات . ارفع شأن المسيحيين بقوة صليبك المحيي . نطلب إليك أيها المسيح إلهنا استجب لنا وارحمنا .

(يارب ارحم)

Grant security, confirmation, and peace to the provinces through Your Goodness. Grant Your mercy and abundance to all the poor of Your people and make our hearts be delighted through the intercession of Your Holy Mother, the Pure Virgin Mary, and St. John the Baptist, and all our fathers the Apostles; we ask You, O Christ our God, hear us and have mercy upon us.
Lord have mercy.

اعط طمأنينة وثباتاً وسلاماً للممالك بصلاحك أنعم لنا بالخصب وبمراحمك لسائر فقراء شعبك ، ولتبتهج قلوبنا . بطلبات أمك العذراء الطاهرة مريم والقديس يوحنا المعمدان ، وكافة آبائنا الرسل قاطبة نطلب إليك أيها المسيح إلهنا استجب لنا وارحمنا .

(يارب ارحم)

+ The priest holds the cross with lit candles and they pray "Lord have mercy Ⲕⲩⲣⲓⲉⲉ̀ⲗⲉⲏⲥⲟⲛ, 100 times"
+ The priest prays the three long litanies:
1- The Peace
2- The Fathers
3- The Congregation
+ The introduction to the creed and the Creed (the whole creed)

+ يرفع الكاهن الصليب وهو مضاء بالشموع و يقولون (يارب ارحم) مئة مرة دمجاً .
+ يقول الكاهن الثلاثة أواشى الكبار وهى:
1- السلامة .
2- الآباء .
3- الاجتماعات .
+ مقدمة قانون الإيمان وقانون الايمان كاملاً إلى آخره .

Aspasmos, Adam

الأبصلمودية آدام

Our Fathers, the Apostles, preached the Gospel of Jesus Christ to all the nations. Their voices reached out all the earth, and their words came to all the countries of the world.

Ⲛⲉⲛⲓⲟϯ ⲛ̀ ⲁⲡⲟⲥⲧⲟⲗⲟⲥ : ⲁⲩϩⲓⲱⲓϣ ϧⲉⲛ ⲛⲓⲉⲑⲛⲟⲥ : ϧⲉⲛ ⲡⲓⲉⲩⲅⲅⲉⲗⲓⲟⲛ : ⲛ̀ⲧⲉ Ⲓⲏⲥ Ⲡⲭⲥ.
Ⲁⲡⲟⲩϧⲣⲱⲟⲩ ϣⲉⲛⲁϥ : ϩⲓϫⲉⲛ ⲡ̀ⲕⲁϩⲓ ⲧⲏⲣϥ : ⲟⲩⲟϩ ⲛⲟⲩⲥⲁϫⲓ ⲁⲩⲫⲟϩ : ϣⲁ ⲁⲩⲣⲏϫⲥ ⲛ̀ ϯⲟⲓⲕⲟⲩⲙⲉⲛⲏ.

نين يوتى إن أبوسطولوس : أفهيؤيش خين نى إثنوس : خين بى إيف أنجيليون : إنتيه إيسوس بيخرستوس .
أبوو خروأوو شيناف : هيجين إبكاهى تيرف : أووه نوو صاجى أففوه : شا أفريجس إن تى إيكوومينى .

آباؤنا الرسل كرزوا فى الأمم بانجيل يسوع المسيح . خرجت أصواتهم على الأرض كلها وبلغ كلامهم إلى أقطار المسكونة .

Liturgy of Blessing the Water	قداس لقان خميس العهد

Deacon
Offer, offer, offer, in order. Stand with trembling. Look toward the east. Let us attend.

Congregation
Through the intercessions of the Theotokos Saint Mary, O Lord grant us, the forgiveness of our sins. We worship You O Christ, with Your good Father, and the Holy Spirit, for You were crucified and saved us. A mercy of peace, a sacrifice of praise.

Priest
(Blessing the water by the cross for the first time)
The love of God the Father; the Grace of the only Begotten Son, our Lord, God and Savior Jesus Christ; and the communion and gift of the Holy Spirit be with you all.

Congregation
And with your spirit.

Priest
(Blessing the water by the cross for the second time)
Lift up your hearts.

Congregation
We have them with the Lord.

Priest
(Blessing the water by the cross for the third time)
Let us give thanks to the Lord.

Congregation
It is meet and right.

Priest
Meet and right, meet and right; truly indeed it is meet and right. We praise You, we exalt You, we bless You, we glorify You, we worship You. We thank You at all times for all Your works You have done for us. You alone are the True God, who exists from the beginning, and who formed water from His heights. Who made the water in the firmament that blesses Your holy name, O King of all creation, Lord Jesus Christ, we worship You. You who sits on the throne of His glory and is worshiped by all the holy powers..

Deacon
You who are seated, stand.

الشماس
تقدموا، تقدموا، تقدموا على الرسم، قفوا برعدة والى الشرق انظروا، ننصت.

الشعب
بشفاعات والدة الإله القديسة مريم، يا رب أنعم لنا بمغفرة خطايانا. نسجد لك أيها المسيح، مع أبيك الصالح، والروح القدس، لأنك صلبت وخلصتنا. رحمة السلام، ذبيحة التسبيح.

الكاهن
(يرشم الماء بالصليب رشم أول)
محبة الله الآب ونعمة الإبن الوحيد ربنا وإلهنا ومخلصنا يسوع المسيح . وشركة وموهبة الروح القدس تكون مع جميعكم .

الشعب
ومع روحك ايضاً.

الكاهن
(يرشم الماء رشماً ثانياً)
ارفعوا قلوبكم.

الشعب
هى عند الرب.

الكاهن
(يرشم الماء رشماً ثالثاً)
فلنشكر الرب.

الشعب
مستحق ومستوجب.

الكاهن
مستحق ومستوجب مستحق ومستوجب لأنه حقاً بالحقيقة مستحق ومستوجب . لأنك بالحقيقة مستحق وعادل ، أكرمك ، أرفعك ، أباركك ، أمجدك ، أسجد لك ، أشكرك فى كل زمان لأجل الخيرات التى صنعتها معنا . أنت الإله الحقيقى وحدك . الكائن منذ البدء الذى أظهر المياه فى علاليه . الذى جعل المياه الكثيرة فى فلك السماء ، هذه تبارك اسمك القدوس يا ملك الخليقة كلها ، يا يسوع المسيح نسجد لك. أيها الجالس على كرسى مجده، الذى تسجد له جميع القوات المقدسة.

الشماس
أيها الجلوس قفوا.

Priest

The angels, the archangels, the principalities, the authorities, the thrones, the dominions, all the serving spirits and all the infinite multitude of angelic powers, who stand before You in fear and trembling, praising Your Majesty.

الكاهن

ان الملائكة ورؤساء الملائكة والرئاسات والسلطات والكراسى والربوات . وكل الأرواح الخدام ، وكل الجمع الغير المحصى من القوات الملائكية هؤلاء القيام أمامك بخوف ورعدة يسبحون عظمتك .

Deacon

Look towards the east.

الشماس

وإلى الشرق انظروا.

Priest

You are He around whom stand the blessed powers; the cherubim and the seraphim thrice glorifying You. Wherefore we also, make us worthy to join their praises and bless you with the voices full of glory saying:

الكاهن

أنت هو الذى يقف حولك القوات الطوباويين : الشاروبيم والسيرافيم هؤلاء يقدسونك ثلاث مرات فى كل حين. ونحن أيضاً اجعلنا مستحقين أن نسبحك معهم ونباركك بأصوات المجد قائلين :

Congregation

The Cherubim worship You, and the Seraphim glorify You, proclaiming and saying, HOLY, HOLY, HOLY, Lord of hosts. Heaven and Earth are full of Your holy glory.

الشعب

الشاروبيم يسجدون لك و السيرافيم يمجدونك ، صارخين قائلين : قدوس قدوس قدوس رب الصاباؤوت ، السماء و الارض مملوءتان من مجدك القدوس.

The priest blesses the water with the cross three times, saying: Agios

يرشم الكاهن الماء ثلاث مرات بالصليب وكل رشم يقول : ⲁ̅ⲅⲓⲟⲥ

Holy, Holy, Holy, You are O Lord and Holy in all things. For You are the True Holy God, Jesus Christ, the Prototokos of all creation, who dwells in the glory of His majesty, whom no body can apprehend the fullness of the Divinity that dwells in Him bodily. You did not consider it robbery to be equal to God, Your Father, but with Your good will You came to earth taking the form of a servant and becoming man in truth. You were incarnate in the undefiled womb of the Holy Theotokos, St. Mary. You who were clothed in purity and never sinned; gave Yourself up to the holy cross for our salvation. You gave us this example, for after supper You arose, took a towel and girded Yourself and poured water into a basin, and began to wash your disciples' feet; and wiped them with the towel with which You were girded. You had given them the ordinance of love and humility, and the remembrance of Your love for mankind. For You said to them, "If I, Your Lord and Master have washed your feet, then you also ought to wash one another's feet. As much as I have done it unto you so you ought to do to one another." You have ordered them to follow Your commandments and Your statutes, for You have said: "love one another, by this shall all men know you are my disciples because you love one another." You also have taught us the love and unity; and You have reconciled us with Your Father. Through washing the disciples' feet and the purity of

قدوس قدوس قدوس أيها الرب وقدوس أنت فى كل شئ ، لأنك أنت الإله القدوس الحقيقى يسوع المسيح الإبن بكر كل الخليقة . الكائن فى مجد عظمته الذى ليس أحد يعرف كمال لاهوته الحال فيه جسدياً . ليس هو اختطافاً ما نويت لتصير مساوياً لله أبيك. لكن بإرادتك وحدك أخذت شكل العبد وصرت إنسانا بالحقيقة ، تجسدت فى بطن الغير الدنسة والدة الإله القديسة مريم . أنت الذى لبست الطهارة ولم تخطئ أبداً ، ودفعت ذاتك إلى الصليب المقدس من أجل خلاصنا . وضعت لنا هذا المثال . إذ قمت من العشاء وأخذت منديلاً اشتديت به ، وصببت ماء فى مغسل وابتدأت تغسل أرجل تلاميذك وتمسحها بالمنديل الذى كنت متزراً به واعطيتهم رسم المحبة وترتيب التواضع وتذكار محبتك للبشر. إذ قلت لهم : أنا غسلت أقدامكم معلماً ورباً ، فيجب عليكم أن يغسل بعضكم أقدام بعض . مثل ما صنعت بكم وكما صنعت بكم إصنعوا أنتم أيضاً ببعضكم بعضاً . وأمرتهم بوصاياك وأوامرك إذ قلت احبوا بعضكم بعضاً ، وبهذا يعلم كل واحد أنكم تلاميذى إذا أحببتم بعضكم بعضاً . وعلمتنا نحن أيضاً المحبة والوحدانية ، وأصلحتنا مع أبيك من جهة غسل أرجل تلاميذك ، ونقاوة هذا

this example, and through Your love and compassion for mankind, You have crowned our freedom. When Peter exalted Your Divinity and refused saying, "You shall never wash my feet", he heard the true case: "If I do not wash you, you have no part with me." Therefore, he cried sincerely saying: "Lord, not my feet only, but also my hands and my head!" and he also heard Your Divine Voice which is full of truth saying, "He who is bathed needs only to wash his feet, but is completely clean." Therefore, we ask and entreat You our Lord Jesus Christ to make us worthy, and dwell in our midst as You were with Your disciples, the holy apostles.

المثال الحقيقى ومن قبل تعطفك ومحبتك للبشر صنعت كمال حريتنا عندما استعظم بطرس لاهوتك وامتنع قائلاً : لا تغسل رجلى إلى الأبد ، فسمع القضية الحقيقية ، إذ لم أغسل قدميك فليس لك معى نصيب ، أما هو بأمانته صرخ قائلاً : يا سيدى ليس رجلى فقط بل ويداى ورأسى ، قدسنى بالكلية . فسمع أيضاً صوتك الإلهى الغير الكاذب : أن الذى استحم لا يحتاج إلا إلى غسل قدميه لكنه كله نقى . من أجل هذا نسأل ونطلب منك يا ربنا يسوع المسيح اجعلنا مستحقين وحل فى وسطنا الآن كما كنت مع تلاميذك الرسل القديسين.

The priest bless the water with the cross and the congregation responds after each time saying (Amen).

ثم يقول الكاهن و يرشم الماء بالصليب و يجاوبه الشعب عند الانتهاء من كل رشم (آمين)

- O You Who blessed at that time, now also bless. Amen.

- Bless this water unto healing, Amen.

- A holy water, Amen.

- A water for the remission of sins, Amen.

- A water of purification, Amen.

- A water for salvation and health of our spirits, bodies and souls, Amen.

- A gift of purity, Amen.

- Love for each other and purity of the senses, Amen.

- That we may be worthy of Your Holy Virtue, which You have taught us through Your love of man, Amen.

- When we wash one another's feet, make us worthy of the inheritance of Your holy disciples, Amen.

- Purify our inner man with the fruits of this Mystery, Amen.

- Grant us the forgiveness of our sins through the indwelling of Your Holy Spirit to purify our spirits, bodies and souls from all defilement, unrighteousness and sin, Amen.

- Grant us the authority to trample on serpents and scorpions and every power of the enemy, and do not permit any evil to overpower us, but grant us wise senses and righteousness; so that we may come before You to receive compassion and mercy, Amen.

- وكما باركت فى ذلك الزمن بارك الآن، آمين

- طهر هذا ليكن ماءً للشفاء، آمين

- ماء مقدساً، آمين

- ماء لغفران الخطايا، آمين

- ماء الطهارة، آمين

- خلاصاً وصحة لأنفسنا وأجسادنا وأرواحنا آمين

- موهبة طاهرة، آمين

- ومحبة لبعضنا بعضاً وحواس نقية، آمين

- لكى نستحق فضيلتك المقدسة. علمنا إياها من قبل محبتك للبشر، آمين

- عندما نغسل أرجل بعضنا بعضاً لنستحق أن نكون فى ميراث تلاميذك الأطهار، آمين

- طهر إنساننا الداخلى بثمرة هذا السـ، آمين

- وانعم لنا بغفران خطايانا بحلول روحك القدوس علينا ليطهر نفوسنا وأجسادنا وأرواحنا . من كل دنس الجسد وكل نجاسة وكل خطية، آمين

- إمنحنا السلطان أن ندوس الحيات والعقارب وكل قوة العدو . ولا تدع شيئاً من الآثام يتسلط علينا . بل انعم علينا بحواس حكيمة وسلوك ذات وقار وأمان لكى نأتى إليك لنجد رحمة أمامك ورأفة، آمين

We ask You O True God, to send Your Holy Spirit the Paraclete upon us and this water, O You who fashioned the

نطلب إليك يا الله الحقيقى لكى ترسل علينا وعلى هذه المياه روحك القدوس الباراقليط. يا جابل

waters, O Jesus Christ our Lord, creator of all; who was crucified for us under Pontius Pilate confessing and saying: "I am the Son of God." We believe that You are the Son of God in truth. Purify this water by the power of Your Holy Spirit to annul the deadly powers of the adversary against us. Rebuke all evil spirits, all sorcery, and all idol worshipping. O our God Jesus Christ, may the power of the adversary flee from this water by the sign of Your Holy cross,

Here the priest blesses the water with the sign of the cross, and says:

- Bring it forth water unto healing, Amen.

- Water unto purification, Amen.

- Water unto remission of sins, Amen.

- Water unto salvation, Amen.

Make us worthy of sonship, that we may cry out towards Your good Father and the Holy Spirit saying:

Our Father Who are in heaven…
The Priest prays the absolution.

Deacon
Let us attend in the fear of God. Amen.

Saved. Amen. And with your spirit. In the fear of God, let us attend.

The priest blesses the basin and the water container three times and says:
Blessed be the Lord Jesus Christ, the Son of God; the sanctification is by the Holy Spirit. Amen

Congregation
Amen, One is the All-Holy Father; One is the All-Holy Son; One is the All-Holy Spirit. Amen.

The highest rank of the priests washes the feet of the other clergy, the deacons and congregation during chanting psalms 15O in the annual tune.

Praise God in all his saints. Alleluia.

المياه، خالق الكل ، يسوع المسيح ربنا الذى صلب عنا فى عهد بيلاطس البنطى . واعترف قائلاً : أنى أنا هو إبن الله . نؤمن أنك أنت هو إبن الله بالحقيقة . طهر هذا الماء بقوة روح قدسك لكى يبطل قوات المضاد القاتل لنا . وينتهر كل الأرواح النجسة. وكل سحر وكل رقية. وكل عبادة الأوثان. فلتهرب من هذا الماء كل قوة المضاد بعلامة صليبك المقدس يا ربنا يسوع المسيح .

(هنا يبارك الكاهن على الماء بالصليب ويقول)

- اظهره ماء الشفاء، آمين

- ماء الطهارة، آمين

- ماء مغفرة الخطايا، آمين

- ماء الخلاص، آمين

واجعلنا مستحقين البنوة لكى نصرخ نحو أبيك الصالح والروح القدس قائلين : يا أبانا الذى ...

يقول الشعب (أبانا الذى فى السموات) ويقول الكاهن التحليل

الشماس
ننصت بخوف الله آمين.

خلصت حقاً ومع روحك، ننصت بخوف الله.

يرشم الكاهن ماء اللقان والطاسة ثلاث رشوم ويقول
مبارك الرب يسوع المسيح إبن الله وقدوس الروح القدس آمين .

الشعب
حقاً واحد هو الآب القدوس . واحد هو الإبن القدوس ، واحد هو الروح القدس آمين . حقاً أومن.

ثم يبل الكاهن الشملة من ماء اللقان ويغسل أرجل الشمامسة ثم الشعب . وأثناء ذلك يرتل الشمامسة المزمور المائة والخمسين بالطريقة السنوية.

Ⲥⲙⲟⲩ ⲉ Ⲫ† سبحوا الله

Psali

ابصالية

Our Lord laid aside His vestments / Took a towel and girded Himself / Poured water into a basin / And washed the disciples' feet.

وضع ربنا ثيابه واشتد بمنديل وصب ماء فى مغسل وغسل أرجل تلاميذه .

Then He came to Simon Peter / To wash his feet / He said unto Him / "You shall never wash my feet."

فجاء أيضاً إلى سمعان بطرس ليغسل قدميه . فقال له لست تغسل لى قدمى إلى الأبد .

Our Savior said to Simon Peter / "I say unto you / If I do not wash you / You have no part with Me."

فقال مخلصنا لسمعان بطرس : أنا أقول لك أنه إن لم تغسل قدميك فليس لك معى نصيب .

Simon Peter said to Him / "O my Lord Jesus Christ / not my feet only / but also my hands and my head!"

قال سمعان لمخلصنا يا ربى يسوع المسيح ليس قدمى فقط بل يدى ورأسى.

And He taught them saying / "I have washed your feet / you also should / wash each other's feet."

وكان يعلمهم قائلاً : أنا غسلت أرجلكم وأنتم أيضاً يجب أن يغسل بعضكم أرجل بعض .

Pray to the Lord on our behalf, our lords and fathers the apostles, and the seventy-two 7:01 AMdisciples, that He may forgive us our sins.

اطلبوا من الرب عنا يا ساداتى الآباء الرسل والاثنين والسبعين تلميذاً . ليغفر لنا خطايانا لأنه مبارك .

(Thanksgiving prayer after blessing of the water)

صلاة شكر بعد اللقان

We give thanks unto You, O Master, Lord, God Almighty, upon every condition, for any condition and in whatever condition, for You have made us worthy to complete Yours Holy Example of the washing of feet at this hour. This You; Your only-begotten Son, our Lord, God, Teacher and Savior Jesus Christ, anointed and taught Your disciples. We ask and entreat Your goodness O Lover of Mankind, forgive our sins and have compassion on us, according to Your great mercy and grant peace on Your Holy Church. Keep us in peace and love with Your fear, alert us to all Your commandments in this generation and forever. Make us all partakers of Your eternal blessings through Yours only-begotten Son Jesus Christ our God, through whom glory, honor, dominion, and worship befit You with Him and the Holy Spirit both now and ever and unto the ages of the ages, Amen.

نشكرك أيها السيد الرب الإله الضابط الكل . نشكرك على كل حال ومن أجل كل حال وفى كل حال . لأنك جعلتنا مستحقين فى هذه الساعة أن نكمل مثال مغسلك المقدس . هذا الذى رسمه وعلمه لتلاميذه إبنك الوحيد الجنس ربنا وإلهنا ومعلمنا ومخلصنا يسوع المسيح ، نسأل ونطلب من صلاحك يا محب البشر تجاوز عن خطايانا الكثيرة وترأف علينا ككثرة مراحمك وانعم لنا فى كل حين بسلامك فى بيعتك المقدسة . احفظنا بسلام ومحبة مع خوفك متيقظين لجميع وصاياك فى هذا الدهر الحاضر وفى الآتى . اجعلنا شركاء لخيراتك الدهرية بإبنك الوحيد يسوع المسيح ربنا . هذا الذى من قبله المجد والاكرام والعز والسجود يليق بك معه والروح القدس المحيي المساوى لك . الآن وكل أوان وإلى دهر الداهرين آمين .

A homily of our Holy Father Saint John Chrysostom

(عظة لأبينا القديس يوحنا ذهبى الفم)

Today, I behold many believers rushing to partake of the awesome mysteries that they may exceedingly benefit. Let me first advise you that you must walk in fear and righteousness as befitting these holy mysteries. My beloved, in this day our Lord Jesus was betrayed; if you then hear that He was

إنى أرى اليوم كثيرين من المؤمنين مسرعين إلى الشركة فى هذه السرائر المملوءة خوفاً ورعدة . لكى يكون الربح مضاعفاً . فارشدكم أنا أولاً بقولى . لكى تسيروا بخوف ورهبة ووجل . كما يحق بهذه السرائر المقدسة . أحبائى أُسلِم السيد

betrayed, do not be disappointed. Let me tell you about whom you shall be disappointed in. Lament and cry over Judas who gave Him up. For He who was betrayed, sits on the right hand of the Father in heaven; and He is also King overall, in an everlasting kingdom. But he who gave Him up, descended into the depths of Hades; there he shall remain unto the end in anticipation of great grief and lament. It is over him you should moan and lament. For our Lord taught us not to grieve over him who endures suffering, but rather to grieve over the evildoer. It is fit to bewail him who does evil more than he who accepts sufferings. Indeed, he who accepts suffering is not evil, but rather he who does evil is wicked. For, being in sufferings leads us to the heavenly kingdom. But evil doing leads us to hell and into punishment. For it is said: "Blessed are they who are persecuted for righteousness' sake, for theirs is the kingdom of heaven." But he who does evil is worthy of punishment and sufferings.

We conclude the homily of our Holy Father saint John Chrysostom, who enlightened our minds and our hearts. In the name of the Father, and the Son, and the Holy Spirit, one God. Amen.

المسيح فى مثل هذا اليوم فاذا سمعتم أنه قد أسلم فلا تعبسوا وجوهكم بل أقول لكم عمن تعبسون . أعبسوا كثيراً وأبكوا جداً على الذى سلمه الذى هو يهوذا . لأن الذى أسلم قد جلس عن يمين الله الآب فى السموات . وهو ملك على الكل ملكاً أبدياً لا إنقضاء له . وأما الذى أسلمه فهبط إلى قاع الجحيم. ويبقى دائماً فيه إلى ما لا نهاية له يتوقع عذاباً أليماً وتنهداً شديداً . على هذا أبكوا ونوحوا . لأن الرب يعلمنا أن لا نحزن على الذى تألم فهو مستحق النوح عليه فى كل مكان أكثر من الذى يقبل الالآم لأنه بالحقيقة ليس رديأ الذى يتألم ٌ بل الذى يفعل الشر بالحقيقة هو الردى لأن قبول الآلام هو الذى يرشدنا إلى ملكوت السموات أما فعل الشر يسبب لنا دخول جهنم والعقاب لأنه يقول طوبى للمطرودين من أجل البر فأن لهم ملكوت السموات وأما فعل الشر فله عقاب وعذاب .

فلنختم عظة أبينا القديس يوحنا ذهبى الفم الذى أنار عقولنا وعيون قلوبنا باسم الآب والإبن والروح القدس الإله الواحد آمين .

Liturgy of The Holy Thursday

قداس يوم
خميس العهد

قداس يوم خميس العهد
Liturgy of the Holy Thursday

+ The Lamb is offered without praying the Agpeya.
+ We do not say ⲁⲗ ⲫⲁⲓ ⲡⲉ ⲡⲓ or Ⲥⲱⲓⲥ ⲁⲙⲏⲛ.
+ The Pauline Epistle is read in the annual tune, and the priest offers incense without kissing.

+ يقدم الحمل بدون صلاة مزامير .
+ لا تقال ⲁⲗ ⲫⲁⲓ ⲡⲉ ⲡⲓ و لا Ⲥⲱⲓⲥ ⲁⲙⲏⲛ
+ يقرأ البولس بطريقته السنوية ويطوف الكاهن بالبخور بدون تقبيل .

The Pauline Epistle
البولس

1 Corinthians 11:23-34

For I received from the Lord that which I also delivered to you: that the Lord Jesus on the same night in which He was betrayed took bread; and when He had given thanks, He broke it and said, "Take, eat; this is My body which is broken for you; do this in remembrance of Me." In the same manner He also took the cup after supper, saying, "This cup is the new covenant in My blood. This do, as often as you drink it, in remembrance of Me." For as often as you eat this bread and drink this cup, you proclaim the Lord's death till He comes. Therefore whoever eats this bread or drinks this cup of the Lord in an unworthy manner will be guilty of the body and blood of the Lord. But let a man examine himself, and so let him eat of the bread and drink of the cup. For he who eats and drinks in an unworthy manner eats and drinks judgment to himself, not discerning the Lord's body. For this reason many are weak and sick among you, and many sleep. For if we would judge ourselves, we would not be judged. But when we are judged, we are chastened by the Lord, that we may not be condemned with the world. Therefore, my brethren, when you come together to eat, wait for one another. But if anyone is hungry,

Ⲁⲛⲟⲕ ⲅⲁⲣ ⲁⲓϭⲓ ⲉⲃⲟⲗ ϩⲓⲧⲉⲛ Ⲡⲟ̅ⲥ̅ ⲙ̀ⲫⲏ ⲉⲧⲁⲓⲧⲏⲓϥ ⲛ̀ⲧⲉⲛ ⲑⲏⲛⲟⲩ : ϫⲉ Ⲡⲟ̅ⲥ̅ Ⲓⲏⲥⲟⲩⲥ ϧⲉⲛ ⲡⲓⲉⲭⲱⲣϩ ⲉ̀ⲛⲁⲩⲛⲁⲧⲏⲓϥ ⲛ̀ϧⲏⲧϥ ⲁϥϭⲓ ⲛ̀ⲟⲩⲱⲓⲕ . Ⲟⲩⲟϩ ⲁϥϣⲉⲡϩ̀ⲙⲟⲧ ⲁϥⲫⲁϣϥ ⲟⲩⲟϩ ⲁϥϫⲟⲥ ϫⲉ ⲫⲁⲓ ⲡⲉ ⲡⲁⲥⲱⲙⲁ ⲉ̀ⲧⲟⲩⲛⲁⲫⲁϣϥ ⲉ̀ϫⲉⲛ ⲑⲏⲛⲟⲩ : ⲫⲁⲓ ⲁⲣⲓⲧϥ ⲉ̀ⲡϫⲓⲛⲉⲣⲡⲁⲙⲉⲩⲓ . Ⲡⲁⲓⲣⲏϯ ⲟⲛ ⲡⲓⲕⲉⲁⲫⲟⲧ ⲙⲉⲛⲉⲛⲥⲁ ⲡⲓⲇⲓⲡⲛⲟⲛ ⲉϥϫⲱ ⲙ̀ⲙⲟⲥ : ϫⲉ ϧⲉⲛ ⲡⲁⲥⲛⲟϥ ⲫⲁⲓ ⲁⲣⲓⲧϥ : ⲥⲟⲡ ⲛⲓⲃⲉⲛ ⲉ̀ⲧⲉⲧⲉⲛⲛⲁⲥⲱ ⲉ̀ⲃⲟⲗ ⲛ̀ϧⲏⲧϥ ⲉⲣⲉⲧⲉⲛⲓⲣⲓ ⲙ̀ⲡⲓⲙⲉⲩⲓ : ⲥⲟⲡ ⲛⲓⲃⲉⲛ ⲉ̀ⲧⲉⲧⲉⲛⲛⲁⲥⲱ ⲉ̀ⲃⲟⲗ ⲛ̀ϧⲏⲧϥ ⲉⲣⲉⲧⲉⲛⲓⲣⲓ ⲙ̀ⲡⲁⲙⲉⲩⲓ .

Ⲥⲟⲡ ⲅⲁⲣ ⲛⲓⲃⲉⲛ ⲉ̀ⲧⲉⲧⲉⲛⲛⲁⲟⲩⲱⲙ ⲉ̀ⲃⲟⲗ ϧⲉⲛ ⲡⲁⲓⲱⲓⲕ : ⲟⲩⲟϩ ⲛ̀ⲧⲉⲧⲉⲛⲥⲱ ⲉ̀ⲃⲟⲗ ϧⲉⲛ ⲡⲁⲓⲁⲫⲟⲧ ⲉⲣⲉⲧⲉⲛϩⲓⲱⲓϣ ⲙ̀ⲫⲙⲟⲩ ⲙ̀Ⲡⲟ̅ⲥ̅ ϣⲁⲧⲉϥⲓ̀ . Ϩⲱⲥ ⲇⲉ ⲫⲏⲉⲑⲛⲁⲟⲩⲱⲙ ⲉ̀ⲃⲟⲗ ϧⲉⲛ ⲡⲁⲓⲱⲓⲕ : ⲟⲩⲟϩ ⲛ̀ⲧⲉϥⲥⲱ ⲉ̀ⲃⲟⲗ ϧⲉⲛ ⲡⲁⲓⲁⲫⲟⲧ ⲛ̀ⲧⲉ Ⲡⲟ̅ⲥ̅ ϧⲉⲛ ⲟⲩⲙⲉⲧⲁⲧⲉⲙⲡ̀ϣⲁ : ⲉϥⲉ̀ϣⲱⲡⲓ ⲉϥⲟⲓ ⲛ̀ⲉⲛⲭⲟⲥ ⲉ̀ⲡⲓⲥⲱⲙⲁ ⲛⲉⲙ ⲡⲓⲥⲛⲟϥ ⲛ̀ⲧⲉ Ⲡⲟ̅ⲥ̅ . Ⲙⲁⲣⲉ ⲡⲓⲣⲱⲙⲓ ⲇⲉ ⲉⲣⲇⲟⲕⲓⲙⲁⲍⲓⲛ ⲙ̀ⲙⲟϥ : ⲟⲩⲟϩ ⲡⲁⲓⲣⲏϯ ⲙⲁⲣⲉϥⲟⲩⲱⲙ ⲉ̀ⲃⲟⲗ ϧⲉⲛ ⲡⲁⲓⲱⲓⲕ : ⲟⲩⲟϩ ⲛ̀ⲧⲉϥⲥⲱ ⲉ̀ⲃⲟⲗ ϧⲉⲛ ⲡⲁⲓⲁⲫⲟⲧ . Ⲫⲏ ⲅⲁⲣ ⲉⲑⲟⲩⲱⲙ ⲟⲩⲟϩ ⲉⲧⲥⲱ ϧⲉⲛ ⲟⲩⲙⲉⲧⲁⲧⲉⲙⲡ̀ϣⲁ : ⲁϥⲟⲩⲱⲙ ⲟⲩⲟϩ ⲁϥⲥⲱ ⲛ̀ⲟⲩϩⲁⲡ ⲛⲁϥ : ϫⲉ ⲙ̀ⲡⲉϥⲇⲓⲁⲕⲣⲓⲛⲓⲛ ⲁⲛ ⲙ̀ⲡⲓⲥⲱⲙⲁ ⲛ̀ⲧⲉ Ⲡⲟ̅ⲥ̅ . Ⲉⲑⲃⲉ ⲫⲁⲓ ⲟⲩⲟⲛ ⲟⲩⲙⲏϣ ϣⲱⲛⲓ ϧⲉⲛ ⲑⲏⲛⲟⲩ ⲟⲩⲟϩ ⲥⲉⲙⲟⲕϩ ⲟⲩⲟϩ ⲥⲉⲉⲛⲕⲟⲧ ⲛ̀ϫⲉ ⲟⲩⲙⲏϣ . Ⲉⲛⲉ ⲁⲛⲉⲣⲇⲓⲁⲕⲣⲓⲛⲓⲛ ⲅⲁⲣ ⲙ̀ⲙⲟⲛ : ⲛⲁⲩⲛⲁϯϩⲁⲡ ⲉ̀ⲣⲟⲛ ⲁⲛ ⲡⲉ . Ⲉϥϯϩⲁⲡ ⲇⲉ ⲡⲉ ⲉ̀ⲣⲟⲛ ⲛ̀ϫⲉ Ⲡⲟ̅ⲥ̅ ⲉϥϯⲥⲃⲱ ⲛⲁⲛ ϩⲓⲛⲁ ⲛ̀ⲧⲉⲛ ϣⲧⲉⲙ ϩⲓⲧⲉⲛ ⲉ̀ⲡϩⲁⲡ ⲛⲉⲙ ⲡⲓⲕⲟⲥⲙⲟⲥ . Ϩⲱⲥ ⲧⲉ ⲛⲁⲥⲛⲏⲟⲩ ⲁⲣⲉⲧⲉⲛϣⲁⲛⲑⲱⲟⲩⲧ ⲉ̀ⲟⲩϩⲉⲙ ⲟϩⲓ ⲛ̀ⲛⲉⲧⲉⲛ ⲉ̀ⲣⲏⲟⲩ . Ⲓⲥ ϫⲉ ⲟⲩⲟⲛ ⲟⲩⲡⲉⲧϩⲟⲕⲉⲣ

1 كورنثوس 11: 23-34

لأنى تسلمت من الرب ما قد سلمته إليكم ، أن الرب يسوع فى الليلة التى أسلم فيها . أخذ خبزاً . وشكر وكسر وقال خذوا كلوا هذا هو جسدى الذى يقسم عنكم. هذا اصنعوه لذكرى . وكذلك الكأس أيضاً بعد العشاء قائلاً : هذه الكأس هى العهد الجديد بدمى اصنعوا هذا كلما شربتم لذكرى . فانكم كلما تأكلون من هذا الخبز . وتشربون من هذه الكأس تبشرون بموت الرب إلى أن يجىء لأن كل من يأكل من هذا الخبز ويشرب من كأس الرب بغير استحقاق يكون مجرماً فى جسد الرب ودمه. فليمتحن الانسان نفسه وهكذا فليأكل من هذا الخبز ويشرب من هذه الكأس . لأن الذى يأكل ويشرب بدون استحقاق . فانما يأكل ويشرب دينونة لنفسه إذ أنه لم يميز جسد الرب . ومن أجل ذلك كثر فيكم المرضى والسقماء وكثيرون يرقدون . لاننا لو كنا حكمنا على أنفسنا لما حكم علينا . وفى دينونتنا هذه انما يؤدبنا الرب . لئلا ندان مع العالم . إذا يا إخوتى حين تجتمعون للأكل فلينتظر بعضكم بعضاً وان كان أحد يجوع فليأكل فى بيته لكى لا يكون

let him eat at home, lest you come together for judgment. And the rest I will set in order when I come. The Grace of God the Father be with you all. Amen	ⲙⲁⲣⲉϥⲟⲩⲱⲙ ϧⲉⲛ ⲡⲉϥⲏⲓ : ϩⲓⲛⲁ ⲛ̀ⲧⲉⲧⲉⲛϣ̀ⲧⲉⲙⲟⲩⲱⲟⲩ̀ⲧ ⲉⲩϩⲁⲡ : ⲡ̀ⲥⲉⲡⲓ ⲇⲉ ⲁⲓϣⲁⲛⲓ ⲉⲓⲉⲑⲁϣⲟⲩ . Ⲡⲓϩ̀ⲙⲟⲧ ⲛⲉⲙ ϯ̀ϩⲓⲣⲏⲛⲏ .	اجتماعكم للدينونة . وأما الأمور الباقية فعند ما أجئ أرتبها . نعمة الله ...

+ The Catholic epistle, Praxis and the Synaxarium are not read.
+ The Trisagion is chanted in the annual tune.
+ The litany of the Gospel is prayed.
+ The Psalm and Gospel are read in the annual tune.

+ لا يقرأ الكاثوليكون ولا الابركسيس ولا السنكسار .
+ تقال الثلاثة تقديسات دمجاً .
+ يقول الكاهن أوشية الانجيل .
+ يرتل المزمور ويقرأ الانجيل بطريقته السنوية .

The Psalm

Ⲯⲁⲗⲙⲟⲥ ⲕ̄ⲃ̄ : ⲇ̄ ⲛⲉⲙ ⲉ̄ Ⲛⲉⲙ ⲯⲁⲗ ⲙ̄ : ⲏ̄

Psalms 22:4, 5, 40:8

You have prepared a table before me in presence of my enemies; who ate my bread, lifted up his heel against me.
Alleluia

Ⲁⲕⲥⲟⲃϯ ⲛ̀ⲟⲩⲧⲣⲁⲡⲉⲍⲁ ⲙ̀ⲡⲁⲙ̀ⲑⲟ ⲉⲃⲟⲗ : ⲙ̀ⲡⲉⲙ̀ⲑⲟ ⲛ̀ⲛⲏⲉⲧϩⲟⲭϩⲉⲭ ⲙ̀ⲙⲟⲓ . Ⲫⲏⲉⲑⲟⲩⲱⲙ ⲙ̀ⲡⲁⲱⲓⲕ : ⲁϥⲧⲱⲟⲩⲛ ⲙ̀ⲡⲉϥϭⲟⲓⲃⲥ ⲉ̀ϩ̀ⲣⲏⲓ ⲉ̀ϫⲱⲓ . ⲁⲗⲗⲏⲗⲟⲩⲓⲁ .

أكسوبتى إنؤو إتترابزا إمبا إمثو إيفول : إمبيه إمثو إنني إتهوج هيج إمموى . في إثؤوأوم إمبا أويك : أفطوأوون إمبيف ثيس إهري إيجوى . ألليلويا .

(مز 22: 4 و5و 40: 8)

هيأت قدامى مائدة مقابل الذين يحزنوننى . الذى أكل خبزى رفع على عقبه . الليلويا

The Gospel

Ⲉⲩⲁⲅⲅⲉⲗⲓⲟⲛ Ⲕⲁⲧⲁ Ⲙⲁⲧⲑⲉⲟⲛ Ⲕⲉⲫ ⲕ̄ⲋ̄ : ⲕ̄ - ⲕ̄ⲑ̄

Matthew 26:20-29

When evening had come, He sat down with the twelve. Now as they were eating, He said, "Assuredly, I say to you, one of you will betray Me." And they were exceedingly sorrowful, and each of them began to say to Him, "Lord, is it I?" He answered and said, "He who dipped his hand with Me in the dish will betray Me. The Son of Man indeed goes just as it is written of Him, but woe to that man by whom the Son of Man is betrayed! It would have been good for that man if he had not been born." Then Judas, who was betraying Him, answered and said, "Rabbi, is it I?" He said to him, "You have said it." And as they were eating, Jesus took bread, blessed and broke it, and gave it to the disciples and said, "Take, eat; this is My body." Then He took the cup, and gave thanks, and gave it to

Ⲉⲧⲁⲣⲟⲩϩⲓ ⲇⲉ ϣⲱⲡⲓ ⲛⲁϥⲣⲱⲧⲉⲃ ⲡⲉ ⲛⲉⲙ ⲡⲓⲙⲏⲧ ⲥ̀ⲛⲁⲩ ⲙ̀ⲙⲁⲑⲏⲧⲏⲥ : ⲟⲩⲟϩ ⲉⲩⲟⲩⲱⲙ ⲡⲉϫⲁϥ ⲛⲱⲟⲩ : ϫⲉ ⲁⲙⲏⲛ ϯϫⲱ ⲙ̀ⲙⲟⲥ ⲛⲱⲧⲉⲛ : ϫⲉ ⲟⲩⲁⲓ ⲉⲃⲟⲗ ϧⲉⲛ ⲑⲏⲛⲟⲩ ⲡⲉⲑⲛⲁⲧⲏⲓⲧ : ⲟⲩⲟϩ ⲉ̀ⲣⲉ ⲡⲟⲩϩⲏⲧ ⲙⲟⲕϩ ⲉ̀ⲙⲁϣⲱ ⲁⲩⲉⲣϩⲏⲧⲥ ⲛ̀ϫⲉ ⲫⲟⲩⲁⲓ ⲙ̀ⲙⲱⲟⲩ ⲉ̀ϫⲟⲥ ϫⲉⲙⲏⲧ ⲁⲛⲟⲕ ⲡⲉ Ⲡⲁ⳪ . Ⲛ̀ⲑⲟϥ ⲇⲉ ⲁϥⲉⲣⲟⲩⲱ ⲡⲉϫⲁϥ : ϫⲉ ⲫⲏⲉⲧⲁϥⲥⲉⲡ ⲧⲉϥϫⲓϫ ⲛⲉⲙⲏⲓ ϩⲓ ⲡⲓⲃⲓⲛⲁϫ ⲫⲁⲓ ⲡⲉⲑⲛⲁⲧⲏⲓϥ : ⲡ̀ϣⲏⲣⲓ ⲙⲉⲛ ⲙ̀ⲫ̀ⲣⲱⲙⲓ ϥⲛⲁϣⲉⲛⲁϥ ⲕⲁⲧⲁ ⲫ̀ⲣⲏϯ ⲉⲧⲥϧⲏⲟⲩⲧ ⲉⲑⲃⲏⲧϥ : ⲟⲩⲟⲓ ⲇⲉ ⲙ̀ⲡⲓⲣⲱⲙⲓ ⲫⲏⲉⲧⲟⲩⲛⲁⲧ ⲙ̀ⲡ̀ϣⲏⲣⲓ ⲙ̀ⲫ̀ⲣⲱⲙⲓ ⲉⲃⲟⲗ ϩⲓⲧⲟⲧϥ : ⲛⲉ ⲛⲁⲛⲉⲥ ⲛⲁϥ ⲡⲉ ⲙ̀ⲡⲟⲩⲙⲁⲥϥ ⲡⲓⲣⲱⲙⲓ ⲉⲧⲉ ⲙ̀ⲙⲁⲩ : ⲁϥⲉⲣⲟⲩⲱ ⲇⲉ ⲛⲁϥ ⲛ̀ϫⲉ Ⲓⲟⲩⲇⲁⲥ ⲫⲏⲉ̀ⲛⲁϥⲛⲁⲧⲏⲓϥ ⲡⲉϫⲁϥ ⲛⲁϥ : ϫⲉ ⲙⲏⲧ ⲁⲛⲟⲕ ⲡⲉ ⲣⲁⲃⲃⲓ : ⲡⲉϫⲁϥ ⲛⲁϥ ϫⲉ ⲛ̀ⲑⲟⲕ ⲡⲉ ⲉⲧⲁⲕϫⲟⲥ . Ⲉⲩⲟⲩⲱⲙ ⲇⲉ ⲁϥϭⲓ ⲛ̀ⲟⲩⲱⲓⲕ ⲛ̀ϫⲉ Ⲓⲏⲥ ⲟⲩⲟϩ ⲉⲧⲁϥⲥ̀ⲙⲟⲩ ⲉ̀ⲣⲟϥ ⲁϥⲫⲁϣϥ : ⲁϥⲧⲏⲓϥ ⲛ̀ⲛⲉϥⲙⲁⲑⲏⲧⲏⲥ ⲡⲉϫⲁϥ : ϫⲉ ϭⲓⲟⲩⲱⲙ ⲫⲁⲓ ⲅⲁⲣ ⲡⲉ ⲡⲁⲥⲱⲙⲁ : ⲟⲩⲟϩ ⲉⲧⲁϥϭⲓ ⲛ̀ⲟⲩⲁ̀ⲫⲟⲧ ⲟⲩⲟϩ ⲉⲧⲁϥϣⲉⲡϩ̀ⲙⲟⲧ ⲁϥⲧⲏⲓϥ ⲛⲱⲟⲩ ⲉϥϫⲱ ⲙ̀ⲙⲟⲥ : ϫⲉ ϭⲓⲥⲱ

(متى 26: 20 - 29)

ولما كان المساء إتكأ مع تلاميذه الاثنى عشر . وفيما هم يأكلون قال لهم الحق أقول لكم : ان واحد منكم يسلمنى . فحزنوا جداً وإبتدأ كل واحد منهم يقول ألعلى أنا هو يارب؟ أما هو فأجاب قائلاً : الذى يغمس يده معى فى الصحفة هو الذى يسلمنى . وان إبن البشر ماض كما هو مكتوب عنه ولكن الويل لذلك الإنسان الذى به يسلم إبن البشر . قد كان خيراً لذلك الإنسان لو لم يولد . فأجاب يهوذا مسلمه وقال : لعلى أنا هو يا معلم؟ فقال له أنت قلت . وفيما هم يأكلون أخذ يسوع خبزاً وباركه وقسمه . وأعطى تلاميذه وقال : خذوا كلوا فان هذا هو جسدى . وأخذ الكأس وشكر وأعطاهم قائلاً : اشربوا من

them, saying, "Drink from it, all of you. For this is My blood of the new covenant, which is shed for many for the remission of sins. But I say to you, I will not drink of this fruit of the vine from now on until that day when I drink it new with you in My Father's kingdom." Glory be to God forever, Amen.

ⲉⲃⲟⲗ ϧⲉⲛ ⲫⲁⲓ ⲧⲏⲣⲟⲩ : ⲫⲁⲓ ⲅⲁⲣ ⲡⲉ ⲡⲁⲥⲛⲟϥ ⲛ̀ⲧⲉ ϯⲇⲓⲁⲑⲏⲕⲏ ⲙ̀ⲃⲉⲣⲓ : ⲉ̀ⲧⲟⲩⲛⲁⲫⲟⲛϥ ⲉ̀ⲃⲟⲗ ⲉ̀ϫⲉⲛ ⲟⲩⲙⲏϣ : ⲉ̀ⲡ̀ϫⲓⲛⲭⲁ ⲛⲟⲩⲛⲟⲃⲓ ⲛⲱⲟⲩ ⲉ̀ⲃⲟⲗ . ϯϫⲱ ⲇⲉ ⲙ̀ⲙⲟⲥ ⲛⲱⲧⲉⲛ ϫⲉ ⲛ̀ⲛⲁⲥⲱ ⲓⲥϫⲉⲛ ϯⲛⲟⲩ ⲉ̀ⲃⲟⲗ ϧⲉⲛ ⲡⲟⲩⲧⲁϩ ⲛ̀ⲧⲉ ⲧⲁⲓⲃⲱ ⲛ̀ⲁⲗⲟⲗⲓ ϣⲁ ⲡⲓⲉ̀ϩⲟⲟⲩ ⲉⲧⲧⲏ : ϩⲟⲧⲁⲛ ⲁⲓϣⲁⲛⲥⲟϥ ⲛⲉⲙⲱⲧⲉⲛ ⲉϥⲟⲓ ⲙ̀ⲃⲉⲣⲓ ϧⲉⲛ ϯⲙⲉⲧⲟⲩⲣⲟ ⲛ̀ⲧⲉ ⲡⲁⲓⲱⲧ . Ⲡⲓⲱ̀ⲟⲩ ⲫⲁ ⲡⲉⲛⲛⲟⲩϯ ⲡⲉ .

هذه الكأس كلكم لأن هذا هو دمى الذى للعهد الجديد الذى يسفك عن كثيرين لمغفرة الخطايا . وأقول لكم انى من الآن لا أشرب من عصير هذه الكرمة إلى ذلك اليوم الذى فيه أشربه معكم جديداً فى ملكوت أبى . والمجد لله دائماً .

Gospel Response

مرد الانجيل

Your body and Your blood; are for the forgiveness of sins; and a new covenant; that You have given to Your disciples.

We have been made worthy; to partake of the tree of life; the true body; and blood of God

Ⲡⲓⲥⲱⲙⲁ ⲛⲉⲙ ⲡⲓⲥⲛⲟϥ ⲛ̀ⲧⲁⲕ : ⲡⲉ ⲡ̀ϫⲱ ⲉ̀ⲃⲟⲗ ⲛ̀ⲧⲉ ⲛⲉⲛⲛⲟⲃⲓ : ⲛⲉⲙ ϯⲇⲓⲁⲑⲓⲕⲏ ⲙ̀ⲃⲉⲣⲓ : ⲉ̀ⲧⲉⲕ ⲧⲏⲓⲥ ⲛ̀ⲛⲉⲕⲙⲁⲑⲏⲧⲏⲥ.

Ⲁⲛⲉⲣ ⲡⲉⲙⲡϣⲁ ⲙ̀ⲡⲓϣϣⲏⲛ ⲛ̀ⲧⲉ ⲡ̀ⲱⲛϧ : ⲉⲑⲣⲉⲛ ⲟⲩⲱⲙ ⲉ̀ⲃⲟⲗ ⲛ̀ϧⲏⲧϥ : ⲉⲧⲉ ⲫⲁⲓ ⲡⲉ ⲡ̀ⲥⲱⲙⲁ ⲙ̀Ⲫϯ : ⲛⲉⲙ ⲡⲉϥⲥ̀ⲛⲟϥ ⲛ̀ⲁⲗⲏⲑⲓⲛⲟⲥ.

جسد ودمك هما لغفران خطايانا وللعهد الجديد الذى أعطيته لتلاميذك .

فاستحققنا شجرة الحياة لنأكل منها الذى هو جسد الله ودمه الحقيقى .

+ **The priest prays the three long litanies**
+ **The Creed is recited**
+ **The prayer of Reconciliation is not prayed**
+ **Continues with "Through the intersession.."**
+ **Continues the liturgy until the end of the Litany of Oblations. The Commemoration of the Saints is not prayed.**
+ **Continues with "As it was.." as usual until the end.**

+ **After communion, the priest does not pray "Our mouths filled..". He prays this litany instead:**

"We thank you, O Lord, Lover of mankind and maker of all good things for our souls. For in this day, You have made us worthy of partaking of your heavenly and immortal Mysteries. That which an eye..."

+ وبعد ذلك يصلي الكاهن الثلاثة أواشى الكبار
+ وقانون الايمان
+ ولا تقال صلاة الصلح
+ بل تقال بشفاعة والدة الاله ..
+ يكمل القداس كالعادة الى اوشية القرابين ولا يقال المجمع و لا الترحيم
+ وبعدها يقال " كما كان .. " الى نهاية القداس

+ وبعد التوزيع لا يصلي الكاهن "فمنا امتلأ فرحاً .." بل يصلي هذه الاوشية :

"نشكرك أيها الرب محب البشر صانع الخيرات لنفوسنا. الذي جعلنا مستحقين في مثل هذا اليوم لأسرارك السمائية والغير المائتة. لأن ما لم تره ..... "

الساعة الحادية عشر من يوم الخميس الكبير
The Eleventh Hour of Thursday of the Holy Pascha

Isaiah 52:13-53:12

Behold, My servant shall understand, and be exalted, and glorified exceedingly. As many shall be amazed at You, so shall Your face be without glory from men, and Your glory shall not be honored by the sons of men. Thus shall many nations wonder at Him; and kings shall keep their mouths shut; for they to whom no report was brought concerning Him shall see; and they who have not heard, shall consider. O Lord, who has believed our report? And to whom has the arm of the Lord been revealed? We brought a report as of a child before Him; He is as a root in a thirsty land; He has no form, nor comeliness; and we saw Him, but He had no form nor beauty. But His form was ignoble, and inferior to that of the children of men; He was a man in suffering, and acquainted with the bearing of sickness, for His face has turned from us; He was dishonored, and not esteemed. He bears our sins, and is pained for us; yet we accounted Him to be in trouble, and in suffering, and in affliction. But He was wounded on account of our sins, and was bruised because of our iniquities; the chastisement of our peace was upon Him; and by His stripes we are healed. All we like sheep have gone astray; everyone has gone astray in his way; and the Lord gave Him up for our sins. And He, because of His affliction, opened not His mouth; He was led as a sheep to the slaughter, and as a lamb before the shearer is silent, so He opened not His mouth. In His humiliation His judgment was taken away; who shall declare His generation? For His life is taken away from the earth; because of the iniquities of My people He was led to death. And I will give the wicked for His burial, and the rich for His death; for He practiced no iniquity, nor craft with His mouth. The Lord also is pleased to purge Him from His stroke. If you can give an offering for sin, Your soul shall see a long-lived seed; the Lord also is pleased to take away from the travail of His soul, to show Him light, and to form Him with understanding; to justify the just one who serves many well; and He shall bear their sins. Therefore He shall inherit many, and He shall divide the spoils of the mighty; because His soul was delivered to death; and He was numbered among the transgressors; and He bore the sins of many, and was delivered because of their iniquities. *Glory be to the Holy Trinity, Amen.*

Isaiah 19:19-25

In that day there shall be an altar to the Lord in the land of the Egyptians, and a pillar to the Lord by its border. And it shall be for a sign to the Lord forever in the land of Egypt; for they shall presently cry to the Lord by reason of them that afflict them, and

(إشعياء النبى 52 : 13 - 53 : 12)

هوذا فتاى يفهم . ويتعالى ويتمجد جداً. كما أن كثيرين يندهشون منك كذلك يهان شكلك ومجدك من الناس . وكذلك تتعجب منه أمم كثيرة وأمامه يسد الملوك أفواههم . لأن الذين لم يتكلموا عنه بين أيديهم يرون . والذين لم يسمعوا يفهمون . يارب من صدق خبرنا . ولمن أستعلنت ذراع الرب . تكلمنا أمامه فإذ هو مثل صبى وكأصل فى أرض عطشى لا صورة له ولا مجد . رأيناه فكان لا منظر له ولا جمال بل شكله حقير ومضنى من بين بنى البشر . رجل أوجاع يعرف ويحمل الأمراض فأنه رد وجهه وأهين ولم يعتد به. هذا الذى حمل خطايانا وتألم عنا. ونحن حسبناه متألماً مضروباً ومعذباً وهو قد جرح لأجل معاصينا . وسحق لأجل آثامنا تأديب سلامنا عليه . وبجراحاته شفينا . كلنا كغنم ضللنا مثل رجل يضل فى طريقه والرب وضع عليه اثم جميعنا . وظلم أما هو فلأجل أنه تألم لم يفتح فاه . مثل خروف سيق إلى الذبح وكحمل صامت أمام الذى يجزه هكذا لم يحرك شفتيه رفع حكمة فى تواضعه وجيله من يقدر أن يصفه. لأن حياته تنزع من على الأرض. من أجل آثام الشعب جاء للموت . وسيعطى المتجاوزى الناموس مجازاة دفنه والاغنياء مكافأة موته. لأنه لم يصنع اثماً ولم يوجد فى فمه غش . أما الرب فشاء أن يشفيه من الجراح. وإذ ما أسلمتم ذواتكم ذبيحة عن الخطية فسترى نفوسكم زرعاً عزه كثير . يريد الرب أن ينزع الالم من نفسه ليريه النور ويصور الفهم ويخلق البر ويتعبد حسناً للجماعة. إذ يحمل خطاياهم . فلذلك أنه يرث الكثيرين . ويقسم غنائم الأقوياء . حيث أسلم نفسه للموت مع الأثمة وهو قد حمل خطايا كثيرين وأسلم من أجل ذنوبهم. مجداً للثالوث القدوس .

(إشعياء النبى 19 : 19 - 25)

فى ذلك اليوم يكون مذبح للرب فى مصر وعمود الرب عند تخومها ويكون علامة أبدية للرب فى كورة مصر . ويصرخون إلى الرب الله من أجل

He shall send them a man who shall save them; He shall judge and save them. And the Lord shall be known to the Egyptians, and the Egyptians shall know the Lord in that day; and they shall offer sacrifices, and shall vow vows to the Lord, and pay them. And the Lord shall smite the Egyptians with a stroke, and shall completely heal them; and they shall return to the Lord, and He shall hear them, and thoroughly heal them. In that day there shall be a way from Egypt to the Assyrians, and the Assyrians shall enter into Egypt, and the Egyptians shall go to the Assyrians, and the Egyptians shall serve the Assyrians. In that day shall Israel be third with the Egyptians and the Assyrians, blessed in the land which the Lord of hosts has blessed, saying, Blessed be My people that are in Egypt, and that are among the Assyrians, and Israel My inheritance. Glory be to the Holy Trinity, Amen.

Zechariah 12:11-14:3, 6-9

In that day the lamentation in Jerusalem shall be very great, as the mourning for the pomegranate grove cut down in the plain. And the land shall lament in separate families, the family of the house of David by itself, and their wives by themselves; the family of the house of Nathan by itself, and their wives by themselves; the family of the house of Levi by itself, and their wives by themselves; the family of Simeon by itself, and their wives by themselves; all the families that are left, each family by itself, and their wives by themselves. In that day every place shall be opened to the house of David and to the inhabitants of Jerusalem for removal and for separation. And it shall come to pass in that day, says the Lord of hosts, that I will utterly destroy the names of the idols from off the land, and there shall be no longer any remembrance of them: and I will cut off the false prophets and the evil spirit from the land. And it shall come to pass, if a man will yet prophesy, that his father and his mother which gave birth to him shall say to him, You shall not live; for you have spoken lies in the name of the Lord: and his father and his mother who gave him birth shall bind him as he is prophesying. And it shall come to pass in that day, that the prophets shall be ashamed, every one of his vision, when he prophesies; and they shall clothe themselves with a garment of hair, because they have lied. And one shall say, I am not a prophet, but I am a farmer, for a man brought me up thus from my youth. And I will say to him, What are these wounds between your hands? And he shall say, Those with which I was wounded in my beloved house. Awake, O sword, against My shepherds, and against the man who is My citizen, says the Lord Almighty; strike the shepherds, and draw out the sheep: and I will bring My hand upon the little ones. And it shall come to pass that in all the land, says the Lord, two-thirds in it shall be cut off and perish; but one-third shall be left in it. And I will

مضايقيهم ويحكم و يكون الرب معروفاً للمصريين ويخاف المصريون الرب فى ذلك اليوم ويقدمون ذبائح وينذرون نذوراً ويضرب الرب المصريين ضربة ويشفيهم شفاء فيرجعون إلى الرب فيستجيبهم ويشفيهم . فى ذلك اليوم يكون طريقه من مصر إلى الأشوريين فيأتى الأشوريون إلى مصر والمصريون إلى الأشوريين ويخدم المصريون الأشوريين فى ذلك اليوم ويكون إسرائيل ثالثاً للأشوريي والمصريين مباركاً فى الأرض التى باركها رب الجنود قائلاً مبارك شعبى مصر والأشوريون وإسرائيل ميراثى . مجداً للثالوث القدوس .

(زكريا النبى 12 : 11- 14 : 3 ، 6- 9)

فيكون فى ذلك اليوم أن النوح يكثر فى أورشليم مثل النوح على بستان الرمان الذى يقلع فى السهل وتنوح الأرض قبائل قبائل على حدتها قبيلة بيت داود على حدتها ونساؤهم على حدتهن وقبيلة بيت ناثان على حدتها . ونساؤهم على حدتهن وقبيلة بيت لاوى على حدتها ونساؤهم على حدتهن وقبيلة بيت شمعون على حدتها ونساؤهم على حدتهن . فى ذلك اليوم يفتح كل مكان لبيت داود وللساكنين فى أورشليم ويكون فى ذلك اليوم قال رب الجنود إنى أمحو إسم الاصنام من الأرض فلا تذكروا بعد وأزيل الأنبياء الكذبة والأرواح النجسة ويكون إذا تنبأ أحد بعد أن أباه وأمه اللذين ولداه يقولان له لا تعيش لأنك تتكلم بالكذب باسم الرب ويربطه أبوه وأمه اللذان ولداه حينما يتنبأ ويكون فى ذلك اليوم أن الأنبياء يخزون كل واحد من رؤياه عند ما يتنبأ ويلبسون مسحاً لأنهم كذبوا بل يقول أنا لست نبياً لأن رجلاً اقتنانى وعلمنى منذ صباى وأقول له ما هذه الجروح التى وسط يديك فيقول لى هذه هى التى جرحت بها فى بيت حبيبى أستيقظ يا سيف على الراعى وعلى الرجل إبن وطنه قال الرب ضابط الكل . اضرب الراعى فتتبدد الخراف وأضع يدى على الرعاة الصغار ويكون فى كل الأرض يقول الرب ان ثلثين يمحيان منها ويضمحلان والثلث يستبقى فيها وأخذ الثلث من النار وأجربه كما تجرب الفضة وامتحنه مثل ما يمتحن الذهب هو يدعو اسمى وأنا استجيبه وأقول هذا شعبى وهو

bring the third part through the fire, and I will try them as silver is tried, and I will prove them as gold is proved: they shall call upon My name, and I will hear them, and say, This is My people: and they shall say, The Lord is my God. Behold, the day of the Lord is coming, and your spoils shall be divided in you. And I will gather all the Gentiles to Jerusalem to war, and the city shall be taken, and the houses plundered, and the women ravished; and half of the city shall go forth into captivity, but the rest of My people shall not be utterly cut off from the city. And the Lord shall go forth, and fight with those Gentiles as when He fought in the day of war. And it shall come to pass in that day that there shall be no light, and there shall be for one day cold and frost, and that day shall be known to the Lord, and it shall not be day, nor night: but towards evening it shall be light. And in that day living water shall come forth out of Jerusalem; half of it toward the former sea, and half of it toward the latter sea: and so shall it be in summer and spring. And the Lord shall be king over all the earth. Glory to the Holy Trinity, Amen.

يقول أنت الرب إلهى هوذا يوم الرب يأتى وتقسم سلبك فيك واجمع كل الأمم على أورشليم للحرب فتؤخذ المدينة وتنهب البيوت وتفضح النساء ويخرج نصف المدينة إلى السبى ولكن بقيه الشعب لا تمحى من المدينة ويخرج الرب ويحارب تلك الأمم كما فى يوم حربة يوم القتال وتقف قدماه فى جبل الزيتون الذى قبالة أورشليم من الشرق. ويأتى الرب إلهى وجميع القديسين معه ولا يكون فى ذلك اليوم نور بل يكون برد وجليد فى يوم واحد ويكون ذلك اليوم معروفاً عند الرب ليس بنهار ولا بليل بل يشرق وقت المساء نور وفى ذلك اليوم يخرج ماء حى من أورشليم نصفه إلى البحر الأول ونصفه الثانى إلى البحر الأخير ويكون فى الصيف وفى الربيع ويكون الرب ملكاً على كل الأرض. مجداً للثالوث القدوس.

Pascha Praise - B (12 times), Page: 7 : تسبحة البصخة B (12 مرة) ، صفحة

The Psalm

Ⲯⲁⲗⲙⲟⲥ ⲙ̅ⲑ̅ : ⲓ̅ⲇ̅

Psalms 49:14

Seeing you have hated instruction, and have cast My words behind you. If you saw a thief, you ran along with him, and have cast in your lot with adulterers. Alleluia

Ⲛ̀ⲑⲟⲕ ⲇⲉ ⲁⲕⲙⲉⲥⲧⲉ ⲧⲁⲥⲃⲱ : ⲟⲩⲟⲅ ⲁⲕⲅⲓⲟⲩⲓ ⲛ̀ⲛⲁⲥⲁϫⲓ ⲥⲁⲫⲁⲅⲟⲩ ⲙ̀ⲙⲟⲕ : ⲁⲕϣⲁⲛⲛⲁⲩ ⲉⲟⲩⲣⲉϥϭⲓⲟⲩⲓ ⲛⲁⲕϭⲟϫⲓ ⲛⲉⲙⲁϥ : ⲁⲕⲭⲱ ⲛ̀ⲧⲉⲕⲧⲟⲓ ⲛⲉⲙ ⲛⲓⲛⲱⲓⲕ . ⲁⲗ.

إنثوك ذيه أكميستيه طا إسفو : أووه أكهيؤوى إننا صاجى صافاهوو إمموك : أكشان ناف إأووريفتشى أووى ناك تشوجى نيماف : أككو إنتيك طوى نيم نى نويك . الليلويا .

(مز 49 : 14)

وأنت قد أبغضت أدبى . وألقيت كلامى إلى خلفك . إذا رأيت سارقاً سعيت معه مع الفسقة جعلت نصيبك . الليلويا .

Introduction to the Gospel, Page: 8 : مقدمة الأنجيل ، صفحة

The Gospel

Ⲉⲩⲁⲅⲅⲉⲗⲓⲟⲛ Ⲕⲁⲧⲁ Ⲓⲱⲁⲛⲛⲏⲛ Ⲕⲉⲫ ⲓ̅ⲅ̅ : ⲕ̅ⲁ̅ - ⲗ̅

John 13:21-30

When Jesus had said these things, He was troubled in spirit, and testified and said, "Most assuredly, I say to you, one of you will betray Me." Then the disciples looked at one another, perplexed about whom He spoke. Now there was leaning on Jesus' bosom one of His disciples, whom Jesus loved.

Ⲛⲁⲓ ⲇⲉ ⲉⲧⲁϥϫⲟⲧⲟⲩ ⲛ̀ϫⲉ Ⲓⲏⲥ ⲁϥϣⲑⲟⲣⲧⲉⲣ ϧⲉⲛ ⲡⲓⲡⲛⲁ : ⲁϥⲉⲣⲙⲉⲑⲣⲉ ⲟⲩⲟⲅ ⲡⲉϫⲁϥ : ϫⲉ ⲁⲙⲏⲛ ⲁⲙⲏⲛ ϯϫⲱ ⲙ̀ⲙⲟⲥ ⲛⲱⲧⲉⲛ ϫⲉ ⲟⲩⲁⲓ ⲉ̀ⲃⲟⲗ ϧⲉⲛ ⲑⲏⲛⲟⲩ ⲡⲉⲑⲛⲁⲧⲏⲓϥ : ⲛⲁⲩⲥⲟⲙⲥ ⲟⲩⲛ ⲟⲩⲃⲉ ⲛⲟⲩⲉⲣⲏⲟⲩ ⲛ̀ϫⲉ ⲛⲓⲙⲁⲑⲏⲧⲏⲥ ⲛ̀ⲥⲉⲉ̀ⲙⲓ ⲁⲛ ϫⲉ ⲁϥϫⲉⲣⲉ ⲛⲓⲙ ⲙ̀ⲙⲱⲟⲩ : ⲛⲁϥⲣⲱⲧⲉⲃ ⲇⲉ ⲛ̀ϫⲉ ⲟⲩⲁⲓ ϧⲉⲛ ⲕⲉⲛϥ ⲛ̀Ⲓⲏⲥ ⲉ̀ⲃⲟⲗ ϧⲉⲛ ⲛⲉϥⲙⲁⲑⲏⲧⲏⲥ : ⲭⲏ ⲉ̀ⲛⲁⲣⲉ Ⲓⲏⲥ ⲙⲉⲓ ⲙ̀ⲙⲟϥ .

(يوحنا 13 : 21 - 4)

ولما قال يسوع هذا قلق بالروح . وشهد وقال: الحق الحق أقول لكم ، ان واحد منكم هو الذي سيسلمني. فكان التلاميذ ينظرون بعضهم إلى بعض ولا يعلمون من عنى منهم . وكان متكئاً فى حضن يسوع واحد من تلاميذه

Simon Peter therefore motioned to him to ask who it was of whom He spoke. Then, leaning back on Jesus' breast, he said to Him, "Lord, who is it?" Jesus answered, "It is he to whom I shall give a piece of bread when I have dipped it." And having dipped the bread, He gave it to Judas Iscariot, the son of Simon. Now after the piece of bread, Satan entered him. Then Jesus said to him, "What you do, do quickly." But no one at the table knew for what reason He said this to him. For some thought, because Judas had the money box, that Jesus had said to him, "Buy those things we need for the feast," or that he should give something to the poor. Having received the piece of bread, he then went out immediately. And it was night. Glory be to God forever, Amen.

Ⲁϥϭⲱⲣⲉⲙ ⲟⲩⲛ ⲉ̀ⲫⲁⲓ ⲛ̀ϫⲉ Ⲥⲓⲙⲱⲛ Ⲡⲉⲧⲣⲟⲥ ⲅⲓⲛⲁ ⲛ̀ⲧⲉϥϣⲉⲛϥ ϫⲉ ⲁϥⲭⲉⲣⲉ ⲛⲓⲙ ⲙ̀ⲙⲱⲟⲩ : ⲡⲓⲙⲁⲑⲏⲧⲏⲥ ⲇⲉ ⲟⲩⲛ ⲉⲧⲉⲙ̀ⲙⲁⲩ ⲉⲧⲁϥⲟⲩⲁϩϥ ⲉϫⲉⲛ ⲑⲙⲉⲥⲧⲉⲛϩⲏⲧ ⲛ̀Ⲓⲏⲥ ⲡⲉϫⲁϥ ⲛⲁϥ ϫⲉ ⲡⲁⲟ̅ⲥ̅ ⲛⲓⲙ ⲡⲉ : ⲁϥⲉⲣⲟⲩⲱ ⲛ̀ϫⲉ Ⲓⲏⲥ ϫⲉ ⲫⲏ ⲁⲛⲟⲕ ⲉ̀ϯⲛⲁⲥⲉⲡ ⲡⲓⲗⲱⲙ ⲛ̀ⲧⲁⲧⲏⲓϥ ⲛⲁϥ ⲛ̀ⲑⲟϥ ⲡⲉ : ⲟⲩⲟϩ ⲉⲧⲁϥⲥⲉⲡ ⲡⲓⲗⲱⲙ ⲁϥⲧⲏⲓϥ ⲛ̀Ⲓⲟⲩⲇⲁⲥ Ⲥⲓⲙⲱⲛ Ⲡⲓⲥⲕⲣⲓⲱⲧⲏⲥ.

Ⲟⲩⲟϩ ⲙⲉⲛⲉⲛⲥⲁ ⲡⲓⲗⲱⲙ ⲧⲟⲧⲉ ⲁϥϣⲉⲛⲁϥ ⲉ̀ϧⲟⲩⲛ ⲉ̀ⲣⲟϥ ⲛ̀ϫⲉ ⲡ̀ⲥⲁⲧⲁⲛⲁⲥ ⲡⲉϫⲉ Ⲓⲏⲥ ⲟⲩⲛ ⲛⲁϥ ϫⲉ ⲫⲏ ⲉⲧ ⲉⲕⲛⲁⲁⲓϥ ⲁⲣⲓⲧϥ ⲛ̀ⲭⲱⲗⲉⲙ ⲡⲁⲓⲥⲁϫⲓ ⲇⲉ ⲙ̀ⲡⲉ ϩ̀ⲗⲓ ⲉ̀ⲙⲓ ⲉ̀ⲣⲟϥ ϧⲉⲛ ⲛⲏⲉⲑⲣⲱⲧⲉⲃ ϫⲉ ⲉⲧⲁϥϫⲟⲥ ⲉⲑⲃⲉ ⲟⲩ : ϩⲁⲛ ⲟⲩⲟⲛ ⲇⲉ ⲛⲁⲩⲙⲉⲩⲓ ⲡⲉ ϫⲉ ⲉ̀ⲡⲓⲇⲏ ⲉ̀ⲣⲉ ⲡⲓⲅⲗⲟⲥⲟⲕⲱⲙⲟⲛ ⲛ̀ⲧⲟⲧϥ ⲛ̀Ⲓⲟⲩⲇⲁⲥ : ϫⲉ ⲁⲣⲏⲟⲩ ⲉ̀ⲣⲉ Ⲓⲏⲥ ⲭⲱ ⲙ̀ⲙⲟⲥ ⲛⲁϥ ϫⲉ ϣⲱⲡ ⲙ̀ⲫⲏ ⲧⲉⲛⲉⲣ ⲭⲣⲓⲁ ⲙ̀ⲙⲟϥ ⲉ̀ⲡ̀ϣⲁⲓ : ⲓⲉ ϫⲉ ⲅⲓⲛⲁ ⲛ̀ⲧⲉϥϯ ⲛ̀ⲟⲩⲉⲛⲭⲁⲓ ⲛ̀ⲛⲓϩⲏⲕⲓ.

Ⲟⲩⲟϩ ⲉⲧⲁϥϭⲓ ⲙ̀ⲡⲓⲱⲓⲕ ⲛ̀ϫⲉ ⲫⲏⲉⲧⲉ ⲙ̀ⲙⲁⲩ ⲁϥⲓ̀ ⲉ̀ⲃⲟⲗ ⲥⲁⲧⲟⲧϥ ⲛⲉ ⲡⲓⲉϫⲱⲣϩ ⲇⲉ ⲡⲉ . ⲟⲩⲱϣⲧ ⲙ̀ⲡⲓⲉⲩⲁⲅⲅⲉⲗⲓⲟⲛ ⲉⲑⲩ̅.

الذى كان يسوع يحبه . فأشار إليه سمعان بطرس بان يسأله من الذى قال عنه؟ فاتكأ ذاك التلميذ على صدر يسوع وقال له يارب من هو؟ أجاب يسوع قائلاً: هو ذاك الذى أغمس أنا اللقمة وأعطيه . فغمس اللقمة وأعطاها ليهوذا سمعان الاسخريوطى . وبعد اللقمة دخله الشيطان . فقال له يسوع ما أنت فاعله فافعله سريعاً . ولم يعلم أحد من المتكئين لماذا قال له ذلك . فظن قوم منهم ، إذ كان الصندوق عند يهوذا ، ان يسوع قال له اشتر ما تحتاج إليه للعيد أو ان يعطى شيئاً للمساكين . أما ذاك فلما تناول اللقمة خرج لوقته وكان ليلاً . والمجد لله دائماً .

Introduction to the Exposition, Page: 9   مقدمة الطرح ، صفحة :

Exposition

The Sun of righteousness shined upon us, and his rays reached all nations of the world; Jesus Christ the true light who shines to everyone coming to the world. The life-giving bread came from heaven and nourished all creation. From the beginning of times, He prepared a table in the wilderness and nourished the people with manna for forty years; They ate and died," so says the Lord. On the eve of that day in which they ate the unleavened bread of Passover, our Lord and Savior Jesus Christ sat there in the upper chamber of Zion with His disciples to celebrate the New Passover which is His very Body that He gave them as a sacrament and the precious Blood, which is superior to the blood offerings. Our Savior took the bread, blessed it, broke it, divided it, and gave it to His disciples saying: Take you eat from this you all. This is My Body that I divide for you and for many for the remission of sins. After that He took the cup, mixed the wine with water and handed it to them saying: Drink from it all of you for this is My blood of the new covenant which is shed for many for the remission of sins. Every time you eat of this bread and drink of this cup you proclaim (preach) my death, confess my

طـرح

شمس البر أضاء شعاعه وبلغ ضياؤه إلى أقطار الأرض . الذى هو يسوع النور الحقيقى الذى يضئ لكل إنسان آتٍ إلى العالم . الخبز السمائى المعطى الحياة المغذى كل صنعة يديه . فى مبدأ الزمان أعد مائدة فى البرية من المن وأعال منها الشعوب أربعين سنة من الزمان فأكلوا وماتوا كقول الرب ، ومائدة جديدة أعدها الإبن فى علية صهيون الأم لما كان عشية ذلك اليوم الذى أكلوا فيه فطير الفصح إتكأ الرب يسوع المخلص فى الموضع العالى هو عليه صهيون وأتكأ معه تلاميذه وكانوا يأكلون الفصح الجديد الذى هو جسده هو بذاته الذى أعطاه لهم بأمر سرى والدم الكريم الحقيقى الذى هو أفضل من دم الحيوانات ، أخذ مخلصنا خبزاً فباركه وهكذا قسمه وناوله لصفوة الرسل قائلاً : خذوا كلوا منه كلكم لأن هذا هو جسدى الذى أقسمه عنكم وعن كثيرين لمغفرة خطاياهم . بعد هذا أمسك كأس الخمر ومزجها بالماء وناولهم قائلاً: خذوا اشربوا من هذه الكأس جميعكم فإن دمى للعهد الذى يهرق عنكم وعن كثيرين لمغفرة خطاياهم . لأن كل مرة تأكلون من

ressurection and remember me until I come. He is the Passover of our salvation. The real Lamb, Christ our Savior said: I say to you I will not drink of this fruit of the vine until that day when I drink it new with you in kingdom of my Father. The Lord said: I say to you, one of you will betray me, and will deliver me to the enemies. And they began to think, each one of them, saying who dares do that? He answered and said: He who dipped his hand in the dish with me will betray me. Then Judas, one of those present said: Is it I? He said to him: You have said it. You have intended evil in your contrariness and dared commit a grave transgression because the Son of God came to save the first man from corruption.

هذا الخبز وتشربون من هذه الكأس تبشرون بموتى وقيامتى وتذكروننى إلى أن أجئ . هذا هو فصح خلاصنا ، الحمل الحقيقى المسيح مخلصنا . قال إنى لا أشرب من هذه الكرمة حتى أشربه معكم جديداً فى ملكوت أبى . قال الرب ان واحداً منكم سيسلمنى فى أيدى المخالفين . فبدأوا يفكرون واحداً فواحداً منهم قائلين مَن الذى يجسر ويفعل هذا ؟ فيهوذا أحد المتكئين قال لعلى أنا هو قال له أنت قلت. فأشار إليه العارف قائلاً : الذى يضع يده معى فى الصحفة . أضمرت الآثم أيها المخالف وتجرأت أنت على أمر ردئ لأن ابن الله أتى ليخلص الإنسان الأول من الفساد .

(North side) Christ our Savior; has come and has borne suffering; that through His Passion; He may save us.

(مرد بحرى) المسيح مخلصنا جاء وتألم عنا لكى بآلامه يخلصنا .

(South side) Let us glorify Him; and exalt His Name; for He had mercy on us; according to His great mercy.

(مرد قبلى) فلنمجده ونرفع اسمه لأنه صنع معنا رحمة كعظيم رحمته .

The Conclusion of the Exposition, Page: 9	ختام الطرح ، صفحة :

| The Conclusion with the Daytime Litanies, Page: 10 without Metanoia for it is after the liturgy | طلبة الصباح ، صفحة : بدون ميطانيات لانها عقب القداس |

BIBLIOGRAPHY

Abdo, Archdeacon Banoub. *The Treasures of Grace (Kenouz El-Neema)*. Abba Makar Church. Imbaba, Giza, Egypt, 2001.

Abnaa El Kanica. *Ϫⲉⲛ Ⲙⲓⲥⲣⲓ ⲠⲒⲬⲰⲘ ⲚⲦⲈ ϮⲆⲒⲆⲐⲎⲔⲎ ⲘⲂⲈⲢⲒ (The Coptic New Testament)*. Cairo, Egypt, 1940.

Amplified Bible, Captures the Full Meaning Behind the Original Greek and Hebrew. U.S.A., 1987.

Azmy, Fr. Abraham, ed. The Book of Agpeya, Virgin Mary and Archangel Michael Church. CT, U.S.A., 2004.

Brenton, Sir, and C. L. Lancelot. *The English Septuagint Bible, Translated from the Greek, Published by Samuel Bagster & Sons, Ltd.* London, 1851.

Coptic Orthodox Church of St. Mark. *ⲠⲬⲰⲘ ⲚⲦⲈ ⲠⲒⲠⲀⲤⲬⲀ ⲈⲐⲞⲨⲀⲂ (The Book of the Holy Pascha)*. NJ, U.S.A., 2004.

Couric, Robert A. *Holy Bible, King James 2000*. Bible League. Kentucky, U.S.A., 2000.

Diocese of Beni Sewef. *Order of the Holy Pascha*. Beni Sewef, Egypt, 1995.

Ekladios, Labib. *The Book of Psalms, Coptic-Arabic*. Cairo, Egypt, 1897.

Esposito, Paul W. *The Logos Bible*. North Charleston, SC: Createspace Independent Publishing Platform, 2012.

Hendrickson. *Holy Bible, Authorized King James Version, 1611 Edition*. Edited by Edition. U.S.A., 2003.

International Bible Society. *Holy Bible, New International Version in Arabic and English*. CO, U.S.A., 1999.

Ishak, Fr. Shenouda Maher. *ⲠⲬⲰⲘ ⲚⲦⲈ ⲚⲒⲮⲀⲖⲘⲞⲤ (Book of Psalms)*. Cairo, Egypt, 1991.

Khalaf, Fr. Ghassan. *The index of the Greek New Testament*. Beirut, Lebanon, 1979.

Makar, Adeeb B. *The Abbreviated Coptic-English Dictionary*. Edited by C. A. St. Antonius Coptic Orthodox Church. and U.S.A., 2001.

Sikkema, Henry. *The Greek Septuagint*, Unbound Bible. U.S.A., 1999.

St. George Church. *The Second Canonical Books*. Sporting, Alexandria, Egypt, 1977.

St. Taklahimanout Church. *Ⲡϫⲱⲙ ⲛ̀ⲧⲉ Ⲡⲓⲡⲁⲥⲭⲁ Ⲉ̅ⲑⲟⲩⲁⲃ (The Book of the Holy Pascha).* Alexandria, Egypt, 1981.

The Bible Society in Lebanon. *Holy Bible, the common translation into Arabic with the second canonical books.* Beirut, Lebanon, 1997.

The Holy Virgin Mary Coptic Orthodox Church. Ⲡⲓⲡⲁⲥⲭⲁ Ⲉ̅ⲑⲟⲩⲁⲃ (The Holy Pascha). Los Angeles, CA, U.S.A., 2000.

The Orthodox Study Bible, New King James Version. Nashville, TN, U.S.A., 1993.

Thomas Nelson Publishers. The Orthodox Study Bible, New King James version. Nashville, TN, U.S.A., 1993.

Van Dyke Arabic Version. Holy Bible, Middle East Bible Society. Cairo, Egypt, 1987.

Virgin Mary Church. Order of the Holy Pascha. Ezbat El-Nakhl, Cairo, Egypt, 2002.

Wahba, Fr, and F. Matthias. *The Book of Agpeya.* Edited by C. A. St. Antonius Church. and U.S.A., 2000.

Wahba, Fr. Matthias F., ed. *Order of the Holy Pascha,* Virgin Mary Church. El-Faggala, Cairo, Egypt, 1970.

Zondervan. Amplified Bible, Captures the Full Meaning Behind the Original Greek and Hebrew, U.S.A. 1987.

«إلَى هُنَا أَعَانَنَا الرَّبُّ».

1 صم 7 : 12

"Thus far the Lord has helped us."
(1Samuel 7:12)